The Papers of
George Washington

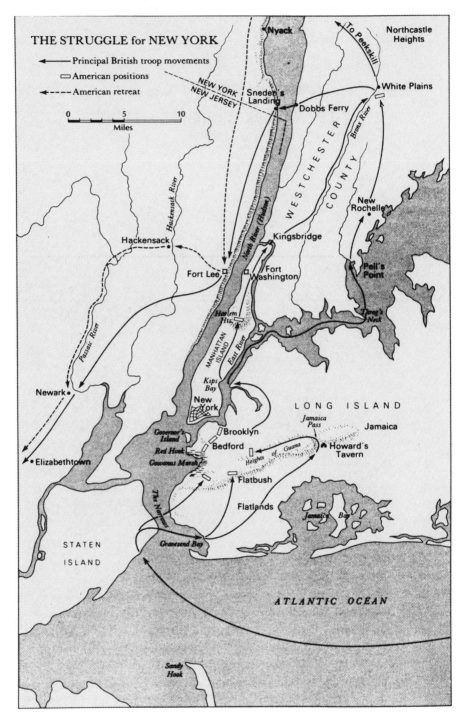

Map 1. The Struggle for New York, 1776. Adapted from 1776: Year of
Illusions *by Thomas Fleming (New York: W. W. Norton & Company, Inc.,
1975). Reproduced by permission of W. W. Norton & Company, Inc.*

The Papers of
George Washington

Dorothy Twohig, *Editor*

Philander D. Chase, *Senior Associate Editor*

Beverly H. Runge, *Associate Editor*

Frank E. Grizzard, Jr., Beverly S. Kirsch, Debra B. Kessler,
and Mark A. Mastromarino, *Assistant Editors*

Revolutionary War Series
6

August–October 1776

Philander D. Chase and Frank E. Grizzard, Jr., Editors

UNIVERSITY PRESS OF VIRGINIA

CHARLOTTESVILLE AND LONDON

This edition has been prepared by the staff of
The Papers of George Washington
sponsored by
The Mount Vernon Ladies' Association of the Union
and the University of Virginia
with the support of
the National Endowment for the Humanities.

THE UNIVERSITY PRESS OF VIRGINIA
Copyright © 1994 by the Rector and Visitors
of the University of Virginia

First published 1994

Library of Congress Cataloging-in-Publication Data
(Revised for volume 6)

Washington, George, 1732–1799.
  The papers of George Washington. Revolutionary War
series.

  Includes bibliographical references and indexes.
  Contents: v. 1. June–September 1775—2. September–
December 1775—[etc.]—v. 6 August–October 1776.
  1. United States—History—Revolution, 1775–1783.
2. Washington, George. 1732–1799—Archives.
3. Presidents—United States—Archives.   I. Chase,
Philander D.   II. Revolutionary War series.   III. Title.
E312.72   1985   973.3   87-403730
ISBN 0-8139-1040-4 (v. 1)
ISBN 0-8139-1538-4 (v. 6)

Printed in the United States of America

Contents

Contents

Maps

Editorial Apparatus

Transcription of the documents in the volumes of *The Papers of George Washington* has remained as close to a literal reproduction of the manuscript as possible. Punctuation, capitalization, paragraphing, and spelling of all words are retained as they appear in the original document. Dashes used as punctuation have been retained except when a period and a dash appear together at the end of a sentence. The appropriate marks of punctuation have always been added at the end of a paragraph. Errors in spelling of proper names and geographic locations have been corrected in brackets or in annotation only if the spelling in the text makes the word incomprehensible. When a tilde is used in the manuscript to indicate a double letter, the letter has been silently doubled. Washington and some of his correspondents occasionally used a tilde above an incorrectly spelled word to indicate an error in orthography. When this device is used the editors have silently corrected the word. In cases where a tilde has been inserted above an abbreviation or contraction, usually in letter-book copies, the word has been expanded. Otherwise, contractions and abbreviations have been retained as written and a period has been inserted after an abbreviation. When an apostrophe has been used in a contraction it is retained. Superscripts have been lowered and if the word is an abbreviation a period has been added. If the meaning of an abbreviation or contraction is not obvious, it has been expanded in square brackets: "H[is] M[ajest]y." Editorial insertions or corrections in the text also appear in square brackets. Angle brackets ⟨ ⟩ are used to indicate illegible or mutilated material. A space left blank in a manuscript by the writer is indicated by a square-bracketed gap in the text [ ]. Deletions from manuscripts are not indicated. If a deletion contains substantive material, it appears in a footnote. If the intended location of marginal notations is clear from the text, they are inserted without comment; otherwise they are recorded in the footnotes. The ampersand has been retained and the thorn transcribed as "th." The symbol for per (℔) is used when it appears in the manuscript. The dateline has been placed at the head of a document regardless of where it occurred in the manuscript.

Since GW read no language other than English, incoming letters written to him in foreign languages were generally translated for his information. Where this contemporary translation has survived, it has been used as the text of the document, and the original version has been included in the CD-ROM edition of the Washington Papers. If there is no contemporary translation, the document in its original language has been used as the text. All of the documents printed in this volume, as well as the routine documents omitted from it and various ancillary materials, may be found in the CD-ROM edition of the papers. The omitted documents are listed in the appendix to this volume.

In the Revolutionary War series, the titles of the documents include current military ranks of persons on duty with the contending armies or mobilized militia units.

Individuals mentioned in the text are identified usually at their first substantive mention and are not identified at length in subsequent volumes. The index to each volume indicates where an identification appears in an earlier volume of the Revolutionary War series.

Symbols Designating Documents

AD	Autograph Document
ADS	Autograph Document Signed
ADf	Autograph Draft
ADfS	Autograph Draft Signed
AL	Autograph Letter
ALS	Autograph Letter Signed
D	Document
DS	Document Signed
Df	Draft
DfS	Draft Signed
L	Letter
LS	Letter Signed
LB	Letter-Book Copy
[S]	Used with other symbols to indicate that the signature on the documents has been cropped or clipped.

Repository Symbols and Abbreviations

CD-ROM:GW	See "Editorial Apparatus"
CSmH	Henry E. Huntington Library, San Marino, Calif.
Ct	Connecticut State Library, Hartford
CtHi	Connecticut Historical Society, Hartford

CtY	Yale University, New Haven, Conn.
DLC	Library of Congress
DLC:GW	George Washington Papers, Library of Congress
DNA	National Archives
DNA:PCC	Papers of the Continental Congress, National Archives
DRC	Riggs Historical Collection, Washington, D.C.
M-Ar	Massachusetts Archives Division, Boston
MdAA	Maryland Hall of Records, Annapolis
MeB	Bowdoin College, Brunswick, Me.
MH	Harvard University, Cambridge, Mass.
MHi	Massachusetts Historical Society, Boston
MWeAt	Westfield Athenaeum, Edwin Smith Historical Museum, Westfield, Mass.
MWiW	Williams College Library, Williamstown, Mass.
N	New York State Library, Albany
NBu	Buffalo and Erie County Public Library, Buffalo, N.Y.
Nh-Ar	State of New Hampshire, Division of Records Management & Archives, Concord
NHi	New-York Historical Society, New York
NjMoNP	Washington Headquarters Library, Morristown, N.J.
NjP	Princeton University, Princeton, N.J.
NN	New York Public Library, New York
NNGL	The Gilder-Lehrman Library, New York
NNebgGW	Washington Headquarters, Jonathan Hasbrouck House, Newburgh, N.Y.
NNPM	Pierpont Morgan Library, New York
PHi	Historical Society of Pennsylvania, Philadelphia
PPAmP	American Philosophical Society, Philadelphia
PPL	Library Company of Philadelphia, Philadelphia
P.R.O.	Public Record Office, London
PWacD	David Library of the American Revolution, Washington Crossing, Pa.
R-Ar	Rhode Island State Library, Rhode Island State Archives, Providence
RG	Record Group (designating the location of documents in the National Archives)
RHi	Rhode Island Historical Society, Providence
RNHi	Newport Historical Society, Newport, R.I.
ViMtV	Mount Vernon Ladies' Association of the Union
ViU	University of Virginia, Charlottesville

Short Title List

Albion and Dodson, *Fithian's Journal.*   Robert Greenhalgh Albion and Leonidas Dodson, eds. *Philip Vickers Fithian: Journal, 1775–1776. Written on the Virginia-Pennsylvania Frontier and in the Army around New York.* Princeton, N.J., 1934.

Aler, *History of Martinsburg and Berkeley County.*   F. Vernon Aler. *Aler's History of Martinsburg and Berkeley County, West Virginia. . . .* Hagerstown, Md., 1888.

Arnold, *History of R.I.*   Samuel Greene Arnold. *History of the State of Rhode Island and Providence Plantations: From the Settlement of the State, 1636, to the Adoption of the Federal Constitution, 1790.* 2 vols. 1859–60. Reprint. Spartanburg, S.C., 1970.

Atwood, *Hessians.*   Rodney Atwood. *The Hessians: Mercenaries from Hessen-Kassel in the American Revolution.* Cambridge, 1980.

Bartlett, *R.I. Records.*   John Russell Bartlett, ed. *Records of the Colony of Rhode Island and Providence Plantations in New England.* 10 vols. Providence, 1856–65.

Baurmeister, *Revolution in America.*   Carl Leopold Baurmeister. *Revolution in America: Confidential Letters and Journals, 1776–1784, of Adjutant General Major Baurmeister of the Hessian Forces.* Translated and annotated by Bernhard A. Uhlendorf. New Brunswick, N.J., 1957.

Bliven, *Battle for Manhattan.*   Bruce Bliven, Jr. *Battle for Manhattan.* New York, 1956.

Bouton, *N.H. State Papers.*   Nathaniel Bouton, ed. *State Papers: Documents and Records Relating to the State of New-Hampshire during the Period of the American Revolution, from 1776–1783. . . .* New Hampshire Provincial and State Papers, vol. 8. 1874. Reprint. New York, 1973.

Boyd, *Jefferson Papers.*   Julian P. Boyd et al., eds. *The Papers of Thomas Jefferson.* 24 vols. to date. Princeton, N.J., 1950–.

Butterfield, *Adams Family Correspondence.*   L. H. Butterfield et al., eds. *Adams Family Correspondence.* 4 vols. to date. Cambridge, Mass., 1963–.

Champagne, *McDougall.*   Roger J. Champagne. *Alexander McDougall and the American Revolution in New York.* Schenectady, N.Y., 1975.

Clark, *George Washington's Navy.*   William Bell Clark. *George Washington's Navy; Being an Account of His Excellency's Fleet in New England Waters.* Baton Rouge, La., 1960.

Clark and Morgan, *Naval Documents.*   William Bell Clark, William James Morgan, et al., eds. *Naval Documents of the American Revolution.* 9 vols. to date. Washington, D.C., 1964–.

Coldham, *American Loyalist Claims.*   Peter Wilson Coldham, ed. *American Loyalist Claims.* Washington, D.C., 1980.

Conn. Hist. Soc., *Collections.*   *Collections of the Connecticut Historical Society.* Hartford, Conn., 1860–.

Cresswell, *Journal.*   Nicholas Cresswell. *The Journal of Nicholas Cresswell, 1774–1777.* New York, 1924.

Dandridge, *Shepherdstown.*   Danske Dandridge. *Historic Shepherdstown.* Charlottesville, Va., 1910.

Davies, *Documents of the American Revolution.*   K. G. Davies, ed. *Documents of the American Revolution, 1770–1783 (Colonial Office Series).* 21 vols. Shannon, Ireland, 1972–81.

Diaries. Donald Jackson and Dorothy Twohig, eds.   *The Diaries of George Washington.* 6 vols. Charlottesville, Va., 1976–79.

Douglas, "Letters."   "Letters Written during the Revolutionary War by Colonel William Douglas to His Wife Covering the Period July 19, 1775, to December 5, 1776." *New-York Historical Society. Quarterly Bulletin,* 12 (1929), 145–54; 13 (1929–30), 37–40, 79–82, 118–22, 157–62; 14 (1930), 38–42.

Ferguson and Catanzariti, *Morris Papers.*   E. James Ferguson, John Catanzariti, et al., eds. *The Papers of Robert Morris, 1781–1784.* 6 vols. to date. Pittsburgh, 1973–84.

Fitzpatrick, *Writings.*   John C. Fitzpatrick, ed. *The Writings of George Washington from the Original Manuscript Sources, 1745–1799.* 39 vols. Washington, D.C., 1931–44.

Force, *American Archives.*   Peter Force, ed. *American Archives.* 9 vols. Washington, D.C., 1837–53.

Ford, *Webb Correspondence and Journals.*   Worthington Chauncey Ford, ed. *Correspondence and Journals of Samuel Blachley Webb.* 3 vols. New York, 1893–94.

Ford, *Writings of Washington.*   Worthington Chauncey Ford, ed. *The Writings of George Washington.* 14 vols. New York, 1889–93.

Freeman, *Washington.*   Douglas Southall Freeman. *George Washington: A Biography.* 7 vols. New York, 1948–57.

Gerlach, *Proud Patriot.*   Don R. Gerlach. *Proud Patriot: Philip Schuyler and the War of Independence, 1775–1783.* Syracuse, N.Y., 1987.

Godfrey, *Commander-in-Chief's Guard.*   Carlos E. Godfrey. *The Commander-in-Chief's Guard: Revolutionary War.* Washington, D.C., 1904.

Graydon, *Memoirs.*   Alexander Graydon. *Memoirs of His Own Time. With Reminiscences of the Men and Events of the Revolution.* Ed. John Stockton Littell. Philadelphia, 1846.

Gruber, "America's First Battle."   Ira D. Gruber. "America's First Battle: Long Island, 27 August 1776." In *America's First Battles: 1776–*

1965, edited by Charles E. Heller and William A. Stofft, 1–32. Lawrence, Kans., 1986.

Gruber, *Howe Brothers.*   Ira D. Gruber. *The Howe Brothers and the American Revolution.* New York, 1972.

Hall, *McGown's Pass.*   Edward Hagaman Hall. *McGown's Pass and Vicinity.* New York, 1905.

Hastings, *Clinton Papers.*   Hugh Hastings and J. A. Holden, eds. *Public Papers of George Clinton. . . .* 10 vols. 1899–1914. Reprint. New York, 1973.

Heitman, *Register.* Francis B. Heitman. *Historical Register of Officers of the Continental Army during the War of the Revolution, April, 1775, to December, 1783.* Washington, D.C., 1914.

"Henshaw's Orderly Book."   "The Orderly Books of Colonel William Henshaw, October 1, 1775, through October 3, 1776." *Proceedings of the American Antiquarian Society,* n.s., 57 (1947), 17–234.

Hinman, *Historical Collection.*   Royal R. Hinman, comp. *A Historical Collection, from Official Records, Files &c., of the Part Sustained by Connecticut, during the War of the Revolution.* Hartford, 1842.

Huth, "Hessian Mercenary."   Hans Huth. "Letters from a Hessian Mercenary." *Pennsylvania Magazine of History and Biography,* 62 (1938), 488–501.

Isham, *Deane Papers.*   Charles Isham, ed. *The Deane Papers.* 5 vols. Collections of the New-York Historical Society, vols. 19–23. New York, 1887–91.

JCC.   Worthington C. Ford et al., eds. *Journals of the Continental Congress.* 34 vols. Washington, D.C., 1904–37.

Johnston, *Campaign of 1776.*   Henry P. Johnston. *The Campaign of 1776 around New York and Brooklyn. Including a New and Circumstantial Account of the Battle of Long Island and the Loss of New York, with a Review of Events to the Close of the Year.* Memoirs of the Long Island Historical Society, vol. 3. Brooklyn, N.Y., 1878.

Johnston, *Harlem Heights.*   Henry P. Johnston. *The Battle of Harlem Heights, September 16, 1776; with a Review of the Events of the Campaign.* 1897. Reprint. New York, 1970.

Jones, *History of N.Y.*   Thomas Jones. *History of New York during the Revolutionary War. . . .* Ed. Edward F. DeLancey. 2 vols. New York, 1879.

Journals of the Council of State of Virginia.   H. R. McIlwaine, Wilmer L. Hall, George H. Reese, and Sandra Gioia Treadway, eds. *Journals of the Council of the State of Virginia.* 5 vols. Richmond, 1931–82.

Kemble Papers.   Stephen Kemble. *The Kemble Papers.* 2 vols. Collections of the New-York Historical Society, vols. 16–17. New York, 1884–85.

Kinnan, *Order Book.* Peter Kinnan. *Order Book Kept by Peter Kinnan, July 7–September 4, 1776.* Princeton, N.J., 1931.

Klein, "Failure of a Mission." Milton M. Klein. "Failure of a Mission: The Drummond Peace Proposal of 1775." *Huntington Library Quarterly,* 35 (1971–72), 343–80.

Laughton, *James's Journal.* John Knox Laughton et al., eds. *Journal of Rear-Admiral Bartholomew James, 1752–1828.* Publications of the Navy Records Society, vol. 6. London, 1896.

Lowell, *Hessians.* Edward J. Lowell. *The Hessians and the Other German Auxiliaries of Great Britain in the Revolutionary War.* 1884. Reprint. Williamstown, Mass., 1975.

Lydenberg, *Robertson Diaries.* Harry Miller Lydenberg, ed. *Archibald Robertson, Lieutenant-General Royal Engineers: His Diaries and Sketches in America, 1762–1780.* New York, 1930.

Mackenzie, *Diary.* *Diary of Frederick Mackenzie; Giving a Daily Narrative of His Military Service as an Officer of the Regiment of Royal Welch Fusiliers during the Years 1775–1781 in Massachusetts, Rhode Island, and New York.* 2 vols. Cambridge, Mass., 1930.

"McMichael's Diary." "Diary of Lieutenant James McMichael of the Pennsylvania Line, 1776–1778." *Pennsylvania Magazine of History and Biography,* 16 (1892), 129–159.

Manders, *Battle of Long Island.* Eric I. Manders. *The Battle of Long Island.* Monmouth Beach, N.J., 1978.

Martin, *Private Yankee Doodle.* Joseph Plumb Martin. *Private Yankee Doodle: Being a Narrative of Some of the Adventures, Dangers and Sufferings of a Revolutionary Soldier.* Ed. George F. Scheer. 1962. Reprint. New York, 1968.

"Mass. Council Journal," Mar.–Sept. 1776 sess. "Records of the Great & General Court or Assembly for the Colony of the Massachusetts Bay in New England Begun and Held at Watertown in the County of Middlesex, on Wednesday the Twenty sixth Day of July 1775." (Microfilm Collection of Early State Records).

Mather, *Refugees of 1776.* Frederick Gregory Mather. *The Refugees of 1776 from Long Island to Connecticut.* Albany, N.Y., 1913.

Mead, *Historie of Greenwich.* Spencer P. Mead. *Ye Historie of ye Town of Greenwich, County of Fairfield and State of Connecticut.* New York, 1911.

Microfilm Collection of Early State Records. Microfilm Collection of Early State Records prepared by the Library of Congress in association with the University of North Carolina.

Middlebrook, *Maritime Connecticut.* Louis F. Middlebrook. *History of Maritime Connecticut during the American Revolution, 1775–1783.* 2 vols. Salem, Mass., 1925.

Minutes of the Albany and Schenectady Committees.		*Minutes of the Albany Committee of Correspondence, 1775–1778. Minutes of the Schenectady Committee, 1775–1779.* 2 vols. Albany, 1923–25.

Moore, *Diary.* Frank Moore.		*Diary of the American Revolution from Newspapers and Original Documents.* 2 vols. New York, 1859.

Morris, *Jay Papers.*		Richard B. Morris et al., eds. *John Jay: The Making of a Revolutionary. Unpublished Papers, 1745–1780.* New York, 1975.

New York Burghers and Freemen.		*The Burghers of New Amsterdam and the Freemen of New York, 1675–1866.* Collections of the New-York Historical Society, vol. 18. New York, 1886.

N.Y. Prov. Congress Journals.		*Journals of the Provincial Congress, Provincial Convention, Committee of Safety, and Council of Safety of the State of New-York, 1775–1776–1777.* 2 vols. Albany, 1842. (Microfilm Collection of Early State Records.)

O'Callaghan and Fernow, *N.Y. Documents.*		E. B. O'Callaghan and Berthold Fernow, eds. *Documents Relative to the Colonial History of the State of New-York.* 15 vols. Albany, 1853–87.

O'Donnell, *Southern Indians.*		James H. O'Donnell. *Southern Indians in the American Revolution.* Knoxville, Tenn., 1973.

"Old Virginia Line."		Lyon G. Tyler. "The Old Virginia Line in the Middle States during the American Revolution." *Tyler's Quarterly Historical and Genealogical Magazine,* 12 (1930–31), 1–43, 90–141, 198–203, 283–289.

Onderdonk, *Suffolk and Kings Counties.*		Henry Onderdonk, Jr. *Revolutionary Incidents of Suffolk and Kings Counties; with an Account of the Battle of Long Island, and the British Prisons and Prison-Ships at New-York.* New York, 1849.

Pa. Archives.		Samuel Hazard et al., eds. *Pennsylvania Archives.* 9 ser., 138 vols. Philadelphia and Harrisburg, 1852–1949.

Palmer, *Biographical Sketches of Loyalists.*		Gregory Palmer. *Biographical Sketches of Loyalists of the American Revolution.* London, 1984.

Papers, Colonial Series.		W. W. Abbot et al., eds. *The Papers of George Washington. Colonial Series.* 8 vols. to date. Charlottesville, Va., 1983–.

Papers, Presidential Series.		W. W. Abbot et al., eds. *The Papers of George Washington. Presidential Series.* 4 vols. to date. Charlottesville, Va., 1987–.

Prince, *Livingston Papers.*		Carl E. Prince et al., eds. *The Papers of William Livingston.* 5 vols. New Brunswick, N.J., 1979–88.

Reed, *Joseph Reed.*		William Bradford Reed. *Life and Correspondence of Joseph Reed.* 2 vols. Philadelphia, 1847.

"Revolutionary Actors."		Jeremiah Colburn, comp. "Documents

and Letters by Actors in the American Revolution." *New-England Historical and Genealogical Register,* 30 (1876), 331–43.

"R.I. Revolutionary Correspondence."   "Revolutionary Correspondence." *Collections of the Rhode Island Historical Society,* 6 (1867), 105–304.

Sabine, *Fitch's New-York Diary.*   William H. W. Sabine, ed. *The New-York Diary of Lieutenant Jabez Fitch of the 17th (Connecticut) Regiment from August 22, 1776 to December 15, 1777.* New York, 1954.

Sabine, *Smith's Historical Memoirs.*   William H. W. Sabine, ed. *Historical Memoirs from 16 March 1763 to 9 July 1776 of William Smith, Historian of the Province of New York.* 2 vols. New York, 1956–58.

Scribner and Tarter, *Revolutionary Virginia.*   William J. Van Schreeven, Robert L. Scribner, and Brent Tarter, eds. *Revolutionary Virginia: The Road to Independence.* 7 vols. Charlottesville, 1973–83.

Scull, *Montresor Journals.*   G. D. Scull, ed. *The Montresor Journals.* Collections of the New-York Historical Society, vol. 14. New York, 1882.

Shewkirk, "Moravian Diary."   Oswald G. Shewkirk. "Occupation of New York City by the British, 1776. Extracts from the Diary of the Moravian Congregation." *Pennsylvania Magazine of History and Biography,* 1 (1877), 133–48, 250–62, 467–68.

Showman, *Greene Papers.*   Richard K. Showman et al., eds. *The Papers of General Nathanael Greene.* 6 vols. to date. Chapel Hill, N.C., 1976–.

Smith, *Letters of Delegates.*   Paul H. Smith et al., eds. *Letters of Delegates to Congress, 1774–1789.* 19 vols. to date. Washington, D.C., 1976–.

Syrett, *Hamilton Papers.*   Harold C. Syrett, et al., eds. *The Papers of Alexander Hamilton.* 27 vols. New York, 1961–87.

Tallmadge, *Memoir.*   Benjamin Tallmadge. *Memoir of Col. Benjamin Tallmadge, Prepared by Himself, at the Request of His Children.* 1858. Reprint. New York, 1968.

Tatum, *Serle's Journal.*   Edward H. Tatum, Jr., ed. *The American Journal of Ambrose Serle, Secretary to Lord Howe, 1776–1778.* San Marino, Calif., 1940.

Taylor, *Papers of John Adams.*   Robert J. Taylor et al., eds. *Papers of John Adams.* 8 vols. to date. Cambridge, Mass., 1977–.

Tilghman, *Memoir.*   *Memoir of Lieut. Col. Tench Tilghman, Secretary and Aid to Washington. . . .* 1876. Reprint. New York, 1971.

Trumbull, *Autobiography.*   John Trumbull. *Autobiography, Reminiscences, and Letters of John Trumbull, from 1756 to 1841.* New York, 1841.

Va. House of Delegates Journal, Oct.–Dec. 1776 sess.   *Journal of the House of Delegates of Virginia.* Williamsburg, Va., 1776.

Va. Senate Journal, Oct.–Dec. 1776 sess.   *Journal of the Senate.* Williamsburg, Va., 1776.

Wade and Lively, *This Glorious Cause.*   Herbert T. Wade and Robert A. Lively. *This Glorious Cause: The Adventures of Two Company Officers in Washington's Army.* Princeton, N.J., 1958.

Ward, *Duty, Honor, or Country.*   Harry M. Ward. *Duty, Honor, or Country: General George Weedon and the American Revolution.* Philadelphia, 1979.

Ward, *War of the Revolution.*   Christopher Ward. *The War of the Revolution.* Ed. John Richard Alden. 2 vols. New York, 1952.

Wharton, *Diplomatic Correspondence.*   Francis Wharton, ed. *The Revolutionary Diplomatic Correspondence of the United States.* 6 vols. Washington, D.C., 1889.

Willcox, *Franklin Papers.*   William B. Willcox et al., eds. *The Papers of Benjamin Franklin.* 28 vols. to date. New Haven, Conn., 1959–.

"Williams' Diary."   "Elisha Williams' Diary of 1776." *Pennsylvania Magazine of History and Biography,* 48 (1924), 334–353; 49 (1925), 44–60.

Wilson, *Heath's Memoirs.*   Rufus R. Wilson, ed. *Heath's Memoirs of the American War.* 1798. Reprint. New York, 1904.

The Papers of George Washington
Revolutionary War Series
Volume 6
August–October 1776

General Orders

Head Quarters, New York, August 13th 1776.
Parole Weymouth.   Countersign York.

Thomas Henly and Israel Keith Esqrs. are appointed Aid-de-Camps to Major General Heath; they are to be respected and obeyed accordingly.[1]

The Court Martial to sit to morrow, for the tryal of Lieut: Holcomb of Capt. Anderson's Company, Col. Johnson's Regiment, under Arrest for "assuming the rank of a Captain & mounting Guard as such."[2]

The Colonels of the several Regiments, or commanding officers, are to send their Quarter Masters to the Laboratory for the Ammunition Cart to be attached to each Regiment with spare Ammunition; to have it posted in some safe and proper place near the Regiment so as to be ready at a moments warning—The Horse and Driver, to be also kept near the regiment. It is the Quarter Master's duty to attend to this and in case of action to see the Cartridges delivered as they are wanted.

The Enemy's whole reinforcement is now arrived, so that an Attack must, and will soon be made; The General therefore again repeats his earnest request, that every officer, and soldier, will have his Arms and Ammunition in good Order; keep within their quarters and encampment, as much as possible; be ready for action at a moments call; and when called to it, remember that Liberty, Property, Life and Honor, are all at stake; that upon their Courage and Conduct, rest the hopes of their bleeding and insulted Country; that their Wives, Children and Parents, expect Safety from them only, and that we have every reason to expect Heaven will crown with Success, so just a cause. The enemy will endeavour to intimidate by shew and appearance, but remember how they have been repulsed, on various occasions, by a few brave Americans; Their Cause is bad; their men are conscious of it, and if opposed with firmness, and coolness, at their first onsett, with our advantage of Works, and Knowledge of the Ground; Victory is most assuredly ours. Every good Soldier will be silent and attentive, wait for Orders and reserve his fire, 'till he is sure of doing execution: The Officers to be particularly careful of this. The Colonels, or commanding Officers of Regiments, are to see their supernumerary officers so posted, as to keep the men to their duty; and it may not be amiss for the troops to know, that if any infamous Rascal, in time of action, shall attempt to skulk, hide himself or retreat from the enemy without orders of his commanding Officer; he will instantly be shot down as an example of Cowardice: On the other hand, the General solemnly promises, that he will reward those who shall distinguish themselves, by brave and noble actions; and he desires every officer to be attentive to this particular, that such men may be afterwards suitably noticed.

General Greene to send for ten of the flat bottomed Boats which are to be kept under Guard at Long Island: No Person to meddle with them, but by his special order.[3]

Thirty seven Men (Sailors) are wanted for the Gallies.

Eighty men properly officered and used to the sea, are wanted to go up to Kingsbridge with the ships and rafts. They are to be furnished immediately and parade with Blankets and Provision, but without Arms, at General Putnam's, at two o'Clock, and take orders from him.

John Gardner of Capt: Trowbridges Company,[4] Col. Huntington's Regiment, tried by a General Court Martial, whereof Col. Wyllys was President and convicted of "Desertion," ordered to receive Thirty-nine lashes.

John Morgan of Capt. Johnson's Company, Col. McDougall's Regiment, tried by the same Court Martial, & convicted of "sleeping on his post," sentenced to receive Thirty lashes.

Francis Claudge of Capt: Speakmans Company,[5] Col. Glovers Regiment, tried by the same Court Martial and convicted of Desertion and re-inlistment—sentenced to receive Thirty nine lashes; thirteen each day successively.

The General approves each of the above Sentences and orders them to be executed at the usual times and places.

The Court of inquiry having reported that Lieut. Mesier had behaved unbecoming an officer to one of superior rank; the Court directed a Court Martial, unless he ask pardon of the officer he affronted: But that officer having represented to the General, that he is willing to pass it over: The General, at his request, orders Lieut: Mesier to be discharged.

After Orders. Col. Miles and Col. Brodhead's Regiments of Riflemen, to discharge and clean their rifles, to morrow at Troop beating, under the inspection of their officers.

Col. Smallwoods and Col. Atlee's Battalions, of Musquetry, to fire at the same time, with loose powder and ball.

Varick transcript, DLC:GW.

1. Israel Keith (1751–1819), a native of Easton, Mass., served as an aide-de-camp to Heath until November 1777 when he became deputy adjutant general for the eastern department. Keith resigned from the army in April 1778 to study law, and in March 1780 he was admitted to practice before the superior court of Massachusetts. Later in 1780 Keith became an aide-de-camp to John Hancock, and after the war he served for several years as adjutant general of the Massachusetts militia.

2. Jacob Holcomb (1741–1820) and John Anderson (1731–1797), both of Hunterdon County, N.J., served as officers in Gen. Nathaniel Heard's brigade of New Jersey militia levies from June to December 1776. For the verdict of Holcomb's court-martial, see General Orders, 15 August. Philip Johnson (1741–1776) of Hunterdon County, a veteran of the French and Indian War, was appointed by the provincial congress on 14 June 1776 as lieutenant colonel of the regiment of militia levies that was raised in Hunterdon and Somerset counties to reinforce the Continental army at New York, and on 1 Aug. he was promoted to colonel of the regiment in place of Stephen Hunt who resigned on grounds of ill health (Force, *American Archives*, 4th ser., 6:1620, 1643, 1657). Johnson was killed in the Battle of Long Island on 27 Aug. when "he received a ball in his breast" while directing the fire of his regiment (ibid., 5th ser., 1:1251).

3. The next day Greene ordered these boats brought to Myford's Ferry on Long Island to transport troops arriving from New Jersey and Connecticut (see Showman, *Greene Papers*, 1:286–87).

4. Caleb Trowbridge (1748–1799) of New Haven was a captain in the 1st Connecticut Regiment during 1775 and continued serving after 1 Jan. 1776 as a captain in Col. Jedediah Huntington's 17th Continental Regiment. Taken prisoner at the Battle of Long Island on 27 Aug., Trowbridge was not released until almost two years later despite Gov. Jonathan Trumbull's persistent efforts to have him exchanged (see GW to Jonathan Trumbull, Sr., 1 Feb. 1777, Trumbull to GW, 27 June 1777, Ct: Trumbull Papers; Trumbull to GW, 26 Feb. 1777, DLC:GW; and Middlebrook, *Maritime Connecticut*, 2:90). In 1781 Trowbridge became captain of the Connecticut privateer *Firebrand* and made two voyages to Holland during which he captured at least two prizes.

5. Gilbert Warner Speakman, who owned a tanhouse in Marlborough, Mass., before the war, served as a captain in Col. John Glover's 14th Continental Regiment from January to December 1776 and as commissary of ordnance for Massachusetts from 1777 to 1780.

From Henry Bromfield

Sir   Boston 13th Augt 1776

I am hond with your Excellencie's Favor of 24th June, wch came to Hand at a time that I was Absent on a Journey in the Country, This wth a great uncertainty whether to undertake the Task Assigned me therein has been the Reason, that I have not returned an earlier Answer, at length however, upon the Consideration of the Delay a Refusal must Occasion, & that the Excuse I might Alledge in my favor might be pleaded by Others who most probable must have been in the same Situation, vizt an Unacquaintedness with the Value of the Various Articles to be Apprised, has determin'd me to Undertake the Trouble in Conjunction with Mr Willm Davis Mercht of this Town on Behalf of Capt. Manly & his Crew, We have spared no Pains to Ascertain the Value of the different Articles; in Order to wch we have Applied to All the Traders & Mechanicks most conversant therein & have from the Information recd from them & Others most capable of giving it, Endeavor'd to make an Estimation as near to Truth as might be, which however it may deviate I am conscious on my Own part cannot be Attributed to Inattention or Neglect, & hope will be such as to meet the Approbation of your Excellency & the Honbe Congress[1]—I have the Honor to be with greatest Esteem & Respect Your Excellencys Most Obedt Humble Servant

                                                      Henry Bromfield

ALS, DLC:GW.

1. Artemas Ward wrote GW on 15 Aug.: "Inclosed is the Invoice of the Brig Nancy with the appraisement of her Cargo; which I received of Mr Bromfield last Monday [12 Aug.] af[ter] the post was gone" (LB, MHi: Ward Papers). Bromfield and Davis's invoice, which is dated 12 Aug., appraises the value of the ordnance stores captured aboard the *Nancy* at £20,530.18.1 (DNA:PCC, item 39). GW enclosed that invoice in his letter to Hancock of 23 August.

To John Hancock

Sir   New York Augt 13th 1776

As there is reason to beleive that but little Time will elapse before the Enemy make their Attack, I have thought It advisable to remove All the papers in my hands respecting the Affairs of the States from this place. I hope the Event will shew the precaution was unnecessary, but yet prudence required that It should be done, Lest by any Accident they might fall into their hands.

They are all contained in a large Box nailed up & committed to the care of Lt Colo. Reed, Brother of the Adjt Genl to be delivered to Congress, In whose Custody I would beg leave to deposit them, untill our Affairs shall be so circumstanced as to admit of their return.[1] The Enemy since my Letter of Yesterday have received a further augmentation of Thirty Six Ships to their Fleet, making the whole that have arived since Yesterday morning Ninety Six. I have the Honor to be with great respect Sir yr most Obed. Servt

Go: Washington

P.S. I would Observe that I have sent off the Box privately that It might raise no disagreable Ideas, & have enjoined Colo. Reed to Secrecy.

G.W.

LS, in Robert Hanson Harrison's writing, DNA:PCC, item 152; LB, DLC:GW; copy, DNA:PCC, item 169; Varick transcript, DLC:GW. The addressed cover includes the notation "⅌ the favor of Col. Reed." Congress read this letter on 17 Aug. (*JCC*, 5:662).

1. GW wrote Hancock on 24 Dec. 1776 asking him to return the headquarters letter books, which he needed for reference (DNA:PCC, item 152). Hancock complied with that request sometime in early January (see Hancock to GW, 1 Jan. 1777, DLC:GW). The remainder of the papers, which included GW's incoming correspondence and other documents that he received as commander in chief between June 1775 and this date, apparently were returned to him the following spring (see GW to Hancock, 18 Aug. 1776; GW to Schuyler, 4 Sept. 1776; and GW to Caleb Gibbs, 3 May 1777, PU: Armstrong Photostats). These papers were much disorganized in the process of packing and moving and were not put in proper order until Richard Varick reorganized GW's wartime papers in 1781 (see Varick to GW, 19 July 1781, and GW to Varick, 21 July 1781, both in DLC:GW).

Bowes Reed (c.1742–1794), a younger brother of Adj. Gen. Joseph Reed, was a lieutenant colonel in the Burlington County, N.J., militia at this time. He was promoted to colonel of the militia on 28 Sept. 1776 and held that rank until March 1778. An attorney like his brother, Bowes Reed was named clerk of the New Jersey supreme court on 6 Sept. 1776 and a justice of the peace in May 1777, and from October 1778 until his death he served as secretary of the state.

From John Hancock

[Philadelphia] 13 August 1776. "I have nothing in Charge from Congress to Communicate to you. Had not the honour of a Letter by the Post, I Judge the Return Express is on the Road, by whom wish to have an Agreeable Accot of the State of the Army."

ALS, DLC:GW.

To Colonel Thomas McKean

Sir   Head Quarters New York 13 Aug. 1776.

In answer to that part of your Letter of the 10th Instt "whether, when a Brigade is drawn up, and the oldest Colonel takes the Right, his Battalion is to be on the right with him; that is, whether the Colonel gives rank to the Battalion"[1] I shall inform you, that to the best of my Military knowledge a Regiment never looses its Rank, consequently can derive none from its Colonel, nor loose any by having the youngest Colonel in the Army appointed to the Comd of it—The oldest Regiment therefore although Commanded by the youngest Colo. is placed on the Right, and the Colonel with it.

I am exceedingly sorry to hear that a Spirit of Desertion prevails among the Pensylvania Association at a time when the Cause of liberty has such a claim upon their Services, and every appearance of danger to it, invites their aid.

I thank you my good Sir for your kind and Affectionate wishes—the day of Tryal, which will, in some measure decide the Fate of America is near at hand, and I am happy in informing of you, that a noble spirit (as far as I can judge of it) seems to pervade this Army—If we should be beaten (our numbers among friends being unequal to those of the Enemy) it will not be, I flatter myself, till after some hard knocks; which will not be very soon recovered of by the Enemy—But that superintending Providence, which needs not the aid of numbers, will lead us I hope to a more fortunate Event.[2] With respect & esteem I am Sir Yr Most Obedt Ser.

Go: Washington

P.S. Perhaps I may not have fully understood the tendency of the question propounded to me, & consequently have given an indecisive answer—the Idea I meant to convey is this, that the Regiment takes Rank from the time it is raised, and[3] can not be depriv'd of that Rank by the change of its Colonel—if therefore three Regiments should be formed into a Brigade the eldest of those Regiments will take the Right, although it is Commanded by the Youngest Colo., but if there shd be no Genl Officer to Comd these three Regiments the Senior Colonel of course does it—not the Colonel of the Senior Regiment—In short, the Rank of a Colonel, & the Rank of a Regiment are distinct things—the first takes Rank from the date of his Commission (when in Service with those of the same denomination) the latter[4] from the time of raising—If three Regiments therefore should be Incamp'd together & no superior Officer to that of Colonl the oldest of the Colonels will Comd those three Regiments. Yrs &c.

Go: Washington

ALS, PHi: McKean Papers. GW addressed the cover of this letter "to Colo. McKean at Amboy."

1. This letter has not been found.

2. GW wrote "Issue" on the manuscript and then changed the word to "Event."

3. At this place in the manuscript, GW wrote and struck out the phrase "never looses its place in the Brigade."

4. GW wrote "other" on the manuscript and then changed the word to "latter."

Letter not found: to Brig. Gen. Hugh Mercer, 13 Aug. 1776. In a letter to GW of 15 Aug., Mercer refers to "your Letters of the 13 & 14."

From a Secret Committee of the New York Convention

Sir   Poughkeepsie [N.Y.] Augt 13th 1776.

Your Excellencys Letter of the 21 Ulto arrived here at a Time when this Committee was dispersed and the Members gone different Ways on different Business—It was however sent by Express to Mr Jay who was then in Connecticut endeavouring to procure Cannon for the Defence of Hudson's River and we have the Pleasure of informing your Excellency that we have obtained ten twelve & ten six pounders with fifty Rounds of Shot for each Cannon—four of the twelves are now at Fort Montgomery.

We have paid a second Visit to the Forts and were pleased to find the Fortifications at the West Point opposite Fort Montgomery going on with Spirit,[1] we think it a most important Post and are confident that if it be well Fortified & defended it will together with Fort Montgomery effectually secure that important Pass—the Attention which General Clinton has paid to that Work as well as other Objects of public concern merit approbation—Several of the Garrison have been put to exercising the Artillery and we hope a Number of good Matrosses will in that Way be made.

The Chain intended for the Sorrelle is arrived and will form a Quarter part of the one designed for Hudson's River, the Iron for the Remainder is come to Hand, and the Smiths begin this Day to Forge it.

We have agreed to fix One End of it at Fort Montgomery and the other at the Foot of a Mountain called Anthony's Nose—it will cross the River Obliquely, and for that Reason be less exposed to the Force of the Tide, & less liable to Injury from the Ships of the Enemy—the Length of the Chain will at least be 2100 Feet. We have purchased and are now fitting out two Sloops each of sufficient Force to manage a Tender, and have appointed Capt. Benson (who will be the Bearer of this Letter) Commander of the one and Capt. Castel of the other[2]—the late Levies have so drained the Country of Men that we fear it will be impracticable to Man these Vessels unless the Officers be permitted to Inlist them from among the Levies—Between fifty and sixty Men for each Vessel will be sufficient—should this Expedient meet with your Excellency's Approbation we flatter ourselves the Vessels would in a very short Time to be fit for Service.

We are much Obliged to your Excellency for communicating to us the agreable Intelligence of the Success attending the Bravery of our Carolina Friends, as well as for your constant and unwearied Attention to the Safety and Defence of this State. We have the Honor to be with the greatest Respect & Esteem—Your Excellencys most Obedt & Very Humbe Servts

By Order of the Committee
Robert Yates Chairman

LS, DLC:GW. For GW's reply to this letter, see his letter to Robert Yates of 17 August.

1. West Point was opposite Fort Constitution.
2. These two captains were Henry Benson and Robert Castle.

From Major General Israel Putnam

Dear Ginrol   tusday Evning [13 August 1776] 8. a. clock

Aftor mr Balor cam to me with your ordor I immedatly went one bord all the roo galles and told them it was your Pesetive ordors that thay proced up the rivor with 2 fier Ships[1] the 2 Rodisland Galles and thes 2 bult hear immedatly waied ancor and proced up the revor the oather 3 have not moved but now aply for 36 men which ware peraded by my quartors for 2 or 3 hours and then went thare way but I beleave thay nevor intend to go and I never intend to Plag my self any mor about them. I am Dear Sir your most obedant humbel Sarvant

Israel Putnam

ALS, MH: Dearborn Collection. The date "Aug. 13th 1776" is written below the dateline on the manuscript in an unidentified handwriting which was added later.

1. See General Orders, this date.

To Major General Philip Schuyler

Dear Sir,   New York Augt 13th 1776.

Your Letter of the 6th Inst. I received this Morning by Bennet. The Reports made by the Emissaries who have been among the Indian Nations, appear not so promising as I could wish. However I trust, as so many have come to the Treaty, their Views are friendly, & tho they may not consent to take an Active Part in our Favor, that they will not Arm against Us.

The Difficulties attending the Vessels fitting for the Lakes, I am well apprized of. My late Letters will inform You, that I have taken Every Measure in my Power to facilitate the Work.

Before this comes to Hand, the Paymaster I expect, will have received a supply of Money. The Extract of Mr Varicks Letter shews It was Much Needed.[1] I have not failed in any Instance to Communicate Your Wants of this Article, *to Congress,* When they have been mentioned to me, Urging at the same Time, Not only the Expediency, but Necessity of keeping the Military Chests constantly furnished. It will be well, for You always to give them Early Notice of What You may have Occasion for, that their Remittances may be adequate. In future I presume they will have the fullest Information upon the Subject, having by some late Resolves enjoined their Commanders in Every Department to transmit them Monthly, a List of the Warrants they Grant, The Paymasters to return a Weekly state of their Military Chests, & the Commissaries & Qur Masters of What they receive. I have not these Regulations by me, but if my Memory serves, they were passed the 2d Inst. & have been forwarded You.[2] I have always laid before Congress, Copies of Your Letters & their Inclosures, where they were of a public Nature or contained Intelligence in any wise Material, Except when advised that You had done It Yourself. I shall here take Occasion to request, That Whenever You write them & Me of the same Things, You Certify Me thereof, to prevent me transmitting useless Information.

In Respect to Colo. Nicolson's Regiment & the Places Where It should be stationed, You certainly can determine better than I, having more in Your Power, Intelligence of the Enemy's Movements & Designs.

I would Observe in Answer to that Part of Your Letter Which mentions, that a Council of Officers & a Court Martial had been Convened & held here to decide upon the Council of those, who had sat at Crown Point, that Your Information is wrong. No Council—No Court of Inquiry—Nor Court-Martial upon that Subject Sir, was Ever convened by my Order or their own Accord. When Intelligence was first received here, that Crown Point was abandoned, It was the Cause of General Alarm & filled the Minds of most who heard It, with no small Degree of Anxiety; Some judging from the Common accepted Opinion and Others from their Knowledge & Acquaintance with It & the Country round about It, that It was of the last Importance to us to possess It, to give us in Conjunction with the Vessels we were about to build, the Superiority of the Lake, & to prevent the Enemy from penetrating into this & the Eastern States. Among

Others, some of the General Officers from their Own Knowledge, & the Rest from the Ideas they had formed, as the Matter was Occasionally mentioned deliver[ed] their Sentiments to this Effect, as did Every Person I heard speak of It at the Time the Account first came. From the Universal Chagrine that took Place, the Regret that Every Person expressed upon the Occasion—the Remonstrance of the Officers, which You transmitted, & Which appeared to contain Many Weighty Reasons, I felt Myself Much Concerned, as Every Body Else did, & Wished According to my Information & Opinion at that Time, the Post had been maintained. I do not wish to dwell longer upon the subject, & therefore shall only add that Your Letter of the 24th Ulto (or at least a Copy of It) was transmitted to Congress, as soon as It was received.[3] Nor shall I have any Objection to sending a Copy of the One before me now when I have an Opportunity to make It out, If It shall be Your Inclination & Request.

I have no News of Importance to Communicate, Unless that the Enemy are daily becoming stronger. On Monday they received an Augmentation of Ninty Eight Ships to their Fleet, with a further Part of the foreign Troops, It is probable.[4] They seem to be Making Great Preparations & We have Reason to expect they are upon the Point of an Attack.

The Letters which Accompany this, You will be pleased to deliver General Gates, Reed and Sinclair.[5] they came to Hand on Sunday, and Wishing You & the Army under Your Command, Health & the Smiles of a Kind Providence on all Your Efforts. I am Dear Sir, Your Most Obedt Servt

Go. Washington

LB, NN: Schuyler Papers; LB, DLC:GW; copy (extract), NHi: Gates Papers; Varick transcript, DLC:GW.

1. GW is referring to the extract of Richard Varick's letter to Schuyler of 4 Aug., which was enclosed in Schuyler's letter to GW of 6 August. See note 1 to that document.

2. See Congress's resolutions of 2 Aug. on this subject in *JCC*, 5:627–28.

3. A copy of Schuyler's letter to GW of 24 July was enclosed in GW's letter to Hancock of 30 July.

4. The previous day was Monday.

5. GW apparently forwarded Hancock's letters to James Reed and Arthur St. Clair of 10 Aug., concerning their promotions to brigadier general (see Hancock's first letter to GW of that date, note 3). The letter or letters to Gates have not been identified. James Reed (1722–1807) of New Hampshire, who

had commanded a regiment since the beginning of the war and had been in the northern department since May of this year, could not assume his duties as a brigadier general because of poor health. "Brigadier General James Reed," Gates wrote Hancock on 2 Sept., "remains so very ill at Fort George, that he will not, I imagine, be again fit for Service this Campaign" (DNA:PCC, item 154). Greatly impaired in hearing and totally blind, Reed returned home to Fitzwilliam, N.H., on 7 Jan. 1777 seeking a cure for his illness, but his doctors could not restore his sight (see Reed to the Continental Congress, 20 Sept. 1788, DNA:PCC, item 42; see also GW to Hancock, 20 Dec. 1776, DNA:PCC, item 152).

From Jonathan Trumbull, Sr.

Sir   Lebanon [Conn.] 13th August 1776
    Your Favour of the 7th Instant, by Mr Root, & the Intelligence it contains has given me great concern & Anxiety—the soon expected Strength of the Enemy & weekness of your Army were equally unforseen and surprizing—tho I never gave credit to the public Accounts of you[r] Numbers, yet I could not suspect they fell so much short of the Numbers proposed as I find they do.
    Immediately upon receipt of your Letter I Summoned my Council of Safety, and Ordered Nine Regiments of our Militia in addition to the Five Western Regiments, Fourteen in the whole to march without loss of Time and join You, under the Command of Oliver Wolcott Esqr. Colo. of the [   ] Regiment as their Brigadier General, who is appointed and Commissioned to that Office.[1] these Orders are accompanied with the most pressing Recommendation of speedily carrying them into Execution, inforced by communicating as much of the Intelligence you was pleased to favour me with of your Situation & danger as I thought prudent and Necessary.
    I have likewise proposed that Companies of Volunteers ⟨cons⟩isting of Able bodied Men not in the Militia should associate ⟨and⟩ March to your assistance, under Officers they should chuse, and have promised them like Wages and Allowance of provisions &C. as the Continental Army receive—some such Companies are formed & I expect more will be, what ever their Numbers may be they will be ordered to join some one of our Militia Regiments, and submit themselves to the Command of their Field Officers while they continue in Service.

Colo. Wards Regiment is on their March to join—I am far from trusting meerly in the Justice of our Cause—I consider that as a Just Ground to Hope for the smiles of Heaven on our Exertions, which ought to be the greatest in our Power.

These fourteen Regiments, sent On the Present Emergency consist of Substantial farmers, whose Business requires their return when the Necessity of their further stay in the Army is Over—And doubt not your attention thereto, and that you will dismis them in whole or in part as soon as you think safe and Convenient.

Capt. Bacon has not been with me tho I have heard of him and that he is returned without going to Rhode Island Capt. Van Buren has been here upon the same Errand, and has procured all the Sail Cloth that was wanted, and part of the Cordage and has a prospect of obtaining the rest of the Cordage in this Colony.[2]

I have notwithstanding forwarded you[r] Letter to Governor Cooke and likewise given him the Intelligence I received from You agreable to your request. I am with Esteem and Regard Sir Your Obedient humble Servant

Jonth; Trumbull

ALS, DLC:GW; LB, Ct: Trumbull Papers. The last three paragraphs of the letter are omitted from the LB.

1. The Connecticut council of safety took these actions on 12 Aug. (see Hinman, *Historical Collection,* 379). Oliver Wolcott, Sr., whom the council of safety commissioned a brigadier general of militia on that date, had been appointed colonel of the 17th Regiment of Connecticut Militia by the general assembly in May 1774 (ibid., 160). The LB, however, reads: "Oliver Wolcott Esqr. Colo. of the 19th Regiment." Wolcott was promoted to major general of militia in 1779 when he defended the state against British raids.

2. Leonard Van Buren was dispatched to Connecticut from Albany by Richard Varick on 3 Aug. to purchase sailcloth and cordage for the American armed vessels being built on Lake Champlain, a mission similar to that of William Bacon who had left Albany for New York five days earlier. Varick instructed Van Buren to inquire for Captain Bacon at Governor Trumbull's house and if he had not yet reached that place, to "leave a Letter for him there, Informing him that You are sent to Connecticut on this Business, & requesting him to desist from purchasing" (Varick to Van Buren, 3 Aug., in Clark and Morgan, *Naval Documents,* 6:36–37). Van Buren subsequently became commissary of forage in the northern department with the rank of major.

To Major General Artemas Ward

Dear Sir,   Head-Quarters New York Augt 13th 1776.

I could not have supposed the Company of Artificers under Capt. Ayres would have insisted on their Wages being augmented in Consequence of their being ordered to this place,[1] the consequences of raiseing their pay would be an Immediate Application from all those in Service as Artificers to be put on the same footing, if not refuse doing Duty any longer than absolutely bound.

But these men understanding the particular branch of makeing Gun Carriages &c. and the absolute necessity we are under for them induces me to order them on at the Wages you mention, and to prevent the Evil abovementioned have concluded to stop them 40 or 50 Miles up the Sound and let them go on with their Business, Norwalk a town in the Western part of a Connecticut situated on the Sound seems a proper Station, to which place you'll please to order them as soon as possible, with their Tools[2] &c. compleat, Necessity obliges me to order on the Company of Artillery which I mentioned in my Letter some time past,[3] both the above Companies may March to Norwich, & from that by Water, they will take in Change the two Sea Mortars wrote for Yesterday, and such other articles as may be bound for this place, If necessary a Company of Artillery might be embodied & put in Continental pay, from among the Inhabitants of and in the Neighbourhood of Boston, in this case Inventory should be taken of such Stores Arms Utensils &c. that are delvd them and the Officers pass their Receipts to be Accountable. I am Sir, Your Most Humble Servt

                                        Go: Washington

LS, in Samuel Blachley Webb's writing, MHi: Ward Papers.

1. For previous correspondence about these artificers, see Ward to GW, 22 July, 4 Aug., and GW to Ward, 29 July.

2. Webb inadvertently wrote "Tolls" on the manuscript.

3. See GW to Ward, 29 July.

From Abraham Yates, Jr.

In Convention of the Representatives of the
Sir State of New York at Harlem Augt 13th 1776.
I am directed by the Convention to return their Thanks to Your Excellency for the Attention You have paid to the removal of suspicious and dangerous Persons from the Environs of the City of New York.[1] Deeply sensible with Your Excellency of the Importance and Necessity of this Measure, the Convention had entered into a Resolution for that purpose previous to their Arrival at this Place[2] but the difficulty of preparing proper Lists, the danger of giving the Alarm to some by the Apprehension of others and the Dilatoriness of Proceedings inseperable from a large Body, together with the great Urgency of our other public Affairs, delayed the Completion of this Business untill Your Excellency had taken it under Your immediate Cognizance. The delicate State of the present Juncture did in the Opinion of this Convention from the nature of the Case fully vest Your Excellency with all the civil Power necessary for the immediate Safety of the Army under your Command and consequently of the american Cause, and considering the great Divisions which have prevailed among the Inhabitants of the State of New York by sparing this House that disagreable Task You have conferred upon them a considerable Obligation.

The Convention, Sir, are at a Loss to conceive on what foundation those Gentlemen who had given their Paroles to a Committee of this House could assume the Opinion that any Dangers would after their Caption result from it. Since evidently the Parole is by that Step entirely dissolved,[3] but as Doubts may remain in their Minds a Resolution is enclosed to Your Excellency which when You shall have made it known to them must certainly obliterate all their Scruples.[4]

I am directed further to inform Your Excellency that the Intelligence with which You have honored them from the Northern Department fully convinces them of the propriety of preserving as much force as possible in the upper Counties. At the same time we hope that the Assistance given to us by the neighbouring States will be effectuall to Defeat the Designs of our Foes in this Quarter.

General Clinton will give Your Excellency full Information with Respect to the Troops under his Command—seven hundred of which are now at the Post to the Northward of Kings Bridge, and more of them would have been there if the essential service of depriving the Enemy of Water did not demand considerable Detachments along the Banks of Hudsons River.

The Convention are very happy that Your Excellency hath attributed to it's proper Cause the omission of a Signature to the Letter which we had the Honor of writing to You on the 9th instant.[5] The fault lay with the Secretaries who in a great Hurry of Business neglected the presenting of it to the President for which we must pray Your Excellency's Excuse.

I am further directed to enclose You the Copy of a Letter from General Scott with relation to one of the Prisoners who hath lately been taken by your Order. And the Copy of our Resolution upon that Subject.[6] I have the Honor to be with great Respect Your Excellency's most Obedient & very humble Servant

By Order.
Abm Yates Junr President P.T.

LS, DLC:GW. A draft of this letter was approved by the convention on the morning of this date. The printed version of the draft is nearly identical to the LS in wording (see *N.Y. Prov. Congress Journals,* 1:570).

Abraham Yates, Jr. (1724–1796), a lawyer and land speculator from Albany, was elected president pro tempore of the convention on 10 Aug. to act in place of Nathaniel Woodhull, who took a leave of absence on that date to serve as brigadier general of the militia forces from Queens and Suffolk counties that had been called out to reinforce the Continental army (ibid., 566). Yates, who represented Albany County in the provincial congresses and conventions from 1774 to 1777, became president of the convention in his own right on 28 Aug. and held that office until 21 Sept. when he went home on leave (ibid., 595, 638, 643). He was a state senator from 1777 to 1790, a Continental loan commissioner from 1777 to 1782, and a member of the Continental Congress from 1787 to 1788.

1. See GW to the New York Convention, 12 August.

2. The convention, which had met at the courthouse at White Plains until 27 July, reconvened at the church in Harlem on 29 July (*N.Y. Prov. Congress Journals,* 1:548). For various resolutions regarding the apprehension of disaffected persons, see ibid., 476–78, 504, 512, 518.

3. The draft version of this letter reads: "is by that effectually destroyed" (ibid., 570).

4. The enclosed resolution of this date declares these paroles to be "totally void as to any obligations thereby laid upon those who have been since the

giving of the said Paroles made prisoners" on GW's orders (DLC:GW; see also *N.Y. Prov. Congress Journals*, 1:570).

5. See GW to the New York Convention, 11 August.

6. John Morin Scott's letter of this date to the president of the convention concerns Willet Taylor of New York City. "He is an infirm man," Scott writes. "His father in law Mr Bogert [John Bogart] a Staunch whig—No difficulty can arise from the Interposition of the Congress in his Affair—I am sure the General [GW] will not be displeased with it. I am told Mr Taylor is willing to give Assurances on Oath. And very probably his Father in Law will undertake for him. For the Sake of his Family, and particularly his wife who is far gone in her pregnancy, I could wish the Convention of the State of New York would do something in the Case—If he is left to me, I must of Course order him to Connecticut—If the Congress will interfere [in] the Affair I will answer for it to the General." The convention's resolution of this date, a copy of which is appended to Scott's letter, empowers Scott with GW's permission "to dispose of Willet Taylor Esquire within this State" (DLC:GW; see also *N.Y. Prov. Congress Journals*, 1:570, and Scott to John McKesson, this date, in Force, *American Archives*, 5th ser., 1:953). GW replied to the convention on 14 Aug.: "I have no Objection to your taking Willet Taylor Esqrs. parole or such other Security as you may esteem Sufficient to prevent him from taking an Unfriendly part agt the United States of America" (LB, in Robert Hanson Harrison's writing, DLC:GW; see also the Varick transcript in DLC:GW).

General Orders

Head Quarters, New York, August 14th 1776
Parole America.   Countersign Liberty.

Alexander Scammell and Lewis Morris Esquires, are appointed Aids-de-Camp to Major General Sullivan; they are to be obeyed and respected accordingly.

The Divisions of the Army, under Major Generals Putnam and Sullivan, having undertaken some special works are to be omitted out of the general detail of Guards and Fatigue for the present.

The General orders three days provision to be cooked immediately, that the Soldiers have their Canteens filled, and be ready to meet the enemy on a short notice.

Such Colonels of Regiments as have not sent for their Ammunition Carts, or drawn for Rum, for the refreshment of their men, in time of action, as pr Order of the 9th Instant, are to do it immediately, and the Quarter Master must take care that it be used properly; the allowance is half a pint pr man.

The Brigadier Generals will please to recollect, that there are a number of spears, at the Laboratory, which will be of great use at the posts, and are waiting to be distributed.

In case of Alarm, the men are immediately to repair to their usual parade, where the Roll is to be called, and then march, join in Battalion, and march to their respective alarm posts— Absentees will be considered as Cowards, and treated as such.

The General flatters himself, that every man's mind and arms, are now prepared for the glorious Contest, upon which so much depends: The time is too precious, nor does the General think it necessary to spend it in exhorting his brave Countrymen and fellow Soldiers to behave like men, fighting for every thing that can be dear to Freemen[1]—We must resolve to conquer, or die; with this resolution and the blessing of Heaven, Victory and Success certainly will attend us: There will then be a glorious Issue to this Campaign, and the General will reward, his brave Fellow Soldiers! with every Indulgence in his power.

The whole Line to turn out to morrow morning and march to their several Alarm posts, in all points ready for action and continue 'till nine o'clock, or further orders.

William Peck and Charles Whiting Esquires, appointed Aids-de-Camp, to Major General Spencer, they are to be respected and obeyed accordingly.[2]

Varick transcript, DLC:GW.

1. "Henshaw's Orderly Book," 217, reads "Yeomen."

2. Charles Whiting (d. 1779) served as adjutant of Col. Samuel Wyllys's 2d Connecticut Regiment from 28 July to 10 Dec. 1775 and as adjutant and a first lieutenant in Wyllys's 22d Continental Regiment from 1 Jan. 1776 to this date. Whiting remained one of General Spencer's aides-de-camp until 14 Feb. 1777, when he became a captain in Col. Samuel Blachley Webb's Additional Continental Regiment.

To James Bowdoin

Sir.   Head-Quarters N. York 14th Augt 1776
Your favor of the 30th Ultimo in behalf of the Honorable Council of the Massachusetts State is duly Received, thro you I beg their Acceptance of most hearty Thanks for their readiness in undertakeing the late Treaty. I likewise congratulate them on

the Success with which it was attended, and wish an early arrival of such of their Tribes as intend Joining Us in the present Controversy, The four under care of Mr Shaw have arrived, and promise to take an Active part with Us, By Intelligence received this morning, from Staten-Island we have the greatest Reason to suppose, a very few days will Determine the fate of this City, a Deserter mentions the Arrival of their whole force, and that it was the Orders of Yesterday to have three days Provisions ready Cooked and be ready at a moments warning—he mentions their numbers to be 26,000—and in General very Healthy,[1] the Army under my command (which amounts to little more than half the number of effective Men) are in good Spirits, and will I hope act becomeing Men fighting for every thing worth liveing for, in this case with the Smiles of Providence I have not a doubt but that we may render a good Account to our Country and Posterity of these Mercenaries. With particular Compliments to the several Members of your Honorable Body, I am Sir with Sentiments of Esteem, Your Most Obedt & Very Hume Servt

Go: Washington

LS (photocopy), in Samuel Blachley Webb's writing, DNA: RG 93, Photocopies of State Records.

1. See the examination of Thomas Givens quoted in note 2 to GW's first letter to Hancock of this date.

To Brigadier General James Clinton

Head Quarters [New York] 14 August 1776. Forwards Clinton's commission as brigadier general in the Continental army.[1] "As the Post you are now at is an Object of great importance, & I am unacquainted with the Officers under you, must request you will remain there, till you hear farther from me."

LS, in Tench Tilghman's writing, CSmH; LB, DLC:GW; Varick transcript, DLC:GW. The cover of the LS is addressed "to The Honble Brigadier General Jas Clinton At Fort Montgomery."

1. Congress made this appointment on 9 Aug. (see *JCC*, 5:641).

From the Continental Congress Secret Committee

Sir　　　　　　　　　　　　　　Philada August 14th 1776

You have annexed an extract of a letter we have just recd from Messrs Clarke & Nightingale Merchts in Providence Rhode Island,[1] this letter was laid before Congress who ordered this Committee to inform your Excellency of the Powder therein mentioned & to desire you woud take possession of it granting a receipt for the same to those who have it in keeping in order that we may Account hereafter for the Value of such part as may be adjudged to the Privateer that retook it. By order & on behalf of the Secret Committee I have the honor to be Your Excellencys Most Obed. Servant

　　　　　　　　　　　　　　Robt Morris, Chair Man

ALS, DLC:GW.

1. The undated extract enclosed with this letter reads: "A few days ago we received intelligence that the sloop Nancy was retaken by the schyler privateer Captain [Charles] Pond and carryed into Fury Inlet Bay on Long Island, we therefore dispatched Captain [Peleg] Potter immediately to make inquiry whether the report was true, he has returned and confirms it and further says She was in possession of the enemy but 5 or 6 days and that she is pillaged of almost every thing; out of All the Arms she had, there is but three Muskets and fifteen pair of Pistols left, they have got two Cutlasses and the 4 swivels on board the privateer—seventy One Cags powder and One Cag salt petre they have Stored in Huntington, also one large Case of Linens Cotton stockings and two or three pieces Cambrick, the Case of Flints Containing 10M are sent forward to New York to his Excellency General Washington, One half Cask powder cont[ainin]g 50 Wt they have put into store at the south side of Long Island—this is all that remains of the Cargo" (DLC:GW).

To Major General Horatio Gates

Dear Sir　　　　　　　　　　New York Augt 14th 1776

I yesterday morning received your Letter of the 29 Ulto by Bennet the Express and am extremely sorry to find the Army is still in a sickly and melancholy State—The precaution taken to Halt the Reinforcements at Skenesborough, which are destined for your Succour, is certainly prudent—they should not be exposed or made liable to the Calamities already too prevailing, Unless in cases of extreme necessity. Doctor Stringer has been here with Doctr Morgan and is now at Philadelphia. I trust he will Obtain some necessary Supplies of Medicine which will enable him under the Smiles of providence, to releive your distresses in some degree.

By a Letter from Genl Ward Two Regiments, (Whitcomb & Phinneys) were to March to your aid last Week[1]—They have happily had the Small pox and will not be subject to the fatal consequences attending that disorder.

I am glad to hear the Vessels for the Lakes are going on with such Industry, Maintaing the Superiority over the Water is certainly of Infinite Importance. I trust, neither Courage nor Activity will be wanting in those to whom the business is committed—If assigned to Genl Arnold, None will doubt of his Exertions.

In Answer to those parts of your letter which so highly resent the conduct of the General Officers here, I would Observe Sir, that you are under a Mistake when you suppose a Council of Officers had sat upon those, who composed the Board at Crown point—When Intelligence was first brought that, that post was evacuated, It spread a Genl alarm and occasioned much anxiety to all who heard It, It being almost universally beleived, that It was a post of the last Importance, and the only One, to give us in conjunction with our Naval force, a Superiority over the Lake and for preventing the Enemy penetrating into this and the Eastern Governments. As this matter was occasionally mentioned—The Genl Officers, some from their own knowledge, & Others from the Opinion they had formed—expressed themselves to that effect as did All I heard speak upon the Subject—Added to this the Remonstrance of the Officers transmitted by Genl Schuyler at the same time the Account was brought, did not contribute a little to authorize the Opinion which was generally entertained—they surely seemed to have some reason for their support, tho It was not meant to give the least encouragement or Sanction to proceedings of such a nature—Upon the whole no Event that I have been Informed of for a long time produced a more general chagrine & consternation—But yet there was no Council called upon the occasion—nor Court of Inquiry—nor Court Martial, as has been Suggested by some. I will not take up more time upon the Subject or make It a matter of further discussion, not doubting but those who determined that the post ought to be Abandoned, conceived It would but promote the Interest of the Great cause we are engaged in, tho Others have differed from them. By the by I wish your description perfectly corresponded with the real circumstances of this Army.

You will have heard before this comes to hand most probably, of the Arrival of Clinton and his Army from the Southward—they are now at Staten Island as are the Whole or the Greatest part of the Hessian & foreign Troops—since Monday Ninety Six Ships came in, which we are Informed is the last division of Lord Howes fleet which touched at Hallifax & by a Deserter, are not to land their Troops—We are in daily expectation that they will make their Attack, All their Movements and the advices we have, Indicating that they are on the point of It. I am Dear Sir Your Most Obedt Servt

Go: Washington

LS, in Robert Hanson Harrison's writing, NHi: Gates Papers; LB, DLC:GW; Varick transcript, DLC:GW.

1. See Artemas Ward to GW, 4 August.

To John Hancock

Sir   New York August 14th 1776

Since I had the honor of addressing you on Monday[1] Nothing of Importance has Occurred here, Except that the Enemy have received an Augmentation to their Fleet of Ninety Six Ships—some Reports make them more: In a Letter I wrote you Yesterday by Lieutt Colo. Reed, I advised you of this, but presuming It may not reach you so soon as this will, I have thought proper to mention the Intelligence again.

Inclosed I have the honor to transmit a Copy of the examination of a Deserter, sent me this morning by Genl Mercer, to which I beg leave to refer Congress for the latest accounts I have from the Enemy. Whether the Intelligence he has given is litterally true, I cannot determine, but as to the Attack we daily expect It.[2]

Your favor of the 10th with Its Inclosures was duly received, and I have Instructed the Several Officers who were promoted, to Act in their Stations as you requested, though their Commissions were not sent.[3]

As we are in extreme want of Tents and Covering for this Army—A Great part of them at Out posts, having nothing to Shelter them—nor Houses to go in, I submit It to Congress, Whether It may not be prudent to remand those that were sent to Boston lately where there are no Troops at present, and If there were, the Necessity for them would not be great, as the Town and Barracks at Several of the posts would be sufficient to receive them.[4]

The Inclosed Letter from Lieutt Colo. Henshaw will discover to Congress his Views and wishes, of which they will consider and determine on, in what ever way they think right and conducive to the public Good—meaning only to lay his Letter before them.[5]

I take the liberty of mentioning that Colo. Varnum of Rhode Island has been with me this Morning to resign his Commission, conceiving himself to be greatly Injured in not having been Noticed in the late Arrangement, & promotions, of Genl Officers. I remonstrated against the Impropriety of the measure at this Time and he has consented to stay till Affairs wear a different Aspect than what they do at present.[6]

11 OClock By a Report Just come to hand from Genl Greene, Twenty Ships more are coming in. I have the Honor to be with Sentiments of the highest respect Sir Yr Most Obedt Servt

Go: Washington

LS, in Robert Hanson Harrison's writing, DNA:PCC, item 152; LB, DLC:GW; copy, DNA:PCC, item 169; Varick transcript, DLC:GW. Congress read this letter on 15 Aug. and the next day referred it to the Board of War (*JCC*, 5:659, 661).

1. See GW to Hancock, 12 August.

2. Thomas Givens, "a Private of the 64 Regt who deserted from Staten Island by Swimming over to Amboy. August 13th 76 at 9 OClock," says in the enclosed document "that all the Troops expected are arrived, That about five hundred Hessians and Six marching Regts arrived yesterday, which having been refreshed at Hallifax are not to be landed at Staten Island but to continue on Board till the Attack be made—That tis supposed the whole force consists of about 26,000 Men—That he heard of no Intention of Attacking Amboy—but that They expected soon to Attack Long Island & New York That three Brigades are to stay on the Island, when the Attack at New York and Long Island be made, [(]Viz.) one opposite Amboy, another at the narrows—and

the third at Elizb. Town point—That the Soldiers are healthy but have no fresh provisions That there were about 9000 effective Men when they left Boston and that 3000 unfit for duty were left behind at Halifax. . . . That Genl Clinton and the Troops from Corolina had arrived & that the 50th Regt were almost cut off at Sullivans Island—That it is in the orders of this day (13th) that the Men be immediately furnished with three days provision ready Cooked and be ready at a Moments warning—That they have Gondlos [that] carry two Guns and 30 Oars each and are designed to Cover the Men when they Land" (DNA:PCC, item 152; see also the slightly different version of Givens's examination in DLC:GW).

GW soon received similar intelligence from another British soldier, John Hammond of the 27th Regiment, who deserted from Staten Island at 8:00 P.M. on 13 August. Hammond says in his examination of this date that he "left the Army preparing to leave the Island—the Battalion Men are all on Board only the Grenadiers & Light Infantry left on the Island The Ships are to be sent up against the Town—thinks all the troops will be landed on Long Island—that they hope to cut us off from the Woods—their Number supposed 25000— ours they think 3 to one—that they mean to land their Men under Cover of Gondolas which have 6 Pounders in them & are built high to cover the Landing—Troops in pretty good Health—no fresh Meat—Hessians are ordinary Troops old & small. They had Orders on Monday [12 Aug.] to cook Provisin for 3 Days on Board the Ships" (DLC:GW).

3. These commissions were enclosed with Hancock's letter to GW of 17 August.

4. For Congress's orders directing the sending of these tents to Massachusetts, see Hancock to GW, 25 June, and GW to Hancock, 27 June (first letter), and note 5.

5. See William Henshaw to GW, 6 July. Congress did not grant Henshaw's wish to be promoted to colonel.

6. Varnum again threatened to resign on 25 Aug. when he wrote GW: "Ever since I waited upon your Excellency; the Expectotion of a Battle hath continued me in my present Command. New Difficulties arising, I can derive no Satisfaction from that Quarter. A Letter from Mr [William] Ellery, enclosed, convinces me that Promotions in the Army are not designed for those, whose Principles are disinterested enough to serve the Continent without. My Disgrace is unalterable fix'd, by confering the 'Detur Digniori' upon those of inferior Standing, without the least Competition of superior Merit. Was Promotion in the Army a Favor, my Tongue and my Pen should be silent: But it is the Just Reward of Merit and Rank. I do not esteem myself obligated to the Public for the Commission I hold, nor for the Greatness of the Pay annexed to it. They can challenge no farther Services from me, whose every Efforts to deserve their good Opinion have been discountenanced. My Continuance here can be of no possible Advantage. The Variety of Incidents that may happen in an Engagement will possible demand my Submission to the Orders of a Brigadier General whose standing 'till lately, hath been subordinate to mine. Disobedience, at a Critical Moment, may loose a Victory which is courting our Embrace. My Pride, is too great ever to bend to Reasons of Policy to the wounding of

my Honor. How cruel the Alternative, to be obliged either to submit to my own Infamy; or, by refusing, incur the Penalties of Death!" (LS, DLC:GW). Ellery's letter has not been identified. Varnum became a brigadier general in February 1777 and remained in the army until March 1779. For additional information about Varnum's rank, see Daniel Hitchcock to GW, 19 Aug. 1776, in CD-ROM:GW.

To John Hancock

Sir   New York Augt 14th 1776
This will be delivered you by Captn Moeballe, a Dutch Gentleman from Surinam, who has come to the Continent with a view of Entering into the Service of the States, as you will perceive by the Inclosed Letters from Mr Brown of Providence and General Greene.[1] What other Letters & Credentials he has, I know not, but at his request have given this Line to Congress to whom he wishes to be Introduced, and where he will make his pretensions known.

I have ordered the Quarter master immediately to write to Mr Brown for the Russia Duck he mentions, with directions to have It Instantly made into Tents there, being in great distress for want of a Sufficient number to cover our Troops.[2] I have the Honor to be Sir Your Most Obedt Servt

Go: Washington

LS, in Robert Hanson Harrison's writing, DNA:PCC, item 152; LB, DLC:GW; copy, DNA:PCC, item 169; Varick transcript, DLC:GW. Congress read this letter on 19 Aug. and referred it to the Board of War (*JCC*, 5:667).

1. These letters have not been identified. Nicholas George Moeballe resigned as a captain in the Dutch service in Surinam on 10 July 1776 and came to America hoping to become a field officer in the Continental army. Congress refused to give him such an appointment apparently because he did not understand English very well. At Moeballe's request the delegates on 6 June 1777 approved a certificate stating "that it was not owing to any fault or bad conduct in him, that Congress did not think it expedient to employ him" (*JCC*, 8:423; see also Moeballe to Congress, 5 June 1777, DNA:PCC, item 42). Moeballe received pay as a captain from the state of Virginia in May 1778 and as a colonel in December 1778 (Gwathmey, *Historical Register*, 556). By 1780 he was living in Holland (see Moeballe to the president of Congress, 19 April 1780, DNA:PCC, item 78).

2. Q.M. Gen. Stephen Moylan wrote Hancock from New York on 6 Sept.: "I am informed that there remains in the hands of Thomas Greene Esqr. of Providence a quantity of Russia Duck, which is ordered by the secret Committee to Lay till farther orders from them, we are here in great want of tents, if

Sir you woud procure an order from Said Committee to have the Duck made up into Tents & forwarded to me, it will be of the greatest service to the army" (DNA:PCC, item 78). Unknown to Moylan, Congress had approved such an order on 30 Aug. (*JCC*, 5:718).

Letter not found: to Brig. Gen. Hugh Mercer, 14 Aug. 1776. In a letter to GW of 15 Aug., Mercer refers to "your Letters of 13 & 14."

From a Secret Committee of the New York Convention

Sir.   Poughkeepsie [N.Y.] Augt 14th 1776.

As we are informed that the little powder belonging to this State is dispersed thro' the Counties for the use of the Militia, we find ourselves under the necessity of requesting an order from your Excellency to Capt. Benson on Mr John R. Livingston for as much powder as may be necessary for our two armed vessels. We have directed him to procure a proper number of hand Granades—there is reason to expect he may be able to purchase them—should he fail in this and the public Stores admit of such a supply we also beg of your Excellency to give him the necessary orders for that purpose. We have the honor to be with the greatest respect and Esteem, Your Excellencys most Obt & hue Sert

By order of the Committee
Robert Yates Chairman

LS, DLC:GW. For GW's reply to this letter, see his letter to Robert Yates of 17 August.

Letter not found: from Lund Washington, 14 Aug. 1776. On 26 Aug. GW wrote Lund Washington: "Your Letter of the 14th is now before me."

General Orders

Head Quarters, New York, August 15th 1776.
Parole Charlestown.   Countersign Boston.

William S: Smith Esqr: appointed to act as Aide-de-Camp to General Sullivan, during the absence of Major Scammell, and to be obeyed and respected accordingly.[1]

Henry Williams of Capt: Parks Company, Colonel Shepard's Regiment convicted by a General Court-Martial whereof Col. Wyllys was President of "Desertion"—sentenced to receive thirty-nine Lashes.

The General approves it, and orders it to be executed at the usual time and place.

Lieut: Holcomb of Capt: Anderson's Company, and Col. Johnson's Regiment, tried by the same Court Martial for "assuming the rank of a Captain, wearing a yellow Cockade, and mounting Guard in that capacity"—it appearing to be done thro' misinformation and want of experience, the Court are of opinion, he should be cautioned by his Colonel, to make himself acquainted with his duty, and that he be released from his arrest.

The General approves thereof and orders that he be discharged.

Mr William Caldwell is appointed Pay Master to Colo. Baldwins Regiment.[2]

Mr John Laurence to the regiment late McDougalls.[3]

The General directs and requests that every officer will see the mens Arms and Ammunition put in order as soon as it clears up;[4] and for that purpose have them paraded and carefully inspected. An enemy often presumes upon neglect at such time, to make an attack.

Mr Robert Prevost Junr appointed Pay Master to Col. Ritzema's regiment.[5]

Col. Glover's regiment to move to morrow to Greenwich, and join General Fellow's Brigade.

General Putnam's Division, to be put into the General detail of duty as before.

Capt: James Chapman to do duty of Major to Col. Tyler's Regiment (late General Parsons's) 'till further orders.

Capt: James Mellen to do the same in Colonel Ward's regiment.[6]

Capt: Thomas Dyer to do the duty of Brigade Major to Genl Parsons's brigade, 'till further orders.

Varick transcript, DLC:GW.

1. William Stephens Smith (1755–1816), a native New Yorker who had been studying law in the city, escaped being captured with Sullivan during the Battle of Long Island twelve days later. Wounded at Harlem Heights on 16 Sept., Smith recovered in time to help delay the British advance toward White Plains in October and to fight at Trenton in December. In January 1777 Smith became lieutenant colonel of Col. William Raymond Lee's Additional Continental Regiment, and in April 1779 he transferred to Col. Oliver Spencer's Additional Regiment. GW appointed Smith inspector and deputy adjutant general of Lafayette's light infantry division on 5 Aug. 1780, and on 6 July 1781 GW named Smith one of his aides-de-camp (see General Orders for those dates). Smith left GW in June 1782 to seek a command on a proposed expedition in the West Indies (see Smith and Matthew Clarkson to GW and GW's certificate of Smith's services, both 24 June 1782, DLC:GW). The expedition was canceled, and in September Smith returned to GW's headquarters to become commissary of prisoners, a position that he held for the remainder of the war (see GW to Smith, 7 Sept. 1782, DLC:GW). From 1785 to 1788 Smith was secretary to the American legation in London. GW appointed Smith federal marshal for New York in 1789, and in 1791 GW made him supervisor of the revenue for the district of New York.

2. William Caldwell of Massachussetts served as paymaster of Col. Loammi Baldwin's 26th Continental Regiment until 31 Dec. 1776.

3. McDougall recommended Laurance for this position in a letter to GW of 9 Aug., saying that Laurance previously had taken "some trouble with the Papers respecting the Payment of my Regiment" (DLC:GW). In response to GW's unfound reply of that date, McDougall wrote GW on 12 Aug. enclosing a recommendation of Laurance, dated 9 Aug., that is signed by the field officers of the 1st New York Regiment "and all the Captains then in Camp" (DLC:GW). John Laurance (Lawrence; 1750–1810), a New York City attorney who emigrated from England in 1767, was McDougall's son-in-law. Commissioned a second lieutenant in the 4th New York Regiment on 1 Aug. 1775, Laurance apparently participated in the Canadian campaign during the following fall and winter. He served as paymaster of the 1st New York Regiment until 21 Nov. 1776 when the state line was rearranged, and on 13 Jan. 1777 he became paymaster of Col. Henry Beekman Livingston's 4th New York Regiment (see Livingston to the New York Committee of Arrangement, 26 Nov. 1776, in Force, *American Archives*, 5th ser., 3:857–58, and O'Callaghan and Fernow, *N.Y. Documents*, 15:209). GW appointed Laurance judge advocate general of the Continental army on 10 April 1777 (see General Orders, that date), and he held that office until 3 June 1782, when Congress accepted his resignation (see *JCC*, 22:314, and Laurance to GW, 16 May 1782, DLC:GW). Laurance was a delegate to the Continental Congress from 1785 to 1787, a member of the U.S. House of Representatives from 1789 to 1793, a federal judge from 1794 to 1796, and a U.S. senator from 1796 to 1800.

4. Ens. Caleb Clap says in his diary that on 14 Aug., "at Evening the most Rain has fallen that we have had this three or four Months" (Clap, "Diary," 250).

5. Robert Provost, Jr. (Prevost; 1737–1796), who previously had been quartermaster of Col. Rudolphus Ritzema's 3d New York Regiment, was recommended by Ritzema and the other field officers of the regiment in a letter to GW of 12 Aug. "as a proper Person for a Regimental Paymaster, he also being a fair Writer and a good Accomptant" (DLC:GW). Provost became paymaster of the 2d New York on 13 Jan. 1777 and served until 1 Jan. 1781.

6. James Mellen (Millen; c.1733–1812), who had been a captain in Col. Jonathan Ward's Massachusetts regiment during 1775, continued serving as a captain in Ward's 21st Continental Regiment after 1 Jan. 1776. Mellen was named acting major on this date in place of Josiah Fay who had died on 8 August. Congress confirmed Mellen's promotion on 25 Sept. (see *JCC*, 5:824), and on 1 Nov. 1776 he became lieutenant colonel of the 9th Massachusetts Regiment. Mellen moved to the 4th Massachusetts Regiment on 1 Jan. 1781, and on 17 Jan. 1783 GW made him lieutenant colonel commandant of the 3d Massachusetts Regiment (see General Orders, that date). Mellen left the army in June 1783.

From Major General Nathanael Greene

Sir   Long Island Augt 15th 1776

It having appeared in Orders that Colo: Hitchcocks's Regiment is to take Possession of the Post opposite to Fort Washington[1] I beg leave to acquaint you that their peculiar Attachment to the old regiments that are here, their thorough Knowledge of the Ground, their Discipline and the good Order in which they are respecting Arms makes me desirous of their remaining here, if it can possibly be dispenced with and absolute Necessity does not require their removal—The most of the Troops that come over here are strangers to the Ground, Undisciplined and badly furnish'd with Arms—They will not be so apt to support each other in Time of Action as those who have long been acquainted, and who are not only attached to each other but to the Place—I have made this Application in Consequence of my own Observations and to evince the Propriety of it send you inclosed the Arrangement for your Inspection[2]—Colo: Hand about Eight OClock yesterday Evening reported that the Hessians were landing on Staten Island to a considerable Number; that after their Landing they paraded upon the Beach and marched up the Hill towards the Flag staf—I have received no

report from him this Morning owning as I suppose to the Inclemency of the Weather, should he not send one speedily I shall
dispatch an Express to inquire the Cause—I have made Choice
of Mr William Blodget and Major William Livingston for my Aid
de Camps should it meet with your Approbation you will please
to signify it [in] Orders[3]—I have the Pleasure to inform you that
the Troops appear to be in exceeding good Spirits and make no
Doubt that if they should make their Attack here we shall be
able to render a very good Account of them—I am carrying into
Execution the late resolve of Congress respecting the removal of
the Cattle dismantling of the Mills, removing the Grain already
thrashed and having that which is still in Sheaf so stacked and
disposed of that in Case of an Attack it may easily be destroyed[4]—The Militia of the County that was ordered here have
not as yet made their Appearance notwithstanding the Promise
I received from the Lieut. Colo: that they should be here last
Night—should they delay coming in any longer than[5] this Day
I am determined not to be trifled with and shall let them feel
my Resentment by vigorous and spirited Exertions of Military
Discipline and those Powers with which I am invested—A Part
of the Militia from the East End of the Island under the Command of Colo: Smith are arrived[6]—I am very sorry that I am
under the Necessity of acquainting you that I am confined to
my Bed with a raging Fever—The Critical Situation of Affairs
makes me the more anxious but I hope thro' the Assistance of
Providence to be able to ride before the Presence of the Enemy
may make it absolutely necessary.[7] I am with respect your Most
Obedt hume Servt

Nathanael Greene

LS, DLC:GW.

1. See General Orders, 12 August.

2. This enclosure has not been identified. Greene's arguments did not dis-
suade GW from moving Hitchcock's regiment (see General Orders, 19 Aug.).

3. GW announced these appointments in the General Orders of the next
day.

4. For the New York convention's resolutions of 20 July regarding the livestock on Long Island, see Nathaniel Woodhull to GW, that date, and note 1.

5. William Smith Livingston, to whom Greene dictated this letter, inadvertently wrote "that" on the manuscript.

6. Josiah Smith (1723–1786) of Moriches Neck, Long Island, was commissioned colonel of a regiment of minutemen in January 1776 by the Suffolk

County committee of safety (see William Smith to the New York Provincial Congress, 24 Jan. 1776, in *N.Y. Prov. Congress Journals*, 1:284). On 20 July the state convention named Smith colonel of a regiment of Long Island militia levies raised to protect the island's livestock, and on 8 Aug. it put his regiment under Greene's command (see ibid., 534, 563–64). Smith's regiment dispersed after the Battle of Long Island and did not reassemble (see ibid., 605, and George Clinton to Henry Beekman Livingston, 5 Oct. 1776, in Hastings, *Clinton Papers*, 1:370).

7. Greene's worsening condition over the next several days obliged GW on 20 Aug. to replace him as commander on Long Island with John Sullivan (see General Orders, that date). Dangerously ill and confined to bed for almost two weeks, Greene missed the Battle of Long Island on 27 Aug. and did not resume his duties fully until sometime in the first week of September.

To John Hancock

Sir   New York Augt 15th 1776

As the situation of the Two Armies must engage the attention of Congress and lead them to expect, that, each returning day will produce some Important Events, This is meant to Inform them that Nothing of Moment has yet cast up. In the Evening of Yesterday there were great movements among their Boats and from the Number that appeared to be passing and repassing about the Narrows, we were Induced to beleive they Intended to land a part of their force upon Long Island, but having no report from Genl Greene, I presume they have not done It. I have the Honor to be with my duties to Congress yr & their most Obedt Servt

Go: Washington

P.S. Your favor of the 13th was received by Yesterdays post—I wrote on Monday by the Return Express as you Supposed.[1]

LS, in Robert Hanson Harrison's writing, DNA:PCC, item 152; LB, DLC:GW; copy, DNA:PCC, item 169; Varick transcript, DLC:GW. Congress read this letter on 16 Aug. (*JCC*, 5:660).

1. See GW's two letters to Hancock of 12 August.

Letter not found: to Walter Livingston, 15 Aug. 1776. Livingston's letter to GW of 7–9 Aug. is docketed "An[swere]d 15. 1776."

From Brigadier General Hugh Mercer

Sir,   Powlis Hook [N.J.] 15 Augt 1776
I was att Eliza. Town when your Letters of the 13 & 14 reached me[1]—The Men who had been prepared to join the Army at N. York lay at New ark—The Posts along the Jersey Shore opposite to Staten Island are sufficiently Guarded—and more Troops are dayly arriving—If you approve of it a Body of four hundred men well accoutred from the Delaware Country may be stationed at Powlis Hook & five hundred of the Jersey men for the Flying Camp at Bergen Town besides what we may Spare to be ready in case of emergency att New ark—Eight Hundred Men will cross to day to join you—if more are necessary please to inform me—I shall be to Night at New ark. I have the honour to be Sir Your excellencys most obed. Sert
                                                        H. Mercer

ALS, DLC:GW.
    1. These letters have not been found.

From Brigadier General Daniel Roberdeau

Sir,   Amboy [N.J.] Augt 15th 1776
In the absence of General Mercer, he being on duty at Elizabeth Town or its neighbourhood, I just now received from one of our posts at South Amboy, two prisoners escaped from the English Fleet—They are inhabitants of Philadelphia and well known to many of us from thence. Their Examination which I forward enclosed may be depended on according to their knowledge.[1] I am Sir Yr most obt hume Serv:
                                                        Danl Roberdeau

LS, PHi: Dreer Collection; copy, enclosed in GW to Hancock, 17 Aug., DNA:PCC, item 152; copy, DNA:PCC, item 169; Sprague transcript, DLC:GW.
    1. The enclosed examinations of Capt. Alexander Hunter and Isaac Farrier are in DNA:PCC, item 152. Nearly identical copies of both documents are in DLC:GW. Hunter, who escaped on 14 Aug. from the *Rockingham*, a transport carrying Hessian soldiers, "informs that he was taken off the Capes of Virginia by a Vessel of Lord Dunmore's on the 8th February 1776. That he was sent to England and put on Board the Rockingham which left St Helens 26 May in Company with the Hessian Fleet. He arrived at the Narrows on Monday last [12 Aug.], and pretending to be a pilot was allowed to go in a small Boat

towards the Hook by which means he escaped. That about 8000 Hessians are arrived and five Thousand more Hessians are expected in a few Weeks—that the whole Force is supposed to be about 26 or 27000. That Lord Dunmore arrived Yesterday, brought but few Men. That the Hessians which arrived on Monday are to land on the Island to refresh and the English were to embark on Board to make room for them, and this he was informed of by a Capt. of the Hessian Fleet. That it is expected an Attack will be made in Eight or Ten days and not before. That it is beleived in the Fleet that General Washington is weak and has not above 15000 Men in New York and Long Island. That he beleives they have no Gallies or Floating Batteries, that they have about Seven two decked Ships and about thirteen of lighter Metal" (DNA:PCC, item 152).

Farrier, a pilot from Philadelphia, who was taken prisoner by the British warship *Viper* on 10 Dec. 1775, says "that on the 17th April he was put on Board the Admirals Ship at Hallifax and continued on Board till he made his Escape. He confirms the Account of Capt. Hunter as to the Number of the Enemy. That it was beleived in the Fleet that General Washington intended making his Stand at New York and was evacuating Long Island. That there is a great deal of Confidence of Success in the Fleet—That the Scotch Troops are extremely incensed agt us and frequently say they will give no Quarter— That it is expected that Burgoyne will in a few days be in the Rear of New York and ready to make a Juncture whenever the Troops land. That he is certain 5000 more Hessians are expected, but he beleives the General will not wait their Arrival before the Attack. That the Brune Frigate and the Centurion of 50 Guns were to go up the North River and that it is a principal Object with them to cut off the Communication between the City of N. York and the Country" (DNA:PCC, item 152).

General Orders

Head Quarters, New York, August 16th 1776
Parole Enfield. Countersign Danvers.

In recommending Pay Masters it is to be observed that no officer can be appointed unless he resigns his former Commission, which he is to do in person at Head Quarters.

Major Livingston, and William Blodget, are appointed Aids-du-Camp to Major General Greene—they are to be obeyed and respected accordingly.

David Astin of Col. Sillimans Regiment and Captain Meads Company,[1] convicted by a General Court-Martial, whereof Col. Wyllys was President of "breaking open a store and stealing Rum, Molasses & Fish,["] sentenced to receive thirty-nine lashes.

John McAlpine & John Hopper of Capt: Smith's Company,[2] Col. Malcom's Regiment convicted by the same Court Martial of "being drunk on their posts"—sentenced to receive thirty lashes each—The General approves the above sentences, and orders them to be put in execution at the usual times and places.

The Orders of the 6th Instant respecting Soldiers abusing people at market, and taking their things, not being known to the troops who have come in since; it is now repeated that the General will punish such offenders severely: And He requires of the officers, who visit the Guards, to see whether the former Order is put up in each guard house, and whether an officer attends at the market agreeable to former orders, & report thereon to their Brigadiers.

Capt: Andrew Billinjo's to do duty as Major to Col. Ritzema's Regiment, 'till further orders.[3]

Unless orders are attended to, and executed, they are of no consequence, and the greatest disorders will insue, the General therefore requests, that the officers would be very careful, not only that the orders be made known to the men, but that they see themselves that they are executed—If every one in his own department would exert himself for this purpose, it would have the most happy effect.

The badness of the weather has undoubtedly prevented an attack, as the enemies troops have been embarked some time, The General therefore directs, that two days Victuals be kept ready dressed by the troops, and their Canteens filled with water; so that the men may be prepared; otherwise in case of an attack they will suffer very much.

All Tents to be struck immediately, on the Alarm being given—viz.: Two Guns at Fort George, Three from Bayards, or Bunker-hill, with a Flag in the day, and a Light at night.

The Divisions of the Army, or Brigades doing seperate duty proving very inconvenient, the whole are to be brought into the General Detail to morrow: The Brigade Majors are to be at Head Quarters, at six o'clock, to settle the detail; and the Major & Brigadier Generals are requested to send, at the same time, a note of the number of men each may want for fatigue, or direct the Engineer having the care of their Works respectively, so to do.

Varick transcript, DLC:GW.

1. Abraham Mead, Jr. (1742–1827), a potter from Greenwich, Conn., was commissioned a captain in the 9th Regiment of Connecticut militia in May

1774, and in June 1776 he was named a captain in Col. Gold Selleck Silliman's regiment of militia levies that reinforced the Continental army at New York. Mead remained on active duty with his company until January 1777 and participated in the major battles of the New York campaign. He became a member of the Greenwich committee of safety on 8 Dec. 1777 and served in that capacity until the end of the war (see Mead, *Historie of Greenwich*, 153–55).

2. Robert Smith (1752–1838), who previously had been a captain in Col. William Malcom's New York City militia regiment, served as a captain in Malcom's regiment of provincial levies from June to late October when he was wounded at the Battle of White Plains. In the spring of 1777 Smith was commissioned a captain in Malcom's Additional Continental Regiment, and on 28 May 1778 Congress appointed him secretary to the Board of War (*JCC,* 11:546). Unwilling to give up his commission, Smith declined to accept that office and remained in the army (see Smith to Henry Laurens, 1, 13 June 1778, DNA:PCC, item 78). He was wounded at the Battle of Monmouth on 28 June 1778, and on 19 Nov. 1778, seeing little prospect that his regiment would take the field again, he submitted his resignation to GW (see Smith to GW, 19 Nov., 5 Dec. 1778, DNA: RG 93, manuscript file nos. 20178, 18279).

3. Andrew Billings (1743–1808), a silversmith from Poughkeepsie, raised a company in Dutchess County in June and July 1775 and served the ensuing campaign as a captain in Col. James Clinton's 3d New York Regiment (see *N.Y. Prov. Congress Journals*, 1:75, 86). During the winter of 1776 Billings raised another company for Continental service, and on 12 April 1776 he and his men were assigned to Col. Rudolphus Ritzema's newly created 3d New York Regiment (see ibid., 297, 308, 392, 405). As the senior captain in Ritzema's regiment, Billings performed the duties of regimental major for several months before his appointment of this date (see Stirling's recommendations for filling vacancies, 22 July 1776, DNA:PCC, item 58). Billings apparently left the army at the end of 1776. In January 1783 GW paid Billings forty guineas for engraving short inscriptions on two cannon that were presented to Rochambeau (see GW to Billings and to Robert Morris, both 22 Jan. 1783, DLC:GW, and *JCC*, 21:1081).

Letter not found: from Benjamin Franklin, 16 Aug. 1776. On 18 Aug. GW wrote to Franklin: "I have been honourd with your favour of the 16th."

To Elbridge Gerry

Dear Sir,   New York Augt 16th 1776.

Your favours of the 3d & 6th have come duly to hand,[1] and Mr Adams's return affords me an oppertunity of acknowledging the receipt of them, & thanking you for the attention paid to the several matters I took the liberty of mentioning as you passed this place.[2]

The Enemy have given us much time to collect our Strength, and erect the necessary Works of Defence—The Militia from Connecticut are coming in fast, and we have received aid from Phila. & that Provence, notwithstanding which if Accts be true the Enemy will out number Us in this Quarter—Our Troops are very sickly but those which are in health are in high Spirits & not at all backward in making the Appeal.

The Flints you were obliging enough to procure (I am told) are arrived—so are the Micmack Indians sent by yr Honble Council. In haste I am Dr Sir Yr Most Obedt Servt

Go: Washington

ALS (photocopy), DLC:GW. The ALS was owned in 1954 by Mr. Herman Warner Williams, director of the Corcoran Gallery of Art. GW addressed the cover to "The Honble Eld. Gerry Esqr. Water Town. Favour'd by the Hon. S. Adams Esq."

1. These letters have not been found.

2. Gerry stopped at New York 18–22 July while traveling home to Massachusetts from Philadelphia, where he was serving in Congress. Gerry's fellow delegate, Samuel Adams, left Philadelphia for Boston on 12 Aug. and reached New York two days later. On this date Sam Adams wrote John Adams from New York that he "found the General [GW] and his family in Health and spirits. Indeed every Officer and Soldier appears to be determin'd. I have not had Opportunity to view the Works here, but I am told they are strong and will be well defended whenever an Attack is made which is expected daily. I see now more than I ever did the Importance of Congress attending immediately to Inlisiments for the next Campaign. It would be a pity to lose your old Soldiers. I am of Opinion that a more generous Bounty should be given. 20 Dollars and 100 Acres of Land for three years [service] at least" (Taylor, *Papers of John Adams*, 4:467–69). Samuel Adams arrived at Boston on 28 August. By that time Gerry apparently had left Massachusetts for Philadelphia where he arrived on 3 Sept. (see John Adams to Abigail Adams, 4 Sept. 1776, in Butterfield, *Adams Family Correspondence*, 2:117–18).

To John Hancock

Sir   New York Augt 16th 1776

I beg leave to inform you that since I had the pleasure of addressing you Yesterday Nothing Interesting between the Two Armies has happened. Things remain nearly in the situation they then were.

It is with peculiar regret and concern that I have an Opportunity of mentioning to Congress the Sickly condition of our

Troops. In some Regiments there are not any of the Field Officers capable of doing duty—In Others the duty extremely difficult for want of a sufficient Number—I have been Obliged to
Nominate some 'till Congress transmit the appointments of
those they wish to succeed to the several Vacancies occasioned by
the late promotions. This being a matter of some consequence I
presume will have their early attention and that they will fill up
the Several Vacancies also mentioned in the List I had the
Honor of transmitting some Few days agoe to the Board of War.[1]
I am Sir with the utmost respect Yr Most Obedt Servt

Go: Washington

LS, in Robert Hanson Harrison's writing, DNA:PCC, item 152; LB, DLC:GW;
copy, DNA:PCC, item 169; Varick transcript, DLC:GW. Congress apparently
read this letter on 19 Aug. (see Hancock to GW, 17 Aug.).

1. See GW to the Board of War, 29 July.

From John Hancock

Philadelphia, 16 August 1776. "I have only time to Acknowledge
the Rect of your Letter of 15th, and to Transmitt the Resolves
pass'd since my last, which you will find Inclos'd."[1]

ALS, DLC:GW.

1. The enclosed resolves of 13, 14, and 15 Aug. include a request that GW
send Congress a copy of the Massachusetts treaty with the St. John's and Mic-
mac Indians, a plan for encouraging Hessians and other foreigners to desert
from the British army, Wuibert's appointment as an assistant engineer, and
orders for Col. James Livingston "to inlist as many companies of Canadians as
are willing to engage in the service" (DLC:GW; see also *JCC*, 5:651, 653–57).

To Frederick Jay

Sir   Head Quarters New York Augt 16th 1776
   In Consequence of my Orders, the undermentioned persons
have been apprehended and are now under a Guard at New
Rochelle or its Neighbourhood.[1] As the sending a Guard thro'
to Govr Trumbull with them would be attended with much
Inconvenience to the public and cannot be agreeable to the
Gentlemen Upon their giving you their Word & Honor to pro-
ceed to Lebanon to Govr Trumbull I am satisfyed to permit

them to go without any other Escort than that of the Officer who will deliver you this. I must beg the favor of you to take the Management of this Business and as soon as it is put upon a proper Footing dismiss the Guard now there. I am with due Respect Sir Yr most obt Servt.

LB, in Tench Tilghman's writing, DLC:GW; Varick transcript, DLC:GW.

Frederick Jay (1747–1799), the younger brother of John Jay, had been an agent in the Dutch East Indies and at Curaçao for a cousin's trading company before setting up his own firm at New York in 1773. Jay became second lieutenant of the "Corsicans" independent militia company in early 1775, and on 14 Sept. 1775 he was commissioned first lieutenant of the "Heart's Oak" company in Col. John Lasher's 1st Regiment of New York Independents (see O'Callaghan and Fernow, *N.Y. Documents*, 8:601–2, and Force, *American Archives*, 4th ser., 3:708). Jay was a member of the New York general assembly from 1777 to 1783. In 1789 he asked GW to name him collector of customs at New York, but GW declined to do so (see Jay to GW, 10 May 1789, in *Papers, Presidential Series*, 2:257–58).

1. The suspected Loyalists named on this list are: "Colo. Philips[,] Jas. Jauncey & his two Sons[,] Joseph Bull[,] Isaac Corsa[,] John Rodgers[,] Ware Branson." Frederick Philipse, Sr. (1720–1786), of Westchester County, a former member of the general assembly and a militia colonel, was paroled by the Connecticut council of safety on 23 Dec. 1776, as were former New York City assemblyman James Jauncey, Sr. (d. 1790), and his sons James and William (see the parole of that date in DNA:PCC, item 67, and Hinman, *Historical Collection*, 400). For efforts to exchange Philipse and James Jauncey, Sr., see GW to William Livingston, 11 May 1777, and GW to the Board of War, 24 Jan. 1778, both in DLC:GW. James Jauncey, Jr. (d. 1777), who had been appointed master of the rolls for the court of chancery in 1774 and a member of the council in 1775, was proposed for exchange with a Pennsylvania officer by the Continental Congress in January 1777, but he died before it could be effected (see *JCC*, 7:52–53, and *N.Y. Prov. Congress Journals*, 1:850–51). Joseph Bull, who apparently was detained because he opposed independence, proved to be a Patriot (see Bull to Henry Remsen, 1 June 1776, in Force, *American Archives*, 4th ser., 6:671–72, and Bull to Nathaniel Woodhull, no date, ibid., 5th ser., 2:109–10). Isaac Corsa (d. 1805 or 1807) of Long Island, a veteran of the French and Indian War, was paroled on 26 Dec. 1776 (see statement of parole, 23–26 Dec. 1776, in DNA:PCC, item 67). "John Rodgers" may be Brig. Gen. Lewis Morris's servant, John Rogers, whom the New York convention on 28 Aug. ordered to be arrested for manifesting "a disposition extremely inimical to the rights and liberties of America." The next day the convention sent Rogers to the Westchester County jail for confinement until further orders (*N.Y. Prov. Congress Journals*, 1:595–96, 600).

From Major William Smith Livingston

Sir   Long Island Augt 16th [1776]

I am desired by General Green to inform your Excellency that Colo: Hand waited upon him this Morning and informed him that the Hessians were landing again Yesterday on the East End of Staten Island to a considerable Number—That there was nothing extraordinary happened—That by the Movements of the Enemy there did not appear any immediate Preparation for an Attack And that three Men of his Regiment last Night Deserted and took with them Six Rifles. I am Your Excellency's Most Obedt Servt

Wm S. Livingston

ALS, DLC:GW.

Greene's other aide-de-camp, William Blodget, wrote GW at 5:00 P.M. on this date: "I am desired to acquaint your Excelly by the General['s] order, that Colonel Hand reports that Thirteen or Fourteen Vessells enterd the Narrows from the Fleet before in New Utrecht Bay—That the Officer of the Ferry Guard says they were all Transports, That their were some Red Coats on board—The Coll says he cou'd not discover many on board those now below—neither have they landed any there to day. That The Camps at the Flaggstaff and Ferry are pretty extensive—he likewise reports That two small vessells of Force went down the Narrows this afternoon" (ALS, DLC:GW).

To the New Jersey Convention

Gentlemen   Head Qrs [New York] Aug. 16. 1776.

I am informed that in consequence of my Letter acquainting you that a number of Persons deemed unfriendly to the Interests of America were suspected of holding a Correspondence with the Enemy from Shrewsbury & its Neighbourhood, Mr Isaac Low late of this City has been apprehended, & is now detained under some kind of Confinement.[1]

Since that time I have received Satisfaction with respect to this Gentleman, who I find has also entered into a Contract with the Congress for the Supply of a great quantity of European Goods—I should therefore be glad that any restraint laid upon him meerly upon my Representation might be removed, & he restored to his former Liberty on such Terms & Conditions as you may think proper if any are necessary.[2] I am with much

Respect & Regard Gentlemen Your most Obed. & Very H'ble
Servt

G.W.

LB, in Tench Tilghman's writing, DLC:GW; Varick transcript, DLC:GW.

1. See GW to Samuel Tucker, 7 August. William Livingston wrote Tucker
on 26 July: "I have authentic Information that some of the most malignant
New York Tories have seated themselves in Shrewsberry; a very improper
place on Account of the facility it affords for keeping up a Communication with
the Enemy. Isaac Lowe, & one Roome are particularly mentioned" (Prince,
Livingston Papers, 1:107–8).

2. The convention complied with this request on 19 Aug. (see Force, *American Archives,* 4th ser., 6:1665). Isaac Low (1735–1791), a New York City merchant who served in the First Continental Congress during 1774 and the New
York provincial congress during 1775, was a political moderate who opposed
independence. Low apparently went to New Jersey after news of the Declaration of Independence reached New York in July, and in September he returned to the British-occupied city, where he lived for the remainder of the
war, serving as president of the chamber of commerce. In 1783 Low moved
to England.

From Major General Philip Schuyler

Dear Sir   Albany August 16th 1776
    About eight last Night I returned to this place after a Month's
Absence; on a Business the most disagreeable to a Man accustomed to Civil Society that can possibly be conceived.

On the 11th Instant, I was honored with your Excellency's
Favor of the 7th, but was unable to answer it from the German
Flatts, altho' I several Times attempted it being ever interrupted
by a Croud of Savages.

Last Evening I received Dispatches from General Gates, Cop-
ies of which I inclose, by which you will percieve that General
Carlton has put it out of our power to have any Intercourse with
him on the Subject Matter contained in the Resolves of the 22d
Ultimo or indeed on any other[1]—With what Degree of Justice
Carlton can bestow the infamous Epithets he has so freely dealt
out in his Orders of the 7th Instant, his barbarous Conduct to
Colonel Allen the infamous Manner in which he engaged the
Savages to act against us last Year; the Murder of the Officers
and Men lately near Isle aux noix in which British Troops were

joined with Savages and other Actions of a like Nature can Witness.[2]

The Works at Fort Stanwix are going on with great Expedition, and by the inclosed Return your Excellency will observe that near eighty Days pork and Flour for the Garrison is in Store there, a considerable Quantity of the latter is on its Way up from Schenectady, and as they had on Monday last twenty three Head of fat Cattle and will receive a constant Supply of fresh Meat, I am under no Apprehensions that the Garrison will be under any Difficulty in the Article of provisions.[3]

The Anchors for the Vessels on Lake Champlain will be procured in this Quarter but we greatly fear to fall short in many of the other Articles, as Capt. Bacon is returned without being able to procure any Thing and not even a Sailor.

Mr Edwards returns this Morning & will engage all the Stockbridge Indians he can, and as you do not direct what pay is to be given we have thought it expedient and as what will best promote the Service and raise these people with the greatest Dispatch, that they should be officered & paid agreeable to the former Resolve of the Commissioners of Indian Affairs and that such as were raised in Consequence of that Resolution should have their pay continued from the Time they were discharged, which is about a Month ago.[4] They shall be disposed of agreeable to your Orders.

Colonels Elmore & Nicholson's Regiments are here they have refused to march until they receive pay and Necessaries—The former they will now have, but where to procure the latter I know not—I will furnish them as well as I can, and keep them here until I receive the Report of two Scouts that are sent one to Oswego, and the other towards Oswegatche.

I shall immediately order Copies of the Transactions of the Commissioners of Indian Affairs at the late Treaty to be made out and transmit them to you—I believe the six Nations will not fall on our Frontiers altho' I believe a few will always join the Enemy in Canada. I have some Matters that concern Officers in the Army to communicate but I am at present too much indisposed to write any more. I am Dr Sir with the greatest Respect Your Excellency's most obedient humble Servant

Ph: Schuyler

P.S. I am just now informed that Lieut. McMichel of Colonel Dayton's Regiment is deserted to the Enemy—I had Information of his Intentions the Evening before I left the German Flatts and sent to have him brought before me but he was supposed to have gone to the Regiment, to which I had ordered him the Day before. Yours &. &. &c.

Ph: Schuyler

ALS, DLC:GW; LB, NN: Schuyler Papers.

1. Schuyler is referring to Congress's resolutions of 22 July empowering departmental commanders to negotiate prisoner exchanges and directing that Ethan Allen and the persons captured with him be exchanged (*JCC*, 5:599; see also GW to Schuyler, 7 Aug.).

The enclosed copies of Gates's letter to Schuyler of 11 Aug. and its enclosures concern the recent attempt by Maj. John Bigelow of the Connecticut independent artillery company to deliver to General Burgoyne copies of Congress's report and resolution of 10 July censuring British treatment of the Americans who surrendered at the Cedars in May (see *JCC*, 5:538–39). The enclosed abstract of Bigelow's journal for 23 July to 10 Aug. is an account of his journey under a flag of truce from Ticonderoga to Île aux Noix, where he encountered a British detachment and was obliged to wait while a British courier carried his dispatch to St. Jean and Quebec (DLC:GW).

Bigelow received no reply from Burgoyne, but he was given a copy of the general order that Gen. Guy Carlton issued at Chambly on 7 Aug., instructing "the Commanding Officers of Corps" to "take special Care, Every one under their Command be informed, that Letters or Messages from Rebels, Traitors in Arms against their King, Rioters, Disturbers of the Public Peace, Plunderers, Robbers, Assassins or Murderers, are on no Occasion to be admitted; that should Emmissaries from such Lawless Men again presume to approach the Army, whether under the Name of Flag of Truce men, or Ambassadors, Except when they come to implore the King's Mercy, their persons shall be immediately seized & Committed to Close Confinement, in order to be proceeded against as the Law directs; their Papers & Letters, for whomsoever Even for the Commander in Chief, are to be delivered to the Provost Marshal that unread & unopened, they may be burned by the Hands of the Common Hangman." Carleton condemns the recent American "Assassination" of Brig. Gen. Patrick Gordon and "the late Notorious Breach of Faith, in resolving not to return the [British] Troops & Canadians taken at St Johns in Exchange for those Rebels who fell into the Hands of the Savages at the Cedars & Quinchen, [and were] purchased from them at a great price & restored to their Country." The blame for such misdeeds, Carleton says, should not "be imputed to the Provincials at large, but to a few wicked & designing Men, who first deceived, then step by Step mislead the Credulous Multitude to the Brink of ruin." Carleton announces that all American prisoners in Canada "who chuse to return home, are to hold themselves in Readiness to embark at a short Notice. . . . They are to look on their respective Provinces as their Prisons & there remain till further Enlarged, or summoned to appear before the Commander in Chief of this Province, or any other Commander in Chief for his Majesty" (DLC:GW). For GW's views on this order, see his letter to Hancock, 20 August.

In his covering letter to Schuyler of 11 Aug., Gates says that Bigelow also brought a letter addressed to "George Washington, *Esqr.*" from Île aux Noix. The resolution of Congress forbidding the receiving of letters so addressed, Gates explains, had not arrived at Ticonderoga before Bigelow departed on his mission (DLC:GW). This letter to GW has not been identified.

2. For the attacks on two American parties near Île aux Noix, see Sullivan to GW, 24 June.

3. The enclosed copy of Henry Glen's provision return for Fort Schuyler, formerly Fort Stanwix, shows that on 13 Aug. there were "180 Barrels of Pork[,] 226 Barrels of Flour & 23 Head Cattle" at the fort (DLC:GW). The previous Monday was 12 August.

4. For the Indian commissioners' resolution of 13 June 1776 regarding the raising of two companies of Stockbridge Indians, see Schuyler to GW, 15 June 1776, n.8. For the discharge of the Stockbridge Indians who had been previously enlisted, see Schuyler to GW, 1 July 1776.

To Jonathan Trumbull, Sr.

Sir　　　　　　　　　　Head Quarters N. York Augt 16th 1776

I have been obliged to trouble you with some more disaffected persons whose residence here was dangerous to the American Interest. I trust I have now done with them, at least for the present, and hope you will excuse the disagreeable necessity I have been under of solliciting your care and attention to provide for them and dispose of them. As the case of these differs in no respect from that of those before I presume they will be put under the same regulations.[1] I am with much respect and regard Your Honor's Most obedient and very humble Servant

　　　　　　　　　　　　　　　　　Go: Washington

LB, Ct: Trumbull Papers; LB, DLC:GW; Varick transcript, DLC:GW.

1. The LB in DLC:GW adds "of those before sent." GW is referring to the regulations given in his letter to Trumbull of 11 August.

From Jonathan Trumbull, Sr.

Sir　　　　　　　　　Lebanon [Conn.] August 16th 1776

Major General Schuyler has requested that two Hundred Seamen may be raised in this state to man the Vessells on the Lake.[1]

as most of our Seamen are marched with the Militia to join your Army, I have to ask the favour of you to permit Capt. David Hawly, and Capt. Frederick Chappel to inlist such Number of Seamen out of our Militia as may be necessary for that Service.[2] I am sir with great Respect Your obedient humble Servant

Jonth. Trumbull

ALS, DLC:GW; LB, Ct: Trumbull Papers. The cover of the ALS includes a note reading "℔ Capt. David Hawly."

1. See Schuyler to Trumbull, 31 July, in Force, *American Archives*, 5th ser., 1:696–97.

2. On 16 Aug. David Hawley (1741–1807) of Stratford and Frederick Chappell (Chapel; c.1746–1789) of New Haven each received £180 from the Connecticut council of safety to raise a crew of seamen for service on the lakes, and both were commissioned captains (Hinman, *Historical Collection*, 380). Hawley, a shipmaster who had traded with the West Indies before the war, went there in 1775 to obtain gunpowder for Connecticut (ibid., 199). On 21 Mar. 1776, while on another trading voyage, his vessel was captured by a British warship in Rhode Island waters. Taken to Halifax, Hawley escaped captivity on 24 April and returned to Connecticut a few weeks later (see the journals of the *Glasgow*, 21 Mar., and the *Rose*, 21–22 Mar., in Clark and Morgan, *Naval Documents*, 4:436, 451, and the *Connecticut Courant, and Hartford Weekly Intelligencer*, 20 May 1776). On 21 Sept. General Arnold appointed Hawley captain of the armed schooner *Royal Savage* on Lake Champlain, and about the same time Frederick Chappell became captain of the row galley *Gates*. The *Royal Savage* was destroyed during the Battle of Valcour Island in October, and the *Gates* was burned at Skenesborough in July 1777 to prevent its capture. Hawley subsequently served as a captain in the Connecticut navy. Given command of the sloop *Schuyler* in April 1777, Hawley took several prizes in Long Island Sound before being captured by a British frigate the following December. Hawley was exchanged by June 1779 when he became captain of the Connecticut sloop *Guilford*. During 1780 and 1781 he commanded a small flotilla of armed boats on Long Island Sound, and in May 1782 he became captain of a Connecticut privateer.

General Orders

Head Quarters, New York, Augt 17th 1776
Parole Falmouth.   Countersign Essex.
Benjamin Durant of Capt: Wadsworth's Company & Col. Bailey's Regiment,[1] convicted by a General Court Martial whereof Col. Wyllys was President, of "getting drunk on Guard," sentenced to receive Thirty Lashes.

Patrick Lion of Capt: Curtis's Company; Regiment late Lear-nad's, convicted by the same Court, of "sleeping on his post"; sentenced to receive Twenty-five lashes.

Benjamin Wallace of Capt: Stewart's, independent Company of New-York Forces convicted by the same Court of "Desertion, and inlisting into another Company," sentenced to receive Thirty-nine lashes.

The General approves the above sentences, and orders them to be executed at the usual time and place.

The General recommends to all commanding officers of divisions, brigades and regiments, in issuing their several orders, to be careful they do not interfere with General Orders, which have been, or may be issued; and those Gentlemen who have not had an opportunity from their late arrival in Camp, to know what have been issued; will do well to inform themselves, and more especially before any special order is issued, which may have a general effect.

The Guard ordered to mount at Lispenard's Brewery, in the evening, to mount in the day also, and march off the parade with the other guards.[2]

Varick transcript, DLC:GW.

1. Although Peleg Wadsworth was commissioned a captain in Col. John Bailey's 23d Continental Regiment on 1 Jan. 1776, he did not accompany the regiment on its recent march from Boston to New York but remained in Boston, where he served as brigade major to the troops there, a position to which Gen. Artemas Ward had appointed him on 22 April (see Artemas Ward to GW, 22 Aug.).

2. GW apparently is referring to the guard that he directed in the General Orders of 26 July to be stationed at Harrison's Brewery on the Hudson River near Leonard Lispenard's house.

Proclamation for the Evacuation of New York

[New York, 17 August 1776]
BY HIS EXCELLENCY GEORGE WASHINGTON, Esquire, General, and Commander in Chief of the Army of the United States of North-America.

WHEREAS a Bombardment and Attack upon the City of New-York, by our cruel, and inveterate Enemy, may be hourly expected: And as there are great Numbers of Women, Children, and infirm Persons, yet remaining in the City, whose Continuance will rather be prejudicial than advantageous to the Army, and their Persons exposed to great Danger and Hazard: I Do therefore recommend it to all such Persons, as they value their own Safety and Preservation, to remove with all Expedition, out of the said Town, at this critical Period,—trusting, that with the Blessing of Heaven, upon the American Arms, they may soon return to it in perfect Security. And I do enjoin and require, all the Officers and Soldiers in the Army, under my Command, to forward and assist such Persons in their Compliance with this Recommendation. GIVEN, under my Hand, at Head-Quarters, New-York, August 17, 1776.

GEORGE WASHINGTON.

Printed broadside, NHi. The imprint at the bottom of the broadside reads: "NEW-YORK—Printed by JOHN HOLT,—in Water-Street." This proclamation was printed in the *Constitutional Gazette* (New York) of 21 August.

From Lord Drummond

Sir   [New York Harbor] August 17th 1776

Being deeply intarested in the welfare of America I think it my Duty to communicate a Matter of Intelligence which I flatter myself may be renderd conducive to the Restoration of a Disirable Peace And in this View I request your Excellency's Permission to land at New York to go to Philadelphia in Order to lay the same before the General Congress.

In the course of a Conversation I have had with Lord Howe I perceive that the powers he is vested with as well as his Disposition for establishing an Equitable and permament Peace are Altogether misunderstood by the Colonies—For in Consequence of a Sketch of some Propositions being offer'd for his Consideration he very frankly assured me he was willing to confer upon those Grounds with any Gentlemen of the Greatest Influence in this Country.

As I am at Liberty to declare his Sentiments I have the Honour to inclose for your Excellency's Information, a Copy of my Corrispondence with his Lordship and of the Propositions referred to in his Letter which are the Motives of my Present Request.[1] Attending in the Boat to be Indulged with your

Answer—I have the Honour to be Your Excellency's Most Obbt Humbe Servant

Drummond

L, DLC:GW. The text and signature of this letter are in an unidentified handwriting, but the docket in Robert Hanson Harrison's writing on the reverse indicates that it is the letter that GW received from Drummond. The address on the manuscript reads: "General Washington &c. &c. &c." The copy of this letter that GW enclosed in his letter to Hancock of 18 Aug. has not been found. Drummond's letter and GW's reply to him of this date were printed by order of Congress in the *Pennsylvania Evening Post* (Philadelphia) of 17 Sept. 1776.

1. Drummond, who had gone to Bermuda for his health in April, returned to New York Harbor on 9 Aug., and the next day he dined with Lord Howe aboard his flagship, the *Eagle* (see GW to Drummond, 23 April 1776, and Tatum, *Serle's Journal,* 61). From his quarters on the sloop *Polly,* Drummond wrote to Lord Howe on 12 Aug. enclosing "the Sketch of Propositions refered to in my late Conversation with your Lordship, which Propositions I have understood the Colonies were disposed not many months ago to make the Basis of a Reconciliation with Great Britain" (DLC:GW). Drummond is referring to the Olive Branch Petition of 5 July 1775. His six-point plan, which allowed each colony's assembly to impose the taxes necessary to pay its allotted share of the empire's expenses, was the same one that he had tried without success to persuade the Americans to accept the previous winter (see "Sketch of Propositions communicated to Lord Howe on the 12th August, 1776," DLC:GW, and Thomas Lynch to GW, 16 Jan. 1776, and note 3). Lord Howe expressed vague approval of Drummond's propositions in his reply to him of 15 August. "As I think they contain matter that upon a conference and cool Discussion might be wrought into a plan of permane[n]t Union," Howe wrote, "I shall with great Satisfaction embrace the first opportunity that may be offered upon those grounds, to promote so desirable an Event" (DLC:GW). Drummond's renewed peace initiative was short-lived. See GW to Drummond, this date, GW to Hancock, 18, 26 Aug., Drummond to GW, 19 Aug., and Hancock to GW, 24 August.

To Lord Drummond

My Lord   Head Quarters New York Augt 17. 1776

I have your Lordships Favour of this Day, accompanied by Papers on Subjects of the greatest Moment, & deserving the most deliberate Consideration.

I can allow much for your Lordships well meant Zeal upon such an Occasion, but I fear it has transported you beyond that Attention to your Parole which comprehends the Character of a Man of strict Honour.

How your Lordship can reconcile your past or present Conduct with your Engagement, so as to satisfy your own Mind, I must submit to your own Feelings, but I find myself under the disagreeable Necessity of objecting to the Mode of Negotiation proposed, while your Lordships Line of Conduct appears so exceptionable.[1]

I shall by Express forward to the Congress your Lordship Letter, & the several Papers which accompanied it.[2] The Result will be communicated as soon as possible.

I am sorry to have detained your Lordship so long, the unavoidable Necessity must be my Apology. I am my Lord, Your Lordships most Obed. & very Hbble Servt.

L, in Joseph Reed's writing, Drummond Castle Papers, Scottish Record Office; LB, DLC:GW; Varick transcript, DLC:GW. The copy of this letter that GW enclosed in his letter to Hancock of 18 Aug. has not been found, but it was printed by order of Congress in the *Pennsylvania Evening Post* (Philadelphia) of 17 Sept. 1776.

1. Before leaving New York for Bermuda in April, Drummond gave his parole of honor that he would not "communicate any information or intelligence whatever" regarding American forces or fortifications and that he would "take every care and precaution to avoid speaking with any British vessel or vessels belonging to the British navy" (*N.Y. Prov. Congress Journals*, 1:419). Drummond violated the latter part of his parole when he visited Lord Howe aboard his ship on 10 Aug. (see Drummond to GW, this date). In addition, while sailing out of New York Harbor in April, Drummond's vessel had been stopped in the Narrows by the British warship *Asia,* and although the *Asia*'s captain, George Vandeput, had immediately released the vessel upon seeing Drummond's parole and had not questioned him or any of the passengers or crew, that incident also was a technical violation of the parole (see Klein, "Failure of a Mission," 371, 373–74). For Drummond's explanation of his behavior, see his letter to GW of 19 Aug., and note 2.

2. See GW to Hancock, 18 August.

To John Hancock

Sir   New York Augt 17th 1776

The circumstances of the Two Armies having undergone no material alteration since I had the honor of writing you last, I have nothing particular or Important to communicate respecting them.

In my Letter of Yesterday I forgot to mention the arrival of

Lord Dunmore here. By the examination of a Capn Hunter who escaped from the Enemy and came to Amboy on the 14th transmitted me by Genl Roberdeau, I am certainly Informed his Lordship arrived on the 13th—The Examination does not say any thing about the Ships he brought with him, It only extends to his Force which It mentions to be weak.

I before now expected the Enemy would have made their Attack—Nor can I account for their deferring It, Unless the Intelligence given by Captn Hunter & Another person who escaped about the same time, is the Cause. to wit—that they are waiting the arrival of Another division of the Hessian Troops which they say is still out. Whether that is the reason of the delay I cannot undertake to determine, but I should suppose things will not long remain in their present state. I have Inclosed a Copy of Genl Roberdeaus Letter and of the Examination of these Two persons, which will shew Congress all the Information they have given upon these Subjects.[1]

I am just now advised by Mr Aires who came from Philadelphia to build the Row Gallies, That Two of our Fire Vessels attempted last night to burn the Enemies Ships & Tenders up the River—he says that they burnt One Tender and One of them boarded the Phenix and was grapled with her for near Ten Minutes, but she cleared herself—We lost both of the Vessels—his Account is not so particular, as I could wish, however I am certain the Attempt has not succeeded to our wishes—In a little time It is probable the matter will be more minutely reported.[2] I have the Honor to be with great respect Sir Your Most Obedt Servt

Go: Washington

LS, in Robert Hanson Harrison's writing, DNA:PCC, item 152; LB, DLC:GW; copy, DNA:PCC, item 169; Varick transcript, DLC:GW.

1. See Daniel Roberdeau to GW, 15 Aug., and note 1.

2. For fuller accounts of this attack on the British warships *Phoenix* and *Rose* and their tenders, see Wilson, *Heath's Memoirs*, 62–63, and the *Phoenix*'s and *Rose*'s journal entries for 16 Aug., in Clark and Morgan, *Naval Documents*, 6:206; see also William Heath to GW, this date. The burned tender was the *Charlotta*.

Benjamin George Eyre, an experienced shipwright who with his two older brothers operated a shipyard at Kensington near Philadelphia, built the frigate *Washington* for the Continental navy earlier this year, and during GW's visit to Philadelphia in late May, he was engaged by GW and Thomas Mifflin to go to New York to build row galleys for the defense of the city and the Hudson River (see GW to Hancock, 7 June 1776, and Eyre's memorial to Congress, 21 May 1777, DNA:PCC, item 41). On 27 Sept. 1776 Q.M. Gen. Stephen Moylan certified that Eyre had "built & completely finished two Gondolas or Row Galleys, one other, is finished all but the smiths work, and one was Left on the Stocks at Newyork entirely Timberd & Rigged. that he was actively employed about the Water frize [chevaux de frise], Sunck in the North River & has been allso employed to appraise sixteen vessells taken up to sink in the North and the east River, that he has gone up to Albany to engage & hurry down plank and boards for the use of the Army" (DNA:PCC, item 41). The three galleys that Eyre completed were the *Lady Washington, Putnam,* and *Independence.* Eyre returned to Philadelphia sometime in October, and on 13 Nov. Congress allowed him $427^{77}⁄90 for his work and expenses in New York (see *JCC,* 6:949, and Eyre's memorials to Congress, 18 Nov. 1776 and 21 May 1777, DNA:PCC, item 41). Eyre served as brigade major of Gen. John Cadwalader's Pennsylvania militia brigade from 1 Dec. 1776 to 29 Jan. 1777, and between 1777 and 1779 he was Continental superintendent of ship carpenters and boat builders, a position in which he proved to be so useful that GW refused to let him resign in December 1778 (see Nathanael Greene to Charles Pettit, 12 Dec. 1778, in Showman, *Greene Papers,* 3:112–13). In 1780 Eyre became lieutenant colonel commandant of the 2d Battalion of Philadelphia militia.

From John Hancock

Sir,   Philadelphia August 17th 1776. 5 O'Clock P.M.
    Your Favour of the 16th Inst: per Post this Minute came to Hand, & shall be laid before Congress on Monday.[1]
    I do myself the Pleasure to enclose sundry Resolves for your Information,[2] and likewise to forward the Commissions ordered by a Resolve of Congress on the 10th Inst., a Copy of which I transmitted in my Letter of that Date. With the most ardent and sincere Wishes for your Health & Prosperity, I have the Honour to be with perfect Esteem Sir your most hble Sert
                                        John Hancock Prest

This morng I Rec'd the Box by Coll Reed, & am Directed by Congress to Take Care of it, which is done.[3]

LS, DLC:GW; LB, DNA:PCC, item 12A. The postscript to the LS is in Hancock's writing.
    1. The following Monday was 19 August.
    2. In the enclosed resolutions of this date, Congress approves a report clearing Brig. Gen. David Wooster of charges of misconduct while he commanded the Continental forces in Canada, appoints an assistant quartermaster general

for the flying camp, directs GW to propose an exchange of the British prisoners who were captured at St. Jean and Chambly for American prisoners captured in Canada, recommends that the Maryland convention "raise & arm two
battalions upon the Continental establishment," and authorizes the sending of
"500 firelocks with bayonets" and other ordnance supplies to the flying camp
(DLC:GW; see also *JCC*, 5:664–66).

3. For the sending of this box of GW's official papers to Philadelphia, see
GW to Hancock, 13 August.

From Major General William Heath

Dear General   Kings bridge Augst 17th 1776
The Last night the Fire Ships & Row Gallies made an attempt,
Upon the Enemys ships, which lay at Anchor up the River,
The Fire ships were well Conducted, the Armed Schooner was
Grappled and Burnt, The Phenix was Grappled for a Bought
Ten minutes, But got herself Clear, The Lady Washington Galley and Independence, were Conducted with Great Judgment
and Bravery, I wish I could Say that the Other Gallies Did any
thing at all The Phenix either Slipt or Cut her Cable The Rose
was left alone, and it is thought might have been Taken, I was
an Eye witness to the whole, and from the Confusion which was
apparent, I am Confident that if an Attempt Should be made
on the Fleet Below, and but one or Two Ships Set on fire their
Confusion would be beyond Description.[1]

I have the Pleasure to Acquaint your Excellency that General
Mifflin has a Bout 500 men at a moments notice, to aid you
in Case of need, they were the last Evening Drawn out when I
reviewed them They are of Colo. Sheas & Magaws Regiments,
and the best Disciplined of any Troops that I have yet Seen in
the Army—I shall this Evening or to morrow Send a Return of
the Troops at this Post, we are Pushing our works with all Dilli-
gence. I have the Honor to be with great Respect your Excellencys Humble Servt

W. Heath

ALS, MH: Sparks Collection.
1. Later this day GW's aide-de-camp Richard Cary replied to Heath: "I am
Commanded by his Excellency to return you his thanks for your favr of this
morning, he is much pleased to hear of the good Behaviour of the Officers &
Men of the Lady Washington & Independence Galleys, and desires You will

inquire into the cause of the inactivity of the other Gallies, and inform him thereof" (MHi: Heath Papers).

Letter not found: to Maj. Gen. William Heath, 17 Aug. 1776. Heath's letter to GW of this date is docketed in Joseph Reed's writing: "Major Genl Heath Kingsbridge Aug. 17 1776 Answerd do."

To Lord Howe

My Lord   Head Qrs New York Augt 17. 1776.

Being authorized by Congress, as their Commanders in every Department are, to Negociate an Exchange of Prisoners, and presuming as well from the nature of your Lordships command, as the Information Genl Howe has been pleased to Honour me with, that the Exchange in the Naval Line will be subject to your Lordships direction,[1] I beg leave to propose the following mode of Exchange for your Lordships consideration, viz. Officers for those of equal Rank & Sailors for Sailors.

If the above proposal should be agreable to your Lordship, I am charged in a particular manner to Exchange any Officer belonging to the British Navy in our hands, & of equal rank, for Lieutt Josiah, who was lately made prisoner in a Ship retaken by the Cerberus Frigate.[2]

The reason my Lord of my being charged to propose the Exchange of Lt. Josiah in preference to that of any Other Officer is, that authentic Intelligence has been received that regardless of his Rank as an Officer, he has not only been Subjected to the duties of a Common Seaman, but has experienced many other marks of Indignity.

As a different Line of Conduct My Lord, has been ever observed to wards the Officers of your Navy who have fallen into our Hands, It becomes not only a matter of right but of duty to mention this to your Lordship, to the end that an enquiry may be made into the case above referred to.

From your Lordships Character for Humanity, I am led to presume, the Hardships Imposed on Lt. Josiah are without either your knowledge or concurrence, and therefore most readily hope that upon this representation, your Lordship will enjoin All Officers under your command to pay such regard to the Treatment of those that may fall into their hands, as their different ranks & situations require and such as your Lordship would wish to see continued by us to those, who are already in our power or who may hereafter by the Chance of War be Subjected to It. I have the Honor to be My Lord with great respect Your Lordships Most Obedt Sevt

G.W.

LB, in Robert Hanson Harrison's writing, DLC:GW; copy, enclosed in GW to Hancock, 21 Aug. 1776, DNA:PCC, item 152; copy, DNA:PCC, item 169; Varick transcript, DLC:GW.

    1. See William Howe to GW, 1 August. For Congress's resolution of 22 July authorizing departmental commanders to negotiate prisoner exchanges, see *JCC*, 5:599.

    2. See Hancock to GW, 8 August.

To Major General William Howe

Sir   Head Qrs New York, Augt 17. 1776

I do myself the honor to transmit the Inclosed Letter from Major French, & at the same time to inform you, that his Exchange for Majr Meigs, whose parole I am advised you have, will meet my approbation—I would take the liberty also to propose an Exchange of any Captn you may chuse for Capn Dearborn whose parole I have heard was delivered you with Major Meig's.[1]

Give me leave to assure you Sir, that I feel myself greatly Obliged by the polite conclusion of your Letter of the 1st Instt, and have a high sense of the honor and satisfaction I should have received from your personal Acquaintance. The different State of the Colonies from what It was last War & which has deprived me of that Happiness, cannot be regretted by any One more than Sir Your Most Obedt Servt

G.W.

LB, in Robert Hanson Harrison's writing, DLC:GW; Varick transcript, DLC:GW.

    1. The enclosed letter from Maj. Christopher French to Howe concerning his proposed exchange has not been identified (see French to GW, 11 Aug.). Congress's resolution of this date approving Maj. Return Jonathan Meigs's exchange for Major French and Capt. Henry Dearborn's exchange for an officer of equal rank was included in the resolutions that Hancock enclosed in his letter to GW of this date (see also *JCC*, 5:665).

From Major William Smith Livingston

Sir   Long Island Augt 17th 1776
   Colo: Hand has this Morning reported to the General that since Yesterday Evening four Vessels of War, one of them the Solbay have sailed from the Fleet at the Narrows—Two Brigs a Sloop and Schooner came in from Sea and the Man of War that lay off the Hook these two Days past came in—The Morning being very Thick he could discern nothing distinctly at the Hook but that late in the Evening of Yesterday some of the Foreign Troops Landed at the Ferry Way on Staten Island.
   I am sorry to inform your Excellency that General Green had a very bad Night of it and cannot bc said to be any better this Morning than he was Yesterday. I have the Honor to be Your most Obedt Servt

                                        Wm S. Livingston

ALS, DLC:GW.

To the New York Convention

Gentn   Head Qrs N. York Augt 17: 1776
   When I consider that the City of New York will in all human probability very soon be the scene of a bloody conflict: I can not but view the great Numbers of Women, Children & infirm persons remaining in It with the most melancholy concern— When the Men of War passed up the River the Shrieks & Cries of these poor creatures running every way with their Children was truly distressing & I fear will have an unhappy effect on the Ears & Minds of our Young & inexperienced Soldiery. Can no method be devised for their removal? Many doubtless are of Ability to remove themselves; but there are Others in a different situation—Some provision for them afterwards would also be a necessary consideration—It would releive me from Great anxiety If your Honble body would Immediately deliberate upon It & form & execute some plan for their Removal and releif in which I will co-operate & assist to the utmost of my power—In the mean Time I have thought It proper to recommend to persons under the above description to convey themselves without

delay to some place of safety with their most valuable Effects.[1] I have the honor &c.

G.W.

LB, in Robert Hanson Harrison's writing, DLC:GW; Varick transcript, DLC:GW. The LB is addressed "to The Honble The Presidt of the Conventn of New York." The convention read this letter on this date, and it is printed in *N.Y. Prov. Congress Journals*, 1:578. That text, which presumably was taken from the unfound receiver's copy, is identical in wording to the LB.

1. See GW's Proclamation for the Evacuation of New York, this date. For the convention's response, see the second letter that Abraham Yates, Jr., wrote to GW on this date.

From Abraham Yates, Jr.

In Convention of the Representatives of the
Sir   State of New York Harlem August 17th 1776
Mr Denning hath made the Convintion Acquainted with your Excellenceys Sentiments upon obstructing the Navigation of the East River between the Grand Battery and Governor's Island. we now take the Liberty of inclosing the Copy of our Resolution for that purpose, which together with this Letter will be handed to your Excellency by the Gentleman of the Committee to whom we make no doubt Sir that you will afford every Assistance in your Power.[1] I have the Honor to be Your most Obedient Humble Servt

Abm Yates Junr President

LS, DLC:GW. The draft of this letter that the convention approved on this date is nearly identical in wording to the LS (see *N.Y. Prov. Congress Journals*, 1:577).

1. William Denning (1740–1819), a New York City merchant who served in the provincial congress and convention from 1776 to 1777, informed the convention on 16 Aug. that William Fundran, who was one of the best pilots in the city, had told him "that the navigation of the East river may be very easily obstructed between the Battery and Nutten [Governor's] island . . . that the depth of water at a particular place which he could point out, did not exceed 5 fathoms; and that the navigation could be obstructed in 4 hours after proper vessels are prepared for that purpose." The convention directed Denning to give this information to GW and to inform him that the convention was willing for the East River to be obstructed if GW thought "it advantageous for the defence of this State" (ibid., 575).

GW's favorable reply, communicated through Denning, prompted the convention to pass the enclosed resolutions of this date: "Whereas it is of the utmost Consequence to the Safety of the City of New York, and the Security of the continental Army now on long Island, that the Communication betwixt that City and the said Island should not be obstructed by the enemies Ships. Resolved, that Captain Anthony Rutgers, Mr William Denning and Mr Patrick Dennis be and they hereby are empowered by this Convention to stop up the Channel betwixt the grand Battery and Nutten Island in case they shall deem the same practicable and that this Convention will defray all the Charges incident to the execution of this Design. Resolved, that General [Lewis] Morris be empowered to purchase a Sloop belonging to Jesse Hunt at New Rochelle and to Order the same to be delivered immediately to the above named Gentlemen at New York loaded with Stone" (DLC:GW; see also *N.Y. Prov. Congress Journals,* 1:577). For evidence that this plan was executed, see General Orders, 24 August.

Denning subsequently became much involved in Continental financial affairs. On 19 July 1776 Congress appointed him one of three commissioners for settling the accounts of New York, and on 30 Mar. 1778 it named him a commissioner of accounts at the Board of Treasury (*JCC,* 5:593; 10:293). Denning was a member of the Board of Treasury from July 1780 to September 1781, and in July 1782 Superintendent of Finance Robert Morris appointed Denning a commissioner for settling the accounts of the quartermaster department (ibid., 16:397; 22:425). Denning served in the New York legislature from 1784 to 1787 and from 1798 to 1808, and he was a member of the U.S. Congress in 1809–10.

From Abraham Yates, Jr.

In Convention of the Representatives of the
Sir   State of New York Harlem 17th Augt 1776
I am directed to inform your Excellency that immediately upon the receipt of your favor of this morning respecting the Women, Children and Infirm persons remaining in the City of New York—The Convention appointed a Committee for the purpose of removeing and provideing for such persons—I inclose a Copy of the Resolves for that purpose and hope you will soon be releived from the Anxiety which their continuence in Town has occationed.[1] And have the Honor to be with verry great Respect Your Most Obedt Hume Servt
                        Abm Yates Junr President

LS, DLC:GW. The draft of this letter that the convention approved on this date is nearly identical in wording to the LS (see *N.Y. Prov. Congress Journals,* 1:578).
  1. The enclosed copy of these resolutions is in DLC:GW (see also ibid.). The committee members were Abraham P. Lott, James Beekman, John Berrien,

and John Campbell. The convention consented to "pay the Expences incident to the removal, and maintenance of such Persons as the said Committee shall think in such indigent Circumstances as not to be able to remove and subsist themselves."

To Robert Yates

Sir   Head Quarters, New York 17 Aug. 1776
   I am favoured with yours of the 13th & 14th inst.[1] and am pleased to find you have been successfull in procuring Cannon for the Defence of Hudsons River; also that there is such a good prospect of effectually securing the Pass at Fort Montgomery, the mention you make of General Clinton's attention to that & other important Objects gives me great satisfaction, & confirms me in the opinion that he is fully qualified for the trust reposed in him by the Congress, in their appointing him a Brigadier— I approve much of the measure for making a number of Matrosses by putting a part of the Garrison to exercising the Artillery, the same steps have been taken here.—If any material advantages can be derived from fitting out the two Sloops you speak of I shall be glad you have undertaken it, tho' I confess they are not very apparent to me at present—I cannot consent to those Vessels being manned from among the Levies, unless absolutely necessary, if the Officers can inlist them out of the Militia I have no objection thereto— I shall comply with your request in furnishing Capt. Benson with a sufficient quantity of Powder for the two Armed Vessels, & am with due Regard & Esteem Sir, Your very Humble Servt

                             Go. Washington

Magazine of American History with Notes and Queries, 6 (1881), 136–37. The letter is addressed to "Robert Yates Esqr. Chairman of the Committee at Poughkeepsie."

   1. See a Secret Committee of the New York Convention to GW, 13, 14 August.

General Orders

Head Quarters, New York, August 18th 1776
Parole Grantham.   Countersign Fairfield.

As nothing contributes so much to the good order and government of troops, as an exactness in discipline, & a strict observance of orders; and as the Army is now arranged into different divisions; those divisions formed into brigades, and the brigades composed of regiments; The General hopes and expects, that the several duties of the Army, will go on with regularity, chearfulness and alacrity: As one means of accomplishing this he desires, that no regiment, brigade or division, will interfere with the duties of another, but walk in their own proper line; the Colonels taking care not to contravene the orders of their Brigadiers; the Brigadiers of their Major Generals; and that the whole pay due attention to the General Orders, which can only be set aside, or be dispensed with by orders of equal dignity.

The army under such a regulation will soon become respectable in itself, and formidable to the foe—It is an incumbent duty therefore, upon every officer of every rank, to be alert and attentive in the discharge of the several duties annexed to his office; his honor, his own personal safety, and for ought he knows, the salvation of his Country, and its dearest priviliges, may depend upon his exertions. Particular Causes[1] may, and doubtless will happen, to render it necessary (for the good of the service) that a change of officers &c.—should be made, from one brigade to another; but when ever there appears cause for this, it will be notified by General, or special Orders.

The General cannot quit the subject, as this may possibly be the last opportunity, previous to an attack, without addressing the private men, and exhorting the troops in general, to be perfoundly silent, and strictly obedient to Orders, before they come to, and also while they are in action, as nothing can contribute more to their Success, than a cool and deliberate behaviour, nor nothing add more to the discouragement of the enemy, than to find new troops calm and determined in their manner. The General has no doubt but that every good Soldier, and all the officers, are sufficiently impressed with the necessity of examining the state and condition of their arms, but his own anxiety on this head impels him to remind them of it after every spell of wet weather, least we should at any time, be caught with arms unfit for immediate use.

The regiments of Militia from Connecticut are to be formed into a Brigade under the command of Brigadier General Wolcot, who is hourly expected; and in the mean time to be under the command of Col. Hinman, the eldest Colonel of the militia.

Though the Fire Ships which went up the North river last Friday Evening, were not so successful as to destroy either of the Men of war, yet the General thanks the officers and men for the spirit and resolution which they shewed in grappling the Vessels before they quitted the Fire Ships; And as a reward of their merit, presents each of those who stayed last, and were somewhat burnt, Fifty Dollars, and Forty to each of the others; And had the enterprize succeeded, so as to have destroyed either of the ships of war, the General could have been generous in proportion to the service.[2]

Varick transcript, DLC:GW.
   1. "Henshaw's Orderly Book," 221, reads "Cases."
   2. The previous Friday was 16 August. For accounts of this engagement, see GW to Hancock and William Heath to GW, both 17 August.

From William Blodget

Sir   Long Island Augt 18. 1776
   Colonel Hands report, mentions no Uncommon movements of the Enemy.

The General desires me to acquaint your Excellency that he finds himself considerably better this Morning than he was Yesterday, and is in hopes in a few days, to be able to go abroad, 'tho still very weak. I am with Respect Humble Servant
                                        Wm Blodget A.D. Camp

ALS, DLC:GW.

To Benjamin Franklin

Sir,   New York Augt 18th 1776.
   I have been honourd with your favour of the 16th, and the several Inclosures contained therein, which are now return'd

with my thanks for the oppertunity of perusing them[1]—I also Inclose you a Letter from Lord Howe, sent out (with others) by a Flag in the Afternoon of yesterday.[2] with it comes a Letter for Lieutt Barrington, who if not among those who broke their Parole, & went of for Canada, is in York, Pensylvania.[3] With very great esteem and respect, I have the honr to be Sir Yr Most Obedt H: Servt

Go: Washington

ALS, PPAmP.

1. Franklin's letter to GW of 16 Aug. has not been found, and its enclosures have not been identified.

2. Howe's letter to Franklin of 16 Aug. concerns peace proposals (see Willcox, *Franklin Papers,* 22:565–66).

3. William Barrington, a lieutenant in the 7th Regiment, had been taken prisoner at Chambly on 18 Oct. 1775. He did not join the other British officers who left Lebanon, Pa., in June 1776, and at this time he was confined in jail at Lancaster (see the Lancaster committee of inspection to the Pennsylvania council of safety, 18 July, in Force, *American Archives,* 5th ser., 1:411–12, and Barrington to the Lancaster committee, 5 Aug., ibid., 761). The Pennsylvania council of safety on 24 Aug. gave the Lancaster committee of inspection permission to take Barrington's parole and to "send him to his brother officers at *York* or *Cumberland* County" (minutes of the Pennsylvania council of safety, 24 Aug., ibid., 1325).

From Major General Nathanael Greene

Sir   Long Island Augt 18th 1776

I have thought proper to communicate to you certain Intilligence which I have recieved from my Brother respecting Captain Grimes, whose Conduct (if I have been rightly informed) does not entitle him to that Place in your Esteem which he now holds, nor to that Confidence which you have thought proper to put in him.

His leaving the Gally at Rode Island in the Time of the Attack, to take Convoy of the Prizes, the Insult which he afterwards gave said Captain, who has ever been held in the highest Esteem, whose Character stands fair and unimpeached; and who has given convincing Proofs of his Courage and Conduct, together with the Information that was given me of his refusing to make the Attack at the Time the Fire Ships went up the River, and the Reluctance that was shewn this Morning to comply with the

Orders given him by General Putnam, induc[e]s me to thinck, that he is much more fond of Parade and shew than he is desirous of signalizing himself in any Action that may be of Service to the Country.

If the Report of his Refusal is founded in Fact, and General Putnam's Orders were not complied with, I think he ought immediately to be put under an Arrest and instantly removed from his Command.[1] I am Your very hume Servt

Nathanael Greene

LS, DLC:GW.

1. This confused report about John Grimes, captain of the Rhode Island row galley *Spit-Fire,* apparently came from Greene's younger brother Christopher, who visited the Long Island camp about this time (see Nathanael Greene to Elihue Greene, 6 Sept. 1776, in Showman, *Greene Papers,* 1:296–97). The captain who recently had abandoned his row galley in Rhode Island was not Grimes but John Hyers of the row galley *Washington.* On 21 July Grimes, in obedience to orders from the Rhode Island assembly, attempted to sail the *Spit-Fire* from Newport to New York in company with the *Washington.* Hyers refused to move his vessel from Newport, however, saying that his crew had left him and that he would not take orders from Grimes in any case. Hearing that Hyers had "planed on Porpos that his men Should Lev him so as to have an Excus for not Goiing" to New York, Grimes sent one of his lieutenants and part of his crew aboard the *Washington* and made the galley's former sailing master, Ebenezer Hill, its new captain (Grimes to Nicholas Cooke, 22 July, in Clark and Morgan, *Naval Documents,* 5:1178–80; see also Cooke to Grimes, 24 July, in "R.I. Revolutionary Correspondence," 158–59). The *Spit-Fire* and *Washington* then proceeded to New York, where they arrived on 28 July (see GW to Hancock, 29 July). The captains and crews of both Rhode Island galleys fought bravely in the engagement with the *Phoenix* and *Rose* on 3 Aug., but neither vessel actively attacked those warships on 16 Aug. when the American galleys and fire ships made a second attempt to destroy them (see Benjamin Tupper to GW, 3 Aug., and Heath to GW, 17 Aug.). The *Spit-Fire* and *Washington* left New York sometime during the next several days and arrived at Providence on 26 Aug. (see the *Providence Gazette; and Country Journal,* 31 Aug.). Ebenezer Hill was commissioned officially as captain of the *Washington* on 19 Dec. 1776. Grimes and Hyers left the Rhode Island naval service by the end of 1776 and subsequently commanded Massachusetts privateers.

To John Hancock

Sir   New York Augt the 18th 1776
I have been honoured with your Favor of the 16th with Its Inclosure and am sorry It is not in my power to transmit Con-

gress a Copy of the Treaty as they require, having sent It away with the Other papers that were in my Hands.

The Resolution they have entered into respecting the Foreign Troops, I am persuaded would produce Salutary Effects, If It can be properly circulated among them. I fear It will be a matter of difficulty—However, I will take every measure that shall appear probable to facilitate the End.

I have the honor to Inclose you for the perusal and consideration of Congress, Sundry papers marked No. 1. to No. 7 Inclusive, the whole of which except No. 2. & 7, My Answers to Lord Drummond & Genl Howe, I received Yesterday Evening by a Flag, and to which I beg leave to refer Congress.[1]

I am exceedingly at a loss to know the Motives and Causes Inducing a proceding of such a nature at this Time and Why Lord Howe has not attempted some plan of negociation before, as he seems so desirous of It. If I may be allowed to conjecture and guess at the Causes—It may be that part of the Hessians have not arrived as mentioned in the examination transmitted Yesterday—or that Genl Burgoyne has not made such progress as was expected, to form a Junction of their Two Armies—Or what I think equally probable—they mean to procrastinate their Operations for some Time, Trusting that the Militia's which have come to our Succour, will soon become tired and return Home as is but too usual with them. Congress will make their Observations upon these Several matters and favor me with the Result as soon they have done.

They will Observe my Answer to Lord Drummond who I am pretty confident has not attended to the Terms of his parole, but has violated It in several Instances—It is with the rest of the papers—but If my Memory Serves me he was not to hold any Correspondence directly or Indirectly with those in Arms against us, or to go into any port or Harbour in America where the Enemy themselves were or had a Fleet or to go on board their Ships.

The Treaty with the Indians is in the Box which Lt. Colo. Reed I presume has delivered before this. If Congress are desirous of Seeing It—they will be pleased to have the Box opened—It contains a variety of papers and All the Affairs of the Army from my First going to Cambridge 'till It was sent away.[2]

This Morning the Phenix and Rose Men of War with Two Tenders, availing themselves of a favourable and Brisk Wind, came down the River and have Joined the Fleet. Our Several Batteries fired at them in their passage but without any good effect that I could perceive. I have the Honor to be with great esteem Sir Your Most Obedt Servt

Go: Washington

LS, in Robert Hanson Harrison's writing, DNA:PCC, item 152; LB, DLC:GW; copy, DNA:PCC, item 169; Varick transcript, DLC:GW. Congress read this letter on 20 Aug. and referred it to a committee of five delegates: Thomas Jefferson, Benjamin Franklin, Edward Rutledge, John Adams, and William Hooper (*JCC*, 5:672).

1. The first five enclosures are copies of Lord Drummond's letter to GW of 17 Aug., GW's reply to Drummond of that date, Drummond's letter to Lord Howe of 12 Aug., Drummond's peace proposals of 12 Aug., and Lord Howe's reply to Drummond of 15 August. Enclosure no. 6 is a copy of Gen. William Howe's letter to GW of 13 Aug. asking if GW objected to the landing at New York of Robert Temple (d. 1784), a resident of Charlestown, Mass., who had recently arrived from England aboard one of the vessels of the British fleet (D, DNA:PCC, item 152; copy, DLC:GW). Enclosure no. 7 is a copy of GW's reply to General Howe of 17 Aug. in which he says that he has no objection to Temple's landing (Df, in Joseph Reed's writing, DLC:GW; copy, DNA:PCC, item 152, and Varick transcript, DLC:GW).

2. For the sending of this box of GW's official papers to Philadelphia, see GW to Hancock, 13 August.

From Major General William Heath

Dear General   Kings-Bridge Aug: 18th 1776

Early this morning the Phoenix Man of War, Rose Frigate & the Two Tenders, came to Sail & stood down the River, keeping close under the East Shore, in order to avoid the Fire of our Cannon; but notwithstanding this Precaution, the Phoenix was thrice Hull'd by our Shot from Mount Washington, & one of the Tenders once—The Rose was Hull'd once by a Shot from Burdit Ferry—They kept their men close, otherwise some of them wou'd have been pickd down by a Party of Rifle-men who were posted on the bank—They fired Grape Shot as they passed, but did no damage save to one Tent—We hope to hear that your Batteries have done the work for some of them[1]—We shall recover some Swivel Guns, Gun Barrels, Shot &c. out of the Wreck of the Tender which was burnt the other night, the Particulars of which shall be transmitted to your Excellency as soon as I can obtain them²—Genl Clinton has about 1400 Men already come in, but their Quarters are so scatter'd, that it will be almost impossible to collect them suddenly, if Occasion shou'd require it—If there are any Spare Tents I earnestly beg for them, if it were but for one Regiment—Genl Clinton has Orders from the Convention of the State of N. York to purchase 10000 feet of Boards, for erecting Sheds &c., but it is uncertain when we shall have them³—I shall tomorrow send for 6 or 700 of Tools, being able to employ that number more than we have at present—The more I view this post the more I am convinc'd of its' Importance.

The Ships have now tryed the Practicability of passing our Works—they have explored every part of the Shore as far as they have gone up the River, and sounded the river in almost every place—Shou'd the Ships rejoin the Fleet without receiving much Damage, I think Howe, will be embolden'd to attempt an Attack some where above this place, thinking that there may be a greater probability of succeeding here, than in the face of so many & strong Works, as have been erected in and around the City—However shou'd his Inclination lead him this Way, Nature has done much for us, and we shall as fast as possible add the Strength of Art—Our Men are in good Health & Spirits, & I dare say will give them a warm reception—I should be glad to have the Carriages for the Four pounders sent forward the moment they are done, as we have not as yet a single Cannon mounted beyond Mount Washington—I have just now received your Excellency's Commands to enquire into the Cause of the Inactivity of some of the Row Gallies, in the late Attack on the enemy's Ships, but as the Gallies have all left this Post and fallen down to the City, I must beg your Excellency to excuse me from that Service. I have the honor to be with the greatest respect Your Excellency's most humble Servt

W. Heath

LS, DLC:GW; ADfS, MHi: Heath Papers.

1. The entry for this date in the *Phoenix*'s journal reads: "At 5 AM Weigh'd and came to Sail in Co his Majestys Ship *Rose*, *Tryal* Schooner and the *Shuldham*, at 20 Minutes past 5 the Rebels Fir'd at us from a Battery on the Eastern Side of the River which we return'd. at ½ past [5] passed through the Channell

on the East side of the Vessels &ca Sunk by the Rebels to block up the Channell between Geffery's Hook and Berdetts Mountain; several Shot was Fir'd [at] us from a Battery upon the Top of the Mountain, after we got through the Channell; At ½ past 6 Fir'd several Broad sides at some Gallies laying close into the Western Shore at ¾ past 6 Commenced Firing at the Batteries upon York Island &ca at ½ past 7 Anchor'd off Staten Island" (Clark and Morgan, *Naval Documents*, 6:225–26; see also the journal of H.M.S. *Rose*, this date, ibid., 225). William Smith says in his *Memoirs* that "a Deserter who had assisted in sinking the Vessels was their Pilot thro' the Gut left unfinished" (Sabine, *William Smith's Memoirs*, 2:3).

2. For this report, see Heath to GW, 20 August. The burned tender was the *Charlotta* (see GW to Hancock, 17 Aug.).

3. For this resolution of 10 Aug., see the *N.Y. Prov. Congress Journals*, 1:567.

Letter not found: to Brig. Gen. Hugh Mercer, 18 Aug. 1776. In a letter to GW of 19 Aug., Mercer refers to "your Excellencys Letter of yesterday."

To the New York Convention

Gentn   New York Augt 18th 1776

I have been honoured with your Letter of the 17th with the Resolution of your honourable Body for obstructing the Channel betwixt the Grand Battery and Nutten Island.[1] Having gone into a considerable Expence for stopping that of the North River, and such as I am not certain I shall be justifyed in, and the Obstructions there being far from compleat, it will not be in my power to engage in the Business you propose, or undertake to Advance any part of the Money which will be necessarily expended in the Execution—At the same time give me leave to assure you Gentlemen that I shall most readily afford you such Assistance as may be derived from the Labour of the Troops here and that can be spared from other Service to facilitate the Design, which will be of great Importance if it can be executed.

I have been also honoured with your favr and Resolution of the same date, and am exceedingly obliged by the ready Attention you have paid to my Recommendation for the removal of the Women & Children and infirm persons from the City.[2] I have the Honor to be with the greatest Respect Yr most obt Sert.

LB, in Tench Tilghman's writing, DLC:GW; Varick transcript, DLC:GW. This letter is printed in the *N.Y. Prov. Congress Journals*, 1:578. That text, which presumably was taken from the unfound receiver's copy, is identical in wording to the LB.

1. See the first letter that Abraham Yates, Jr., wrote to GW on 17 August.
2. See Yates's second letter to GW of 17 August.

From Major General Philip Schuyler

Dear Sir　　　　　　　　　　Albany August 18th 1776

Your Excellency's favor of the 13th Instant was Delivered me about nine Last Evening.

I am very Confident that you have pursued Every measure in your power, to releave our wants in this Quarter, and to Facilitate the works going on to the Northward; we have people in every Quarter Attemping to procure the variety of Articles, that are wanted, but after all, We shall fall Considerably short, nor did I ever doubt, but that your Excellency had Communicated to Congress, the Difficulties we Laboured under for the want of money, I Assure you that I all ways have and shall Continue to Advise them in time, of the Necessity of Supplies of Cash; The resolves you mention have not been sent me, nor any about raising Troops for three years, Except that the Officers are to have the same Allowance for recruting.

I cannot upon recurring to my Letter of the 6th Instant, perceive that I intimated the Least doubt of your Excellencys not having Communicated to Congress, such part of my Letters, as were Necessary for them to know, I shall strictly Comply with your order and Advise You of any Information which I at the same time send You and them.

If your Excellency will please to reperuse my Letter of the 6th Instant, I belive you will Find, that it is in no part suggested, that a Court of Inquiry, or Court Martial was Convened at New York, upon the Subject alluded to, I was informed that a Council of Officers had Convened at New York, I was Advised of what was their decision. I was Chagrined and had the Information been as I thought it, I belive your Excellency will do me the Justice to think That I should have had too much reason to be so.

As the movement of the Army from Crown point to Tyonderoga was so Generally Condemned at New York, It is more then probable that Congress must have heard it, and I therefore wish, that every thing I have said on the Subject, should be Communicated to them, I frankly Confess that I first moved the Matter, and that were the Question to be again Ajetated, I should still Continue of the same Sentiments, unless better reasons Could be given against it, than those I have Adduced in support of my Opinion, and then I should have most readily Acquiesced, or if your Excellency, without having given any reasons for it, had ordered me to move the Army back to Crown point, I should have Obeyed without Hesitation or a Murmur, well knowing that the orders of my Superior Officer are on no Account to be Contested.

I Assure you, my dear Sir, that I very reluctantly entered on a Command, in which I foresaw as many Difficulties as I have Experienced, I easily Conceived that a people whom it had been necessary to Inspire with Jealousy of the men in power in Great Britain, and those Employed by them in this Injured Country, would also be Easily Induced, by Artful and Designing men to Transfer part of that Jealousy to the Servants of the public here, my Conjectures were well founded, for Suspicion and Envy have Followed me, from the Moment I came To the Command, I have experienced the Most Illiberal abuse, in many of the Colonies, and even in the Army I Commanded, and if any Accident should happen to the Northward, the same spirit that has Imputed The Misfortunes in Canada to me, will Impute that also to me, I have Intreated Congress to Cause a Minute Enquiry to be made into my Conduct,[1] and I Trust, if it is done, that I shall not only be Honorably Acquited, but that Judicious men will discover in me the Honest man and the Faithfull American. But as Envy even in that Case, will not Cease, nor Melevolence withold its Slander, I am Determined to Quit The Army, As soon as my Conduct has been Enquired into and Evince myself in private Life what I have Strove to do in public; the Friend of my Injured Country.

Soon after Colo. Daytons regiment marched to Johnson Hall, some of the Officers broke open the Doors and Carried away a very Considerable Quantity of Effects, Contrary to mine and Colo. Daytons Orders, soon after my Arrival at the German Flatts, I was Informed of this by some of the Officers, who wished an Enquiry, that the Innocent might not share The Scandal with the Guilty, I ordered a Court Martial on Lieut. McDonald, Witnesses with respect to his Conduct being On the spot, he was Tryed and broke, in the Course of his Tryal it appeared that a number of others were Concerned, and I ordered Lieut. Colo. White, & Capts. Ross and Patterson down from Fort Stanwix, the two Captains Delivered me the paper No. 1, in Answer to which I advised them Candidly to Narrate the Whole Transaction No: 2 is their Narrative, and No: 3 Contains an Account of what they took, No. 4 with the paper Inclosed in it is what Colo. White Delivered me. As I was Apprehensive that a public Conviction of so many Officers, would reflect to much Disgrace on our Troops, I chose to defer any further proceeding untill I should advice with your Excellency. permitt me therefore to Intreat your Opinion, wether it will be prudent for me to Accept of the Concessions, they Offer to make at the head of the Regiment, and thus to Bury the Affair, or wether I ought to have them Tryed, please to return the papers above Alluded To, as I have not time to make Copys of them.[2]

Inclose your Excellency, Copy of a Letter from Colo. Dayton with Copy of a paper Inclosed in it, he has changed the name of Fort Stanwix, The Messesaga Indians Mentioned in the paper, Live on the west side of Lake Ontario, and of those the Savages, who made our people prisoners at the Cedars, were Chiefly Composed.[3]

Only five Quire of Cartridge paper Could be procured, which I have sent Colo. Dayton, we are greatly in want of that Article, Capt: Varick informs me that he has wrote to your Excellency for it, it is not to be had any where, nearer than New York, General Gates also presses me in a Letter of the 16th Instant for that Article, please to order it to be sent with all expedition. I also Inclose a Copy of a Letter from General Arnold.[4]

As I Cannot possibly find time to make two Copies of the Transaction at the Late Treaty, I have mentioned to Congress, that I had sent one to you, to be Transmitted, after perusal to them.[5]

Also Inclose Copy of a Letter from Genl Arnold which gives me a state of our naval force on Lake Champlain.

Your Excellency's Letter of the 10th Instant to Capt. Varick is Just come to hand but not any of the Articles Mentioned in the return are as yet Arrived. I am Dr Sir with unfeigned Esteem and Respect Your Excellency's most Obedient Humble Servant

Ph: Schuyler

LS, DLC:GW; LB, NN: Schuyler Papers.

1. See Schuyler to Hancock, 16 Aug., DNA:PCC, item 153.

2. These enclosures, which have not been identified, apparently were returned to Schuyler. Lt. William McDonald, who was commissioned a second lieutenant in Col. Elias Dayton's 3d New Jersey Regiment in March 1776, was cashiered on 1 August. For McDonald's arrest, see Schuyler to Dayton, 22 July, in Force, *American Archives*, 5th ser., 1:511. Lt. Col. Anthony Walton White and captains John Ross (1752–1796) and Thomas Paterson were not tried for their offenses. Assisted by GW, White became lieutenant colonel of the 4th Continental Dragoons in 1777 and served until 1782 (see GW to White, 20 Mar. 1777, DLC:GW). Ross, a physician from Burlington, N.J., remained a captain in the 3d New Jersey Regiment until the spring of 1779 when he became major of the 2d New Jersey Regiment. Ross served as brigade inspector of the New Jersey brigade from October 1779 to November 1780 and retired from the army on 1 Jan. 1781. In 1782 Ross was a lieutenant colonel in the New Jersey militia, and from 1781 to 1789 he was state naval officer at Burlington. GW named Ross collector of customs there in 1789. Paterson served as a captain in the 3d New Jersey Regiment until 4 Sept. 1778 when he resigned his commission on account of his health (see Paterson to GW, that date, DNA: RG 93).

3. Dayton changed the name of Fort Stanwix to Fort Schuyler. Dayton's letter to Schuyler of 15 Aug. concerns the recent desertion of Lt. Edward McMichael and two other men to the British and the shortages of ammunition and money in his regiment. "McMichael," Dayton says, "knows our Situation respecting Ammunition which he will most certainly discover to them [the British]—We have now only 2160 Musket Cartridges and no paper or thread to make any more[.] I hope Cash will very soon be sent to us, as I wish neither Officers or Soldiers should have any cause to complain as they both do at present having near four Months' pay due" (DLC:GW). Dayton enclosed a copy of the "Information given by Richd Bell & Samuel Freeman concerning the Scout which went from Fort Schuyler to Oswego" and back to Fort Schuyler between 7 and 15 August. Their party was ambushed by the Missisauga Indians about six miles from Oswego, and only Bell, who was a guide, and Freeman, a soldier, escaped (DLC:GW).

4. "Capt. Varick," Arnold says in his letter to Schuyler of 8 Aug. from Skenesboro, "has been very active and industrious in procuring the Articles for the Navy[.] many are arrived at Tyonderoga, and proper Steps taken to procure the others. The Carpenters go on with great Spirit—The eight Gondalos will be compleated in a few days[.] One Row Gally is gone to Tyonderoga, and will soon be fitted and armed, three others will be launched in ten days or a fortnight—Four others will be set up in a few days great part of the timber being cut—Iron, Sails, Cordage and Anchors will be wanted in a few days" (DLC:GW).

5. Schuyler enclosed with this letter a transcript of the proceedings of the conference that he and two other Indian commissioners held with representatives of the Six Nations at German Flats from 8 to 13 August. GW forwarded that document to Congress with his letter to Hancock of 23

August. For the text of the transcript, see Force, *American Archives*, 5th ser., 1:1035-49.

To Jonathan Trumbull, Sr.

Sir   New York Augt 18th 1776

I have been duly honored with your favor of the 13th inst. and at the same time that I think you and your Honble Council of Safety highly deserving of the thanks of the States for the measures you have adopted in order to give the most early and speedy succour to this Army, give me leave to return you mine in a particular manner.

When the whole of the reinforcements do arrive, I flatter myself we shall be competent to every exigency, and with the smiles of Providence upon our arms and vigorous exertions, we shall baffle the designs of our inveterate Foes formidable as they are—Our situation was truly alarming a little while since; but by the kind interposition and aid of our Friends is much bettered.

You may rest assured Sir, that due consideration shall be had to the several Militia Regiments that have come & are marching to our assistance, and that they shall be dismissed as soon as circumstances will admit of it. I trust as long as their is occasion for their service, that the same spirit and commendable zeal which induced them to come will influence their continuance— I sincerely wish it was in my power to ascertain the particular period when they would be needed, that they might not be detained one unnecessary moment from their homes and common pursuits. But as this cannot be done; as the approaching contest and trial between the two Armies will most unquestionably produce events of the utmost importance to the States; as the issue, if favorable, will put us on such a footing as to bid defiance to the utmost malice of the British Nation and those in alliance with her, I have not a doubt but they will most readily consent to stay, and chearfully forego every present and temporary inconvenience so long as they shall be necessary.

I am happy Capt. Van Buren has succeeded so well in the business he was upon, it being of great consequence for us to fit out and maintain our vessels on the Lake.

On the night of the 16th two of our Fire Vessels attempted to burn the Ships of War up the River. One of them boarded the Phœnix of 44 Guns and was grappled with her for some minutes, but unluckily she cleared herself—The only damage the Enemy sustained was the destruction of one Tender. It is agreed on all hands that our people engaged in this affair behaved with great resolution and intrepidity. One of the Captains— Thomas—it is to be feared perished in the attempt, or in making his escape by swimming, as he has not been heard of—His bravery entitled him to a better fate—Though this enterprise did not succeed to our wishes, I incline to think it alarmed the Enemy greatly—For this morning, the Phœnix and Rose with their two remaining Tenders taking the advantage of a brisk and prosperous gale with a favorable tide, quitted their stations and have returned and joined the rest of the Fleet—As they passed our several Batteries they were fired upon, but without any damage that I could perceive.

The whole of the British Force in America, except those employed in Canada, are now here; Clinton's arrival being followed the last week by that of Lord Dunmore who now forms a part of the Army we are to oppose. His coming has not added but little to their strength. I have the honor to be with great respect Sir Your most obedient Servant

Go: Washington

LB, Ct: Trumbull Papers; LB, DLC:GW; Varick transcript, DLC:GW.

General Orders

Head Quarters, New York, August 19th 1776.
Parole Georgia.   Countersign Hartford.
John Green of Capt: Johnsons Company and late Col. McDougall's Regiment, convicted by a General Court Martial, whereof Col. Wyllys is President, of "breaking out of his quarter guard and being absent two days"—ordered to receive Thirty-nine Lashes. The General approves the sentence, and orders it to be executed at the usual time and place; and the prisoner to be then returned to his quarter guard.

The Court Martial to sit to morrow, for the tryal of Lieut. Hubbel[1] of the regiment late Col. McDougall's—The Judge Advocate will be informed of the witnesses by General Putnam.

A Subaltern's Guard to go over to morrow, to relieve the Guard at Hoebuck ferry.[2]

Col. Hitchcock's Regiment to move to morrow, to Burdetts ferry, and relieve the party now there; they are to join General Mifflins Brigade, and receive Orders from Major General Heath, agreeable to General Orders of the 12th Instant.[3] General Putnam will order boats.

The Adjutants of such regiments as have lately come in to apply at the Adjutant General's office for Blank Returns which they are to fill up and bring in at orderly time—viz.: Eleven O'Clock every Saturday.

After this day, a Major to mount at the Main Guard, at the Grand Battery, instead of a Lieut: Colonel.

Varick transcript, DLC:GW.

1. "Henshaw's Orderly Book," 222, reads "Lieutenant Hobby." For the charges against Caleb Hobby and his acquittal, see General Orders, 4, 22 August.

2. The Hoboken ferry crossed the Hudson River from the town of Hoboken in New Jersey to Col. Leonard Lispenard's house on Manhattan Island, which was about half a mile from GW's headquarters at the Mortier house.

3. For Nathanael Greene's protest against this order, see his letter to GW of 15 August. "Great Changes and Alterations have lately been made," Hitchcock wrote Col. Moses Little on 15 August. "It gives me much Uneasiness that your Regiment is not going with mine. . . . The General thinks however they [the enemy] will attempt to take & occupy the River on both Sides there & consequently has ordered two more of the established Regiments there; if they come (& come they certainly will in a few Days) I will defend the Place as long as I can; they have certainly been embarking for a Day or two; I am yet fully of the Belief they will Land on Long Island for One of their Places & where else I don't know, but I'm fully persuaded, in more Places than One" (Johnston, *Campaign of 1776*, pt. 2, 75–76).

From Lord Drummond

Sir   sloop Polly Augt 19th 1776

While attending in the Boat on the 17th I was favoured with yours of that Date, and in Answer to those Points it seemd to allude to I coud then only return a verbal Message by Mr Tighlman which I flatter myself woud remove the Suspicions you entertained. As my first Motive for asking Lord Howes Permission to land at New York, was to give me an Opportunity of explaining myself to your Excellency on the Subject of my Parole in Relation to my Return to this Place—so the Hope I entertained of effecting it in this Way, made me perhaps too negligent in not saying any thing on that Subject in my Letter to you.[1]

Aware however of the Possibility of not being able to obtain an Interview with your Excellency—I had taken the Precaution to prepare a Letter to Colonel Moylan on that subject, and which I read to Mr Tighlman on his Delivering me that from your Excellency but which I forbore delivering as not thinking it sufficiently explicit.

But shoud Suspicions on any other Point in the Parole have arisen, I have only to beg that Your Excellency will have the goodness to permit me to a Personal Interview with You, which will either afford me an Opportunity of exculpating myself, or will place me in a Situation to suffer that Treatment which must follow an Infraction of Parole. I have the Honour to be Sir Your most Obt and most Humble servant,

Drummond

I enclose My Letter to Colol Moylan which I have alluded to together with the Logbook.[2]

ALS, DLC:GW; ADfS, Drummond Castle Papers, Scottish Record Office; copy, enclosed in GW to Hancock, 26 Aug. 1776, DNA:PCC, item 152; copy, DNA:PCC, item 169.

1. See Drummond to GW, 17 August.

2. "Finding I am disappointed in waiting on Genl Washington, and thanking him personally," Drummond says in his letter to Stephen Moylan of 17 Aug., "I should think myself very wanting in Duty was I not to do it in this manner and inform him how much I had benefitted by the permission he was good enough to give me of going to sea for the Recovery of my Health.

"In compliance with the terms of my Parole I have avoided every Port, where there was a likelyhood of my falling in with any of the English ships of War, and in consequence have not been Spoke to by any Vessell falling within the description of the Parole from the time of my departure from the [Sandy] Hook till my arivall off that place on the Night of the 9th when I was boarded by a boat from one of the Frigates belonging to the English Fleet, who took the Entire Management of the Vessell.

"I was now for the first time to my surprise Informed of the English Fleet and Army being at this place as the intelligence I had before my departure from the West Indies was that the Destination of the Fleet was more to the Southward and not at New York" (Drummond Castle Papers, Scottish Record Office). The enclosed logbook of Drummond's voyage has not been identified.

GW did not grant Drummond an interview or respond to this letter. For Drummond's further efforts to defend himself, see his letters to GW of 9 Dec.

1776 (Drummond Castle Papers, Scottish Record Office) and 14 Nov. 1778 (Collections of Lord Fairfax of Cameron, Gays House, Holyport, Maidenhead, Berkshire, England).

Letter not found: from Maj. Gen. Nathanael Greene, 19 Aug. 1776. In a letter to Hancock of 20 Aug., GW says that he received "a Letter from Genl Greene Yesterday Evening."

To John Hancock

Sir   New York Augt the 19: 1776

I have Nothing of moment to communicate to Congress, as things are in the situation they were when I had last the Honor of addressing them.[1]

By a Letter from Genl Ward of the 12th, I find that Whetcombs Regiment on the 8th, and Phinneys on the 9th, Marched from Boston for Ticonderoga.

Governor Trumbull also in a Letter of the 13th, Advises me that Wards Regiment in the service of the States was on the March to this Army, and that he and his Council of Safety had in the Whole, Ordered Fourteen Militia Regiments to reinforce us. Three of them have arrived, & amount to about a Thousand & Twenty men. When the whole come in, we shall be on a much more respectable footing than what we have been, but I greatly fear If the Enemy defer their Attack for any considerable time, they will be extremely Impatient to return Home, and If they should, we shall be reduced to distress again: he also adds, that Captn Van Buren who had been sent for that purpose, had procured a sufficient supply of Sail Cloth for the Vessels to be employed in the Lake and a part of the Cordage in that State, and had a prospect of getting the Remainder.

As there will be a difficulty in all probability to circulate the papers designed for the Foreign Troops, and many miscarriages may happen before It can be Effected, It may be proper to furnish me with a larger Quantity than what I already have.[2]

Inclosed I have the honor to transmit you a Genl Return of Our Whole force at this Time in which are comprehended the Three Regiments of Militia above mentioned. I am sorry It should be so much Weakned by Sickness—The Return will shew you How It distresses us.[3] I have the Honor to be Sir with great respect Your Most Obedt

Go: Washington

P.S. The post Just now arrived, has brought a further Supply of papers for the Hessians, which makes my requisition unnecessary.

LS, in Robert Hanson Harrison's writing, DNA:PCC, item 152; LB, DLC:GW; copy, DNA:PCC, item 169; Varick transcript, DLC:GW. Congress read this letter on 20 Aug. (*JCC*, 5:691).
     1. See GW to Hancock, 18 August.
     2. These papers, which probably had been sent with Hancock's letter to GW of 16 Aug., were German translations of Congress's resolution of 14 Aug. offering 50 acres of land and the free exercise of religion and civil liberties to any foreign mercenary who deserted from the British army (see *JCC*, 5:653–55). For efforts to distribute copies of the resolution on Staten Island, see Hugh Mercer to GW, this date, n.1, and GW to Hancock, 26, 29 August.
     3. This return has not been identified.

To Major General William Heath

Sir   Head Quarters [New York] 19. Aug. 1776
     I received yours of yesterday's date—The ships of War & Tenders were fired at from the Batteries here as they passed, and I suppose received similar damages to what they met with from the Forts at Mount Washington & Burdit Ferry. I shall not be able to spare any Tents for Genl Clinton at present owing to the very small Stock on Hand, with regard to their Quarters being so scattered I can only say, that I think it of less consequence the Case should be so circumstanced there than here, at this time— I have wrote to Colo. Knox this morning, desiring him to have the Carriages for four poundrs ready & sent forward with all expedition.[1]
     When I directed you to inquire into the Cause of the inactivity of some of the Row Gallies it was upon a presumption they were near you, as they are now come down to the City I shall give further Orders respecting that Affair.[2] I am Sir Your very humble Servt

Go: Washington

LS, in Tench Tilghman's writing, MHi: Heath Papers. The cover is addressed to "Major General Heath—Kings Bridge."

1. GW's letter to Knox of this date has not been found.

2. See General Orders, 21 August.

From Lord Howe

Sir, Eagle off Staten Island, August the 19th 1776.

Concurring in the Proposition you have been pleased to make in your Favor of the 17th for an Exchange of Prisoners in my Department, viz. Officers for those of equal Rank, and Sailors for Sailors; I will take the Liberty to propose an Officer of the same Rank to be exchanged for Mr Josiah, when he arrives.

The Cerberus being absent, I have no other Information respecting the Situation of Mr Josiah, than what is communicated in your Letter. But the matter, you may be assured, shall be inquired into, and every Attention paid to the Rules of Propriety, as well as the Dictates of Humanity, on all such Occasions.

Principles and Conduct form the true Distinction of Rank amongst Men: Yet without a competent Habit in the Manners of the World, they are too liable to meet with unmerited Disregard. But Insult and Indignities to Persons of whatever Rank, who are become Parties in these unhappy Disputes, cannot be justified, and are, I persuade myself, as much disapproved of, by every Officer under my Command, as they can never cease to be by me. I am, with great personal respect, Sir, Your most obedient humble Servant

Howe

LS, DLC:GW; copy, enclosed in GW to Hancock, 21 Aug. 1776, DNA:PCC, item 152; copy, DNA:PCC, item 169. The LS is addressed to "General Washington."

Letter not found: to Col. Henry Knox, 19 Aug. 1776. GW wrote to William Heath on this date: "I have wrote to Colo. Knox this morning."

From Colonel Henry Knox

May it please Your Excellency   New York Augt 19 1776
I understood that some few Cannon were to be taken from Mount Washington for Kings Bridge for the present—we find great difficulty in procuring the Carriages for General Fellowss encampment—the Greatest part of which I hope will be Completed to day and tomorrow after which we will turn our whole endevors to Complete those for Kings Bridge.[1] I am with Great Respect Your Excellencys Most Obt & Humble Sert

Henry Knox

ALS, MHi: Heath Papers. GW's aide-de-camp Richard Cary sent this letter to Heath with a brief covering letter (see Cary to Heath, this date, MHi: Heath Papers).

1. See Heath's request for these carriages in his letter to GW of 18 August.

From Brigadier General Alexander McDougall

Sir.   Tuesday 1 OClock. [19 August 1776]
The Substance of the examination of the woman which your excellency directed me to take, is as Follows vizt That her name is Mary Debeau; that She lived with Mr John Livingston about 18 months ago; and resided two weeks in Newyork, before She went to Staten Island, the day the man of warr passed up the River.[1] That She embarked with 7 men good livers in appearance, & 8 or 9 women, & ten Children, landed to the right of the Fleet & army; and that no person Questioned her or her Companions there, about her or their business, or on any other Subject.[2] That her errand there, was to See her husbands mother. She can give no account of the state of the army on the Island nor precisely where she staid. That She left that, on Sunday last in the afternoon, in Company with 10 or 11 men, and women and passed the Fleet on her left; and landed at the foot of Leary's Street; (where the Ferries to Powles Hook are kept) between 7 & 8 last night and that the boat was not examined in crossing the Bay, nor any of the passengers Questioned when they landed. That her Husband John Debeau is in our Service; (She thinks in the first Battalion of Militia.) That she knows not the name of any of her companions, who went down or came

up with her, except; one Cassens, who said he lived lately near the exchange. That from what she could collect the business of her Companions down, was to Secure a place of retreat, & those who came up to take their Famil[i]es out of Town. She answers So evasively, that I am at loss to determine her true Character. I have However had her Searched by matrons for Papers; but found none. From her appearence and deportment; I am inclined to conclude, she is a follower of the Enemy's army. And as the Committee of the Town is composed of Persons from every Quarter of the Town, I s[u]bmit it to your excellency, whether they will not be most likely to Search this matter, to the Bottom; and discover her fellow passengers; if her Story be true. I have the Honor to be Your excellency's very Humble servant

Alexr McDougall

ALS, DLC:GW. Samuel Blachley Webb docketed this letter: "From B. Genl McDougall Augt 19. 1776." Although that date was a Monday, it apparently is correct, because McDougall says that Mrs. Debeau left Staten Island the previous Sunday afternoon (presumably 18 Aug.) and arrived in nearby New York City "between 7 & 8 last night."

1. The *Phoenix* and *Rose* went up the Hudson River on 12 July.

2. McDougall inadvertently wrote "subsect" in the manuscript.

From Brigadier General Hugh Mercer

Sir,   New Ark [N.J.] 19 Augt 1776

This will be delivered at Head Quarters by Mr Ludwick; whom I sent for to Amboy in consequence of your Excellencys Letter of yesterday[1]—Inclosd is some Intelligence that may be of Consequence[2]—I am pushing on Troops to Bergen to the Amount of one Thousand—I hear the 3rd Virga Regt is on the March to join the Army—please to signify your Intentions as to the Disposition of such Virga Troops as may arrive—whether they are to proceed on to N. York or remain in the Flying Camp. I have the honour to be Sir Your excellencys Most obed. Sert

H. Mercer

ALS, DLC:GW.

1. This letter has not been found. Christopher Ludwick (Ludwig; 1720–1801), a native German who had served in the Austrian and Prussian armies before establishing himself as a gingerbread baker at Philadelphia in 1754, was a volunteer in the flying camp. When Ludwick arrived at headquarters later

this day, GW engaged him to distribute copies of Congress's resolution of 14 Aug. offering inducements to German deserters (see GW to Hancock, this date). "Mr. Ludwig the bearer of this," Joseph Reed wrote William Livingston on this date, "puts his Life in his Hand on this Occasion in order to serve the Interests of America. We cannot doubt your kind Advice & Assistance as to Mode but must beg it may not be communicated farther least a Discovery may be made which must prove fatal to Mr. Ludwig" (Prince, *Livingston Papers*, 1:119–20). In a brief letter to Livingston of 22 Aug., GW writes: "The Inclosed is left open for your perusal in hopes that you will be able to facilitate the design" (ALS, MHi: Livingston Papers). Although that enclosure has not been identified, it probably concerned Ludwick's mission. Ludwick crossed to Staten Island on the night of 22 Aug. but "returned disappointed" to Elizabeth the next day (Livingston to Mercer, 23 Aug., ibid., 124). Ludwick may have been more successful a few days later (see GW to Hancock, 26 Aug.).

During the following fall and spring, Ludwick attempted to persuade Hessian prisoners of war to defect to the American cause (see Hancock to GW, 16 Nov. 1776, DLC:GW, and Ludwick to Congress, 8 Mar. 1777, DNA:PCC, item 41). On 3 May 1777 Congress appointed Ludwick superintendent of bakers and director of baking for the Continental army, and he served as such until 1782 (see *JCC*, 7:323–34; 19:159; Ludwick to Congress, March 1785, DNA:PCC, item 41; and GW's certificate for Ludwick, 12 April 1787, DLC:GW).

2. Mercer enclosed the 18 Aug. examination of a Captain Britton, whose brig had carried 400 light horsemen from Halifax to Staten Island, and the undated examination of Jonathan Woodman, Isaac Osborne, and Robert Peas, seamen who had been captured by the British warship *Cerberus* in June and recently had escaped from a transport in New York Harbor (both are in DLC:GW).

Britton says: "From the best intelligence that he could collect, there are about Seven Hundred Light Horse on Staten Island, it is thought there are about twenty five Thousand Effective Men Eleven Thousand of which are Hessians—The General report was that they intended to attact Long Island first and if possible to Storm the Fort opposite the City in Order to prevent their Shippin[g] being Anoy'd when the Attack is made on New York.

"The Hessians were Landing on Staten Island as fast as possible when he left it—and from a conversation he had with several Hessian Officers he has no doubt from Proper encouragement & opportunity they would Join the Americans. That Capt. Talbot of the Niger with two other Frigates had received Orders to go round the East end of Long Island into the Sound in Order to cut off the communication between Long Island & the Main. That it is generally thought They mean to Attack Long Island with their Grenadiers and Light Infantry, and at the same time to send the remainder of their Army up the North River and Land above the Town by which means they expect to secure General Washington & the Army without firing a Shot. That Capt. Britton beleives the Attack is only delay'd untill a favourable Wind and Tide offers as they intended it on Saturday Morning last [17 Aug.], that they are certain of Success as they are of Opinion our Men will not Stand more than one Fire, that the mode of Attack is to give one Fire and then rush on with Fix'd Bayonets. That a number of Boats from Long Island came over with fresh Provisions and intelligence during his confinement, and that a Negro from Statend Island goes over to the Jersey shore every night to receive Letters lodged in some Private Place, and that he beleives they have daily intelligence of all our Movements.

"A Negro escaped from Statend Island this morning who says that all the Troops from this Quarter, were to march on Wednesday next [21 Aug.], and to be replaced by Hessians" (DLC:GW).

The three seamen say in their examination "that the Phenix man of War was grappled by one of Our Fire Ships & Narrowly escaped being burnt— That the Ships in their passage down received some Shots & the Phenix had One Man killed. That on Thursday night last a Boat came from the Phenix down to the Fleet, a Lieutt in which received a Cannon Ball through his thigh from One of Our Batteries—The Accounts as to the Number of the Enemies Troops are Various—That the Army is sickly especially Ld Dunmore's who brought but 106 Black & White with him—That Genl Clinton's Conduct at Charles Town is much blamed—he is accused of Cowardice & some say he will be hanged. That before 9 OClock Boats are suffered to pass through the Fleet without Interruption—That they have built about 20 New flat Bottom Boats— Every Ship besides having One. That last Week several Troops were embarked—some Yesterday & the Ships that received them all unmoored. That the Hessian Troops appear old & Indifferent. That the Highlanders seem very desirous of deserting, Three of whom have been lately taken in the Attempt & hanged & one Shot" (DLC:GW).

From Brigadier General Daniel Roberdeau

New-Ark[1] [N.J.] Augst 19th 1776
Sir   half past 11 OClock A.M.
The Post rider just past through here with a very incredible story which he told with great Confidence vizt that you had received a Flag from Lord Howe "proposing to retire with the Fleet and Army and that he was willing to settle the present dispute on any terms you should ask" for which he quoted the Authority of an Officer in your Army who told him that he might spred the News without the least reserve for that the Officer offered to sware to the truth for that he had it from you. As this Intelligence might have a tendancy to lull the Inhabitants I thought it duty to make it the subject of an Express without consulting Genl Mercer who is gone forwards towards Amboy. I am Sir Yr most obt huml. Sert

Danl Roberdeau

The Intelligencer further informed that the Reason of this hasty move from Ld Howe was news from England of a Rumpus wt. France.

ALS, DLC:GW.
1. Roberdeau first wrote "Woodbridge" on the manuscript and then struck it out and wrote "New-Ark."

To Brigadier General Daniel Roberdeau

Sir   Head Qrs N. York Augt 19th 1776
 I Received your favor of this date and thank you for the Intelligence thereby communicated.

The Report propagated by the post Rider, is totally destitute of truth in every instance, & as It may have the fatal tendency you seem but too Justly to apprehend, I beg Sir, that you will take Such Steps to contradict & Suppress It, as you shall think most likely to effect It.[1] I am &c.

G.W.

LB, in Robert Hanson Harrison's writing, DLC:GW; Varick transcript, DLC:GW.
1. GW also refutes this false report in the General Orders for 20 August.

From Major General Artemas Ward

Sir   Boston 19 August 1776.
 Your Letter of the twelfth Instant I received Saturday Evening;[1] I gave immediate attention to your Orders, and as it was judged extremely difficult, if not impracticable, to convey the Mortars by land, I gave Orders to the proper persons to prepare every thing necessary for conveying them by water, and to work day and night until they were compleated. This day they will go on board of Lighters to Sandwich from which place they are to be conveyed over the narrow neck of land to a place called Buzzards Bay,[2] where they will be put on board two Lighters and conveyed to Rhode Island, from thence, keeping near the land, to New york. I ordered they should be put on board two Vessels for the greater safety that if one should meet with any misfortune the other might perhaps go safe. I have given Mr Davis,

Deputy Barrack Master, the care of them as he was well acquainted with Coast, and have directed him to make all possible
dispatch in conveying the Mortars with their Appertenances to
New york.[3] An Invoice of them is as follows, 2 Sea Mortars with
upper and under Beds. 1 Truck Carriage. 1 Dozen Handspikes.
4 Iron Crows. 2 Spruce Poles for a pair of Sheers.[4] 2 Hoisting
Tackles. 3 Guys. 2 Pair of Slings. 4 Luff Tackles. 2 Coils of small
Cordage. I have ordered Ensign Gould with his party, (who
were going to New york by land,) to go on board the Vessels as
a Guard, lest the Enemy should send their Boats from some of
their Cruisers and attack the Lighters.

Great is our Solicitude for you and the Army under your
Command at New york, as we are in constant expectation of
the Enemy's making a violent attack. May the God of Armies
give You Success! I am Your Excellency's Obedient Humble
Servant

Artemas Ward

LS, DLC:GW; LB, MHi: Ward Papers.

1. The previous Saturday was 17 August. On the manuscript of the LS,
quotation marks that may have been added later appear around the words "I
received Saturday evening."

2. Crossing the base of Cape Cod peninsula was preferable to the long,
time-consuming voyage around the cape.

3. For Lt. Col. Joshua Davis's difficulties in moving these mortars from Nor-
wich, Conn., to New York, see his letter to GW of 10 September. See also
Joseph Eayres's report to Artemas Ward, c.30 Aug., and Davis to Ward, 2
Sept., in MHi: Ward Papers.

4. These two poles were to be fastened together to form a hoisting appa-
ratus.

To Lund Washington

Dear Lund,   New York Augt 19th 1776.

Very unexpectedly to me, another revolving Monday is arrived before an Attack upon this City, or a movement of the Enemy—the reason of this is incomprehensible, to me—True it is
(from some late informations) they expect another arrival of
about 5000 Hessians;[1] but then, they have been stronger than
the Army under my Command; which will now, I expect, gain
strength faster than theirs, as the Militia are beginning to come
in fast, and have already augmented our numbers in this City

and the Posts round about, to about 23,000 Men. The Enemy's numbers now on the Island and in the Transports which lay off it, are by the lowest Accts 20,000 Men by the greatest 27,000 to these the expected (5000) Hessians are to be added.

There is something exceedingly misterious in the conduct of the Enemy—Lord Howe takes pains to throw out, upon every occasion, that he is the Messenger of Peace—that he wants to accomodate matters—nay, has Insinuated, that he thinks himself authorized to do it upon the terms mentioned in the last Petition to the King of G: Britain[2]—But has the Nation got to that, that the King, or his Ministers will openly dispense with Acts of Parliament—And if they durst attempt it, how is it to be accounted for that after running the Nation to some Millions of Pounds Sterlg to hire and Transport Foreigners, and before a blow is struck, they are willing to give the terms proposed by Congress before they, or we, had encountered the enormous expence that both are now run to—I say, how is this to be accounted for but from their having received some disagreeable advices from Europe; or, by having some Manouvre in view which is to be effected by procrastination. What this can be the Lord knows—we are now passed the Middle of August and they are in possession of an Island only, which it never was in our power, or Intention to dispute their Landing on.[3] this is but a small step towards the Conquest of this Continent.

The two Ships which went up this River about the middle of the past Month, came down yesterday, sadly frightned I believe, the largest of them, the Phœnex (a 44. Gun Ship) having very narrowly escaped burning the Night before by two Fire ships which I sent up; one of which was grapnal'd to her for Ten Minutes, in a light blaze, before the Phœnex could cut away so as to clear herself. the other Fire ship run on board of the Tender near the Phœnex, & soon reduced her to Ashes. We lost no lives in the Attempt unless the Captn of the Ship which made the attempt upon the Phœnex perish'd. We have not heard of him since, but it is thought he might have made his escape by Swimming, which was the Plan he had in contemplation.

As the Collection of Mercers Bonds has not been put into the hands of Colo. Peyton, I have no objection to your undertaking of it if Colo. Tayloe has none; accordingly, I inclose you a Letter to him on this Subject, which you may forward, & act agreeable to his Instructions, and appointment.[4] I do not recollect enough of the Tenor of the Bonds to decide absolutely in the case of Majr Powell. true it is the design of making the Bonds carry Interest from the date, was to enforce the punctual payment of them; or, to derive an advantage if they were not. The Circumstances attending his going to Hampton, & the time when he did, I know not. He knew that those Bonds were payable to Tayloe & me—he knew that they became due (to the best of my recollection) the first of December, & should have tendered the Money at that time in strictness[5]—however if you have the Collection, in all matters of that kind take Colo. Tayloe's, or (which I believe will be the same think) Mr Jas Mercer's opinion as it will be impossible for me to determine these matters at the distance I am, and under the hurry of business I am Ingaged In.

There is no doubt but that the Honey locust if you could procure Seed enough, & that Seed would come up, will make (if sufficiently thick) a very good hedge—so will the Haw, or thorn, and if you cannot do better I wish you to try these—but Cedar or any kind of ever Green, would look better; howr, if one thing will not do, we must try another, as no time ought to be lost in rearing of Hedges, not only for Ornament but use.

Adams's Land you will continue to Rent to the best advantage, for I believe it will turn out, that I made bad worse, by attempting to save myself by taking that pretty youths debts upon myself.[6] As Lord Dunmore and his Squadron have joind the Fleet at Staten Island, you will, I should think, have a favourable oppertunity of sending of your Flour, Midlings, Ship stuff &ca—Corn will, more than probably, sell well sometime hence—especially if your Crops should be as short as you apprehend—If your Ship stuff & Middlings should have turnd Sower it will make exceeding good Bisquet notwithstanding. Your Works abt the Home House will go on Slowly I fear as your hands are reduced, & especially if Knowles fails.[7] remember that the New Chimneys are not to smoke. Plant Trees in the room of all dead ones in proper time this Fall. and as I mean to have groves of Trees at each end of the dwelling House, that at the South end to range in a line from the South East Corner to Colo. Fairfax's, extending as low as another line from the Stable to the dry well, and towards the Coach House, Hen House, & Smoak House as far as it can go for a Lane to be left for Carriages to pass to, &

from the Stable and Wharf. from the No. Et Corner of the other
end of the House to range so as to Shew the Barn &ca. in the
Neck—from the point where the old Barn used to Stand to the
No. Et Corner of the Smiths Shop, & from thence to the Servants Hall, leaveng a passage between the Quarter & Shop, and
so East of the Spinning & Weaving House (as they used to be
called) up to a Wood pile, & so into the yard between the Servts
Hall & the House newly erected—these Trees to be Planted
without any order or regularity (but pretty thick, as they can at
any time be thin'd) and to consist that[8] at the North end, of lo-
custs altogether. & that at the South, of all the clever kind of
Trees (especially flowering ones) that can be got, such as Crab
apple, Poplar, Dogwood, Sasafras, Lawrel, Willow (especially
yellow & Weeping Willow, twigs of which may be got from Philadelphia) and many others which I do not recollect at present—
these to be interspersed here and there with ever greens such
as Holly, Pine, and Cedar, also Ivy—to these may be added the
Wild flowering Shrubs of the larger kind, such as the fringe
Tree & several other kinds that might be mentioned. It will not
do to Plant the Locust Trees at the North end of the House till
the Framing is up, cover'd in, and the Chimney Built—otherwise it will be labour lost as they will get broke down, defaced
and spoil'd, But nothing need prevent planting the Shrubery at
the other end of the House.[9] Whenever these are Planted they
should be Inclosd, which may be done in any manner till I
return—or rather by such kind of fencing as used to be upon
the Ditch running towards Hell hole—beginning at the Kitchen
& running towards the Stable & rather passing the upper
Corner—thence round the Dry Well—below the necessary
House, & so on to the Hollow by the Wild Cherry tree by the
old Barn—thence to the Smiths Shop & so up to the Servants
Hall as before described. If I should ever fulfil my Intention it
will be to Inclose it properly—the Fence now described is only to
prevent Horses &ca. injuring the young Trees in their growth.

As my Greys are almost done, and I have got two or three
pretty good Bays here, I do not Incline to make an absolute Sale
of the bay horse you mention—But if Mr Custis wants him, &
you and he can fix upon a price, he may take him at such valuation; paying the Money and using him as his own; subject however to return him to me if I should hereafter want him and will

repay him his money—by this means he will (if it should not prove an absolute Sale) have the use of the Horse and I, the use of the money.

Before I conclude I must beg of you to hasten Lanphire about the addition to the No. End of the House, otherwise you will have it open I fear in the cold & wet Weather, and the Brick work to do at an improper Season, neither of which shall I be at all desirous of. My best wishes to Milly Posey and all our Neighbours and friends. with sincere regard I remain Dr Lund, Yr affecte Friend

Go: Washington

ALS, CSmH.

1. See the examination of Capt. Alexander Hunter quoted in Daniel Roberdeau to GW, 15 Aug., n.1.

2. See Lord Drummond to GW, 17 Aug., and note 1. GW is referring to the Olive Branch Petition of 5 July 1775.

3. On the manuscript GW first wrote "the possession of" and then, striking out those words, he wrote "their Landing on."

4. For a discussion of the collection of these bonds which GW and John Tayloe had received at the sale of George Mercer's lands in Fauquier and Frederick counties, Va., during November 1774, see Lund Washington to GW, 29 Oct. 1775, n.7. See also Lund Washington to GW, 24 Nov., 17, 23, 30 Dec. 1775, 8, 15 Feb. 1776; GW to Tayloe, 11 Dec. 1775, 12 Mar. 1776; and Tayloe to GW, 6 Feb. 1776.

Although GW's enclosed letter to Tayloe of this date has not been found, GW transcribed a significant portion of it in his letter to Francis Lightfoot Lee and Ralph Wormeley, Jr., of 20 June 1784, in which he summarizes his involvement in the sale of Mercer's lands. That extract, which is dated "New York Augt 19th 1776," reads: "A Letter which I received from Mr Lund Washington by the last Post informs me, that no person (by your order) has yet applied for Colo. Mercers Bonds in his hands. That frequent tenders of money in discharge of them are made to him—and that he thinks, if it was agreeable to you & me, he could collect the debts which are due, without much difficulty, or neglect of my business.

"I have never had a wish that this business should be placed in his hands, not so much because I was fearful of its interfering with my business, as because I was unwilling to have it thought I had a mind to favor a relation or friend with the Commission—& therefore recommended Colo. Peyton—but as the latter has not entered upon the collection (from what cause I know not) I shall have no objection to Mr Lund Washington's doing it if you desire it, and he will do it upon as easy terms as Colo. Peyton, or any other proper person would undertake it for" (ALS [photocopy], DLC:GW).

5. At the sale of George Mercer's lands, Leven Powell (1737–1810), a successful merchant in Loudoun County, Va., gave GW and Tayloe bonds dated

26 Nov. 1774 for £182 and £40 Virginia currency to secure his purchases, and on 4 April 1776 Powell redeemed both bonds, paying the £222 principal and £14.16 in interest that had accumulated since 1 Dec. 1774. Powell was the third of the forty-five purchasers recorded in Lund Washington's account book who discharged his debt. The last of the outstanding bonds was redeemed in November 1779 (see Lund Washington's account book, 1762–85, MdAN). Powell, who was a close friend of GW, served as a major in the Loudoun County militia from 1775 to January 1777, when on GW's recommendation Powell was appointed lieutenant colonel of Col. William Grayson's Additional Continental Regiment (see Powell to GW, 29 Jan. 1777, PHi: Gratz Collection). Powell resigned his commission in November 1778 for reasons of health (see Powell to GW, 28 Nov. 1778, PHi: Dreer Collection). He served in the Virginia house of delegates in 1779, 1787 to 1788, and 1791 to 1792, and he was a member of the U.S. Congress from 1799 to 1801.

6. For a discussion of GW's difficulties with Daniel Jenifer Adams and the land in Charles County, Md., that Adams gave GW in partial discharge of his debt to him, see GW to Lund Washington, 20 Aug. 1775, n.4. See also Lund Washington to GW, 5, 15, 29 Oct., 3, 10, 17 Dec. 1775, 17, 31 Jan., 15 Feb. 1776, and Thomas Stone to GW, 16 Jan. 1776.

7. For bricklayer John Knowles's previous illness and injury, see Lund Washington to GW, 22, 29 Oct., 3, 10, 17 Dec. 1775. Knowles was still working at Mount Vernon in the 1780s.

8. On the manuscript GW struck out "of all" before "that."

9. The southern addition to the Mount Vernon mansion, which included a study and a master bedroom, had been completed by the end of 1775. House carpenter Going Lanphier began work earlier this year on the northern addition, which was to include a banquet hall, but it was not finished until after the war.

General Orders

Head Quarters, New York, August 20th 1776.
Parole Hampton.   Countersign Gates.

Nathaniel Mun of Capt. Peters's Company, Col. Reads Regiment, convicted by a General Court Martial whereof Col. Wyllys is President of "Desertion and reinlistment into another corps."

James Mumford of Capt. Ledyards Company, Regiment late Col. McDougall's convicted by the same Court Martial of the same crime.

Alexander Moore, Serjeant in Capt. Conway's Company,[1] Col. Wynd's Battalion convicted by the same Court Martial of "Desertion."

Christopher Harpur of the same Company and Battalion, convicted by the same Court Martial of the same crime. Each of the above prisoners were sentenced to receive thirty nine lashes.

The General approves the sentences, and orders them to be executed at Guard mounting, to morrow morning, at the usual place.

The troops lately arrived are informed that it is contrary to General Orders, to fire in camp; such Firelocks as are loaded, and the charges cannot be drawn, are to be discharged at Retreat beating in a Vulley under the inspection of an officer. The officers of such troops are desired and required to prevent all the firing in the camp, as it tends to great disorder.

The regiments of militia, now under the Command of Col. Hinman, from Connecticut, are in case of alarm, to parade on the grand parade, and there wait for orders.

The officers who have lately come into Camp are also informed that it has been found necessary, amidst such frequent changes of Troops to introduce some distinctions by which their several ranks may be known—viz.: Field Officers wear a pink or red cockade—Captains white or buff—Subalterns green—The General flatters himself every Gentlemen will conform to a regulation which he has found essentially necessary to prevent mistakes and confusion.

The trial of Lieut: Hubbel is postponed 'till tomorrow.[2]

The General Court Martial to set on Thursday, as a Court of enquiry, into the conduct of Adjutant Brice of Col. Smallwood's Battalion, charged with "disobedience of orders and disrespectful behaviour to his commanding officer."[3]

The General being informed, to his great surprize, that a report prevails and is industriously spread far and wide that Lord Howe has made propositions of peace, calculated by designing persons more probably to lull us into a fatal security;[4] his duty obliges him to declare that no such offer has been made by Lord Howe, but on the contrary, from the best intelligence he can procure—the Army may expect an attack as soon as the wind and tide shall prove favourable: He hopes therefore, every man's mind and arms, will be prepared for action, and when called to it, shew our enemies, and the whole world, that Freemen[5] contending on their own land, are superior to any mercenaries on earth.

The Brigadiers are to see the Spears in the different works, under their command, kept greased and clean.

General Sullivan is to take the command upon Long Island, 'till General Greene's State of health will permit him to resume it, and Brigadier Lord Stirling is to take charge of General Sullivans division 'till he returns to it again.

Edward Tilghman Esqr. is appointed as an Assistant Brigade Major to Lord Stirling; the duty of the whole division being too great for one officer—He is to be respected and obeyed accordingly.[6]

Varick transcript, DLC:GW.

1. John Conway (1743–1802) of Woodbridge, N.J., became a captain in Col. William Winds's 1st New Jersey Regiment in November 1775. Wounded at the Battle of Germantown on 4 Oct. 1777, Conway was named major of the 4th New Jersey Regiment later that month, and the next year he transferred to the 3d New Jersey. In July 1779 Conway became lieutenant colonel of the 1st New Jersey Regiment. A court-martial on 28 Aug. 1780 acquitted him of charges of disobeying orders and ungentlemanlike conduct (see General Orders, that date), and he retired from the army at the end of that year.

2. "Henshaw's Orderly Book," 223, reads "Lieutenant Hobby." For Caleb Hobby's court-martial, see General Orders, 4, 19, 22 August.

3. The following Thursday was 22 August. Jacob Brice (Bryce), who had become adjutant of Col. William Smallwood's Maryland regiment in March 1776, was tried on this charge a few days later (see General Orders, 24 Aug.). Brice apparently was acquitted, for during the Battle of Long Island on 27 Aug., he was captured by two British light-horse officers and escaped by shooting the soldier guarding him (extract of a letter from New York, 31 Aug. 1776, in Force, *American Archives*, 5th ser., 1:1250). On 10 Dec. 1776 Brice was commissioned a captain in the 3d Maryland Regiment, and on 1 Jan. 1780 GW appointed him brigade major and inspector of the 1st Maryland Brigade (see General Orders, that date). In August 1780 Brice was wounded and captured in the American defeat at Camden, South Carolina. After his exchange Brice joined the 4th Maryland Regiment as a captain, and on 1 Jan. 1783 he transferred to the 1st Maryland Regiment, where he remained until the end of the war.

4. See Daniel Roberdeau to GW, 19 August.

5. "Henshaw's Orderly Book," 223, reads "those Men."

6. Edward Tilghman (1751–1815), a cousin of Tench Tilghman, enlisted as a private in the Philadelphia associators earlier this year and apparently marched with them to Perth Amboy in July. A capable young attorney who had studied law at the Middle Temple in London, Tilghman served only briefly as assistant brigade major of Stirling's brigade before returning to Philadelphia

to resume his legal practice. Although Tilghman subsequently became one of the most renowned lawyers in the city, he consistently refused to serve in public office.

From Colonel Lewis Duboys

New Windsor [N.Y.]
May it please your Excellency   20th August 1776
I received your Excellency's Letter of the 9th of August and agreeable to your Order have procured Returns of all the Officers of the Regiment under my Command of the Men inlisted by them (except three Captains who are at present in New York) The Number which as yet they have been able to inlist consists of thirty Men; 23 of which are well Armed and will be ready to march on Saturday next agreeable to your Excellency's Order.[1]

At a meeting of the Officers this Day they requested me to petition your Excellency that you would be pleased to order them into immediate Service at New York or wherever your Excellency may think fit. As the Country is very much drained of Men every Man that can any way be spared being already in the Service. they think that if they were in present Service they might not only have an Opportunity of exerting themselves to the utmost of their power, but might also compleat their Company's out of the Militia whenever it is thought expedient to grant them that Liberty.

They all express the most ardent Zeal for the Service, and are unwilling to be Idle at this important Crisis. I am your Excellencys most Obedient humble Servant

Lewis Duboys

ALS, N; Sprague transcript, DLC:GW. The addressed cover of the ALS is in DLC:GW.

1. The following Saturday was 24 August.

From the Greenwich Committee of Safety

Greenwich in the State of Connecticut
Sir   Augt 20th 1776.
The Authority Selectmen & Comttee of this Town have yesterday reced from his Honor the Governor of sd state, a requisition

dated the 12th instant, to embody all the householders not obliged to do duty in any Training Band, in order to march forthwith to N. York to Join the Army under your Excellency's Command. we thereupon warned all the able Bodied men in the Town to assemble at 6 O'Clock this morning, but as the mallitia is already gone into the service, & this Town hath been pretty much drained of men in the progress of the war, we find there are now but few fit to go, & those few badly Equipped, the householders having been at different times Striped of their fire Arms to supply those who turned out in the Defence of their Country. All which being maturely considered by the sd Authority &ca it was Judged most proper to advise your Excellency of our difficulties, in order to know from yr Excelly whether the service requires the whole of the few Men remaining in this Town to be raised immediately, & if so whether they can be supplied with Arms on their arrival at York.

As the Bearer, Doctor Mead a Member of the Comttee will deliver this,[1] we think it superfluous to add any more further than that we are with the greatest Esteem Your Excellency's Obedt huml. servts

Per order of the Authority &ca
John Mackay Chairman pro: Temp.

LS, in John Mackay's writing, DLC:GW.

1. Amos Mead (1730–1807), a physician who had served as a surgeon with the Connecticut troops at Ticonderoga during the French and Indian War, was a member of the general assembly from 1770 to 1776, 1778 to 1781, 1785, 1787 to 1788, and 1790 to 1793. He was also a member of the Connecticut Ratifying Convention in 1788.

To John Hancock

Sir New York Augt 20th 1776

I was yesterday Morning favoured with yours of the 17th, accompanied by Several Resolutions of Congress, and Commissions for Officers appointed to the late Vacancies in this Army.

I wrote some days ago to Genl Schuyler, to propose to Genls Carleton & Burgoyne an Exchange of prisoners in consequence of a former Resolve of Congress authorizing their Commanders in each Department to negociate One.[1] That of Major Meigs for Major French, and Captain Dearborn for any Officer of equal rank, I submitted to Genl How's consideration by Letter on the 17th, understanding their paroles had been sent him by Genl Carleton, but have not yet received his Answer upon the Subject.

In respect to the Exchange of the prisoners in Canada, If a proposition on that head has not been already made, and I believe It has not, the Inclosed Copy of Genl Carleton's Orders transmitted me under Seal by Major Bigelow, who was sent with a Flag to Genl Burgoyne from Tyconderoga with the proceedings of Congress on the breach of Capitulation at the Cedars & the Inhuman treatment of our people afterwards, will shew It is unnecessary, as he has determined to send them to their own provinces there to remain as prisoners, Interdicting at the same time All kind of Intercourse between us & his Army, except such as may be for the purpose of Imploring the Kings Mercy. The Assassination he mentions of Brigadr Genl Gordon is a fact entirely new to me, and what I never heard of before. I shall not trouble Congress with my Strictures upon this Indecent, Illiberal and Scurrilous performance so highly unbecoming the Character of a Soldier and a Gentleman, Only observing that Its design is somewhat artfull, and that each Boatman with Major Bigelow was furnished with a Copy.[2]

I have also transmitted Congress a Copy of the Majors Journal, to which I beg leave to refer them for the Intelligence reported by him on his return from the Truce.[3]

By a Letter from Genl Greene Yesterday Evening he informed me, he had received an Express from Hog Island Inlet advising that 5 of the Enemy's Small Vessells had appeared at the Mouth of the Creek with some Troops on board—also That he had heard Two pettiaugers were off Oister Bay, the whole supposed to be after live Stock and to prevent their getting It, he had detached a party of Horse & Two Hundred & Twenty men among them, Twenty Rifle men.[4] I have not received further Intelligence upon the Subject.

I am also advised by the Examination of Captn Britton, Master of a Vessel that had been taken, transmitted me by Genl Mercer, that the Genl Report among the Enemy's Troops was when he came off, that they were to Attack Long Island and to secure Our Works there If possible at the same time that Another part of their Army was to land above this City[5]—This Information is corroborated by many other Accounts and is probably true— Nor will It be possible to prevent them landing on the Island, As Its great Extent affords a variety of places favourable for that purpose, and the Whole of our Works on It are at the end opposite to the City. However we shall attempt to harrass them as much as possible which will be all that we can do. I have the Honor to be with Sentiments of the greatest esteem Sir Yr Most Obed. Servt

Go: Washington

LS, in Robert Hanson Harrison's writing, DNA:PCC, item 152; LB, DLC:GW; copy, DNA:PCC, item 169; Varick transcript, DLC:GW. Congress read this letter on 22 Aug. and referred it to the Board of War (*JCC*, 5:695).

1. See GW to Schuyler, 7 August.

2. For Guy Carleton's order of 7 Aug., see Schuyler to GW, 16 Aug., n.1. The copy of the order enclosed with this letter is incorrectly dated 4 Aug. (DNA:PCC, item 152). Patrick Gordon, lieutenant colonel of the 29th Regiment, was appointed an acting brigadier general in Canada by Carleton in June 1776. On 25 July Gordon was ambushed and fatally wounded near Chambly by Lt. Benjamin Whitcomb's scouting party (see Whitcomb's journal, 14 July–6 Aug. 1776, DLC:GW). Carleton's order, Matthias Ogden wrote Aaron Burr on 11 Aug., is "truly ridiculous. . . . But there is one part of it in which I think they in some measure accuse us justly: I mean that of assassinating, as they term it with too much truth, Brigadier-General *Gordon*. He was shot by the *Whitcomb* I mentioned in my last, who had been sent there as a spy. The act, though villa[i]nous, was brave, and a peculiar kind of bravery that I believe *Whitcomb* alone is possessed of. He shot *Gordon* near by their advanced sentinel; and, notwithstanding a most diligent search was made, he avoided them by mere dint of skulking" (Force, *American Archives*, 5th ser., 1:901; see also extract of a letter from Albany, 12 Aug. 1776, ibid., 923).

3. John Bigelow (1739–1780) of the Connecticut independent artillery company was at the British outpost on Île aux Noix from 28 July to 8 August. "I observed during my Stay there," he says in his journal, "that they paraded, at different times, their officers in an ostentatious Manner, and with the manifest Intent to lead me into the Belief of their being very numerous, but I do not think that I saw above forty of them during the whole time, and more than sixteen together. They displayed the very same Pageantry, respecting five or six Batteaus, appearing exceedingly busy in carrying some Timber to the Isle, merely to shew themselves, and give their preparations a formidable Appearance. They have been employed about building a very large Bake House & perhaps for the same Reason. All the new Batteau's I cou'd see about the Island amounted to no more than Twelve. They talk much of Hessians and Hanoverians, but I saw none" (Bigelow's Journal, 23 July–10 Aug. 1776, DNA:PCC, item 152; see also the copy in DLC:GW).

Bigelow, who was a native of Hartford, Conn., served as a volunteer under Arnold at Ticonderoga in May 1775, and in January 1776 he raised his independent artillery company in Connecticut. During the fall of 1776 Bigelow commanded the artillery on Mount Independence near Ticonderoga (see Gates's general orders, 15 Oct. 1776, in Force, *American Archives*, 5th ser., 3:528). Bigelow declined appointment as major of Col. Samuel Wyllys's 3d Connecticut Regiment in February 1777 (see Hinman, *Historical Collection*, 408), and during the ensuing months he apparently served in the militia. In March 1778 Governor Trumbull appointed Bigelow to superintend the making of clothing for Continental troops, and the council of safety directed him to procure clothing for the state's Continental officers (ibid., 527–28, 533).

4. This letter has not been found. Hog Island (now called Centre Island) is at the mouth of Oyster Bay on the north side of Long Island.

5. For Captain Britton's intelligence of 18 Aug., see Hugh Mercer to GW, 19 Aug., n.2.

From John Hancock

3 oClock P.M.

Sir　　　　　Congress Cham[be]r [Philadelphia] 20 Augst 1776

Your Letter by Express with its several Inclosures I yesterday Rec'd, & yours by Post this moment come to hand; I have laid the whole before Congress, & am directed to keep the Express;[1] I shall therefore only by the Return of the Post Inclose you Two Commiss[ion]s which please to order to be Deliver'd;[2] Referring all other matters to be Sent by the Express. I have the hon. to be Your most Obedt sert

John Hancock Prest

ALS (photocopy), ViU: Gwathney Autographs Collection microfilm; ALS, sold by Sotheby, Parke-Bernet, item 271, 27–28 Feb. 1974.

1. On 19 Aug. Congress read GW's second letter to Hancock of 12 Aug., and on this date it read GW's letters to Hancock of 18 and 19 Aug. (*JCC*, 5:667, 672, 691). Congress detained the express rider, because it was discussing the papers concerning Lord Dunmore that GW had enclosed in his letter of 18 Aug. (see Hancock to GW, 24 Aug.).

2. The commissions are probably those for James Chapman and Thomas Dyer, both of whom Congress promoted to major on this date (ibid., 667–68).

From Major General William Heath

May it Please your Excellency   Kingsbridge Augst 20th 1776

I have the Pleasure to Inform you, that we have taken out of the wreck of the Tender lately burnt up the north River,[1] The following Cannon Vizt One Six Pounder, Two Three Do One Two Do and Ten Swivels, One Cabooses[2] and Apron, Two Cutlasses, Two Gun Barrels, One Crow bar and 4 Gapp[l]in[g]s and Chains, Lieut. Landon of Colo. Nicolls Regiment with Two of the Company to Which he belongs went off and Towed the Wreck on Shore Under the Fire of the Cannon of the Ships, a Cannon Ball Passing within a few Inches of his Head, He is an Undaunted officer, and with great Fatigue Has Taken these Cannon out of the water, I therefore beg leave to recommend this Service in Particular to your Excellency notice and if you Should think Some Reward Proper to be Given, it will be gratefully received by the Adventurers and Perhaps Prompt Others to daring Actions.[3] I have the Honor to be with great respect your Excellencys most Humble Servt

W. Heath

ALS, DLC:GW.

1. For the burning of the British tender *Charlotta* on the night of 16 Aug., see GW to Hancock, 17 August.

2. A caboose is a cookroom or kitchen on the deck of a small vessel.

3. Richard Langdon became a first lieutenant in Col. Isaac Nicoll's regiment of Orange County minutemen in March 1776.

General Orders

Head Quarters, New York, August 21st 1776.
Parole Kingsbridge.   Countersign Jersey.

Adjutant Taylor to do the duty of Brigade Major to General McDougall's Brigade during Major Platts illness; he is to be obeyed and respected accordingly.[1]

Lieut: Hobby of Capt: Hyatts Company, Regiment late General McDougalls, tried by a General Court Martial whereof Col. Wyllys was president for misbehaviour in leaving one of the Hulks in the North River; was acquitted and the complaint reported groundless—Ordered that he be discharged from his arrest.

A Court of inquiry to sit on Friday at Mrs Montagnies, upon Capt: McCleave, Stanton and Tinker, charged with backwardness in duty, up the North River last week, and misbehaviour on Sunday last when the Men of war came down the river[2]— Court to consist of the following persons, & meet at ten O'Clock—General McDougall President. Col. Malcom. Lt Col. Shepard. Lt Col. Wesson[.] Major Brooks. Capt. Peters[.][3] Capt: Van Dyck.[4] Members. The Judge Advocate to attend and all witnesses.

Fifty men properly officered to parade every morning at six O'Clock at General Putnam's; there to take Orders from him; Not to bring arms—These to be continued every day till further orders.

Fifty men also for fatigue to parade to morrow morning properly officered on the Grand parade without Arms—take orders from Capt: Post.

Ten Men with one Subaltern, who have been used to the Sea, to parade at General Putnams this afternoon, two OClock, to proceed to Kingsbridge, up the North River—take three days provision.

The like number for the same service, to parade to morrow morning, Six o'Clock, at General Putnam's quarters—take three days provision; both parties parade without arms.

Twenty men, with a Subaltern, to parade for fatigue, to morrow morning without Arms, on the Grand parade to proceed to Bayard hill, and work upon the well—take orders from the person who has the direction of digging the well.

Varick transcript, DLC:GW.

1. Andrew Taylor was appointed adjutant of McDougall's 1st New York Regiment on 18 Mar. 1776, and on 18 June the provincial congress commissioned him a second lieutenant (*N.Y. Prov. Congress Journals*, 1:498). Taylor remained in the 1st New York Regiment until November when he became an assistant quartermaster general with the rank of major. On 4 Dec. 1776 Taylor was recommended to the New York committee of safety as a person well qualified to obstruct the Hudson River near Newburgh (ibid., 735). Stationed at Newburgh, Taylor became by September 1777 a deputy quartermaster general with the rank of colonel. He apparently retired from that office in 1779.

2. The previous Sunday was 18 Aug., and the following Friday was 23 August. Joseph Reed discusses this inquiry in a letter to William Heath of this date: "The Captains of the Row Gallies having much resented the Suspicions formed of them for their Behaviour up the River as well as when the Men of

War passed this Place—intimated to the General [GW] that they supposed the Situation of the Times could not admit of a Trial or they should call for one. The General has thought proper to take them at their Offer & ordered a Court of Inquiry to set next Friday—As you seemed to be of Opinion there was a Failure of Duty when they went up last Week—the General desires you would collect such Evidence of their Behaviour as you think will put the Matter in its proper Light & send the Witnesses down here by that Day at 10 oClock. As Genl Mifflin seems to have been particularly attentive to their Behaviour the General thinks his Testimony may be of Service & would have him attend if he can be spared" (MHi: Heath Papers; see also Heath to Mifflin, 22 Aug., MHi: Heath Papers).

3. This member of the court may be Andrew Peters, a captain in the 13th Continental Regiment, or Nathan Peters, a captain in the 3d Continental Regiment. Both officers were stationed at New York at this time.

4. Abraham C. Van Dyke (Van Dyck; b. 1718), a New York City resident who had been a marine lieutenant during the French and Indian War, commanded the Grenadier Company in Col. John Lasher's regiment of militia independents from September 1775 to July 1776, when his company became part of Lasher's regiment of New York levies. Earlier this year Van Dyke's men had built the circular Grenadier battery on the Hudson River near the city (see General Orders, 29 April 1776), and during the American retreat from New York in September, Van Dyke was taken prisoner there. He was exchanged in April 1778, and on GW's recommendation, Congress on 24 July 1780 appointed Van Dyke lieutenant of marines aboard the sloop *Saratoga* (see Elias Boudinot to GW, 22 April 1778, DNA:PCC, item 152; GW to the Board of Admiralty, 29 May 1780, DNA:PCC, item 37; and *JCC*, 17:612, 650–51, 661). Van Dyke resigned his commission in November 1780.

To John Hancock

Sir   New York Augt the 21st 1776

Inclosed I have the Honor to transmit you a Copy of my Letter to Lord Howe as well on the Subject of a Genl Exchange of prisoners in the Naval Line, as that of Lieutt Josiah in particular, and of his Lordships Answer, which for Its matter and manner, is very different from Genl Carletons Orders which were forwarded Yesterday.[1]

The Situation of the Armies being the same, as when I had the pleasure of addressing you last, I have Nothing special to communicate on that head, nor more to add, than that I am with all possible respect Sir Your Most Obedt Servt

Go: Washington

LS, in Robert Hanson Harrison's writing, DNA:PCC, item 152; LB, DLC:GW; copy, DNA:PCC, item 169; Varick transcript, DLC:GW. Congress read this letter on 23 Aug. and referred it to the Board of War (*JCC,* 5:698).

1. See GW to Lord Howe, 17 Aug., and Lord Howe to GW, 19 August. Congress on 23 Aug. directed the Board of War to publish both letters (*JCC,* 5:698).

To Major General William Heath

Head Quarters New York 21st Augt 1776

Sir   8 OClock P.M.

Inclosed I transmit you Copy of a Letter which I have this Moment recd from Genl Livingston at Elizabeth Town.[1] You will perceive by it that the Enemy are upon the point of striking the long expected Stroke, and as part of the Information seems to intimate that the Attack may be up the North River as well as at the lower posts, I have only to recommend to you to be as well prepared as possible for this important Event. Should any other Intelligence of Moment come to hand you may depend it shall be immediately communicated to you by Sir Yr most obt Servt

Go: Washington

LS, in Tench Tilghman's writing, MHi: Heath Papers. The cover is addressed "to The Honble Major Genl Heath at Kings Bridge."

1. See William Livingston to GW, this date.

From Brigadier General William Livingston

Elizabeth Town [N.J.]

May it please Your Excy   Augt 21st 1776

In the utmost Haste, I must inform you that very providentially, I sent a Spy last Night on Staten Island to obtain Intelligence of the movements of the Enemy, as many Things apparently new was seen from our Lines—He has this Moment returned in safety—The Substance of his Information I must give you in short—He went on the Island about Midnight and got undiscovered to the House of the Person to whom he was sent, who informed him—That the whole Force of the Enemy of every kind was 35000 Men, 15000 of whom were left on the Island, but all the rest Embarqued.

That they expected to attack every Hour, he thinks this Night at farthest—It was to be on Long Island, & up the North River—That the 15000 Men were to land & attack at Bergen Point, Elizabeth Town Point and at Amboy.[1]

He has heard the Orders read & heard the Generals talk of it—The Waggons are all laid out & ready—That they appear very determined & will put all to the Sword—They are in great want of Provision—Pork tolerably good but flour exceedingly bad—They have eat up all the Cattle and are now killing & barrelling up all the Horses they meet with.

All the field Pieces are taken on Board except two—The Informant may be depended on, being employed by the General and carries his Baggage—He has been employed in purchasing Cattle—He has given £10 for a Cow and 10 Dollars for a Sheep—That the Tories on the Island are very illy treated lately, so that the Inhabitants who at first were so pleased, would now be willing to poison them all—They take from them every Thing they choose, and no one has any Thing they can call their own.[2] I am with great respect Your Excellencies Most Hble Servt

Wil: Livingston

LS, DLC:GW; copy, enclosed in GW to Hancock, 22 Aug. 1776, DNA:PCC, item 152; copy, MHi: Heath Papers; copy, DNA:PCC, item 169. The addressed cover of the LS includes a note signed by Livingston that reads: "The Bearer is to pass all Ferries & Posts and to be hastened with all speed."

1. In a postscript to a short letter that GW wrote to Livingston on 22 Aug., he says: "I believe the Attempt, if any, upon the Jerseys by the Foreigners will be nothing more than a diversion to withdraw your Aid from this place" (ALS, MHi: Livingston Papers).

2. An anonymous American correspondent at New York wrote on 22 Aug.: "The night before last, a lad went over to *Staten-Island,* supped there with a friend, and got safe back again undiscovered; soon after he went to General *Washington,* and upon good authority reported, that the *English* Army, amounting to fifteen or twenty thousand, had embarked, and were in readiness for an engagement; that seven ships of the line, and a number of other vessels of war, were to surround this city, and cover their landing; that the *Hessians,* being fifteen thousand, were to remain on the Island, and attack *Perth-Amboy, Elizabeth-Town Point,* and *Bergen,* while the main body were doing their best here; that the Highlanders expected *America* was already conquered, and that they were only to come over and settle on our lands, for which reason they had brought their churns, ploughs, &c.; being deceived, they had refused

fighting, upon which account General *Howe* had shot one, hung five or six, and flogged many.

"Last evening, in a violent thunder-storm, Mr. [   ] (a very intelligent person) ventured over. He brings much the same account as the above lad, with this addition, that all the horses on the Island were, by *Howe's* orders, killed, barrelled up, and put on board, the wretches thinking that they could get no landing here, and of consequence be soon out of provision. That the Tories were used cruelly, and with the Highlanders were compelled to go on board the ships to fight in the character of common soldiers against us. The *British* Army are prodigiously incensed against the Tories, and curse them as the instruments of the war now raging" (Extract of a Letter from New-York, Dated August 22, 1776, in Force, *American Archives*, 5th ser., 1:1111–12).

To Brigadier General William Livingston

Sir   Head Quarters [New York] Aug. 21t 1776.
⟨I a⟩m much obliged to you for your Favour of this Date— The Intelligence is important, & I shall take every necessary Measure to avail myself of it. Should any new Intelligence arrive you will please to forward it with the same kind Expedition you have used on this.

We have made no Discovery of any Movements here of any Consequence. I am with much Regard Sir Your most Obed. Hbble Sert

Go: Washington

LS, in Joseph Reed's writing, MHi: Livingston Papers.

To Major General Philip Schuyler

New York Augt 21. 1776.
On Monday I received your Favor of the 16th inst. with Its several Inclosures.[1] The Time You were in Treaty I can readily conceive, was sufficiently irksome & disagreeable. However, If the Good Consequences Which You meant should be produced from It, You will think It was extremely well spent.

General Carlton's Orders for their Indecent, Illiberal Scurrility, are equal If not superior to any Thing I have seem, & are such as I could not have expected from a Person of his High Rank. He holds forth a Language very different from General

Howe as You would perceive by the Copy of his Letter I transmitted You.[2] The Assassination of General Gordon, is a Matter entirely new—having Never heard of It before. The Paper made up as a Letter & directed to me, Which Major Bigelow brought with him, Only Contained a Copy of the Orders.

I am Glad the Works at Fort Stanwix are Going on so well & that they have so Much Provision in Store. In a little Time I hope they will be strong & Compleat.

By a Letter from Governor Trumbull he informs Me, that a Captn Van Buren had procured a sufficient Quantity of Sail Cloth & a part of the Cordage wanted for the Gallies, in Connecticut, & that the Rest of the Cordage would be probably Obtained there.[3] Upon the whole I hope Necessaries to fit them Out, will be Obtained one Way or Other.

The inclosed Letter from Colo. Stark was transmitted and referred to Me by General Gates in Order that I might determine upon the Subject of It.[4] I should suppose the Value of Rations should be sett[l]ed with the Commissary Or Submitted to Congress for their Decision. I do not con-ceive It with me, to give any Direction in this Instance, & therefore thought It right, to give Notice of It by this the first Opportunity.

Since my last of the 13th Nothing worthy of Mention has occurred in this Quarter, Unless the Ships of War having left their Stations up the North River & Joined the Fleet again is considered as such. On Sunday Morning they came down with their remaining Tenders.[5] It is more than probable, that an Attempt by two of our Fire Vessels to destroy them a Night or two before contributed to their Departure. The Enterprize tho' conducted with spirit & Resolution did not succeed to our Wishes, Only One Tender having been destroyed. The Phœnix was Grapled for some Minutes but cleared herself without Damage. I am Dr Sir, Your Most Obedt Servt

Go: Washington

LB, NN: Schuyler Papers; LB, DLC:GW; copy (extract), NHi: Gates Papers; Varick transcript, DLC:GW. The LB in DLC:GW contains some minor variations in wording.

1. The previous Monday was 19 August.

2. GW is referring to William Howe's letter to him of 1 Aug., a copy of which was enclosed in GW to Schuyler, 7 August.

3. See Jonathan Trumbull, Sr., to GW, 13 August.

4. See John Stark's letter to Gates of 5 Aug., which is quoted in Gates to GW, 7 Aug., n.5.

5. The previous Sunday was 18 August.

General Orders

Parole Johnson.

Head Quarters, New York, August 22nd 1776.
Countersign Kingstown.

Varick transcript, DLC:GW.

To John Hancock

Sir   New York Augt 22d 1776

I do myself the Honor to transmit Congress, a Copy of a Letter I received yesterday Evening by Express from Genl Livingston—Also Copies of three Reports from Colo. Hand.[1]

Though the Intelligence reported by the Spy on his return to Genl Livingston, has not been confirmed by the Event he mentions, an Attack last night, there is every reason to beleive that One is shortly designed. The falling down of Several Ships Yesterday Evening to the Narrows crouded with men—Those succeeded by Many more[2] this morning, And a great number of Boats parading around them as I was just now Informed, with Troops—are all circumstances Indicating an Attack, and It is not Improbable It will be made to day. It could not have happened last night, by reason of a Most violent Gust.[3]

We are making every preparation to receive 'em, and I trust, under the Smiles of providence with our own exertions, That my next, If they do attack, will transmit an Account that will be pleasing to every Friend of America and to the rights of Humanity. I have the Honor to be with all possible respect Sir Your Most Obedt Servt

Go: Washington

LS, in Robert Hanson Harrison's writing, DNA:PCC, item 152; LB, DLC:GW; copy, DNA:PCC, item 169; Varick transcript, DLC:GW. Congress read this letter on 26 Aug. (*JCC*, 5:700).

1. GW enclosed copies of William Livingston's letter to him of 21 Aug. and three short letters that Col. Edward Hand, who was at the Narrows, wrote to

Col. John Nixon on that date (all in DNA:PCC, item 152). In his first letter to Nixon, Hand reports that "twelve small Vessels and two Men of War came in from Sea late yesterday Evening. The small Craft and one of the Men of War joined the Fleet at the watering place[.] Some of the Blue Coated Gentry embarked yesterday Afternoon below the Narrows and then moved up. The Admiral had a large Company on Board in the Evening, his Ship was ornamented by displaying a Variety of Colours on the Occasion." In the second letter, written at 9:00 A.M., Hand says: "Since I reported this Morning 19 Transports have been filled with Men and they still continue to embark." Hand's third letter, written at 5:00 P.M., reads: "There are at least 14 Sail of Transports, some of them crouded with Men, now under sail, and more from the Noise are hoisting Anchor. These under sail move down as fast as they get from among the Fleet."

Ambrose Serle, who was aboard Lord Howe's flagship the *Eagle,* says in his journal that on 20 Aug., "all the Captains in the Fleet, belonging to the Men of War, met on board the Eagle, and had long Consultation with the Admiral [Howe]. Every thing now begins to look extremely serious." On the evening of 21 Aug. the captains returned to the *Eagle* to receive orders for landing troops on Long Island the following day (Tatum, *Serle's Journal,* 70–71).

2. The LB reads "Several more."

3. An anonymous American correspondent at New York wrote on this date: "The thunder-storm of last evening was one of the most dreadful I ever heard; it lasted from seven to ten o'clock. Several claps struck in and about the city; many houses damaged; several lives lost" (Extract of a Letter from New-York, Dated August 22, 1776, in Force, *American Archives,* 5th ser., 1:1111–12; see also Tatum, *Serle's Journal,* 71; Albion and Dodson, *Fithian's Journal, 1775–1776,* 214–16; and Shewkirk, "Moravian Diary," 145–46).

From John Hancock

Sir   Philadelphia 22d Augst 1776

Congress not having Come to a full Determination upon the Subject of your Letter by the Express, he is still Detain'd, I shall so soon as the Resolutions are perfected Dispatch him with them[1]—Your favr of 20th I have rec'd, & is before Congress with its Inclosures.

I have now only to Inclose you several Resolves pass'd yesterday in Congress, to which beg Leave to Refer you.[2] I have the honour to be with all possible respect Sir Your most Obedt servt
                                    John Hancock Presidt

The three Gentln who Came from Virginia, for the Apprehending of whom you issued a Warrant, were taken at Eliza.

Town, & deliver'd me yesterday by a party of the Light horse, and are now under Guard, will be Examin'd this Day.[3]

ALS, PHi: Gratz Collection.

1. Hancock is referring to GW's letter to him of 18 Aug. concerning Lord Drummond's peace proposals. For Congress's response, see Hancock to GW, 24 August.

2. The enclosed resolutions of 21 Aug. concern Basil Bouderot's trial for murdering Samuel Holden Parsons's brother, capital punishment for persons "found lurking as Spies in, or about the Fortifications or Encampments of the Armies of the United States," appropriation of $500,000 for the army at New York, procurement of cannon for Gates's army, continuance of Artemas Ward as eastern department commander, and procurement of copper (DLC:GW; see also *JCC*, 5:692–94).

3. The warrant of 17 Aug., which Robert Hanson Harrison signed by GW's command, directs Jacob Shafer of New York City to apprehend Thomas Reed, Patrick Ballantine, and Robert Gilmour "late of the Colony of Virginia . . . who passed from the above said City this morning to Powles Hook" and who "are persons unfriendly to the rights and liberties of the United States of America and are carr[y]ing on sundry malpractices against the interest of said States." Shafer was to take the prisoners to Philadelphia and deliver them to the president of Congress (ADS, sold by Parke-Bernet Galleries, catalog 1190, item 31, 30–31 Oct. 1950; the ADS was sold again by Sotheby, Parke-Bernet, catalog 4158, item 79, 3 Oct. 1978). Congress resolved on this date to send the prisoners to the Pennsylvania council of safety for examination (*JCC*, 5:695), and on the reverse of the warrant Hancock instructs the officers of the prisoners' guard to carry out that order. No record of the council's action on this matter appears in its minutes.

To Major General William Heath

Dr Sir,　　　　　　　　　　　　　　New York Augt 22d 1776.

As the Enemy must pass this place before they can attempt the Posts above, and as your Troops there, are new augmented, I would have you pick out a body of about Eight hundred or a thousand light active men, and good Marksmen (Including the light Infantry and Riflemen) ready to move this way upon the appearance of the Shipping coming up, or upon the commencement of the Canonade of any of our Works.

By the time these Troops get in to the flat grounds of Harlem they will be able (especially if you send a Horseman or two on before for Intelligence which will be proper) to determine whether the Ships Intend higher up than this Neighbourhood and regulate themselves accordingly.

There is a road out of the Harlem flat Lands that leads up to the Hills & continues down the North River by Bloomingdale—Delancys &ca[1] which road I would have them March as they will keep the River in sight and pass a tolerable Landing place for Troops in the Neighbourhood of Bloomingdale. this Detachment should bring a couple of light field Pieces.

I think two, or even four pieces of Cannon might be spared from Fort Washington to the Post ovr the Bridge[2]—But query whether it might not do to run them from thence when occasion shall seem to require it as that Post never can be attacked without sufficient notice to do this—Colo. Knox will have four Carriages ready for that place immediately if we have not other Imployment upon hand—which General Putnam who is this Instant come In seems to think we assuredly shall this day as there is a considerable Imbarkation on board of the Enemy's Boats. I shall therefore only add that you should delay no time in forming your Detachment for our Aid—or your own Defence as Circumstances may require. Yrs &ca in haste

Go: Washington

ALS, MHi: Heath Papers.

1. Oliver De Lancey (1718–1785), a prominent merchant and Loyalist who had been a member of the governor's council since 1760 and receiver general of the colony since 1763, lived in a mansion at Bloomingdale, a village on the west side of Manhattan Island about seven miles north of New York City. The mansion was burned by Patriots in 1777, and in 1779 the state confiscated all of De Lancey's property. De Lancey raised a Loyalist brigade of 1,500 men for the defense of Long Island in September 1776 and commanded it with the rank of brigadier general until 1783. After the war he moved to England.

2. GW is referring to King's Bridge (see Heath to GW, 18 Aug.).

From Major General William Heath

Kingsbridge Augt 22nd 1776
Dear General   half Past 2 oClock A:M.

I have the Honor this moment to receive yours of the last Evening Inclosing Copy of a Letter from Genl Livingston.

I can Assure your Excellency that every thing in my Power

shall be Done to be in Readiness, either to receive the Enemy here or to afford you Aid, Fort Washington is in Good order, but our works here are not yet Compleated, and we are as yet Entirely without any Cannon mounted—General Mifflen Seems Unwilling, that any Should be removed from Mount Washington but I think to order up at least Two this Day we have 15 or 1600 men here, who are Excellent marksmen, and nature has Given us Proper Ground for them, we have received a number of Boards, and shall Put up sheds Immediately in order to Draw our men together being at present much Scattered.[1] I have the Honor to be with great respects your Excellencys most Humble Servt

W. Heath

General Clinton is gone Down to view the most Important Posts and to Raise a sufficient number of militia to defend them if Such a number Can be Mustered, and give orders for Securing the Stocks &c.

P.S. I have this moment seen the Orders from the Adjt Genl to Genl Mifflin The Detachment will march immediately but Your Excellency will consider our Situation. W.H.

ADfS, MHi: Heath Papers.

1. At this place in the manuscript, Heath wrote and then struck out the phrase: "If the Bakers are at Liberty in the City I should be Glad that, a."

From Major General William Heath

Kingsbridge Aug: 22nd 1776

Dear General   2 O'Clock P.M.

I have the honor this moment to receive your Orders for augmenting the Detachment designed for your Aid—Genl Mifflin, Clinton & myself an Hour or Two Ago had determined upon the same Plan, and think our Selves happy in having the same order'd by your Excellency—The Detachment shall be got ready with all Expedition, & Officer'd with the best Officers which we have, Genl Mifflin will command them—If the Commissary Genl has a Quantity of hard biscuit on hand I cou'd wish to have some sent here immediately, if he has not that a Quantity may be baked for us if possible—As we have not Ovens as yet

built in Genl Clinton's Brigade, and the Men with great Difficulty obtain their bread from day to day we are about building
Ovens as fast as the materials can be procured. I have the honor
to be With great Respect Your Excellency's most Humble Servt
W: Heath

ADfS, MHi: Heath Papers.

From Richard Peters

Sir. War Office [Philadelphia] Augt 22d 1776
I have put under the Care of the Bearer's, Part of the Philadelphia Light Horse, five hundred thousand Dollars to be sent
to Ticonderoga for the Use of the Northern Army.[1] As it might
save Expence & be more expeditious, I have desired the Gentlemen, to call at Head Quarters & take your Excellency's Opinion & Directions as to the Propriety of sending the Money by
Water; the River being now cleared of the Enemy's Ships.
Should you think it best to send their Charge by Water, the
Gentlemen will either accompany it themselves, or submit to
your Excellency's Appointment of another Guard with Pleasure,
as some of them are desirous of returning tho' two are inclinable
to proceed the whole Way. I have troubled you on this Head by
the Advice of the Board of War & have the Honour to be with
great Esteem & Respect your very obedt & most hble Servt
Richard Peters Secy

ALS, MH: Dearborn Collection.
1. Congress made this appropriation on 15 Aug. (*JCC,* 5:659).

From Major General Artemas Ward

Sir Boston 22 August 1776
Your Excellency's letter of the thirteenth Instant came to hand
last Evening; and agreeable to your Directions I shall order
Capt. Burbeck with his Company of Artillery, and the Company
of Artificers, to march as soon as possible for Norwich and from
thence to go by water to Norwalk, and New york. I am Your
Excellency's most Obedient Humble Servant
Artemas Ward

Postscript: Major Wadsworth, was appointed Major of Brigade to this Division of the Army the 22 Day of April, and when the Continental Regiments were ordered to New york, and Ticonderoga, as the Brigade was divided, I directed him to do duty as Brigade Major to the Regiments that are ordered in to take the place of the Continental Regiments, until further Orders.

LS, DLC:GW; LB, MHi: Ward Papers.

From Abraham Yates, Jr.

In Convention of the Representatives of the
Sir   State of New York Haerlem August 22d 1776
The Convention of this State have received Information from one of the Deputies of the City and County of New York, of a Report Prevailing amongst the Army, "that if the fortune of War should oblige our Troops to abandon that City, it should be immediately burnt by the retreating Soldiery, and that any Man is authorized to set it on fire."

The Convention will chearfully submit to the fatal Necessity of destroying that Valuable City whenever Your Excellency shall deem it essential to the Safety of this State or the general Interest of America—Yet the Duty which they owe to their Constituents obliges them to take every possible Precaution that Twenty thousand Inhabitants may not be reduced to Misery by the wanton Act of an Individual.

They therefore entreat the favor of Your Excellency to take such Measures in preventing the evil Tendency of such a Report as You shall deem most expedient.[1] I have the Honor to be Your Excellency's most Obedient and very humble servt

By Order.
Abm Yates Junr President

LS, DLC:GW; Df (mutilated), N: New York Provincial Congress Revolutionary Papers. The convention read and approved the draft of this letter on this date, but the text does not appear in the journal (*N.Y. Prov. Congress Journals,* 1:584).

1. For GW's response, see his letter to the New York convention of 23 August.

General Orders

Head Quarters, New York, August 23rd 1776.
Parole Charlestown.　　　　　　　　Countersign Lee.

The Commissary General is directed to have five days Bread baked, and ready to be delivered: If the Commissary should apply to the commanding officers of regiments, for any Bakers, they are to furnish them without waiting for a special order.

The General was sorry yesterday to find, that when some troops were ordered to march, they had no provisions, notwithstanding the Orders that have been issued.[1] The men must march, if the service requires it, and will suffer very much if not provided: The General therefore directs, all the Troops to have two days hard Bread, and Pork, ready by them; and desires the officers will go through the encampment, and quarters, to see that it be got and kept.

The General would be obliged to any officer, to recommend to him, a careful, sober person who understands taking care of Horses and waiting occasionally. Such person being a Soldier will have his pay continued, and receive additional wages of twenty Shillings ℔ Month—He must be neat in his person, and to be depended on for his honesty and sobriety.

The officers of the militia are informed, that twenty-four Rounds are allowed to a man, and two Flints; that the Captains of each Company should see that the Cartridges fit the bore of the gun; they then are to be put up in small Bundles; All the Cartridges except six; writing each mans name on his bundle, and keep them safely 'till the Alarm is given, then deliver to each man his bundle; the other six to be kept for common use. In drawing for ammunition, the commanding officers should, upon the regimental parade, examine the state of their regiments, and then draw for Cartridges, and Flints, agreeable to the above regulation. Capt: Tilton will assist them in their business, and unless in case of alarm, they are desired not to draw for every small number of men, who may be coming in.

The Enemy have now landed on Long Island, and the hour is fast approaching, on which the Honor and Success of this army, and the safety of our bleeding Country depend. Remember officers and Soldiers, that you are Freemen, fighting for the blessings of Liberty—that slavery will be your portion, and that of your posterity, if you do not acquit yourselves like men: Remember how your Courage and Spirit have been dispised, and traduced by your cruel invaders; though they have found by dear experience at Boston, Charlestown and other places, what a few brave men contending in their own land, and in the best of causes can do, against base hirelings and mercenaries—Be cool, but determined; do not fire at a distance, but wait for orders from your officers—It is the General's express orders that if any man attempt to skulk, lay down, or retreat without Orders he be instantly shot down as an example,[2] he hopes no such Scoundrel will be found in this army; but on the contrary, every one for himself resolving to conquer, or die, and trusting to the smiles of heaven upon so just a cause, will behave with Bravery and Resolution: Those who are distinguished for their Gallantry, and good Conduct, may depend upon being honorably noticed, and suitably rewarded: And if this Army will but emulate, and imitate their brave Countrymen, in other parts of America, he has no doubt they will, by a glorious Victory, save their Country, and acquire to themselves immortal Honor.

The Brigade Majors are immediately to relieve the Guards out of the regiments order'd to Long Island, from other regiments of the brigade, and forward such Guards to the regiments.

Major Newbury's Col. Hinmans, Major Smiths, Col. Cook's, Col. Talcots, Col. Baldwin's and Major Strong's Regiments of Connecticut Militia to parade this evening precisely at five OClock on the Grand parade—Major Henly will attend and shew them their alarm posts, and direct them in manning the lines.[3]

When any of the Field Officers for Picquet, or Main Guard, are sick, or otherwise incapable of the duty, they are immediately to signify it to their Brigade Major—but the General hopes that triffling excuses will not be made, as there is too much reason to believe has been the case.

Varick transcript, DLC:GW.

1. For these orders regarding provisions, see General Orders, 16 August. The marching troops were reinforcements for Long Island (see GW to Hancock, this date).

2. "Henshaw's Orderly Book," 226, adds "of Cowardice."

3. "Our Connecticuit Militia have Come in Bravely," Col. William Douglas

wrote his wife on this date. "Twelve Regt. were on the Grand Perade at one time yesterday. almost one half of this Grand Army now Consists of Connecticut Troops. the Militia are a fine Set of Men. I,m fully of the opinion that if the enemy attempt to Carry this Citty by Storm it will Cost them very Deer. they may Burn it, but they Cant Take it, and it is of no Service to them to Destroy it" (Douglas, "Letters," 13:81).

Roger Newberry (Newbury; 1735–1814) of Windsor, who commanded the 1st Regiment of Connecticut militia, was promoted to colonel of militia in 1777 and brigadier general of militia in 1781. Seth Smith subsequently served as lieutenant colonel of regiments of militia levies raised to defend Connecticut in 1777 and 1778 (Hinman, *Historical Collection*, 276, 314). Jonathan Baldwin (1722–1802) of Waterbury was lieutenant colonel of Col. James Wadsworth's 10th Regiment of Connecticut militia (ibid., 215). Simeon Strong of Burlington was commissioned major of the 15th Regiment of Connecticut militia in March 1775 (ibid., 163).

To John Hancock

Sir   New York Augt 23. 1776

I beg leave to inform Congress that Yesterday morning & in the course of the preceeding night, a considerable body of the Enemy amounting by report to Eight or Nine thousand, and these all British, landed from the Transport Ships mentioned in my Last at Gravesend Bay on Long Island, and have approached within three miles of our Lines, having marched across the Low, cleared Grounds, near the Woods at Flat Bush where they are halted from my last Intelligence.[1]

I have detached from hence, Six Battallions as a reinforcement to our Troops there,[2] which are all that I can spare at this Time, not knowing but the Fleet may move up with the Remainder of their Army and make an Attack here on the next Flud Tide. If they do not, I shall send a further reinforcment should It be necessary, and have ordered five Battallions more to be in readiness for that purpose. I have no doubt, but a little Time will produce some Important events. I hope they will be happy—The Reinforcement detached yesterday went off in high spirits, and I have the pleasure to Inform you that the whole of the Army, that are effective & capable of duty, discover the same and great chearfulness. I have been Obliged to appoint Major Genl Sullivan to the command on the Island, owing to Genl Green's Indisposition, he has been extremely Ill for several days and still continues bad.

By Wednesday Evening's post, I received a Letter from Genl Ward Inclosing a Copy of the Invoice of the Ordinance Stores taken by Captn Manly with the appraisemt of the same made in pursuance of my direction founded on the Order of Congress which I do myself the Honor of transmitting.[3]

You will also receive the Treaty between the Commissioners and the Indians of the Six Nations and Others, at the German Flats, which Genl Schuyler requested me to forward by his Letter of the 18 Instt. I have the Honor to be with great respect Sir Your Most Obedt Servt

Go: Washington

LS, in Robert Hanson Harrison's writing, DNA:PCC, item 152; LB, DLC:GW; copy, DNA:PCC, item 169; Varick transcript, DLC:GW. Congress read this letter on 26 Aug. and referred it to the Board of War (*JCC,* 5:700–701).

1. Ambrose Serle says in his journal that "about 15,000 Troops" landed on Long Island on 22 August. "The Disembarkation was effected upon the flat Shore, near Gravesend, without the least Resistance. . . . Every thing, relative to the Disembarkation, was conducted in admirable Order, and succeeded beyond our most sanguine Wishes" (Tatum, *Serle's Journal,* 71–72).

General Howe wrote Lord George Germain on 3 Sept. that the whole landing force, which included Donop's Hessian corps and forty cannon, landed "in two hours and a half under the direction of Commodore Hotham, Lieutenant-General Clinton commanding the first division of the troops. The enemy had only small parties on the coast, who upon the approach of the boats retired to the woody heights commanding a principal pass on the road from Flatbush to their works at Brooklyn. Lord Cornwallis was immediately detached to Flatbush with the reserve, two battalions of light infantry and Colonel Donop's corps with six field-pieces, having orders not to risk an attack upon the pass if he should find it occupied, which proving to be the case his lordship took post in the village, and the army extended from the ferry at the narrows through Utrecht and Gravesend to the village of Flatland" (Davies, *Documents of the American Revolution,* 12:216–18; see also Lord Howe to Philip Stephens, 31 Aug. 1776, in Clark and Morgan, *Naval Documents,* 6:373–77, and *Kemble Papers,* 1:84–85).

2. This reinforcement included Col. Gold Selleck Silliman's regiment of Connecticut militia levies, Col. Samuel Miles's regiment of Pennsylvania riflemen, Col. John Tyler's 10th Continental Regiment, and Col. Jedediah Huntington's 17th Continental Regiment (see Silliman to his wife, 24 Aug., in Johnston, *Campaign of 1776,* pt. 2, 52–53; Miles's journal, ibid., 60–61; and Sabine, *Fitch's New-York Diary,* 25).

3. Artemas Ward's letter to GW of 15 Aug. is quoted in Henry Bromfield to GW, 13 Aug., n.1. The previous Wednesday was 21 August. For Congress's resolution of 17 June 1776 regarding this appraisement, see *JCC,* 5:454.

To Major General William Heath

Sir   Head Quarters New York 23d Augt 1776

Yesterday Morning the Enemy landed at Gravesend Bay upon Long Island, from the best Information I can obtain, to the Number of about Eight Thousand. Colo. Hand retreated before them, burning as he came along, several parcels of Wheat, and such other Matters as he judged would fall into the Enemy's Hands. Our first Accounts were, that they intended, by a forced March, to surprize Genl Sullivan's (who commands during the Illness of Genl Green) Lines, whereupon I immediately reinforced that post with Six Regiments. But they halted last Night at Flat-Bush. If they should attack General Sullivan this day, and should shew no Disposition to attack me likewise, at the making of the next Flood, I shall send such further Reinforcements to Long Island as I may judge expedient, not chusing to weaken this post too much, before I am certain that the Enemy are not making a Feint upon Long Island to draw our Force to that Quarter when their real Design may perhaps be upon this. I am Sir Yr most obt Servt

Go: Washington

The Flood Tide will begin to make about Eleven Oclock, at which time, if the Detatchment ordered yesterday, were to move to the high, and open Grounds about Mr O. Delancy & Bloomingdale, they would be ready to come forward, or return back, as occasion should require it will give them a little Exercise— and shew them wherein they are wanting in any matter.

LS, in Tench Tilghman's writing, MHi: Heath Papers; LB, DLC:GW; Varick transcript, DLC:GW. The postscript of the LS is in GW's writing. The cover of the LS is addressed "to The Honble Major Genl Heath at Kings-Bridge."

From Major General William Heath

Kingsbridge Augst 23rd 1776

Dear General   half past One oClock P:M.

I am so unhappy as not to receive your Letter Untill this moment, having been all this forenoon with the Engineers viewing the Ground & laying out the works, But upon Sight of your Letter I have ordered the Detachment Here to Parade and march for Mount Washington as Soon as Possable, And the Detachment at that place which Consists of near Eight Hundred to march forward agreable to your Excellency's Direction.[1]

I hope Soon to hear Good News from Long Island, I have never been afraid of the force of the Enemy, I am more So of their Arts, They must be well watched, They like the Frenchman look one way and Row the other, However I trust that they will not find Americans deficient either in fortitude or Policy—A floating Bridge or number of Boats Seems to be highly necessary for a Communication on Harlem River I submit to your Excellency's Consideration whether Some of the Fire rafts (as they are Called) might not be Employd to advantage for this Purpose. I have the Honor to be with great respect your Excellencys Hbl. Servt

W. Heath

ALS, DLC:GW; ADfS, MHi: Heath Papers.
1. Heath wrote Thomas Mifflin at 2:00 P.M. on this date: "Being out with the Engineers I Did not receive the Enclos'd Untill Just now I have Ordered the Detachment here to Parade Immediately and march as far Down as your Post, you will Immediately march the Detachment at your Post forward as far as you may think Proper agreable to his Excellency's direction Colo. Nickolls [Isaac Nicoll] who commands the Detachment here will halt at your Post unless there should be an Alarm, when he will follow as fast as possible, if all should be Quiet he is to return before Evening" (MHi: Heath Papers; see also Heath to Nicoll, this date, MHi: Heath Papers).

To the New York Convention

Gentlemen   Head Quarters New York 23d Augt 1776
I am favoured with yours of the 22d acquainting me with a Report now circulating "that if the American Army should be obliged to retreat from this City, any Individual may set it on fire."

I can assure you Gentlemen, this Report is not founded upon the least Authority from me. On the contrary[1] I am so sensible of the Value of such a City and the Consequences of its Destruction to many worthy Citizens & their Families that nothing but the last Necessity and that such as should justify me to the whole World, would induce me to give Orders for that purpose.

The unwillingness shewn by many Families to remove notwithstanding your and my Recommendation may perhaps have led some persons to propagate the Report with honest and innocent Intentions. But as your Letter first informed me of it, I cannot pretend to say by whom or for what purpose it has been done.

As my Views with Regard to the Removal of the Women and Children have happily coincided with your Sentiments and a Committee appointed to carry them into Execution,[2] I submit it to your Judgment whether it would not be proper for the Committee to meet immediately in this City and give Notice of their Attendance on this Business. There are many who anxiously wish to remove but have not the means. I am with much Respect & Regard Gentn yrs &ca.

LB, in Tench Tilghman's writing, DLC:GW; LS (mutilated), in Joseph Reed's writing, N: New York Provincial Congress Revolutionary Papers; Varick transcript, DLC:GW. The LS was badly damaged in the New York State Library fire of 1911, leaving only a very small amount of readable text and GW's signature. The convention read this letter on 24 Aug., and the text of the LS is printed in the *N.Y. Prov. Congress Journals*, 1:588.

1. The LS reads "On the other Hand" (ibid.).

2. For the appointment of this committee, see Abraham Yates, Jr., to GW, 17 Aug. (second letter), and note 1.

From Major General John Sullivan

Dr Genll   Long-Island Augt 23d 1776.

This Afternoon the Enemy formed & attempted to pass the Road by Bedford a smart fire between them and the Rifle Men ensued, the Officer sent off for a Reinforcement which I ordered down Immediately, a number of Musketry came up to the Assistance of the Rifle Men whose fire with that of our field peices caused a Retreat of the Enemy our Men followed them to the House of Judge Lefferds, where a number of them had taken Lodgings drove them out and Burnt the House and a number of other Buildings Contiguous, they think they kill'd a number & as Evidence of it they produce three Officers Hangers a Carbine & one Dead Body with a considerable Sum of Money in Pocket, I have ordered a party out for Prisoners to night—

we have driven them half a Mile from their former Station, these things argue well for Us and I hope are so many preludes to a General Victory.[1] Dr Genl I am wt. much Esteem Yr Very Huml. Servt

Jno: Sullivan

Copy, in Samuel Blachley Webb's writing, enclosed in GW to Hancock, 24 Aug. 1776, DNA:PCC, item 152; LB, MHi: Sullivan Papers; copy, DNA:PCC, item 169. The text of Webb's copy is fuller than the LB and apparently closer to the text of the letter that GW received and read.

1. For other accounts of this day's skirmishing about the village of Flatbush, see Extract of a Letter from New York, 24 Aug., in Force, *American Archives,* 5th ser., 1:1144; Sabine, *Fitch's New-York Diary,* 26–27; James Chambers to his wife, 3 Sept. 1776, in *Pa. Archives,* 2d ser., 10:306–8; and the diary of a Hessian officer in Lowell, *Hessians,* 60–61. The road running north from Flatbush to Bedford went through one of the four strategically important passes in the Heights of Guana, beyond which lay the American line of forts and parapets that defended Brooklyn. The houses that the Americans burned in Flatbush belonged to Leffert Lefferts, Jeremiah Vanderbilt, and Evert Hegeman.

General Orders

Head Quarters, New York, August 24th 1776.
Parole Jamaica.   Countersign London.

All the intrenching tools are to be collected, and delivered in to the store. Officers who have given receipts will be called upon, as they are answerable for them if there should be any deficiency.

The General has appointed William Grayson Esqr. one of his Aide-du-Camps; he is to be obeyed and respected accordingly.

In Case of action, any orders delivered by Col. Moylan Quarter Master General, as from the General, to be considered as coming from him, or as delivered by an Aide-du-Camp.

The Adjutants of the Connecticut Militia, are directed to make themselves acquainted, with parapet firing; and the other officers of those Corps would do well to attend to it, and practice their men every day: Their Honor and Safety will much depend upon their avoiding any confusion in manning the lines.

The Court Martial of which Col. Wyllys was President is dissolved.

The Brigade Majors, in forming the new one, to be careful to have it full; and officers, who can attend.

The Court Martial to proceed at their first sitting to the tryal of Adjutant Brice of Col. Smallwoods Battalion, charged with "Disobedience of orders."

The changing of the regiments occasioning some difficulties in the duty—The Brigade Majors are to send, by the Orderly Serjeant, every morning, a duty return of the officers and men in their respective brigades.

The passage of the East-River being obstructed in such a manner, with Chevaux-de-Frizes &c., as to render it dangerous for any Vessels to attempt to pass, The Sentinels along the river, contigious to where the obstructions are placed, are to hail and prevent any Vessels attempting to pass, otherways than between the Albany Pier, and a Mast in the river, which appears above water nearly opposite.

Varick transcript, DLC:GW.

To John Hancock

Sir,   New York Augt 24th 1776.

The irregularity of the Post prevents your receiving the early and constant Intelligence it is my Wish to communicate. This is the third Letter which you will, probably, receive from me by the same Post. The first was of little or no consequence, but that of yesterday gave you the best Information I had been able to obtain of the Enemy's Landing, and movements upon Long Island.[1] Having occasion to go over thither yesterday, I sent my Letter to the Post Office at the usual hour (being informed that the Rider was expected every moment and wou'd go out again directly) but in the Evening, when I sent to enquire, none had come in.

I now Inclose you a report made to me by Genl Sullivan after I left Long Island Yesterday.[2] I do not conceive that the Enemys whole Force was in motion, but a detach'd Party rather—I have sent over four more Regiments with Boats, to be ready, either to reinforce the Troops under General Sullivan, or to return to this place if the remainder of the Fleet at the Watering place should push up to the City, which hitherto (I mean since the Landing upon Long Island) they have not had in their power to do on Acct of the Wind, which has either been a head, or too small, when the Tide has served. I have nothing further to trouble the Congress with at present than that I am theirs, and your Most Obedt Hble Servt

Go: Washington

ALS, DNA:PCC, item 152; LB, DLC:GW; copy, DNA:PCC, item 169; Varick transcript, DLC:GW. Congress read this letter on 26 Aug. and referred it to the Board of War (see the docket on the ALS, and *JCC*, 5:700–701).

1. See GW to Hancock, 22, 23 August. Congress read all three letters on 26 Aug. (ibid.).

2. See Sullivan to GW, 23 August.

From John Hancock

Sir,   Philada August 24th 1776

The late Conduct of Lord Drummond is as extraordinary, as his Motives are dark and mysterious. To judge the most favourably of his Intentions, it should seem, that an overweening Vanity has betrayed him into a criminal Breach of Honour. But whether his Views were upright, or intended only to mislead and deceive, cannot at present be a Matter of any Importance. In the mean Time, I have the Pleasure to acquaint you, that Congress highly approve of the Manner in which you have checked the officious & intemperate Zeal of his Lordship. Whether his Designs were hostile, or friendly, he equally merited the Reproof you have given him; and I hope for the future he will be convinced, that it is higly imprudent to attract the Attention of the Public to a Character, which will only pass without Censure, when it passes without Notice.

The Congress having considered the Matter thoroughly are of Opinion to decline taking any public or farther Notice of his Lordship, or his Letters; and particularly as you have so fully expressed their Sentiments on the Subject in your Letter to him.[1] It was the Consideration of this point that induced Congress to detain the Express till now. I have the Honour to be with perfect Esteem and Regard Sir your most obedt and very hble Sert

John Hancock Presidt

LS, DLC:GW; LB, DNA:PCC, item 12A.
1. See GW to Drummond, 17 Aug., and GW to Hancock, 18 August.

From Major General William Heath

Dear General   Kingsbridge Augst 24th 1776

In Order to Ease Head Quarters as much as Possible, And on Account of our Distance from thence, General or Garrison Court Martials have been Appointed at this Post for the Tryal of Offenders, Brigadier General Mifflen has Sent me the Inclosed this Day, But I pause Untill I Know your Excellency's Pleasure (which I Desire you would be pleased to Signify as Soon as Convenient) whether the before mentioned Offender and all Others Except in very Extraordina[r]y Cases in deed, Are to be Tryed by Court Martials appointed here or refered to those appointed from Head Quarters.[1]

A very Considerable Quantity of Sails & Rigging Striped off the Vessels lately Sunk near Mount Washington at present Remains there, I Submit to your Excellency's Determination if it would not be well to Send them further up the River where they might be Safely Stored, as it Cannot be Done here, the Stores being wanted for Other uses.

On the 21st Instant the Body of a man was Taken up at Burditts Ferry, The Commanding Officer there not being able to find any Civil Authority Appointed a Court of Enquiry to Consider the Cause of his Death, who reported the Enclosed. The Body was afterwards Buried, And the money & Effects are in the Hands of Colo. Ward[.] It Since appears that Hardenbrook (for that was his Name) was by Occupation a Carpenter belonging to the City of New York, who has been heretofore Employed by Dunmore and Tryon and for whom he retained an Affection, That upon the Day of the Ships falling Down the River he Attempted to get on Board of them But found a Watery Grave, the reward of Such Unrighteousness, I am told that he has a Brother in the City who is a Staunch friend to American Liberty, and who I suppose is as yet Unacquainted with the Fate of his Brother.[2]

The Detachment from the Two Brigades, amounting to Ten or Eleven Hundred men, with Surprising Alertness Almost Instantly turned out on yesterday and Marched Some Miles towards the City, And this Day upon the Flood Tide formed upon their Parades, The Officers and men appeared greatly Disapointed on Yesterday when they were told that the Enemy were not moving and that they might return to their Quarters, The men grow more Sickly as your Excellency will See by the Returns.[3] I have the Honor to be with great respect your Excellencys most Humble Servt

W. Heath

ALS, DLC:GW; ADfS, MHi: Heath Papers.

1. In the enclosed letter of this date, Thomas Mifflin requests Heath "to appoint a General Court Martial as soon as possible for Tryal of Lieutenant [John] Priestly of Col. Magaws Battalion Cap. [John] Beat[t]y's Company, who is chargd by his Captain with making Use of indecent abusive & traiterous Expressions against his Brother Officers & his Country" (DLC:GW). Heath replied to Mifflin on this date that because Priestly was "charged not only of makeing Use of Indecent and Abusive, but also of traiterous Expressions against his Country," the request for a court-martial had been referred to GW (MHi: Heath Papers). With GW's approval Priestly was subsequently tried by a court-martial at Fort Washington (see GW to Heath, 26 Aug., and Heath to Mifflin, 27 Aug., MHi: Heath Papers). The court-martial apparently acquitted Priestly, for on 12 Oct. 1776 he was promoted to captain in Magaw's 5th Pennsylvania Regiment, and on 16 Nov. 1776 he was taken prisoner with the regiment at Fort Washington. After his exchange in August 1778, Priestly returned to civilian life.

2. The enclosed report of the court of inquiry has not been identified. Theophilus Hardenbrook (Hardenbrock) was a house carpenter in New York City in 1769 (see *New York Burghers and Freemen*, 539–40). Ambrose Serle says in his journal that on 18 Aug., the day that the *Phoenix* and *Rose* returned down the Hudson River past the American batteries at Fort Washington and Burdett's Ferry, "a young Man came off from the Shore in a Canoe, and got on board the Ships. . . . A Captain Hornneck, an Engineer, who came off with him, was drowned by the Canoes striking against the Rose. They tried to save the poor Gentleman, but in vain, as they could not stay for him, being in the midst of the Rebels' Fire. This was regretted as a capital Loss" (Tatum, *Serle's Journal*, 68). Maj. Carl Leopold Baurmeister, adjutant of the Hessian forces, says that the engineer was named Freudenberg and that he drowned while trying to swim to Staten Island at Decker's Ferry (Baurmeister to Baron von Jungkenn, 2 Sept. 1776, in Baurmeister, *Revolution in America*, 31–42).

3. These returns have not been identified. Mifflin says in his letter to Heath of this date: "I have orderd the two Battalions to parade at Eleven OClock, the Time of Low Water: that We may be ready to march if necessary. Cap. [Jotham] Horton gave the Alarm Yesterday through Misinformation—If we discover any Movement of the Enemy you will hear 3 Cannon. A heavy Firing was seen & heard from our post last Night suposd to have happend at long Island—50 Cannon beside small Arms were heard" (DLC:GW).

To Major General Philip Schuyler

Dear Sir   New York Augt 24th 1776.

I received Your Favor of the 18th with its several Inclosures on Thursday by Mr Allen.[1]

My Letter of the 13th does not, nor was It meant to contain the most distant Hint of Your Entertaining Doubts or Suspicions of my Not having communicated to Congress, such Parts of your Letters as were Material. It was only designed to answer Yours, where You say, since my Arrival here, You had not written to them on Military Affairs, supposing Whatever Information You might Give & Which was Necessary for them to know would be communicated by me.[2] My Request to be advised of the Information You might Give Congress of any Matters Whereof You wrote me at the same Time, was to prevent my sending them unnecessary Intelligence & the Trouble of sending Needless Copies & Extracts made out.

I am in Hopes the Articles mentioned in the Letter to Captn Varrick, will have come to Hand before this[3]—Also those contained in the inclosed List, shipped on Board the Schooner Union, Philo Sandford, Master the 19th instt as the Qr Mastr Genl has reported to Me.[4]

The Treaty with the Indians agreeable to Your Request, I have transmitted to Congress.[5]

It Gives me Pleasure to find the Vessels for the Lakes are in such Forwardness & Going on with such Industry. I Yet hope we shall have a Navy there, equal to Every Exigency & that will be superior to those the Enemy can build. Captns Hawley & Chappel are now here with Permission from Govr Trumbull & Myself to inlist, If they can, Two hundred Seamen out of the Militia just sent from the State of Connecticut.[6] How they will succeed, I cannot determine.

I wish You had proceeded in such Way, as Your own Judgment & Inclination led, in the Case referred to Me for my Advice respecting Colo. Dayton's Officers. I am sorry that Persons of their Rank & of their Connections, should have Given into such dishonorable & disgraceful Practices, & feel Myself a Good Deal concerned, for themselves, & their Friends. But as the Matter is with Me to determine. As the Making Concessions at the Head of the Regiment, would not answer any purpose, but that of

Rendering them Objects of Ridicule & Contempt—As they could never after Claim & support that Authority Over their Inferiors, that is necessary to Good Governmt & Discipline—As Public Justice and a Regard to our Military Character requires That Matters of this Nature should meet with Every possible Discouragement. As My Conduct might Otherwise be deemed reprehensible & to deter Others from a Conduct Which is but too prevalent I cannot but advise that the several Persons concerned, be subjected to the Trial of a Court-Martial. If the Court should think they ought to be broke & dismissed the Service, Colo. Dayton, his Major & Other Officers, will recommend such as will be proper Persons to fill the Vacancies Occasioned by their Removal.

On Wednesday Night & Thursday Morning a Considerable Body of the Enemy said to be Eight or Nine thousand, landed at Gravesend Bay on Long Island. They have approached within about three Miles of our Lines & Yesterday there was some Skirmishing, between a Detachment from theirs & a Party from our Troops. Their Detachment were obliged to Give Ground, and were pursued as far as where they had a Post at Judge Leffords, His House & Outhouses served as Quarters for them & were burnt by our People. We sustained no Loss in this Action, that I have heard, Except, having two Men slightly[7] wounded. Our People say the Enemy met with More. they found one dead Body in the Habit of a Soldier, with a Good Deal of Money in his Pocket, & Got three Hangers & a Fuzee. I am Dr Sir, Your Humble servt

Go. Washington.

P.S. Our Party threw a Shell from a Howitz Which fell on & bursted in a House, where several of them were; Whether they were injured by It We have not learned. A Firing has been heard this Morning, but know Nothing of the Event.

LB, NN: Schuyler Papers; LB, DLC:GW; Varick transcript, DLC:GW.

1. The previous Thursday was 22 August.
2. See Schuyler to GW, 6 August.
3. See GW to Richard Varick, 10 August.
4. Q.M. Gen. Stephen Moylan's return of items sent to Albany on the *Union* by Asst. Q.M. Gen. Hugh Hughes is dated 19 August. It lists 60 doubleheaded shot for eighteen-pound cannon, 80 doubleheaded shot for twelve-pounders, 80 doubleheaded shot for nine-pounders, 100 doubleheaded shot for six-

pounders, 30 reams of musket cartridge paper, 9 bullet molds, and a little more than thirty-three hundredweight of grapeshot (DLC:GW).

5. See GW to Hancock, 23 August.

6. See Jonathan Trumbull, Sr., to GW, 16 August.

7. The copyist inadvertently wrote "shightly" on the manuscript.

To Jonathan Trumbull, Sr.

Sir   New York Augt 24th 1776

On thursday last[1] the Enemy landed a body of Troops supposed to amount, from the best accounts I have been able to obtain, to eight or nine thousand men at Gravesend Bay on[2] Long Island, ten miles distant from our works on the Island, and immediately marched through the level and open lands to Flat-Bush where they are now incamped. They are distant about three miles from our Lines, and have woods and broken grounds to pass, which we have lined, before they can get to them—Some skirmishings have happened between their advanced Parties and ours in which we have always obtained an advantage—What the real designs of the Enemy are I am not yet able to determine; my opinion of the matter is, that they mean to attack our works on the Island and this City at the same time; and that the Troops at Flat Bush are waiting in those plains till the wind and tide, which have not yet served together, will favor the movement of the Shipping to this place—Others think they will bend their principal force against our Lines on the Island; which, if carried, will greatly facilitate their designs upon the City—This also being very probable, I have thrown what force I can over, without leaving myself too much exposed here; for our whole numbers, if the intelligence we get from Deserters be true, falls short of that of the Enemy, [consequently, the Defence of our own Works, and the Approaches to them is all we can aim at. This then in a Manner leaves the whole Island in possession of the Enemy,][3] and of course, of the supplies it is capable of affording them.

Under these circumstances would it be practicable for your Government to throw a body of about one thousand, or more, men across the sound to harrass the Enemy in their rear or upon their flank? This would annoy them exceedingly, at the same time that a valuable end, to wit, that of preventing their parties securing the Stocks of Cattle &c. would be answered by it. The Cattle to be removed or killed.

The knowledge I have of the extraordinary exertions of your State, upon all occasions, does not permit me to require this, not knowing how far it is practicable, I only offer it therefore as a matter for consideration, and of great public utility if it can be accomplished—The Enemy, if my intelligence from Staten Island be true, are at this time rather distressed on account of provisions: if then we can deprive them of what the Island affords much good will follow from it.[4]

The Foreigners are yet upon Staten Island—The British Troops are upon Long Island, and on Ship board. With very great Respect and Esteem I remain Sir Your most obedient humble Servant

G. Washington

LB, Ct: Trumbull Papers; LB, DLC:GW; Varick transcript, DLC:GW.

1. The previous Thursday was 22 August.

2. The copyist inadvertently wrote "or" on the manuscript.

3. The copyist inadvertently omitted the text within square brackets. It is supplied from the LB in DLC:GW.

4. Joseph Reed wrote a similar letter to Trumbull on this date: "There can be no doubt but before this reaches you you will have heard that the Enemy have landed a considerable body of men on Long Island within 7 miles of our Lines. We cannot yet determine whether the main body of the Army is landed with a view to make a general attack on that side, or whether it is a large detachment sent to draw off our attention from this place while they proceed up with their Fleet and principal Force—The success has been various in the little skirmishes we have had, but our Troops have generally drove them back.

"Before his Excellency rode out this morning he directed me to acquaint you with our Situation, and to submit to your consideration, whether it would be possible to transport a body of men (say 1000) to Long Island below the Enemy with a view to divide their Force and make a diversion—His Excellency is not insensible that a great part of the Western Militia are now in this Camp, but he supposes it might be possible that the Eastern Militia might be employed in such a service. I should illy express the General's intentions, if what I have said should be construed into an order or even a request, unless in your own judgment & those with whom you think proper to consult, it should stand fully approved: nor will our operations be governed in the least by a dependence on such a measure—But at the same time the great advantages arising from it are so extremely obvious that I need not enlarge upon them" (Ct: Trumbull Papers).

General Orders

Head Quarters, New York, August 25th 1776.
Parole Marlborough.   Countersign Newtown.

A special Court Martial to sit this day at twelve OClock, at Mrs Montagnies for the tryal of Lieut: Col. Zedwitz, charged with "carrying on a treasonable correspondence with the enemy"; to be composed of a Brigadier General and twelve Field Officers—General Wadsworth to preside.[1]

The General Order against working on Sunday is revoked the time not admitting of any delay.[2] The same number of fatigue men to turn out, as yesterday, this afternoon at three OClock, as well Militia as other troops.

Col. Smallwood to command Lord Stirling's Brigade during his absence on Long Island.[3]

Varick transcript, DLC:GW.

1. For the proceedings of Herman Zedwitz's court-martial on this and the next day, see DLC:GW; see also Force, *American Archives*, 5th ser., 1:1159–62. The principal evidence against Zedwitz was an intercepted letter that he had written to Gov. William Tryon on 24 Aug., offering in return for £2,000 sterling in hard gold to procure accurate intelligence about the American forces from "a gentelman wich is allways near the general and has the opportunity To See all the general Returns of the Strenght of the Armee, where and how Strong the detachements are Comanded." Zedwitz also informed Tryon of American efforts to induce Hessians to desert, an alleged plot "to Spoil the Watering place" on Staten Island with "14 Botles of Stof Black as an Ink," and his expectation of soon being appointed "Trugh gen. Washington Recommendation . . . as full Colonel and Comander of the 3 forts on the Nort River 65 Miles from hear." Although Zedwitz says in the letter that "de World will Certenly Blame my Caracter, by Serving in an Armee and giving the Enemy Intelligence," he insisted at his court-martial that he only had written Tryon "such storys as he might believe without any intention on my part of performing." The court did not accept that explanation, and on 26 Aug. it found Zedwitz guilty and sentenced him to be cashiered from the army (DLC:GW).

2. For this earlier order, see General Orders, 3 August.

3. Stirling on this date took command of a brigade on Long Island consisting of Col. Samuel Miles's and Col. Samuel Atlee's Pennsylvania regiments, two regiments of Pennsylvania levies from the flying camp, and two regiments of New York levies (see Sullivan's orders, this date, in "Henshaw's Orderly Book," 229–30).

Orders to Major General Israel Putnam

[Headquarters, New York, 25 August 1776]

It was with no small degree of concern I percieved yesterday a scattering, unmeaning & wasteful fire, from our people at the enemy, a kind of fire that tended to disgrace our own men as soldiers, and to render our defence contemptible in the eyes of the enemy; no one good consequence can attend such irregularities, but several bad ones will inevitably follow on it; Had it not been for this unsoldierlike and disorderly practice, we have the greatest reason imaginable to believe, that numbers of deserters would have left the enemys army, last year, but fear prevented them from approaching our Lines then, and must forever continue to operate in like manner whilst every soldier concieves himself at liberty to fire when & at what he pleases. This is not the only nor the greatest evil resulting from the practice; for as we do not know the hour of the enemy's approach to our lines but have every reason to apprehend that it will be sudden & violent, whenever attempted; we shall have our men so scattered & (more than probable) without ammunition, that the consequences must prove fatal to us: besides this there will be no possibility of distinguishing between a real and false alarm.

I must therefore Sir, in earnest terms, desire you to call the Colonels & commanding officers of corps, (without loss of time) before you; and let them afterwards do the same by their respective officers, and charge them, in express & positive terms, to stop these irregularities, as they value the good of the service, their own honor, and the safety of the army; which under God, depends wholly upon the good order & government that is observed in it.

At the same time, I would have you form a proper line of defence, round your incampment and works, on the most advantageous grounds; Your guards which compose this are to be particularly instructed in their duty; & a Brigadier of the day to remain constantly upon the lines, that he may be upon the spot to command, & see that orders are executed. Field officers should also be appointed to go the rounds & report the situation of the guards; no person to be allowed to pass beyond the guards without special orders in writing.

By restraining the loose, disorderly & unsoldierlike firing be-

fore mentioned, I do not mean to discourage Partizan & scouting parties; on the contrary I wish to see a spirit of this sort
prevailing, under proper regulation & officers either comm[is-
sione]d or non comm[issione]d (as cases shall require) to be directed by yourself or licens'd by the Brigadier of the day, upon
the spot, to be sent upon this service. Such skirmishing as may
be effected in this manner will be agreable to the rules of propriety, & may be attended with salutary effects; inasmuch as it will
inure the troops to fatigue & danger; will harrass the enemy,
may make prisoners & prevent their parties from getting the
horses & cattle from the interior parts of the island, which are
objects of infinite importance to us, especially the two last.

All the men not upon duty, are to be compelled to remain in,
or near their respective camps or quarters, that they may turn
out at a moments warning; nothing being more probable than
that the enemy will allow little enough time to prepare for the
attack: The Officers also, are to exert themselves to the utmost
to prevent every kind of abuse to private property, or to bring
every offender, to the punishment he deserves; shameful it is to
find that those men, who have come hither, in defense of the
rights of mankind, should turn invaders of it by destroying the
substance of their friends.

The burning of houses, where the apparent good of the service is not promoted by it; & the pillaging of them, at all times, &
upon all occasions, is to be discountenanced and punished with
the utmost severity; In short it is to be hoped, that men who
have property of their own, & a reguard for the rights of others,
will shudder at the thought of rendering any man's situation, to
whose protection he had come, more insufferable than his open
and avowed Enemy would make it, when by duty & every rule
of humanity they ought to aid, & not oppress, the distress'd in
their habitations.

The distinction between a well regulated army, & a mob, is the
good order & discipline of the first, & the licentious & disorderly
behaviour of the latter; Men, therefore, who are not employed,
as mere hirelings, but have step'd forth in defence of every thing
that is dear & valuable, not only to themselves but to posterity,
should take uncommon pains to conduct themselves with uncommon propriety & good order; as their honor reputation &c.
call loudly upon them for it.

The wood next red hooks should be well attended to; put some of the most disorderly rifle men into it; The militia or most indifferent troops (those I mean which are least tutored & seen least service) will do for the interior works, whilst your best men should at all hazards prevent the enemy's passing the wood; & approaching your works; The woods should be secured by abatties &c. where necessary to make the enemys approach, as difficult as possible; Traps & ambuscades should be laid for their parties if you find they are sent out after cattle &c.[1] Given under my hand at Head Quarters this 25th day of Augt 1776.

Go: Washington

LB, in William Grayson's writing, DLC:GW; Varick transcript, DLC:GW.

GW on 24 Aug. put Putnam in general command of the American forces on Long Island. "General Putnam," Joseph Reed wrote his wife on that date from New York City, "was made happy by obtaining leave to go over—the brave old man was quite miserable at being kept here" (Reed, *Joseph Reed*, 1:220). Sullivan retained immediate command of the American troops on the island outside the fortifications at Brooklyn.

1. GW is referring to the wooded Heights of Guana, which lay a short distance south and east of the Brooklyn lines.

General Orders

Head Quarters, New York, August 26th 1776
Parole Newcastle.   Countersign Paris.

Six hundred men properly officered, from General Wolcot's Brigade, to parade to morrow morning, at six o'clock, on the Grand Parade, without arms for fatigue: Four hundred to take directions from General McDougall, and two hundred from Lieutt Fish; and the same number to be continued 'till the works are completed; to leave work at young flood, and go on again at the ebb.

The General is very anxious for the state of the arms and ammunition, the frequent rains giving too much reason to fear they may suffer; He therefore earnestly enjoins officers and men to be particularly attentive to it and have them in the best order.

Varick transcript, DLC:GW.

From Timothy Edwards

Stockbridge [Mass.]

May it please your Excellency   Augt 26. 1776

Upon my return home from the treaty at the German-Flatts, the 17 Inst., I communicated the contents of your letters, of the 7th & 10 Inst., to the Indians of this place, then at hand— On the 23 Inst:, being generally collected from their various dispersions, they resolved to join the army under Major Genl Schuyler—The main body of them propose to march tomorrow—As some are yet at their hunting and fishing grounds the number that will engage, cannot be ascertained—Genl Schuyler has doubtless informed your Exellency, That as you had been silent about the terms and mode of engaging them he advised to execute the plan adopted by the Commissioners of Indian affairs for this department, in June last: A copy of what was then sent you[1]—This I have followed—Any services which I can execute you may be assured shall be undertaken with alacrity. I am Your Exellencies most respectful, obedient humble Servant

Timth. Edwards

ALS, DLC:GW.

1. See Schuyler to GW, 15 June and 16 August.

To John Hancock

Sir   New York Augt 26th 1776

I have been duly honoured with your favors of the 20th & 24th and am happy to find my Answer to Ld Drummond has met the approbation of Congress. whatever his views were, most certainly his conduct respecting his parole is highly reprehensible.

Since my Letter of the 24th, All most the whole of the Enemies fleet have fallen down to the Narrows, and from this circumstance—the Striking of their Tents at their Several Encampments on Staten Island from time to time previous to the departure of the Ships from thence, we are led to think, they mean to land the Main Body of their Army on Long Island and to make their Grand push there. I have ordered over considerable reinforcements to our Troops there, and shall continue to send more as circumstances may require. There has been a little skirmishing & Irregular firing kept up between their and our advanced Guards, in which Colo. Martin of the Jersey Levies has received a Wound in his Breast which It is apprehended will prove mortal[1]—A private has had his Leg broke by a Cannon Ball, and Another has received a Shot in the Groin from their Musquetry—This is all the damage they have yet done us—What they have sustained is not known.

The Shifting & changing, the Regiments have undergone of late, has prevented their making proper returns, and of course put it out of my power to Transmit a Genl One of the Army—However I beleive, our Strength is much the same that It was when the last was made,[2] with the addition of Nine Militia Regiments more from the State of Connecticut averaging about 350 Men each these are Nine of the Fourteen Regiments mentioned in my Letter of the 19th Our people still continue to be very sickly.

The papers designed for the Foreign Troops have been put into several Channels in order that they might be conveyed to 'em, and from the Information I had yesterday, I have reason to beleive many have fallen into their Hands.

I have Inclosed a Copy of Lord Drummond's Second Letter in answer to mine,[3] which I received since I transmitted his First & which I have thought necessary to lay before Congress that they may possess the whole of the Correspondence between us, and see how far he has exculpated himself from the charge alleged against him—The Log Book he mentions to have sent Colo. Moylan, proves nothing in his favor. That shews he had been at Bermuda, & from thence to some other Island & on his passage from which to this place the Vessel he was in was boarded by a pilot who brought Her into the Hook, where he found the British Fleet, which his Lordship avers he did not expect were there, having understood their destination was to the Southward. I have the Honor to be with great respect Sir Your Most Obedt Sert

Go: Washington

LS, in Robert Hanson Harrison's writing, DNA:PCC, item 152; LB, DLC:GW; copy, DNA:PCC, item 169; Varick transcript, DLC:GW. Congress read this letter on 28 Aug. (*JCC*, 5:710).

1. Col. Ephraim Martin recovered from his wound.

2. The general return of the army at New York that GW enclosed in his letter to Hancock of 19 Aug. has not been identified.

3. See Drummond to GW, 19 August.

To Major General William Heath

Dr Sir   Head Quarters New York Aug. 26th 1776

I have now before me your letters of the 23rd & 24th of this Inst.; with respect to the detachment I directed on the 23rd, I concieve it to be highly expedient that they be kept in the most perfect readiness to act as the circumstances of affairs may render necessary; the present appearance of things seems to indicate an intention in the enemy to make their capital impression on the side of Long Island; but this may possibly be only a feint, to draw over our troops to that quarter, in order to weaken us here; As to the floating bridge you have mentioned for keeping Open the communication on Harlem river, I entirely approve of the Application of the fire rafts to that purpose provided they will Answer the design, to which you intend to convert them; I should think that a General or Garrisson Court martial at your quarters for the tryal of offenders (in cases not capital) would be useful and proper; The Qur M. Genl informs me he has sent up a person last week for the purpose of securing the sails and rigging taken from the vessels lately sunk near Mount Washington.

I have spoke to some gentlemen on the subject of Hardenburgh's death who (I make no doubt) will convey the account to his brother. I am Sir Yr Most Obedt

Go: Washington

LS, in William Grayson's writing, MHi: Heath Papers. The cover of the LS is addressed "to Majr Genl Heath at King's bridge."

From Major General William Heath

Dear General   Kingsbridge Aug: 26th 1776

I have just had the Honor to receive your's of this day's Date, & shall continue in the most perfect readiness, the Detachment designed for your Aid if Occasion should require it—I will further confer with the Brigadier Generals & Engineers, on the Probability of the Fire Rafts answering the Purpose of a floating Bridge, It is my own, as well as Genl Clinton's Opinion that they will, and it was also the Opinion of Col: Putnam on Saturday last[1] that they cannot be employed to better purpose.

Our Works are going on briskly, but we are rather weak in Teams, I have this day sent down Boats to bring up the Gun Carriages[2]—Monsieur St Martin our Engineer conducts very well, he is knowing & useful in his Department.[3]

I have been Yesterday & this day, much unwell, Pain in my Side & Head, & something feaverish I hope it will pass off, I am determined to shake it off if possible. I have the honor to be with great Respect Your Excellency's most humble Servt

W. Heath

P.S. Col. Thomas this moment comes in, & says he hears that One Ship & Two Frigates have entered the Sound, & that an Express is gone to the Congress of New York—doubtless by this Your Excellency has an Acct of it.[4]

W.H.

ADfS, MHi: Heath Papers.

1. The previous Saturday was 24 August.

2. Henry Knox wrote Heath on 24 Aug.: "I send you Lt [David] Preston of the artillery to mount the Guns and get the Implements & ammunition to the post at Kings Brid⟨ge⟩ you will please to give him such direct⟨ions⟩ as you think proper—you must give him men as it is utterly imposs⟨ible⟩ for us to spare one from this place [New York] You must also find a Boat for the Carriages &c. as Genl Putnam refuses to let one go from this" (MHi: Heath Papers).

3. At GW's direction Joseph Reed wrote Heath on 17 Aug. recommending St. Martin to his notice "as he may be of some Service at your Post & is not so immediately wanted here" (MHi: Heath Papers).

4. The British frigates *Brune* and *Niger* and brig *Halifax* were sailing to the western entrance of Long Island Sound "to prevent Supplies being sent through that Channel to the Town of New York" (disposition of British warships in North America, 13 Aug., in Clark and Morgan, *Naval Documents,* 6:167–69; see also the *Connecticut Journal* [New Haven], 28 Aug.). On 27 Aug. the New York convention read a copy of the letter that Erastus Wolcott wrote to the Saybrook committee of safety on 24 Aug. reporting that three British warships had passed New London heading west in Long Island Sound. In response the convention resolved to inform GW "that the committee of South-old at the east end of Nassau [Long] island, have mounted four cannon as field pieces, vizt: 3 6-pounders, and 1 3-pounder, to prevent depredations of the

enemy along the Sound, and to enable the inhabitants to make a stand at certain passes, and that His Excellency be requested to send a sufficiency of powder, ball and cartridge paper for the said cannon, to the care of Col. Livingston" (*N.Y. Prov. Congress Journals,* 1:593–94; see also Henry Beekman Livingston to GW, 30 Aug.).

From Major General Philip Schuyler

Dear Sir   Albany August 26th 1776

I am honored with your Excellency's Favor of the 21st Instant inclosing Colo: Stark's Letter to General Gates.

On the 16th Instant I wrote to Congress, desiring that the Money to be allowed for Rations in this Department might be determined—That I had refused to do it until ordered by your Excellency or by Congress, and gave my Reasons for it[1]—I have not yet been honored with their Answer—I was perfectly right in my Conjecture that if I did it, I should either incur the Censure of Congress or the Blame of the Army, the latter would have happened, for I should not have estimated a Ration so high as the Field Officers and the Commissary have done, concieving that it may be furnished at a Rate considerably less.

The Sail Cloth and part of the Cordage from Connecticut passed this Yesterday on its way to Tyonderoga.

Colonel Nicholson and Colonel Elmore's Regiments, (Copies of whose Returns I inclose) are to march to Day into Tryon County.[2] As by our latest Accounts the Enemy are not constructing any Vessels of Force at St Johns, I begin to apprehend that they build Batteaus merely to amuse us, as they can easily convey them into the St Lawrence to transport Troops &c. to the Westward and that they will attempt, as the Indians suggest, to penetrate by the Way of Oswego—I have ordered Scouts to be kept out continually towards that place and also towards Oswegatche and have desired General Gates to send others to that part of the St Lawrence above Montreal, that we may have the earliest Intelligence if any Troops should be filing off to the Westward.

We are greatly distressed for Musket Ball and Cartridge paper; that lately come up being all for Cannon Cartridges—please to order up what can be spared from your Quarter, as also forty Horn Lanthorns and what Bullet Moulds can be procured.

Inclose your Excellency Copy of a Return of our Naval Force; which since the Date of that Return is I believe augmented with three Stout Gallies of seventy three Feet Keel and one or more Gondaloes.[3]

General Gates has promised me a Return of the Army and in the mean Time, has sent me the Commissary's Return of Issues Copy of which I inclose[4]—General Gates advises me that since the 13th about 300 Massachusetts Militia have joined and that [there][5] are between 12 & 1500 Connecticut Militia at Skenesborough and the sixth Battalion of pennsylvanians at Crown point, and that those are not included in the Return. I am Dr Sir with every respectful Sentiment Your Excellency's Most Obedient Hume Servant

Ph: Schuyler

LS, DLC:GW; LB, NN: Schuyler Papers.

1. See Schuyler to Hancock, 16 Aug., DNA:PCC, item 153.

2. These returns, which are in DLC:GW, indicate that Col. Samuel Elmore's Connecticut state regiment was considerably stronger than Col. John Nicolson's New York regiment. Elmore's return, docketed 21 Aug., shows 26 commissioned and staff officers, 42 noncommissioned officers, and 436 privates, of whom 277 were present and fit for duty and 112 were on command mostly at Fort George. Nicolson's return of 20 Aug. shows 21 commissioned and staff officers, 16 noncommissioned officers, and 243 privates, of whom 89 were present and fit for duty and 83 were on command.

3. The enclosed list of Continental armed vessels on Lake Champlain, dated 18 Aug., shows twelve vessels on the lake, including one sloop, three schooners, seven gundalows, and one row galley. Those vessels had a total of 67 cannon, 94 swivel guns, and 485 crewmen (DLC:GW).

4. This return from Elisha Avery, deputy commissary at Ticonderoga, shows that 7,202 men, including artillerymen, militia, and crews of three vessels, drew provisions on 12 and 13 August. Schuyler also enclosed a copy of Avery's return of provisions and other stores at Ticonderoga on 13 Aug. (DLC:GW).

5. This word appears in the LB.

To Major General Artemas Ward

Sir.   Head Quarters N. York 26th Augt 1776.

I am now to Acknowledge the Recpt of yours of the 15th and 19th Instant and am much obliged for your care and dispatch in forwarding the Two Sea Morters which I wish may come safe to hand, The number and Strength of the Enemy and the many different posts we have to occupy together with the late Manœvre's of General Howe render it utterly impossible for me to relieve you by sending a General Officer from this to take Command in Boston, Congress seeing the Situation pass'd the enclosed Resolve,[1] and I cannot but hope you will conclude to keep the Command 'till something decisive is done with our formidable Enemy in this Quarter, who have landed most of their Army on Long Island and advanced part of them as far as Flatt Bush within three Miles of our Works. between them & the Works is a Ridge of Hills covered wt. Woods[2] in which I have posted a large Body of the Army, which have once repulsed an advanced party of them in an attempt to get thro—and I cannot but hope will prevent or at least weaken them much should they effect their purpose of passing. I am Sir Your Most Hume Servt

Go: Washington

LS, in Samuel Blachley Webb's writing, MHi: Ward Papers.

1. Congress requested in its resolution of 21 Aug. that Ward continue commanding the eastern department until further orders if his health permitted (*JCC,* 5:694).

2. GW is referring to the Heights of Guana.

To Lund Washington

Dear Lund,   New York Augt 26th 1776.

Your Letter of the 14th is now before me[1]—You are fully acquainted with my unwillingness to be concerned in Vessels, but if you cannot dispose of my Flour in the Country (which I should much prefer) you must then do the best you can with it, without waiting for particular Instructions from me, as the distance is too great to do this; and you know I shall not disapprove of any thing you do (although it should not turn out well) as I am perswaded you mean to do for the best.

If the Freight of Flour to Hispaniola is 20/ pr Barrl it will certainly be Cheaper to take a part of the Vessel than give this, as the Vessel might, if thought necessary, be Insured with the Cargo. You can best judge how you will be able to pay the £300 and comply with other Ingagements—In short I leave the whole matter to you, and had rather you would act in these matters as you shall from your own judgment, and the advise of those you can rely on, think best than refer things to me as the time which it takes to write & obtain an answer may, and often will, disconcert a good Scheme.

If the Flour was not in danger of Spoiling, I should think the keeping of it longer might be no disadvantage as it may, probably, be more Saleable sometime hence & can be Ship'd in greater safety in the course of the Winter than Now—But apropos! is there not an Imbargo upon Provisions of all kinds? It runs in my head that there is; if so how can you Ship Flour? Upon the whole, I again repeat, do as you please with respect to the purchasing of a fifth of Harpers Vessel[2] as also in the disposition of the Flour and Corn—as well as other things—The first part of the Summer has been very dry at this place but for the last Fortnight we have had scarce any thing but Rain.

I wish most ardently you could get the North end of the House covered in this fall, if you should be obliged to send all over Virginia, Maryland, & Pensylvania for Nails to do it with. Unless this is done it will throw every thing exceedingly backward—retard the design of Planting Trees as mentioned in my last,[3] & perhaps be the means of spoiling another Frame; besides keeping the House in a disagreeable littered Situation. It is equally my Wish to have the Chimneys run up—In short I would wish to have the whole closed in [(]if you were even to hire many Workmen of different kinds to accomplish it).

The Enemy on Wednesday night, and thursday last, landed a pretty considerable part of their Force on long Island; at a place called Graves end bay about Ten Miles from our Works on the Island; and Marched through the Flat & level Land, which is quite free of Wood, till they (or part of them) got within abt three Miles of our Lines, where they are now Incampd; A Wood & broken ground lying between Us. What there real design is I know not; whether they think our Works round this City are too strong, and have a Mind to bend their whole force that way—or whether it is intended as a feint—or is to form part of their Attack, we cannot as yet tell—however I have strengthend the Post as much as I can, to prevent a Surprize, and have lined the Wood between them and Us, from whence some Skirmishes have ensued and lives lost on both sides. A few days more

I should think will bring matters to an Issue one way or other or else the Season for Action will leave them as we [are] verging close upon September.

I am not at all surprized that our Numbers should be so much magnified with you, when in the very Neighbourhood they are thought to be double what they really are—but this you may be assured of, that our numbers are a good deal short of those of the Enemy, who have this further great advantage of us that by knowing their own points of Attack, they can regulate matters accordingly, where as we are obliged, as far as we are able, to be prepared at all points. Our Officers and Men (such as are fit for duty) seem to be in good Spirits, but we are exceedingly Sickly, more so than the Army has been at any one time since I have Commanded it. I have no doubt however, at least I am flattered into a belief, that Victory, if unfortunately it should decide in favour of the Enemy will not be purchased at a very easy rate.

I, in behalf of the Noble cause we are Ingaged in, and myself, thank with a grateful Heart all those who supplicate the throne of grace for success to the one & preservation of the other. That being from whom nothing can be hid will, I doubt not, listen to our Prayers, and protect our Cause and the supporters of it, as far as we merit his favour and Assistance. If I did not think our struggle just, I am sure it would meet with no assistance from me—and sure I am that no pecuniary Satisfaction upon Earth can compensate the loss of all my domestick happiness and re- quite me for the load of business which constantly presses upon and deprives me of every enjoyment.

Remember me kindly to all friends, & to Milly Posey, and be assured that I am sincerely and truly Dr Sir Yr Most Affecte

Go: Washington

ALS, CtHi: Hoadly Collection.

1. This letter has not been found.

2. John Harper was a merchant in Alexandria. Dixon and Hunter's edition of the *Virginia Gazette* [Williamsburg] for 22 Nov. 1776 says: "On the 16th in- stant was stranded on Cape Henry, the brigantine Beckey, or Lady Washing- ton, laden with flour and bread, from Alexandria, bound to Charlestown in South Carolina, Captain's name Harper." It is not known whether or not that cargo included any of GW's flour.

3. See GW to Lund Washington, 19 August.

From Joshua Wentworth

Sir,   Portsmouth [N.H.] Augt 26. 1776

I have the pleasure to advise the arrival at this Port a Prize Ship named the Nelly Frigate, (Lyonel Bradstreet mastr) from the Bay of Honduras, for London, Lading with a Cargo, of 120,000 feet Mahogany Logs and Forty Tons chip't & unchipt Logwood, sent in by the Hancock Capn Tucker & the Franklyn Capt. Skimmer, in the Service of the United Colonies the Vessel & Cargo the property of Inhabitants of Great Brittian, I have Libled her & shall persue to Trial &ca.[1]

The Trial on the recapture of the Brigt. Elizabeth, taken by Comr Manly & others in the service of the Continent & bound for Halifax, ended the 22d Inst.[2] The Jury acquited her & Cargo, which appearing so directly Contarary to the resolves of Congress & the Law of this Colony; That I conceiv'd it my Duty to appeal; in Justice to the Continent & Captors, which I hope Your Excellency will approbate, part of the Claimants (notwithstanding the verdict is in their favor) are desireous of compromiseing with the Captors, and offer them their full Quota, of Salvage Which is, the one third of half the Value of Vessel & Cargo, we havg establish'd that the Enemy were in Possession more than ninty six hours,[3] but the flagrant error in the Jury, forbid my conceedg to any compromise, for the Captors, as in that Case I must have surrender'd the Just Claim of the Continents, added to which there was taken with the said Brigt. a Mr Jackson, a Mr Keighley & Mr Newton, passengers, with their Effects, & Those Effects are Intended, (as the resolves of Congress expressd) to supply the enemy, & become forfited—yet they were releas'd with the rest of the Cargo. Each Claim is seperate, shou'd Your Excellency recommend my compromissg with those Claimants who are Esteem'd friendly, I shall Comport with it, but as your last favor desired my persuing the line of Duty pointed out by the Laws of the Continent,[4] I shall steedily attend toe them, unless otherways directed—From a principle of Humanity I cou'd wish the suffering Claimants cou'd be releived, but I think it out of the line of my Duty to help them— In a few days I shall forward the appeal to the Secretary of Congress and fully advise him thereon, and shou'd he think it necessary Shall attend the Trial at Philadelphia or elswhere that may be appointed.[5]

The Nelly Frigate, is a Ship of 305 Tons mounts 2 three pounders & 4 Two pounders.

This Eastern Country are anxiously concern'd for Your Excellencys Success in the Important Battle, expected to have taken place 'ere this; which God Grant has Terminated in favor of this Distress'd Country. remain'g with due respect Yr Excellencys Most obt & Very hume Servt

Josh. Wentworth

I shd not have troubled your Excellency wt. this business, cou'd I devine where my friend Mr Moylans residence is, un'til wch Yr Excellency will excuse me.

ALS, DLC:GW.

1. The *Nelly Frigate* was captured east of the Virginia capes on 6 Aug., and a prize crew was directed to take it to Boston. Adverse winds and the necessity of avoiding British cruisers caused the *Nelly Frigate* to put into Portsmouth on 20 Aug., and before the ship could proceed to Boston, Wentworth brought suit in the New Hampshire admiralty court to have it and its cargo sold there, an action that angered John Bradford, the prize agent for Massachusetts, who wanted the sale to occur at Boston where he would collect a commission on it (see Clark, *George Washington's Navy*, 178–79). Bradford about this time sent Capt. Samuel Tucker and a crew to bring the *Nelly Frigate* to Boston, but they returned without the ship (see Bradford to Hancock, 29 Aug., in Clark and Morgan, *Naval Documents*, 6:346). The *Nelly Frigate* and its cargo were sold at Portsmouth before 6 Nov. (see John Langdon to Hancock, that date, ibid., 7:58–59).

2. For the capture and recapture of the *Elizabeth* and the dispute over its disposal, see Winthrop Sargent to GW, 7 April, and note 1; GW to Hancock, 25–26 April, and note 10; and GW to Wentworth, 15 June 1776, and note 1.

3. Congress resolved on 5 Dec. 1775 that in cases of recaptured vessels, the prize money was to be one-half of the value of the vessel and cargo if it had been in enemy hands for more than ninety-six hours. The prize money was reduced proportionately for shorter periods of enemy control. One-third of the prize money was allotted to the officers and crewmen who made the recapture, and the balance went to the owner of their vessel, in this case the Continental government (*JCC*, 3:374–75, 407).

4. See GW to Wentworth, 15 June 1776.

5. Robert Hanson Harrison replied to Wentworth on 10 Sept.: "Removed at such a distance as his Excellency is, and Involved in a multiplicity of Important business, It is impossible for him to give directions about or to pay attention to the Continental Armed Vessels at the Eastward—Therefore, at the same time that he doubts not but your conduct is right respecting the Appeal, he

apprehends you should correspond with the Marine Committee appointed by Congress in all matters that may occur in your department, presuming that they were appointed & are intended for that purpose. His Excellency can only repeat what he has already said, that the Laws prescribed by Congress, are the only Rules by which you can conduct yourself—It is not his wish nor in his power to give any orders or advice authorizing a deviation or departure from them—If in any instances hardships of a peculiar nature cast up—Congress & Congress alone have it in their power to releive, on proper representation being made" (DLC:GW). On 14 Oct. 1776 Congress reversed the decision of the New Hampshire admiralty court but ruled that the owners need pay the United States and the recaptors only one-twelfth of the value of the ship and cargo. The United States' share of the prize money was remitted to the owners of the goods, leaving them to pay one-thirty-sixth of the value of the ship and cargo to the recaptors (*JCC*, 6:870–73).

General Orders

Head Quarters, New York, August 27th 1776.

Parole [   ].   Countersign [   ].

Varick transcript, DLC:GW.

Sgt. Peter Kinnan of Col. Ephraim Martin's regiment of New Jersey militia levies, which was stationed on Long Island, wrote in his orderly book under this date: "This being the day of the attack on Long Island, the orders were all verbal" (Kinnan, *Order Book*, 88).

Lieutenant Colonel Robert Hanson Harrison to John Hancock

Sir   New York Augt 27. 1776 Eight OClock. P.M.

I this minute returned from our Lines on Long Island where I left his Excellency the General. From him I have It in command to Inform Congress that Yesterday he went there & continued till Evening when from the Enemy's having landed a considerable part of their Forces and many of their Movements, there was reason to apprehend they would make in a little time a Genl Attack. As they would have a Wood to pass through before they could approach the Lines, It was thought expedient to place a number of Men there on the different Roads leading from whence they were stationed in order to harrass and annoy them in their March—This being done, early this Morning a

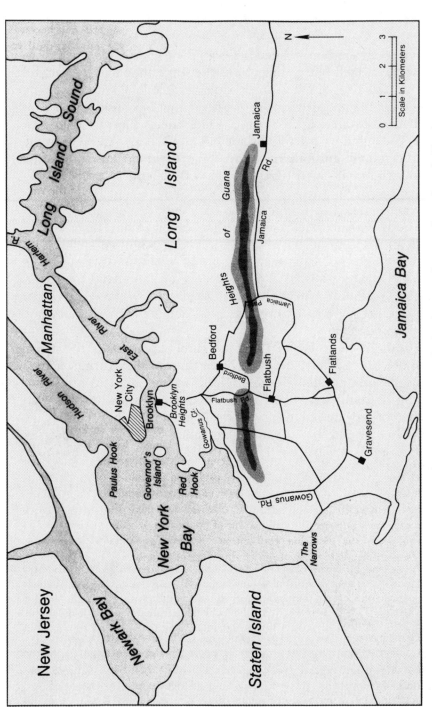

Map 2. The Battle of Long Island, 27 August 1776. From America's First Battles, 1776–1965, ed. Charles E. Heller and William A. Stofft, cartographer Laura Kriegstrom Poracsky (Lawrence: University Press of Kansas, 1986). Reproduced by permission of the University Press of Kansas.

Smart engagement ensued between the Enemy and our Detachments,[1] which being unequal to the force they had to contend with, have sustained a pretty considerable loss—At least many of our Men are missing, among those that have not returnd are Genls Sullivan & Lord Stirling—The Enemy's loss is not known certainly, but we are told by such of our Troops that were in the Engagement and that have come in,[2] that they had many killed and wounded—Our party brought off a Lieutt, Sergt, and Corporal with 20 privates prisoners.[3] While These Detachments were engaged, a Column of the Enemy descended from the Woods and marched towards the Center of our Lines with a design to make an Impression, but were repulsed—This Evening they appeared very numerous about the Skirts of the Woods where they have pitched Several Tents, and his Excellency Inclines to think they mean to attack and force us from our Lines by way of regular approaches rather than in any other manner.[4]

Today Five Ships of the Line came up towards the Town where they seemed desirous of getting, as they turned a long time against an unfavourable Wind,[5] and on my return this Evening[6] I found a Deserter from the 23d Regmt, who Informed me that they design as soon as the Wind will permit 'em to come up, to give us a Severe Cannonade and to Silence our Batteries, If possible. I have the Honor to be in great Haste Sir Your Most Obedt

Rob. H. Harrison.

ALS, DNA:PCC, item 152; LB, DLC:GW; copy, DNA:PCC, item 169; Varick transcript, DLC:GW. The LB includes a note that reads "A Simr letter to Gl Mercer." The LB differs in wording from the ALS at several places. For significant variations, see notes 1, 2, 4, and 6.

The account of the Battle of Long Island that Harrison gives in this letter indicates that as of early evening on this date GW was not fully informed about the disastrous events that had occurred several hours earlier on the Heights of Guana. That heavily wooded ridge, which lay from one-and-a-half to three miles outside the Brooklyn lines, was defended during the battle by about thirty-five hundred Americans. Lord Stirling commanded a force at Gowanus Pass at the western end of the ridge, and General Sullivan commanded forces at Flatbush and Bedford passes, located respectively about two and three miles east of Gowanus Pass. Jamaica Pass, about six miles east of Gowanus Pass, was guarded only by five mounted militia officers.

During the early morning hours on this date, the main body of General

Howe's army, consisting of about ten thousand men, outflanked the American positions on the Heights of Guana by crossing Jamaica Pass. Capturing the five militia officers posted there, the British force proceeded undetected along the north side of the ridge toward Brooklyn in order to cut off the Americans at the other three passes. Meanwhile, on the south side of the ridge, Gen. James Grant with about five thousand British troops made a diversionary attack on Gowanus Pass, and Gen. Philip von Heister with about four thousand Hessians threatened Flatbush and Bedford passes. Distracted by those maneuvers, Sullivan and Stirling were not aware that the main British force was behind them until about nine o'clock in the morning when Howe's flanking column reached the village of Bedford near Bedford Pass and gave a signal for a general attack. In the ensuing fighting, which lasted until about two o'clock in the afternoon, the British and Hessians routed the Americans, killing two to three hundred of them and taking 1,097 prisoners including Stirling and Sullivan. British and Hessian losses totaled 63 men killed, 283 wounded, and 21 captured (see Force, *American Archives*, 5th ser., 1:1256–59). Washington observed the battle from a vantage point within the Brooklyn lines and received his first reports from officers and soldiers who straggled into those lines.

For published accounts of the Battle of Long Island, see Freeman, *Washington*, 4:153–75; Gruber, "America's First Battle"; Johnston, *Campaign of 1776;* Manders, *Battle of Long Island;* and Ward, *War of the Revolution*, 1:211–37.

1. The LB adds: "which continued with Intermissions till the Afternoon."

2. The LB reads: "that were engaged & that got off."

3. Lt. John Ragg of the 2d Regiment of Marines was captured with his detachment on Gowanus Road by the Delaware Regiment when the British mistook the blue-uniformed Delaware troops for Hessians. For the sending of these prisoners to Connecticut, see Heath to GW, 30 Aug., and note 5.

4. The LB reads: "This Evening they appeared very numerous about the Skirts of the Woods next to our Lines where they pitched many Tents, and his Excellency Inclines to think they mean to attack & to make an Impression by regular Approaches rather than in any other manner." General Howe says in his letter to Lord George Germain of 3 Sept. that "the grenadiers and 33rd regiment being in front of the column soon approached within musket shot of the enemy's lines at Brooklyn, from whence these battalions without regarding the fire of cannon and smallarms upon them pursued numbers of the rebels that were retiring from the heights so close to their principal redoubt and with such eagerness to attack it by storm that it required repeated orders to prevail upon them to desist from the attempt. Had they been permitted to go on, it is my opinion they would have carried the redoubt, but as it was apparent the lines must have been ours at a very cheap rate by regular approaches I would not risk the loss that might have been sustained in the assault and ordered them back to a hollow way in the front of the works out of the reach of musketry" (Davies, *Documents of the American Revolution*, 12:216–18).

5. To divert American attention from Howe's attack, Sir Peter Parker sailed from Staten Island toward New York City this morning with the warships *Preston, Renown, Asia, Roebuck,* and *Repulse*. "The Wind veering to the Northward

soon after the Break of Day," Lord Howe wrote to Philip Stephens four days later, "the Ships could not be moved up to the Distance proposed." The *Roebuck* "was the only Ship that could fetch high enough to the Northward to exchange a few random Shot with the Battery on Red Hook. And the Ebb [tide] making strongly down the River soon after, I ordered the Signal to be shewn for the Squadron to anchor" (Clark and Morgan, *Naval Documents*, 6:373–77).

6. The LB reads: "& on my return to Head Quarters to Night."

From John Hancock

Sir   Tuesday 6 oClock P.M. Philada 27 Augst 1776
I am this moment favd with yours of yesterday's Date, which I shall in the Morng Communicate to Congress.

I inclose sundry Resolves of Congress to which beg leave to Refer you,[1] & am with much Respect, Sir Your most obed. srt
                                                    John Hancock Prest

ALS, NjP: General Manuscripts.
1. Hancock enclosed copies of Congress's resolution of 26 Aug. concerning pensions for disabled American officers, soldiers, marines, and sailors and its resolution of 27 Aug. offering land to foreign officers who quit the British service (DLC:GW; see also *JCC*, 5:702–5, 707–8).

From Major General William Heath

Kingsbridge Augst 27th 1776
Dear General   8 oClock A:M.
By Express this moment, I am Informed that Two Ships and One Brig are Just Come to Anchor above Frog Point near the New City—I have Instantly Detached Colo. Graham with his Regiment with orders to prevent their Landing to Pillage or Burn,[1] I Imagine that more ships will follow them—But whether their Plan is only to Block up the Sound or to make a Diversion on this Side, Time must Discover, I have Given orders for Two Six pounders to be Brought from mount washington to this Post,[2] we Suffer here Extreemly for Horses not a Single One at this Post to Send on Express, General Mifflin Acquaints me that He Cannot Spare Either Horse or waggon from that Post, I beg that two or three may be Ordered here.[3]

An Ammunition Cart or Two Such as have been Provided for

Each Regiment at New York would be very Servicable Here, and I think the Same Reason holds good here as there that each Regiment should have One. I Have the Honor to be with great respect your Excellencys most Humble Servt

W. Heath

ADfS, MHi: Heath Papers.

1. Throg's Neck, also called Frog's or Throck's neck, is in the southeast corner of the present-day Bronx. Lying between the East River and Long Island Sound, this strategically important peninsula was bordered by creeks and marshes on the north and west at the time of the Revolutionary War, making it virtually an island during high tides. Most of Howe's army landed there on 12 Oct. 1776.

Heath says in his memoirs that on this date "several barges full of men landed on New City Island, and killed a number of cattle. Two companies of the [Graham's] regiment, immediately on their arrival, ferried over to the island. The enemy carried off one man and 14 cattle—the remainder of the cattle were secured" (Wilson, *Heath's Memoirs,* 65). City Island is in Long Island Sound about a mile and a half northeast of Throg's Neck. Heath's orders to Graham of this date are in MHi: Heath Papers.

Morris Graham, a colonel in the Dutchess County militia, was named by the New York convention on 17 July to command a regiment of militia levies from his county, which was assigned to Gen. George Clinton's brigade (see *N.Y. Prov. Congress Journals,* 1:528). Accused of retreating without orders at the Battle of White Plains, Graham was tried and acquitted by a court-martial on 2–4 Nov. (see the court-martial proceedings in Hastings, *Clinton Papers,* 1:413–16; George Clinton to GW, 29 Oct. 1776, ibid., 394; and General Orders, 1, 8 Nov. 1776). During 1777 and 1778 Graham commanded various regiments of militia levies that supported the Continental army. On 1 Aug. 1777 George Clinton ordered Graham to reinforce Schuyler at Albany (ibid., 2:149–51). In May 1778 Graham was stationed at White Plains where he gathered intelligence about the British forces in and around New York City, and on 8 Aug. 1778 GW attached Graham's regiment to the light infantry corps commanded by Gen. Charles Scott (see General Orders, that date).

2. See Heath to Thomas Mifflin, this date, MHi: Heath Papers.

3. GW's aide-de-camp Richard Cary wrote Heath on 1 Sept. informing him that GW "has directed the Qr Mr Genl to furnish you with the Horses wanted" (MHi: Heath Papers).

General Orders

Head Quarters, New York, August 28th 1776
Parole Sullivan.   Countersign Stirling.

Varick transcript, DLC:GW.

Peter Kinnan wrote in his orderly book under this date: "No orders this day that ever came to hand" (Kinnan, *Order Book*, 88).

From Major General Horatio Gates

Sir,   Tyconderoga August 28th 1776.

Yesterday I had the Honour to receive your Excellencies Letter of the 14 Instant which is all I have been favoured with since that of the 19th of July. I have at length the Satisfaction to send a pretty correct General Return of the Army in this Part of the Northern District of America; a Copy of my last Letter to General Schuyler, which is in the Packet, will explain the Return to your Excellency.[1] I also enclose my Orders and Instructions to Lieutenant Whitcomb who went from hence the [   ] Instant upon a Scout towards St Johns Chamble &c. The Report of his last Scout, which General Sullivan sent him upon has already been sent to General Schuler, who has doubtless transmitted it to your Excellency.[2] As the Small-Pox is now perfectly removed from the Army, I shall in consequence of the Intelligence received of the Motions of the Enemy immediately assemble my principal Strength to maintain this Important Pass, and hope General Waterbury, in a Week at farthest, will be able to come with the three Row-Gallies to Tyconderoga, and proceed the Instant they arrive and are fitted to join General Arnold upon the Lake. In the mean Time, we are exerting our utmost Industry to Fortify this Post, a Plan of which is Inclosed.[3] The Weather of Late has been so uncommonly Wet and Stormy for the Season, that we are much retarded in our Works. As the Enemy feel alike the Inclemency of the Season, I hope we shall be prepared for them when they come. My Orders to Brigadier General Arnold your Excellency will find in the Packet;[4] he read and entirely approved them before he left Tyconderoga. I hope they are the Sentiments of your Excellency and the most Honourable the Congress upon that Momentous Command.

As the Newhampshire, and Connecticut Militia have come without Tents much Time is Lost by those Regiments in covering themselves. It happens very Fortunately, that Mount Independence affords an Ample Supply of Materials for Huts,[5] otherwise those Corps must soon have felt great distress—The Massachusetts Militia are arrived, well supplied with excellent Tents, and a Sufficiency of good Camp Utensils. This in our present Circumstances is a great Help to us; and does that Province much Honour.

Governour Trumbull acquaints me he has forwarded 1000 falling Axes and two Loads of Cloathing.[6] His Excellency has, from the beginning of the Misfortunes of this Army, done every thing in his Power to reestablish it in Health and Power. Too much cannot be said in his Praise. Your Excellency must long ere this, have received from General Schuyler the Report of Major Biggelow, who returned with the Flag of Truce from Isle-Aux-Noix.[7] As I constantly Report every extraordinary Occurrence to General Schuyler, I take it for granted there is no Delay with him in forwarding them to your Excellency and the Congress. I have ordered Commissary Avery to forward to Colonel Trumbull the Returns and Reports that are proper to be made in his Department and Doctor Morgan has, before this, shewn your Excellency my letter to him of the 22nd Instant.[8]

I am pleased at the Account General Schuyler gives me of 513 Thousand Dollars being arrived at Albany, from Philadelphia, it is much wanted both there, and here, as The Militia were promised their Mileage and Billetting-Money at Number Four but no Money was sent there to pay them. This neglect caused much murmuring amongst them, and was very near stopping their March from Thence. I wish good Care was taken not to make any Promises to Troops, but such as are punctually performed. I apprehend this Promise was made by the Legislature at Water-Town. I have the Honour to be Your Excellencys most Obedient Humble Servant

Horatio Gates

LS, DLC:GW; ADfS, NHi: Gates Papers.

1. The enclosed return of 24 Aug. and the copy of Gates's letter to Schuyler of 26–27 Aug. are in DLC:GW. The return shows that the five infantry brigades in the vicinity of Ticonderoga contained 490 commissioned officers, 63

staff officers, 691 noncommissioned officers, and 9,157 rank and file, of whom 4,899 rank and file were present and fit for duty. Capt. Stephen Badlam's artillery corps had 142 officers and men, but only 48 of its 96 matrosses were present and fit for duty. The infantry detachments at Crown Point, Fort George, and Skenesboro had a total of 129 commissioned officers, 18 staff officers, 187 noncommissioned officers, and 2,134 rank and file, of whom 1,500 were present and fit for duty. "Notwithstanding the Number victualed, we want Men," Gates says in his letter to Schuyler. "More than one half that Eat, do not act—The Sick, the Lame and Lazy, you well know, make an unreasonable Proportion in our Army." Schuyler enclosed copies of this letter and return in his letter to GW of 31 August.

2. A copy of Benjamin Whitcomb's journal for his scouting trip to St. Jean between 14 July and 6 Aug. was enclosed in Gates's letter to GW of 7 August. The copy of the instructions to Whitcomb of 19 Aug. that Gates enclosed with his letter of this date is in DLC:GW. Mindful that Whitcomb had ambushed and killed a British officer on his earlier trip, Gates forbade him "to fire upon, to kill, to wound, to scalp, or, in any way, to injure the Life or person of any one engag'd in the service of the Enemy, Except, in your own Defence. . . . 'Tis not by Sacrificing a few unhappy Victims, who may fall into our hands, that the important Controversy between G: Britain & this Country is to be settled."

3. Although the enclosed plan of Ticonderoga has not been identified, it probably was a version of the map of the fort and its dependencies that John Trumbull, the deputy adjutant general for the northern department, drew during this month. See Trumbull, *Autobiography,* 33.

4. The enclosed copy of these orders of 7 Aug. is in DLC:GW. Gates instructed Arnold to station his fleet at Split Rock or Isle aux Têtes (Ash Island) and not to go farther north. "The Preventing the Enemy's Invasion of our Country," Gates writes, "is the ultimate End of the important Command, with which you are now intrusted. It is a defensive War we are carrying on; therefore, no wanton Risque, or unnecessary Display of the Power of the Fleet, is, at any Time, to influence your Conduct."

5. Mount Independence was on the eastern shore of Lake Champlain across from the fort at Ticonderoga. Three of Gates's brigades were camped on this hill, which was being cleared and fortified to protect the main fort.

6. See Jonathan Trumbull, Sr., to Gates, 12 Aug., in Force, *American Archives,* 5th ser., 1:925.

7. For Maj. John Bigelow's intelligence, see Schuyler to GW, 16 Aug., and note 1, and GW to Hancock, 20 Aug., and note 3.

8. Gates sent Dr. John Morgan a copy of his letter to Egbert Benson of 22 Aug., in which Gates complains that Dr. Samuel Stringer, whom he had sent to New York on 29 July to procure medicines for the northern army, "is gone a preferment hunting to the Congress at *Philadelphia,* while the troops here are suffering inexpressible distress for want of medicines. I entreat, sir, you will instantly lay this letter before General *Washington,* and receive his commands for sending a supply of medicines to Doctor [Jonathan] Potts, at *Lake George*" (Force, *American Archives,* 5th ser., 1:1114).

From Abraham Yates, Jr.

In Convention of the Representatives of the
Sir State of New York at Harlem Augt 28th 1776
I am commanded by the Convention to enclose to Your Excel-
lency the Copy of a Letter they received last Evening from Gen-
eral Woodhull[.][1] The Convention are of Opinion that the
Enemy may be prevented from getting the Stock and Grain on
Long Island, if the Regiments under the Command of Colo.
Smith and Colo. Remsen be sent to join General Woodhull. That
this Junction may be effected and how Major Lawrence (who is
a Member of this Convention and the bearer hereof) will inform
Your Excellency.[2] I have the Honor to be with the greatest Respect Your Excellency's most Obedient & most humble servant

By Order.
Abm Yates Junr President

LS, DLC:GW; Df (mutilated), N: New York Provincial Congress Revolutionary
Papers. The convention approved the draft earlier on this date (see *N.Y. Prov.
Congress Journals*, 1:595).

1. The enclosed copy of Nathaniel Woodhull's letter to the convention of
27 Aug. reads: "I am now at Jamaica [Long Island] with less than one hundred
men, having bro't all the Cattle from the westward and Southward of the Hills;
and have Sent them off with the Troops of Horse, with Orders to take all the
rest Eastward of this place, to the Eastward of Hempsted Plains, and to put
them into the Fields, and Set a Guard over them—The Enemy I am informed
are entrenching from the Heighths near Howards Southward. I have now
received yours with several Resolutions which I wish was in my power to put
in Execution—But unless Colo. Smith And Remsen mentioned in yours join
me with their Regiments or some other Assistance immediately, I shall not be
able; for the People are all moving Eastward and I cannot get any Assistance
from them—I shall continue here as long as I can in Hopes of a Reinforcement—but if none comes soon I shall retreat & drive the Stock before me into
the woods—Colonels Smith & Remsen I think can't join me—Unless you can
Send me some other assistance, I fear I shall soon be obliged to quit this
place" (DLC:GW).

Howard's Inn was near the Jamaica Pass in Heights of Guana. The letter to
which Woodhull refers is the one that the convention sent him on 26 Aug.,
enclosing resolutions that it had passed on 24 Aug. in response to news of the
British landing on Long Island. In those resolutions the convention orders all
the livestock south of the Heights of Guana in Queens County to be moved to
"the fields at east end of Hemstead Plains" and directs Woodhull to "take post"
with his brigade of Queens and Suffolk county militia "on the high grounds
running through Nassau [Long] island, as near to the enemy as he may think
expedient, for the purpose of opposing their incursions." If it seemed that

the British would "gain possession of those heights," Woodhull was to retreat, "removing and destroying the stock and the grain, and dismantling the mills" (ibid., 588, 590).

2. On 24 Aug. the convention had sent two of its members, William Smith of Suffolk County and Samuel Townshend of Queens County, to confer with GW about the removal of livestock from western to eastern Long Island and to submit to his "consideration the propriety of ordering" colonels Josiah Smith's and Jeromus Remsen's regiments of New York militia levies, which were attached to Gen. John Nixon's brigade at Brooklyn, to reinforce Woodhull's brigade (ibid., 588). Smith and Townshend reported on 26 Aug. that GW "seemed well pleased" with the convention's actions "but said *he was afraid it was too late.*" GW assured them, nevertheless, "that he would immediately give orders that Col. Smith's and Remsen's regiments should march into Queens county to join Genl. Woodhull; and as to calling out any more of the militia, he asked what time we thought it would take to have the militia of Westchester county embodied? We told him we thought at least 4 or 5 days; upon which he made no reply" (ibid., 589–90).

Although the Battle of Long Island on 27 Aug. prevented Smith's and Remsen's regiments from reinforcing Woodhull, the convention continued to pursue the matter. After approving the draft of this letter on this date, the convention ordered Cornelius Van Wyck, a member from Queens County, to "repair immediately to Flushing to gain intelligence of the situation of the enemy and what places are now occupied by Genl. Woodhull" and find "the most suitable place for the reinforcement to join Genl. Woodhull to land" (ibid., 595). Woodhull, however, wrote the convention from Jamaica on this date: "As to Colos. Smith and Remsen's regiments, they cannot join me, for the communication is cut off between us" (ibid., 596).

Jonathan Lawrence (1737–1812), of Newtown, Long Island, represented Queens County in the provincial congress and convention between 1775 and 1777. At this time he was on leave from the convention, serving as brigade major of Woodhull's militia brigade, and he had come from Woodhull's camp the previous day to inform the convention about the brigade's situation (ibid., 595–96). Settling in Dutchess County after Newtown was occupied by the British, Lawrence served in the state senate from 1777 to 1783 and on the state's council of appointment from 1778 to 1779 and from 1782 to 1784. During the summer of 1778 he apparently participated in the Rhode Island expedition (Mather, *Refugees of 1776*, 442–43).

Jeromus Remsen, Jr. (1735–1790), of Queens County was appointed by the New York convention on 13 Aug. as colonel of a regiment of militia levies from Kings and Queens counties (*N.Y. Prov. Congress Journals,* 1:568). Remsen's regiment was attached to Gen. John Nixon's brigade at Brooklyn until the American evacuation of Long Island on 30 Aug., when it was assigned to Gen. George Clinton's brigade at King's Bridge (ibid., 568, 603–4). The regiment dispersed over the next several days, however, and it was not reorganized (ibid., 605; see also Heath to GW, 31 Aug. [third letter]).

To Abraham Yates, Jr.

Sir   Long Island Augst 28th 1776

I was just now honored with your favor of this date with Genl Woodhulls Letter & should esteem myself happy were it in my power to afford the assistance required; but the enemy having landed a considerable part of their force here & at the same time may have reserved Some to attack New York, it is the opinion not only of myself but of all my General Officers I have had an opportunity of consulting with that the men we have are not more than competent to the defence of these Lines & the Several posts which must be defended—This reason & this only prevents my complying with your request—I Shall beg leave to mention in confidence that a few days ago upon the Enemys first landing here, I wrote to Governor Trumbull recommending him to throw over a body of a 1000 men on the Island to annoy the enemy in their rear If the state of the Colony would admit of it[1]—Whether it will be done I cannot determine, that Colony having furnished a large proportion of men I was & Still am doubtfull whether it could be done—If it could I am Satisfied it would from the zeal & readiness they have ever shewn to give every possible Succour—I am hopefull they will be in a condition to do it, & if they are[,] those troops I doubt not will be ready & Willing to give Genl Woodhull any assistance he may want—But cannot the Militia effect what he wishes to do? They I believe must be depended on in the present instance for relief. I have the honor to be Yours &c.

                                        Go. Washington

Transcript, MH: Sparks Papers. The New York convention read this letter late this afternoon, and it is printed in the *N.Y. Prov. Congress Journals,* 1:599. That text, which presumably was taken from the unfound receiver's copy, is nearly identical in wording to the Sparks transcript.

1. See GW to Jonathan Trumbull, Sr., 24 August.

General Orders

                         Head Quarters, New York, August 29th 1776

Parole [   ]   Countersign [   ].

One Orderly Serjeant from each regiment in General Wadsworths, General Wolcot's and General Fellows's Brigades, and one from Col. Knox's Command, to attend daily at Head Quarters until further orders.

The commanding officers of each company, in the several regiments in this post, are strictly required to attend, to the orders that have been given, by the Commander in Chief, from time to time, to see that their respective Rolls are looked over, and the orders of the day published to their whole company. And as it is the pleasure of the Commander in Chief of the Continental Forces, that all Soldiers that pass from Long Island here without passes, should immediately be sent back. All the Guards especially, and all others, belonging to the Army in this post, are required to take up all soldiers coming from Long Island without passes signed by a proper officer, and send them immediately back to Long Island.

The Colonels or commanding Officers of each regiment must take care that the arms and ammunition of each soldier be in good order; that they be equipped and constantly ready for action. They must be particularly attentive to see that the Cartridges suit their peices.

All the guards, and also all others belonging to the Army, are to be vigilant in taking up, and confining, all persons guilty of disorderly firing, or firing without leave. All the guards supplied by general detail, are to be punctually on the Grand Parade by eight o'clock in the morning, and in case any Brigade Major does not punctually bring on the men, he is to furnish, the Brigadier of the day is to report him immediately, and if such Brigade Major is delayed by the negligence of an Adjutant, he is to put such Adjutant immediately under an arrest.

It is hoped that every officer and soldier, in this post, will exert himself for the good of the service, to the utmost; and as there are many intrenchments, now begun that are unfinished, that necessity requires should be immediately completed; it is justly expected, that every brave man will exert himself to complete every needful fortification.

Varick transcript, DLC:GW. The order of this date concerning the evacuation of the sick from Long Island that is printed with GW's general orders in Johnston, *Campaign of 1776*, pt. 2, 30–31, was probably issued by Gen. Israel Putnam (see Fitzpatrick, *Writings*, 5:497, n.14).

Council of War

[Long Island, 29 August 1776]

At a Council of War held at Long Island, Augt 29. 1776. Present His Excellency, The Comander in Cheif[.] Majors General Putnam[,] Spencer. Brigrs Genls Mifflin[,] McDougall[,] Parsons[,] Scott[,] Wadsworth[,] Fellows.

It was submitted to the consideration of the Council whether under all circumstances It would not be Eligable to Leave Long Island & Its Dependencies & remove the Army to New York— Unanimously agreed in the Affirmative for the following reasons.

1st Because Our advanced party had met with a defeat & the Wood was lost where we expected to make a principal Stand.

2d The great Loss sustained in the death or Captivity of Several valuable Officers and their Battallions or a Large part of them had occasioned great confusion and discouragement among the Troops.

3d The Heavy rains which fell Two days & Nights with but Little Intermission had Injured the Arms & Spoiled a great part of the Ammunition, and the Soldiery being without Cover & Obliged to lay in the Lines were worn out and It was to be feared would not be retained in them by any Order.[1]

4 From the Time the Enemy moved from Flatbush, Several large Ships had attempted to get up as supposed into the East River to cut off our Communication, by which the whole Army would have been destroyed, But the Wind being N.E. could not affect It.

5th Upon consulting with persons of knowledge of the Harbour they were of Opinion that Small Ships might come between Long Island & Governors Island where there are no Obstructions and which would cut off the communication effectually, and who were also of Opinion the Hulks sunk between Governors Island & the City of New York were no sufficient Security for Obstructing that passage.

6. Though our Lines were fortified with some strong Redoubts, yet a Great part of them were weak being only abbattied with Brush and affording no strong cover, so that there was reason to apprehend they might be forced, which would have put

our Troops in confusion & havg no retreat, they must have been cut to peices or made prisoners.[2]

7. The Divided state of the Troops rendered our defence very precarious, and the duty of defending long and extensive Lines at so many different places without proper conveniences & cover so very fatiguing that the Troops had become despirited by their Incessant duty and watching.

8 Because the Enemy had sent several Ships of War, into the sound, to a place called flushing bay, and from the information recieved that a part of their troops were moving across Long Island, that way, there was reason to apprehend, they meant to pass overland, & form an encampment above Kings bridge, in order to cut off & prevent all communication between our army, & the country beyond them or to get in our rear.[3]

D, in Robert Hanson Harrison's and William Grayson's writings, DLC:GW; DS (extract), in Joseph Reed's writing, DLC:GW; copy, enclosed in GW to Hancock, 31 Aug. 1776, DNA:PCC, item 152; copy, DNA:PCC, item 169; Varick transcript, DLC:GW. The unsigned document in DLC:GW is in Harrison's writing except for the eighth reason, which is in Grayson's writing. Reed's extract omits the reasons and is signed by all members except John Fellows and GW.

John Morin Scott is the only council member who is known to have expressed reservations about retreating. "I was summoned," Scott wrote John Jay on 6 Sept., "to a Council of War at Mr. Philip Livingston's house on Thursday 29th ult. never having had reason to expect a proposition for a retreat till it was mentioned. . . . As it was suddenly proposed, *I as suddenly objected to it,* from an aversion to giving the enemy a single inch of ground; but *was soon convinced by the unanswerable reasons for it.* They were these. Invested by an enemy of above double our number from water to water, scant in almost every necessary of life and without covering and liable every moment to have the communication between us and the city cut off by the entrance of the frigates into the East River between (late) Governor's Island and Long Island; which General McDougall assured us from his own nautic experience was very feasible. In such a situation we should have been reduced to the alternative of desperately attempting to cut our way [through] a vastly superior enemy with certain loss of a valuable stock of artillery and artillery stores, which the continent has been collecting with great pains; or by famine and fatigue have been made an easy prey to the enemy. In either case the campaign would have ended in the total ruin of our army" (Johnston, *Campaign of 1776,* part 2, 36–39).

For Joseph Reed's alleged role in persuading GW to call this council of war, see Reed, *Joseph Reed,* 1:226–27n; Graydon, *Memoirs,* 166; and Freeman, *Washington,* 4:172–73, n.218. For an account of the retreat from Long Island, which was executed successfully during the ensuing night, see GW to Hancock, 31 August.

1. "You may judge of our situation," Scott wrote Jay on 6 Sept., "subject to almost incessant rains, without baggage or tents and almost without victuals or drink, and in some part of the lines the men were standing up to their middles in water" (Johnston, *Campaign of 1776*, pt. 2, 36–39; see also Graydon, *Memoirs*, 165; Martin, *Private Yankee Doodle*, 27–28; Skewkirk, "Moravian Diary," 147–48; and the *New-York Journal; or, the General Advertiser*, this date).

2. The place in the lines where Capt. Alexander Graydon of the 3d Pennsylvania Regiment was posted "was low and unfavourable for defence. There was a *fraised* ditch in its front, but it gave little promise of security, as it was evidently commanded by the ground occupied by the enemy, who entirely enclosed the whole of our position, at the distance of but a few hundred paces" (Graydon, *Memoirs*, 165; see also Scott to Jay, 6 Sept., in Johnston, *Campaign of 1776*, pt. 2, 36–39; Wade and Lively, *This Glorious Cause*, 216; Martin, *Private Yankee Doodle*, 27; and Tallmadge, *Memoir*, 10).

3. For intelligence about these warships near the western entrance to Long Island Sound, see Heath to GW, 26 Aug., and note 4. Flushing Bay, located on the northwest coast of Long Island, is a shallow inlet of the East River.

To John Hancock

Sir   Long Island Augt 29: 1776. ½ after 4. A.M.
     I was last night honoured with your favor of the 27th accompanied by sundry Resolutions of Congress. Those respecting the officers &c. that may be wounded in the service of the States are founded much in Justice, and I should hope may be productive of many salutary consequences—As to the Encouragement to the Hessian Officers, I wish It may have the desired effect, perhaps It might have been better, had the offer been sooner made.
     Before this you will probably have received a Letter from Mr Harrison of the 27th advising of the Engagement between a Detachment of our Men and the Enemy on that day. I am sorry to inform Congress that I have not yet heard either of Genl Sullivan or Lord Stirling, who they would observe were among the missing after the Engagement—Nor can I ascertain our Loss, I am hopefull part of our Men will yet get in, several did Yesterday morning—That of the Enemy is also uncertain—The Accounts are various—I incline to think they suffered a good deal—Some Deserters say five Hundred were killed and Wounded—There was some Skirmishing the greatest part of Yesterday between parties from the Enemy and our People—In

the Evening It was pretty smart—The Event I have not yet learned.[1]

The Weather of late has been extremely wet. Yesterday It rained severely the whole afternoon which distressed our people much, not having a sufficiency of Tents to cover them, and what we have not got over yet. I am in hopes they will All be got to day and that they will be more confortably provided, tho the great scarcity of these Articles distresses us beyond measure not having any thing like a sufficient Number to protect our people from the Inclemency of the Weather and which has occasioned much sickness and the Men to be almost broke down. I have the Honor to be with great respect Sir Your Most Obedt Servt

Go: Washington

LS, in Robert Hanson Harrison's writing, DNA:PCC, item 152; copy, DNA: PCC, item 169.

1. Capt. Alexander Graydon says that on 28 Aug. "there was an incessant skirmishing kept up in the day-time between our riflemen and the enemy's irregulars; and the firing was sometimes so brisk, as to indicate an approaching general engagement. This was judiciously encouraged by General Washington, as it tended to restore confidence to our men, and was, besides, showing a good countenance to the foe" (Graydon, *Memoirs*, 165–66; for other accounts of this skirmishing, see Martin, *Private Yankee Doodle*, 27; Tatum, *Serle's Journal*, 80; Moses Little to his son, 1 Sept., in Johnston, *Campaign of 1776*, pt. 2, 43–44; and Gold Selleck Silliman to his wife, 29 Aug., ibid., 54).

From Major General Philip Schuyler

Dear Sir   Albany August 29th 1776
Yesterday I was honored with your Excellency's Favor of the 24th Instant.

The Articles mentioned in your Letter to Captain Varick are arrived and forwarded to Tyonderoga—Those sent by Philo Sentford are not yet arrived, detained I suppose by Northerly Winds which have prevailed for some Days.[1]

Our Carpenters at Skenesborough sicken very fast—Captain Titcomb's Company from the Massachusetts Bay consisting of fifty had only ten at Work on the 25th Instant[2] and many of the others were also incapable of Duty—We have however got so far a Head of the Enemy in our Naval Force that I hope they will not be able to equal it this Campaign, notwithstanding the Indisposition of our Carpenters.

The Reasons your Excellency assigns for proceeding against the Officers of Colonel Dayton's Regiment by Court Martial are incontrovertable.

I am happy to learn that our Troops had the Advantage in the Skirmish on Long Island—Indecisive as these little Rencounters are, they are however attended with good Consequences—The Express advises us that before he left New York and after he had received the Letter for me Accounts arrived that we had killed and taken sixty of the Enemy with six Field pieces—I hope it may be confirmed.

Congress have ordered me to make Enquiry of and to bring to Tryal the persons concerned in the plunder of General prescott's and Captain Anstruther's Baggage—I am informed by Lieut: Colonel Brown that Lieutenant Johnson last Year of Captain Lamb's Artillery Company and now in some Corps at New York was principally concerned in taking Anstruther's.

As the Evidences are in this Quarter, your Excellency will judge of the propriety of sending Johnson up, or ordering the Witnesses down.[3]

Most of the Stockbridge Indians inclined to go to New York— I ordered them provisions and I believe they are now on their passage.

The Committee of this place did not chuse to send the Boards Mr Hughes wrote for on their Risk—They informed me of this, and I did not hesitate to assure them that they would be considered as shipped on the public Account—This Day they informed me, that not more than ten thousand Boards were as yet gone and that they could not prevail on any more Masters of Sloops to carry them further than peek's Kill—Apprehensive that you would be greatly distressed for Shelter for the Men, I have requested them, if they cannot do otherwise to send them to peek's Kill, and to advise Colonel Moylan, of the Number that will be landed there, by this Express.[4]

I percieve that Congress has resolved on inlisting Men to serve three Years—I fear very few Recruits will be obtained in the Country at this Time, and very few out of the Army, if the Inlistments are not attempted until the Time of those now engaged is nearly expired—Would it not be well immediately to appoint recruiting Officers in every Corps to enlist those for three Years, who are now engaged until the Fall or Winter only—In the Course of three Months an alert Officer will have it in his power with the Bounty he may be authorized to give to engage a good Number—The Home-Sickness begins to prevail about the Middle of October, and when that unconquerable Distemper once takes place every Consideration gives Way to it—I shall communicate my Ideas on this Subject to Congress in a Letter I have occasion to write them to Day.[5] I am Dr Sir with Every Affectionate wish Your Excellencys Most Obedient Humble Servant

Ph: Schuyler

LS, DLC:GW; LB, NN: Schuyler Papers. The extract mentioned in note 4 has not been found.

1. See GW to Richard Varick, 10 Aug., and the list of articles sent to Albany aboard Philo Sandford's schooner *Union,* 19 Aug., cited in GW to Schuyler, 24 Aug., n.4.

2. "Captain *Titcomb's* company of carpenters," David Waterbury wrote Gates from Skenesboro on 25 Aug., "are all sick, except four, and applied for discharges. The tools they brought with them are private property, and they mean to carry them off" (Force, *American Archives,* 5th ser., 1:1154). Titcomb's company apparently arrived at Skenesboro on 24 July, and by 23 Aug. it had built a row galley and was working on another one. Titcomb was promised command of the second row galley, but it apparently was not finished before his company disbanded (see Arnold to Schuyler, 24 July, Gates to Arnold, 23 Aug., and Arnold to Gates, 23 Aug., in Clark and Morgan, *Naval Documents,* 5:1197–98; 6:283; and Gates to Waterbury, 2 Sept., in Force, *American Archives,* 5th ser., 2:127).

3. Congress on 30 July directed Schuyler to investigate charges that "some licentious persons" had plundered Gen. Richard Prescott's baggage after his capture in Canada the previous November (*JCC,* 5:618). The accused included Col. James Easton and Lt. Col. John Brown, who asserted their innocence and demanded a court of inquiry (see Arnold to Hancock, 1 Feb. 1776, DNA:PCC, item 162; Easton to Hancock, 8 May 1776, DNA:PCC, item 78; Brown to Congress, 26 June 1776, DNA:PCC, item 153; and *JCC,* 4:313–14, 5:485). Although Schuyler requested Gates in a letter of this date to convene a court of inquiry on the charge against Brown, no formal investigation was conducted before Brown resigned from the army in March 1777 (Force, *American Archives,* 5th ser., 1:1221–22; see also Brown to Gates, 3 Sept., 1–2 Dec. 1776, ibid., 2:143, 3:1158–60; Gates to Brown, 2 Dec. 1776, ibid., 1160; Brown to Hancock, 10 Dec. 1776, DNA:PCC, item 78; GW to Schuyler, 19 Feb. 1777, NN: Schuyler Papers; *JCC,* 7:181).

William Anstruther (d. 1778), a captain in the 26th Regiment, was among the officers captured with Prescott (see list of British officers on vessels near

Montreal, 21 Nov. 1775, DLC:GW). On 17 Aug. 1776 Congress read a letter from Lt. Martin Johnson of that date, in which he admitted having in his possession a diamond ring belonging to Anstruther but denied breaking open his trunk. Johnson "found the ring," he said, "sometime after the garrison capitulated, and thought it to be a prize." Congress ordered Johnson to deliver the ring to the secretary of the War Office, who was to send it to Anstruther (ibid., 5:664). Johnson, who had served in Canada during the previous fall and winter as first lieutenant of Capt. John Lamb's independent New York artillery company, was appointed first lieutenant of Capt. Alexander Hamilton's independent New York artillery company in February 1776. Hamilton informed the New York convention on 12 Aug. 1776 that Johnson had been promoted "to a captaincy of one of the row-gallies, (which command, however, he has since resigned, for a very particular reason)" (Syrett, *Hamilton Papers*, 1:187–88). The reason probably was Johnson's involvement in plundering Anstruther's baggage.

4. At GW's direction, Robert Hanson Harrison on 3 Sept. sent Stephen Moylan a copy of this paragraph. "His Excellency," Harrison wrote Moylan in his covering letter of that date, "desires that you will take measures not only for getting those [boards] they have sent to Peeks Kill down to King's Bridge or some place near It, But also that you will exert yourself to have a pretty considerable quantity provided as many will be wanted in all probability to Shelter the Troops that may be stationed there & at the posts about It" (DLC:GW). Asst. Q.M. Gen. Hugh Hughes requested these boards in a letter to the Albany committee of correspondence of 18 Aug., which the committee read three days later (*Minutes of the Albany and Schenectady Committees*, 1:527; see also Schuyler to GW, 2 Sept., and note 2).

5. Schuyler's letter to Hancock of this date is in DNA:PCC, item 153.

From Lord Stirling

My dear General   Eagle, August 29th 1776.

I have now an Oppertunity of informing you of what has happened to me Since I had last the pleasure of Seeing you; about 3 oClock in the morning of 27th I was Called up and Informed by General Putnam that the Enemy were advanceing by the Road from flat Bush to the Red Lyon,[1] and ordered me to March with the two Regiments nearest at hand to Meet them; these happend to be Haslets & Smallwoods, with which I accordingly Marched, and was on the Road to the Narrows Just as the day light began to appear, we proceeded to within about half a Mile of the Red Lyon and there met Col: Atlee with his Regiment who Informed me, that the Enemy were in Sight, indeed I then Saw their front between us and the Red Lyon, I desired

Colonel Atlee to place his Regiment on the left of the Road and to wait their Comeing up, while I went to form the two Regiments I had brought with me, along a Ridge from the Road up to a peice of wood on the Top of the Hill, this was done Instantly on very Advantageous ground. Our Opponents advanced and were fired upon in the Road by Atlee's, who after two or three Rounds retreated to the wood on my left and there formed,[2] by this time Kichline's Rifle Men arrived, part of them I placed along a hedge under the front of the Hill, and the rest in the front of the wood.[3] The troops opposed to me were two Brigades of four Regiments Each under the Command of General Grant; who advanced their light Troops to within 150 yards of our Right front, and took possession of an Orchard there & some hedges which extended towards our left;[4] this brought on an Exchange of fire between those troops and Our Rifle Men which Continued for about two hours and the[n] Ceased by those light troops retireing to their Main Body. In the Meantime Capt. Carpenter brought up two feild peices which were placed on the side of the Hill, so as to Command the Road and the Only Approach for some hundred Yards; on the part of General Grant there were two feild peices one Howitz advanced to within three Hundred yards of the front of our Right and alike detachment of Artillery to the front of our left on a riseing Ground, at About 600 yards distance, one of their Brigades, formed in two lines opposite to our Right and the other Extended in one line to top of the Hills in the front of our left, in this possition we stood Cannonadeing each other 'till Near Eleven oClock, when I found that General Howe with the Main Body [of] the Army was between me and Our Lines, and saw that [the] only Chance of Escapeing being all made prisoners,[5] was to pass the Creek near the Yellow Mills, and in order to render this the more practicable I found it Absolutely Necessary to Attack a Body of Troops Commanded by Lord Cornwallis posted at the House near the Upper Mills; this I Instantly did, with about half of small-woods first ordering all the other troops to make the best of their way thro' the Creek,[6] we Continued the Attack a Considerable time the Men haveing been rallied and the Attack renewed five or Six Several times, and were on the point of driveing Lord Cornwallis from his Station, but large [Succours][7] arriveing rendered it impossible to do more than to provide for Safety, I endeavoured to get in between that House and fort Box,[8] but on Attempting it I found a Considerable body of Troops in my Front, and Several in pursuit of me on the Right & left & a Constant fire-ing on me, I immediately Turned the point of a Hill which Cov-ered me from their fire, and I was soon out of the Reach of my pursuers; I soon found that it would be in Vain to Attempt to make my Escape, and therefore went to Surrender my self to General De Heister Commander in Cheif of the Hessians.[9]

AL, DLC:GW; copy, enclosed in GW to Hancock, 31 Aug. 1776, DNA:PCC, item 152; copy, DNA:PCC, item 169. Stirling was a prisoner aboard Lord Howe's flagship, the *Eagle* (see Tatum, *Serle's Journal*, 80–82). This letter was brought to GW by Gen. John Sullivan, who had been paroled by his British captors (see GW to Hancock, 31 Aug.).

1. The Red Lion Tavern stood about three miles south of the Brooklyn ferry at the junction of Gowanus Road, which ran from Brooklyn to the Nar-rows, and Martense Lane, a narrow road leading southeast through the Heights of Guana toward Flatbush.

2. For Col. Samuel John Atlee's account of these events, see his journal entry for 27 Aug. in Force, *American Archives*, 5th ser., 1:1251–55. For other accounts, see extract of a letter from a Marylander [Mordecai Gist], 30 Aug., ibid., 1232–33; extract of a letter from New York, 1 Sept., ibid., 2:107–8; Sa-bine, *Fitch's New-York Diary*, 30–31; and Samuel Holden Parsons to John Adams, 29 Aug., in Taylor, *Papers of John Adams*, 5:4–7.

3. Lt. Col. Peter Kachlein (Kechlein; 1722–1789) commanded the militia regiment that had been raised in Northampton County, Pa., during July as part of the state's quota for the flying camp. Kachlein's men arrived on Long Island on 26 Aug., and in the fighting on Gowanus Road this day, many of them, including Kachlein, were captured. A native of Heidelburg, Germany, Kachlein emigrated to America in 1742 and soon settled at the site of Easton, Pennsylvania. From 1774 to 1775 he was a member of the Northampton County committee of observation and the Pennsylvania convention. On 22 May 1775 Kachlein was named captain of the Easton company of associators, and on 17 July 1776 he became lieutenant colonel of the county's flying camp regiment. After the Battle of Long Island, Kachlein remained in captivity until he was paroled on 29 Dec. 1776. He was exchanged in August 1778 and became Northampton's county lieutenant in March 1780.

4. Maj. Gen. James Grant commanded his own 4th Brigade, which con-sisted of the 17th, 40th, 46th, and 55th regiments, and Brig. Gen. James Ag-new's 6th Brigade, which consisted of the 22d, 43d, 54th, and 63d regiments. Grant's force also included the 42d Royal Highlanders, two New York provin-cial companies, and a Royal Artillery detachment with ten guns (see William Howe to George Germain, 3 Sept., in Davies, *Documents of the American Revolu-tion*, 12:216–18).

5. The words within square brackets are taken from the copy in DNA:PCC, item 152.

6. The retreating troops crossed Gowanus Creek and its extensive marshes to the Brooklyn lines, while Stirling with five companies from Col. William Smallwood's Maryland regiment covered their retreat and tried to escape up the Gowanus Road by attacking the 2d Grenadiers and 71st Highlanders who had blocked the road behind him near the Cortelyou house. "Most of our Generals," an anonymous American participant wrote on 1 Sept., "were upon a high hill in our [Brooklyn] lines, viewing us with glasses. When we began our retreat, they could see the enemy we had to pass through, though we could not. Many of them thought we would surrender in a body, without firing. When we began the attack, General *Washington* wrung his hands, and cried out, *Good God! What brave fellows I must this day lose!*" (Force, *American Archives*, 5th ser., 2:107–8; for other accounts of this action, see extract of a letter from a Marylander [Mordecai Gist], 30 Aug., ibid., 1:1232–33; Sabine, *Fitch's Diary*, 30–31; and Martin, *Private Yankee Doodle*, 26.

7. Although this word is struck out on the manuscript of the AL, it appears in the copies in DNA:PCC.

8. Fort Box, which presumably was named for Gen. Nathanael Greene's brigade major Daniel Box, was a small redoubt located at the southeastern end of the Brooklyn lines near the head of Gowanus Creek.

9. Leopold Philipp, Freiherr von Heister (d. 1777), an elderly lieutenant general in the service of the landgrave of Hesse-Cassel, commanded the division of Hessian troops, containing about eighty-six hundred men, that arrived at Staten Island on 12 Aug. (see Atwood, *Hessians*, 51–57). On 25 Aug. Heister landed on Long Island with two Hessian brigades totaling about four thousand men and relieved Cornwallis's troops at Flatbush. During the Battle of Long Island, Heister's corps attacked the American detachment at Flatbush Pass and moved west to assist in cutting off Stirling's force on Gowanus Road. An officer of considerable battlefield experience but only moderate abilities, Heister was criticized increasingly by General Howe over the next four months for his seeming lack of aggressiveness and alleged indulgence of plundering. Howe's complaints and news of the Hessian defeat at Trenton on 26 Dec. 1776 convinced the landgrave to recall Heister in April 1777. Heister left America the following July, and in October he reached Cassel, where he died the following month (see ibid., 61–65, 103–13).

General Orders

Head Quarters, New york, August 30th 1776.
Parole Liberty.   Countersign Hancock.

All commanding Officers of regiments are to parade on their regimental parade, this evening at five o'Clock, examine the state of their men's ammunition and arms, get them in the best Order—All damaged Cartridges are to be returned and in this case fresh ones drawn without farther order. The Returns of the regiments are to be made as soon, and as exact as possible. No Arguments can be necessary at such a time as this, to induce all officers to a strict attention to this duty.

The constant firing in the Camp, notwithstanding repeated Orders to the contrary, is very scandalous, and seldom a day passes but some persons are shot by their friends—Once more therefore the General entreats the officers to prevent it, and calls upon the Soldiers to forbear this practice—Peices that cannot be drawn are to be discharged in a Volley, at Retreat Beating, and not otherwise, and then by command of the officer.

The loss of two General Officers by the late Action having occasioned a necessary change in the brigades; the Brigade Majors are to attend ten OClock to morrow to receive a new arrangement.

As the Tents are wet, and Weather unfavorable, the troops are to remain in the City till further Orders; those not supplied with Barracks, to apply to Mr Roorbach, Barrack Master: Officers and Men are charged to see, as little damage as possible, done to houses where they are quartered.

General Wadsworth to send two Regiments from his Brigade, to reinforce Col. Sergeant at Horns hook, as soon as possible.

In case of an Alarm this evening, which may be expected from the nearness of the enemy, and their expectation of taking advantage of the late rains, and last nights fatigue;[1] the following disposition is to take place and the regiments are to parade accordingly—General Mifflin's to parade on the Grand Parade, they are then to join the regiments lately composing Lord Stirlings Brigade, and the whole to parade on the parade lately assigned by him to them; these are to act under General Mifflin as a Reserve Corps. The regiments of General Nixon's Brigade are to join General Spencer's division who will assign them their alarm posts—The Jersey Troops to join General McDougall's Brigade, and parade at, or near, said ground.

Varick transcript, DLC:GW; Df, in Joseph Reed's writing, owned (1989) by Ms. Nancy A. Bergh (Marnan Collection), Minneapolis, Minnesota.

1. For the previous night's retreat from Long Island to New York City, see the proceedings of the council of war, 29 Aug., and GW to Hancock, 31 August. "In the morning," Rev. Ewald Gustav Schaukirk of New York wrote in his diary entry for this date, "unexpectedly and to the surprise of the city, it was found that all that could come back was come back; and that they had

abandoned Long Island. . . . It seemed a general damp had spread; and the sight of the scattered people up and down the streets was indeed moving. Many looked sickly, emaciated, cast down, &c.; the wet clothes, tents—as many as they had brought away—and other things, were lying about before the houses and in the streets to dry; in general everything seemed to be in confusion" (Skewkirk, "Moravian Diary," 148).

From William Duer

sir   In Committee of Safety Harlem Augt 30th 1776
By Order of the Committee of Safety of this State I transmit to your Excellency the Examination of Daniel Redfeild in order that such Measures may be pursued for baffling the Enemy's Operations, as your Prudence shall dictate[1]—I have likewise to inform your Excellency that on Yesterday Morng one Lounsbery in Westchester County who had headed a Body of about 14 Tories was kill'd by an Officer nam'd Flood, on his Refusal to Surrender himself Prisoner—That in his Pocket Book was found a Commission sign'd by Genl Howe to Major Rogers empowering him to raise a Battalion of Rangers with the Rank of Lt Colo. Commandant; That annext to this was a Warrant to this Lounsberry sign'd by Major Rogers appointing him a Captain of one of these Companies.

Likewise a Muster Roll of the Men already enlisted—The Committee of Safety will transmit to your Excellency certified Copies of all these Papers, as early as possible.[2] I am sir by Order Your most Obedt Hble Servt

Wm: Duer

ALS, DLC:GW.
  1. Daniel Redfield (1728–1788), a shipowner from Killingworth (now Clinton), Conn., says in the enclosed copy of his 29 Aug. examination that he was held on the British brig *Halifax* for a short time after the *Halifax* captured and burned his sloop in Long Island Sound on 26 August. From the *Halifax*'s pilot Redfield learned that the *Halifax* and two frigates "were to anchor in Flushing Bay, and that the Enemys design was to land Part of their Forces from Long Island, and that some Ships of War &cc. were to run up the North River and to land another Body of Men at or near Kingsbridge that they intended to make a Junction of their Forces, and did not doubt by these Means to cut off all Communication with our Army both by Land, and Water, and oblige them to Surrender for Want of Provisions. . . . They [do] not intend to make an Attack upon the City" (DLC:GW).
  2. William Lounsbury was killed on 28 Aug. near Mamaroneck, N.Y., by a

detachment of Westchester County militia commanded by Capt. John Flood, whom the New York convention the next day rewarded with $20 for his action against such "a notorious enemy to the cause of America." One of Lounsbury's recruits was wounded, and four were captured (*N.Y. Prov. Congress Journals,* 1:599–600). The documents in Lounsbury's pocketbook have not been identified.

To Major General William Heath

New York, 30 August 1776. "As Numbers of the Militia are going off without Licence, I desire you will stop all such at Kings bridge, as are not furnished with regular Discharges."[1]

LS, in Tench Tilghman's writing, MHi: Heath Papers.
1. Heath wrote the captain of the main guard at King's Bridge later on this date, instructing him "to Stop all Soldiers Coming from the City Except Such as have Proper Discharges, you are to Post Two Sentries on the Bridge that none may Escape" (MHi: Heath Papers).

From Major General William Heath

Dear General   Kingsbridge Augst 30th 1776
A Sloop from Red Hook (up the North River)[1] has Just Come to Anchor near this Place, having on Board about 4 Tons & half of Gun Powder made at Livingstons Mills which was to be Deliver'd to your Excellency at New York, but the master has Stoped here Untill He Knows your Pleasure where to Land it.[2]
A very Extraordinary Report has Just Spread here, that whether True or false we are as yet uncertain That Long-Island is Evacuated by Our Troops.[3]
The Ships in the East River fall Down yesterday afternoon to Hunts Point, where they now lie at anchor.[4]
I have just Sent the Prisoners Taken on the 27th Instant to Connecticut.[5]
I am in Anxiety Untill I hear from you and am with great respect your Excellencys most Humble Servt
                                                W. Heath

ADfS, MHi: Heath Papers.
1. Heath apparently is referring to Lower Red Hook Landing (now Barrytown) on the east bank of the Hudson River in Dutchess County near the

inland town of Red Hook. The other Red Hook, which the Americans fortified, is on New York Harbor at the western end of Long Island.

2. "The General," Joseph Reed wrote Heath later on this date, "desires you
will detain the Powder you have received till further Order at Kings bridge
except 1 Ton to be sent down—the Remainder to be procured occasionally"
(MHi: Heath Papers).

3. Joseph Reed explains the reasons for evacuating Long Island in his letter
to Heath of this date (MHi: Heath Papers).

4. Hunt's Point, which is bounded by the East and Bronx rivers, was in the
part of Westchester County that is now the Bronx. The British warships *Halifax, Niger,* and *Brune* anchored on 29 Aug. in Flushing Bay, a mile or two south
of Hunt's Point (see the logs of the *Halifax,* 29, 31 Aug., and the *Niger,* 30–31
Aug., in Clark and Morgan, *Naval Documents,* 6:355, 370–71).

5. For the capture of Lt. John Ragg's detachment during the Battle of Long
Island, see Robert Hanson Harrison to Hancock, 27 Aug., and note 3. For the
sending of these prisoners to Fairfield, Conn., on this date, see Heath to Nathan Umstead and Heath to the Fairfield Committee of Inspection, both 29
Aug., and Heath to the Commissary of Provisions, 30 Aug., MHi: Heath Papers. The Fairfield committee of inspection wrote GW on 25 Sept., informing
him that, agreeable to his directions communicated by his secretary, it had sent
Lieutenant Ragg and his servant to Middletown, Conn., and the other twenty-
one prisoners to Wallingford, Conn., "where they are placed in the Parishes
in the interior part of the County agreable to Rules of Congress. . . . As we
could find no Rule of Congress how the charges of marching them were to be
defrayed; We took a Guard of a Sergeant and Six from our Battery, and advanced them a penny a Mile for their support—Whether we have done right
or not we do not know—The Men we were sensible could not be marched
without support—We should therefore take it as a favor if your Excellency
would direct us to whom we are to look for their billiting for 11 Days, and the
advanced Money for marching them to the places of their destination" (LS,
written and signed by Thaddeus Burr, DLC:GW). The expense account for
£14.6.½ enclosed with the committee's letter is also in DLC:GW. No reply to
that letter has been found.

From Lieutenant Colonel
Henry Beekman Livingston

Sagg Harbour [N.Y.]

May it please Your Excellency   30th August 1776

On Thursday Last I received an Express from Captain Davis
Stationed at Montauk Point notifying me, that he had discovered three saild of the Enemy making for the Point, that they
had hoisted out their Boats to the Number of ten or twelve he
susspected with design to land and Carry off Stock: After giveing

the orders I thought necessary to Captains Roe, and Griffin, I set out for the Point,[1] On my Arrival in the Evening at Captain Davis'es Station, I found three Vessels which I took to be Frigates from twenty to thirty Guns, a Brig we immagined a Prize, and a Small Sloop, Close in with the Land; at 7 OClock in the Evening one of the Frigates the Brig and the Sloop made for the Continent south West of New London where they anchered under the Shore, the Other Two Ships Bore away for Block Island. On Saturday Morning the three Vessels under the Eastern Shore, takeing advantage of the Tide of Flood and a fair wind Sailed up the Sound as far as Huntington, about Sixty Miles from hence the tide and wind makeing against them they were obliged to come to an Anchor. how far they have since proceeded is uncertain, but suppose the Communication by water between this and New York is now Cut off, the Ships off Block Island still Continue to Cruise there; we immagine by their movements that they wait the Arrival of a Fleet[2]—I have just received an Account of My Colonels promotion to the Rank of Brigadier General, as next in Rank to him in the Regiment I should [have] Transmitted Your Excellency a General Return of the whole: But my remote distance from the *Major* part of the Regiment together with the uncertainty whether it is Your Excellencies Intention I Should succeed him has prevented me.[3]

The Inclosed is a true state of the Detatchment Your Excellency was pleased to honour me with the command of.[4] My respects wait on Mrs Washington. I remain Sir Your Excellencies most Obedient Humble Servant

Henry B: Livingston

P:S: Any Command your Excellency pleases to honour me with will be forwarded by the Bearer Lieutenant Smith of Captain Roes Company.[5]

My Dear General I have just received an Account by express that the Communication between us and New York is Cut off and that your Excellencies attempts to dislodge the Enemy have hitherto been Successless I have dispatched an Account of this Matter to his Excellency Govenor Trumbull of Conecticut.[6] If it meets with Your Excellencies approbation I should think notwithstanding the Ships in the Sound we shall be able in a few Days to get a Body of men from Conecticut whose Attack on the

Back of Our Enemies from this way may be a means of Distressing them much: they have now poss[ess]ion of Jamaica and Hemstead plains consequently this Country is exposed to their Ravages, the Communication at Hellgate is not Yet Cut off, I wait with impatience for Your Excellencies Commands. Yours Afftely

Henry B: Livingston

The publick spirit of this Country has reduced its Militia to nothing.

ALS, DLC:GW.

The village of Sag Harbor is on the southeastern peninsula of Long Island about thirty-five miles from Montauk Point.

1. The detachment from Col. James Clinton's 2d New York Regiment that Livingston commanded in eastern Long Island during the summer of 1776 consisted of John Davis's, Daniel Roe's, and Daniel Griffing's companies. John Davis (d. 1782) of East Hampton, Long Island, was a first lieutenant in James Clinton's 3d New York Regiment from June 1775 to April 1776, when he raised a company and became a captain in Clinton's new 2d Regiment. In November 1776 Davis was named a captain in Livingston's newly formed 4th New York Regiment. Davis was wounded at the Battle of Stillwater in September 1777, and in April 1780 he was promoted to major of the 4th New York. In December 1780 Gov. George Clinton sent Davis to Long Island to impress clothing and blankets (see Clinton to Davis, 22 Dec. 1780, in Hastings, *Clinton Papers*, 6:510–12). Davis was captured at Sag Harbor by the British in November 1781 and was treated as a spy. He died in captivity at New York a short time later allegedly of starvation or poisoning (see anonymous letter to George Clinton, 16 Dec. 1781, ibid., 7:584–85, and Mather, *Refugees of 1776*, 96, 217, 324).

Daniel Roe (1740–1820) of Brookhaven, Long Island, a veteran of the French and Indian War, served as captain of a company of Suffolk County minutemen from December 1775 to April 1776, when he raised a company for Continental service and was assigned to Clinton's 2d New York Regiment (see *N.Y. Prov. Congress Journals*, 1:232, 421, 424, and Mather, *Refugees of 1776*, 991). On 20 Sept. 1776 Roe led an expedition to Brookhaven to seize Loyalist leaders and remove his and other families to Connecticut, and on 28 Oct. 1776 he again raided the town, capturing two sloops (see Livingston to GW, 24 Sept., and Onderdonk, *Suffolk and Kings Counties*, 54, 62). Although Roe accepted a captaincy in Livingston's 4th New York Regiment in November 1776, he apparently left the army a short time later (see Mather, *Refugees of 1776*, 530, 699, 1016–17).

Daniel Griffing (1736–1822) of Southold, Long Island, another veteran of the French and Indian War, became a captain in Clinton's 3d New York Regiment in June 1775 and continued as a captain in Clinton's 2d Regiment from April to November 1776. Disappointed at not being promoted, Griffing apparently resigned his commission in January 1777 (see Griffing to the New York convention, December 1776 and 4 Jan. 1777, in the *N.Y. Prov. Congress Journals,* 2:329, 392, and Mather, *Refugees of 1776,* 368, 1014–16). Griffing became a privateer captain later in the war.

2. The frigate *Cerberus* and sloop *Merlin* were stationed off Block Island at this time. The three vessels that sailed up Long Island Sound apparently were the frigates *Brune* and *Niger* and the brig *Halifax.*

3. Congress appointed James Clinton a brigadier general on 9 Aug. (see General Orders, 12 Aug.). Livingston did not take command of the main part of the 2d New York Regiment in the Hudson highlands. Retreating with his detachment to Saybrook, Conn., on 2 Sept., he remained with it on the Connecticut coast until November when he became colonel of the 4th New York Regiment.

4. This return has not been identified.

5. George Smith (1749–1822) of Smithtown, Long Island, an attorney who had graduated from the College of New Jersey in 1770, served as a second lieutenant under Capt. Daniel Roe in the 2d New York Regiment from April to November 1776. Smith continued in that rank in the 4th New York Regiment until 5 Oct. 1777, when he was appointed deputy judge advocate general for the northern department, an office that he held until 1 April 1780 (see Smith to Congress, 21 April 1787, DNA:PCC, item 42). In November 1778 Smith and a cousin led a raiding party that seized a prominent Loyalist at Brookhaven, and in the fall of 1780 Smith was allowed to return to Long Island, where he apparently acted as an American spy (see the *Royal Gazette* [New York], 2, 9 Dec. 1778, and Mather, *Refugees of 1776,* 569, 928–29).

6. This news was received by Rev. Samuel Buell of East Hampton, who was with Livingston at Sag Harbor. At Livingston's urging, Buell wrote Governor Trumbull on this date informing him "that the Ministerial Army (Supposed to be about Sixteen thousand) Are on this Side our Army upon the Island, have lined across the Island from the Sound to the South Side, So that we on the East End, can have no access to our Army. . . . The Enemy have 200d Horse Their riders were to Dine the Day before Yesterday at *Hempstead*—They have the Command of the west End of the Island intirely." Buell suggested that Trumbull send "a Number of Troops" to reinforce eastern Long Island as Livingston did also in a letter that he wrote to Trumbull of this date (DLC:GW). Trumbull enclosed copies of these letters in his letter to GW of 31 Aug.–1 September.

From the New York Committee of Safety

In Committee of Saf⟨ety⟩ at Kingsbridge
Sir   the 30th August 1776
    In our way to Fishkill agreable to an adjournment of the Convention, we are informed that the Army is removed from Long Island to the City of New York—an anxiety to know the fact, as

well as to be informed wether you think any measures necessary for us to take—Induces us to trouble your Excellency at this time for an answer hereto—We have ordered last Night all the Militia of the Counties of Ulster, Dutchess, Orange and Westchester to be ready at a Minutes warning, with five days provisions.[1]

We shall wait the return of our Messenger at this place, and are, Sir Your Most Obedient & Verry Hume Servt

Abm Yates Junr President

LS, DLC:GW. The draft of this letter that the committee of safety approved at the beginning of its session on this date contains only minor differences in wording (see *N.Y. Prov. Congress Journals*, 1:602).

1. For this order, see ibid., 601. The convention, which had adjourned on 29 Aug., reconvened in the Episcopal church at Fishkill on 5 Sept. (ibid., 600, 609).

To Abraham Yates, Jr.

Sir   New York Augt 30th 1776

Your favr of this date is just come to hand. Circumstanced as this Army was in respect to Situation Strength &c., it was the unanimous advice of a Council of General Officers to give up Long-Island, and not by divideing our Force be unable to resist the Enemy in any one point of Attack, this reason added to some others, particularly the fear of haveing our Communication cut of from the Main (of which there seemed to be no Small probability) and the extreame fatigue our Troops were laid under in guarding such extensive Lines, without proper Shelter from the weather, induced the above Resolution.[1]

It is the most intricate thing in the World Sir to know in what manner to conduct ones self with Respect to the Militia, if you do not begin many days before they are wanted to raise them, you cannot have them in time, if you do they get tired and return, besides being under very little Order or Government whilst in Service—However if the Enemy have a design of serveing of Us at this place as we apprehended they meant to do on Long-Island—it might not be improper to have a body in readiness to prevent or retard a Landing of them on the East of Harlem River, if need be—In haste & not a little fatigued, I remain with great Respect & Esteem Sir Yr Most Obedt Hume sert

G.W.

LB, in Samuel Blachley Webb's writing, DLC:GW; Varick transcript, DLC:GW. The New York committee of safety read this letter at the beginning of its session on 31 Aug., and it is printed in the *N.Y. Prov. Congress Journals*, 1:603. That text, which presumably was taken from the unfound receiver's copy, is nearly identical in wording to the LB.

1. See the proceedings of the council of war for 29 August.

General Orders

Head Quarters, New York, August 31st 1776.
Parole Harlem.   Countersign Flushing.

Major Livingston, charged with having ordered a negroe to fire on a Soldier of Capt: Newcomb's Regiment is ordered to be confined and brought to trial: But the General is sorry to see Soldiers, defending their Country, in time of imminent danger, rioting and attempting to do themselves justice.[1]

The Plunderers of Lord Stirling's house, are ordered to restore to the Quarter Master General, what they have taken, in failure whereof they will certainly be hanged.[2]

It is the Generals orders that the remainder of Lutz's and Kachlein's Battalions be joined to Hands Battalion; that Major Huys be also under the special command of Col. Hand;[3] that then those Battalions, with Shee's, Col. Magaw's, Col. Huchinson's, Col. Atlee's, Col. Miles, Col. Wards Regiments be brigaded under General Mifflin, and those now here march, as soon as possible, to Kingsbridge.[4] The Quarter-Master will supply waggons if to be spared, if not, to apply to Lieut: Achbolt on the North River, Boat Station; or Ensign Allen on the East; who will supply boats.[5] A careful officer with a small guard to attend them. Major Lord will supply, from General Walcot's Brigade, an officer and six men to each boat, to bring boats back, except those that are ordered to stay.

Both officers and soldiers are informed that the Retreat from Long Island was made by the unanimous advice of all the General Officers, not from any doubts of the spirit of the troops, but because they found the troops very much fatigued with hard duty and divided into many detachments, while the enemy had their Main Body on the Island, and capable of receiving assistance from the shipping: In these circumstances it was thought unsafe to transport the whole of an Army on an Island, or to engage them with a part, and therefore unequal numbers; whereas now one whole Army is collected together, without Water intervening, while the enemy can receive little assistance from their ships; their Army is, and must be divided into many bodies, and fatigued with keeping up a communication with their Ships; whereas ours is connected, and can act together: They must affect a landing under so many disadvantages, that if officers and soldiers are vigilant, and alert, to prevent surprise, and add spirit when they approach, there is no doubt of our success.

Ebenezer Gray is appointed Brigade Major to General Parsons.[6]

The following disposition is made of the several Regiments, so as to form Brigades, under the commanding officers respectively mentioned.

Genl: [Samuel Holden] Parsons: [Jedediah] Huntington, [William] Prescot[t], [Jonathan] Ward, [John] Durkee, [John] Tyler.[7]

Gen: [Alexander] McDougall: McDougall, [Rudolphus] Ritzema, [William] Smallwood, [Charles] Webb, Artificers.[8]

Gen: [John Morin] Scott: [John] Lasher, [William] Malcom, [Samuel] Drake, [Cornelius] Humphrey.

Gen: [James] Wadsworth: [Samuel] Chapman,[9] [Comfort] Sage, [Samuel] Selden,[10] [Fisher] Gay, [Philip Burr] Bradl[e]y.

Comdt [Gold Selleck] Silliman: Silliman, [Jabez] Thompson, [Ichabod] Lewis, [John] Mead, [Benjamin] Hinman.

Gen: [John] Nixon: [James Mitchell] Varnum, [Moses] Little, [Daniel] Hitchcock, Nixon, [John] Bailey.

Gen: [James] Clinton: [John] Glover, [Joseph] Read, [Loammi] Baldwin, [Ebenezer] Learned.[11]

Gen: [Nathaniel] Heard: [Philip Van] Cortlandt, [Philip] Johnson, [Silas] Newcomb, Freeman [David Forman], [Ephraim] Martin.

Gen: [John] Fellows: [Jonathan] Holman, [Simeon] Cary, [Jonathan] Smith.[12]

Comdt [William] Douglass: Douglass, [Jonathan] Pettiborne

[Pettibone], [John] Cook, [Matthew or Elizur] Talcott, [Samuel] Chapman.[13]

Comdt [John] Chester: Chester, [George] Pitkin,[14] [Jonathan] Baldwin, [Simeon] Strong, [Roger] Newburry [Newberry].

Comdt [Paul Dudley] Serjeant [Sargent]: Serjeant, [Epaphrus] Sheldon,[15] [Matthew or Elizur] Talcot.

They are to chuse out capable, active and spirited persons, to act as Brigade Majors, who will be allowed for their service.

The General hopes the several officers, both superior and inferior, will now exert themselves, and gloriously determine to conquer, or die—From the justice of our cause—the situation of the harbour, and the bravery of her sons, America can only expect success—Now is the time for every man to exert himself, and make our Country glorious, or it will become contemptable.

Commanding Officers of regiments, are to take care to have hard Bread and Pork for two days kept by them constantly— The neglect of former orders, in this respect, has occasioned some of the hardships the troops have lately sustained—If there is any delay at the Commissary's, good officers will compose and quiet their men, and mention it by way of letter to the General.

Varick transcript, DLC:GW; Df, DNA: RG 93, Orderly Books, vol. 15. Volume 15 contains drafts of the general orders for 31 Aug. to 4 Oct. 1776, parts of which are in Adj. Gen. Joseph Reed's writing. The first two paragraphs of the draft for this date are in his writing as are the dateline and the words "Parole" and "Countersign." Reed's writing in the other drafts is indicated in the source notes to the appropriate general orders.

GW's reorganization of his army on this date shows the diversity of the forces under his immediate command. They included 25 Continental regiments, 5 state regiments, 23 regiments of militia levies, and 14 Connecticut militia regiments in addition to artificers and artillery. The Continental regiments were distributed among the brigades commanded by Mifflin, Parsons, McDougall, Nixon, James Clinton, and Sargent. Miles's and Atlee's Pennsylvania state troops and Andrew Ward's Connecticut state regiment were assigned to Mifflin's brigade. Smallwood's Maryland state regiment was in McDougall's brigade, and Bradley's Connecticut state regiment was in Wadsworth's brigade. Scott's brigade consisted of four regiments of New York militia levies. Five more regiments of New York levies made up George Clinton's brigade, which is not mentioned in these general orders. Heard's brigade was composed of five regiments of New Jersey levies, and Fellows's brigade contained three regiments of levies from Massachusetts. Three of the six regiments of Connecticut levies were in Wadsworth's brigade. The commanders of the other three regiments of Connecticut levies—Silliman, Douglas, and

Chester—were given commands of temporary brigades, each of which consisted of the commanding officer's regiment of levies and three or four Connecticut militia regiments. Two other Connecticut militia regiments were joined with Sargent's 16th Continental Regiment to form Sargent's brigade. One Connecticut militia regiment may have been in Wadsworth's brigade (see note 9).

1. William Smith Livingston apparently was not convicted of this charge. Silas Newcomb was colonel of a regiment of New Jersey militia levies.

2. For the court-martial of the accused plunderers, see General Orders, 5, 11 September. Stirling's well-furnished mansion, which he had inherited from his parents, stood at the corner of Broad and Beaver streets.

3. These Pennsylvania flying camp regiments were understrength before the Battle of Long Island, and during the battle Kachlein's and Lutz's regiments lost many men, including the two commanding officers who were captured. Lt. Col. Nicholas Lutz (Lotz; 1740–1807) of Reading, Pa., commanded the Berks County regiment of flying camp troops in the absence of its colonel, Henry Haller. A native of the German Palatinate who had come to Pennsylvania as a youth, Lutz in 1775 was named chairman of the Berks County committee of observation and lieutenant colonel of the county's 3d Regiment of associators, and on 2 July 1776 he became lieutenant colonel of the regiment raised for the flying camp. Lutz remained a British prisoner until he was paroled in April 1777. He was exchanged in September 1779 and served from 1780 to the end of the war as commissioner of forage for Berks County.

Major Huys is William Hay (d. 1812) of Londonderry, Pa., who commanded Col. James Cunningham's Lancaster County regiment of flying camp troops until Cunningham arrived in late September. Hay began his Revolutionary War career in May 1775 as first lieutenant of a company of Londonderry associators who styled themselves the "Liberty Company." On 8 July 1776 he was elected captain of one of the Lancaster County companies raised for the flying camp (see Bartrem Galbraith to the Lancaster Committee of Observation, that date, in Force, *American Archives*, 5th ser., 1:121). Hay became major of Cunningham's regiment on 18 Aug. and its lieutenant colonel on 30 August. Although Hay left on furlough on 27 Sept., he returned to the regiment by early November and apparently served to the end of the year. Later in the war Hay became a commissary of forage in the quartermaster department.

4. Haslet's regiment of Delaware Continentals is added to Mifflin's brigade in the general orders for the following day.

5. Edward Archibald, who had been an ensign in Col. John Glover's Massachusetts regiment during 1775, was a first lieutenant in Glover's 14th Continental Regiment during 1776, and John Allen was one of the regiment's ensigns at this time. Archibald subsequently served as a captain lieutenant in Col. John Lamb's 2d Continental Artillery from 1 Jan. 1777 to 25 June 1781.

6. Ebenezer Gray (1743–1795) of Windham, Conn., who had been a second lieutenant in the 3d Connecticut Regiment during 1775, became on 1 Jan. 1776 a first lieutenant and regimental quartermaster in the 20th Continental Regiment. Gray served as Parsons's brigade major apparently until 18

Mar. 1777, when he was appointed major of the 6th Connecticut Regiment (Hinman, *Historical Collection,* 423). Promoted to lieutenant colonel on 15 Oct. 1778, Gray held his commission until June 1783, transferring to the 4th Connecticut Regiment on 1 Jan. 1781 and the 3d Connecticut Regiment on 1 Jan. 1783.

7. Col. Samuel Wyllys's 22d Continental Regiment is included in Parsons's brigade in the general return of Continental army at New York for 14 Sept. (DNA: RG 93, Revolutionary War Rolls, 1775–83).

8. The regiment of artificers was commanded by Col. Jonathan Brewer.

9. Samuel Chapman (1722–1803) of Toland, Conn., a veteran of the French and Indian War, was appointed a militia colonel by the Connecticut general assembly in June 1775, and his 22d Regiment was one of the fourteen militia regiments that the council of safety ordered to New York on 11 Aug. 1776 (see Hinman, *Historical Collection,* 184, 378–79). The listing of Chapman's regiment in both Wadsworth's and Douglas's brigades in these general orders indicates some confusion about its assignment. Although Douglas does not include Chapman's regiment among the ones under his command that he names in a letter to his wife of 7 Sept., the army's general return for 14 Sept. shows it in his brigade and not in Wadsworth's brigade (see note 13 and the general return for the Continental army, 14 Sept., DNA: RG 93, Revolutionary War Rolls, 1775–83). Chapman's assignment is reversed in the general return for 21 Sept., where his regiment appears in Wadsworth's brigade and not in Douglas's brigade (see the general return for the Continental army, 21 Sept., in DNA: RG 93, Revolutionary War Rolls, 1775–83). Chapman's regiment was discharged from Continental service on 25 Sept. (see GW to Trumbull, 26 Sept.).

10. Samuel Selden (1723–1776) of Hadlyme, Conn., colonel of one of the six regiments of Connecticut militia levies, was captured at Kip's Bay on 15 Sept. and died of a fever on 11 Oct. while a prisoner in New York City.

11. James Clinton's brigade, which was stationed in the Hudson highlands, apparently included five companies of the 2d New York Regiment, which Clinton had commanded before his recent promotion to brigadier general (see General Orders, 12 Aug.). The remainder of the 2d New York Regiment was with Lt. Col. Henry Beekman Livingston in eastern Long Island (see Livingston to GW, 30 Aug.).

12. Jonathan Smith (1741–1802) of Lanesborough, Mass., was appointed colonel of the Berkshire County regiment of militia levies on 26 June 1776 and served until their enlistments expired on 1 December. Smith subsequently represented Berkshire in the Massachusetts General Court for several terms, and he was a delegate to the state's constitutional ratifying convention in 1788.

13. William Douglas (Douglass; 1742–1777) of Northford, Conn., colonel of a regiment of Connecticut militia levies previously assigned to Wadsworth's brigade, wrote his wife on 7 Sept.: "I have three Regt. of Militia in my Brigade, and they give me much Fateague and Trouble on act. of the officers not knowing and Doing their Duty. Cols. Cook, Pettebone & Talcutt are the Comdr. the Sick I Discharge others Desert and the Regt. will Soon be reduc,d to but a Sma[ll] number. there is no Subordination among them, which I fere will

Finally ruing the Army. they had much better never come to assist us than Leave us in Such a Scandalous manor. . . . many of them would Sell amarica to git home" (Douglas, "Letters," 13:119–20).

A younger brother of Col. John Douglas, William Douglas served during the French and Indian War as a sergeant in the provincial forces, and after the war he made a fortune as a shipmaster sailing out of New Haven to the West Indies. Commissioned a captain in the 1st Connecticut Regiment in May 1775, Douglas took part in the invasion of Canada that fall, and during the siege of St. Jean he commanded an armed vessel. In November 1775 General Montgomery appointed Douglas commodore of the small American fleet on Lake Champlain, but Schuyler replaced him in May 1776 when it became evident that Douglas would not soon return from an extended furlough (see the *Connecticut Journal* [New Haven], 22 Nov. 1775, and GW to Schuyler, 24 April 1776, n.1). In May 1776 the Connecticut general assembly named Douglas major of Col. Andrew Ward's state regiment, and on 14 June it appointed him colonel of one of the six regiments of militia levies ordered to New York. Douglas's men helped to cover the American retreat to the Brooklyn lines during the Battle of Long Island on 27 Aug., and on 15 Sept. they attempted unsuccessfully to defend positions at Kip's Bay. Douglas's levies served through December, participating in the battles of Harlem Heights and White Plains. On 1 Jan. 1777 Douglas became colonel of the 6th Connecticut Regiment. His health soon deteriorated, and he died at Branford, Conn., on 28 May 1777.

Jonathan Pettibone (1710–1776) of Simsbury, Conn., who had been colonel of the 18th Regiment of Connecticut militia since the spring of 1774, marched his men to New York during late August in company with Chapman's regiment (see Pettibone and Chapman to Jonathan Trumbull, Sr., 20 Aug. 1776, in Force, *American Archives*, 5th ser., 1:1085). Pettibone died on 26 Sept., the day after GW discharged his regiment (see GW to Trumbull, 26 Sept.). The Connecticut militia at New York at this time included the 6th Regiment commanded by Col. Elizur Talcott (1709–1797) of Glastonbury and the 23d Regiment commanded by Col. Matthew Talcott of Middletown. It is not known which of these regiments was assigned to Douglas's brigade and which to Sargent's brigade. For a discussion of the confusion about the assignment of Chapman's Connecticut militia regiment, see note 9.

14. George Pitkin (1729–1806) of East Hartford, Conn., who had served with the Continental army during 1775 as lieutenant colonel of the 4th Connecticut Regiment, was at this time lieutenant colonel of the 19th Regiment of Connecticut militia. Pitkin apparently marched his regiment to New York in late August and returned home a short time later because his health would not permit him to endure camp duty (see Pitkin to Jonathan Trumbull, Sr., 15 Aug., in Force, *American Archives*, 5th ser., 1:970). Maj. Nathaniel Terry commanded the regiment in Pitkin's absence. Continuing ill health obliged Pitkin to resign his militia commission in December (see Pitkin to Trumbull, 16 Dec. 1776, ibid., 3:1250).

15. Epaphrus Sheldon (1753–1850) of Torrington, Conn., who was appointed major of the 17th Regiment of Connecticut militia in May 1774, com-

manded that regiment at New York during August and September 1776 in the absence of Col. Oliver Wolcott and Lt. Col. Ebenezer Norton (see Hinman, *Historical Collection,* 160, and the general returns for the Continental army, 14, 21 Sept., in DNA: RG 93, Revolutionary War Rolls, 1775–83). Sheldon became a lieutenant colonel by March 1777, and by January 1778 he was colonel of the 17th Regiment of militia (see Hinman, *Historical Collection,* 303, 427).

To John Hancock

Sir   New York Augt 31st 1776

Inclination as well as duty would have Induced me to give Congress the earliest Information of my removal and that of the Troops from Long Island & Its dependencies to this City the night before last, But the extreme fatigue whic⟨h⟩ myself and Family have undergone as much from the Weather since the Engagement on the 27th[1] rendered me & them entirely unfit to take pen in hand—Since Monday[2] scarce any of us have been out of the Lines till our passage across the East River was effected Yesterday morning & for Forty Eight Hours preceding that I had hardly been of[f] my Horse and never closed my Eyes so that I was quite unfit to write or dictate till this Morning.

Our Retreat was made without any Loss of Men or Ammunition and in better order than I expected from Troops in the situation ours were—We brought off all our Cannon & Stores, except a few heavy peices, which in the condition the earth was by a long continued rain, we found upon Trial impracticable— The Wheels of the Carriages sinking up to the Hobs, rendered it impossible for our whole force to drag them—We left but little provisions on the Island except some Cattle which had been driven within our Lines and which after many attempts to force across the Water we found Impossible to effect, circumstanced as we were—I have Inclosed a Copy of the Council of War held previous to the Retreat, to which I beg leave to refer Congress for the Reasons or many of them, that led to the adoption of that measure.[3] Yesterday Evening and Last night a party of our Men were employed in bringing Our Stores, Cannon, Tents &ca from Governors Island, which they nearly compleated— Some of the Heavy Cannon remain there still, but I expect will be got away to day.

In the Engagement on the 27th Generals Sullivan & Stirling

were made prisoners; The former has been permitted on his parole to return for a little time—From My Lord Stirling I had a Letter by Genl Sullivan a Copy of which I have the Honor to transmit—That contains his Information of the Engagement with his Brigade—It is not so full and certain as I could wish; he was hurried most probably as his Letter was unfinished[4]— Nor have I been yet able to obtain an exact account of Our Loss, we suppose It from 700 to a Thousand, killed & taken—Genl Sullivan says Lord Howe is extremely desirous of seeing some of the Members of Congress for which purpose he was allowed to come out & to communicate to them what was passed between him & his Lordship—I have consented to his going to Philadelphia, as I do not mean or conceive It right to withold or prevent him from giving such information as he possesses in this Instance.[5]

I am much hurried & Engaged in Arranging and making new Dispositions of our Forces, The Movements of the Enemy requiring them to be immediately had, and therefore have only time to add that I am with my best regards to Congress Their & Your Most Obedt He Servt

Go: Washington

LS, in Robert Hanson Harrison's writing, DNA:PCC, item 152; LB, DLC:GW; copy, DNA:PCC, item 169; Varick transcript, DLC:GW. Congress read this letter on 2 Sept. and referred it to the Board of War (*JCC,* 5:723).

1. The LB reads: "(as much from the weather as any thing else) since the incampment of the 27th."

2. The previous Monday was 26 August.

3. See the proceedings of the council of war for 29 August.

4. See Stirling to GW, 29 August.

5. Sullivan, who arrived in Philadelphia on 2 Sept., told Delegate Josiah Bartlett "that Lord Howe expressed himself very desirous of an accommodation with America, without any more bloodshed; [and] that he was very willing to meet, at almost any place, a number of the members of Congress (as private gentlemen, for he could not own any such body as Congress) to try if they could make any proposals for an accommodation." That message was unwelcome because it put the delegates in a serious dilemma. "If the Congress," Bartlett wrote William Whipple on 3 Sept., "should accept of the proposed conference, only on a verbal message, when at the same time Lord Howe declares he can consider them only as private gentlemen, especially when we are certain he can have no power to grant any terms we can possibly accept; this I fear will lessen the Congress in the eye of the public, and perhaps at this time intimidate people when they see us catching hold of so slender a thread to

bring about a settlement. On the other hand, General Sullivan's arrival from Lord Howe with proposals of an accommodation, with 30 falsehoods in addition, are now spread over this City, and will soon be over the Continent, and if we should refuse the conference, I fear the Tories, and moderate men, so called, will try to represent the Congress as obstinate, and so desirous of war and bloodshed that we would not so much as hear the proposals Lord Howe had to make, which they will represent (as they already do) to be highly advantageous for America, even that he would consent that we should be independent provided we would grant some advantages as to trade. Such an idea spread among the people, especially the soldiers at this time might be of the most fatal consequence" (Smith, *Letters of Delegates*, 5:94–95). Congress on 6 Sept. appointed a committee to confer with Lord Howe (see *JCC*, 5:738; see also Hancock to GW, 8 Sept., and note 2). For its subsequent negotiations, see Franklin to GW, 8 Sept. and Edward Rutledge to GW, 11 September.

From Major General William Heath

Dear General   Kingsbridge, Augst 31th 1776
   Ever Since my arrival at New york I have considered this Post to be the Key of the Island, and Consequently of great Importance[.] Its Importance at this Time is apparently Enhanced, And much more is necessary to be Done than we Can Possibly Do with our few Scattered Troops, General Clintons five Regiments Consist of near 1400 Rank and file fit for Duty Two Hundred of that number are on Command with General Mifflen 300 are at mount Washington and Colo. Grahams Regiment Remains near Hunts Point, to Prevent the Enemys Landing near That Place (And Indeed I think there is a greater Probability that a Body of the Enemy may be Thrown Over from Flushing to Hunts Point than at any other Place, and the Disaffected on Long Island Can in a few Hours Collect a Sufficient number of Boats with those belonging to the Ships to Set over a Considerable Body of Troops in a short Time). After Deducting these Several Detachments the Remainder is short of 800 & these in Scattered Quarters at present—which Puts it out of Our Power to Throw up So many works as I could Wish to See, But our greatest want is that of artificers and Tools, for the Building of Several Stores for Provisions[,] Magazines, Sheds for the Troops, Bake House &c. which are much wanted and if the artificers are not now wanted at the City some of them might be well Employd here, We are also in Great want of an Artillery officer or Two,

Colo. Knox has lately Sent to this Post Lieut. Preston upon whose arrival I ordered fifty active young men to be Draughted for the artillery Service[.] the Lieut. has been Sick ever Since, The Detachment Can do nothing being destitue of an Instructor and wholly unacquainted with Cannon[.] Capt. Horton at mount Washington having Sent a Detachment with General Mifflen has it not in his Power to Aid us.[1]

If the Quarter Master General has any Planks at the City, proper for Platforms they are much wanted here as it Does not appear that Mr Cranch Can Obtain any this way Short of Albany—which Cannot be got here under Several days and are Immediately wanted.[2]

I think the Evacuating of Long Island was a wise and Prudent Manoeuvre, and that it is now much more in Our Power to Defeat the Enemy than before, I regret nothing Save their acquisition of So much fresh Provisions, and our Loss of So much Labour, your Excellency will permit me again to repeat, that I think there is great Probability that the Enemy will Throw over a Body of Troops from Flushing or Some where near that Place as it Can be Done with the greatest Ease—But shou'd your Excellency think otherwise I will immediately upon Signification thereof order Col. Graham's Regiment up here. I have the Honor to be with the greatest respect your Excellency's most Humble Servt.

ADf, MHi: Heath Papers.

1. David Preston of Massachusetts was a second lieutenant in Knox's artillery regiment from December 1775 to November 1776. Jotham Horton (d. 1795) served as a first lieutenant in Col. Richard Gridley's Massachusetts artillery regiment from May to December 1775 and became a captain-lieutenant in Knox's regiment on 1 Jan. 1776. Horton was taken prisoner when Fort Washington fell to the British on 16 Nov. (see Horton to Knox, 3 Jan. 1777, NNGL: Knox Papers). He subsequently served as a captain in the 3d Continental Artillery Regiment until September 1778, when he resigned his commission.

2. GW's aide-de-camp Richard Cary wrote Heath the next day that GW had "desired Colo. Moylan to place an Assistant Qr Mastr up at Kingsbridge to supply such Articles as are necessary which would thereby save much trouble to all parties, & particularly to the General, as a considerable part of his time is taken up in reading Letters from different Quarters upon such subjects, which at this time is far from being agreeable to him. Should such an Assistant Qr Mr be placed at Kingsbridge it is presumed care will be taken that no applications be made to him for any articles but only such as cannot be dispensed with" (MHi: Heath Papers).

Nathaniel Cranch (c.1780) of Boston, a nephew of John Adams's brother-in-law Richard Cranch, was a clerk in the quartermaster general's department from 1775 to the spring of 1780, when he returned to Boston and died in a fall during a storm (see Richard Cranch to John Adams, 22 July 1776 and 26 April 1780, in Butterfield, *Adams Family Correspondence*, 2:57–58, 3:325–29, and note 5).

From Major General William Heath

Dear General   Kingsbridge, Augst: 31st 1776

What Fatality Attends the Sinking of the[1] Chevaux De Frise I cannot tell, I was Extremely Uneasy yesterday at the Delay, I went to the Place, Called Capt. Cooke on Shore, told him every moment was precious, and that if any Benifit was ever to be reaped from them it would Probably be Soon, He told me that they met with many & Great Dificulties, that the night before last one of the Vessells which was fitted for Sinking, Drove with her Anchors nearly Down to the Glass House, I have Just this moment Received the Inclosed from Colo. Hutchinson, How the Rapidity of the Current Should be but Just now discovered I cannot tell[.][2] I wish Colo. Putnam if he Can be Spared may Still Superinte[n]d this Business, or Such other Order be Taken as your Excellency shall think Proper—Judge Morris this moment Informs me that Troops have been Seen at New Town.[3] I have the Honor to be with great respect your Excellency most Humble Servt

W. Heath

ADfS, MHi: Heath Papers.

1. Heath neglected to strike the word "our" at this place on the manuscript when he changed the wording.

2. Col. Israel Hutchinson wrote Heath on this date from Mount Washington "that Capt. Cooke sunk a Cheveaux D Fries which is now floating down the River He has been with me this Morng and tells me that it is His Opinion that the current is so rapid that all Endeavours of the Kind will not stop the River" (MHi: Heath Papers). Capt. Robert Cook commanded the row galley *Lady Washington*. The glass house, which opened as a bottle manufactory in 1758 and subsequently became a tavern, was about four miles up the Hudson from New York City.

3. Richard Morris (1730–1810) of Mount Fordham in Westchester County, a younger brother of Lewis Morris and a half brother of Gouverneur Morris, was judge of the royal vice-admiralty court for New York, New Jersey, and Connecticut from 1762 to 1775, when he resigned his office over the objec-

tions of Governor Tryon. On 2 Aug. 1776 Morris declined to become judge of the state admiralty court, telling the convention that "he most heartily joined with his countrymen, and was ready to support them with his life and fortune; but that from the situation of his family and property, the remainder of his life was necessary for attention to his own affairs" (*N.Y. Prov. Congress Journals,* 1:554). In 1778, however, Morris accepted a seat in the state senate, and the next year he became chief justice of the state supreme court, on which he served until he retired from public life in 1790.

From Major General William Heath

Aug: 31st 1776

Since Enclosing—Col. Remsen's Regiment are here, they say their Time of Engagement is up this Day many of them are desirous, to go over and if possible save their Families & Effects,[1] Should be glad to know your Excellency's Pleasure in this respect—They say they mean to return, I cannot answer for them—I suppose the like Applications will be made by many of Col. Smith's Men—I beg an immediate Answer to this particular if your Excellency pleases—Numbers of Sick are also moving this Way, should be glad also to know if they who are really so are to pass, & whether passes from Colonels are to be valid, not knowing in this time of hurry to whom your Excellency, has deligated that power in every Condition. Your's as before

W. Heath

Df, MHi: Heath Papers.

1. Col. Jeromus Remsen's militia levies wished to return to their homes in Kings and Queens counties on Long Island. Many of them subsequently evacuated their families to the mainland in order to escape British occupation of the island.

From Major General William Heath

Kingsbridge Augst 31st 1776

Dear General   7 oClock in the Evening

I have this moment received Information that a Large Body of the Enemy appeared Opposite to Hunts Point Just before Sun Sit and Pitched their Tents on an Hill to the number of 100 or more[.] it is also Said that numbers of men have been Put on Board the Ships, this Day, I have Ordered the Regiments to lie on their Arms &c. I have the Honor to be &c. with great respect your Excellencys most Humb. Servt

W. Heath

ADfS, MHi: Heath Papers.

To Major General William Heath

Dr Sir Head Quarters New York Augt 31st 1776.

I have reciev'd your letter of this day,[1] and concur with you in sentiment as to the probability of the Enemy's endeavoring to land their forces at Hunts point, or some place not far distant from it; in order to prevent such an attempt from being carried into execution, I have sent up General Mifflin with the troops he brought from your quarters strengthened by a reinforcement; with this assistance, I hope you will be able to defeat their intentions; I beg you will exert yourself to the utmost of your abilities on this momentous occasion; In particular I must request of you, that the cheveux de frise be immediately sunk; was it in my power to send you Col. Putnam, I would willingly comply with your request but we have so much business for him here, that he cannot by any means be spared; Colo. Knox has directed Capt. Bryan to go up immediately; he recommends him as a good officer & equal to any that he has in the artillery;[2] As to passes signed by Colos. of Regiments they are not to be permitted; none but those under the hand of a Brigadier general or one of superior rank, are to have any reguard paid to them unless you hear something farther from me on that subject. I am Sir Yr Most Obedt Servt

Go: Washington

LS, in William Grayson's writing, MHi: Heath Papers.

1. This letter responds to matters contained in Heath's first and second letters to GW of this date.

2. GW apparently is referring to David Briant (Bryant; d. 1777) of Massachusetts, who had been a captain lieutenant in Knox's artillery regiment since the previous December. Continuing in the 3d Continental Artillery after 1 Jan. 1777, Briant was promoted to captain on 10 May and died on 12 Sept. 1777 of wounds he received the previous day during the Battle of Brandywine.

From Lieutenant Colonel
Henry Beekman Livingston

South Hold [N.Y.]

May it please Your Excellency   31st August 1776

I have since I wrote to You Yesterday received by Express an Account which may be depended upon that General Woodhull was taken a Prisoner by our Enemies on wednesday Last. Their Troop of Horse is considerd by the Inhabitants to the westward of Huntington as an insurmountable Obstacle to their ever Obtaining their freedom independant of Great Brittain, many have been prevaild with by the Disaffected to us to solicit Pardons from Lord Howe, and they are circulateing at a Great rate. Our Communication is cut Off from New York by Land and there are 3 Ships a Brig and a Sloop that endeavour to intercept it by water, So many reports daily Circulate here with respect to the Strength & advantageous Situation of our Enemies that it is very dificult to give Your Excellency a distinct account[.] they are now possesed of Hemstead-Plains their Horse are Continually employd in disarming the Inhabitants but do them no other Injury General Woodhull was taken a Prisoner by them and Treated Cruelly by them After he was taken he received a wound in his Head and much uncivil Language and Finally Committed Close Prisoner to Jamaica Goal[1]—Our Enemies are plentifully supplied with fresh Provisions which togather with the precarious Situation I am in has induced me to March My Detachment to the westward in Order to Harrass their forageing Parties I have endeavourd to prevail upon the Comittees of the Different Towns to raise their Malitia and have Also sent an Express to Governor Trumbull requesting his Aid: for if some encouragement is not Given to the Country People they will be intirely passive. I am Your Excellencies Most Obt Servt

Henry B: Livingston

I expect to be at Huntington in about three Days. we begin Our March tomorrow Morning I hope for Your Excellences Approbation.

ALS, DLC:GW. The addressed cover includes the notation "Per Lt. [George] Smith Express."

1. Nathaniel Woodhull was captured near Jamaica, N.Y., on 28 Aug. by the

17th Light Dragoons, whom General Howe on that date had detached with the 71st Highlanders to pacify eastern Long Island. The *Connecticut Journal* (New Haven) for 4 Sept. says that Woodhull "for refusing to give up his side Arms, was wounded on the Head with a Cut[l]ass, and had a Bayonet thrust thro' his Arm." On 9 Sept. William Warne informed the New York committee of safety "that one of the lighthorsemen told he had taken Genl. Woodhull in the dark in a barn; that before he would answer when he spoke to the General, he had cut him on the head and both arms" (*N.Y. Prov. Congress Journals,* 1:617; for another account of this incident, see Onderdonk, *Suffolk and Kings Counties,* 36–41). Woodhull was moved about this time to a British transport in New York Harbor, and on 6 Sept. he was sent ashore to a hospital at New Utrecht, where he died on 20 Sept. (Sabine, *Fitch's New-York Diary,* 40, 143).

From the New York Committee of Safety

Philipse's Manor Augt 31st 1776
Sir   In Committee of Safety for the State of New York

We had the Honor of your Excellency's Letter of Yesterday,[1] And see the Weight of the Reasons which induced You to quit the Lines on Long Island. We acknowledge the difficulty of managing the Militia so as to render them Usefull, which is in some Measure owing to their being ill appointed and unused to Camps and of Consequence suffering more than those who have got into a regular way of providing against Inconveniences.

We are so fully satisfied of the Enemies Design to land above New York and of the Mischiefs that will result therefrom, that we cannot by any Means advise Your Excellency to trust for its prevention to any Militia, which we can at this time call out— who after the great Drafts we have already made cannot be expeditiously collected[,] will be ill Armed[2] and we fear some of them not so well affected as we would wish—We know no Country so capable of being defended as that above the Bridge; should the Enemy once occupy it we have Reason to dread the Consequences. We take the Liberty to hint these Things to Your Excellency, tho' we are pursuaded they have not escaped Your Observation in Order to convince our Constituents and the rest of the Continent engaged in the same Cause that we are willing to make any Sacrifices which the general Interest demands.

We enclose a Resolution for the removal of the Cattle from the Island of New York which Your Excellency will cause to be executed if You think it necessary as we have no force that we can trust with it's execution[3]—We cannot but hope that the Commissary will give every relief to the Inhabitants by purchasing from them all the Stock that are fit for the use of the Army.

We have directed Colo. Smith to go to long Island in Order to destroy the Cattle which will otherwise serve as a Supply to the Enemy. If by calling in the out Posts the force of our Army is so much concentred,[4] that any part of them could safely be spared. We are fully persuaded that three thousand Rangers would be very usefully employed on long Island and not only harrass the Enemy but prevent their foraging Parties from ever getting beyond the Plains which extend quite across the Island and by that means save at least two thirds of it from the Enemy.

Your Excellency knows how to pardon on the Score of our Anxiety for the general Welfare—our stepping somewhat out of the regular Line and suggesting such Ideas as our knowledge of the Country induces us to believe useful. We have the Honor to be Your Excellency's most Obedient and very humble servants

By Order.

Abm Yates Junr President

LS, DLC:GW. The draft of this letter that the committee of safety approved earlier on this date is nearly identical in wording to the LS (see *N.Y. Prov. Congress Journals*, 1:603).

1. See GW to Abraham Yates, Jr., 30 August.

2. The draft reads: "can not be expeditiously collected well—ill armed" (*N.Y. Prov. Congress Journals*, 1:603).

3. The committee of safety resolved on this date "that the Inhabitants of New York Island and those parts of Westchester County which are most exposed to the Depredations of the Enemy do forthwith drive their Horned Cattle, Horses—Hogs and Sheep into the Interior part of this State; And that General Washington be requested to make this Order Public and give all possible Assistance in carrying it into Execution when he shall think necessary" (DLC:GW; see also *N.Y. Prov. Congress Journals*, 1:603).

4. The draft reads "concentrated."

From Major General Philip Schuyler

Dr Sir   Albany August 31st 1776

I am this Moment favored with a Letter from General Gates, Copy of which I do myself the Honor to inclose you, together with a Copy of a Return and sundry original Letters from Officers of our Army prisoners in Canada.[1]

The Musket Cartridge paper mentioned in your Excellency's last is not yet arrived[2]—Every Thing that can be procured here or any where in the Country is instantly sent.

I am so accustomed to ill Usage that I am not surprised that General Gates should be informed that I had ordered the Regiments he mentions to be stopped on their March—This Report is only a perversion of an Order of mine of the seventeenth Instant sent to General Waterbury, Copy of which now inclose[3]—The Information on which it was founded is corroborated by a Letter of the 22d August, with which Governor Trumbull has honored me, and which was delivered me after I had began this Letter, in which he says "Innoculation for the small pox I find has been practised by Troops on the March to join your Army—I hope a practice so pernicious in every Respect will be discouraged—I have taken the Liberty to suggest my Fears and Sentiments to General Gates on this Subject—Indeed Sir if it is not timely restrained it appears to me it must prove fatal to all our operations and may ruin the Country."[4]

I never neglect laying all Letters & papers which I receive from General Gates or from any other Quarter, that ought to be transmitted, before your Excellency or Congress.

The two persons mentioned in General Gates's Letter to have come from Dartmouth College, have not yet informed me of their Business.[5]

As I could not procure any regular Returns of what provision was with the Army and on the Communication, and as it was necessary that I should be informed of it, on the 20th Instant I wrote to General Gates on the Subject, Extract of my Letter your Excellency will see in the inclosed to Mr Trumbull, as well as what Answer has been given to it by Mr Avery, and my Resolutions thereon which I trust will meet with your Approbation—Your Excellency will please after perusal, to order the Letter to be sealed and delivered.[6]

In my last, I informed your Excellency that the Stockbridge Indians had determined to go to New York.[7] Many of them have changed their Resolutions and arrived here Yesterday on their Way to Tyonderoga. I am Dear Sir Most respectfully Your Excellency's Most Obedient Hum. Servant

Ph: Schuyler

LS, DLC:GW; LB, NN: Schuyler Papers.

1. Copies of Gates's letter to Schuyler of 26–27 Aug. and his return of 24 Aug. also were enclosed in Gates's letter to GW of 28 Aug. (see note 1 to that document). The letters from the imprisoned officers, Gates writes Schuyler, "are all, (General Thompsons excepted) wrote in so extraordinary a Stile and Manner, that I think the Authors must be either Suborned by the Enemy, or the Letters themselves a Forgery; for I can no other way, Account for Officers writing such Letters. They ought to be sent without Delay to Congress" (DLC:GW). GW forwarded these letters with his letter to Hancock of 4 September. William Thompson's unaddressed letter of 5 Aug., which probably was written to Maj. Peter Scull, is in DNA:PCC, item 159, and Capt. Ebenezer Sullivan's letter to John Sullivan, Capt. Thomas Theodore Bliss's letter to Rev. William Emerson, and Capt. Ebenezer Green's letter to Col. Israel Morey, all dated 14 Aug., are in DNA:PCC, item 78. The three captains, who were taken at the Cedars in May, condemn Congress for not procuring their release by ratifying Arnold's cartel with Capt. George Forster, and they exonerate Forster of charges that he mistreated American prisoners.

2. See GW to Schuyler, 24 Aug., and note 4.

3. "I am just now told," Gates writes in his letter to Schuyler of 26–27 Aug., "that the two Continental Regiments [from Boston] are stop'd by your order on their March from Number four [Charlestown, N.H.] hither; as I am assured by the Authority of the Massachusetts Government that they were perfectly cleansed at Boston, from all Infection after Inocculation, I have ordered them to March here [Ticonderoga] without Delay" (DLC:GW). Schuyler's orders of 17 Aug. direct Gen. David Waterbury "to dispatch three or four trusty Officers to the different roads which the Militia take in their way to Skeensborough, with positive Orders to remove all Officers and Soldiers infected with the Small Pox to a distance from the roads, no excuse is to be taken, no plea of danger to the infected is to be attended to, the Life of individuals is not to be put into Competition with that of the States. . . . They are also strictly to forbid any Officer or Soldier, or any other person whatsoever that has lately had the Small Pox from Joining the army unless such person can produce a certificate from some surgeon or Physician, countersigned by the Committee or magistracy of the town in which such surgeon or Physician resides, and sworn to by the Party himself, that there is no danger of communicating the Infection" (DLC:GW).

4. For the full text of Trumbull's letter, see Force, *American Archives*, 5th ser., 1:1115–16.

5. These two unidentified men, who brought Gates's letter of 26–27 Aug. to Albany, subsequently gave Schuyler a copy of Dartmouth president Eleazar Wheelock's memorial to Congress, requesting financial support for the Indian boys enrolled at the college. Schuyler wrote Hancock on 2 Sept., recommending that Congress make "some Allowance for those Boys" (DNA:PCC, item 153), and on 19 Sept. the delegates appropriated $500 for that purpose (*JCC*, 5:787).

6. In his letter of 20 Aug. to Gates, Schuyler writes: "It is impossible for me to judge of what provisions, &c., may be wanted with the Army and at the different posts, without returns from the Commissaries, &c. These must come

to me through the proper channel. Mr. [Walter] *Livingston* is the Deputy Commissary-General in this department; and in the absence of Mr. *Trumbull*, the Commissary-General, he is to furnish me with a general return, made out of the returns of the Commissaries at the different posts. This he cannot do, unless the Commissaries at those posts send him the returns. Be pleased to order Mr. *Avery* immediately and weekly to make returns to Mr. *Livingston*, that I may know how the Army is supplied with provisions. If he should refuse this, you will be pleased immediately to advise me thereof, that I may take proper steps to enforce a compliance with my orders" (Force, *American Archives*, 5th ser., 1:1083–84). Commissary Elisha Avery, a Gates protégé who refused to acknowledge Walter Livingston's authority, sent Schuyler two returns, copies of which were enclosed in this letter: a return of provisions on hand at Ticonderoga on 23 Aug. and a return of the number of men who drew provisions there on 24 Aug., supplemented by estimates of the rations drawn by the men at Crown Point and Skenesboro and aboard the vessels on Lake Champlain (DLC:GW). The letter that Schuyler enclosed for Trumbull has not been identified.

7. See Schuyler to GW, 29 August.

From Brigadier General John Morin Scott

Sir   New York Augt 31st 1776

As I heard there was a Council of War this Morning[1] and I was not summoned to attend it, I chose to confine myself to my Duty as Brigadier of the day; in which by the Tardiness of the Guards; I spent three hours on the parade. Will You give Me Leave, Sir, as a Regard to the Interest of my Country compels Me to it, to give You my Sentiments at this important hour. I beleive that in Spite of the precautions that have been taken to shallow the Entrance into the East River, the Enemies Ships may force their Way into it. Should that not be the Case they have the Command of the City from Long Island. Their Ships perfectly command the North River. I have reason to believe that their Troops are filing off to the Eastward; and I make no doubt that under Cover of their Ships of War, now in the Sound; they will throw a large Body of Troops into West Chester County; and possess themselves of the Heights opposite to Kings bridge woods. By this Manœuvre, we shall be encircled with the same Kind of danger that We had Reason to apprehend on the other side of the Water; the Apprehension of which induced Us to retreat. I know of no Expedient to prevent it, but to put our Gallies & armed Vessels, which I hear are ordered round into the North River, into the Eastern mouth of the passage between this Island and Westchester County.[2] By this Means the Communication between both may be mainta[i]ned Then a strong Garrison in the Kings bridge Works & Woods; and Retreat of the rest of the Army into West Chester County. The City will in that Case be evacuated. I have very little Apprehension that the Enemy will attempt to land in it while We are here; as I think they can drive Us out of it with out that Risk; and we never I am convinced can prevail on the Troops to stand a Bombardment & Canonade—They will be sacrificed to no purpose if they should. Many of them already, as I am informed have deserted. I am also told they are extreamly discontented for the Want of pay & provisions. God knows what will be the Issue. But I think that the Method I propose will prevent the Enemies encircling us; and enable us to keep up a Communication with the eastern States when perhaps the Interruption that will be given us by the Ships of War will soon deprive Us of that Advantage from the Western States; to support which nevertheless with some Detour it might be well to attend to our forts in the Highlands. You will I hope, Sir, pardon the Liberty I have taken. It proceeds from an hearty Zeal in the Cause of my Country, and a real Desire to contribute towards making this Campaign both glorious to yourself and promotive of the Weal of America. I am Sir with the greatest respect Your Excellency's most obedient Servant

Jno: Morin Scott

May I ask of You, Sir, to be careful of this Letter as it contains my Sentiments and my Brigade Major's immediate Attendance at Head Quarters renders it impossible for Me to retain a Copy.[3]

ALS, DLC:GW.
  1. No formal council of war was held at New York on this date.
  2. Scott is referring to Harlem River.
  3. Scott's brigade major was Nicholas Fish.

From Jonathan Trumbull, Sr.

Sir   Lebanon [Conn.] 31st August[–1 September] 1776
Adjutant General Reed's Letter of the 24th Instant came to hand Tuesday Morning the 27th—Yours of the same Date Yesterday.[1]

On receiving the former I advised with my Council; We concluded to send Benja. Huntington Esqr. one of my Council, with Direction to take with him Majr Ely at New London, an Officer there well acquaint[ed] with the People on Long Island, to proceed there and consult and agree with some of the sure friends, of our Cause, with secrecy as far as the Circumstances would admit, for a Number of their Men, assured Friends and well acquainted on the Island, to join with a body from this State, if Possible to accomplish your wishes, to cause a Diversion to the Enemy to Harrass them on their rear, and to prevent their excursions in pursuit of the Provisions the Island affords—I hear they Sailed for the Island Yesterday—His return is expected the beginning of next Week.[2]

If he succeeds according to our hopes[3] no Exertions of this State, I trust, will be wanting at this critical conjuncture to harrass and to keep the Enemy at Bay—to gain Time and every Advantage the case may admit—Shall give the earliest intelligence of our proceedings, that you may Cooperate with our Designs—The race is not to the Swift nor the Battle to the Strong—It is nothing with God to help, whether many, or with those that have no Power—He hath so ordered things in the Administration of the Affairs of the World, as to encourage the Use of Means; and yet so, as to keep Men in Continual Dependence upon him for the efficacy and Success of them—to make Kings and all men to know the reins of the World are not in their hands, but that there is *one* above who sways and governs all things here below.

I am closing, a Post comes in, and brings the Letters, Copies of which are enclosed[4]—Now expect Mr Huntington's speedy return—Have sent for my Council, my own thoughts and such[5] as come to me are to Send forward four or Five of the Companies now Stationed at New London, with Four Field peices I hope six peices, to join those men which may be ready for the Service on Long Island, 4 or 5 Companies to follow from New London as soon as they can be marched Down; and also to order on other Companies to take the Places of such as are removed from thence.

I am inclined to think, we shall fall upon some measure similar to what is mentioned,[6] No Delay can be admitted at this critical Moment. please to give me the earliest intelligence, how we may best serve agreable to your Desires.

Shall send in the Morning this intelligence, to Governor Cooke of Providence, and ask his assistance in the best way he shall think the Circumstances of that State will admit.

1st Sepr. Enclosed is Copy of Another Letter dated Yesterday from Southold—that you may Observe the Contents[7]—I hope to pursue our Measures so as to stop the Enemy getting in to Suffolk County. I am, with Esteem and Regard Your Excellency's Most Obedient Humble Servant

Jonth; Trumbull

ALS, DLC:GW; LB, Ct: Trumbull Papers.

1. For Joseph Reed's letter to Trumbull of 24 Aug., see GW to Trumbull, that date, n.4.

2. Benjamin Huntington (1736–1800), a lawyer from Norwich, became a member of the Connecticut council of safety in May 1775. He also served in the state's house of representatives from 1771 to 1780 and was its clerk in 1776 and 1777 and its speaker in 1778 and 1779. Elected to the Continental Congress in January 1780, Huntington attended as a delegate later that year and in 1782, 1783, and 1788. He was a member of the state senate from 1781 to 1790 and from 1791 to 1792, and he served in the U.S. Congress from March 1789 to March 1791. John Ely of Saybrook at this time was major of Col. Erastus Wolcott's state regiment stationed at New London and Groton.

3. The LB adds: "shall proceed with vigour to put the same in execution."

4. Trumbull enclosed copies of Col. Henry Beekman Livingston's and Rev. Samuel Buell's letters of 30 Aug. requesting him to send reinforcements to Long Island (DLC:GW; see also Livingston to GW, 30 Aug., n.6).

5. The LB reads: "and such of my Council."

6. On 1 Sept. the council ordered Col. Erastus Wolcott to embark for Long Island as soon as possible with his state regiment which was stationed at New London and Groton and to take six field pieces from the forts at those places. The council also directed the commanding officers of eight militia regiments to prepare to go to Long Island (Hinman, *Historical Collection*, 383).

7. This letter from the Suffolk County committee of safety reads: "We are sorry to Acquaint you that we have Rec'd several Expresses from the Middle of this Island Acquainting us of the Regular Troops having Sorrounded Our Lines at the West End and Stop'd our Communication to the Army & Provinshal Congress, their Scouting Party Consists of about *300* Light horse & *400* foot together with a Number of Tory Recruits & to all appearance are about Penetrating into this County, as they have already Marched as far as the Western part of Hemstead Plains where they took Prisoner Brigadier Genl Nathaniel Woodhull Comr in Chief of the Militia of this Island—We must beg the favour of you to Aid & Assist us with Men and Ammunition as our Men are

Chiefly drawn off and are now in the Army so that we are not able to raise more than *750* Men in the whole County that are Capable to bare Arms—if you think proper to Send us Men which we think we realy need, we must beg you would send what Provisions you think they will want, all but fresh which we Can make out to Supply them with—by the best accts we Can learn of the Strength of the Regular Army now Landed on this Island, they Consist of about *15000* or *20000* Men" (DLC:GW).

General Orders

Head Quarters, New York, septembr 1st 1776.
Parole Hartford.   Countersigns Boston.

It being necessary there should be an Arrangement of the troops, in order that they may act with union and firmness— The Army, as brigaded yesterday, is now arranged in three Grand Divisions, under the following officers (Viz.) Major Genl Putnam to command the following brigades. Parsons's[,] Clinton's[,] Scott's[,] Fellow's[,] Silliman's.

The centre Divisions, under Genl Spencer and Genl Green the former to command the whole untill Genl Green's recovery. (viz.) Nixon's[,] McDougall's[,] Heard's[,] Wadsworth's[,] Douglass's[,] and Chester's.[1]

Genl Heath's to consist of Genl Mifflin's Brigades and Genl George Clinton's.

The centre Division to hold themselves in readiness to march immediately to Harlem, to prevent the enemy's landing on this Island.

Samuel Augustus Barker, to act as Major to the Brigade under Col. Douglass; Benjamin Talmadge Brigade Major to Colo. Chester.[2]

Col. Haslett's Regiment to march to join Genl Mifflin, to whose Brigade he is to belong.

Varick transcript, DLC:GW; Df, DNA: RG 93, Orderly Books, vol. 15.

1. Col. Paul Dudley Sargent's name appears at the end of this list in Kinnan, *Order Book*, 93, and "Williams' Diary," 48:335.

2. Samuel Still Augustus Barker (1756–1819) of Branford, Conn., served as adjutant of Col. William Douglas's regiment of Connecticut militia levies from June to December 1776, when he became adjutant and a first lieutenant in Douglas's 6th Connecticut Regiment. Barker was promoted to captain in May 1780, and during 1781 he was named brigade major and subinspector of the

1st Connecticut Brigade. He resigned from the army on 13 April 1782 and later settled in Dutchess County, New York.

Benjamin Tallmadge (1754–1835), who managed GW's secret service between 1778 and 1783, was born at Brookhaven, Long Island, and after graduating from Yale in 1773, he became superintendent of the high school at Wethersfield, Connecticut. Abandoning plans to study law, Tallmadge joined Col. John Chester's regiment of Connecticut militia levies in June 1776 as a lieutenant and adjutant. He was named brigade major of Gen. James Wadsworth's brigade on 11 Oct. 1776 (see General Orders, that date), and on 14 Dec. 1776 he was commissioned a captain in the 2d Continental Light Dragoon Regiment. Promoted to major in April 1777, Tallmadge remained with that regiment until the end of the war, participating in numerous skirmishes and raids and becoming deeply involved in intelligence work. In 1778 Tallmadge began conducting a highly useful correspondence with American agents in New York City, and in September 1780 he played an important role in uncovering Arnold's treason (see Tallmadge, *Memoirs*, 29, 35–39). In November 1780 Tallmadge led a raid on Fort St. George, Long Island, for which he was commended by Congress (see ibid., 39–42, and *JCC*, 18:1121–22). After the war Tallmadge became a businessman in Litchfield, Conn., and from 1801 to 1817 he was a member of the U.S. Congress.

From Major General William Heath

Dear General   Kingsbridge Sept. 1–1776

The Appearance of the Enemy on Long Island the last Evening, near Newtown, Induced Genl Mifflin to leave Col. Hand's Battalion at Harlem, & proceed with the other Battalions over Kingsbridge, & take Post on the Heights on the East side of Harlem River, towards Morrisania—Consequently Mount Washington has only Col. Hutchinson's Regiment, & a Detachment of 300 Men for it's Defence—It is the Opinion of the General Officers here, that all the Troops which marched Yesterday with Genl Mifflin from the City should be posted over the Bridge, towards Morrisania &c. on the Heights, & that Your Excellency should be sollicited, if the Service will admit of it, To order a Battalion down to Harlem, & that Col. Hand may take post towards Hunt's Point, & that another Battalion may be ordered, to Mount Washington, This is submitted to Your Excellency's Determination—We are now going to reconnoitre the Ground, & the Enemy's Situation as far as we may be able to do it—I have Ordered Col. Hutchinson to push the Sinking the Chevaux de Frise, all in his Power—If your Excellency should want Teams & an Order for impressing them should be sent here, I suppose a number may be obtained—A number of Boats are immediately wanted to form a Bridge over Harlem River Opposite Mount Washington—I have the Honor to be with great Respect your Excellency's most humble Servt

Wm Heath

ADfS, MHi: Heath Papers.

To Major General William Heath

Sir   New York Sept. 1st 1776

I received your favor of this date and Intend this Evening to go to Harlem and see whether the situation of Things will admit of the several Detachments and Dispositions you mention, so that every place necessary to be maintained should have measures taken for their defence. I should suppose that Hutchinsons Regiment & the 300 Men you say are at Mount Washington, will do to Garrison It for the present and will be equal to any force that will be brought against It, If they keep a good look out & do not suffer a Surprize—This you must strongly press upon them to guard against.

As It is of great consequence to gain Intelligence of the Enemies designs, and of their Intended Operations, I cannot but recommend your attention to this Subject and that you will concert some measures with Genl Clinton for establishing a channel of Information. I apprehend that his General acquaintance with most of the people in the Colony will give him an Opportunity of fixing upon suitable persons and in whom a confidence may be reposed to embark in this Business and who from their connections on the Island and the assistance of their Friends there might obtain frequent Accounts that would be usefull and of great advantage—perhaps some might be got who are really Tories for a reasonable reward to undertake It—Those who are Friends would be preferable If they could manage It as well—I will not add more upon the Subject, but heartily wish you and Genl Clinton could fall upon some mode to carry into execution a Scheme of this sort.

We are in extreme Want here of a Number of Horses & Teams to transport Baggage &c. from place to place and therefore have

Inclosed a Warrant authorizing you or any substituted by you to Impress them[1]—If they can be procured Immediately by Hiring It would be better, but If not, I beg you will take the most early means to send them down by Impressing them. they must be had at all events.

If there is a possibility of procuring Boats for Harlem river It shall be done. I am Sir Yr H. Servt

Go: Washington

LS, in Robert Hanson Harrison's writing, MHi: Heath Papers.

1. The enclosed impress warrant of this date, written by Robert Hanson Harrison and signed by GW, is in MHi: Heath Papers.

From Major Joseph Ward

Sir   Boston 1 September 1776.

Your Excellency's Letter of the twentysixth of August came by the last Post; General Ward being out of Town, I have transmitted the Letter with the inclosed Resolve of Congress to him.

I am sorry to inform your Excellency that Captain Burke in the armed Schooner Warren on the twentysixth of August was taken by a British Frigate about ten leagues without this Bay. Captain Ayers in the armed Schooner Lynch was in Company with the Warren but made his escape, and brought this intelligence.[1]

We hear with inexpressible Pleasure of the Repulse which our Troops under Your Excellency's Command gave the Enemy, and most ardently pray that it may be a prelude to the total Defeat of those infamous tools of the most infamous Tyrant. I have the Honour to be Sir Your Excellency's most Obedient Humble Servant

Joseph Ward

ALS, DLC:GW.

1. The *Warren* was captured by the British warship *Liverpool* off Cape Ann (see Artemas Ward to GW, 29 July 1776, n.2). John Ayres of Marblehead, Mass., who had been captain of the *Lynch* since 1 Feb. 1776, again eluded capture at sea by the British on 27 September. He received a Continental navy commission as captain on 10 Oct. 1776 but was discharged from command in February 1777 after refusing to sail his vessel unarmed (see Clark, *George Washington's Navy*, 182–83, 197–98).

Letter not found: from John Augustine Washington, 1 Sept. 1776. On 22 Sept. GW wrote to Washington: "I have had no Letter from you since the date of my last saving the one of Septr the 1st."

To Abraham Yates, Jr.

Sir   New York Septr 1st 1776

I was yesterday honoured with your favor of that date[1] and should have answered It by the return of the person who brought It, had I not been engaged then in a Multiplicity of Business which occasioned me to forget It till he was gone.

In respect to the Cattle on this Island, I shall desire the Commissary to purchase as many of them from the Inhabitants as he can conveniently and will afford every assistance the situation of affairs will admit of, to have the remainder secured; But as to those on Long Island, It is impossible for me to take any measures or give any assistance to prevent their falling into the Enemies hands—I am persuaded the Number of Rangers you mention, were they to exert themselves might be of service and annoy the foraging parties of the Enemy not a little—But Sir I cannot spare any men for that purpose—Tho our Force is called in from the Out posts & collected upon this Island—Yet It will not be more than competent to the defence of the Several Lines necessary to be maintained. nor is It perhaps by any means so great as common estimation & report make It.

I am extremely Obliged by your Opinion on the defensible state of the Grounds above Kingsbridge tho they had not escaped my observation—Their Importance I am fully sensible of, and as far as the critical situation of Things will allow, their defence shall be attended to, to prevent If possible the Enemy from possessing them. I have &c.

G.W.

P.S. As the posts at Kings Bridge are of such great Importance, I think It will be well and extremely necessary to be favoured with your friendly exertions in affording every aid in your power for their defence—Cannot some more Militia be prevailed on to give their assistance & in whom you can confide? I will not enlarge, being fully assured you will do all you can.

LB, in Robert Hanson Harrison's writing, DLC:GW; Varick transcript, DLC:GW. The New York committee of safety read this letter on 3 Sept., and it is printed in the *N.Y. Prov. Congress Journals,* 1:604–5. That text, which presumably was taken from the unfound receiver's copy, is nearly identical in the wording to the LB.

1. See the New York Committee of Safety to GW, 31 August.

General Orders

Head Quarters, New York, septemb: 2nd 1776.
Parole Effingham.   Countersign Putnam.

The General hopes, after the inconveniencies that have been complained of, and felt, that the commanding Officers of Corps will never, in future, suffer their men to have less than two days provisions, always upon hand, ready for any emergency—If hard Bread cannot be had, Flour must be drawn, and the men must bake it into bread, or use it otherwise in the most agreeable manner they can. They are to consider that all the last war in America, no Soldier (except those in Garrison) were ever furnished with bread ready baked, nor could they get Ovens on their march—The same must be done now.

The brigades under Genl Spencer, are still to keep themselves in readiness to march at the shortest notice; but in the mean time are to have regimental and brigade parades assigned them, in case of an Alarm before they move—These parades not to interfere with any of those in Genl Putnam's Division; to avoid which, the officers commanding them are to consult him, and each other, that they may be disposed of to the best advantage.

When regiments march away in future, the officers are to see that the men take their tent-poles in their hands—All their Tin-Camp-Kettles, and see the Tents tied up carefully, and a sufficient guard left to take care of them.

The Brigades of Genl Putnam's Division, are to furnish fifty men, to attend at the Hospital, upon Dr Morgan, to whom their names are to be returned.

Varick transcript, DLC:GW; Df, DNA: RG 93, Orderly Books, vol. 15.

Kinnan, *Orderly Book,* 95, includes another paragraph at the end of this day's general orders: "The Gen'l hopes the several officers, both superior and inferior, will now exert themselves and gloriously determine to conquer or die. From the justness of our cause, the situation of the harbor, and the bravery of her sons, America, thro' the blessing of God, can only expect success; now is the time for every man to exert himself and make our country glorious or become contemptible."

To John Hancock

Sir   New York Septr the 2d 1776

As my Intelligence of late has been rather unfavourable and would be received with anxiety & concern, peculiarly happy should I esteem myself, were It in my power at this time, to transmit such information to Congress, as would be more pleasing and agreable to their Wishes—But unfortunately for me— Unfortunately for them, It is not.

Our situation is truly distressing—The check our Detachment sustained on the 27th Ulto, has dispirited too great a proportion of our Troops and filled their minds with apprehension and despair—The Militia instead of calling forth their utmost efforts to a brave & manly opposition in order to repair our Losses, are dismayed, Intractable, and Impatient to return. Great numbers of them have gone off; in some Instances, almost by whole Regiments—by half Ones & by Companies at a time—This circumstance of Itself, Independent of others, when fronted by a well appointed Enemy, superior in number to our whole collected force, would be sufficiently disagreable, but when their example has Infected another part of the Army—When their want of discipline & refusal of almost every kind of restraint & Government, have produced a like conduct, but too common to the whole, and an entire disregard of that order and subordination necessary to the well doing of an Army, and which had been Inculcated before, as well as the nature of our Military establishment would admit of, our condition is still more alarming, and with the deepest concern I am obliged to confess my want of confidence in the Generality of the Troops. All these circumstances fully confirm the opinion I ever entertained, and which I more than once in my Letters took the liberty of mentioning to Congress, that no dependence could be put in a Militia or other Troops than those enlisted and embodied for a longer period than our regulations heretofore have prescribed. I am persuaded and as fully convinced, as I am of any One fact that has happened, that our Liberties must of necessity be greatly hazarded, If not entirely lost If their defence is left to any but a permanent, standing Army I mean One to exist during the War—Nor would the expence Incident to the support of such a body of Troops as would be competent almost to every exigency, far exceed that which is daily Incurred by calling in succour and New Inlistments and which when effected are not attended with any good consequences. Men who have been free and subject to no controul cannot be reduced to order in an Instant, and the privileges & exemptions they claim and will have Influence the conduct of others and the aid derived from them is nearly counterbalanced by the disorder, Irregularity and confusion they occasion—I cannot find that the Bounty of Ten Dollars is likely to produce the desired effect—When men can get double that sum to engage for a month or two in the Militia & that Militia frequently called out, It is hardly to be expected—The addition of Land might have a considerable influence on a permanent Inlistment.[1] Our number of men at present fit for duty are under 20,000—they were so by the last returns and best accounts I could get after the Engagement on Long Island—since which Numbers have deserted—I have ordered Genl Mercer to send the Men Intended for the Flying Camp to this place, about a 1000 in number, and to try with the Militia, if practicable, to make a diversion upon Staten Island.[2] Till of late I had no doubt in my own mind of defending this place nor should I have yet If the Men would do their duty, but this I despair of—It is painfull and extremely grating to me to give such unfavourable accounts, but It would be criminal to conceal the truth at so critical a juncture—Every power I possess shall be exerted to serve the Cause, & my first wish is, that whatever may be the event, the Congress will do me the Justice to think so. If we should be obliged to abandon this Town, ought It to stand as Winter Quarters for the Enemy? They would derive great conveniences from It on the one hand—and much property would be destroyed on the other—It is an important question, but will admit of but little time for deliberation—At present I dare say the Enemy mean to preserve It if they can—If Congress therefore should resolve upon the destruction of It, the Resolution should be a profound secret as the knowledge of It will make a Capital

change in their plans. I have the Honor to be with great esteem
Sir Your Most Obedt Servt

Go: Washington

LS, in Robert Hanson Harrison's writing, DNA:PCC, item 152; LB, DLC:GW;
copy, DNA:PCC, item 169; Varick transcript, DLC:GW. Congress read this letter on 3 Sept. and resolved itself into a committee of the whole to consider its
contents (*JCC*, 5:733).

1. Congress on 16 Sept. doubled the bounty and resolved to grant lands to
officers and soldiers engaged for the duration of the war (*JCC*, 5:762–63; see
also Hancock to GW, 24 Sept.).

2. No written orders to Mercer on these matters have been found. Mercer
did not launch a raid on Staten Island until 16 Oct. (see Mercer to GW, that
date; see also GW to Mercer, 5 Sept., and Mercer to GW, 7 Sept.).

From Commodore Esek Hopkins

Sir   Providence Septr 2nd 1776

I am Order'd by the Marine Committee to get the Valuation
of the Stores that I brought from New Providence,[1] and as part
of them was sent to Newyork by your Order should be glad you
would Order Mr Knox, or some other of your Officers to put a
Value on them, and order them to transmit such Valuation to
me as soon as Convenient.

Sir Should be extremely oblig'd to you if you have Settled a
Cartell with Admiral or General Howe, if you would endeavour
to get one Mr Henry Hawkings who was taken out of the Sloop
L'Aaimable Marie Peter Douville Master the 20th May last, off
Shrewsberry Inlet near Sandy Hook, and I believe is now on
board the Phœnix, and I hear acts as a common hand—he is
young man and a near kinsman of mine, and his Father and
Mother are very A[n]xious to get him Exchang'd.[2]

I can send a Prisoner of almost any Rank that may [be] required for him.

Your assistance in this matter will very much oblige Sir Your
most humbl. Servt

E.H.

LB, RHi: Hopkins Papers.

1. For the cannon that Hopkins captured at New Providence, see GW to
Hopkins, 14, 25 April, Hancock's first letter to GW, 20 April, and Hopkins to
GW, 22 May 1776.

2. The *L'Amiable Marie*, commanded by Pierre Douville (Du Ville; 1745–1794), was returning to Providence from France with a cargo of gunpowder when it was captured by a British cruiser (see Nicholas Brown & Co. to Plombard and Legris & Co., 6 June 1776, in Clark and Morgan, *Naval Documents,* 5:396–97). The *Providence Gazette; and Country Journal* for 31 May 1777 says that Hawkins was killed while on board the *Phoenix* "in her Passage up the North River last Summer, by a Shot from one of our Batteries." In March 1777, however, Lord Howe ordered the captain of the *Phoenix* to free Hawkins and permit him to return to Providence (see Peter Parker to Nicholas Cooke, 14 Mar. 1777, in Clark and Morgan, *Naval Documents,* 8:107–8). Henry Hawkins may be the privateer captain of that name who sailed out of Philadelphia between 1779 and 1782.

From Major General Philip Schuyler

Dear Sir   Albany September 2d 1776
    I have received a Requisition from General Gates for 2 Lb. Binding and 2 Lb. large Wire, 6 Lb. of Emery and six Screw plates, none of which can be procured here or any where in this part of the Country—Your Excellency will please to order these Articles to be sent by the first Conveyance.[1]
    Yesterday a Gentleman from the Committee of this City waited on me, and advised me that a person, who was sent up to purchase Boards by the Assistant Q. M. General had procured a Quantity from a Master of a Sloop and had engaged that he should have the Advantage of carrying them down in his own Vessel & represented farther that a very considerable Time would elapse before they could reach New York in that Way as there are several Sloop Loads and requesting my Advice on the Occasion. Conceiving that you are in immediate Want of the Boards, I advised that they should be sent down in any Vessels they could procure to carry them—I mention this lest it should be thought that I had interfered in the Quarter Master General's Department.[2]
    I am sorry that Dr Morgan has put me under the Necessity of Writing him the inclosed but as I am resolved not to be insulted by any person worthy of my Notice, I could not pass over the false and scandalous assertion in Silence—I have met with the most unjust cruel and ungenerous Treatment, I have it amply in my power to justify every part of my Conduct, and I hope the

Enquiry which I have intreated Congress to be made into it, will evince to the World how hardly I have been dealt by.[3]

Some of the Captains in Colo: Nicholson's Regiment have inlisted so very few Men that I durst not venture to sign Warrants for their pay—The Excuse they make is that with the Bounty allowed by Congress they could not engage any Men, as it was so greatly inferior to what was given to the Militia. I am with Sentiments of the greatest Regard & Esteem Your Excellency's most obedient humble Servant

Ph: Schuyler

LS, DLC:GW; LB, NN: Schuyler Papers.

1. These articles were included on a list of needed items that Schuyler recently had received from Morgan Lewis, deputy quartermaster general of the northern department (see Schuyler to Gates, 1 Sept., in Force, *American Archives*, 5th ser., 2:110–11).

2. The informant may be Jeremiah Van Rensselaer, whom the Albany committee of correspondence on 21 Aug. appointed chairman of a committee charged with obtaining the boards requested by Asst. Q.M. Gen. Hugh Hughes (*Minutes of the Albany and Schenectady Committees*, 1:527, 537; see also Schuyler to GW, 29 Aug., and note 4).

3. Schuyler's letter to Dr. John Morgan of 1 Sept. is an angry reaction to a report by Schuyler's close friend Dr. Samuel Stringer that Morgan had accused Schuyler of "making a Fortune out of the public." Denouncing that charge as "equally false & injurious," Schuyler challenged Morgan to prove it. "My patrimonial Estate," Schuyler writes, "afforded me a genteel Competency . . . and that Man is both a Scoundrel & a Lyar that insinuates that it is since encreased by either dishonest, dishonorable or any indirect practice" (Gerlach, *Proud Patriot*, 191). Morgan tried to mollify Schuyler in his reply of 6 Sept. by saying that Stringer had misrepresented his views, but Schuyler was more inclined to believe his friend Stringer (see ibid., 191–92).

From Jonathan Trumbull, Sr.

Sir   Lebanon [Conn.] Sept. 2d 1776

Since my last of the 31st ultmo have resolved to throw over upon Long Island a Thousand or fifteen hundred Troops, and the necessary orders are accordingly gone forth—and expect the same will be immediately Effected[1]—have likewise wrote to Governor Cooke to afford what Assistance in his Power for the same purpose[2]—Thought it expedient to give your Excellency the earliest Intimation of this Movement, that you might be able to Direct in what manner they may best Cooperate with the other Troops in serving the General Cause & frustrating the Intentions of our Enemies upon that Island.

As we have various accounts but no certain Intteligence respecting the Situation of our Armies, we are anxious to learn the Perticulars. Remain Sir with the highest Esteem and Regard your most Obedt humble Servt

Jonth; Trumbull

LS, DLC:GW; LB, Ct: Trumbull Papers.

1. The Connecticut council of safety on 1 Sept. ordered eight militia regiments and Col. Erastus Wolcott's state regiment to prepare to go to Long Island. Later on this date, however, the council learned of the American retreat to New York and directed Wolcott not to embark his men until he received further orders (see Hinman, *Historical Collection*, 383, and Trumbull to Cooke, 5 Sept., in "R.I. Revolutionary Correspondence," 167–68).

2. For Rhode Island's response to this request, see Nicholas Cooke to GW, 6 September.

General Orders

Head Quarters, New York, sept: 3rd 1776.
Parole Vernon.   Countersign Mifflin

The General most earnestly requests, that the several Brigadiers, and Commandants of Brigades, get their respective Corps in the best order as soon as possible and for this purpose they should join in Brigades as soon as can be, on a parade appointed for that purpose.

The Brigade, Majors according to the new arrangement are to attend every day for orders while they stay in town if they should march to reinforce Genl Mifflin's & McDougall's Brigades, they will fix upon one to come to Head Quarters every day for orders.

Genl Fellow's Brigade to furnish a Captain, two subs. & fifty men, for Boat duty, 'till further orders, to parade at Head Quarters, and receive Orders at eight OClock, every morning.

Some instances of infamous Cowardice, and some of scandalous Plunder, and Riot, having lately appeared, the General is resolved to bring the offenders to exemplary punishment—the notion that seems too much to prevail of laying hold of property not under immediate care, or guard, is utterly destructive of all

Honesty or good Order, and will prove the ruin of any Army, when it prevails—It is therefore hoped the Officers will exert themselves, to put a stop to it on all future occasions. If they do not, e'er long Death will be the portion of some of the offenders.

The state of the Ammunition and Arms, should be a subject of constant attention to every officer.

The General hopes the justice of the great cause in which they are engaged, the necessity and importance of defending this Country, preserving its Liberties, and warding off the destruction meditated against it, will inspire every man with Firmness and Resolution, in time of action, which is now approaching— Ever remembring that upon the blessing of Heaven, and the bravery of the men, our Country only can be saved.

The General orders a return of every regiment to be made immediately, and delivered to the Brigadier, or Commandant of the brigade, so that the Brigade Returns may be made at twelve O'Clock to morrow.

The near approach of the enemy, obliges the Guards to be doubled—the several Brigade Majors are immediately to settle the duty of their Brigades, according to their strenght—This is confined to Genl Putnam's division.

After Orders. Capt: Hezekiah Holdridge of Col. Wyllys's Regt appointed to act as Major of said regiment; for the present.

Varick transcript, DLC:GW; Df, in Joseph Reed's writing, DNA: RG 93, Orderly Books, vol. 15. The two passwords in the draft are not in Reed's writing.

From Major General Horatio Gates

Sir,   Tyconderoga 3rd September 1776.

This will be presented your Excellency by Major Hubley, who acted as Brigade Major to the Baron De Wedtke, being desirous to go to Philadelphia upon his Private Affairs, I have granted him permission, He is a Young Gentleman of Character in his Profession, and as such I introduce him to your Excellency.[1]

Brigade Major Scull accompanies Major Hubley, he goes to New York at the request of Brigadier General Thompson as your Excellency will be acquainted by General Thompsons Letter to Major Scull of the 6th of August from Quebe[c].[2]

Nothing extraordinary since my Last to your Excellency has

occurred here. The Fleet under General Arnold down the Lake is Increased to Twelve Sail Carrying Sixty Seven pieces of Cannon, The Three Row Galleys, and one more Gondola, will be ready to Join The Fleet in ten or fifteen Days at farthest The Excessive Rains has caused so much Fever and Ague at our Dock Yards at Skeensborough that the Ship Carpenters are almost all Sick which has very much retarded the finishing the Row Gallies.

I expect every Hour to hear from General Arnold, and the Return of my Scouts towards Canada I then shall immediately make a Report to your Excellency. with great Respect I am Your Excellencies Most Obedient Humble Servant

Horatio Gates

Copy, NHi: Gates Papers.

1. Adam Hubley, Jr. (c.1744–1793), became a lieutenant in the 1st Pennsylvania Regiment in October 1775 and accompanied it to Canada the following winter. On 31 July 1776 Hubley was sent from Ticonderoga to Fort George to inventory the possessions of the recently deceased Baron de Woedtke (see John Trumbull to Peter Gansevoort, that date, in Force, *American Archives*, 5th ser., 1:698). Hubley skirmished with Hessian troops near Fort Washington on 9 Nov. 1776 (see extract of an anonymous letter, 8–9 Nov. 1776, ibid., 3:601–2), and on 6 Dec. 1776 he was appointed major of the 10th Pennsylvania Regiment. Hubley transferred to Col. Thomas Hartley's Additional Continental Regiment on 12 Jan. 1777, but two months later he returned to the 10th Pennsylvania Regiment to be its lieutenant colonel. Named lieutenant colonel commandant of the "new" 11th Pennsylvania Regiment in June 1779, Hubley participated in Sullivan's expedition later that year. He resigned his commission in February 1781 (see Hubley to GW, 3 Feb. 1781, DLC:GW).

2. Gates may be referring to the letter that William Thompson wrote on 5 Aug. apparently to his brigade major Peter Scull, an unaddressed copy of which was enclosed in Schuyler to GW, 31 August. In it Thompson reports the impending release of American prisoners in Canada and requests: "If you can obtain leave of the commanding Officer, I would be glad you would meet me at New-York, with my Papers that I may get all my accounts settled on my arrival there" (DNA:PCC, item 159). Peter Scull (1753–1779), who was commissioned a second lieutenant in Thompson's Pennsylvania rifle regiment in July 1775 and a captain in Col. John Shee's 3d Pennsylvania Regiment the following January, became Thompson's brigade major in March 1776. In January 1777 Scull joined Col. John Patton's Additional Continental Regiment as a major. He resigned his commission in January 1778, and after declining offers to become a deputy inspector general or an assistant secretary to GW, he accepted appointment as secretary to the Continental Board of War in November 1778 (see GW to Scull, 5 Jan. and 19 Mar. 1778, DLC:GW; GW to Arthur St. Clair, 10 April 1778, CSmH; Scull to GW, 14 April 1778, PHi: Gratz Collection; and *JCC*, 12:1077, 1101, 1107). Scull resigned that office in August

1779 (ibid., 14:1009), and he died at sea the following November while sailing to France for his health (see John Jay to Arthur Lee, 26 Jan. 1780, in Morris, *Jay Papers,* 713–14).

From John Hancock

Sir,   Philada Sepr 3d 1776.
I do myself the Honour to enclose you sundry Resolves, by which you will perceive that Congress having taken your Letter of the 2d Inst. into Consideration, came to a Resolution, in a Committee of the whole House, that no Damage should be done to the City of New York.

I have sent Expresses to order the Battalions up to Head Quarters agreeably to the Resolves herewith transmitted; & likewise to the several States to the Northward of Virginia to send all the Aid in their Power to the Army.[1] I have the Honour to be, with perfect Esteem & Regard, Sir your most obed. & very hble Servant

John Han⟨cock⟩

LS, DLC:GW; LB, DNA:PCC, item 12A. The signature of the LS is mutilated.

1. The first of the enclosed resolutions of 3 Sept. informed GW that "the Congress would have especial Care taken, in case he should find it necessary to quit New York, that no damage be done to the said City by his Troops on their leaving it; the Congress having no doubt of being able to recover the same, tho^ the Enemy should for a time obtain Possession of it" (DLC:GW; see also *JCC,* 5:733). In a second resolution Congress ordered three Continental regiments from Virginia, two from North Carolina, and one from Rhode Island to march immediately to reinforce the army at New York and recommended that the Massachusetts General Court send a militia regiment to Rhode Island to replace the regiment taken from that state. Congress also recommended that the states north of Virginia send "all the aid in th⟨eir⟩ power" to GW's army (DLC; see also *JCC,* 5:733–34, and Hancock to Certain Continental Officers and to Certain States, 3 Sept., in Smith, *Letters of Delegates,* 5:95–97).

From Major General William Heath

Dear General   Kingsbridge Sept. 3d 1776
I find many of the Soldiers belonging to the Battalions, that suffered the Most, in the late Action on Long Island much

Dispirited, & often uttering Expressions that they have lost their Officers, lost their Blankets, & have no money, & the like, I could wish that your Excellency would just think of the matter, & if the Paymaster has Money in the Treasury, that they may be paid— I am confident that at this Time it would answer a very good purpose, & if agreeable to your Excellency, should be glad that I might have it in my power to inform them, that it shall soon be done.[1]

Genl Clinton acquaints me that near one half of the Detachment, from his Brigade which are at Mount Washington are sick, & principally for the want of Covering, on which Account they have suffered much, he sollicits that your Excellency would order a Battalion (or part of one) to that post who have Tents, or if you should not think that proper, that his Men at that post may have Tents allowed them of which he says there are a number in the Store.

I have without Loss of time in Consort with General Clinton been endeavouring to effect what your Excellency was pleased to hint in your last, I think our Prospect appears promising.[2]

I consider our present Situation on several accounts, one that requires the Exertions of all the Abilities of the most able Generals—a well connected Plan must connect & direct our opperations—I ever have been, I still am confident that we may defeat the Enemy; but Art & Stratagem must be our pole Star, & Vigilance & Alertness our Compass.

As great numbers of the Troops are daily marching from the City, & taking post in places where it will be impossible for them suddenly to erect Bake Houses, I beg leave to suggest to your Excellency, whether it would not be highly expedient, to keep all the Bakers in the City, baking of hard Bread, which may be easily conveyed a little back, & may prove of vast advantage—at some critical Time. I have the honor to be with great Respect your Excellency's most humble Servt

W. Heath

P.S. As a very considerable Alteration has lately been made in what was at first considered as my Division by the removal of Genl Fellows's Brigade, & other Regiments, I should be glad to be informed, what Brigades or Regiments are to receive Orders from me & where the Division Line is to Terminate.

W. Heath

ADfS, MHi: Heath Papers.

1. Paymaster Gen. William Palfrey wrote Heath on this date: "As I expect a large Sum of Money by the Way of Dobbs's ferry soon—the General has directed me to deposit it somewhere in your Neighbourhood" (MHi: Heath Papers). For the subsequent payment of the troops, see GW to Heath, 8 September.

2. See GW to Heath, 1 September.

To Brigadier General Hugh Mercer

Dr Sir   N. York Septr 3. 1776

From the present complexion of our Affairs It appears to me of the utmost Importance & that the most Salutary consequences may result from our having a strong Encampment at the post on the Jersey side of the North River, opposite to Mount Washington on this Island—I therefore think It adviseable & highly necessary that you detach such a Force from Amboy & Its dependencies under the Command of an Officer of Note, Authority & influence, with a Skilfull Engineer to lay out such additional Works as may be Judged Essential & proper & the situation of the Ground will admit of—they should be begun & carried on with all possible diligence and dispatch.[1]

It will be proper that a considerable Quantity of Provision should be collected for the maintenance & support of the Camp, & for this purpose I wish you to have proper measures adopted to procure It & have It deposited there & at places of Security not far distant.

As the Continl Officer now at this post will take rank & the command, probably of any you may send, Unless he should be a Genl Officer, I think & wish if you have One that possibly be spared & in whose Judgemt, activity & Fortitude you can rely, that he may be appointed to the command rather than an Officer of Inferior rank. I am &c.

G.W.

LB, in Robert Hanson Harrison's writing, DLC:GW; Varick transcript, DLC:GW.

1. Mercer received GW's orders this night and ordered a detachment commanded by Brig. Gen. James Ewing to begin enlarging the works on the Palisades above Burdett's Ferry across the Hudson River from Fort Washington (see Mercer to Hancock, 4 Sept., DNA:PCC, item 159). Begun in mid-July,

these works were called Fort Constitution at this time but were renamed for Maj. Gen. Charles Lee on 19 October. The fort was captured by the British on 20 November.

Letters not found: from Brig. Gen. Hugh Mercer, 3 Sept. 1776. On 5 Sept. GW wrote to Mercer: "I have been favoured with your Two Letters of the 3 Instt."

From Colonel Rufus Putnam

Sir   Blooming dale September the 3d 1776
    according to your Exelencies order I have Reconnoitered every part about the Island of New york and the main as Farr as Frogs point and on a full Vew Find the Enimy have Such a Veriety of places to Chuse out of that its Imposable to prevent there Landing When they please they have Such guides and Intiligence of our movements that they Can always avoid or Surprize any parties that are Posted to oppose there Landing there army is So Numerious that they Can always attack any Devition [division] of our army with a Superour force. and yet while our army is Extended from N. york to kings Bridge tis Nesesary to have a Body of Reserve at this place. But I Can not think it would be Best nor have we time to make fortification Sence the moment any Quarter is attack the whole Body of Reserve I Conclude will be ordered to Support it: I Should advise the throwing obstructions in the way of Landing that they have one weeks provition [provision] always with them and teams Ready to Carry there Bagage whereever the Service Requiers.
    I mentioned to your Exelency that I thought your army Should be Collected to gather in Some advantagous place where Supplys might be had and a Camp Fortified in Such a maner as the Enimy dare not attack or if they did must be Repulsed and I think So Still if it Be posable to Effect it. and to defend the passage of the North River which I take to be the Cappital object and at the Same time keep open a Communication with the Eastern and Southern Collonies—is to post the army from Burdet landing on the Jersey Shore—Mount Washington and the Hights South as far as Col. Morrises House on Harlem River[1] the Hights we now possess are at kings Bridge and as farr South

as the three trees—the Batteries on the Jersey Side to be Filled with guns the Battery on the Rocks Below Mount Washington Compleated a new one Builded Below the Hill opposit the Sunken Vessels. these well filled with guns and ammunition. if the Gallies also aforded there asistence would Render it Very Difiquilt for Ships to pass if they attempted to force this post I think they must be Beat. if they Deteached into the Country on either hand it must Scattere there army in Such a maner that your Excelency Must Drub them. But if Supplys Cannot be had at this place at the high lands there may Both by land and Warter. I think there has Ben Some Proff the Ships Dare not attempt that pasage but they are not prepaired to Defend against a land army this is Surly worth attention for if they possess them Selves of this passage we Shall be in a Bad Box for my Sentiments about that place I Referr your Exelency to Ld Stearlings Reports Last May.[2] I know that this Doctrenn gives up york to Distru[c]tion and Exposes many other towns to be Ravaged by them But what are 10: or 20 towns to the grand object if they once pass the Highlands I See no way to prevent the Juncetion of there armys Burgoyne Need Never Come from Cannada if How gits to albany our Northern army Must Quit Ticondorroga or fall a Sacrefize. I am your Exelencies most obedient Humble Servent

Rufus Putnam

ALS, DLC:GW. At the head of this document Putnam wrote: "The Report of R. Putnam—Engeneer."

1. Roger Morris (1727–1794), a native of Yorkshire, England, who had served with GW on the Braddock campaign in 1755, married Mary Eliza Philipse, a wealthy New York heiress, in 1758, and in 1765 he built a beautiful house, now known as the Jumel Mansion, on the highest ground in upper Manhattan, about a mile south of the site of Fort Washington and about three miles north of the village of Harlem. GW used Morris's mansion as his headquarters from 15 Sept. to 21 October. Morris, who sat on the New York council from 1765 to 1775, sailed to London in May 1775 after declaring his Loyalist sympathies. He returned to New York in December 1777, and on 1 Jan. 1779 he became inspector of Loyalist claims with the rank of provincial colonel. Morris left America at the end of the war and settled permanently in Yorkshire.

2. See Stirling to GW, 1 June 1776.

General Orders

Parole America.   Countersign Shelbourne.

It is with amazement and concern, the General finds, that the men of every regiment, are suffer'd to be constantly rambling about, and at such distances from their respective quarters and encampments, as not to be able to oppose the enemy in any sudden approach.[1] He therefore not only commands, but most earnestly exhorts the Colonels and commanding officers of Corps, as they value their own reputation, the safety of the Army, and the good of the cause, to put an immediate, and effectual stop to such an unsoldierlike, and dangerous practice; as one step towards the accomplishment of which, he orders and directs that all those who shall be absent without leave be immediately punished.[2]

The sick of the several regiments of Militia are to be discharged if they are well enough to get home, and choose to be discharged—All the other sick are to be provided for in such a manner, and in such places, as the Director General of the Hospitals & the several regimental Surgeons shall think best for them. In giving these discharges particular care is to be taken by the Colonels and General Walcott to see that none but those who are really sick be dismissed and that the discharges be given in writing by Genl Walcott.

The General does in express and peremptory terms, insist upon exact returns of the several regiments, and other Corps, and the Brigadiers and officers commanding Brigades, are to see that this order is complied with, without delay; as it is essentially necessary for the General to be acquainted with the exact state of the army.

Col. Glover, during the absence of Genl Clinton, is to be considered as Commandant of his Brigade, and to be obeyed accordingly.

The increased number of waggons will in future admit of more regularity in marching the regiments than has yet prevailed—Whenever therefore a regiment is ordered to march they should get their Baggage in readiness, but not move it 'till conveniencies are provided. The Qr Master of the regiment should then overlook it & stop all heavy, useless lumber, and the

Commanders of regiments would do well, to take particular Care in this matter. No Colonel is to seize any boat, or waggon, by his own Authority, on Penalty of having his baggage turn'd out and left.

The Brigade Majors are ordered to have their Brigade Returns immediately made, or the General will put the Delinquents in Arrest; unless the Adjutants fail in their duty, and they put such Adjutants in Arrest.

The Brigade Majors both standing and temporary are hereafter punctually to attend at eleven O'Clock at Head Quarters. There has been of late a shameful remissness in some of them.

Varick transcript, DLC:GW; Df, DNA: RG 93, Orderly Books, vol. 15. The last three paragraphs of the general orders in the draft are in Joseph Reed's writing.

1. The draft reads: "as to render it impossible to collect them under Arms in time to oppose the Enemy in any sudden Approach." See also Kinnan, *Order Book*, 97, and "Williams' Diary," 48:338.

2. The draft reads: "he orders and directs that the rolls be called over three times a day, and that all those who shall be absent without Leave be immediately punished." See also Kinnan, *Order Book*, 98, and "Williams' Diary," 48:338.

The next day Edward Tilghman wrote General Heath on behalf of Joseph Reed: "It is with infinite Amazement and Concern the General [GW] finds, that Men of almost every Regiment are sufferd to ramble and straggle from their respective Quarters and Encampments, so that in Case of an Alarm, wh. we have great Reason hourly to expect, it will be impossible for them to be so effectually collected, as to be able to repel the crafty and enterprizing Enemy. As it is of the last Importance that so dangerous a Practice should be speedily corrected, he begs of you to bend your Attention to this Subject particularly, and recommends that henceforth the Rolls in each Regiment be called over three Times a day, and the Delinquents instantly punished; that no Soldier be permitted on any Acct to quit his Quarters without Leave, and at any Rate only a few at a Time.

"The daily Complaints of the most unbounded Licentiousness of the Troops, in plundering and destroying every thing they can lay their Hands on, gives his Excellency the utmost uneasiness, and will unless speedily put an End to, prove the disgrace and destruction of the Army. The Genl is surprized that Freemen engaged in the glorious Cause of Liberty, and fighting in Defence of every thing that is dear to them, should inconsiderately plunge into such infamous and atrocious Crimes, while our mercenary Enemy, the tools of Tyranny and Oppression, exhibit almost a perfect pattern of Regularity. You will therefore not only take Care to convince the Soldiers how truly abominable such Behavior is, but by the most steady and regular discipline, prevent these Irregularities in future.

"Upon your attention to these Matters the good of the Cause depends, and the Genl rests assured that you will embrace every opportunity of removing the present causes of complaint.

"Tis his Excellency's order that a copy of this Letter be given to each Brigade Major who is to *see that the contents of it are communicated to his Brigade, and at the same time inform the Men from the Genl, that every offender will be certainly and severely punished*" (MHi: Heath Papers).

To Colonel Fisher Gay

Sir   New York Sept. 4th 1776

Whether you do not get the General Orders, with that regularity which is to be wished or whether (which is hard to suppose) you do not attend to them, I will not undertake to determine; But it is a melancholy truth, that Returns, essentially necessary for the Commanding Officer to govern himself by, & which might be made in an hour after they are Calld for where care and Order are Observed, are obtained with so much difficulty. Nor can I help regretting that not only regular Returns, but that orders in instances equally important should be so little attended to. I therefore address my self to you in this manner, requesting in Express & peremptory terms, that you do without delay make out & return to the Adjutant General's Office immediately an exact state of the regiment or Corps under your Command, and that the like return be given in every Saturday at Orderly time without fail. I also desire in terms equally express, that you do not suffer the men of your Corps to straggle from their Quarters, or be absent from camp without leave, and even then, but few at a time. Your own Reputation—the safety of the Army, & the good of the Cause depends, under God, upon our vigilance & Readiness to oppose a Crafty & enterprizing enemy, who are always upon the watch to take advantages. to prevent straggling let your Rolls be called over three times a day, & the delinquents punished. I have one thing more to urge, and that is, that every attempt of the men, to Plunder Houses, Orchards, Gardens &c. be discouraged not only for the Preservation of property & sake of good Order, but for the Prevention of those fatal Consequences which usually follow such Diabolical practices. In Short Sir, at a time when every thing is at stake, It behoves every man to Exert himself. It will not do for the Commanding Officer of a Regiment to Content himself with barely giving Orders, he should see (at least know) they are executed. he should call his men out frequently and Endeavour to impress them with a Just and true sense of their duty, & how much depends upon subordination and Discipline—Let me therefore not only Command but Exhort you & your Officers, as you Regard your Reputation your Country, and the sacred Cause of Freedom in which you are engaged, to manly & Vigorous exertions at this time each striving to excell the Other in the respective duties of his department. I trust it is unnecessary for me to add further and that these & all other Articles of your duty you will Execute with a Spirit & punctuallity becoming your Station. I am Sir Your Most Obt Servant

G.W.

LB, in Caleb Gibbs's writing, DLC:GW; Varick transcript, DLC:GW.

The signed letter sent to Gay apparently fell into British hands because General Howe's secretary Frederick Mackenzie includes a full copy of it in his diary entry for 17 Sept. and says it "was taken from an original, signed by him [GW]" (Mackenzie, *Diary*, 1:54–55). Ambrose Serle writes in his journal entry for 18 Sept. that "a curious Letter was intercepted, or rather taken with its Bearer, from Washington to some of his Rebel-Officers, upbraiding them with Want of Courage and Want of Discipline, and reproaching them that a Band of mercenary Hirelings (which is the best Name he can bestow upon his lawful Sovereign's Forces) should so far excel them in both. The Letter, as it ought, will be published" (Tatum, *Serle's Journal*, 108). The letter apparently was not published at that time, however.

To John Hancock

Sir   New York Septr 4th 1776

Since I had the Honor of addressing you on the 2d Our affairs have not undergone a change for the better, nor assumed a more agreable aspect than what they then wore. The Militia under various pretences of sickness &c. are daily diminishing & in a little time I am persuaded, their number will be very inconsiderable.

On Monday night a Forty Gun Ship passed up the Sound between Governor's & Long Island & Anchored in Turtle bay. In her passage she received a discharge of Cannon from our Batteries but without any damage & having a favourable wind

& Tide soon got out of their reach. Yesterday morning I dispatched Majr Crane of the Artillery with Two Twelve pounders & a Howitz to annoy her, who hulling her several times forced her from that Station & to take shelter behind an Island where she still continues.[1] There are several other Ships of War in the sound with a good many Transports or Store Ships, which came round Long Island, so that that communication is entirely cut off. The Admiral with the main body of the Fleet is close in with Governor's Island.

Judging It expedient to guard against every Contingency as far as our peculiar situation will admit, and that we may have resources left, If obliged to abandon this place, I have sent away & am removing above Kingsbridge All our Stores that are unnecessary & that will not be immediately wanted.

I have inclosed several original Letters from some of our Officers, prisoners at Quebec which fell into Genl Gates's hands & were transmitted by him to Genl Schuyler who sent them to me—Genl Gates adds that the persons who brought them said Genl Burgoyne had sent Messages to the Inhabitants upon the Lakes, inviting their continuance on their farms & assuring them that they should remain in security.[2]

The post master having removed his Office from the City to Dobb's ferry, as It is said, makes It extremely inconvenient, and will be the means of my not giving such constant & regular Intelligence as I could wish.[3] Can not some mode be devised by which we may have a pretty constant & certain Intercourse & communication kept up? It is an Interesting matter and of great importance and as such I am persuaded will meet with due attention by Congress.

I have transmitted the Copy of Genl Gates's Letter as sent me by Genl Schuyler, from which Congress will discover all the Information I have respecting Genl Burgoyne's message and my latest Intelligence from Tyconderoga, with the returns of the Army there[4]—Those of the Army here It is impossible to obtain till the hurry and bustle we are now in are a little over. I have &c.

G.W.

P.S. Congress will perceive by Genl Gates's Letter, his want of Musquet Cartridge paper,[5] It is impossible to supply him from hence, they will therefore be pleased to order what he wants, If

It can be procured, to be immediately sent him from Philadelphia.

LB, in Robert Hanson Harrison's writing, DLC:GW; copy, DNA:PCC, item 169; Varick transcript, DLC:GW. Congress read this letter on 6 Sept. and referred it to the Board of War (*JCC,* 5:738–39).

1. On the morning of 2 Sept. the British frigate *Rose* covered the landing of troops on Governors Island, and that night it sailed up the East River with a number of flatboats to the mouth of Newtown Creek near Turtle Bay. The next morning the *Rose* moved a short distance farther up the river to Blackwell's (now Roosevelt) Island, which was seized by British troops that afternoon (see the Journal of H.M.S. *Rose,* 2–3 Sept., in Clark and Morgan, *Naval Documents,* 6:666; Lydenberg, *Robertson Diaries,* 95–96; Mackenzie, *Diary,* 1:37–39; and Wilson, *Heath's Memoirs,* 68). The *Rose* sustained only minor damage from the American cannonade. "A great Firing was heard last night from the Town upon the Rose & the Boats," Ambrose Serle says in his journal entry for 3 September. "One Shot passed through the Rose, and another beat off one of her anchors, without doing any other Damage. The Rebels fired two Pieces of Ordnance upon her to-day from a Battery opposite Bushwyck; and wounded two or three Men. The Boats got safe into Newtown Creek, and, as 'tis supposed, unperceived by the Enemy, through the favorable Darkness of the Night" (Tatum, *Serle's Journal,* 90–91).

2. These letters were enclosed in Schuyler's letter to GW of 31 August.

3. The New York committee of safety ordered New York Postmaster General Ebenezer Hazard to Dobbs Ferry on 30 Aug. (*N.Y. Prov. Congress Journals,* 602).

4. For Gates's letter to Schuyler of 26–27 Aug. and his return of 24 Aug., see Gates to GW, 28 Aug., n.1, and Schuyler to GW, 31 Aug., nn.1 and 3. Gates says in his letter that some frontier settlers had informed him "that the Enemy were straining every Nerve to come and attack us; that they had large Boats, or Gondolas, which carried each a Brass 24 Pounder. and that they made no Doubt of being an Overmatch for us upon the Lake" (DLC:GW).

5. "I am astonished," Gates writes, "at not receiving the Musket Cartridge-Paper which I wrote for so repeatedly, and so long ago. I desire you will spare neither Pains nor Cost to send it here. . . . One hundred Reams of Musket cartridge Paper is as little as should be sent immediately" (DLC:GW).

To Lieutenant Colonel Henry Beekman Livingston

Sir   [New York] Sept. 4. 1776

In answer to both your favours just receivd by Lieut. Smith[1] I can only say, that circumstanced as we both are at present it is not in my power to give you any other instructions for your

Conduct than that you pursue every step which shall appear to you necessary & judicious for annoying & harrassing the Enemy, & to prevent their forraging, & while those measures are in any degree effectual I would wish to have you continue on the Island, but as soon as you find you can be of no longer service I would have you make your retreat to the main without farther delay—You will take care to have Boats so provided as to secure your Retreat in the best manner possible. I am with due Regards Sir Your very hum. Servt

G.W.

LB, in Tench Tilghman's writing, DLC:GW; Varick transcript, DLC:GW.

1. See Livingston to GW, 30 and 31 August.

To Major General Philip Schuyler

Dear Sir   New York septr 4. 1776.

Your Favors of the 29th & 31st Ulto with their several Inclosures have been duly received.

I sincerely Wish the Event of the Skirmish on Long Island had been as favorable as reported to You. Hurried & Involved in a Multiplicity of Buisiness, I cannot give You a particular Detail of It, I shall only add that we lost in killed wounded & Prisoners, from 700 to a thousand Men. Among the Prisoners are General Sullivan & Lord Stirling. The Enemy's Loss has not been asscertained Yet, But there is Reason to beleive from the Continuance of the Action & the Heavy Firings between them & Lord Stirling's Detachmt, that It was considerable. We have been informed so by Deserters. They Overpowered our People by their Numbers & Constant Reinforcements.[1]

When I have an Opportunity & Circumstances will admit, I will enquire after Lieut. Johnson & Order him to Albany.

I am extremely Obliged for Your Interposing to have the Boards sent down. I have informed the Quarter Master General & directed him, to take Measures for Obtaining a large Supply, as I have Grounds to Apprehend many will be wanted.[2]

The short Inlistment of our Troops has been the Source of some of our Misfortunes & of Infinite Trouble and Difficulty already, And I am not Without Apprehension that sooner or later must prove of fatal Consequence. I have wrote my Sentiments very fully to Congress upon this Subject, two or three Times—In a late Letter, I have urged the Expediency of a permanent Army during the War.[3] The Necessity is too Obvious to require Arguments to prove It. I think It will be adviseable to recruit out of the present Army as fast as possible. But I fear the Progress will be but small. The Bounties Given by the different States to raise their Quotas of Men for so short a Time, must have a pernicious Tendency. Many will refuse to inlist, as that allowed by Congress is so low, in Hopes of Exacting more.

The Letters from our Officers in Canada transmitted by General Gates I have sent to Congress with the Return You inclosed.[4] I have also perused & delivered Your Letter to the Commissary, having sealed It first, & Wish Matters to be so ordered as to promote the service.

Observing that General Gates in his Letter to You mentions his Want of Cartridge Paper for Musquets I have wrote to Congress & requested them to supply It if possible, having none here or but Very little, And have also directed the Quarter Master General to send up some Grind stones, not knowing Whether they can be had at Albany.[5] I am Dr Sir With Great Esteem, Your Most Obedt Servt

Go: Washington.

P.S. Your Letter preceeding the two last came to Hand When I was sending away My Papers & being put up with them after a Cursory Reading I don't relect It sufficiently to Answer.[6]

Being almost certain that We shall have Occasion for a large Quantity of Boards for Barracks & shelter for the Troops, Which will be posted at Kings bridge, In Its Vicinity & Over the River opposite the Works erected at the Upper End of this Island, I wish to be informed, If they can be supplied & shall be Glad those who undertake It, will begin to Hurry 'em down, with all Expedition to the Nearest Landing place to the Bridge.

G.W.

LB, NN: Schuyler Papers; LB, DLC:GW; copy, NHi: Gates Papers; Varick transcript, DLC:GW.

1. The favorable report to which Schuyler refers in his letter to GW of 29 Aug. concerns the skirmish at Bedford Pass on 23 Aug., not the Battle of Long Island on 27 Aug., which GW discusses in this letter (see Sullivan to GW, 23

Aug.; GW to Schuyler, 24 Aug.; and Robert Hanson Harrison to Hancock, 27 Aug.).

2. For GW's directions to Q.M. Gen. Stephen Moylan, see Robert Hanson Harrison to Moylan, 3 Sept., quoted in Schuyler to GW, 29 Aug., n.4.

3. See GW to Hancock, 2 September.

4. See GW to Hancock, this date, and note 4.

5. See GW to Hancock, this date, and note 5. Gates also requested grindstones in his letter to Schuyler of 26–27 Aug. (DLC:GW).

6. GW is referring to Schuyler's letter of 26 August. The LB in DLC:GW reads "recollect" instead of "relect."

From Abraham Yates, Jr.

In Committee of Safety for the State of
Sir   New York—Fishkill Septr 4th 1776.

I enclose to your Excellency by the order of the Committee of Safety, a copy of a report which relates to a part of your Letter of the first Instant, respecting the calling out more of the Militia of this State for the purpose of reinforcing the Posts at Kings Bridge—It is with extreme concern that the Committee of Safety see their Inability to assist further in maintaining those important posts; they flatter themselves that the Reasons which they have offered will appear As Satisfactory to your Excellency as they did to the Committee.[1]

I am however directed to assure your Excellency that the whole Militia of the Counties of Ulster Orange Dutches and West Chester shall be ready to march whenever your Excellency or General Clinton shall think it absolutely necessary—And to inform you that the Committee of Safety will immediately exert themselves in arming with Lances, all Such of the well Affected Militia, as are destitute of Arms.[2] I have the Honor to be most respectfully Sir your most obedient humble Servant

By Order
Abm Yates, Jun. President

LS, DLC:GW. The draft of this letter that the committee of safety approved late this afternoon contains only a few minor variations in wording (see *N.Y. Prov. Congress Journals*, 1:606–7; see also note 2).

1. The enclosed report of this date gives three reasons for not calling out additional militia from Orange, Dutchess, Westchester, and Ulster counties: "1st That from the best Information they have been able to obtain the number of Armed and well affected Militia in the said Counties do not exceed three

thousand one hundred; the number of disarmed & disaffected Persons, two thousand three hundred, and the Number of Slaves two Thousand three hundred—From a Comparison of these Numbers and from our firm opinion that the disaffected only wait an Opportunity of rising; that General Howe is actually endeavouring to enlist Men in most of those Counties, and that our Enemies would not scruple to Stir up our Slaves to bear arms against us, it would be [extremely hazardous] to the internal Peace of the said Counties to draw out at present any more of their Militia.

"2d That from the Situation of the County of West Chester, which borders both on the Sound and Hudsons River, and the Counties of Dutches Ulster and Orange, on the North River (the Channel of which we have no reason to think sufficiently obstructed) the Enemy might Land to the Northward of our Posts at Kings Bridge, and take possession of those Counties, without any possibility of a Resistance from the Militia.

"3d That from the want of Tents or sufficient Houses the Militia would be extremely exposed to the Inclemencies of Weather, and other Hardships; which added to the Arts of the Tories in Construing into a Defeat the late Prudent retreat from Long Island; and the present inconvenient Season of the year, would we fear prove too Severe a Trial for the Virtue and patriotism of Common Soldiers, and disgust them so as to prevent their being of Service to the State on a Still more critical Occasion—This appears to have been lately the Case both of the Militia and New Levies on Nassau [Long] Island" (DLC:GW; see also *N.Y. Prov. Congress Journals,* 1:606).

2. The draft reads: "as are at present destitute of firearms" (ibid., 606–7).

General Orders

Head Quarters, New-York, septr 5th 1776
Parole Chatham.   Countersign Maryland.

The Brigade Majors immediately to settle a Court Martial, making an allowance for the Absence, or Indisposition, of any officers. They are to meet at the Brick-House near the encampment late of Genl McDougall, to morrow at ten O'Clock. Notice to be given accordingly. They are first to try the scoundrels, who have been detected in pillaging, and plundering, Lord Stirling's, and other property.

Such as were directed by yesterday's Orders to apply to Genl Walcott for discharges are in future to apply to the Brigadiers under whom their regiments are ranged.

Varick transcript, DLC:GW; Df, in Joseph Reed's writing, DNA: RG 93, Orderly Books, vol. 15. The two passwords in the draft are not in Reed's writing.

From Major General Nathanael Greene

Dear Sir   New York Island Sept. 5 1776

The critical situation in which the Army are in, will I hope sufficiently Apologize for my troubleing your Excellency with this Letter. The Sentiments are dictated I am sure by an honest mind, A mind who feels deeply Interested in the Salvation of his Country; and for the honnor and Reputation of the General under whom he serves.

The Object under consideration, is whether a General and speedy retreat from this Island is Necessary or not. to me it appears the only Eligible plan to oppose the Enemy successfully and secure our selves from disgrace. I think we have no Object on this side of Kings Bridge. Our Troops are now so scatterd that one part may be cut off before the others can come to their support. In this Situation suppose the Enimy should Run up the North River several Ships of force and a Number of Transpo⟨rts⟩ at the same time, and effect a Landing between the Town and middle division of the Army. Another party from Long Island should land right oppisite. these two parties form a Line across the Island and Entrench themselves. The two Flanks of this Line could be easily supported by the Shiping. the Center fortified with the Redoubts would render it very difficult if not impossible to cut our way through. At the time the Enemy are Executeing this movement or Manouvre, they will be able to make sufficient diversions if not real lodgments to render it impossible for the Center and uper Divisions of the Army to afford any assistance here. Should this Event take place⟨,⟩ and by the by I dont think it very improbable, Your Excellency will be reduced to that situation which every prudent General would wish to avoid⟨;⟩ that is of being Obligeed to fight the Enemy to a disadvantage or Submit.

It has been agreed that the City of Newyork would not be Tenable if the Enimy got possession of Long Island & Govenors Island. they are now in possession of both these places.[1] Notwithstanding I think we might hold it for some time, but the Annoyance must be so great as to render it an unfit place to Quarter Troops in. If we should hold it, we must hold it, to a great disadvantage. The City and Island of Newyork, are no Objects for us, we are not to bring them in Competition with the General Interest of America. Part of the Army already has met with a defeat, the Country is struck with a pannick, any Cappital loss at this time may ruin the cause. Tis our business to study to avoid any considerable misfortune. And to take post where the Enemy will be Obligd to fight us and not we them. The sacrafice of the Vast Property of Newyork and the Subburbs I hope has no influence upon your Execellencys measures. Remember the King of France when Charles the fifth Emperor of Germany invaded his Kingdom, he lead [laid] whole Provinces waste; and by that policy he starvd and ruind Charles Army, and defeated him without fighting a Battle.[2] Two thirds of the Property of the City of Newyork and the Subburbs belongs to the Tories. We have no very great Reason to run any considerable risque for its defence. If we Attempt to hold the City and Island and should not be able finally We shall be wasteing of time unnecessarily and betray a defect of Judgment if no worse misfortune Attends it.

I give it as my Oppinion that a General and speedy Retreat is absolutely necessary and that the honnor and Interest of America requires it. I would burn the City & subburbs—and that for the following Reasons—If the Enemy gets possession of the City, we never can Recover the Possession, without a superior Naval force to theirs. It will deprive the Enemy of An Opportunity of Barracking their whole Army together which if they could do would be a very great security. It will deprive them of a general Market. the price of things would prove a temptation to our people to supply them for the sake of the gain, in direct violation of the Laws of their Country. All these Advantages would Result from the destruction of the City. And not one benefit can arise to us from its preservation that I can conceive off. If the City once gets into the Enemies hands, it will be at their mercy either to save or destroy it, after they have made what use of it they think proper.

At the Retreat I would Order the Army to take post part at Kings Bridge and part along West Chester Shore where Barracks may be procurd for that part of the Army that are without Tents—I must confess I am too Ignorant of the Ground to form much Judgment about posting the Troops. Your Excellencys superior Judgment formd from your own observation upon the ground, will enable you to make a much better Disposition, than I can conceive off.

If my Zeal has led me to say more than I ought, I hope my good Intentions may Atone for the Offence. I shall only add that these Sentiments are not dictated from fear, nor from any Apprehensions of personal danger. But are the Result of a cool and deliberate survey of our situation, and the necessary measures to extricate us from our present difficulties. I have said nothing at all about the temper and dispositions of the Troops and their Apprehensions about being sold. This is a strong intimation that it will be difficult to get such Troops to be have with proper Spirit in time of Action if we should be Attackt.

Should your Excellency agree with me, with respect to the two first points, that is, that a speedy and General Retreat is necessary; and also that the City & Subburbs should be burnt, I would Advise to call a General Council upon that Question and take every General Officers Oppinion upon it. I am with due respect your Excellencys most Obedient humble Servant

N. Greene

ALS, DLC:GW. The text in angle brackets is mutilated.

1. The British landed at Governors Island on the morning of 2 Sept., three days after the retreating Americans moved the island's small garrison to New York.

2. Francis I (1494–1547) of France lost a series of wars to the Holy Roman Emperor Charles V (1500–1558) during the first half of the sixteenth century.

To Major General William Heath

Dear Sir,   New York. Septr 5th 1776.

As every thing, in a manner, depends upon obtaining Intelligence of the Enemys motions, I do most earnestly entreat you and Genl Clinton to exert yourselves to accomplish this most desireable end. leave no stone unturn'd, nor do not stick at expence to bring this to pass, as I never was more uneasy than on Acct of my want of knowledge on this Score.

Keep besides this precaution, constant lookouts (with good Glasses) on some commanding heights that looks well on to the other shore (& especially into the Bays, where Boats can be concealed) that they may observe more particularly in the Evening if there be any uncommon movements—much will depend upon early Intelligence, & meeting the Enemy before they can Intrench. I should much approve of small harrassing Parties, stealing as it were, over in the Night, as they might keep the Enemy alarm'd & more than probably bring off a Prisoner from whom some valuable Intelligenc[e] may be obtain'd.

Your Command lays in the two Brigades of Mifflin and Clinton, from whom let me have, & without delay, exact returns— as far as you find it convenient to advance any of those Men so far your authority extends.

Let me entreat your particular attention to the Stores &ca sent up to the Posts above. I am Dr Sir Yr Most Obedt Servt

Go: Washington

ALS, ViU.

To Brigadier General Hugh Mercer

Dr Sir   New York Septr 5. 1776

I have been favoured with your Two Letters of the 3 Instt and observe what you have done in consequence of my Instructions. When I wrote for Troops to be sent to the post opposite Mount Washington, I did not Immagine you would have so many to spare[1]—About a Thousand under Genl Ewen [Ewing] in addition to those already at the post, I think will be fully competent to Its defence & such works as may be necessary to erect, & will also be sufficient to carry them on. More I conceive will be unnecessary & may be better employed elsewhere. I am Dr Sir &c.

G.W.

P.S. You will be pleased to keep in view the matter I mentioned to you about Staten Island, Esteemg a Diversion there if It can be effected will be of great service.[2]

LB, in Robert Hanson Harrison's writing, DLC:GW; Varick transcript, DLC:GW.

1. See GW to Mercer, 3 September. Mercer's two letters to GW of that date have not been found.

2. For this proposed raid on Staten Island, see GW to Hancock, 2 Sept., and note 2.

From Jonathan Trumbull, Sr.

Sir   Lebanon [Conn.] Septemr 5th 1776

Since my last to You[1] I have received Intelligence that since our Troops retreated from the West End of Long Island the Militia have disbanded themselves, laid down their Arms, and are making their Submission to Genl How, and that all Ideas of Opposition *there* are at an End, two Companies of Continental Troops that were stationed there are arrived at Saybrook;[2] in this Situation we cannot hope to make a Diversion there to any purpose with what Force we can throw over. We can only assist such as chuse to retire from the Island in getting off their persons and Effects, which to the utmost of our power will be done.

I have now ordered such of the remaining Regiments of Militia in this State as can be spared from the immediate Defence of the Sea Coast to march towards New York with all Expedition, that they may be ready, if wanted, to join and support the Army under your Command, make a Diversion either on the Main or on Long-Island, or cover the Country, and if not necessary for any of these purposes, that they, or such part of them as shall be thot proper, may relieve, and take the places of an equal Number of the Militia of this State now in Service, whose Interest greatly suffers by their Absence, as well as the general Interest of the Country.

I have also ordered the Two Regiments of light Horse which did not before march with Colo. Seymour to march towards New York, and rendezvous at or near Westchester, where they are to attend your Orders, and perform such Duty as You shall prescribe either by scouring the Country, and preventing or suppressing any risings of our internal Enemies, in which Service it is apprehended they may be particularly usefull, or any other Duty they are capable of, or to join the Army, and act with them, if you shall judge it necessary and expedient.[3]

The critical Situation of Affairs at this Juncture, and the Information in your favour of the 24th Ulto that your Numbers were yet outdone by the Enemy, has induced me to order these Regiments on this Service, that Nothing may be wanting on our part to the Support and Defence of the Rights & Liberties of the rising States of America.

I have likewise taken the Liberty to propose to the General

Assembly of the Massachusetts Bay and Governor Cooke of Rhode Island, to send forward a part of their Militia, as may be most convenient for them, to join and assist the Army under Your Command.[4] I am informed by Governor Cooke that *they* have a Regiment there nearly raised, and that the state of Rhode Island is ready to co-operate to the extent of their power in every Measure necessary for our common Defence.

I have it likewise in Contemplation, if practicable to procure a sufficient naval Force to clear the Sound of the Enemys Ships now in it, and have proposed the Matter to Governor Cooke, and requested of him to join their Force with ours, and ask the Concurrence of Commodore Hopkins with such part of the Continental Fleet as are ready & capable to act. I beg leave to ask your Opinion whether a plan of this Nature be practicable and usefull, and in Case it should be attempted whether a Number of Seamen may not be draughted from the Army to assist in the Enterprize.[5] I am, Sir, with every Sentiment of Respect and Esteem Your obedient humble Servant

Jonth; Trumbull

ALS, DLC:GW; LB, Ct: Trumbull Papers.

1. See Trumbull to GW, 2 September.

2. For the retreat of Lt. Col. Henry Beekman Livingston's Continental detachment from Long Island on 2 Sept., see Livingston to GW, 11 September.

3. On this date the Connecticut council of safety directed all of the light horse stationed east of the Connecticut River to march to Westchester, and the next day it ordered nine regiments of militia to join the light horse there (see Hinman, *Historical Collection*, 384–85). Maj. Ebenezer Backus commanded these light-horse reinforcements, which consisted of the 2d and 4th regiments, and on 10 Sept. the council appointed Gurdon Saltonstall brigadier general of the new militia reinforcements (see ibid., 386). Trumbull introduced each of these commanders to GW in separate brief letters of 11 Sept. (Ct: Trumbull Papers).

4. See Trumbull to the Massachusetts General Court, 6 Sept., in Force, *American Archives*, 5th ser., 2:205–6, and Trumbull to Cooke, 5 Sept., in "R.I. Revolutionary Correspondence," 6:169–70.

5. Trumbull discusses his plan to clear Long Island Sound in his letter to Cooke of 5 Sept., ibid.

From Abraham Yates, Jr.

In Convention of the Representatives of the State
Sir   of New York—Fish Kill, Septr 5th 1776

I am directed by the Convention of this State to transmit to your Excellency a Copy of a Resolution which they entreat may be carried into Execution with all possible Dispatch.[1]

It is with Extreme Concern that we find ourselves under the disagreable necessity of having recourse to this unhappy but necessary expedient or of troubling your Excellency with a Commission of this Nature—But the critical Situation of this State, the total want of Brass Field pieces, and our inability to have this Resolve executed by the City of New York,[2] on account of their absence from the City, reduces us to the present Dilemma, either of adopting this Measure—or of neglecting the public Safety.

They therefore trust that your Excellency's Zeal for the public Service will induce you to pardon the Liberty they take of troubling you on this Occasion. I have the Honor to be with great respect your Excellency's obedient humble Servant

By order
Abm Yates Junr President

LS, DLC:GW. The draft of this letter that the committee of safety approved late this afternoon contains only a few minor variations in wording (see *N.Y. Prov. Congress Journals*, 1:611; see also note 2).

1. The convention's resolution of this date authorizes and requests GW "to cause all the Bells in the different Churches and public Edifices in the City of New York to be taken down, and removed to New Ark in New Jersey, with all possible Dispatch, that the Fortune of War may not throw the Same into the Hands of our Enemy, and deprive this State, at this critical period, of that necessary tho' unfortunate resource for Supplying our want of Cannon" (DLC:GW; see also *N.Y. Prov. Congress Journals*, 1:610).

2. The draft reads: "and our inability to have this resolve executed by the committee of the city of New-York" (ibid., 611).

General Orders

Head Quarters, New York, sept: 6th 1776.
Parole Pitt.   Countersign Camden.

David Henly Esqr: is appointed Depy Adjt General until further orders, and is immediately to repair to General Spencer's division to regulate the several Returns and do the other duties of said office, extending his care to the division under Genl Heath. he is to be obeyed and respected accordingly.

Col. Glover, Commandant of Genl Clinton's Brigade, is to recommend a suitable, active officer, for Major of Brigade, in Major Henly's stead.

The General expects the Majors of Brigade, to be very active and careful, to get their Brigades in the best order; to bring on their Guards and Fatigue Parties early; see the proper reliefs marched off; Returns made, and to march with the Brigade to the Alarm Posts, as frequently as possible—The Adjutants being under their particular direction, they are to see that they do their duty and put them in Arrest where they fail in it.

The Majors of Brigade and Adjutants are reminded, that the returns are all expected in to morrow, both regimental and brigade, in order to complete the General Return. Any one who fails will be noticed in public orders.

The General is resolved to put a stop to plundering, and converting either public, or private property, to their own use when taken off, or found by any soldiers—He therefore calls upon all the officers, to exert themselves against it, and if the Colonels, or other officers of Regiments see, or know, of any Horses, Furniture, Merchandize, or such other Property, in the hands of any officer or soldier; and do not immediately take hold of it, giving immediate notice of it to the Brigadier General; such Officer will be deemed a party, brought to a Court Martial, and broke with Infamy: For let it ever be remembered, that no plundering Army was ever a successful one.

Varick transcript, DLC:GW; Df, in Joseph Reed's writing, DNA: RG 93, Orderly Books, vol. 15. The two passwords in the draft are not in Reed's writing.

From Nicholas Cooke

Sir,   Providence September 6th 1776.

The Necessity which caused the unexpected Evacuation of Long-Island hath alarmed the General Assembly of this State, as it seems that Communications cannot be kept open with an Island where the Enemy's Ships can approach. This hath filled us with Apprehensions for the Town of Newport and the Island of Rhode-Island, which are of so great Importance to this and the other United States. Upon which the Assembly have thought proper to appoint John Collins, Joshua Babcock, and Joseph Stanton Esquires a Committee to wait upon your Excellency, to acquaint you with the State of this Government, and to confer with you upon the best Measures to be taken for its Defence, and with Respect to the Island of Rhode Island. I beg the Favour of your Excellency to treat them with the most entire Confidence, and have no Doubt but that the same Disposition which hath always induced you to manifest your Regard to this State will induce you to give us your best Advice and Assistance.[1]

Upon receiving Information of the landing of the Enemy upon Long-Island, and a Letter from Governor Trumbull acquainting us with your Request that a Body of Men might be thrown upon the East End of that Island, this State ordered the whole Brigade with the Two Gallies and a sufficient Quantity of Provisions and Ammunition to proceed to that Island, and ordered them to be replaced by the Militia of the State. We exerted ourselves to get them in Readiness, and some of them were under Orders to proceed, when we received the most uncertain and aggravated Accounts of the Evacuation of Long-Island, which occasioned us to stop the Men until we could receive Intelligence to be depended upon; which we did not gain until the last Evening.[2] I beg Leave to observe to your Excellency the Advantages that may accrue to the common Cause from the several States having early and authentick Intelligence of all Matters of Importance that shall happen, and to request your Excellency to favour us with Accounts of every Thing material. I have the Honor to be with every Sentiment of Esteem and Respect Sir Your Excellencys Most obedt humble Servant

Nichs Cooke

LS, DLC:GW; Df, R-Ar.

1. This recently appointed committee arrived at GW's headquarters on 13 Sept. and conferred with him during the next two days (see Bartlett, *R.I. Records,* 7:609; GW to Cooke, 17 Sept., and Joshua Babcock to Cooke, 21 Sept., in Force, *American Archives,* 5th ser., 2:442–43).

Joseph Stanton, Jr. (1739–1807), of Charlestown, R.I., represented Kings (later Washington) County in the general assembly almost continuously between 1768 and 1790, when he became a U.S. senator. A veteran of the French and Indian War, Stanton served as colonel of a state regiment from December 1776 to November 1777. In 1779 he was appointed a brigadier general of militia, and in 1788 he was promoted to major general. Stanton returned to the general assembly in 1794, and in 1801 he was elected to the U.S. Congress, where he served until his death.

2. On 2 Sept. the general assembly ordered the two regiments that composed the state garrison brigade to proceed with a detachment of artillery to Long Island "for the protection of the inhabitants and the stock" (Bartlett, *R.I. Records,* 7:606). For the subsequent orders given to these regiments, see William Bradford to GW, 14 September.

To John Hancock

Sir   New York Septr 6th 1776

I was last night honored with your favor of the 3d with sundry Resolutions of Congress, and perceiving It to be their Opinion and determination that no damage shall be done the City in case we are obliged to abandon It, I shall take every measure in my power to prevent It.

Since my Letter of the 4th nothing very material has occurred, unless It is that the Fleet seem to be drawing more together and all getting close in with Governor's Island. Their designs we can not learn, nor have we been able to procure the least information of late of any of their plans or Intended Operations.

As the Enemy's movements are very different from what we expected and from their large Encampments a considerable distance up the Sound, there is reason to beleive they Intend to make a landing above or below Kings bridge & thereby to hem in our Army and cut off the communication with the Country, I mean to call a Council of Genl Officers to day or to morrow & endeavour to digest and fix upon some regular and certain System of conduct to be pursued in order to baffle their efforts and counteract their Schemes, and also to determine on the expediency of evacuating or attempting to maintain the City and the Several posts on this Island—The result of their Opinion & deliberations I shall advise Congress of by the earliest Opportunity which will be by Express, having It not in my power to communicate any Intelligence by post as the Office is removed to so great a distance and entirely out of the way.

I have Inclosed a List of the Officers who are prisoners and from whom Letters have been received by a Flag. we know there are others not Included in the List.[1]

Genl Sullivan having Informed me that Genl Howe was willing that an exchange of him for Genl Prescot should take place, It will be proper to send Genl Prescot—immediately—that It may be effected.

As the Militia Regiments in all probability will be impatient to return and become pressing for their pay, I shall be glad of the direction of Congress, whether they are to receive It here or from the Conventions or Assemblies of the respective States to which they belong. On the One hand, the Settlemt of their Abstracts will be attended with trouble and difficulty—On the other they will go away much better satisfied and be more ready to give their aid in future, If they are paid before their departure.

Before I conclude, I must take the liberty of mentioning to Congress the great distress we are in for want of Money—Two Months pay, and more to some Battallions, is now due the Troops here without any thing in the Military chest to satisfie It. This occasions much disatisfaction and almost a general uneasiness. Not a day passes without complaints and the most Importunate and urgent demands on this head. As It may Injure the service greatly, and the want of a regular supply of Cash produce consequences of the most fatal tendency, I entreat the attention of Congress to this subject, and that we may be provided as soon as can be with a Sum equal to every present claim.[2]

I have wrote to Genl Howe proposing an Exchange of Genl McDonald for Lord Sterling and shall be extremely happy to obtain It as well as that of Genl Sullivan's for Genl Prescott,[3] being greatly in want of them and under the necessity of appointing protempore, Some of the Cols. to command Brigades.

I have the Honor to be with the highest respect Sir Yr Most Obedt Servt

Go: Washington

P.S. As Two Regiments from N. Carolina & 3 Regimts more from Virga are ordered here, If they could embark at Norfolk &c. and come up the Bay with Security, It would Expedite their arrival & prevent the Men from a Long Fatiguing March—This however should not be attempted If the Enemy have Vessels in the Bay and which might probably Intercept 'em.[4]

LS, in Robert Hanson Harrison's writing, DNA:PCC, item 152; LB, DLC:GW; copy, DNA:PCC, item 169; Varick transcript, DLC:GW. Congress read this letter on 9 Sept. and referred it to the Board of War (*JCC*, 5:747).

1. The list of prisoners was omitted from this letter by accident (see Hancock to GW, 8 Sept.). GW enclosed the list in his letter to Hancock of 11 Sept., but it has not been identified.

2. Congress responded to this request on 9 Sept. by resolving that "500,000 dollars be sent to the pay master general, for the use of the army at New York" (*JCC*, 5:747).

3. See GW to Howe, this date.

4. The LB reads: "If the Enemy have Vessels that could take them & that are in the Bay." For Congress's resolution of 3 Sept. concerning these reinforcements, see *JCC*, 5:733–74. The three Virginia regiments, which were commanded by Brig. Gen. Adam Stephen, sailed up the Chesapeake Bay later this month, but they were delayed on the Delaware River until late October when they again were ordered to join GW (see the Virginia Navy Board to Adam Stephen, 11 Sept., in Clark and Morgan, *Naval Documents*, 6:784, and Richard Peters to GW, 24 Oct.). On 16 Sept. Congress gave the North Carolina council of safety permission to delay the march of that state's two regiments (*JCC*, 5:762). No North Carolina troops joined GW until the following spring.

To Major General William Heath

Dear Sir   New York Sepr 6th 1776.

The present posture of our Affairs, the Season of the year, and many other reason's which might be urged, renders it indispensably necessary that some Systematic plan should be form'd, and, as far as possible pursued, by us—I therefore desire that immediately upon receipt of this Letter you will let Genls Mifflin & Clinton know that I desire to see them with you, at this place, (Head Quarters) at Eight Oclock to morrow Morning—Let them know (which may be done by shewing each of them this Letter) the business they are called together for, in order that their thoughts may be turnd as much as possible to the Subject.[1]

It might be well for neither of you to mention your coming hither (least, if the Enemy should have notice of the Generals being absent from their Posts some advantages might be taken of it) but it will be very proper to leave directions with the next Officers in Comd in case an Enemy should appear what they are to do that no confusion may arise. I am Dr Sir Yr Most Obedt

Go: Washington

P.S. Do not fail to bring exact returns of the two Brigades with you—and the two Jersey Regiments at Fort Washington. a perfect knowledge of our strength being indispensably necessary to the determining upon any Plan.

ALS, MHi: Heath Papers.

1. For an account of this council of war, see GW to Hancock, 8 September. See also Wilson, *Heath's Memoirs*, 68.

From Major General William Heath

Dear General   Kingsbridge Sept. 6th 1776

I have to acknowledge the Honor of the receipt of your favor of yesterday I was in Hopes this morning to have Given you Some fresh Intilligence, but have not yet Receiv⟨ed⟩ it but Still Expect it, as we have undoubtedly a Spy on the Island, Every necessary and Proper preparation having been made for that Purpose the Last night, and it is rather too Early in the morning as yet to receive our Expected Intilligence, General Clinton Went Down yesterday to Froggs Point and Posted the Light Horse (Ten in number) in the most Proper place, to act as Videtts,[1] the General took Two Compani⟨es⟩ Down with him with whom he Intended to make an Excursion on Long Island, but found one of the Ships Opposite to that Point, and a Small Encampment of the Enemy (Highlanders) on the Opposite Shore on the Point that forms Flushing Harbour above White Stone,[2] and at this Place he Could not obtain a Single Boat for the Purpose, He Sent one of the Company Back, the other to East Chester, from whence Colos. Nicolls & Dubois (two approved officers) were to Endeavour to Send a Party on to the Island the Last or this night, as should appear most advisiable The General while there was Informed, that an officer of Colo. Smith Regiment (and for whom he Left Orders to Come to this place if he could be found) had Come over from the Island the Day before and Said that the Enemy had Impressed 5 or 600 Teams in order to Convey their Flatt Bottomd Boats from Red Hook to New Town, and that he understood that the Day before the militia had been Called together to Know who would Engage for the King &c. but did not Know the Success This officer Stopt over in the Evening to get his Clothing & Returnd in the morng By others it has been Said that the Enemys Head Quarters are at Newtown,[3] The moment I receive further Intilligence it shall be Transmitted to your Excellency. I have the Honor to be with great respe[c]t your Excellencys most Humble Servt

W. Heath

ADfS, MHi: Heath Papers.

1. Heath on 5 Sept. ordered a chain of vedettes and sentinels to be formed at Morrisania, Hunt's Point, and Throg's Point (see Wilson, *Heath's Memoirs*, 68).

2. Whitestone, Long Island, is on the East River a short distance east of College Point, which lies on the east side of Flushing Bay.

3. Newtown, Long Island, served as General Howe's headquarters beginning 31 Aug. (see Lydenberg, *Robertson Diaries*, 95).

From Major General William Heath

Dear General   Kingsbridge Sept. 6. 1776

Since Enclosing my other Letter I am informed that several Houses are left with large Quantities of valuable Furniture (in particular at Delancy's) which are in danger it is said of being plundered, there were also on that Farm about Ten Horses, more than half of which are already taken away—Such practices surely ought to be restrained—Wou'd it not be much better for the Quarter Master General, to take the Horses into his Custody, than to have them thus plundered away, I beg that there may be one General Order respecting this matter, as it will prevent such abuses as ought not to be practised, and puts a Stop to continual Complaints, I wish to know your Excellency's pleasure on this Account. I have the honor to be &c.

Wm Heath

ADfS, MHi: Heath Papers.

From Major General William Heath

King's Bridge Sepr 6th 1776.

Dear General   3 oClock P.M.

Colonels Nicoll DuBois & Drake[1] are just come in and give the following Information vizt That one Mr Cornwall of Cow Neck came over to Frogg's Point the last Night (Co[r]nwall is a stanch Friend to the Liberties of America, a Relation to Comfort Sands Auditor General of the State of New York) and says that he is a Soldier in the Militia of Cow Neck, under the Command of Capt. Stephen Thorn of that Place who held a Commission as Capt. of that Militia under the Governor of New York. That (he) Thorn waited upon General How to resign his Commission who told him that such as held Commissions under Government & resigned them would be severely punished, upon which he continues with his Company of Militia to guard the Coast at Cow Neck altho he appears to be friendly to our Cause, and allows all Persons to Land and pass without Mollestation.[2]

Co[r]nwall further says that the Enemys Main Body is at Bedford, that they have impressed from 1000 to 1500 Waggons & Carts to transport their Baggage Boats &ca—This Account is also confirmed by a Letter from one Mr Stephen Sands of Cow Neck to his Brother Richard Sands at New Rochelle both of whom are esteemed Friends to our Cause[3]—Co[r]nwall further adds that he heard Capt. Thorn say that the Enemy woud land in two Places between Hell Gate and Frogg's Point, one of which he supposed would be a feint Vizt that meant the latter Place— That the Militia was to be mustered To morrow to give an Opportunity for raising Recruits for the King who were to be commanded by Colo. Ludlow.[4]

Cornwall goes on to the Island again this Night—Capt. Thorns Company may be taken with the greatest Ease; but we fear that at present it would rather diserve the Cause.

Colonels Nicoll and Drake are returned to their Posts that not a Moment may be lost in this Important Business—We are also informed by the same Channel that one Kissam—a late Tory Member of the Assembly of this State is employed in distributing Royal Pardons to the Inhabitants of Long Island.[5] I have &ca

Wm Heath

ADfS, MHi: Heath Papers.

1. Although Joseph Drake of New Rochelle had resigned his commission as a colonel in the Westchester County militia on 24 July in a dispute over military precedence, he readily obeyed the New York committee of safety's resolution of 27 Aug. directing him to call out immediately "as many of the militia . . . as he shall think sufficient to watch the motions of the enemy's ships now in the Sound, and to prevent all communication with the disaffected inhabitants" (*N.Y. Prov. Congress Journals*, 1:593; see also ibid., 537, 556, 565, 597, 598).

2. Cow Neck, now called Manhasset Neck, is on the northwestern shore of Long Island between Manhasset Bay and Hempstead Harbor. James and Aspinwall Cornwell of Cow Neck served in Capt. Stephen Thorn's militia company during 1775 and signed the Queens County association in January 1776 (see Mather, *Refugees of 1776*, 1051). Aspinwall Cornwell served as an ensign in Capt. John Sand's Great Neck and Cow Neck militia company from October 1775 to March 1776 when he was promoted to second lieutenant (see O'Callaghan and Fernow, *N.Y. Documents*, 15:286). Stephen Thorn of Hempstead remained loyal to the British crown throughout the war. His property, including a 371–acre farm and two sloops, was confiscated by the state, and he settled in Nova Scotia after 1783 (Palmer, *Biographical Sketches of Loyalists*, 861).

Comfort Sands (1748–1834), a wealthy New York merchant who was building a house in New Rochelle, served in several provincial congresses and state assemblies and was state auditor general from 1776 to 1782. During much of the war Sands was a major provisions contractor for the Continental army. In 1782 Sands joined Walter Livingston, William Duer, and Daniel Parker in forming Sands, Livingston & Co., a firm that held a contract for provisioning West Point and the moving army. About the same time Sands began furnishing GW's household supplies. Sands's reluctance to cooperate in meeting the army's changing needs, however, soon led GW to seek new contracts (see GW to Robert Morris, 31 Oct., 1782, DLC:GW; see also Sands, Livingston, Duer, & Parker to Morris, 11 Sept. 1782, in Ferguson and Catanzariti, *Morris Papers*, 6:356–64).

3. Stephen and Richardson Sands were brothers of Comfort Sands. Richardson Sands (1754–1783), who lived in Philadelphia, was a partner in Comfort Sands & Co.

4. Gabriel George Ludlow (c.1736–1808), who commanded the Queens County militia at the beginning of the Revolutionary War, was arrested as a suspected Loyalist by order of the Continental Congress in January 1776 and was sent to Philadelphia (see *JCC*, 4:27–28, 114, and *N.Y. Prov. Congress Journals*, 1:289). Obtaining his release a short time later, Ludlow did not return to

Queens County until General Howe's army landed on Long Island in August, when he raised 700 men to reinforce Gen. William Erskine at Jamaica, New York. At this time Ludlow was recruiting a battalion for Gen. Oliver De Lancey's Loyalist brigade, and he subsequently commanded that battalion with rank of colonel until 1783. Ludlow's property, which included 144 acres on Long Island and 17,000 acres in Ulster County, was confiscated by the state during the war, and he subsequently settled at Carleton, New Brunswick (see Palmer, *Biographical Sketches of Loyalists*, 509–10).

5. Daniel Kissam (d. 1782) of Cow Neck was a judge of the court of common pleas for Queens County, and in 1774 he became a member of the county's committee of correspondence. As a member of the New York general assembly in 1775, Kissam voted against approval of the acts of the first Continental Congress, and in January 1776 he was among the suspected Long Island Loyalists arrested by order of Congress (*JCC*, 4:27–28, 114). Kissam's 330–acre Long Island farm was confiscated by the state later in the war.

To Major General William Howe

Sir.   Head Quarters New York, Sepr 6th 1776.

By a letter from Majr Genl Sullivan, while on Long Island, & which he acquainted me was wrote by your permission,[1] I was inform'd it would be agreable to exchange that gentleman for Majr Genl Prescott, & Brigadr Lord Stirling for any Brigadr of yours in our possession.

In consequence of this intelligence, I have wrote to Congress, requesting that Genl Prescott may be sent here, that this proposal may be carried into execution[.][2] We have no Brigadr of yrs a prisoner with us, except Genl McDonald taken in North Carolina, whom I am willing to exchange for Lord Stirling; & shall be glad to know your pleasure on the subject.[3] I have the honor to be Sir Yr Most Obed. Servt

G.W.

LB, in William Grayson's writing, DLC:GW; two copies, P.R.O., 30/55, Carleton Papers; Varick transcript, DLC:GW.

1. This letter has not been identified.

2. See GW to Hancock, this date. The copies in the P.R.O. read: "that this part of the Proposal may be carried into Execution."

3. For the defeat and capture of Brig. Gen. Donald McDonald at the Battle of Moore's Creek on 27 Feb. 1776, see Joseph Reed to GW, 23 Mar. 1776, and note 1.

To Jonathan Trumbull, Sr.

Sir   New York Septemr 6th 1776

I have been honored with your favor of the 31st ulto and am extremely obliged by the measures you are taking in consequence of my recommendatory letter. The exertions of Connecticut upon this, as well as every other occasion, do them great honor, and I hope will be attended with successful and happy consequences. In respect to the mode of conduct to be pursued by the Troops that go over to the Island, I cannot lay down any certain rule; it must be formed and governed by circumstances and the discretion of those who command them.

I should have done my self the honor of transmitting you an account of the engagement between a detachment of our Troops and the Enemy on Long Island on the 27th and of our retreat from thence, before now, had it not been for the multiplicity of business I have been involved in ever since, and being still engaged, I cannot enter upon a minute and particular detail of the affair—I shall only add, that we lost, in killed, prisoners & wounded, from 700 to a thousand men. Among the prisoners are General Sullivan & Lord Stirling. The enclosed list will shew you the names of many of the Officers that are prisoners.[1] The action was chiefly with Troops from Jersey, Pensylvania, the lower Counties and Maryland and Colo. Huntington's regiment. They suffered greatly, being attacked and overpowered by a number of the Enemy greatly superior to them—The Enemy's loss we have not been able to ascertain, but we have reason to believe it was considerable, as the engagement was warm and conducted with great resolution and bravery on the part of our Troops. During this engagement a deep column of the Enemy descending from the wood attempted an impression upon our Lines, but retreated immediately on the discharge of a Cannon and part of the Musquetry from the Line nearest to them. As the main body of the Enemy had encamped not far from our Lines and I had reason to believe they intended to force us from them by regular approaches which the nature of the ground favored extremely, and at the same time meant by the Ships of war to cut off the communication between the City and the Island, and by that means keep our Men divided and unable to oppose them any where, by the advice of the Genl Officers, on the night of the 29th I withdrew our Troops from thence without any loss of men and but of little baggage.[2] I have the honor to be very respectfully Sir Your most obedient Servant

Go: Washington

LB, Ct: Trumbull Papers; LB, DLC:GW; Varick transcript, DLC:GW.

1. This list has not been identified.

2. For fuller accounts of these events, see Robert Hanson Harrison to Hancock, 27 Aug., and the proceedings of the council of war, 29 August.

To Abraham Yates, Jr.

Sir   Head Quarters New York. Sept. 6th 1776.

I have now before me your letter of the 4th Instt inclosing the report against ordering out any more of the militia from the counties of Orange, Dutchess, West Chester or Ulster—The reasons alledged by the Commee, to whom this mattter was referred, are entirely satisfactory to me, and therefore I do not expect a compliance with that part of my letter which respects this matter. I have the honor &C.

G.W.

LB, in William Grayson's writing, DLC:GW; Varick transcript, DLC:GW. The New York committee of safety read this letter on 9 Sept., and it is printed in the *N.Y. Prov. Congress Journals*, 1:615. That text, which presumably was taken from the unfound receiver's copy, is nearly identical in the wording to the LB.

General Orders

Head Quarters, New York, sept: 7th 1776.

Parole Temple.   Countersign Liberty.

John Davis of Capt. Hamilton's Company of Artillery, tried by a Court Martial whereof Col. Malcom was President, was convicted of "Desertion" and sentenced to receive Thirty-nine lashes.

Levi Webster, of Capt. Hydes Company, Col. Wyllys's Regt, convicted by the same Court Martial of the same offence, sentenced to the same punishment.

The General approves the sentence, and orders them to be executed, on the regimental parade, at the usual hour in the morning.

A Court Martial, consisting of a Commandant of a brigade, two Colonels, two Lt Cols.—two Majors & six Captains to sit to morrow at Mrs Montagnie's to try Major Post of Col. Kacklien's Regt "For Cowardice, in running away from Long-Island when an Alarm was given of the approach of the enemy.["] The same Court Martial also to try John Spanzenberg Adjutant of the same regiment, for the same offence, and likewise Lieut. Peter Kacklein.[1]

Benjamin Stone appointed Quarter Master, William Adams appointed Pay Master; Nathaniel Webb Adjutant of Col. Durkee's Regiment. Daniel Tilden Esqr: to do duty as Captain 'till further orders.[2]

Richard Sill appointed Pay Master to Col. Tylers Regimt.[3]

Major Lee is desired to do the duty of Brigade Major in Major Henly's stead, 'till an appointment is made.

Varick transcript, DLC:GW; Df, in Joseph Reed's writing, DNA: RG 93, Orderly Books, vol. 15. In the draft the two passwords and the phrase concerning Lt. Peter Kachlein at the end of the fourth paragraph are not in Reed's writing.

1. Michael Probst was appointed major of Lt. Col. Peter Kachlein's regiment of Northampton County, Pa., associators on 17 July 1776, and John Spangenberg (c.1748–1824) was named the regiment's sergeant major on that same date. Peter Kachlein, Jr., a son of Lieutenant Colonel Kachlein, served as a second lieutenant in his father's regiment. For the verdicts on these defendents, see General Orders, 10 September. Probst became lieutenant colonel of the 3d Regiment of Northampton County militia by May 1777, and Spangenberg served on the frontier in 1781 as quartermaster of the county's 2d Regiment.

2. These appointments in Col. John Durkee's 20th Continental Regiment expired on 31 Dec. 1776. Benjamin Stone (d. 1820), of Atkinson, N.H., apparently had been a first lieutenant in Col. John Waldron's New Hampshire regiment at the siege of Boston during the previous winter. Stone was commissioned a captain in the 3d New Hampshire Regiment in November 1776 and served until May 1779. William Adams, who had been an ensign in the 6th Connecticut Regiment during 1775, was appointed a first lieutenant in the 20th Continental Regiment on 1 Jan. 1776. He became paymaster of the 4th Connecticut Regiment on 1 Jan. 1777 and received commissions as a second lieutenant in July 1777 and a first lieutenant in May 1779. Adams was transferred to the 1st Connecticut Regiment on 1 Jan. 1781, but the following 13 April he was cashiered for failing to join that regiment (see General Orders, that date). Nathaniel Webb (1737–1814) of Windham, Conn., had been adjutant of the 8th Connecticut Regiment before becoming a first lieutenant in the

20th Continental Regiment on 1 Jan. 1776. He was named a captain in the 4th Connecticut Regiment on 1 Jan. 1777 and retired on 1 Jan. 1781. Daniel Tilden (1743–1833) of Lebanon, Conn., who had been a first lieutenant in the 3d Connecticut Regiment during 1775, was a first lieutenant and adjutant in the 20th Continental Regiment from 1 Jan. 1776 until his promotion on this date. Tilden apparently served as a militia officer after 1776.

3. Richard Sill (1755–1790) of Lyme, Conn., previously had been quartermaster of Col. John Tyler's 10th Continental Regiment. Sill became paymaster of the 8th Connecticut Regiment on 1 Jan. 1777 and a first lieutenant in that regiment in December 1777. Transferred to the 1st Connecticut Regiment on 1 Jan. 1781, Sill was promoted to captain the following April, and in September 1781 he became an aide-de-camp to Lord Stirling. After Stirling's death in January 1783, Sill returned to his regiment and served until the following June.

To John Hancock

Sir   New York Septr 7th 1776

This will be delivered you by Captn Martindale & Lieutt Turner who were taken last Fall in the Armed Brig Washington, & who with Mr Childs the 2d Lieutt have lately effected their escape from Hallifax.

Captn Martindale and these Two Officers have applied to me for pay from the 1st of January till this time, But not conceiving myself authorized to grant It, however reasonable It may be, as they were only engaged till the Last of Decemr at their instance I have mentioned the matter to Congress & submit their case to their consideration.[1] I have the Honor to be with profound respect Sir Your Most Obedt Servt

Go: Washington

LS, in Robert Hanson Harrison's writing, DNA:PCC, item 152; LB, DLC:GW; copy, DNA:PCC, item 169; Varick transcript, DLC:GW. Congress read this letter on 13 Sept. and referred it to the Board of War (*JCC,* 5:755).

1. For the capture of the *Washington* off Cape Ann on 4 Dec. 1775, see William Watson to GW, 30 Oct. 1775, n.3, and GW to Hancock, 14 Dec. 1775. On 11 Dec. the brig's officers and crew were put aboard a British warship bound to England (see Intelligence from Boston, 17 Dec., enclosed in Richard Dodge to GW, 16 Dec. 1776). Although threatened with trial as pirates, the prisoners were pardoned in England, and the following spring they sailed on another warship to Halifax to await exchange. On 19 June several prisoners, including Sion Martindale, Moses Turner, and James Childs, escaped from the Halifax jail. The three officers returned to Plymouth, Mass., where William

Watson informed them that their commissions had not been renewed and referred them to GW (see Clarke, *George Washington's Navy*, 184–85). In October
Congress granted the three officers a total of about $717 for expenses, pay,
and rations (see ibid., 186, and *JCC*, 5:758; 6:867, 883).

From Brigadier General Hugh Mercer

Sir,   Amboy [N.J.] 8 oClock A.M. 7th Sept. 1776
I have been confined two days by a fever which has not left
me—it is a great mortification that I have it not in my power to
attend at Head Quarters—it would however have been impossible for any Officers from this place to be in Time at New York—
By some Neglect of the Messenger your letter was not delivered
till 7 this morning.[1]

General Roberdeau waits on your Excelle[n]cy to know the
Result of your Determinations and to inform you of the State of
the Troops in the New Jerseys.

My Ideas of the operations for this Campaign are to prevent
the Enemy from executing their Plan of a Junction between the
Armies of Howe & Burgoin—on which the Expectations of the
King and Ministry are fixed.

We should keep N. York if possible—as the Acquiring of that
will give Eclat to the Arms of Britain—Afford the Soldiers good
Quarters—and furnish a Safe harbour for the fleet—If it even
could be retaind A month or two—keeping the feild so long in
this Climate may be supposd to affect the health of European
Troops very much. On the other hand a free and Safe Communication with the Countries from whence supplies of Men & Provisions can come to your Army is a consideration of superior
moment to any other.

How far both those objects may be within the compass of your
Excellencys Force I cannot pretend to judge—having a very inadequate knowledge of the particulars necessary to found an
Opinion upon. I have not seen Col. Rawlings but gave General
orders att all the Posts along the Jersey Shore—that the Troops
from Mary Land should proceed immediately to N. York.[2]

I hope to be able very soon to effect some enterprize on Staten
Island—when we have a Sufficient Number of men for the Flying Camp to dispose along the different Posts—but the Militia
are not the Men for such a Purpose—Four Colonels were with

me some Nights ago to inform that their men would fight the Enemy on this Side—but would not go over to Staten Island. I have the honour to be Sir Your Excellencys Most obed. Servt

Hugh Mercer

ALS, DLC:GW. GW replied to this letter on 8 September.

1. No letter requesting Mercer to attend the council of war held at headquarters on this date has been found. For an account of the council's decisions, see GW to Hancock, 8 September.

2. Moses Rawlings (1745–1809), who had joined Capt. Michael Cresap's Maryland rifle company as a lieutenant in June 1775 and had become captain of the company when Cresap died in October, was appointed lieutenant colonel of Col. Hugh Stephenson's Maryland and Virginia rifle regiment by Congress on 27 June 1776 (see *JCC*, 5:486). Stephenson having died in August, Rawlings marched the regiment north to New York during this month, and commanded it at Fort Washington, where he was wounded and captured when the fort fell to the British on 16 Nov. (see GW to Henry Laurens, 21 Aug. 1778, DNA:PCC, item 152). After being exchanged in December 1777, Rawlings "found his efforts to collect his regiment ineffectual and that he was drawing pay without doing duty; he therefore determined to resign which he did in June 1779" (Rawlings to the Continental Congress, 28 Nov. 1785, DNA:PCC, item 41; see also Rawlings to GW, August 1778, DNA:PCC, item 41, and 2 June 1779, DNA: RG 93, Manuscript File no. 20186). In September 1779 Rawlings was named commander of prisoners at Fort Frederick, Md., and he apparently served in that capacity until 1783.

Letter not found: from Robert Morris, 7 Sept. 1776. On 12 Sept. GW wrote to Morris: "I have been honored with your favr of the 7th Inst."

General Orders

Head Quarters, New York, sept: 8th 1776.
Parole Grayson.　　　　　　　　　Countersign Tilghman.

Alexander McIntire of Capt. Newall's Company,[1] James Butler of Capt: Dalley's Company[2] and John Knowlon of Capt. Maxwell's Company, all of Col. Prescotts Regiment tried by a Court Martial, whereof Col. Malcom was President, and acquitted of "plundering a Celler belonging to a Citzen of New-York"—each ordered to be discharged, and join their regiments.

Ames Reed Corporal in Capt. Vancleavers Company,[3] Regiment late Col. Johnson's, tried by the same Court Martial, and convicted of "Speaking disrespectfully and villifying the Commander in Chief"—sentenced to receive Thirty-nine Lashes, at different days successivly, thirteen each day, and reduced to the ranks.

John Lillie of Col. Knox's Regt of Artillery, Capt. Hamilton's Company, convicted by the same Court Martial of "Abusing Adjt Henly, and striking him"—ordered to receive Thirty-nine lashes in the same manner.

The General approves the above sentences and orders them to be put in execution at the usual time & place.

The General directs, that in future, in case of any Soldier detected in plundering, the Brigadier General, or Colonel, or commanding Officer of the regiment immediately call a Court Martial, and have the offenders tried and punished without delay.

Varick transcript, DLC:GW; Df, in Joseph Reed's writing, DNA: RG 93, Orderly Books, vol. 15. The two passwords in the draft are not in Reed's writing.

1. Jonathan Nowell (1747–1821) of York, District of Maine, served as a captain in Col. James Scammans's Massachusetts regiment before becoming a captain in Col. William Prescott's 7th Continental Regiment on 1 Jan. 1776.

2. No captain of this name served under Prescott. Butler apparently belonged to Capt. Samuel Darby's company.

3. Benjamin Van Cleve (Van Cleaf; 1747–1836) of Maidenhead, N.J., who previously had been a first lieutenant in the Hunterdon County militia, became a captain in Col. Philip Johnson's regiment of New Jersey militia levies in June 1776 and served until December. Colonel Johnson had been killed in the Battle of Long Island on 27 August. Van Cleve was promoted to major in the Hunterdon County militia on 15 Mar. 1777, and the following fall he commanded a temporary guard of one hundred men at the public stores at Trenton. Van Cleve resigned his commission on 13 Nov. 1777 to serve in the state assembly, to which he was elected frequently until 1805.

To Brigadier General James Clinton

Sir   New York 8th Sept. 1776

I have this day wrote to the President of the Convention of New York[1] requesting that an Aid of Six hundred Militia may be sent to you from the Counties of Ulster & Orange or any other that is more proper and convenient, for the purpose of assisting you either in the defence of the Highlands in Case they should be attacked or of constructing New Works and Fortifications, by which they may be rendered more secure. However whether you receive this Reinforcement or not I must intreat you in the strongest Manner to exert yourself to the utmost of your Abilities in making those two posts at the Highlands as defensible as possible. Their great Importance must be obvious to every person. I am Sir yr.

LB, in Tench Tilghman's writing, DLC:GW; Varick transcript, DLC:GW.
    1. See GW's first letter to Abraham Yates, Jr., of this date.

From Brigadier General James Clinton

Fort Montgomery [N.Y.]
May it Please Your Excellency   Septr 8th 1776
    Inclosed I Send you A Return of the Number of men at Each of the Fortifications in the Highlands And A Return of the Artillery Stores and Ordinance at Each place.[1]
    we are at Present Buissily Employed in Fortifying the Post on the South Side of the Pouplops Kill we have four twelve Pounders Mounted there and Expects Soon to have More[2] we are Likewise Employed in Building three Barracks Viz. one at Fort Constitution one at the South Side of the Said Kill and the other at Red Hook Near Peeks Kill A Post Ordered to be Fortified by the Provincial Congress where there is A Major and about 150 Men of my Brothers Brigade[3] we are very Much in want of the Barracks but we have no Nails to finish them I have Sent an Order to the Q. M. Genl for such Nails as we want and am in hopes he Can suply us.
    Our Men is but Indifferently Suplyed with Arms though I have taken what pains I Could to procure them and get them Repaired by the Armourers we have Near our Compliment if they were but good but many of those Sent here by the Different Committees and those taken from the Disafected persons in Dutchess County were as bad arms as ever I Seen and Can Never be Made Suitable for A Regt as their Bores are Small & Barrells thin & Weak But we are Determind to make them answer as well as we Can there was A Committee from Congress here a few Days Ago to Inspect our works and See what Necessaries were wanting for the Garrisons A Return of which I give them[4] Your Excellency will see by the Inclosed Returns that our

Fortifications is but Scarce of men in Case of an Attack. I am Your Excellencys Most Obedient Humble Servant

James Clinton Brigr General

ALS, MH: Sparks Collection.

1. These returns have not been identified, but for a report of the number of troops in the Hudson highlands at this time, see note 4.

2. This post on Popolopen Creek subsequently was named Fort Clinton (see George Clinton to GW, 23 July).

3. The fort that the provincial congress on 8 Aug. authorized to be constructed at Roa Hook near Peekskill was called Red Hook at this time and later became known as Fort Independence (see *N.Y. Prov. Congress Journals,* 1:563). Maj. Israel Thompson commanded the three companies stationed there (see Thompson to George Clinton, 20 Aug., in Hastings, *Clinton Papers,* 1:317–18).

4. The New York committee of safety on 2 Sept. appointed a committee of four members to visit forts Constitution and Montgomery in order to gain "a full and clear view of these important fortresses" (*N.Y. Prov. Congress Journals,* 1:604). Clinton informed the committee that there were 764 men in the Highlands, including 398 at Fort Montgomery and 216 at Fort Constitution (ibid., 1:613). After hearing the committee's report on 5 Sept., the convention resolved on 7 Sept. to reinforce the forts with 600 militia levies from Albany, Dutchess, Ulster, and Orange counties (ibid., 611, 613–14).

From Benjamin Franklin

Sir   Philada Sept. 8. 1776

The Congress having appointed Mr Adams, Mr Rutledge & my self, to meet Lord Howe, and hear what Propositions he may have to make, we purpose setting out to-morrow, and to be at Perth Amboy on Wednesday morning, as you will see by the enclosd, which you are requested immediately to forward to his Lordship;[1] and if an Answer comes to your hands, that you would send it to meet us at Amboy. What we have heard of the Badness of the Roads between that Place & New York, makes us wish to be spar'd that part of the Journey. With great Respect & Esteem, I have the honour to be, Sir, Your Excy's most obedt & most humble Servant

B. Franklin

ALS, CtY.

1. For the appointment of this committee, see GW to Hancock, 31 Aug., n.5, and Hancock to GW, this date, n.2. Franklin's enclosed letter to Lord Howe of this date informs Howe that the committee would be at Perth Amboy about nine o'clock in the morning on Wednesday 11 Sept. and requests him

to set a time and place for a meeting to discuss his peace proposals (see Willcox, *Franklin Papers,* 22:591–93). GW conveyed that letter to Howe with a brief
covering letter on 9 Sept., and the next day Howe replied to GW, asking him
to forward his answer to Franklin, in which he says that he would meet the
committee on 11 Sept. "at the house on Staten Island opposite to Amboy, as
early as the few conveniencies for travelling by land on Staten Island will
admit" (see GW to Howe, 9 Sept., and Howe to GW, 10 Sept., both in DLC:GW,
and Howe to Franklin, 10 Sept., in Willcox, *Franklin Papers,* 22:597–98). For
the results of the meeting, see Edward Rutledge to GW, 11 September.

To John Hancock

Sir   New York Head Qrs Septr 8th 1776
    Since I had the honour of addressing you on the 6th Instt I
have called a Council of the General Officers in order to take a
full & comprehensive view of our situation & thereupon form
such a plan of future defence as may be immediately pursued &
subject to no other alteration than a change of Operations on
the Enemy's side may occasion. Before the Landing of the Enemy on Long Island, the point of Attack could not be known or
any satisfactory Judgemt formed of their Intentions—It might
be on Long Island—on Bergen, or directly on the City, this
made It necessary to be prepared for each and has occasiond an
expence of labour which now seems useless & is regretted by
those who form a Judgement from after knowledge: But I trust
men of discernment will think differently, and see that by such
works & preparations we have not only delayed the Operations
of the Campaign till It is too late to effect any capital Incursion
into the Country, but have drawn the Enemy's forces to one
point and obliged them to decline their plan, so as to enable us
to form our defence on some certainty. It is now extremely obvious from all Intelligence—from their movements, & every other
circumstance that having landed their whole Army on Long
Island, (except about 4,000 on Staten Island) they mean to inclose us on the Island of New York by taking post in our Rear,
while the Shipping effectually secure the Front; and thus either
by cutting off our Communication with the Country oblige us to
fight them on their own Terms or Surrender at discretion, or by
a Brilliant stroke endeavour to cut this Army in peices & secure
the collection of Arms & Stores which they will know we shall

not be able soon to replace. Having therefore their System unfolded to us, It became an important consideration how It could be most successfully opposed—On every side there is a choice of difficulties, & every measure on our part, (however painfull the reflection is from experience) to be formed with some apprehension that all our Troops will not do their duty. In deliberating on this great Question, it was impossible to forget that History—our own experience—the advice of our ablest Friends in Europe—The fears of the Enemy, and even the Declarations of Congress demonstrate that on our side the War should be defensive, It has been even called a War of posts, that we should on all occasions avoid a general Action or put anything to the risque unless compelled by a necessity into which we ought never to be drawn. The Arguments on which such a System was founded were deemed unanswerable & experience has given her sanction—With these views & being fully persuaded that It would be presumption to draw out our young Troops into open Ground against their superiors both in number and discipline, I have never spared the Spade & Pickax: I confess I have not found that readiness to defend even strong posts at all hazards which is necessary to derive the greatest benefit from them. The honour of making a brave defence does not seem to be a sufficient stimulus when the success is very doubtfull and the falling into the Enemy's hands probable: But I doubt not this will be gradually attained. We are now in a strong post but not an Impregnable one, nay acknowledged by every man of Judgement to be untenable unless the Enemy will make the Attack upon Lines when they can avoid It and their Movements Indicate that they mean to do so—To draw the whole Army together in order to arrange the defence proportionate to the extent of Lines & works would leave the Country open for an approach and put the fate of this Army and Its stores on the Hazard of making a successfull defence in the City or the issue of an Engagement out of It—On the other hand to abandon a City which has been by some deemed defensible and on whose Works much Labor has been bestowed has a tendency to dispirit the Troops and enfeeble our Cause: It has also been considered as the Key to the Northern Country, But as to that I am fully of opinion that the establishing of Strong posts at Mount Washington on the upper part of this Island and on the Jersey side opposite to It with the assistance of the Obstructions already made, & which may be improved in the Water, that not only the Navigation of Hudsons River but an easier & better communication may be more effectually secured between the Northern & Southern States. This I beleive every one acquainted with the situation of the Country will readily agree to, and will appear evident to those who have an Opportunity of recurring to good Maps. These and the many other consequences which will be involved in the determination of our next measure have given our minds full employ & led every One to form a Judgement as the various Objects presented themselves to his view. The post at Kingsbridge is naturally strong & is pretty well fortified, the Heights about It are commanding and might soon be made more so. These are Important Objects, and I have attended to them accordingly—I have also removed from the City All the Stores & Ammunition except what was absolutely necessary for Its defence and made every Other disposition that did not essentially interfere with that Object, carefully keeping in view untill It should be absolutely determined on full consideration, how far the City was to be defended at all events. In resolving points of such Importance many circumstances peculiar to our own Army also occur, being only provided for a Summers Campaign, their Cloaths, Shoes and Blankets will soon be unfit for the change of weather which we every day feel—At present we have not Tents for more than ⅔d, many of them old & worn out, but if we had a plentiful supply the season will not admit of continuing in them long—The Case of our Sick is also worthy of much consideration—their number by the returns forms at least ¼ of the Army. policy and Humanity require they should be made as comfortable as possible—With these and many other circumstances before them, the whole Council of Genl Officers met yesterday in order to adopt some Genl line of conduct to be pursued at this Important crisis.[1] I intended to have procured their separate Opinions on each point, but time would not admit, I was therefore Obliged to collect their sense more generally than I could have wished. All agreed the Town would not be tenable If the Enemy resolved to bombard & cannonade It—But the difficulty attending a removal operated so strongly, that a course was taken between abandoning It totally & concentring our whole strength for Its defence—Nor were some a little Influenced in their opinion to whom the determn of Congress was known, against an evacuation totally, as they were led to suspect Congress wished It to be maintained at every hazard—It was concluded to Arrange the Army under Three Divisions, 5000 to remain for the defence of the City, 9000 to Kingsbridge & Its dependancies as well to possess & secure those posts as to be ready to attack the Enemy who are moving Eastward on Long Island, If they should attempt to land on this side—The remainder to occupy the intermediate space & support either—That the Sick should be immediately removed to Orange Town, and Barracks prepared at Kingsbridge with all expedition to cover the Troops.[2]

There were some Genl Officers in whose Judgemt and opinion much confidence is to be reposed, that were for a total and immediate removal from the City, urging the great danger of One part of the Army being cut off before the other can support It, the Extremities being at least Sixteen miles apart—that our Army when collected is inferior to the Enemy's—that they can move with their whole force to any point of attack & consequently must succeed by weight of Numbers if they have only a part to oppose them—That by removing from hence we deprive the Enemy of the Advantage of their Ships which will make at least one half of the force to attack the Town—That we should keep the Enemy at Bay—put nothing to the hazard but at all events keep the Army together which may be recruited another Year, that the unspent Stores will also be preserved & in this case the heavy Artillery can also be secured[3]—But they were overruled by a Majority who thought for the present a part of our force might be kept here and attempt to maintain the City a while longer.

I am sensible a retreating Army is encircled with difficulties, that the declining an Engagemt subjects a General to reproach and that the Common cause may be affected by the discouragement It may throw over the minds of many. Nor am I insensible of the contrary Effects if a brilliant stroke could be made with any probability of Success, especially after our Loss upon Long Island—But when the Fate of America may be at Stake on the Issue, when the wisdom of Cooler moments & experienced men have decided that we should protract the War, if possible, I cannot think it safe or wise to adopt a different System when the Season for Action draws so near a Close—That the Enemy mean to winter in New York there can be no doubt—that with such an Armament they can drive us out is equally clear. The Congress having resolved that It should not be destroyed nothing seems to remain but to determine the time of their taking possession—It is our Interest & wish to prolong It as much as possible provided the delay does not affect our future measures.

The Militia of Connecticut is reduced from 8000 to less than 2,000 and in a few days will be merely nominal—The arrival of some Maryland troops &c. from the flying Camp has in a great degree supplied the loss of men, but the Ammunition they have carried away will be a loss sensibly felt—The impulse for going Home was so irresistable it answered no purpose to oppose It— tho I would not discharge, I have been obliged to acquiesce & It affords one more melancholy proof how delusive such dependencies are.

Inclosed I have the honor to transmit a Genl Return, the first I have been able to procure for some time—Also a report of Captn Newell from Our Works at Horn's Hook or Hell Gate[4]— their situation is extremely low and the Sound so very narrow that the Enemy have 'em much within their Command. I have the Honor to be with great respect Sir Yr Most Obed. Servt

Go: Washington

P.S. The Inclosed Informatn this minute came to Hand, I am in hopes we shall henceforth get regular Intelligence of the Enemies Movements.[5]

LS, in Robert Hanson Harrison's writing, DNA:PCC, item 152; LB, DLC:GW; copy, DNA:PCC, item 169; Varick transcript, DLC:GW. Congress read this letter on 10 Sept. and referred it to the Board of War (*JCC*, 5:748–49).

1. No record of the proceedings of this council of war has been found. The council did not include Gen. Hugh Mercer (see Mercer to GW, 7 Sept.).

2. Tench Tilghman wrote Q.M. Gen. Stephen Moylan on 9 Sept.: "His Excellency [GW] commands me to desire that you would without loss of time set about preparing a sufficient Quantity of Boards, Scantlin and every Material necessary for the Building of Barracks at Kings bridge and the posts thereabouts. His Reasons for pressing you to exert yourself at this time are, that the North River down which most of the Articles must come, is now entirely free from any Obstruction by the Enemy, but how long that may continue is uncertain. The Season advances fast, when it would be impossible for the Troops to

lay in Camp, even if they were all supplied with Tents and had a sufficient Stock of Blankets and other warm Cloathing, but you well know that in the Article of Tents, at least one third part of the Army are unprovided, and those that we have are worn and bad, as to bedding and other Cloaths they are in a manner destitute. We have every Reason to fear and suppose that the great naval Force of the Enemy will oblige us to quit this City whenever they please to make an Attack upon it. We must then depend upon Barracks for Shelter, and for that Reason his Excellency calls upon you and your Deputies to exert yourselves in the most strenuous Manner in collecting such a Stock of Wood for the Building and Brick or Stone and Lime for the Chimneys and Ovens as will enable you in a short time to provide comfortable Covering for the Men at the different posts" (DLC:GW).

3. Nathanael Greene was a prominent proponent of immediately evacuating the city. For further arguments on this point, see Greene to GW, 5 Sept.; Certain General Officers to GW, 11 Sept.; the proceedings of the council of war, 12 Sept., and Heath to GW, 13 Sept.; see also GW to Hancock, 11, 14 September.

4. The enclosed general return has not been identified. Capt. Eliphelet Newell's report to Col. Henry Knox, written at 9 A.M. on this date, concerns the British attempt to destroy the American redoubt at Horn's Hook. GW reinforced that post as the mainstay of the defense of Hell Gate after the Battle of Long Island (see General Orders, 30 Aug.), and the British began building a battery directly across the East River from the redoubt on 4 Sept. (see Mackenzie, *Diary*, 1:38, 40). "I wou'd inform you" Newell writes Knox on this date, "that the enemy has open'd two 3 gun Batterys & have At least 4 Royals [small mortars] & have very much damag'd two plat-forms & the breast-works are very much shatter'd they have also broke our Limbers they have sent a shott through one of our Large Carriage's one of Colo. Sergents Regt is kill'd & two or three wounded but we have none lost or wounded they continue to keep up a very severe Bombardment & Cannonade their Ordnance is 12 & 24 p[ounde]rs I shou'd think it nessesary that there should be carpenters sent here to repair platforms. . . . P.S. we can bring but two guns to bear upon them" (DNA:PCC, item 152). For other accounts of this action, see Mackenzie, *Diary*, 41–43, Tatum, *Serle's Journal*, 95, and George Clinton to Abraham Yates, Jr., this date, in Hastings, *Clinton Papers*, 1:338–42.

5. The enclosed letter that Col. Isaac Nicoll wrote General Heath on this date from New Rochelle reads: "We have sent one Samuel Hunt on Long Island a young Man I think will answer every purpose he is sent after it tis uncertain when he will return, but this Evening there is one Mr Sands to be Over, who can give us a particular Account, there is one Wm Tredwell and another person from Goshen in Orange County, the latter unknown to me crosst here 4 or 5 days ago Mr Tredwell is a Disaffected person & all his Friends live on long Island—I understand that his brothers are warmly engaged against us & I am well persuaded he will go thro' the whole of their Camps, he is expected over every hour, I have secured the Horses & intend to secure them, put them apart, & bring them, to you as soon as they cross— we will be able to get all we want from them—The News collected since I saw

you is that the main body of their Army is at New-Town, & Lord Howe [General Howe] keeps that as Head Quarters, that all the Waggons as far Eastward as they have been able to go, is presst & carried to New Town, and that every Horse fit for the Troops is presst & taken away from their proper Owners without any respect of Persons—They talk of raising three Regiments one to be a Regiment of Rangers, to be commanded by Major Rodgers [Robert Rogers], and if the People will not turn out Volunteers they will draft them—They had their Genl Muster yesterday, but raised no recruits on account of the Weather, At which meeting they agree'd to keep but Two Senteries on Cow Neck—one at long Point, and the other at Watch point which makes it safe to cross, It is said there is three Regiments at Flushing, One at Jamaica" (DNA:PCC, item 152).

William Treadwell (1747–1818), a physician and merchant from North Hempstead, Long Island, and Benjamin Ludlum of Goshen, N.Y., were examined by George Clinton on 13 Sept. and by a committee of the New York convention the next day (see Clinton to Abraham Yates, Jr., 13 Sept., in Hastings, *Clinton Papers*, 1:346, and *N.Y. Prov. Congress Journals*, 1:626). For their statement of 15 Sept. giving additional intelligence about British activities on Long Island, see Hastings, *Clinton Papers*, 1:347–48.

From John Hancock

Sir,   Philada Sepr 8th 1776. Sunday 6 OClock P.M.

I am this Minute honored with your Favour of the 6th Inst.; and am to acknowledge the Receipt of your several Favours to that Date.

The Congress, concurring with the Proposal of exchanging Generals Prescot & McDonald for Genls Sullivan & Stirling, have authorized the Board of War to send the two former to you for that Purpose, as soon as possible.[1]

In Consequence of the Message which Genl Sullivan delivered to Congress from Lord Howe, respecting a Conference with some of their Members, they have, after great Debate, been Induced to pass the first Resolution of the 5th of Sepr; and have since appointed three Gentlemen on that Business, as you will observe by a subsequent Resolution, to which, without any Comment, I beg Leave to refer you. But in Order to prevent similar Messages for the future, they have passed a Resolve directing the Mode in which all Applications shall hereafter be made, either to Congress, or the Commander in Chief of the Army, and to which only any Attention is to be paid. I beg Leave to refer you to the Resolve itself, as the future Rule of your Conduct with Respect to every such verbal Application, until it shall be altered, or you shall hear further from Congress on the Subject.[2]

The List of Officers, who are Prisoners with the Enemy, which you mention as enclosed in your Favour of the 6th, it is probable, was thro Hurry omitted, as it has not come to Hand.[3]

Before this reaches you, a Supply of Money will doubtless be arrived, it being now two Days since it was sent. Henceforth you will be more regularly supplied with that Article.

The Congress have ordered a large Stock of Cloth here to be immediately made up into Tents, and to be forwarded to you with all possible Dispatch. They have likewise ordered some Duck in the Eastern States be made into Tents & sent you.[4]

Tomorrow Morning I will lay your Letter before Congress and acquaint you immediately of the Result. Genl Sullivan went from here two Days ago. The Committee to wait on Lord Howe will set out tomorrow Morning for New-York.

The interesting State of our Affairs, and the Anxiety of Congress to hear from you as often as possible, will naturally suggest to you the Propriety of giving them all the Information in your Power, as often as your important Concerns will admit of it.

My most ardent and incessant Wishes attend you, that you may still rise superior to every Difficulty, and that your great & virtuous Ex[e]rtions on Behalf of your Country, may be crowned with that Success, which from the Supreme Being's Love of Justice, and the Righteousness of our Cause, in Conjunction with our own Endeavours, it is not irrational to expect.

I am to request you will direct Major Hausackre to repair to this City as soon as possible to take the Command of the German Battalion, of which he is appointed Colonel, being extremely wanted.[5] I have the the Honour to be with every Sentiment of Respect & Esteem Sir your most obed. & very hble Sert

John Hancock Presidt

LS, DLC:GW; LB, DNA:PCC, item 12A. The LB omits the last paragraph.

1. Hancock enclosed a copy of Congress's resolution of 4 Sept. approving this exchange (DLC:GW; see also *JCC*, 5:735), but he did not include the resolution of 5 Sept. ordering the Board of War to send Richard Prescott and Donald McDonald under escort to GW (see ibid., 736).

2. For a discussion of the background of these resolutions, see GW to Han-

cock, 31 Aug., n.5. The first enclosed resolution of 5 Sept. requests Sullivan to inform Lord Howe that "this Congress being the Representatives of the free and independant States of America, cannot, with Propriety, send any of its Members to confer with his Lordship in their private Characters; but, that ever desirous of establishing Peace on reasonable Terms, they will send a Committee of their Body to know whether he has any Authority to treat with Persons authorized by Congress for that Purpose, in Behalf of America; and what that Authority is, and to hear such Propositions as he shall think fit to make respecting the same." The second enclosed resolution of 5 Sept. directs Hancock to inform GW that "no Proposals for making Peace between Great Britain and the United States of America, ought to be received or attended to, unless the same be made in Writing, and addressed to the Representatives of the said States in Congress, or Persons authorized by them; And if Application be made to him by any of the Commanders of the British Forces on that Subject, that he inform them, that these United States, who entered into the War only for the Defence of their Lives and Liberties, will cheerfully agree to Peace on reasonable Terms, whenever such shall be proposed to them in Manner aforesaid." Congress appointed Benjamin Franklin, John Adams, and Edward Rutledge to the conference committee on 6 Sept. (DLC:GW; see also ibid., 737–38). On 7 Sept. Congress resolved to send copies of these resolutions to GW (see ibid., 743).

3. This list, which has not been identified, was enclosed in GW's letter to Hancock of 11 September.

4. Congress on 30 Aug. resolved that "the duck, in the hands of Mr. Green, at Rhode Island, be made up into tents, and forwarded, with all possible expedition" to GW. On that date Congress also ordered James Mease, commissary of Pennsylvania troops, to purchase all the linen in Philadelphia and have it made into tents as soon as possible (see ibid., 718–19). When Mease reported on 4 Sept. that the only suitable cloth he could find in the city was a parcel of light sailcloth in the hands of the marine committee, Congress ordered that committee to deliver it to him and directed the secret committee to request the Continental agents in the eastern states to purchase duck and "other cloth fit for tents" (ibid., 735).

5. Nicholas Haussegger (d. 1786), who emigrated to America from Hanover, Germany, about 1744, served as an officer in the French and Indian War before moving to Lebanon, Pa., in 1764. On 4 Jan. 1776 he was commissioned a major in the 4th Pennsylvania Regiment, and on 17 July Congress named him colonel of the German Regiment, which he commanded until he retired in the summer of 1778 (see ibid., 571, 734–35). Hancock also enclosed with this letter copies of Congress's resolutions of 6 Sept. appointing John Paul Shott a captain in the Continental army and 7 Sept. filling vacancies in the 2d Pennsylvania Regiment that resulted from Arthur St. Clair's recent promotion to brigadier general (DLC:GW; see also ibid., 740, 746).

To Major General William Heath

Dear Sir.   Head Quarters New York Sept. 8th 1776.
I have lately reciev'd information (on which I can in some measure rely) that it is impracticable for carriages to pass from Harlem point or any of the landing places contiguous to it, towards King's bridge any other way than along the public roads; I should therefore concieve it would be highly expedient to throw every impediment and obstruction in the ways leading from the above mentioned places as also in the roads leading from Morrissena & Delancy's mills, & indeed any other, which you concieve there is a probability of the enemy's making use of, in order to prevent or at least delay them in the conveyance of their artillery: In some places it may be necessary to fell trees across the roads; in others I would recommend deep pits to be dug; in short I must request you will have them broke up & destroy'd in such a manner as to render them utterly impassable; N.B. I mean those roads within your district leading from King's bridge down to the points on which it is suppos'd the enemy will land.[1] I am Sir Yr Most Obedt Servt

Go: Washington

P.S. As the money is now arrived, you will order to be delivered in all the pay abstracts for July & Augt.[2]

LS, in William Grayson's writing, MHi: Heath Papers; LB, DLC:GW; Varick transcript, DLC:GW. The LB does not include the postscript concerning pay abstracts.

1. Robert Hanson Harrison reiterated these instructions in a letter that he wrote to Heath on the evening of 9 Sept. (MHi: Heath Papers).

2. For Heath's previous request for payment of the troops, see his letter to GW of 3 September.

To Brigadier General Hugh Mercer

Sir   Head Quarters New York Sept. 8th 1776
I have received your letter by Genll Roberdeau of the 8th of Sept.,[1] and am sorry to hear of your indisposition, which however I hope will in a Short time be removed; There has nothing very material pass'd in this Quarter since you were here; still matters wear so critical an aspect, that I have determined to Call

over Colo. Ward's regiment from the post Opposite mount Washington; you will therefore be pleased to detatch so many of the Troops under your Command, as will make up this deficiency, & still keep Genll Ewings compliment of fifteen hundred men intire[2]—Notwithstanding this Assistance I shall still stand in need of two or three thousand men to reinforce the posts here, & am anxious for the Arrival of the Maryland & Virginia troops, which are on their march to this place; I shall be glad you will immediately inform me by Express, where they are, & when I may with Certainty expect them; I could wish they were pushd forward with all Possible Expedition; Genll Roberdeau will Communicate to you, the result of the Council, also any other thing material which are not mentioned in this letter. I am Sir Your Most Obbt Servant;

G.W.

P.S. I desire you will direct the Engineer to Expedite the Works (to the Utmost of his Abilities) which are necessary for the defence of Genll Ewings Post.

G.W.

LB, in Caleb Gibbs's writing, DLC:GW; Varick transcript, DLC:GW.

1. Mercer's letter is dated 7 September.

2. For the previous stationing of Gen. James Ewing's detachment at this fort, see GW to Mercer, 3, 5 September. Col. Andrew Ward's regiment subsequently was attached to the brigade commanded by Col. Paul Dudley Sargent (see General Orders, 18 Sept.).

From Major General Philip Schuyler

Dear General   Albany Septr 8th 1776

Yesterday I was honored with your two Favors of the 20th Ultimo and 4th Instant, the former Mr pallasier, the latter by Mr Allen.[1]

Mr Pallasier will leave this for Tyonderoga to Morrow Morning.

Notwithstanding the Retreat from Long Island, I am still in Hopes, that the Enemy will not be able to accomplish their Intentions, and that you will in the End reap those Laurels which you so highly merit.

General Gates in a Letter just received from him observes "that as the Fleet is large and mounts a great Number of Cannon and the Body of Troops here very considerable, it is immediately necessary that fifteen Tons of powder, ten of Lead with Flints and Cartridge paper in proportion should be sent to this post." I have taken the Liberty to transmit this Request directly to Congress, supposing that you would not be able to comply with it— Should I be mistaken and your Excellency be able to order up any of these Articles you will please to advise Congress thereof.[2]

By the inclosed papers your Excellency will percieve that we are threatned with an Enemy from the Westward—I have requested the Committee of this County to order the Militia to march—They have directed half of the whole Militia of the County immediately to move to Tryon County and I have requested General Gates to hold three Regiments in readiness to march.[3]

Colonel Dayton cannot be short of Salt provisions as he mentions, unless the Commissary at his post has made a false Return—He has had a constant Supply of fresh Meat since his last Return, Copy whereof I now inclose.[4]

Inclose an Account of what Boards have gone from here, by comparing that with the Account of what is received, the Quarter Master General will know what Number may be at peek's-Kill and on their Way down[5]—I shall order all to be sent that can be collected, but I fear they will be very inconsiderable as not many Boards have been sawed lately—My Mills that used to cut from forty to fifty thousand Boards of fourteen Feet long have not cut one this Year, as I was under a Necessity of sending my Oxen to the Army—That has been the Case with several others—Should you want Timber for the Buildings, I believe it might be procured here and sent down in Sloops.

Should you stand in Need of small Craft to convey Troops from one Quarter to the other they might be brought from Lake George, I believe fifty could be spared. I am Dr Sir with the greatest Esteem your Excellency's most obedient humble Servt

Ph: Schuyler

P.S. I have advised Congress of the Information given me by Colonel Dayton.[6]

LS, DLC:GW; LB, NN: Schuyler Papers.

1. GW's letter to Schuyler of 20 Aug. introduces Christophe Pélissier (b. 1728), a French Canadian whom Congress recently had made an engineer. "Presuming It will be more agreeable to him," GW writes, "and also more benificial to the States, to employ him in the Northern Department on the Works at Tyonderoga, those opposite & such Others as You may conceive Necessary to be erected, I have directed him to wait on You for that purpose & to put himself under Your Command" (LB, NN: Schuyler Papers). A native of Lyon, France, who had emigrated to Canada about 1752, Pélissier became director of an ironworks near Trois Rivières in 1767, and when American forces invaded Canada in late 1775, he enthusiastically supported them, supplying munitions and other stores for the attack on Quebec. Having accepted an American commission as colonel for the Trois Rivières district, Pélissier was obliged to leave Canada when the American army retreated in June 1776. On 20 July he petitioned Congress to provide him a means of supporting himself and assisting the American cause (see Pélissier to Congress, that date, DNA:PCC, item 78). Nine days later Congress appointed Pélissier an engineer with the rank of lieutenant colonel and sent him to GW (*JCC*, 5:615). Pélissier served at Ticonderoga as an assistant engineer under Col. Jeduthan Baldwin until late December when he returned to Congress to solicit promotion to chief engineer at Ticonderoga (see Schuyler to Hancock, 30 Dec. 1776–1 Jan. 1777, DNA:PCC, item 153). Congress referred his request to GW, who declined to act on it (see *JCC*, 7:60, and GW to Hancock, 5 Feb. 1777, DNA:PCC, item 152). Dissatisfied with that response, Pélissier sailed to Lyon by March 1777, and except for a brief visit to Canada in 1778, he remained in France until his death sometime before 1799 (see Schuyler to Hancock, 8 Mar. 1777, DNA:PCC, item 153, and Pélissier to Congress, no date, DNA:PCC, item 78).

2. For Gates's letter to Schuyler of 5 Sept., see Force, *American Archives*, 5th ser., 2:185–86. After receiving Schuyler's letter to Hancock of this date, Congress on 14 Sept. resolved to send 15,000 tons of powder, 20,000 flints, 10 tons of lead, and 100 reams of cartridge paper to Ticonderoga (see Schuyler to Hancock, 8 Sept., DNA:PCC, item 153, and *JCC*, 5:756, 758).

3. Schuyler enclosed a copy of Col. Elias Dayton's letter to him of 4 Sept. from Fort Schuyler covering a letter to Dayton of that date from Thomas Spencer at Oneida, who reported rumors of an impending Indian attack on the Mohawk Valley. Spencer had received word from Onondaga that 700 Indians at Oswego commanded by Walter Butler were planning to strike various settlements in the valley. Dayton also included another letter of 4 Sept. written by Spencer on behalf of the Onondaga chiefs requesting assistance from the Mohegan tribe in New England (DLC:GW). For Schuyler's letter to Gates of 7 Sept. concerning reinforcements for Tryon County, see Force, *American Archives*, 5th ser., 2:220. For the drafting of the Albany County militia, see the *Minutes of the Albany and Schenectady Committees*, 1:546–47.

4. Dayton writes in his letter to Schuyler of 4 Sept. that "we are pretty well supplied with Flour but scant of salt provision" (DLC:GW). The enclosed copy of Henry Glen's return of provisions at Fort Schuyler on 13 Aug. shows 180

barrels of pork, 226 barrels of flour, 23 head of cattle, and 467 soldiers victualed (DLC:GW).

5. GW forwarded this account, which has not been identified, to Q.M. Gen. Stephen Moylan (see GW to Schuyler, 12 Sept.).

6. See Schuyler to Hancock, this date, DNA:PCC, item 153.

To Abraham Yates, Jr.

Sir.   [New York, 8 September 1776]

I have just reciev'd the resolve of your Convention respecting the removal of the bells belonging to the different churches & public edifices in this City, to New ark in the Province of New-Jersey;[1] The measure I highly approve of, & shall accordingly have it carried into execution.

I have lately been coversing with Genl Clinton concerning the defence of the forts on the high lands, who agrees with me in sentiment, that the force already there, is by no means sufficient;[2] I should therefore concieve it would be greatly in advancement of the service, if you would cause a reinforcement of Militia amounting to about six hundred, to be sent there from the Counties of Ulster and Orange or any other that may be most proper & convenient; They may be usefully and importantly imploy'd, as well in the defence of the Highlands, in case they should be attacked, as in erecting new works and fortifications, by which they may be rendered more secure. I am Sir yr most Obed. Servt

G: Washington

LS, in William Grayson's writing, owned (1986) by Mr. Kenneth E. Goddard, Palos Verdes Estates, Calif.; LB, DLC:GW; Varick transcript, DLC:GW. Although the LS has no dateline, it is docketed "Sept. 8. 1776," and the LB and Varick transcript are dated 8 September. The New York committee of safety read this letter on 9 Sept., and the text of the LS is printed in the *N.Y. Prov. Congress Journals*, 1:616, with a dateline reading: "Head-Quarters, New-York, Septr. 8th, 1776."

1. For the New York convention's resolution of 5 Sept. on this subject, see Yates to GW, that date, and note 1.

2. See GW to James Clinton and James Clinton to GW, both this date.

To Abraham Yates, Jr.

Sir   New York 8th Sepr 1776

I wrote you this Morning by your Express, but forgot to mention[1] a Matter of Consequence. It being determined to remove our Sick to Orange Town, we shall want four large Albany Sloops for that purpose.[2] The fatigue of travelling that Distance by land, would not only be more than the Patients could bear, but we have full Employ for our Waggons in transporting Baggage, Tents &ca for the Troops from hence to our out posts. I must therefore beg the favor of your Honble Body to procure the above Number of Vessels and send them down with as much Dispatch as possible to this City. I am with Respect Yr most obt Servt.

P.S. I shall be glad to know by Return of the Express when I may probably expect the Sloops down. There are several now on the lower parts of the River with Boards perhaps you might engage them to come this way, which woud save time.

LB, in Tench Tilghman's writing, DLC:GW; Varick transcript, DLC:GW. The New York committee of safety read this letter on 9 Sept., and it is printed in the *N.Y. Prov. Congress Journals,* 1:616. That text, which presumably was taken from the unfound receiver's copy, is nearly identical in the wording to the LB.

1. The text in the *N.Y. Prov. Congress Journals* reads "omitted mentioning" (ibid.).

2. The decision to move the sick and wounded in the hospital at New York up the Hudson River to Orange Town (now Orangeburg), N.Y., had been made by the council of war of the previous day (see GW to Hancock, this date; see also John Morgan to GW, 12 Sept.).

General Orders

Head Quarters, New-York, sept: 9th 1776.

Parole Mifflin.   Countersign Putnam

Elias Matthew appointed Quarter Master to Tyler's regiment.[1]

Gardiner Carpenter appointed Pay Master to Colonel Huntington's regiment.[2]

The Colonels, or commanding officers of regiments, or Pay Masters where appointed, are immediately to prepare and send in, their Pay Abstracts, for the Months of July & August—The Pay Master will attend at his old Office at Mr Lispenard's on

Thursday and Friday to receive those of the division under General Putnam. A time and place will be appointed in General Orders to morrow to receive those of Genl Heath's & Spencer's divisions.[3]

Mr Adjutant Bradford, to do the duty of Brigade Major to Genl Nixons Brigade, during Major Box's illness.[4]

The Maryland Brigade being ordered to march, Genl Fellows's to supply 250 Men in their stead, 'till further Orders.[5]

The several Brigade Majors are required to have their men, on the Grand parade, at eight O'Clock, every Monday[6] precisely, or they will be publickly reprimanded. The late relief of the Guards is a Subject of general Complaint—No failure of duty in the Adjutant will execuse, unless the Adjutant is put in Arrest.

Varick transcript, DLC:GW; Df, in Joseph Reed's writing, DNA: RG 93, Orderly Books, vol. 15. The two passwords in the draft are not in Reed's writing.

1. Elias Mather of Connecticut served as quartermaster of Col. John Tyler's 10th Continental Regiment until 1 Jan. 1777, when he became quartermaster of the 6th Connecticut Regiment. Commissioned a second lieutenant in the 6th Connecticut Regiment on 15 Nov. 1778, Mather remained in the army until September 1780.

2. Gardner Carpenter (1749–1815) of Connecticut was paymaster of Col. Jedediah Huntington's 17th Continental Regiment until December 1776.

3. The following Thursday and Friday were 12 and 13 September. Times and places for receiving Heath's and Spencer's abstracts are given in General Orders, 11 September.

4. William Bradford, Jr. (1752–1811), of Bristol, R.I., a son of deputy governor William Bradford, was adjutant and a second lieutenant in Col. Daniel Hitchcock's 11th Continental Regiment. The younger Bradford was named a temporary aide-de-camp to Gen. Charles Lee on 29 Oct. 1776 (see General Orders, that date). In December 1776 he was appointed major of Col. Benjamin Tallman's Rhode Island state regiment (see Bartlett, *R.I. Records*, 8:64, 74), and in January 1777 he became major of Col. Henry Sherburne's Additional Continental Regiment, in which he served until he retired on 1 Jan. 1781 (see GW to Sherburne, 12 Jan 1777, RNHi).

5. At GW's request Robert Hanson Harrison wrote Heath at 8:15 P.M. on this date, informing him that "all the Mary land Troops that were here yesterday were ordered to march to day and Join the Troops at Kings Bridge & It's dependencies—Three Companies more arrived this Evening which are also ordered to march to Morrow Morning" (MHi: Heath Papers).

6. The draft reads "every M[o]rning." See also "Williams' Diary," 48:340.

From Major General William Heath

Dear General   Kingsbridge Sept. 9th 1776.

By Two Persons who Came from Long-Island this morning (who we have Employed for the purpose of Secret Intelligence) we are Informed That the Enemy are Encamped in three Divisions, One at Newtown which is Head Quarters, One at Flushing, and One at Jamaica The Hessians are at Newtown,[1] That 1500 waggons are Employed in Bringing aCross the Boats &c. That an Attack will Soon be made Some where East of Hell Gate, That Their advance Guards are no further than White Stone, Except a party of 25 Scotch men who are at Great Neck.

By another Person That Three Pilots are Gone to Pilot 30 Sail of Transports up the Sound, that these Pilots are the Same who lately Piloted the Ships and Brig, That Two attacks will be made, One at Harlem and the Other Eastward of that Place,[2] That if Capt. Thorn lately mentioned to your Excellency, has any Friendship for us, it is through Fear.[3]

That by the Best accounts General Wood[hu]ll is Dead of the wounds which He received after He was taken, I wish to have the Troops Designed by your Excellency for this Post Sent forward, that a proper Disposition may be made, I fear that this Important Post will be too Long neglected, it is undoubtedly the Key of the Island and altho mount Washington and its Environs should be Impregnable yet they never Can Secure the Communication to the Eastward and Northward it might be Done here. I have the Honor to be &c.

W. Heath

ADfS, MHi: Heath Papers.

1. For a detailed account of the deployment of the British and Hessian troops on Long Island at this time, see Mackenzie, *Diary,* 1:39–40.

2. At flood tide on the night of this date, the British brought these transports undetected through Hell Gate, and at daybreak on 10 Sept. two battalions of light infantry were ferried to Montresor's and Buchanan's islands, nearly opposite Harlem, where the British encountered virtually no Continental resistance (see ibid., 43; see also Tatum, *Serle's Journal,* 96).

3. For previous intelligence regarding Capt. Stephen Thorn, see Heath's third letter to GW of 6 September.

From Major General Philip Schuyler

Dear Sir   Albany September 9th 1776

At half after ten this Morning I received a Letter from General Gates, Copy whereof I inclose your Excellency.[1]

As it is most probable that the Enemy are attempting to cross the Lake, I have therefore thought it necessary to apply to the Neighbouring Counties of the New England States, and those of Ulster and Dutchess in this, to order their Militia to march up—As soon as they arrive I shall either move with what part may go to the Northward or with those to the Westward as may be most necessary—This can however only be determined by farther Intelligence from General Gates and Colo: Dayton which I momently expect to receive.

The Cartridge paper arrived here on the second Inst: was sent forward on the third and arrived at Fort George on the 5th at Night, and was probably forwarded from thence on the 6th.[2]

I am informed that the Army is in the greatest Distress for Medicines—As every Misfortune and Want they labour under is imputed to me, so is this—I am heartily tired of Abuse and was in Hopes that Congress would have ordered an Enquiry into my Conduct—I requested it most earnestly on the sixteenth of last Month, but have not yet been honored with an Answer—I will no longer suffer the public Odium, since I have it most amply in my power to justify myself, and shall therefore resign my Commission as soon as I return from Tyonderoga or Tryon County, of this I shall advise Congress that Orders may be given for a General Officer to reside in this place, without which the Service will suffer—But in doing this I shall never forget the Duty I owe to my Country, and if I can by Advice or any other Means promote the Weal of it, none will do it with more Alacrity.[3] I am Dr Sir with every Sentiment of Esteem and Respect Your Excellency's most obedient humble Servant

Ph: Schuyler

LS, DLC:GW; LB, NN: Schuyler Papers. Schuyler wrote similar letters to Hancock and the New York committee of safety on this date (see DNA:PCC, item 153, and *N.Y. Prov. Congress Journals,* 1:621–22).

1. The enclosed copy of Gates's letter to Schuyler of 6 Sept. contains an extract from the letter that Lt. Col. Thomas Hartley wrote to Gates earlier

on that date from Crown Point, reporting that "there has been a very heavy cannonading down the Lake all this Morning it is undoubtedly between our Fleet and the Enemy so that you may prepare accordingly—I have sent down a Boat just now to know more particularly" (DLC:GW). The firing proved to be a "small action at *Windmill-Point*." Unfavorable winds on Lake Champlain prevented Hartley from receiving accurate reports of it until 10 Sept. (see Hartley to Gates, 7, 8, 10 Sept., in Force, *American Archives*, 5th ser., 2:222–23, 251, 278).

2. In the enclosed letter from Gates to Schuyler of 6 Sept., Gates expresses great vexation at not receiving any musket cartridge paper at Ticonderoga (DLC:GW).

3. Schuyler's letter to Hancock of 16 Aug. is in DNA:PCC, item 170. Schuyler offered his resignation to Congress in a letter to Hancock of 14 Sept. (DNA:PCC, item 153; see also Schuyler to GW, 16 Sept.). For Congress's efforts to supply the northern department with medicines, see *JCC*, 5:622, 781, 812–13, 822–23.

To Jonathan Trumbull, Sr.

Sir   Head Quarters N. York Septemr 9th 1776

I have the honor of your favor of the 5th instant and am sorry to say that from the best information we have been able to obtain, the people on Long Island have, since our evacuation, gone generally over to the Enemy, and made such concessions as have been required: some through compulsion I suppose but more from inclination—As a diversion on the Island has been impracticable under these circumstances, I think you have done well in assisting the removal of the persons and effects of our Friends from thence.

I observe, with great pleasure, that you have ordered the remaining Regiments of Militia that can be spared from the immediate defence of the Sea Coast to march towards New-york with all expedition—I cannot sufficiently express my thanks, not only for your constant ready compliance with every request of mine, but for your own strenuous exertions and prudent forecast in ordering matters so, that your force has generally been collected and put in motion as soon as it has been demanded.

With respect to the Militia both Horse and Foot, I am of opinion that they will render us more service by rendezvousing at different places along the Sound in Westchester County and thereabouts, than by coming directly to this city—It will not only give the Enemy who are extending their Encampments up the

Island an idea of our force along the Coast, but if they should attempt a landing above Kingsbridge they will be in readiness to join our force about that place, the Horse particularly whose rapid motion enables them to be, in a short time, at any point of attack[1]—Besides, the difficulty of procuring Forrage upon this Island for any number of horses is an objection to their being stationed here. I fear the Militia, by leaving their homes suddenly, and in a manner unprepared for a long absence may have sustained some injury. To this cause I must, in a great measure, impute their impatience to return and the diminution of their number at this time to about two thousand. Their want of discipline, unwillingness, nay refusal[2] to submit to that order and regularity essential in all Armies, indulgences claimed and allowed them, infecting the rest of the Troops more or less, have been of pernicious tendency, and occasioned a good deal of confusion and disorder—But Sir, these things are not peculiar to those of any particular State. They are common to all Militia, and what must be generally expected. For men who have been free and never subject to restraint or any kind of controul, cannot be taught the necessity, or be brought to see the expediency of strict discipline in a day.

I highly approve of your plan and proposition for raising such a naval force as will be sufficient to clear the Sound of the Enemy's Ships of War. If Admiral Hopkins will join you, I should suppose it not only practicable but a matter of certainty, and if it can be effected many valuable and salutary consequences must result from it—As to draughting Seamen from the Continental Regiments it cannot be done, as their number have been reduced so low already by taking men from them for the Gallies, Boats and other purposes, that some of them have hardly any thing but the name: besides, I must depend chiefly upon them for a successful opposition to the Enemy. If it can be done out of the Militia I shall not have the least objection, and heartily wish the enterprize, whenever attempted, may be attended with all possible success.[3] The Enemy's Ships can receive no reinforcements but such as go round Long Island, as our works at Hellgate will prevent their sending any Ships that way. They are sensible of their importance, and yesterday opened two three Gun Batteries to effect their destruction, but as yet have not materially damaged them, and they must be maintained, if possible.

The more secrecy and dispatch that can be used in collecting the Naval Force, the more likely the enterprize will be to succeed. I have the Honor to be with very great Esteem Sir Your most obedient Servant

G. Washington

P.S. The nearer the Militia and Horse keep on the Sound towards Kingsbridge, the better, as they will be ready to oppose any landing of the Enemy and also to receive orders for reinforcing any Posts on this side in case of necessity.

LB, Ct: Trumbull Papers; LB, DLC:GW; Varick transcript, DLC:GW.

1. Robert Hanson Harrison informed General Heath of this arrangement in a letter written at 8:15 P.M. on this date. Heath was instructed to inquire if any of the Connecticut militia or horsemen were "in West Chester or any where near Kings bridge & take such measures for regulating their Motions & conduct as may be most serviceable & beneficial and most likely to give the speediest aid In case of an Attack" (MHi: Heath Papers).

2. The LB in DLC:GW reads: "I may add refusal."

3. The LB in DLC:GW includes here the sentence: "Secresy & dispatch will be most likely to give It a happy Issue." The similar sentence in the next paragraph is omitted in that document.

From Abraham Yates, Jr.

Sir   Fishkill [N.Y.] Sepr 9th 1776.

Your Excellency's letters of the 8th instant this moment arrived, and we are happy to inform you that the Resolutions inclosed have anticipated your Excellency's recommendation relative to a reinforcement for the fortresses in the highlands,[1] and although we have done every thing in our power to raise them with dispatch, we are apprehensive that the whole will not arrive there within less than fourteen days, and that all this week will elapse before any of them will be got at the post.

The vessels for the sick shall be procured as soon as possible and sent to the City of Newyork; for which purpose, we have directed every vessel[2] down the river to be impressed, until the number required is procured, and ordered two others from Fishkill landing, lest the vessels might be small and four of them insufficient; their dispatch will depend upon wind and weather; we suppose however, they may be down by Wednesday and

Thursday next.[3] I have the honour to be with the greatest respect Your Excellency's most obedient & humble servant

By Order

Abm Yates Junr President

LS, DLC:GW. The draft of this letter that the New York committee of safety approved earlier on this date contains only a few minor variations in wording (see *N.Y. Prov. Congress Journals,* 1:616; see also note 2).

1. In the enclosed resolutions of 7 Sept., the New York convention authorizes the sending of 600 militia reinforcements to forts Constitution and Montgomery and various tools and ordnance stores to Fort Montgomery (DLC:GW; see also *N.Y. Prov. Congress Journals,* 1:613–14).

2. The printed draft reads "every empty vessel."

3. In response to GW's second letter to Yates of 8 Sept., the committee of safety on this date directed Gen. James Clinton "to despatch a whale boat well armed, with a proper officer, early to-morrow morning, to proceed towards New-York, with orders to impress four of the first large convenient sloops they may meet with" and send them to the city to remove the sick to Orange Town. John Moore, a member of the convention, was authorized at the same time to impress two sloops in the vicinity of Fishkill landing for the same purpose (ibid., 616–17). The following Wednesday and Thursday were 11 and 12 September.

General Orders

Head Quarters, New-York, sept: 10th 1776.

Parole Marblehead.   Countersign Orange.

Major Popst of Col. Kackleins Battalion having been tried by a Court Martial whereof Col. Silliman was President on a charge of "Cowardice and shamefully abandoning his post on Long-Island the 28th of August"; is acquitted of Cowardice but convicted of Misbehaviour in the other instance—he is therefore sentenced to be dismissed the Army as totally unqualified to hold a Military Commission.

Adjutant Spangenburg and Lieut: Kacklein tried for the same Offence were acquitted. The General approves the sentence as to Spangenburg and Kacklein, and orders them to join their regiment: But as there is reason to believe farther Evidence can soon be obtained with respect to the Major—he is to continue under Arrest 'till they can attend.[1]

The Brigade Major of the day, to carry the Parole and Countersign, to the several Guards, as formerly; taking care that it be done early.

The Brigade Majors are directed to have the several regiments join in Brigade as often as possible, and to be very careful that they are thoroughly acquainted with their Alarm-posts and the Lines they are to mann.

The General observes with great concern, that too little care is taken, to prevent the men straggling from their quarters, and encampments, so that in case of a sudden Attack, it will be difficult to collect them; he therefore most anxiously desires, both Officers and Men, would attend to it, and consider, how much their safety, and success depends upon their being at hand, when wanted—The order for calling the Roll three times a day, is to be punctually obeyed, and any officer omitting it, will be brought to a Court-Martial.[2]

Great Complaints are made of the Adjutants, as being irregular and remiss in duty—The General informs them, that he expects an alacrity and dispatch of business, equal to the importance of their situation, and will certainly make some examples, if (which he sincerely hopes may not be the case) there should be any farther reason for complaint.

The Court Martial to sit to morrow, for the trial of Capt. Rapaljee, confined by Col. Lasher, for refusing to do duty.[3]

Major Scammell is appointed a temporary Assistant, to the Adjutant General, and is to repair to Genl Heath's division[4]— He is to be obeyed and respected accordingly.

Varick transcript, DLC:GW; Df, in Joseph Reed's writing, DNA: RG 93, Orderly Books, vol. 15. The two passwords in the draft are not in Reed's writing.

1. Major Probst apparently was exonerated because by the spring of 1777 he was lieutenant colonel of a Northampton County, Pa., militia regiment.

2. For this order, see General Orders, 4 Sept., n.2.

3. Jacques Rapalje (Rapelje) of Long Island was named a captain of militia levies by the Kings County committee of safety on 19 June 1776, and he received his commission from the New York provincial congress eight days later (see Force, *American Archives*, 4th ser., 6:974, and *N.Y. Prov. Congress Journals*, 1:508). The charge made against Rapalje by his regimental commander, Col. John Lasher, apparently was not proven, and later this month he was captured by the British (see Force, *American Archives*, 5th ser., 2:875).

4. Adj. Gen. Joseph Reed wrote General Heath on this date that "the great extent of the army, and the confusion consequent thereupon, for want of a sufficient number of experienced officers, has induced the General to appoint Major *Henley* Deputy Adjutant-General, and Major *Scammel* as assistant to me in my department" (ibid., 275).

From Brigadier General James Clinton

Fort Montgomery [N.Y.]

May it Please your Excellency   septr 10th 1776

Yours of the 8th of this Inst. I just Receiv'd and am Glad to hear your Excellency has Ordered a Reinforcement of Six hundred men which I hope will be Sufficient and are as Many as we Can find Barrack room for if the three Barracks were finish'd that I have Order'd to be built. I hope the Quarter Master General can supply me with the Nails—Agreeable to an Order sent him, and if not already sent, he may send them with one of the four sloops that goes Down to bring the sick from the Hospital in New-York to Orange Town.

We are as busy in fortifying these Garrisons with the other Posts as fast [as] Possible and order all the Garrison out every Day both offrs & Soldrs, Except those on Guards and the Sick, & a very few number of Cooks, and those Detach'd in the Artillery who are employd daily in makeing Cartriges, &c. and learning the Artillery Exercise, for which I have as yet exempt'd them from any other kind of Duty In order to encourage them to learn.

I have likewise Recd two Letters this Day from Congress Copies of them you have Inclos'd[1]—I have Just now Stopt Capt. Dirck Schuylers Sloop from Albany, and Sent her Down to New-York to Remove the Sick to Orange-Town—I have Orderd Lieutt Henry Pawling, of the 2nd New-York Regmnt, to proceed Down the River with a Whale-Boat and 11 Men, to Press the first Three Good Sloops that he Meets wt., for the Same Purpose.[2] I am Your Excellency's Most Obedt Humble Servt

James Clinton B. Genl

LS, DLC:GW.

1. The New York committee of safety drafted a letter to Clinton on 9 Sept. informing him of its resolution to send 600 militia to reinforce the Highlands and requesting him to send an officer down the Hudson River to impress four sloops for removing the sick from New York City to Orange Town (see *N.Y. Prov. Congress Journals*, 1:616–17). The second document apparently was the impress warrant of that date (ibid., 617).

2. Henry Pawling (1752–1836) became a first lieutenant in Col. Lewis Du-boys's 5th New York Regiment on 21 Nov. 1776. He was captured at Fort Montgomery on 6 Oct. 1777 and remained a prisoner for nearly three years before rejoining his regiment (see officer's petition to George Clinton, 24 May

1780, in Hastings, *Clinton Papers*, 5:750–52). Transferred to the 2d New York Regiment on 1 Jan. 1781, Pawling was promoted to captain in that regiment on 6 Nov. 1782 and served until the end of the war.

From Joshua Davis

Norwick [Conn.] Septr 10 1776

I tak liberty to Inform your Excy of my Safe arival Into Norwick last Evning, With two Sea Mortors after A long Detention in giting up the Sound by Reason Of the Enemy & Contarary Wind, altho I have Indavord to Mak all despach in my power, & from The best advice I Can git hear togather with my one [own] Judgment think it Not prudent to Com any farther By Warter Am Now making Preparation to Bring them by land, With all Possabel Expedition. Persuant to my orders from the Honrbl. Majr Ginerl Ward As I Expectd when I left boston to Com up to york By Warter not Knowing the Sound was blockd up Did not bring money to pay the Vessels pilots & Sundary Othe[r] Chargs that will arise if your Exelency Think proper, plas to order me one hunrd Pound, or if more, for which I mirst [must] give an Account, I hop to your Sattisfaction.[1] any orders your Exelency Shall be plasd to Send, Shall be Thankfully Recived & puntually obayd By your Most obedant huml. Sert

Josha Davis

P.S. Capt. Burbeck Compy with Earghtean of ginl Lees gard is with me which I belive will be Serfictiant help. The Rest of the troops I Shall Send forward.

Sene I Wrote the Above I understand thare is Danger On Som Part of the Road from this to Newyork As I find it Vary Difugalt to provid for one hunrd & thirty men Being out of provition I Send parte Forward, & Keek [keep] only What is Mentioned above only Serfitiant to hoist a mortor Submit thar farther Safty to yr Exely Better Judgment.

ALS, ViMtV; Sprague transcript, DLC:GW. Although Robert Hanson Harrison docketed the ALS, "Col. Joshua Davis's Letter 10 Sepr 1776 Ansd 12th," the reply of that date has not been found. The Sprague transcript does not include the postscripts.

1. Gen. Artemas Ward's aide-de-camp Joseph Ward wrote Davis on 18 Aug. directing him to "convey two Sea Mortars with their appertenances across the land from Sandwich to Buzzards Bay" and from thence by water to New York

(Clark and Morgan, *Naval Documents,* 6:222). Davis informed General Ward on 2 Sept. that he had arrived with the mortars at New London the previous day and was disappointed to learn that two British warships and two tenders recently had gone up Long Island Sound toward New York. "I am in Greait Consarn—But None Discurregd," Davis wrote Ward. "I am Now Waiting for a Wind am Deturmined to Push up the Sound as far as I Can With All Possabel Safty & Despach the Communecation being Intierly Cut of by Warter betwen this place & N. york. . . . In Som Way or annothe Will Persew the Matter untill I land the morters if possabel" (MHi: Artemas Ward Papers). On 12 Sept. GW issued a warrant for $333⅓ to pay Davis's expenses in bringing the mortars from Boston (warrant book no. 2, DLC:GW).

From John Hancock

Sir   Congress Chamber [Philadelphia] 10th Sepr 1776
    Your Letter of 8th Inst. is now under the Consideration of Congress; as soon as they have come to a Determination upon it the Result shall be transmitted you, in the mean time Congress being Apprehensive that their former Resolution of 3d Int was not rightly understood, have directed me to Send you the foregoing, by which you will perceive that their wish is to preserve N. York & leave the time of Evacuatg it to yor Judgment.[1] I beg leave to Refer you to the Resolve, not havg time to Add, but that I am, Sir your very hume set

John Hancock P⟨residt⟩

ALS, N: Signers Collection. Part of the signature is mutilated.
    1. Congress's resolution of 10 Sept. directs Hancock to inform GW that "it was by no means the Sense of Congress in their Resolve of the third instant respecting New York, that the Army or any part of it should Remain in that City a Moment longer than he shall think it proper for the publick Service that Troops be Continued there" (DLC:GW; see also *JCC,* 5:749).

From Major General William Heath

Kingsbridge Sept. 10th 1776
Dear General   half past 6 O'Clock P.M.
    I have just returned from Frog's Point, Hunt's point & Morrisania—I find the Enemy have been all this Day landing Troops on Montrosure's Island where there appears to be a very large Number of them & Senteries posted all round the Island.[1]
    In Addition to 150 Men sent down this morning near to

Hunt's point—I have this Evening ordered 200 as a Piquet to rendezvouz, at the Widow Morrises,[2] & have ordered General Clinton's Brigade to lie on their Arms, the Inclosed I received a few minutes ago, from Genl Clinton[3]—I think the Enemy mean to land soon, & that in Two or Three places—I think the Troops beyond this place vastly insufficient for the post as yet, but having once & again mentioned it, think that I have done my Duty, and am determined to make the best Defence in my power, if it should be with only One Thousand Men.[4] I have the honor to be With great Respect Your Excellency's Most humbl. Servt

Wm Heath

ADfS, MHi: Heath Papers.

1. In a letter of this date addressed "to General Heath or General Miflin," Gen. Alexander McDougall reports: "Early this morning about 1000 of the Enemy landed on montresours Island; and its probable many more will be landed there for the Conveniency of landing on the main, or to raise a Battery to facilitate their Landing at morisenia" (MHi: Heath Papers). British officer Frederick Mackenzie says in his diary entry for this date that "at daybreak the 1st and 2nd Battalions of Light Infantry embarked in flatboats . . . and landed on Montresor's and Buchannan's Islands, nearly opposite Haerlem. . . . There were not more than 20 Rebels on the Islands, who retired and made their escape as soon as they saw our people landed. The possession of these Islands facilitates the landing of the Army on York Island, and will protect the boats which may have occasion to pass through Hellgate, or come down from Flushing or Whitestone" (Mackenzie, *Diary*, 1:43).

2. Sarah Gouverneur Morris (c.1714–1786), widow of Lewis Morris, Jr., was the wealthy Loyalist owner of Morrisania and mother of Gouverneur Morris.

3. George Clinton wrote Heath from New Rochelle on this date, informing him that he had canceled a small expedition to Long Island the previous night because a British brig and three tenders "lay in a Line directly opposite to the Place we must have Landed. . . . The Brigg has now besides the Tenders four Sloops & as nearly as I can guess about twenty Boats, all which have been collected since ten o'clock this Morning; from the Number of Men seen on Board it is apprehended they intend to make an Expedition ag't this Shore this Evening." In a postscript Clinton adds: "This Moment the Brigg & other Vessells came under way with Boats in Tow & are standing up towards Troggs Point; their Number dont exceed 20" (Hastings, *Clinton Papers*, 1:343–45).

4. Robert Hanson Harrison replied to Heath on 11 Sept. that GW was "fully sensible that you are deficient in Men which is not only the case of your post but of every Other, and which he well knew would inevitably be the consequence, when It was determined that our defence should be divided and extended to so many Objects—This having been determined on, and the point of Attack uncertain, our attention must be had to every part where It is likely to fall—That you may be reinforced, his Excelly has Issued Orders for Colo.

[Andrew] Wards Regiment at Burdets Ferry immediately to cross and be under your direction—he also desires that you would send out & get Informn,
If you can of the Connectt Militia & Light Horse & give them orders to advance as fast as possible & take such Stations as you shall think most proper"
(MHi: Heath Papers).

From Jonathan Trumbull, Sr.

Sir   Lebanon [Conn.] Septemr 10th 1776
    When Your Excellency was pleased to request the Militia of
this State to be sent forward with all possible expedition to reinforce the Army at New York,[1] no time was lost to expedite their
march, and am happy to find the spirit and zeal that appeared
in the people of this State to yield every assistance in their power
in the present critical situation of our affairs. The season indeed
was most unfavorable for so many of our Farmers and Labourers to leave home. Many had not even secured their harvest.
The greater part had secured but a small part of their hay, and
the preparation for the crop of winters grain for the ensuing
year totally omitted; but they (the most of them) left all to afford
their help in protecting and defending their just rights and Liberties against the attempts of a numerous army sent to invade
them. The suddeness of the requisition, the haste and expedition required in the raising, equipping and marching such a
number of men after the large draughts before made on this
State engrossed all our time and attention. On such a sudden
demand of the Militia Your Excellency could not expect to find
them all compleatly officered with either Field, or Commission
Officers, when you consider that many of both were just before
engaged in the service in the eight Regiments we had so lately
raised—At that time the Assembly could not think it proper to
supply their places in the Militia by appointing other Officers in
the room and stead of those who only had left the Militia for a
few months service in the Army, then to return: beside, it cannot
be expected but on such a sudden call as this, many officers may
be sick, or at present unfit for service, or some necessary hindrance which may prevent their going forward at this time—
And if in these cases we had undertaken to appoint and commission Field Commission Officers and Subalterns in the room or
places of those absent or otherwise hindred, in a little time we

should soon have the greatest part of our Militia to become Officers: for when once formally appointed and commissioned they must remain, and the others in whose room they are appointed, when they return, would be out of the Militia, and totally useless; beside many other inconveniences which might follow; and as it is necessary that every Company be properly officered, at least in proportion to their numbers, and that those who do the duty of an officer in a particular rank, be considered and treated as an officer of the rank in which he does duty. To explain myself, A Colonelcy is vacant, the Lieutenant Colonel must act for the present Company as Colonel, the Major as Lieut. Colonel, the eldest Captain in the regiment as Major; & if a Captaincy is vacant the first Lieutenant and when they return they will of course be reduced to their former rank in the Militia at home to act as Capt. and so in succession—This is the only way I can possibly imagine to releive the difficulty—Our Militia set out with those ideas, they were encouraged by them, and we could conceive of no difficulty to the Public, either in point of expence or expediency, for the vacancy to be filled up in this way, and to do the duty, take the rank and receive the pay during the present service—This I am induced to suggest to Your Excellency, as I am informed a great uneasiness has arisen by means of those who had taken rank in the manner above proposed, and have been surprised and obliged to relinquish their claim. I can conceive of no possible method beside to supply and fill up these vacancies. Am persuaded it will be agreeable to this State and will be attended with the least inconveniences of any method which occurs, and will give great satisfaction to the Militia who have joined your Army, as well as those now going forward, and should be extremely sorry to have any damp on the spirits of so many who have in this critical time sacrificed their interest beyond most others on the present occasion—Therefore should be much obliged to Your Excellency, if no insuperable objections should arise, which at present do not occur to me, if orders might be given for our Militia to be filled up with officers proper to take rank in Succession in the respective Regiments, in manner as above proposed, for the present campaign, And am With the greatest respect and Esteem your Excellency's Most obedient humble Servant.

LB, Ct: Trumbull Papers.

1. See GW to Trumbull, 7 August.

General Orders

Head Quarters, New-York, sept. 11th 1776.
Parole Ulster.   Countersign Albany.

Robt Williams of Col. Glovers Regiment is appointed Pay Master to said regiment.[1]

William Arnold and Samuel Clark of Capt. Smith's Company,[2] Col. Smallwood's Regiment—Daniel Donovel of Capt. Hardenberg's Company,[3] tried by a Court Martial whereof Col. Malcom was President, on a charge of "plundering the House lately occupied by Lord Stirling"—Donovel was convicted of the crime and sentenced to receive Thirty-nine Lashes—the others acquitted—The General approves the sentence, orders the latter to join their regiments and Donovel to be whipp'd to morrow, on the Grand parade, before the Guards march off—The Provost Marshal to see it executed, Col. Ritzema's Regt being removed.

Peter Richards, Serjeant in the General's Guard convicted by the same Court Martial of "Abusing and striking Capt. Gibbs," sentenced to be reduced to the ranks, and whipped Thirty-nine Lashes.[4] The General approves the sentence, and orders it to be executed, to morrow morning, at the head of the company at eight o'Clock.

Col. Palfrey Pay Master will receive the Pay-Abstracts agreeable to yesterday's Orders of Genl Spencer's Division, at General McDougall's quarters, near Harlem on Saturday and Sunday— Of General Heath's division at his Head-Quarters at any time.[5]

The commanding Officers of Col. Silliman's, Col. Lewis, Coll Mead's and Col. Thompson's Regts to examine the state of the Ammunition of their regiments, it being reported that their men on Guard last night were deficient.

John Christy of Col. Humphrey's Regt convicted by a Court Martial whereof Col. Malcom was President of "Desertion"—ordered to receive Thirty-nine lashes—The General approves the sentence, and orders it to be executed, to morrow, at the usual time & place.

Such regiments whose Pay-Masters have not been named in General Orders, are by their Field Officers, immediately to recommend suitable persons, to the General, for that office—Every recommendation is to be signed by the Field Officers of the regiments who are present.

Varick transcript, DLC:GW; Df, in Joseph Reed's writing, DNA: RG 93, Orderly Books, vol. 15. The two passwords in the draft are not in Reed's writing.

1. Robert Williams (1753–1834), a native of Boston who had taught at the Roxbury Latin School after graduating from Harvard College in 1773, served as paymaster of Col. John Glover's 14th Continental Regiment until the end of 1776. Appointed an ensign in Col. William R. Lee's Additional Continental Regiment on 24 April 1777, Williams became paymaster of that regiment the following June. He transferred to Col. Henry Jackson's Additional Continental Regiment in April 1779 and continued serving under Jackson in the 9th Massachusetts Regiment during 1781 and 1782, the 4th Massachusetts during the first ten months of 1783, and Jackson's Continental regiment from November 1783 to June 1784. Williams was promoted to first lieutenant in April 1782.

2. Samuel Smith (1752–1839) served as a captain in Col. William Smallwood's Maryland regiment from 14 Jan. 1776 until his appointment as major of the 4th Maryland Regiment on 10 December. Promoted to lieutenant colonel on 22 Feb. 1777, Smith was wounded the following October during the defense of Fort Mifflin, for which Congress on 4 Nov. 1777 resolved to honor him with an "elegant sword" (*JCC*, 9:862). Smith resigned from the army in May 1779 and later became major general of the Maryland militia.

3. The draft reads: "Daniel Donovel of Capt. Hardenburgh's Compy Col. Ritzma's Regt John Andrews of Capt. Gilman's Company." Jeremiah Gilman commanded a company in Col. John Nixon's 4th Continental Regiment.

4. Peter Richards (d. 1781), who previously had been a sergeant in Col. Asa Whitcomb's 6th Continental Regiment, joined the commander in chief's guard on 12 Mar. 1776. Richards was reported to be "on command" with GW on 27 Nov. 1776 (see Godfrey, *Commander-in-Chief's Guard*, 238).

5. For the previous orders regarding Spencer's and Heath's pay abstracts, see General Orders, 9 September. The following Saturday and Sunday were 14 and 15 September.

Letter not found: to the Continental Congress Committee of Conference or Edward Rutledge, 11 Sept. 1776. In a letter of this date to GW, Rutledge, who was a member of the committee, refers to "your Favour of this Morning."

Letter not found: from the Continental Congress Committee of Conference, 11 Sept. 1776. In a letter to GW of this date, Edward Rutledge says: "We wrote you about 2 Hours ago by the Post."

From Certain General Officers

May it please your Excellency   September 11. 1776

The Situation of the Army under your Excellency's Command is in our Opinions so critical & dangerous that We apprehend a Board of General Officers should be immediately calld for the purpose of considering it.[1]

We do not mean to condemn as unwise or imprudent any Measures which have heretofore been taken; but We conceive a Reconsideration of an important Question determined at the last Board of General Officers to be absolutely necessary to satisfy our own Apprehensions & the Apprehensions of many excellent Field Officers & others from the Dispositions now making by the Advice of that Board.[2]

We know the Danger & bad Policy of giving Way to Applications for the Reconsideration of common Propositions, which may have been solemnly determined; but the present Case is of such Magnitude & is big with such Consequences to All America that a Breach of common Forms & even the Risque of establishing wrong precedents should in our Opinions be now overuled.

What we have to offer to Your Excellency in general Council proceeds not from Fear of personal Danger nor the Expectation of deriving to ourselves any Honor & Reputation from a Change of Measures—it proceeds from a Love of our Country and a determined Resolution to urge the best & wisest Measures: & finally to execute if possible even erroneous Ones which on cool dispassionate Reconsideration cannot be avoided.

Nathanael Greene M.G.

Thomas Mifflin B.G.

Jno. Nixon B.G.

Rezin Beall B.G.[3]

Saml H. Parsons B.G.

James Wadsworth B:G:

I think it a mark of Wisdom to reconsider Opinions, upon Subjects of high Importance when ever so many respectable Gentn request it as have signed above me. I therefore heartily concur with them in the Application abovementioned.

Jno: Morin Scott B.G.

DS, in Thomas Mifflin's writing, DLC:GW; Varick transcript, DLC:GW. Scott's postscript to the DS is in his writing.

1. See the proceedings of the council of war held on 12 September.

2. For the decisions made by the council of war that met on 7 Sept., see GW to Hancock, 8 September.

3. Rezin Beall (1723–1809), who was brigadier general of the Maryland militia forces in the flying camp, previously had commanded an independent company of troops raised for the defense of Maryland, and he had been wounded during an engagement with Lord Dunmore's forces at St. George Island, Md., in July 1776. A resident of Little Paint Branch in Prince George's County, Beall visited Mount Vernon in February 1774 and applied unsuccessfully for the job of leading the expedition that GW sent to the Ohio Valley to secure his land claims on the Ohio and Kanawha rivers (see *Diaries*, 3:232).

To John Hancock

Sir   New York Septr 11th 1776

I was yesterday honored with your favor of the 8th Instt accompanied by Sundry Resolutions of Congress, to which I shall pay the strictest attention and in the Instances required make them the future Rule of my conduct.

The Mode of Negotiation pursued by Lord Howe I did not approve of, But as Genl Sullivan was sent out upon the business and with a Message to Congress, I could not conceive myself at liberty to interfere in the matter as he was in the character of a prisoner and totally subject to their power and direction.

The List of prisoners before omitted thro hurry, is now inclosed, tho It will probably have reached Congress before this.[1]

I shall write by the first Opportunity for Major Hawsaikse to repair to Philadelphia, he is in the Northern Army and will also mention the several Appointments in consequence of Coll Sinclair's promotion.[2]

As soon as Generals Prescott and McDonald arrive, I shall take measures to advise Genl Howe of It, that the proposed exchange for Genl Sullivan & Lord Stirling may be carried into execution.

Since my Letter of the 8th, Nothing material has occurred, except that the Enemy have possessed themselves of Montezores Island and landed a considerable number of Troops upon It. This Island lies in the Mouth of Harlem river which runs out of the Sound into the North River and will give the Enemy an easy opportunity of landing either on the Low Grounds of Morrisania, If their views are to seize & possess the passes above Kingsbridge, or on the plains of Harlem, If they design to Intercept and cut off the communication between our several posts. I am making every disposition and arrangement that the divided State of our Troops will admit of, and which appear most likely and the best calculated to oppose their Attacks, for I presume there will be several. How the Event will be, God only knows; But you may be assured that Nothing in my power, circumstanced as I am, shall be wanting to effect a favourable and happy Issue.

By my Letter of the 8th you would perceive that Several of the Council were for holding the Town conceiving It practicable for some time—Many of 'em now, upon seeing our divided State, have altered their Opinion and allow the expediency and necessity of Concentring our whole force or drawing It more together. convinced of the propriety of this measure, I am ordering our Stores away, except such as may be absolutely necessary to keep as long as any Troops remain, that If an evacuation of the City becomes Inevitable, and which certainly must be the case, there may be as little to remove as possible.

The Inclosed packet contains Several Letters for particular Members of Congress and for some Gentlemen in Philadelphia. They came to hand Yesterday and were brought from France by a Captn Leviz lately arrived at Bedford in the Massachusetts State. I must request the favor of you to open the packet and to have the Letters put into a proper channel of Conveyance to the Gentn they are addressed to.[3] I have the honor to be with the highest esteem Sir Your Most Obedt Servt

Go: Washington

LS, in Robert Hanson Harrison's writing, DNA:PCC, item 152; LB, DLC:GW; copy, DNA:PCC, item 169; Varick transcript, DLC:GW. Congress read this letter on 13 Sept. and referred it to the Board of War (*JCC,* 5:755).

1. This list, which GW had intended to enclose in his letter to Hancock of 6 Sept., has not been identified.

2. For Congress's resolutions regarding these appointments, see Hancock to GW, 8 Sept., n.5. No letter from GW to Nicholas Haussegger has been found.

3. This packet apparently contained letters from Silas Deane brought by a Captain Leavey or Levy who sailed out of Bordeaux in late July or early August (see Elbridge Gerry to Joseph Trumbull, 12 Sept., and Caesar Rodney to

George Read, 13 Sept., in Smith, *Letters of Delegates*, 5:144–46, 154–55; and Deane to Robert Morris, 30 July, 4 Dec. 1776, in Isham, *Deane Papers*, 1:170, 399–402).

From Lieutenant Colonel Henry Beekman Livingston

Saybrook [Conn.]
May it please your Excellency   11th Septr 1776

Since my last by Lieutenant Smith I have been able to collect no assisstance,[1] the Malitia of Southold about one Hundred and fifty in number deserted me at the River Head on my way to Huntington haveing heard that long Island was given up to the Enemy, Colonel Mulford was gathering the Malitia of South and East Hampton when this Report (industriously Circulated by our Enemies) was spread among them, in Vain I endeavoured to remove the Falacy: Colonel Smiths Regiment haveing been dismissed by their Colonel, arrived in small Parties and Confirmed the Report, I received at the same time Letters from the Town of Huntington praying me for *Gods Sake* not to advance any farther, as they had already submitted to the Enemy, and much feared Terms would not be granted them Should I proceed any farther, these Considerations togather with a fear that Our Retreat might be cut off as I had engaged no Boats to take off the Troops induced me to determine a Retreat which was effected on the 2d of September In three Hours after we arrived at this Place since that time I have almost Constantly been employed in Assisting the unfortunate Inhabitants of Long Island to remove their Stocks[2]—On my way from the River Head hearing that the disaffected in and about Huntington were disarming Our Freinds I took the same method and have Collected about 236 Small Arms have also Brought Off 6 Peices of Ordnance one 9 one 12 and 4 Six Pounders all unmounted 5 Qr Casks Powder 2½ Boxes of Ball 190 Cartouch Boxes 160 Powder Horns filled 153 Bayonets[3]—before I left Long Island The Towns of East Hampton and Southampton had sent for their Pardons to Lord How since I have left it they have almost universally taken the Oath of Allegiance to his Britanick Majesty tendered to them by Colonel Gardiner I have since taken him and have him now in Custody at this Place with two others Governor Trumbull has appointed a Committee to examine them and if they Merit the Indulgence to permit them the liberty of a Town in Connecticut on their Parole,[4] the Governor has also sent about 280 Men to My Assistance as my own are not to be depended on their Connections being on Long-Island, twenty one deserted on the day of our Retreat since that many others; this has reduced the Detatchment to a Trifle I propose sailing from this Place for Huntington tomorrow Morning and hope to have an Opportunity of being Serviseable the whole of the Troops I Shall have with me will be about 420 I am thus particular as I understood Your Excellency was informed I had a greater Number, I beleive if 10,000. Men were sent on the East End of Long Island they woud give a verry unexpected turn to Affairs the Division would Certainly surprize our Enemies, I would not have had the presumtion to Mention this had I not heard it was Your Excellencies Intention, they are now perfectly Secure their whole attention is bent on their Operations at New York. I send enclosed a True State of the Detatchment under my Care[5] & remain with respect Your Excellencies Most Obt Humble Servant,

Henry B: Livingston

P.S. The inclosed are the Proclamations of Generals How and Erskin which I intercepted at River Head.[6]

ALS, DLC:GW.

1. See Livingston to GW, 31 August.

2. Livingston marched his detachment west from Southold to Riverhead, N.Y., on 1 Sept., and the next day he evacuated Long Island, ferrying his men across the sound to Saybrook on the Connecticut coast (see Livingston to the Connecticut Council of War, 4 Sept., in Force, *American Archives*, 2:170). David Mulford, Sr. (1722–1778), of East Hampton, who had held a commission as an officer since 1748, was named colonel of the 2d Regiment of Suffolk County militia in August 1775. After Gen. Nathaniel Woodhull was captured on 28 Aug. 1776, Mulford took command of the militia at Huntington. He was forced to swear an oath of allegiance to the king on 7 Sept. but subsequently took refuge in Connecticut (see Mather, *Refugees from Long Island*, 476–77, 992, 997).

3. For the disposal of these items, see Livingston to Jonathan Trumbull, Sr., 11, 14 Sept., in Force, *American Archives*, 5th ser., 2:296–97, 336–37.

4. Abraham Gardiner (1721–1782), a member of the East Hampton committee of correspondence in 1774 and a signer of the Suffolk County associa-

tion in 1775, received a commission from Governor Tryon to administer British loyalty oaths to his neighbors after the Battle of Long Island. On 9 Sept., however, Gardiner transported his family and livestock to Saybrook, where he was arrested by Livingston. Gardiner apparently was exonerated by the examining committee because in March 1777 the state of New York reimbursed him for his cost in moving to Connecticut (Mather, *Long Island Refugees*, 116–17, 351–52, 770–71).

5. The enclosed return of 12 Sept. shows that Livingston's detachment contained 13 commissioned officers, 1 adjutant, 25 noncommissioned officers, and 224 rank and file, of whom 178 rank and file were present and fit for duty, 2 on furlough, 16 on command, and 28 deserted. The detachment had 320 good and 60 bad arms. In a note on the return, Livingston writes: "I Shall be joined tomorrow by Captain [Christopher] Leffingw[el]l's independant Company of 50 Men and three Companies of Colonel Wolcuts [Erastus Wolcott's] Regiment 60 Men each by Gove[r]nor Trumbulls Order they are Command[ed] by Major [John] Ely who is Commanded to act in Concert with me" (DLC:GW).

6. General Howe's proclamation of 23 Aug. offers pardon and protection to the loyal inhabitants of Long Island who had been "forced into rebellion" and encouragement to "those who choose to take up arms for the restoration of order and good government within this Island" (Force, *American Archives*, 5th ser., 1:1121). Brig. Gen. William Erskine's proclamation of 29 Aug. calls upon the inhabitants of Suffolk County to lay down their arms and provide the British troops with cattle, wagons, and horses. If they fail to show "a dutiful submission in all respects," Erskine warns, he will march his troops "without delay into the country" and lay "waste the property of the disobedient, as persons unworthy his Majesty's clemency" (ibid., 1211–12). William Erskine (1728–1795), who entered the British army in 1743 and served as a major of light dragoons in Germany during the Seven Years' War, was knighted by George III in 1763 when he presented colors captured by his regiment. Named lieutenant colonel commandant of the 1st Battalion of the 71st Regiment in 1775, Erskine sailed to America in the spring of 1776 as commander of the 42d and 71st regiments with the rank of brigadier general, and during the Battle of Long Island he commanded a brigade. After the battle General Howe appointed Erskine commanding officer for the eastern part of Long Island, and on 7 Oct. 1776 he became quartermaster general of Howe's army (see William Howe to George Germain, 3 Dec. 1776, in Force, *American Archives*, 5th ser., 3:1054–55). Erskine served as quartermaster general until he returned to England in the summer of 1779. He also participated in Tryon's raid on the Connecticut coast during the spring of 1777 and commanded troops at various other times during his stay in America. Erskine was promoted to major general in 1779 and lieutenant general in 1787.

To Brigadier General Hugh Mercer

Sir   New York Sept. 11th 1776

I have received your favour by Colo. Weedon.[1] As it seems every day more Probable that the Posts at Kingsbridge will be occupied by this Army & the principal defence made there, I have orderd Colo. Bradlys Regiment to move from Bergen. As that Post does not seem to be an Object of the Enemys Attention I am in doubt whether it is necessary for you to replace this Regiment or leave it to the remaining troops—as you best know what number there are from your Camp at that Post I must leave it to you to direct a further supply or not as under all Circumstances you think best & necessary—We find a moving Camp will require a great[er] Number of waggons than was expected. If Mr Biddle could engage about 50 of the common Country waggons or in proportion of the Philadelphia Teams to go up to Burdetts ferry, it would greatly releive us, The Idea of impressing is very disagreable & only to be adopted in Case of the most urgent Necessity[2]—The Enemy is taking Post on the Islands about Hellgate so as to make a landing with the greater Ease & Convenience. We are endeavouring to give them a suitable Reception & hope they will not be able to execute their Scheme. I am Sir Your Most Obbt Humbe Servant

G.W.

LB, in Caleb Gibbs's writing, DLC:GW; Varick transcript, DLC:GW.

1. This letter has not been found. George Weedon (c.1734–1793), a tavern keeper from Fredericksburg, Va., served under GW in the Virginia Regiment as an ensign beginning in September 1755. Weedon was promoted to lieutenant in July 1757 and captain-lieutenant in May 1762, and after the French and Indian War he became a captain in the Spotsylvania County militia. When the Spotsylvania Independent Company was formed in December 1774, Weedon was named its captain, and on 12 Jan. 1776 the Virginia convention commissioned him lieutenant colonel of the 3d Virginia Regiment. In August the Continental Congress promoted Weedon to colonel and ordered him to march the 3d Virginia Regiment to New York, where, after arriving at GW's headquarters on this date, it was stationed at Harlem Heights. GW appointed Weedon acting adjutant general in January 1777, and a month later Congress made him a brigadier general. In the spring of 1778 Weedon left active service after a long dispute about rank. He retained his Continental commission, however, and on returning to Virginia he was active in supervising the militia's resistance to British raids up the James and Potomac rivers. His forces participated

in the Virginia campaign of 1781 and were present at the Battle of Yorktown. Weedon resigned his commission in July 1783.

2. Acting on orders from Mercer, Deputy Q.M. Gen. Clement Biddle previously had impressed nearly three hundred wagons, about half of which arrived at Burdett's Ferry on the night of 4 September. GW then "orderd a number of them to be discharged & a part to be sent over" to Fort Washington (Biddle to Heath, 5 Sept., MHi: Heath Papers). Clement Biddle (1740–1814), a prominent Philadelphia merchant who in 1775 had helped raise a company of volunteers called the Quaker Blues, was appointed by Congress on 8 July 1776 to be deputy quartermaster general of the flying camp with the rank of colonel. Gen. Nathanael Greene made Biddle one of his aides-de-camp in November 1776, and GW named him commissary general of forage in July 1777. Biddle resigned from the army in June 1780, but at Greene's urging, he accepted appointment as quartermaster general of the Pennsylvania militia in September 1781. During the 1780s and 1790s Biddle transacted much of GW's personal business in Philadelphia, and in 1789 GW appointed him U.S. marshal of Pennsylvania.

From Edward Rutledge

My dear Sir

Brunswick [N.J.] Wednesday Evening
[11 September 1776] 10' O'clock

Your Favour of this Morning is just put into my Hands[1]—in Answer I must beg Leave to inform you that our Conferrence with Lord Howe has been attended with no immediate Advantages—He declared that he had no Powers to consider us as Independt States, and we easily discover'd that were we still Dependt we would have nothing to expect from those with which he is vested—He talk'd altogether in generals, that he came out here to consult, advise, & confer with Gentlemen of the greatest Influence in the Colonies about their Complaints, that the King would revise the Acts of Parliament & royal Instructions upon such Reports as should be made and appear'd to fix our Redress upon his Majesty's good Will & Pleasure— This kind of Conversation lasted for several Hours & as I have already said without any Effect[2]—Our Reliance continues therefore to be (under God) on your Wisdom & Fortitude & that of your Forces—That you may be as succesful as I know you are worthy is my most sincere wish—I saw Mrs Washington the Evening before I left Philadelphia, she was well—I gave Mr Griffin a Letter from her for you[3] The Gentlemen beg their Respects— God bless you my dear Sir. Your most affectionate Friend

E. Rutledge

We wrote you about 2 Hours ago by the Post.[4]

ALS, DLC:GW. Robert Hanson Harrison docketed this letter: "From Edwd Rutledge Eqr. Septr 1776." The Continental Congress committee conferred with Lord Howe on Wednesday, 11 Sept. (see note 2).

1. This letter, which may have been addressed to the committee of conference, has not been found.

2. For other accounts of this meeting, which was held earlier this day on Staten Island across from Perth Amboy, see the minutes in Willcox, *Franklin Papers*, 22:598–605; the committee's report to Congress, 17 Sept., in *JCC*, 5:765–66; and Lord Howe to Lord George Germain, 20 Sept., in Davies, *Documents of the American Revolution*, 12:225–27.

3. Rutledge apparently gave this letter, which has not been found, to Deputy Adj. Gen. Samuel Griffin at Perth Amboy on the way to or from the meeting with Lord Howe.

4. This letter from the committee has not been found.

General Orders

Head Quarters, New York, sept: 12th 1776.
Parole Franklin.   Countersign Congress.

The difficulty of procuring Milk, and other proper Food for the sick, has induced the General to establish an Hospital, where those Necessaries can be procured in plenty—The regimental Sick are therefore to be immediately mustered for this purpose—One of the Hospital Surgeons will attend with the regimental Surgeon—such as are able to remove themselves will be allowed so to do, under the care of a proper officer—A suitable officer, not under the rank of a Captain, is to be appointed by the Brigadier, out of each Brigade, to attend such sick of each Brigade, as cannot remove themselves; they are, under the Advice of the Surgeon, who also attends, to see that all proper care is taken for their comfort, while removing, and afterwards.

The same Court Martial which tried Major Popst to try Major Hetfield, charged with "Making a false Report of the Guards."[1]

As the care of the sick is an object of great Importance, The General directs, that a person, not under the rank of a Captain, be also appointed in like manner, in each Brigade, who shall be empowered to procure Necessaries for them, and Monies furnished for that purpose; he taking care that the utmost regularity and Care be used.

John Porter Esqr: is appointed Paymaster to Col. Ward's Regiment, in the Continental service.[2]

Varick transcript, DLC:GW; Df, in Joseph Reed's writing, DNA: RG 93, Orderly Books, vol. 15. The two passwords in the draft are not in Reed's writing.

1. Moses Hatfield (Hetfield) of Orange County, N.Y., who had commanded a company of minutemen during 1775 and had become major of one of the county's militia regiments in February 1776, was appointed major of Col. Samuel Drake's regiment of New York militia levies on 10 June 1776. Hatfield was released from arrest on 14 Sept., and ten days later he was captured at Montresor's Island. After his exchange in April 1778, he was appointed commissary of hides for the army at New York. GW accused Hatfield of being a double spy in January 1780, and that month a court of inquiry investigated him for graft (see GW to William Irvine, 1 Jan. 1780, 9 Jan. 1780 [second letter], PHi: Irvine Papers; GW to Heath, 12 Jan. 1780, MHi: Heath Papers; and GW to Moses Hazen, 24 Jan. 1780, DLC:GW). The Board of War removed Hatfield from office the following June (see Timothy Pickering to George Clinton, 30 June 1780, in Hastings, *Clinton Papers*, 5:898–99). He subsequently served in the Orange County militia, becoming a lieutenant colonel in March 1783.

2. John Porter of Massachusetts served as paymaster of Col. Jonathan Ward's 21st Continental Regiment until the end of the year when he secured commission as a captain in the 13th Massachusetts Regiment. Porter was promoted to major in May 1777, and he transferred to the 6th Massachusetts on 1 Jan. 1781. In October 1782 a court-martial convicted Porter of overstaying his leave of absence, and GW denied his petition to be reinstated in the service (see General Orders, 12 Oct. 1782, and Jonathan Trumbull, Jr., to Calvin Smith, 25 Oct. 1782, DLC:GW; see also Porter to GW, 9 April 1788, and GW to Porter, 30 April 1788, DLC:GW, and *JCC*, 32:170).

Council of War

[New York, 12 September 1776]
At a Council of War held at Gen. McDougals Qua⟨rters⟩[1] Sept. 12. 1776.

Present His Excelly Gen. Washington. Major Gen. Puttnam[,] Heath[,] Spencer[,] Green[,] Brigr Gen. Mifflin[,] Parsons[,] McDougal[,] Nixon[,] Wadsworth[,] Scott[,] Fellows[,] Clinton.[2]

The General read a Letter signed by some general Officers proposing that there should be a Reconsideration of the Matter determined in Council last week with Respect to the State & farther Disposition of the Troops.[3]

The Question was put whether the Determination of last Week Should be reconsidered & the Opinions as follow.

To reconsider		To adhere
Gen. Beall	Gen. McDougal	Gen. Spencer
Gen. Scott	Gen. Parsons	Gen. Clinton
G. Fellows	Gen. Mifflin	Gen. Heath.[4]
G. Wadsworth	Genl Green	
Gen. Nixon	Gen. Puttnam	

It was considered what Number of Men are necessary[5] to be left for the Defence of Mount Washington & its Dependencies agreed that it be 8000.

D, in Joseph Reed's writing, DLC:GW; two copies, NHi: McDougall Papers, Varick transcript, DLC:GW. The mutilated text within angle brackets is supplied from the documents in the McDougall Papers, which are certified by Richard Varick as true copies of Reed's manuscript, one made on 13 Feb. 1782 and the other made on 15 Mar. 1782.

1. After the Battle of Long Island, Alexander McDougall's brigade headquarters apparently was at Mrs. Catharine Benson McGown's house or tavern, located a short distance south of the village of Harlem on the post road that ran between King's Bridge and New York City (see Champagne, *McDougall*, 113, and Hall, *McGown's Pass*, 14–15).

2. Although Brig. Gen. Rezin Beall's name does not appear on this list, his inclusion among the voters listed near the end of the document indicates that he was present at this council of war.

3. See Certain General Officers to GW, 11 September. For the decisions of the council of war held on 7 Sept., see GW to Hancock, 8 September. Following this paragraph in the manuscript, Reed struck out a paragraph that reads: "The Question Whether this Army should take principal Post at Kingsbridge & the Neighbourhood with a V[i]ew of evacuating New York whenever it shall be found difficult or impracticable to maintain the City—was considered & debated with great Solemnity & Attention."

4. This vote to reconsider the previous council's decision to hold New York City apparently was understood to be a rescinding of that decision and an approval of the city's evacuation (see Wilson, *Heath's Memoirs*, 69, and GW to Hancock, 14 Sept.). For George Clinton's and William Heath's reasons for dissenting from the majority on this question, see Clinton to GW, c.12 Sept., and Heath to GW, 13 September.

5. At this place in the manuscript, Reed struck out the phrase "for the Posts at Burdets Ferry."

From Brigadier General George Clinton

[c.12 September 1776]

In Consequence of a Motion made in a late Counsel of Genl Officers (in which Contrary to former Determination) it was advised that the City of Newyork shoud be evacuated & that the Disposition of the Army shoud be changed & that those who adhered to the former Opinion shoud assign their Reasons for defending the City as one of those I now begg leave to lay before your Excellency the following.

1st Tho' the City of Newyork if attacked & Bombarded both by Sea & Land may perhaps not be defensible yet the ⟨h⟩eights contiguous to & which Command it in my Opinion are & in this I am warranted by the Extensive & strong Works erected there last Spring & Summer[.] The whole Island is broken Land very capable of Defence[.] By the Genl Return our Numbers far exceed the Enemy & tho we have many Sick yet suposing them to have none our Fit for Duty is equal to or may exceed the whole Number they can bring to Action leaving only small Numbers to defend Long & Staten Islands.[1] The City is of great Value in itself yet its Importance is much enhanced when we consider if possessed by the Enemy it furnishes them with a safe Harbour through the Winter for thier Fleet Barracks & good Quarters for their Troops add to this A Safe & Happy Assylum for the disafected by which their army will (In all probabillity) be greatly Recruited.

2d The City & Posts near it if possessed by the Enemy may be so strengthned [(]& the Works nearly compleated for them) considering the Advantages they already have in the Possession of Long Island as to render it with a few Men only defensible agt any Force we can send against it of Consequence their Possession of the City will not tend much to weaken or divide their Army (One Capital Reason given for evacuating the City.).

3dly If the City & Posts near it are evacuated Paulus Hook & Other Works on the Jersy Shore must of Course also fall into the Hands of the Enemy and almost the whole Eastern Extent of that State lay exposed to the Ravages of our Cruel Enemy from whence they may with Ease & safety draw great Supplies for their Army.

4thly The same Reasons which are given for abandoning the

City &c. will hold for our retreating before the Enemy to the Highlands—They have the Command of the Water. They can transport their Army from Place to Place by Water with much more Expedition than we can ours by Land this is our Misfortune & shoud they (possessed of the City which will at all Times afford them a safe & commodious Retreat) move their Army or Part of it up the Sound to Mamarioneck or even farther Eastward they may with almost equal Ease draw a Chain of Works across to the North River & cut off our Communication with the Country as they coud by the last Disposition of our Army.

5thly The Reason urged most Strongly by those who advised the evacuating the City &ca was that by holding the City our Army so disposed as to secure a Retreat to the Country must be divided & of Course we must fight the Enemy by Detachments & this the best Writers say is Dangerous I am not much Read in the Art of War Common Reason however teaches me that if the Enemy attacks the Country in various Places by Parties too strong for the Militia we must detach Parts of our Army to such Places to defend them or suffer the Inhabitants to be plundered & ruined And I will readilly submit to the World to determine whether a Country if unprotected by our Army will readilly draw out their Militia to reinforce it leaving their Famillies without any Degree of Defence or Safety. But

6thly Was there any Weight in the Reason the Disposition of the Army advised by those Gentlemen almost equally divides it with the former & one single Movement of the Enemy up the Sound will necessarilly throw our Divissions farther a Part—We are to hold Fort Washington on the Island to secure this the Highlands near Colo. Morris's & Bourdetts Ferry And the Heights North & East of King's Bridge & the whole of this Arangement must depend on the Obstruction in Hudson's River opposite Fort Washington being sufficient to prevent the Enemy passing up the River in which I have no Faith—The Works at Bourdets Ferry are in my Opinion not Tenable if the Enemy are possessed of Newyork they may approach it with Ease & carry it by a Regular Seige—It is commanded by a Neighbouring height—We can have no Army there to fight them without our weakning that in this Quarter. Those Works once in the Enemys Possession they command Fort Washington & their Fleet will the River in which Case they form their intended Junction with the

Northern Army & lay the whole State under Contribution nor shall we [be] able to pass the River to give any Succor to the States of New Jersy or Pensylvania.

Upon the whole our Army is superior to theirs—We have near 30000 including Sick—their utmost Number dont exceed 25000—We are possessed of Strong Works to abandon them & fly before an Inferior Number of the Enemy will enspirit them & dishearten our Soldiery & the Country which latter will look upon their Army no longer as their Defence—We will with Justice loose their Confidence & support—They will abandon the Cause & We cant without their Aid Support it.

Having in a Counsel of General Officers joined in Opinion with a large Majority that the City of Newyork ought not be evacuated by our Troops & that the following Disposition of the Army woud be proper for the Defence of the City or Heights which are contiguous to & command it, The Island & for securing a Communication with the Country, towit, 5000 Men for the City & Posts near it 6000 to be posted at or near Harlem & 9000 At the Heights near King's Bridge & Fort Washington & the most advantageous Posts near the later Place & that Bridges of Communication shoud be immediately thrown across Harlem River And being afterwards in Consequence of a Representation in Writing directed to your Excellency subscribed by 7 or 8 Genl Officers[2] (all of whom were present at the former Counsel & most of them agreed to in above Opinion) summoned to attend a Second Counsel for the Purpose of reconsidering the Question & for re[s]cinding the former Resolution with.

ADf (incomplete), DLC: James and George Clinton Papers.

1. The preceding two sentences are written in the margin of the draft next to this paragraph, and although Clinton fails to indicate their exact location in the text, their content suggests this placement.

2. See Certain General Officers to GW, 11 September. For the decisions of the council of war held on 7 Sept., see also GW to Hancock, 8 September.

To Brigadier General James Clinton

Sir   Head Quarters New York 12th Sepr 1776

I have before me your two Letters of the 8th and 10th Inst. the first inclosing Returns of the Number of Men and Ordnance and Artillery Stores at Forts Montgomery and Constitution; the last, Copies of two Letters from the Convention of the State of New York, by which it appears they had ordered in 600 Militia as a Reinforcement to the two posts, and which I hope will put them in a proper State of Defence.[1]

I ordered Colo. Knox to provide and forward the different Articles wanted by you in the Ordnance Department, but he informed me, that from the present unsettled State of our Magazine and Laboratory (many of our Stores being removed and on their way to Kingsbridge and Mount Washington) he could not comply at once with the whole of the demand, but would send what he could conveniently collect.

The Convention of New York having appointed Mr Schenk to provide what Articles they found wanting at their late Review of your Works and Stores (and which include many of the Articles you wrote for) I hope, as he will make it his particular Business, that he will collect many Articles, which Colo. Knox from the present hurry of our Affairs cannot attend to.[2] And if they should both provide the same things, your Stores will only be the fuller. I have again ordered the Quarter Masr Genl to send up the Nails with all possible Expedition.

The Convention having ordered an Armourer with proper Tools to be fixed at Your posts, I hope what Arms are at present out of Repair will soon be made fit for Use.[3] We must make every shift with our old Arms, till we can get better supplied. I am Sir Yr most obt Servt

Go: Washington

LS, in Tench Tilghman's writing, NNPM; LB, DLC:GW; Varick transcript, DLC:GW.

1. The LB reads: "which I hope will prove sufficient to put them in a proper State of Defence."

2. John Schenk, Jr. (1758–1845), of Poughkeepsie, who had served as captain of a company of Dutchess County minutemen during 1775 and had been promoted to major in April 1776, was appointed by the convention on 7 Sept. to act as agent for procuring and forwarding nails, entrenching tools, and various ordnance supplies to Fort Montgomery (see *N.Y. Prov. Congress Journals*, 1:415, 614). Schenk wrote Abraham Yates, Jr., on 9 Sept. accepting the appointment, and he appeared before the state committee of safety the next day to receive its orders (see Force, *American Archives*, 5th ser., 2:260). For the expanded list of military stores that Schenk was directed on that date to fur-

nish for the highland forts, see *N.Y. Prov. Congress Journals,* 1:618; see also GW to Abraham Yates, Jr., this date.

3. The convention took this action on 7 Sept. (see ibid., 614).

Letter not found: to Joshua Davis, 12 Sept. 1776. The letter that Davis wrote to GW on 10 Sept. is docketed in part "Ansd 12th."

Lieutenant Colonel Robert Hanson Harrison
to John Hancock

Sir   Head Qrs New York Septr 12th 1776

His Excellency being called from Head Quarters to day on business of Importance which prevents his Writing,[1] I therefore do myself the honor to inform Congress of what has happened since his Letter of Yesterday.

Last Evening the Enemy transported a number of Men from Buchanans to Montezors Island, and by their several movements more strongly indicate their Intention to land somewhere about Harlem or Morrisania—most likely at both at the same time. This Morning One of the Ships that has been for some time in the Sound moved down towards Hell Gate, but the tide leaving her, she could not get near enough to bring her Guns to bear upon our Fortification. If she means to attack It, It is probable she will warp in the next tide. Their Batteries have kept up a pretty constant fire against our's at that place, but without any considerable effect. This Morning they opened a New One.[2]

I do not recollect any other material occurrence and shall only add That I have the Honor to be with the highest respect Sir Your Most Obedt Servt

Rob. H. Harrison

ALS, DNA:PCC, item 152; LB, DLC:GW; copy, DNA:PCC, item 169; Varick transcript, DLC:GW. Congress read this letter on 14 Sept. and referred it to the Board of War (*JCC,* 5:757).

1. GW attended the council of war of this date.

2. Frederick Mackenzie says in his diary that two battalions of the British 1st Brigade crossed to Buchanan's and Montresor's islands on the morning of 11 Sept. "to support the Light Infantry and secure the posts there. The Rebels appear numerous on the opposite shores, which probably made it necessary to reinforce them. A good deal of firing at the Batteries at Hellgate. The Rebels have thrown some of their Shells very well. We had some men wounded there. A great number of the Country small Craft, are collecting at Flushing for the

service of the Army." On this date, Mackenzie says, "The two other Battalions of the 1st brigade passed over to the Islands. The fire is still kept up on both sides at Hellgate; but that of the Rebels slackens. We had four or five men wounded there this day. The Brune frigate, came down the Sound, and Anchored above Montresor's Island" (Mackenzie, *Diary,* 1:44).

From John Morgan

May it please Your Excellency   New York Sepr 12. 1776.

Agreeable to Orders I have been into the County of Orange & collected seven Members of Committee, & spent the whole of Yesterday & part of this day in viewing the Country, & looking out for proper Coverings for the reception of the Sick & Wounded. I am sorry to report that in a circuit of 14 Miles in that County, I cannot find or hear of any suitable Accomodations, for more than about 100 Sick. No Country can be worse provided in all respects; & the places proposed are remote from any Landing.[1]

From the knowledge I have of New-Ark, I am perswaded it is a place infinitely superior in all respects for the Establishment of a Genl Hospital. There are but 4 Miles of Land Carriage required; all the rest is Water Carriage. The Houses are numerous large & Convenient. If it be objected that they are full of Inhabitants from N. York, so is every Hovel thro' Orange County; & as to the Town of Orange, I cannot find that there is room for One Sick person without incommoding Some One or other.

After this report, which is grounded on the most careful Inquiry & Inspection, I wait your Excellencys further orders. but if I may be permitted to offer my Sentiments it is, that no time be lost in applying to the Committee at New-Ark by requisition for Room for the Sick; & if your Excellency thinks proper, I will immediately repair with all dispatch to urge the Matter without delay—or proceed in any other Way your Excellcy may see fit. I am, Yr Excellencys Most obedt & very humble Servt

John Morgan

ALS, DLC:GW.

1. John Haring of Orange Town wrote Gen. George Clinton on this date: "Doctor Morgan has been up here to look for a place for the sick and wounded; at the time I was with him I Could not think of a proper place but since he has been gone it has been suggested to me that the new Court House

in Haverstraw precinct would answer, and am of Opinion it is the suitablest place in our part of the County. I should be Glad if you would mention it as such, it is a spacious Building and stands upon somewhat of a rising Ground. In our town-ship I am Convinced, there can be no place Got, without turning a number of Distressed persons out of Doors, almost every House here is filled and Crowded with people who fled out of the City" (Hastings, *Clinton Papers,* 1:345–46).

To Robert Morris

Sir   Head Quarters N. York 12th Sepr 1776

I have been honored with your favr of the 7th Inst. upon the Subject of Tents for this Army.[1] That you might receive proper Information of the Number wanted, I directed the Quarter Master General to return you an Estimate, whose Office it is to provide them. His Report you will find in the inclosed Letter which I beg leave to refer you,[2] and requesting that the greatest Dispatch may be used in having them made and forwarded. I have the Honor to be with the greatest Respect Sir Your most obt Servt

G.W.

LB, in Tench Tilghman's writing, DLC:GW; Varick transcript, DLC:GW. The LB is addressed "to Robt Morris Esq: Chairman Secret Committee of Congress."

1. This letter has not been found.
2. Neither Q.M. Gen. Stephen Moylan's report nor the enclosed letter has been identified.

From Richard Peters

Sir.   War Office [Philadelphia] Septr 12th 1776

By Direction of Congress to the Board of War I have procured two of the Philadelphia Light Horse to conduct the Generals Prescott & Macdonald to your Excellency to be exchanged agreeable to the Resolve of Congress for the Generals Sullivan & Lord Sterling.[1] I have directed the Gentlemen of the Escorts to stop short at some safe Place on the Road & send off an Express to your Excellency for your Directions in the Matter. The Generals are on their Parole not to attempt an Escape or take any Step contrary to the Rules of War, but to deliver themselves to your Excellency for your proper Disposal of them until their Exchange can be effected. I have the Honor to be Your obedt humble Servt

Richard Peters Secy

ALS, DLC:GW.

1. For Congress's resolutions of 4 and 5 Sept. regarding this exchange, see *JCC*, 5:735–36. For Congress's payment of some of the expenses incurred in sending the two generals to New York, see ibid., 818, 844.

To Major General Philip Schuyler

Dear Sir   Head Qurs New York septr 12th 1776.

I Yesterday Evening received Your Favor of the 8th instant with Its Inclosures.

You were right in supposing me unable to comply with General Gates's Request; I am by no Means provided to supply so large a Demand & am Glad You Transmitted his Application immediately to Congress.

The Papers You inclosed but too strongly indicate the Hostile Intentions of the Indians. However I trust if they should attempt an Incursion upon the Frontiers, that the Force You will be able to oppose to 'em will be sufficient to repel their Attacks & prevent their doing much Mischief.

I have deliver'd the Returns of Boards & Plank, to the Qr Master Genl, who will examine them & pay whatever is due, as soon as proper Accounts are rendered him. As We shall have Occasion for a Great Quantity, I must request Your Assistance, in furnishing Every supply in your Power. Neither Timber or Boats will be wanted.[1]

I am Exceedinly hurried by a Variety of Buisiness now before me, And shall only add, That I am, Dr Sir with Great Respect Your Most Obedt Servt

Go: Washington.

LB, NN: Schuyler Papers; LB, DLC:GW; Varick transcript, DLC:GW.

1. On this date Q.M. Gen. Stephen Moylan wrote Robert Hanson Harrison: "I have given a bill of Scantlin to a man who engages to get as much as will be wanted for the Barracks, between this & Peekskill, So that I dont think it necessary for the General to mention any thing at present, relative to the Timber" (DLC:GW).

From Major General Philip Schuyler

Dear Sir   Albany september 12th 1776

Yesterday I was favored with a Letter from General Gates of the 7th instant, continued to the 8th, Covering the Information given by a Hessian Deserter & Copy of his Capitulation, Copies whereof I do Myself the Honor to inclose.[1]

General Gates informs Me "No Intelligence that can be depended upon, has Yet arrived from the Fleet, Scouts & Parties are out by Land & by Water to make Discoveries."

Part of the Militia of this County are now in this Town & schenectady & more are daily coming in, I have not heard a Line from Colo: Dayton, since that of the 4th instant, I have therefore requested the Militia to remain here, untill I shall be enabled to Judge, which Way It will be proper to March them. I am Dr Sir, most respectfully Your Excellencys Obedt Humble servt

Ph: Schuyler

LS, DLC:GW; LB, NN: Schuyler Papers. Robert Hanson Harrison inadvertently docketed the LS: "Septr 12. Gen. Schuyler. Ansd 12." GW replied to Schuyler on 20 September.

1. The enclosed copy of the 5 Sept. examination of Anthony Fasselabord, a trooper in the Brunswick Dragoon Regiment Prinz Lüdwig who deserted at Montreal on 24 June, gives an account of the arrival and deployment of German troops in Canada (DLC:GW). Gates's letter to Schuyler of 7–8 Sept. has not been identified.

To Abraham Yates, Jr.

Sir   Head Qrs New York Septr 12th 1776

I yesterday received the favor of your Letter of the 9th with Its several Inclosures and am extremely happy that your Honbe Body had anticipated my recommendation by resolving on an Augmentation of Six hundred men to the Garrisons in the Highlands—the Importance of those posts demands the utmost attention, and every exertion to maintain them.

The Vessels for the removal of the Sick are not yet arrived. Their Present situation gives me great anxiety. As the wind is now favourable I would fain hope that a sufficient number will come down to day to take in the whole. If they do not my distress will be much Increased.

Genl Clinton in a Letter of the 8th transmitted me a List of

Artillery & Ordnance Stores wanted at Forts Montgomery & Constitution, which Included the Several Articles you have determd to procure, Except those mentioned below. I directed that they should be sent up, but as the situation of our Affairs at this Time may not perhaps admit of It, I think It will be prudent for Mr Schenk whom you have appointed an Agent in this Instance, to get all he can[1]—Should he be able to obtain the supply you have voted necessary—and Genl Clinton's demand be complied with also, no damage will be done—Our stores will not be too large. I have the Honor to be with great respect Sir Your Most Obedt Sert

Go: Washington

Intrenching Tools[,] Iron Carriages[,] Cannon Harness[,] Armourer with his Tools.

LS, in Robert Hanson Harrison's writing, NBu; LB, DLC:GW; Varick transcript, DLC:GW.

1. See GW to James Clinton, this date.

General Orders

Head Quarters, New-York, sept: 13th 1776.
Parole Newark.   Countersign Amboy.

Serjeant Clements, late of the General's Guard, convicted by a Court Martial whereof Col. Malcom was Presdt, of "Remissness of duty"—is ordered to be reduced to the ranks. The General approves the sentence and orders that he be sent back to the regiment from which he was taken.

The visiting officer has again reported that the men from Col. Silliman's, Col. Lewis's, and Col. Thompson's Regiments, go upon guard, deficient in Ammunition and with bad Arms—The General hopes the officers of those regiments will immediately attend to it.

Simon Learned, late Lieutenant in Learned's Regiment, having resigned his Commission as Lieutenant, is appointed Paymaster to said regiment.[1]

Genl Fellow's Brigade to remove into the adjoining Out Houses, and raft the boards which compose their present Encampment, to Kingsbridge, or such part of them, as may be deemed necessary by him.

A disappointment with respect to a proper place for the removal of the sick, in some measure vacates the Order of yesterday, and the following is now to be attended to, and obeyed— The situation of the Army rendering it difficult to make that provision for the relief and support of the sick in the City of New-York which their cases may require—In Order the most speedy and effectual manner to remove the sick to some place where they can be supplied with every thing necessary for them, the General directs the Surgeons of each Brigade, under the immediate Inspection of the Brigadiers, to examine the state of the sick, and to make a list of the names of such as they suppose can remove themselves to the Brigadier General of the Brigade, who is desired to send such Convalescent persons to some convenient place in the Neighbourhood of New-York, to be chosen by, and be under the care of, a discreet Officer, and one of the regimental Surgeons, who is, in the most prudent manner, to make the necessary provision for the reception and support of such Convalescent Persons, who are immediately to be returned to their regiments when their health will admit of their doing duty. Such as are so ill as not to be able to remove themselves, are to be collected under the care of another officer of the like Rank, in one place and notice given to the Director General of the Hospital, that they may be taken proper care of. In each of the above cases, the superintending officer is permitted to lay out money, in the most frugal manner, for the comfortable Subsistence of his sick, which will be allowed him on rendering his account.

Mr Hendrick Fisher is appointed Paymaster to Col. Prescott's regiment.[2]

Charles Hobby Hubbard Esqr: to Col. Serjeant's Regt until the person arrives who is designed for that office.[3]

Varick transcript, DLC:GW; Df, DNA: RG 93, Orderly Books, vol. 15. Except for the passwords, the first part of the draft through the second sentence of the fifth paragraph is in Joseph Reed's writing.

1. Simon Learned (Larned; 1753–1817) served as a second lieutenant in Col. Jonathan Brewer's Massachusetts regiment during 1775, and on 1 Jan. 1776 he became a first lieutenant in Col. Ebenezer Learned's 3d Continental Regiment. Appointed a first lieutenant and adjutant of the 4th Massachusetts Regiment on 1 Jan. 1777, Learned was promoted to captain in March 1778. A year later he was named a brigade major, and in 1782 he became an aide-

de-camp to Gen. John Glover. After Learned's military service ended in June 1783, he settled in Pittsfield, Mass., as a merchant. He served in the U.S. House of Representatives from 1804 to 1805, and during the War of 1812 he was colonel of the 9th Infantry Regiment.

2. Hendrick Fisher, Jr., of Bound Brook, N.J., who had been a first lieutenant in the 1st New Jersey Regiment since 16 Dec. 1775, served as paymaster of Col. William Prescott's 7th Continental Regiment until late November when he was named a first lieutenant in the new 1st New Jersey Regiment. Fisher resigned in September 1780.

3. Charles Holby Hubbard of Massachusetts was killed on 23 Sept. during an attempt to recapture Montresor's Island.

To Major General William Heath

Dr Sir,   New York Sepr 13th 1776.

Before this Letter can reach you, the Brigade under Colo. Chester's Command no doubt has reached you, but unless more assistance of Waggons and Teams are sent I cannot undertake to say when you will get a further reinforcement—let me entreat therefore that Genl Clinton and yourself will exert yourselves in getting, by Impressment, or otherwise, a parcel of Teams to come to our Assistance.[1]

The Brigades which I mean to Send to you are these following, and which I mention, that your disposition of them may be thought of in time, taking into consideration that Sheas Magaws & Haslets, will return to their former Station at Mt Washington under the immediate Comd of their old Brigadier,[2] Mifflin, but in lieu of these Regiments, it is possible when we get removed from hence you may get an equivalt numbe⟨r⟩.

	Officers	R. & File[3]
Parsons's	400	1221
Scott	284	963
Wadsworth	334	1195
Fellows	272	1122
Silliman	367	677
Douglas's	347	744
Chester	513	1178
Total	2517	7100
		2517
		9617

I must also beg that you will have the Vessels that go up with Stores &ca immediately dispatch'd back to this place. you cannot conceive how we are put to it for conveniences to transport the Sick—the Stores—the Baggage &ca—In short we are hazarding every thing in a confused way. Let there be the most vigilant lookout kept. you know I suppose that four More Ships two of the⟨m⟩ 40 odd Guns are gone up the East River.[4] I am Yr Most Obedt Servt

Go: Washington

ALS, MHi: Heath Papers. The portions of the text enclosed within angle brackets are mutilated in the manuscript.

1. Adj. Gen. Joseph Reed wrote on the cover of this letter: "The Waggons some of which have taken Sick contrary to Orders are to be sent back immdy we shall want every Waggon here."

2. GW inadvertently wrote "Brigagier" on the manuscript.

3. In the manuscript these columns are broken between two pages following the entry for Silliman's brigade. Subtotals of "1657" and "5178" are "Brought up" to the top of the respective columns on the second page under headings reading "Officrs" and "R. & F. fit for duty."

4. On the afternoon of this date, the British warships *Phoenix* and *Roebuck,* accompanied by the frigates *Orpheus* and *Carysfort,* sailed about three miles up the East River to the mouth of Bushwick Creek on the Long Island side of the river. The *Phoenix* lost one man to the fire of American batteries on Manhattan Island. None of the ships returned fire, but the American batteries were answered by British batteries on Governors Island and at Brooklyn (see Tatum, *Serle's Journal,* 99–100; Lydenberg, *Robertson Diaries,* 97; and Mackenzie, *Diary,* 1:45; see also the logs of the *Carysfort, Orpheus,* and *Roebuck* for this date in Clark and Morgan, *Naval Documents,* 6:805–6, 839).

From Major General William Heath

Kingsbridge

m[a]y it Please your Excellency   Sept. 13th 1776

Being so unhappy as to Differ in Sentiment from a Majority of the Honble Board of General Officers of the Army of the United States of america, in the Important Question whether, a Former Determination of the Board Should be reconsidered, and the City of new York no⟨w⟩ be Evacuated,[1] and Some of the General officers Desiring that the reasons of the Gentlemen Differing in Sentiment from the Majority might be Stated, I Do most Freely and Heartily State mine, which I am ready to avow and Declare to the World.

1st objtn to the Evacuating the City, Because it gives Such unspeakable advantage to the Enemy, In all Invasions of a Country, a wise and Politick General will if Possible early avail himself of Some Place of Importance, Free and Easy of access to navigation and if Possible at the Conflux of the most Considerable Rivers, where He Can with Ease form His Magazines, fortify and Secure the Place for a Safe retreat in Case of necessity for an Assylum for his Sick & Wounded, and for the advantage of winter Quarters, all of which are Capital objects in the views of a Commander And Clear it is that the City of New York has from the very first Landing of the Enemy at Staten Island been the Object of their Commanders, Their Manoeuvre from Staten Island, to Long Island Together with the whole of their Present manoeuvres, are but So many Clear and Striking Evidences of it, The City and it[s] Environs being Surrounded with a great variety of works, has much Pusselled the enemy, The City being their object as I have before observed, Their whole Attention has been Centering to obtain the Possession of it which has Induced them to Keep their Fleet & army, as much as Possible together, and with all this Collected Force they have Discovered a Diffidence (fortifyed as our Camp has been) of Attacking us— The City being now about to be Put into their Hands, Gives them almost (not to Ennumerate) every advantage which they Can wish to Have, and leads to my

2nd objtn Because it gives the Enemy a unspeakable advantage, to Attack Differant States with great Ease and Advantage, 1st Because Having got Possession of the City—well Fortified a Small Garrison will be Sufficient to defend it, which will Enable them to Employ almost their whole Force against the Neighbouring States, where they will ravage the Country, Disarm the Inhabitants, and Derive to themselves many advantages, and Compel us unavoidably to Detach our Army which is a Manoeuvre often Times very Dangerous and in the Present Case will Serve only to Fatigue and Harrass our Troops.

3rdly Because it will Give the Enemy an Oppertunity to Infest our Sea Coast, with nearly the whole of their Ships of war, as they will be no Longer necessary, Here to Cover the Landing of

Troops or Guarding the Transports and Storeships in the Harbour, which will now Ride in Safety at the wharves.

4thly Because from its Centrical Situation as a Safe Rendezvous for the Enemies Ships & Troops both Winter, and Summer the giveing them the City Entire, will afford them a great advantage, by winter as well as Summer Campaigns to Annoy and Distress the United States, both northward & Southward.

5thly Because I think it will greatly Dispirit both the army, and Country, Partly at this Time and much more So when they Come to Se[e] and Hear, that the Enemy are making Excursions both Eastward & Southward, which I think a man need nither be a Prophet or Son of a Prophet to fore See.

6thly Because, I think our Situation, (having So many works Thrown up) and numbers if Properly Disposed of as would have Enabled us to have Kept the Enemy at Bay, Untill the Campaign was Spun out, as the Enemy have all along Discovered no great fondness for Attacking our Lines I think that if the Army had been Posted Immediately (after) agreable to the Determination of the Preceeding Board, of Genl officers,[2] The Enemy would not have Dar'd to attacke us, and if they had, would have met with a Rebuff.

The foregoing with Several others are the reasons for my being against a Reconsideration of a former Determination If your Excellency should Desire any further Explination of the Last objection as to our being in ability to Keep the Enemy at Bay I am ready to Do it.

I am Unhappy when I Differ from others in Sentiment, Especially those who I revere for their wisdom and Knowledge and more So if it be on Matters of vast Importance, But I must act agreable to the Dictates of my Own reason, and Cannot give up my own Opinion untill I am Convinced by better reasons than my own, that I am mistaken. I have the Honor to be with great respect your Excellencys most Humble Servt

W. Heath

ADfS, MHi: Heath Papers.

1. See the proceedings of the council of war for 12 September.

2. For the decisions of the council of war held on 7 Sept., see GW to Hancock, 8 September.

From the Massachusetts General Court

Sir   State of Massachusetts Bay Sepr 13th 1776.

The General Assembly of this State have for some days past, been anxiously expecting the particulars of the late attack upon the Continental Army under your Excellency's more immediate Command; but the accounts hitherto received, have been vague, & uncertain.

It is the earnest desire of the Assembly, at this important crisis, to furnish you with every needed Assistance in their power; and having just received a Letter from Govr Trumbull, proposing the raising a part of our Militia for this important purpose, and soon after a Letter from the Honble Congress to the same effect, as also a Resolve of Congress relative to this matter,[1] they have ordered a fifth part of the Militia, not already in the service (the remote Counties, and some Sea-Port Towns excepted) to be immediately drafted out and to march with all possible dispatch, to your assistance; excepting one Battalion ordered to Rhode Island, in consequence of the Resolve beforemention'd.

Our Troops will gladly receive, upon their route, your Excellencys orders for their destination, as the Express returns. A Copy of our Resolve, respecting said Draft, is inclosed.[2] As we cannot furnish Tents for these Troops, Your Excellency, will provide for them; perhaps 4000 Men. We shall subsist them 'till their arrival at Horse neck, and depend upon your Excellency's giving orders for their receiving rations after that time. We ardently wish you victory over the Enemies of the American States, and remain, with great respect, Your Excellency's Most obedt humble Serts

Jer: Powell Presidt[3]

LS, DLC:GW; LB, M-Ar: Revolution Letters; Df, M-Ar: Revolution Letters; two copies, M-Ar: Journals of the House of Representatives. According to the extracts from the minutes of the house of representatives and council that appear at the end of the draft, it was approved by both bodies earlier on this date.

1. See Jonathan Trumbull, Sr., to the Massachusetts General Court, 6 Sept., in Force, *American Archives*, 5th ser., 2:205–6, and Hancock to Certain States, 3 Sept., in Smith, *Letters of Delegates*, 5:96–97. For Congress's resolutions of 3 Sept., see *JCC*, 5:734.

2. The enclosed resolution of 11–12 Sept. is in DLC:GW (see also "Mass. Council Journal," Mar.–Sept. 1776 sess., 545–49). The council on 16 Sept.

named Benjamin Lincoln commander of these reinforcements (see ibid., 586).

3. Jeremiah Dummer Powell (1720–1784) of North Yarmouth, District of Maine, served in the Massachusetts house of representatives from 1745 to 1766 and then on provincial council until 1774, when he refused appointment to the mandamus council by Gen. Thomas Gage. Powell was named to the state council on 30 May 1776, and he remained a member until his death, serving as council president from 1776 to 1781.

General Orders

Head Quarters, New-York, sept: 14th 1776.
Parole Bristol.   Countersign Roxbury.

The Court of Inquiry on Major Hatfield, not having been able to proceed he is released from his arrest, until they can attend.

The General is exceedingly anxious that every Soldier should be well provided with Ammunition, and desires, that every officer will be careful to see there is no deficiency in this respect, as it is highly probable they may soon be called to Action.

It is so critical a period, and so interesting to every true lover of his Country, that the General hopes that every officer & Solider will now exert himself to the utmost—it is no time for ease or indulgence—the Arms of the men, the Condition of the sick, care to prevent Imposition in order to avoid danger and duty— Vigilance of Sentries and Guards, are all now requisite—We have once found the bad consequences of a surprize; let the utmost Care be used to prevent another—For this purpose, the General directs that none be put out as sentries at night but pick'd men; that they be visited every half hour, and every motion of the enemy narrowly watched.

General Wadworth's Brigade to furnish two Sentries upon the road, to prevent Waggons, in the public Service, going out empty, or carrying sick.

Benjamin Haywood, late Lieutenant in the 4th Regiment, is appointed Paymaster to said regiment.[1]

Capt. Brown is excused from duty, on account of his assisting the Quarter-Master General.

Varick transcript, DLC:GW; Df, in Joseph Reed's writing, DNA: RG 93, Orderly Books, vol. 15.

1. Benjamin Haywood had been commissioned a second lieutenant in Col. John Nixon's 4th Continental Regiment on 1 Jan. 1776.

From William Bradford

State of Rhode Island &c.

Sir   Bristol September 14th 1776

Governor Cooke having entered the Hospital for Inoculation it becomes incumbent upon me to acquaint your Excellency that upon the Receipt of a Letter of the 3d instant from Mr President Hancock inclosing several Resolves of the General Congress, One of them ordering One of the Continental Battalions in this State to march immediately to New York and requesting the Massachusetts-Bay to send a Regiment of their Militia to replace it and another recommending it to all the States Northward of Virginia to furnish all the Aid in their Power to the Army at New York, I summoned the Committee appointed to act in Cases of Emergency during the Recess of the General Assembly to meet who have taken every necessary Measure to forward the March of the Battalion ordered to New York. Part of them will proceed this Day and the Remainder to Morrow.[1]

The Committee not having it in their Power to afford so speedy an Aid in any other Way have requested Col. Richmond who commands the other Continental Battalion in this State to hold it in Readiness to march at the shortest Notice. And he accordingly will proceed with his Battalion to New York as soon as he shall receive Intelligence that the Regiment from the Massachusetts hath entered this State. To replace it the Committee have Ordered a Battalion of Militia of Seven Hundred Men to be raised and embodied.[2] I have the Honor to be with great Esteem and Respect Sir Your Excellency's Most obedient and Most humble Servant

William Bradford Deputy Governor

LS, DLC:GW; Df, R-Ar.

1. See Hancock to Certain States, 3 Sept., in Smith, *Letters of Delegates,* 5:96–97. For Congress's resolutions of that date regarding reinforcements for New York, see *JCC,* 5:734. The regiment that the committee ordered to march immediately to New York was the one commanded by Col. Christopher Lippitt.

2. This regiment, which was enlisted for three months, was commanded by Col. John Cooke (see Arnold, *History of R.I.,* 2:384). The regiment of Massachusetts militia that marched to Rhode Island was commanded by Col. Joseph Cushing.

To John Hancock

Sir   New York Septr 14th 1776.

I have been duly honored with your favor of the 10th with the Resolution of Congress which accompanied It, and thank them for the confidence they repose in my Judgement respecting the evacuation of the City. I could wish to maintain It, Because I know It to be of Importance,[1] But I am fully convinced that It cannot be done, and that an attempt for that purpose if persevered in, might & most certainly would, be attended with consequences the most fatal and alarming in their nature. Sensible of this, Several of the Genl Officers since the determination of the Council mentioned in my last, petitioned that a Second Council might be called to reconsider the propositions which had been before them upon the Subject.[2] accordingly I called One on the 12th when a large Majority not only determined a removal of the Army prudent but absolutely necessary, declaring they were entirely convinced from a full and minute inquiry into our Situation, that It was extremely perilous and from every movement of the Enemy and the Intelligence received, their plan of Operations was to get in our rear, & by cutting off the Communication with the Main, oblige us to force a passage thro em on the terms they wish, or to become prisoners in some short time for want of necessary supplies of Provision. We are now taking every method in our power to remove the Stores &c. in which we find almost insuperable difficulties. They are so great & so numerous, that I fear we shall not effect the whole before we meet with some interruption. I fully expected that an Attack somewhere would have been made last Night. In that I was disappointed, & happy shall I be If my apprehensions of One to Night or in a day or two, are not confirmed by the Event. If It is deferred a little while longer I flatter myself All will be got away, and our Force be more concentred & of course more likely to resist them with success.

Yesterday afternoon Four Ships of War, Two of Forty & Two of Twenty eight Guns went up the East River, passing between Governors and Long Island, and Anchored about a Mile above the City opposite Mr Stivansents where the Rose Man of War was laying before.[3] The design of their going not being certainly known, gives rise to various Conjectures—Some supposing they are to cover the landing of a part of the Enemy above the City— Others that they are to assist in destroying our Battery at Horn's Hook, that they may have a free and uninterrupted Navigation in the Sound—It is an Object of great importance to them, and what they are industriously trying to effect by a pretty constant Cannonade & Bombardment.

Before I conclude, I would beg leave to mention to Congress, that the pay now allowed to Nurses for their attendance on the sick, is by no means adequate to their services—the consequence of which is, that they are extremely difficult to procure, Indeed they are not to be got, and we are under the necessity of substituting in their place a Number of Men from the respective Regiments, whose service by that means is entirely lost in the proper line of their duty, and but little benefit rendered to the Sick. The Officers I have talked with upon the Subject, All agree that they should be allowed a Dollar ⅌ Week, and that for less they cannot be had.[4] Our Sick are extremely numerous and we find their removal attended with the greatest difficulty; It is a matter that employs much of our time & care, and what makes It more distressing, is the want of proper & convenient places for their reception. I fear their sufferings will be great and many, However nothing on my part that Humanity or policy can require shall be wanting to make them comfortable so far as the State of things will admit of. I have the Honor to be with great respect Sir Your Most Obedt Sert

Go: Washington

LS, in Robert Hanson Harrison's writing, DNA:PCC, item 152; LB, DLC:GW; copy, DNA:PCC, item 169; Varick transcript, DLC:GW. Congress read this letter on 16 Sept. (*JCC,* 5:760).

1. The LB reads: "Because It is known to be of Importance."

2. See Certain General Officers to GW, and GW to Hancock, both 11 September.

3. The *Rose,* which had sailed up the East River on 2 Sept., was anchored near the mouth of Bushwick Creek at this time (see GW to Hancock, 4 Sept.; Mackenzie, *Diary,* 1:38–39; and the logs of the *Carysfort, Orpheus,* and *Roebuck,* 13 Sept., in Clark and Morgan, *Naval Documents,* 6:805–6, 839). For the sailing of the four warships up the East River to join the *Rose,* see GW to Heath, 13 Sept., n.4. Petrus Stuyvesant (1727–1805) lived at Petersfield on the East River in one of three country houses in the Bowery area that had been owned by Gov. Petrus Stuyvesant during the previous century.

4. Congress approved this wage on 9 Oct. (see *JCC,* 6:858).

From Major General William Heath

Kingsbridge Septr 14th 1776

Dear General 3 oClock P.M.

I am Just returned (much Fatigued) from East Chester Bay, where I have been with Genl Clinton and Colonel Chester to Reconnoitre the Ground.

I have the Honor this moment to receive yours of this Day, and have Immediately ordered all the Teams here or that Can be Procured to be Sent to you[1]—Would to God that the Business of a Certain Department, was Performed with alertness, I wish it may not Prove the Loss of many Stores if nothing worse.

your Excellency is Pleased to mention the Brigades which you mean to Send to this Post, I find upon Looking over the List, that all Except one are new Levies or Militia, Such are the Troops now Posted here, Except Three or four Regiments— Three of which your Excellency is pleased to order away—your Excellency will Please to Permit me with all Humility to ask if it be Safe, To trust a Post Considered of So much Importance by the Board of General Officers, Almost Entirely to new Troops, a great Part of whom Know Little of Discipline, and have as yet very few works for their Defence, I Flattered my Self that we should have had a Proportion of the Disciplined Troops here I wished no more, your Excellency is Sensible how Difficult it is to manage New Troops Especially So great a Body of them[2] and how Dangerous must it be to trust so many out Posts as there are in this Post to inExperianced Sentinels.

I am Just Informed that a number of militia and Light Horse, are on their march from Connecticut I have this Day ordered 200 men to relieve Colo. Nixon at Morrissania.

Colo. Hutchinson has Sent the Inclosed to me and Urges an answer before he makes up [h]is abstract.[3] your Excellency will please to give Such Direction as you may think Proper. I have the Honor to be with great respect your Excellencys most Humble Servt

W. Heath

ADfS, MHi: Heath Papers.

1. Heath is referring to GW's letter to him of 13 September. On this date Heath ordered Asst. Q.M. Gen. Hugh Hughes "immediatly to engage and Impress All the Waggons & Teams that you possibly can; which with those

here, you are to send to Newyork, where they are extreamly wanted—The Vessells also which come up with Stores Baggage &ca must be unloaded without Delay and sent down" (MHi: Heath Papers).

2. At this place in the manuscript Heath struck out the following text: "and General Clinton as well as my Self are truly Disapointed, And when there are So many Established Regiments from the State to which I belong, your Excellency will not be Surprised if I Should wish to have Some of them, Since a like Passion is Discovered, in another Gentleman, who I am well Pleased should be gratified, and should think myself Happy under a like gratification if it were not Prejudicial to the Service. I have this Day Releived General Nixons Disciplined Regiment from an Important Post with a Detachment of 200 men one Half new Levies."

3. This enclosure has not been identified.

General Orders

Head Quarters, New York, septr 15th 1776.
Parole Essex.   Countersign Kingsbridge

Varick transcript, DLC:GW; Df, DNA: RG 93, Orderly Books, vol. 15.

General Orders

Head Quarters, Harlem-Heights, sept: 16th 1776.
Parole Bell.   Countersign Maryland.

The Arrangement for this night.

Genl Clinton to form next to the North River, and extend to the left—Genl Scott's Brigade next to Genl Clinton's—Lt Col. Sayer of Col. Griffith's Regt with the three Companies intended for a reinforcement to day, to form upon the left of Scott's Brigade[1]—Genl Nixon's—Col. Serjeant's division, Col. Weedon's and Major Price's Regts[2] are to retire to their quarters and refresh themselves, but to hold themselves in readiness to turn out [at] a minute's warning[3]—Genl McDougall to establish proper guards against his Brigade upon the height, and every Regiment posted upon the Heights, from Morris's house to Genl McDougall's Camp, to furnish proper Guards to prevent a Surprize; Not less than twenty men from each regiment—Genl Putnam commands upon the right-flank to night—Genl Spencer from McDougall's Brigade up to Morris's house—Should the

Enemy attempt to force the pass to night, Genl Putnam is to apply to Genl Spencer for a reinforcement.[4]

Varick transcript, DLC:GW; Df, DNA: RG 93, Orderly Books, vol. 15.

GW had moved his headquarters the previous day to Roger Morris's house on Harlem Heights, the high rocky terrain at the northern end of Manhattan Island lying west and north of the village of Harlem and the Harlem Plains. Morris's handsome Georgian mansion, which stands on a bluff overlooking the Harlem River at present-day 160th Street and Edgecomb Avenue, was on the post road three and a half miles south of King's Bridge and about a mile and a half north of the "Hollow Way," a narrow valley at the southern end of the defensive lines that the Americans established on Harlem Heights after retreating there on 15 September. For an account of that retreat, see GW to Hancock, this date. For an account of the Battle of Harlem Heights which occurred on this date, see GW to Hancock, 18 September. GW's headquarters remained at Morris's house until 21 October.

This day's general orders concern GW's reorganization of his forces on Harlem Heights in anticipation of an attack by General Howe's army which had landed on Manhattan Island the previous day and had established its advanced posts about two miles south of the "Hollow Way" (see GW to Hancock, this date). GW had deployed three divisions on the heights during the evening of 15 September. The southernmost positions overlooking the "Hollow Way" were manned initially by General Greene's division, which included Nixon's, Sargent's, and Beall's brigades, Col. George Weedon's as yet unbrigaded regiment and the recently arrived detachment of Maryland Continentals commanded by Maj. Thomas Price (see John Chilton to an unknown correspondent, 17 Sept., in "Old Virginia Line," 92–94). Between Greene's division and Morris's house GW had placed General Putnam's division consisting of George Clinton's, Scott's, Heard's, Douglas's, and McDougall's brigades, and General Spencer's division consisting of Fellows's, Silliman's, Wadsworth's, and Mifflin's brigades (see Johnston, *Harlem Heights*, 49–50, 64–65, 143).

1. These companies of the 1st Maryland Regiment of flying camp troops apparently were commanded by Lt. Col. Henry Shyrock (c.1736–1814), a Washington County saddler and tavern keeper, whom the Maryland convention had appointed major of the regiment on 27 June 1776 and its lieutenant colonel on 7 August. Shyrock was named lieutenant colonel of the 6th Maryland Regiment in December and resigned his commission on 17 April 1777. He became assistant deputy quartermaster general for Washington County in June 1778, a purchasing agent there in 1779, and county commissary for horses in 1781. Charles Greenberry Griffith (1744–1792), a planter from Frederick County, was appointed lieutenant colonel of the 1st Maryland flying camp on 27 June and became its colonel on 30 July. Griffith left the army in January 1777 and subsequently held various local offices in Frederick County. He was a member of the lower house of the Maryland assembly from 1781 to 1783 and from 1787 to 1788.

2. Thomas Price of Frederick, Md., who had commanded a rifle company at Cambridge from August to November 1775, was appointed major of Col. William Smallwood's Maryland regiment in January 1776.

3. The word "at" appears in the draft.

4. This pass may be the place about three fourths of a mile south of Morris's house where the post road between New York City and King's Bridge ascended Harlem Heights.

To John Hancock

Head Qrs at Col. Roger Morris's House
Sir   Septr 16th 1776

On Saturday about Sunset Six more of the Enemy's Ships, One or Two of which were men of War; passed between Governors Island & Red Hook and went up the East River to the Station taken by those mentioned in my Last[1]—In half an Hour, I received Two Expresses, One from Col. Serjeant at Horn's Hook (Hell Gate) giving an Account that the Enemy to the amount of Three or Four Thousand had marched to the River & were embarking for Barns's or Mont[r]esors Island where Numbers of them were then Incamped; the other from Genl Mifflin, that uncommon & formidable movements were discovered among the Enemy, which being confirmed by the Scouts I had sent out, I proceeded to Harlem where It was supposed, or at Morisania opposite to It, the principal attempt to land would be made[2]— However Nothing remarkable happened that night—But in the morning they began their Operations—Three Ships of War came up the North River as high [as] Bloomingdale which put a total stop to the removal by Water of any more of our provision &c. and about Eleven OClock those in the East River began a most severe and Heavy Cannonade to scour the Grounds and cover the landing of their Troops between Turtle-Bay and the City, where Breast Works had been thrown up to oppose them.[3] As soon as I heard the Firing, I road with all possible dispatch towards the place of landing when to my great surprize and Mortification I found the Troops that had been posted in the Lines retreating with the utmost precipitation and those ordered to support them, parson's & Fellows's Brigades, flying in every direction and in the greatest confusion, notwithstanding the exertions of their Generals to form them. I used every means in my power to rally and get them into some order but my attempts were fruitless and ineffectual, and on the appearance of a small party of the Enemy, not more than Sixty or Seventy, their disorder increased and they ran away in the greatest confusion without firing a Single Shot[4]—Finding that no confidence was to be placed in these Brigades and apprehending that another part of the Enemy might pass over to Harlem plains and cut off the retreat to this place, I sent orders to secure the Heights in the best manner with the Troops that were stationed on and near them, which being done, the retreat was effected with but little or no loss of Men, tho of a considerable part of our Baggage occasioned by this disgracefull and dastardly conduct[5]—Most of our Heavy Cannon and a part of our Stores and provisions which we were about removing was unavoidably left in the City, tho every means after It had been determined in Council to evacuate the post, had been used to prevent It. We are now encamped with the Main body of the Army on the Heights of Harlem where I should hope the Enemy would meet with a defeat in case of an Attack, If the Generality of our Troops would behave with tolerable bravery,[6] but experience to my extreme affliction has convinced me that this is rather to be wished for than expected; However I trust, that there are many who will act like men, and shew themselves worthy of the blessings of Freedom. I have sent out some reconoitring parties to gain Intelligence If possible of the disposition of the Enemy and shall inform Congress of every material event by the earliest Opportunity. I have the Honor to be with the highest respect Sir Your Most Obedt Sert.

L, in Robert Hanson Harrison's writing, DNA:PCC, item 152; LB, DLC:GW; copy, DNA:PCC, item 169; Varick transcript, DLC:GW. Congress read this letter on 17 Sept. (*JCC*, 5:779).

At the end of the letter sent to Hancock, Harrison wrote and signed a note that reads: "The above Letter is nearly a Copy of a rough One sketched out by his Excellency this Morning & who Intended to sign It, but having rode out & his return or where to find him, Incertain I have sent It away without" (DNA:PCC, item 152). For the alarm that called GW away from his headquarters, see GW to Hancock, 18 September.

1. See GW to Hancock, 14 September. Five transports sailed up the East River on Saturday evening, 14 Sept., and anchored at the mouth of Bushwick Creek about six or seven o'clock (see the journals of the *Carysfort* and *Roebuck*, that date, in Clark and Morgan, *Naval Documents*, 6:822–23, 839, and Tatum, *Serle's Journal*, 102–3).

2. No written reports to GW from Sargent or Mifflin on the evening of 14 Sept. have been found. British Capt. Frederick Mackenzie says in his journal entry for 15 Sept.: "Orders were given last night for the four brigades encamped in the Environs of Newtown, to strike their tents at 2 o'Clock this

morning, load their baggage, form at the head of their Encampments, with their blankets and two days provisions, and wait for orders. Some other preparatory movements were also ordered, and executed. At 4 this Morning the Brigade of Guards marched to Newtown where they waited for orders. In this situation we all expected to have received orders to proceed towards Hellgate, and either to have embarked there or at some place farther to the right, in order to make a descent on that part of New York Island opposite; but were much surprized at receiving orders to march towards Bushwick" (Mackenzie, *Diary,* 1:46; see also Lydenberg, *Robertson Diaries,* 97, and Baurmeister, *Revolution in America,* 48). Barns's Island is one of several names given to Buchanan's (now Ward's) Island, which is adjacent to Montresor's (now Randall's) Island in the Hell Gate portion of the East River.

3. The British warships *Renown, Repulse,* and *Pearl* and the schooner *Tryal* were sent up the Hudson River early on 15 Sept. to divert American attention from the landing that Howe's army was preparing to make on the east side of Manhattan Island (see William Howe to George Germain, 21 Sept., in Davies, *Documents of the American Revolution,* 12:227–29, and Lord Howe to Philip Stephens, 18 Sept., in Clark and Morgan, *Naval Documents,* 6:885–90; see also the journals of the *Pearl* and *Renown,* 15 Sept., ibid., 844, 861, and Tatum, *Serle's Journal,* 103).

Shortly after noon about four thousand British and Hessian soldiers in flatboats crossed the East River from Bushwick Point on Long Island and landed on Manhattan Island at Kip's Bay, a small inlet located at the foot of present-day East 34th Street. By 5:00 P.M. about nine thousand more troops were ashore (see Mackenzie, *Diary,* 1:47–49; *Kemble Papers,* 1:88; Lydenberg, *Robertson Diaries,* 97–98; and Ward, *War of the Revolution,* 1:242–44). The preliminary cannonade was delivered by the warships *Phoenix, Roebuck, Rose, Carysfort,* and *Orpheus,* which were anchored two to three hundred yards off shore (see each ship's journal entry for 15 Sept., in Clark and Morgan, *Naval Documents,* 6:839–41, 849; Mackenzie, *Diary,* 1:46–47; and Tatum, *Serle's Journal,* 103). "It is hardly possible to conceive," Midshipman Bartholomew James of the *Orpheus* writes, "what a tremendous fire was kept up by those five ships for only fifty-nine minutes, in which time we fired away, in the Orpheus alone, five thousand three hundred and seventy-six pounds of powder. The first broadside made a considerable breach in their works, and the enemy fled on all sides, confused and calling for quarter, while the army landed, but, as usual, did not pursue the victory, though the rebels in general had left their arms in the intrenchment" (Laughton, *James's Journal,* 31).

4. The LB reads "Sixty or Seventy in Number." Col. William Douglas, whose brigade of Connecticut militia and militia levies occupied crudely dug entrenchments a short distance south of Kip's Bay, wrote his wife three days later, that during the British cannonade, "my Left wing gave way which was form,d of the militia. I Lay myself on the Right wing, wateing for the [British landing] boats untill Capt. Printice [Jonas Prentice] Came to me and told if I ment to Save my Self to Leave the Lines for that was the orders on the Left and that they had Left the Lines. I then told my men to make the best of their way as I then found I had but about ten Left with me. . . . we then had a Mile to Retreat Through as hot a fire as Could well be made but they mostly over shot

us. the Brigade was then in Such a Scatter,d poster [position] that I Could not Collect them and I found the whole Army on a Retreat" (Douglas, "Letters," 13:122; see also Martin, *Private Yankee Doodle*, 32–41).

Brig. Gen. Samuel Holden Parsons marched three of the Continental regiments in his brigade north from Corlear's Hook to reinforce the troops under attack near Kip's Bay. On Murray Hill about a half a mile west of the bay, Parsons met GW, who directed him to keep his troops in order and bring them forward. As the brigade approached the top of the hill from the west, British grenadiers were advancing up its eastern slope from Kip's Bay, and Parsons heard GW shout "Take the walls!" and then add "Take the corn-field!" referring to a field on the nearby post road connecting New York City and King's Bridge. "Immediately from front to rear of the brigade," Parsons later testified, "the men ran to the walls, and some into the corn-field, in a most confused and disordered manner." Parsons "used his utmost endeavour to form the brigade into some order upon that ground, but the men were so dispersed he found it impossible" (report of the court of inquiry on Col. John Tyler, 26 Oct. 1776, in Force, *American Archives*, 5th ser., 2:1251–54). Quickly routing Parsons's and Fellows's brigades, the British grenadiers seized the hill, cutting the post road, and then they halted to wait for the rest of Howe's army to land at Kip's Bay (see *Kemble Papers*, 1:88; Mackenzie, *Diary*, 1:47–48; Lydenberg, *Robertson Diaries*, 97–98).

William Smallwood says in a letter to the Maryland convention of 12 Oct. that during the Kip's Bay landing, "sixty [British] Light Infantry, upon the first fire, put to flight two brigades of the *Connecticut* troops—wretches who, however strange it may appear, from the Brigadier-General down to the private sentinel, were caned and whipped by the Generals *Washington, Putnam,* and *Mifflin,* but even this indignity had no weight, they could not be brought to stand one shot" (Force, *American Archives*, 5th ser., 2:1011–14). Heath says in his memoirs that the poor showing of the troops on 15 Sept. so exasperated GW that he "threw his hat on the ground, and exclaimed, 'Are these the men with which I am to defend America?'" (Wilson, *Heath's Memoirs,* 70). George Weedon wrote John Page on 20 Sept. that GW "was so exhausted" by his efforts to rally the retreating Americans at Kip's Bay, "that he struck Several Officers in their flight, three times dashed his hatt on the Ground, and at last exclaimed 'Good God have I got such Troops as Those.' It was with difficulty his friends could get him to quit the field, so great was his emotions" (Ward, *Duty, Honor or Country,* 59). These stories, which apparently were based on "camp gossip," cannot be substantiated by eyewitness accounts (see Freeman, *Washington,* 4:194, n.118).

5. Howe's delay in moving his troops beyond Murray Hill until late afternoon enabled GW to reform the disorganized American brigades on the Bloomingdale Road a short distance west of the hill and use that road and the upper part of the post road to evacuate nearly all of his army to Harlem Heights before Howe's forces extended their lines across the island to the Hudson River and occupied New York City later that evening (see the report of the court of inquiry on Col. John Tyler, 26 Oct. 1776, in Force, *American Archives*, 5th ser., 2:1251–54; William Smallwood to the Maryland Convention,

12 Oct. 1776, ibid., 1011–14; Mackenzie, *Diary*, 1:49–50; Lydenberg, *Robertson Diaries*, 98–99; and *Kemble Papers*, 1:88).

6. The LB reads "with tolerable resolution." For criticism of GW's decision to defend Harlem Heights and to fight "*a war of posts*," see Graydon, *Memoirs*, 174–75.

From John Hancock

Sir,   Philada Sepr 16th 1776.
   The Congress having at different Times passed sundry Resolves relative to a Variety of Subjects, I do myself the Honour to enclose you a Copy of the same, as necessary for your Information & Direction.[1]
   The Resolve of the 12th respecting Colonel Trumbull, will I trust be satisfactory, & prove the Means of his continuing in an office of such Importance to the Army, and which he has hitherto discharged with the greatest Fidelity & Success. I have the Honour to be with perfect Esteem & Respect Sir your most obed. & very hble Ser.

John Hancock Presidt

LS, DLC:GW; LB, DNA:PCC, item 12A.
   1. Hancock enclosed copies of various resolutions dated 10, 12, and 14 Sept., all of which are in DLC:GW (see also *JCC*, 5:749, 752–54, 757–58). The enclosed resolution of 10 Sept. clarifies Congress's intention to leave any decision to abandon New York City to GW's discretion. In one of the resolutions of 12 Sept., Congress reaffirms its resolve of 8 July giving Commissary Gen. Joseph Trumbull power to supply the northern army by upholding his "Right to direct the Operations of his Department both as Contractor and Issuer of Provisions." The other resolutions of 12 Sept. concern the appointment of a deputy adjutant general and deputy quartermaster general for the northern department and the payment of militia at New York. The resolutions of 14 Sept. deal with rations for militia officers, winter quarters and ammunition supplies for the northern army, procedures to compel discharged soldiers to return all Continental arms, ammunition, and other property, and various personal matters regarding individual officers.

From Richard Peters

War Office [Philadelphia] Septr 16th 1776
   The Board of War have directed me to lay the foregoing Memorial of the Second Lieutenants of the Virginia Regiments before your Excellency for your Opinion & Advice thereon which

the Board request you will communicate to them as soon as convenient.[1] I have the Honor to be Your most obedt humble Servt

Richard Peters Secy

ALS, DLC:GW.

1. Congress read this undated and unsigned petition from the second lieutenants of the 1st Virginia Regiment on 14 Sept. and referred it to the Board of War (*JCC*, 5:760). Addressed to Congress, the document expresses the petitioners' view that promotion of lieutenants should be based on date of commissioning rather than rank within companies, because, they say, their way to future advancement has been blocked by the many first lieutenants who have been "put over their heads" while they were on active duty and unable to seek "that preferment in their different Counties, which their services and friends would probably have procur'd them" (DNA:PCC, item 42).

That argument is refuted explicitly in an undated and unsigned petition addressed to GW about this time by the first lieutenants of the 3d Virginia Regiment. "Yr Memorialists," they write, "woud humbly represent to yr Excellency the Mode by which the Troops were raised in Virginia. . . . Every first Lieutt took Command, & succeeded to a Company before any Second Lieutenant, altho the Commission of the 2d Lieut. was of elder date. The dating of Commissions of the Virgina Officers being from the Completion of the Companies, was the reason why any Second Lieut. bore a Commission of an elder date than a first Lieutenant. . . . Till very lately, no Second Lieutenant entertained an Idea, of ranking before a first Lieutenant—on the contrary, many of the eldest Second Lieutenants have (where Vacancies happened) received first Lieutenants Commissions; & many first Lieutenants, bearing Commissions of younger date than Second Lieutenants, have seceeded to Companies, without the smallest Objection on the part of the second Lieutenants, & this even in the Regiment to which the Petitioners belong" (DLC:GW).

GW returned the second lieutenants' petition with his reply to the Board of War of 30 Sept., in which he says: "Having considered the inclosed Memorial which you were pleased to transmit for my advice thereon, I beg leave to inform you, that in my Opinion, the service will be most advanced in general cases, by directing promotions in a Regimental Line. However I should think this had better be practised than Resolved on, always exercising a right of promotion on account of extraordinary merit or preventing a succession to office where It is wanting and the person claiming unfit for it" (LS, in Robert Hanson Harrison's writing, DNA:PCC, item 152; see also the LB in DLC:GW and the Varick transcript in DLC:GW).

From Major General Philip Schuyler

Dear Sir   Albany Septr 16. 1776.

I do myself the Honor to inclose You Copies of General Arnolds & Colo: Dayton's Letters, In Consequence of the Intelligence they contain, I have dismissed the Militia.[1]

Yesterday I transmitted to Congress, Copies of the Papers here mentioned, together with my Resignation, and have advised them that I shall continue to act as usual, until such a Time is Elapsed, In Which a General Officer can be sent here, If they think It necessary that one should reside here, Which I supposed could not exceed a Fortnight, Immediately after Which I propose Attending my Duty in Congress.[2]

As there is not sufficient Water at this Season to raft Boards to this Place from the Mills, Which border on Hudsons River above this, they must be brought Part of the Way by Land, which will Considerably enhance the price, & Of which I have adviced the Quarter Master General.

I am informed that the Term for which De Haas's Maxwells & Winds Regiments were engaged, expires the Beginning of October & I fear the soldiers will not remain in the Service after that; If they leave Tyonderoga, It will not only weaken but greatly dispirit our Troops. I sincerely wish Congress would take some Measures, If possible to detain these people, untill the Season shall be so far advanced, as that there will be no Prospect of the Enemy attempting any Thing in this Quarter until Another Year.

Your Excellency's Favor of the 12th instant Mr Allen delivered Me Yesterday. I am Dr Sir Most respectfully & sincerely Your Obedient Humble servt

Ph: Schuyler

LS, DLC:GW; LB, NN: Schuyler Papers.

1. The enclosed copies of Arnold's letters to Gates of 7 and 8 Sept. and Col. Elias Dayton's letter to Schuyler of 11 Sept. are in DLC:GW. Arnold reports that on 3 Sept. he arrived with his fleet at Windmill Point near the northern end of Lake Champlain, but anticipating a British attack, he withdrew on the morning of 8 Sept., to Isle La Motte, about seven miles to the south, where he believed "the best Stand" could be made. Dayton writes from Fort Schuyler that he has been unable to confirm the recent rumors of an impending Indian raid on the Mohawk Valley and concludes that no enemy force is "on their way" from Oswego (see Schuyler to GW, 8 Sept., and note 3).

2. Schuyler's letter to Hancock of 14 Sept. is in DNA:PCC, item 153. On 2 Oct. Congress resolved that Schuyler be requested to "continue the command which he now holds" and assured "that the aspersions, which his enemies have thrown out against his character, have had no influence upon the minds of the members of this house . . . and that, in order effectually to put calumny to silence, they will, at an early day, appoint a committee of their body, to enquire fully into his conduct, which, they trust, will establish his reputation in the opinion of all good men" (*JCC,* 5:841).

Letter not found: from Samuel Washington, 16 Sept. 1776. On 5 Oct. GW wrote to his brother Samuel: "Your favour of the 16th of last Month came safe to hand."

General Orders

Head Quarters, Harlem Heights, sept: 17th 1776.
Parole Leitch.   Countersign Virginia.

The General most heartily thanks the troops commanded Yesterday, by Major Leitch, who first advanced upon the enemy, and the others who so resolutely supported them[1]—The Behaviour of Yesterday was such a Contrast, to that of some Troops the day before, as must shew what may be done, where Officers & soldiers will exert themselves—Once more therefore, the General calls upon officers, and men, to act up to the noble cause in which they are engaged, and to support the Honor and Liberties of their Country.

The gallant and brave Col. Knowlton, who would have been an Honor to any Country, having fallen yesterday, while gloriously fighting, Capt. Brown is to take the Command of the party lately led by Col. Knowlton—Officers and men are to obey him accordingly.

The Loss of the Enemy yesterday, would undoubtedly have been much greater, if the Orders of the Commander in Chief had not in some instances been contradicted by inferior officers, who, however well they may mean, ought not to presume to direct[2]—It is therefore ordered, that no officer, commanding a party, and having received Orders from the Commander in Chief, depart from them without Counter Orders from the same Authority; And as many may otherwise err through Ignorance, the Army is now acquainted that the General's Orders are delivered by the Adjutant General, or one of his Aid's-De-Camp, Mr Tilghman, or Col. Moylan the Quarter Master General.

Brigade Majors are to attend at Head Quarters, every day at twelve O'Clock, and as soon as possible to report where their several Brigades and Regiments are posted. If many regiments have not been relieved, for want of the attendance of their Brigade Majors for Orders;[3] It is therefore the Interest and Duty of every Brigadier to see that his Brigade Major attends at twelve

O'Clock at Noon, and five in the afternoon; and they are to be careful to make the Adjutants attend them every day.

The several Major & Brigadier Generals are desired to send to Head-Quarters an Account of the places where they are quartered.

Until some general Arrangement for duty can be fixed, each Brigade is to furnish Guards, who are to parade at their respective Brigadier's quarters, in such proportions as they shall direct.

Such regiments as have expended their Ammunition, or are otherwise deficient, are immediately to be supplied, by applying to the Adjutant General for an Order—but the regiment is to be first paraded, and their Ammunition examined, the commanding officer is then to report how such deficiency has happened.

Varick transcript, DLC:GW; Df, in Joseph Reed's writing, DNA: RG 93, Orderly Books, vol. 15.

1. For an account of the Battle of Harlem Heights on 16 Sept., see GW to Hancock, 18 September. Andrew Leitch (c.1750–1776), merchant from Dumfries, Va., who had visited at Mount Vernon with his wife in April 1775, commanded the Prince William County Independent Company before he was commissioned a captain in the 3d Virginia Regiment on 5 Feb. 1776 (see *Diaries*, 3:313–14, 322–23). Although no record of his promotion to major has been found, Leitch apparently succeeded Thomas Marshall as major of the 3d Virginia Regiment after Congress on 13 Aug. promoted Marshall to lieutenant colonel (see *JCC*, 5:649). Leitch died of his wounds on 1 or 2 Oct. (see GW to Hancock and GW to Samuel Washington, both 5 Oct.).

2. For the failure of GW's plan to cut off a detachment of British light infantrymen by having Knowlton's and Leitch's men march behind them, see GW to Hancock, 18 Sept., n.1.

3. The word "If" is struck out in the draft.

To Nicholas Cooke

Sir   Head Qrs at Colo. Morris's House Septr 17th 1776

I received the honor of your favor of the 6th Inst. by Messrs Collins, Babcock & Stanton, and should have acknowledged It before now, had I not been prevented by the peculiar Situation of our Affairs.

I communicated my Sentiments to those Gentn upon the Subject of your Letter and the several propositions that were before me,[1] who I doubt not will make a full and due report of the same to you and your Honble Assembly: However I shall take the liberty of adding, that the divided State of our Army, which when collected in One body is inferior to that of the Enemy—their Having landed almost the whole of their force on Long Island, and formed a plan of cutting off all communication between that and the City of New York, which we had but too good reasons to beleive practicable and easy to effect with their Ships of War, made It necessary and prudent to withdraw our Troops from the former, that our chance of resistance and opposition might be more probable and likely to be attended with a happy Issue.

I feel myself much concerned on account of your Apprehensions for the Town of Newport and the Island of Rhode Island, and should esteem myself peculiarly happy were It in my power to afford means for their Security and that of the State in General, or to point out such measures as would be effectual for that purpose; But circumstanced as I am, It is not possible for me to grant any Assistance, nor can I with propriety undertake to prescribe the mode which will best promote their defence. This must depend on such a variety of circumstances, that I should suppose you and the Assembly who are in the State will be much more competent to the Task than what I or any person out of It can be, and therefo⟨re⟩ I can only recommend that you will pursue such steps as you in your Judgement shall think most conducive to that end, observing that It appears to me a matter of extreme difficulty (If practicable) to prevent the Enemy's Ships doing damage to every Island accessible to 'em, unless the passes between them and the Main are so narrow as to oblige them to come very near such Batteries as may be erected for their annoyance on commanding Ground.

I cannot sufficiently express my thanks for the readiness you and your Assembly manifested in ordering Troops &c. to Long Island on hearing of my request to Governor Trumbull upon that Subject. At the time that I made It, I conceiv⟨ed⟩ the plan of much Importance, and that many valuable and salutary consequences might have resulted from It, But as Things have undergone a material change since, It may not be improper to consider and be satisfied of some facts, which ought to be clearly known, previous to any attempt to carry It into Execution & on which the success of It will greatly depend—such as an entire conviction of the friendly disposition of the Inhabitants on the Island—the Number that would Join the Troops that might be sent over—The lengths they would go—the Support they would & can give, and whether a retreat from thence, could be safely effected in case It should be necessary—These matters and others which a more minute consideration of the plan will present to your view, should be well weighed and digested & which I thought It my duty to mention especially as the Scheme had originated with me—My Anxiety and concern for the Inhabitants at the East end of the Island, who have been represented always as friendly & well attached to the cause of the States, prompt me to wish them every assistance, but If the Efforts you could make in conjunction with Governor Trumbull would not promise almost a certainty of success, perhaps they might tend to aggravate their misfortunes—The Committee stated sundry propositions respecting this expedition—such as If any thing was attempted where a Stand should be made? This must be left to the discretion of those who command—nor can I spare an Officer for that purpose or recommend One—What Number of Men should be sent? & what proportion from the Massachusetts—The Number necessary will depend upon the force they will have to oppose & the assistance they would derive from the Islanders—the proportion from the Massachusetts on the will of the legislature, or voluntary Engagement of the people in the service—What Artillery they should have? I am of Opinion the Artillery would be subject to loss without any great advantage resulting from It—They also asked whether any Frigates should be sent &c.? As the Enemy have now the free and entire command of the Sound, and many Ships of War in it, they will be much more liable to be taken, than they would have been some time ago, and when It was proposed by Governor Trumbull to make an attempt upon the Ships above Hell Gate. In this Instance However I do not conceive my self at liberty to say any thing peremptory one way or other, having no power over the Frigates.

I am sensible of the force of your Observation, that the Common Cause might be benefited by the Several States receiving early and authentic Intelligence of every material occurrence. permit me at the same time to assure you, that I often regret my incapacity in this instance, and that the neglect does not arise from want of Inclination or thro inattention, but from the variety of Important matters that are always pressing upon and which daily surround me.

Before I conclude I shall take this Opportunity to inform you, that having received certain Information that the Enemy's plan of Operations was to pass from Long Island and Land in our Rear with their Army, to cut off all communication with the Country, and for which they were making every possible disposition, A Council of Genl Oficers determined last Week on a removal of the Army from the City in order to prevent the fatal consequences which must inevitably ensue If they could have executed their Scheme, resolving at the same time, that every appearance of defence should be kept up till Our Sick, Ordinance & Other Stores could be removed.[2] This was set about with the greatest Industry and as to the Sick was compleatly effected, but on Sunday morning before we had accomplished the removal of all our Cannon, provision & Baggage, they sent three Ships of War up the North River whereby the Water carriage was totally stopped, the Ships Anchoring not far above the City. and about Eleven OClock those that were laying at Turtle Bay or rather below It in the East River, being Six or Seven in Number besides some Transports, began and continued for some Time a most severe and Heavy Canonade to scour the Ground and cover the Landing of their Troops. I had gone the Night before to the Main body of the Army which was posted on the plains and Heights of Harlem, apprehending from many uncommon and great movements among the Enemy that they meant to make an attack there that Night, or to land on the East side of Harlem River. As soon as the firing began, I rode with all possible dispatc⟨h⟩ towards the place of landing where Breast Works had been thrown up, and to my great surprize and mortification found the Troop⟨s⟩ that had been posted in the Lines retreating with the utmost precip[it]ation and disorder and those ordered to support them, notwithstanding the exertions of their Brigadiers, Parsons & Fellows, to form them, running away in the most disgraceful and shamefull manner, nor could my utmost efforts rally them or prevent their flight. This scandalous conduct occasioned a loss of Several Tents and Other Baggage which Otherwise would have been easily secured— The remainder of the Troops that were in the City got out and the retreat of the whole was effected with the loss of but very few Men, not more than three or four that I have heard of were made prisoners, & only One or two killed. I am now Encamped on the Heights above mentioned which are so well calculated for defence, that I should hope If the Enemy make an Attack and our Men will behave with tolerable resolution, they must meet with a repulse if not a total defeat. They advanced in sight Yesterday in several large bodies, but attempted Nothing of a General nature—Tho in the forenoon there were some smart skirmishes between some of their parties and detachments sent out by me, in which I have the pleasure to inform you our Men behaved with bravery and Intrepidity, putting them to flight when in Open Ground and forcing them from posts they had Seized Two or three times. from some of their wounded Men which fell into our Hands, the appearance of blood in every place where they made their Stand and on the fences they passed,[3] we have reason to beleive they had a good many killed & wounded, tho they did not leave many on the Ground—In number our Loss was very inconsiderable, but in the fall of Lieutt Colo. Knolton I consider It as great, being a brave and good Officer and It may be increased by the death of Major Leitch of the Virginia Regiment who unfortunately received Three Balls thro his side.[4] Having given you a Summary Account of the situation of our Affairs & in such manner as circumstances will admit of I have only to add that I have the honor to be with Sentiments of the highest esteem Sir Your Most Obedt Servt

Go: Washington

P.S. The Committee have expressed their apprehensions of being Obliged to abandon the Island of Rhode Island & Newport & requested my Opinion—At present I can see no cause for It, & the propriety of the measure must depend upon circumstances—But I should suppose they ought to be very pressing & the Necessity great before they ought to be given up. Most certainly no Immaginary Ills or Necessity should lead to such a measure—At this Time the danger can only be Ideal—and If the Enemy persevere in their plans here & our Men behave as they should do, I am persuaded they will not have an Opportunity to employ their attention elsewhere this Campaig⟨n.⟩

LS, in Robert Hanson Harrison's writing, R-Ar; LB, DLC:GW; Varick transcript, DLC:GW. The few mutilated portions of the text of the LS are supplied within angle brackets from the LB.

1. The LB reads "before us."
2. GW is referring to the council of war that met on 12 September.
3. The LB reads "as they passed."
4. For a fuller account of the Battle of Harlem Heights, see GW to Hancock, 18 September.

To Colonel John Glover

Sir.   Head Quarters Col. Morriss's Sept. 17th 1776.
On the receipt of your letter communicating the intelligence from Col. Durkie, respecting the desertion of the militia from Powles hook, I have ordered Col. Williams regiment of militia, amounting to about five hundred men, to march immedy, as a reinforcement to Col. Durkie; Col. Knox will direct what shot & shells, are to be sent over, & I shall give orders that boats be prepared to transport the waggons.[1] Col. Putnam has marked out some works, near Burdetts ferry in order to defend & secure that post; These I request and desire may be carried on with all possible expedition; I think your incampment on the low grounds is altogether improper, and ought to be removed immediately to the heights as I am clear of opinion that when you are attacked by the enemy, it will be in your rear. Yr hhble Servt
                                                        Go: Washington

P.S. Col. Glover will send the letters to Col. Durkie & Genl Mercer immediately.[2]

LS, in William Grayson's writing, owned (1993) by Mr. Joseph Rubinfine, West Palm Beach, Florida.

1. Glover's letter, which has not been found, apparently reported the panic-stricken retreat of Col. John Duychinck's regiment of Middlesex County, N.J., militia from Paulus Hook to Bergen on the morning of 16 Sept., when the British warship *Renown* fired several broadsides at that post (see the *Renown's* journal entry for that date, in Clark and Morgan, *Naval Documents,* 6:861, and Extract from a Journal Kept by the Chaplain of Colonel Durkee's Regiment, 15–23 Sept., in Force, *American Archives,* 5th ser., 2:460–62). The flight of the militia left only "about three hundred effective men" of Col. John Durkee's 20th Continental Regiment at Paulus Hook (ibid.).

William Williams (1730–1811), a successful merchant from Lebanon, Conn., and a son-in-law of Gov. Jonathan Trumbull, was colonel of the 12th Connecticut Regiment of militia, one of the nine militia regiments that the state council of safety recently had ordered to march towards New York. At this time, however, Williams was in Philadelphia attending the Continental Congress, to which he had been elected in October 1775, and in his absence Lt. Col. Obadiah Hosford (Horsford) commanded the regiment (see Conn. Hist. Soc., *Collections*, 8:159, and Force, *American Archives*, 5th ser., 2:909–10). Williams was reelected to Congress in October 1776, and in December, citing the overwhelming pressures of his civil duties, he resigned his commission as colonel of the 12th Regiment. A member of the Connecticut house of representatives from 1757 to 1776 and from 1781 to 1784, Williams served as its speaker in 1775 and from 1781 to 1783. He was elected to Congress in 1783 and 1784 but did not attend.

2. GW apparently is referring to unidentified letters written to these officers by William Grayson on 16 Sept. (see Mercer to GW, this date, and Glover to GW, 18 Sept.).

To Major General William Heath

Sir.   Head Quarters Col. Morriss[']s Sept. 17th 1776.
    Some advices lately recieved from Powle's hook, has made it necessary that Col. William's regiment, should march to that post as a re-inforcement to Col. Durkie; it will be proper therefore they should be immedy put in motion towards Mount Washington, where they are to cross. Yr hhble Servt
                                                    Go: Washington

LS, in William Grayson's writing, MHi: Heath Papers.

From Brigadier General Hugh Mercer

Sir,   Perth Amboy [N.J.] 17th Sept. 1776 4 P.M.
    I receved just now the favour of Col. Graysons Letter of Yesterday[1] and in consequence shall send off a Detachment of the Men inlisted for the Flying Camp—to Powlis Hook—The Melitia of Pennsylva. and New Jersey stationed on Bergen and at Powlis Hook have behaved in a scandalous Manner—running off from their Posts on the first Cannonade from the Ships of the Enemy—Att all the Posts we find it difficult to keep the Melitia to their duty—By some Accounts recived to day—the Enemy met with a repulse from your Troops—I beg leave to congratulate your Excellency on the Success and hope it will Animate our

Army to act more generally with the Spirit of Freemen. I have the honour to be Sir your Excellencys Most obedt Sert

H. Mercer

ALS, DLC:GW.

1. This letter has not been identified.

General Orders

Head Quarters, Harlem-Heights, Sept: 18th 1776.

Parole Jersey.   Countersign Newport.

The Brigade Majors are immediately to settle a Court Martial for the trial of prisoners; to meet at the white house near Head Quarters.[1]

Commanding Officers of regiments, and all other officers, are charged in the strictest manner, to prevent all plundering, and to seize every Soldier carrying Plunder, whether belonging to the same regiment or not, or on whatever pretence it is taken, and the General positively commands, that such plunderer be immediately carried to the next Brigadier or commanding officer of a regiment, who is instantly to have the offender whipped on the spot.

The Regimental Surgeons are to take care of their own sick for the present, until the General Hospital can be established on a proper footing—They are to keep as near their regiments as possible, and in case of Action to leave their Sick under the care of their Mates, and be at hand to assist the wounded.

Under the pretence of ranging or scouting, the greatest irregularities and excesses have been committed, the General therefore forbids in the most express manner, any such parties, but by his leave, or of the Brigadier General of the day in writing & then always to be under the direction of an officer—The General does not mean to discourage patrolling and scouting Parties, when properly regulated, on the other hand he will be pleased with, and accept the services of any good officers, who are desirous of being thus employed, and will distinguish them.

Genl Parsons, Genl Scott's and Col. Sergeant's Brigades are to march over Kingsbridge and take General Heath's Orders for encamping—Col. Shee, Magaw, Haslett, and the regiment under Col. Brodhead, are to return to Mount Washington, and be under the immediate Care of Genl Mifflin.

Col. Wards Regiment from Connecticut, may for the present, be annexed to the Brigade commanded by Col: serjeant.

Genl Mifflin's, McDougall's, Heard's, Wadworth's, and Fellow's Brigades, and the Brigades under the Command of Cols. Silliman & Douglass, are to have each a regiment in the Field this evening, by Mr Kortright's house.[2]

Varick transcript, DLC:GW; Df (incomplete), in Joseph Reed's writing, DNA: RG 93, Orderly Books, vol. 15. The two passwords in the draft are not in Reed's writing.

1. The white house apparently stood where present-day St. Nicholas Avenue meets 160th Street (Johnston, *Harlem Heights,* 93). "Williams' Diary," 48:343–44, reads: "to meet at the Brick House back of the Lines immediately[.] Orderly Sergts. from Genl. McDugals General Parsons Genl. Nixons General Wadsworth General Heards Colo. Duglass & Colo Sillimans brigade to attend at Head Quarters every Day." The latter sentence is struck out in the draft.

2. The draft ends: "by Mr Cortrights House back of." "Williams' Diary," 48:344, reads: "by McCartrights House back of the Lines at 5 O'Clock this afternoon as Piquet Advance Posts the whole to be under the command of Brigadier Generals who are to see thay are properly posted from the North River round to the Encampment above the Road.

"Genl. McDougal Brigadier of the Day & to appoint the Field officers of the Picquet. All Fireing in Camp is Expressly forbid but under the Direction of an Officer at Retreat Beating Any offender to be immediately seized & receive 10 Lashes by order of the nearest Brigadier or Colo. of a Regiment.

"An exact return of each Regt. to be given to the Adjutant General Without Delay noticing the Number of Men Killed & Wounded in the Late Skirmish on the 16th.

"The Brigadiers & Officers commanding Brigades are to settle with the Quarter Master General for the Waggons which may be necessary to do the Ordinary Dutys of the Brigade & the latter is to Furnish them accordingly."

Gen. Joseph Spencer's headquarters was at a house rented by Lawrence Kortwright in the area east of present-day Amsterdam Avenue near 148th Street. The grand parade ground of the army was in an adjoining field (Johnston, *Harlem Heights,* 93).

From Colonel John Glover

Sir   Burdit's ferry Sept: 18. 1776.

The express I sent off to Genl Merser is this moment returned being obliged to go to Amboy to find him. Inclosed is his letter to your Excellency.[1]

Col. Bawldwin's Regit is much in want of tents, there being none to be had here, nor any barns but what are taken for the sick. The men by being so much exposed, I fear will be all sick, & very soon unfit for duty.

The enemy are forming an encampment on the edge of the North River, about one mile below the ground where the Battle was fought on Monday last.[2] I have moved the Brigade up the hill about one & half from the ferry. Col. Bradley's Regt is posted between my Brigade & Pawles Hook. The Asia man-of-war passed by that post nine o'clock this morning; Col. Durke saluted her with 5 shots, 32 pounders, which was not returned.[3] Col. Durke expects to be reinforced with 500 men from Gen. Merser, when he hopes to defend the fort should he be attacked. I am with duty & respect Your Excellencys most obedient Huml. Sert

John Glover

Transcript, NN: Bancroft Collection.

1. See Mercer to GW, 17 September.
2. The previous Monday was 16 September.
3. The British warship that passed Paulus Hook this morning was the *Renown* (see Tatum, *Serle's Journal*, 108; see also Extract from a Journal Kept by the Chaplain of Colonel Durkee's Regiment, in Force, *American Archives*, 5th ser., 2:460–62).

To Colonel John Glover

Head Quarters, Col. Morriss's, September 18, 1776.
Sir: The inconveniences Col. Baldwin's regiment must of necessity be exposed to, for the want of tents, is a circumstance I can only lament but cannot remedy; to supply them from this place is altogether out of my power, as one half of the brigades from here are in the same situation; all I can say on the subject is to recommend to you, the building of huts in the most convenient manner the nature of the case will admit of, to answer the present purpose, until proper barracks can be erected; where these huts are to be placed, as also the propriety of continuing your present encampment so far distant from the ferry as a mile and a half, will be determined upon the spot by Gen. Green and yourself; he is gone to visit your quarters to day.[1] I am, etc.

Fitzpatrick, *Writings*, 6:70.

1. Greene took command of the American forces in New Jersey on 17 Sept.

and made his headquarters at Fort Constitution (later called Fort Lee) at Burdett's ferry (see Greene to Nicholas Cooke, 17 Sept., in Showman, *Greene Papers*, 1:300–302).

To John Hancock

Head Qrs at Colo. Roger Morris's House

Sir   Septr 18th 1776

As my Letter of the 16th contained Intelligence of an Important nature, and such as might lead Congress to expect, that the evacuation of New York and retreat to the Heights of Harlem in the manner they were made, would be succeeded by some other Interesting event, I beg leave to inform them, that as yet nothing has been attempted upon a large and general plan of Attack.

About the time of the posts departure with my Letter, the Enemy appeared in several large bodies upon the plains about Two & a half miles from hence. I rode down to our advanced posts to put matters in a proper situation if they should attempt to come on. When I arrived there, I heard a firing which I was informed was between a party of our Rangers under the Command of Lieutt Col. Knolton, and an advanced party of the Enemy. Our Men came in & told me that the body of the Enemy, who kept themselves concealed consisted of about three Hundred as near as they could guess. I immediately ordered three Companies of Colo. Weedons Regiment from Virginia under the command of Major Leitch & Col. Knolton with his Rangers, composed of Volunteers from different New England Regiments, to try to get in their Rear, while a disposition was making as If to attack them in front, and thereby draw their whole attention that way. This took effect as I wished on the part of the Enemy. On the appearance of our party in front, they immediately ran down the Hill, took possession of some fences & Bushes and a Smart firing began, but at too great a distance to do much execution on either side. The parties under Colo. Knolton & Major Leitch unluckily began their attack too soon, as It was rather in flank than in Rear. In a little time Major Leitch was brought off wounded, having received Three Balls thro his side, and in a short time after Colo. Knolton got a wound which proved mortal. Their Men however persevered &

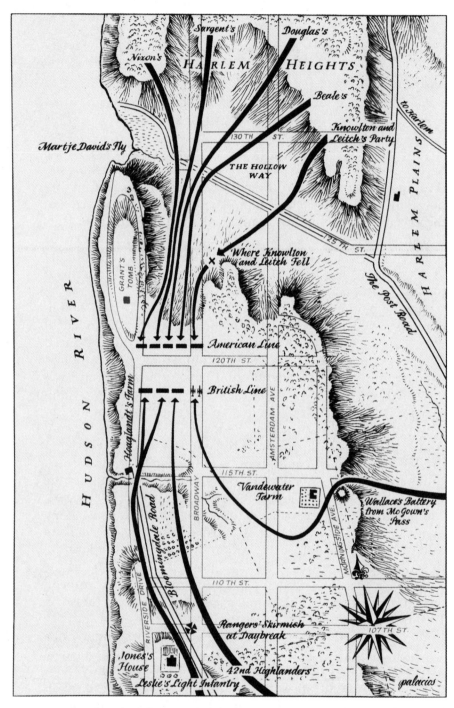

Map 3. The Battle of Harlem Heights, 16 September 1776. From Battle for Manhattan *by Bruce Bliven, Jr. (New York: Henry Holt and Company, 1956). Reproduced by permission of the cartographer, Rafael D. Palacios, Isla Verde, Puerto Rico.*

continued the Engagement with the greatest resolution.[1] Finding that they wanted a support, I advanced part of Colo. Griffiths and Colo. Richardson's Maryland Regiments with some detachments from the Eastern Regiments who were nearest the place of Action. These Troops charged the Enemy with great Intrepidity and drove them from the Wood into the plain, and were pushing them from thence, (having silenced their fire in a great measure) when I judged It prudent to order a Retreat, fearing the Enemy (as I have since found was really the case) were sending a large Body to support their party.[2] Major Leitch I am in hopes will recover, But Colo. Knolton's fall is much to be regretted, as that of a brave & good Officer. We had about Forty wounded, the Number of Slain is not yet ascertained, but It is very inconsiderable. By a Serjeant who deserted from the Enemy & came in this Morning, I find that their party was greater than I immagined—It consisted of the 2d Batallion of Light Infantry, a Batallion of the Royal Highlanders & Three Companies of the Hessian Rifle Men, under the command of Brigadr Genl Leslie. The Deserter reports that their loss in Wounded & Missing was Eighty Nine, and Eight killed—In the latter, his Account is too small as Our people discovered and buried double that Number.[3] This Affair I am in hopes will be attended with many salutary consequences, as It seems to have greatly inspirited the whole of our Troops. The Serjeant further adds, that a Considerable body of Men are now encamped from the East to the North River, between the Seven & Eight mile Stones under the command of Genl Clinton—Genl Howe he beleives has his Quarters at Mr Apthorps House.[4] I have the Honor to be with Sentiments of the highest regard & esteem Sir Yr Most Obedt Sert

Go: Washington

P.S. I should have wrote Congress by Express before now, had I not expected the post every Minute which I flatter myself will be a sufficient Apology for my delaying It.

The late losses we have sustained in our Baggage & Camp necessaries have added much to our distress which was very great before, I must therefore take the Liberty of requesting Congress to have forwarded as soon as possible such a supply of Tents, Blankets, camp Kettles and Other Articles as can be collected. We cannot be ovrstocked.

G.W.

LS, in Robert Hanson Harrison's writing, DNA:PCC, item 152; LB, DLC:GW; copy, DNA:PCC, item 169; Varick transcript, DLC:GW. Congress read this letter on 20 Sept. (*JCC*, 5:787). A somewhat condensed and partially altered version of this letter appears in Dixon and Hunter's edition of the *Virginia Gazette* (Williamsburg) for 4 Oct. 1776 as an "*extract of a letter from a General officer, who was present at the time of action.*"

Although the action of 16 Sept. described in this letter has become known as the Battle of Harlem Heights, it consisted, as GW wrote Nicholas Cooke on 17 Sept., only of "some smart skirmishes" between detachments of the two contending armies. This indecisive little engagement raised the Americans' morale, however, by reassuring them in the wake of the previous day's debacle at Kip's Bay that many of their soldiers could and would fight bravely and well against British and Hessian regulars in small unit actions. For general accounts of this engagement, see particularly Johnston, *Harlem Heights*, 44–91; Blivin, *Battle for Manhattan*, 83–100; Freeman, *Washington*, 4:197–203; and Ward, *War of the Revolution*, 1:246–52.

1. Joseph Reed says in a letter to his wife, Esther De Berdt Reed, of 17 Sept. that on the morning of 16 Sept. "an Acct. came that the Enemy were advancing upon us in three large Columns—we have so many false Reports that I desired the General [GW] to permit me to go & discover what Truth there was in the Acct. I accordingly went down to our most advanced Guard [Knowlton's rangers] & while I was talking with the Officer, the Enemy's advanced Guard fired upon us at a small Distance, our men behaved well stood & return'd the Fire till overpowered by numbers they were obliged to retreat. . . . Finding how things were going I went over to the General to get some support for the brave Fellows who had behaved so well—by the Time I got to him the Enemy appeared in open view & in the most insulting manner sounded their Bugle Horns as is usual after a Fox Chase. I never felt such a sensation before, it seem'd to crown our Disgrace. The General was prevailed on to order over a Party to attack them & as I had been upon the Ground which no one else had it fell to me to conduct them—an unhappy Movement was made by a Regt. of ours which had been ordered to amuse them [the British] while those I was with expected to take them in the Rear—but being diverted by this the Virginia Regimt. with which I was went another course; finding there was no stopping them I went with them the new Way—& in a few Minutes our brave Fellows mounted up the Rocks & attacked them; then they ran in Turn— each Party sent in more Succours so that at last it became a very considerable Engagement & Men fell on every side" (Johnston, *Harlem Heights*, 134–36). Reed's letter to his wife of 22 Sept., contains a somewhat different version of these events, in which he says that Knowlton's and Leitch's attempt to cut off the British detachment "was unhappily thwarted . . . by some Persons calling to the Troops & taking them out of the Road I intended" (ibid., 136–39).

The first skirmish of the day occurred near the British advanced posts in the vicinity of present-day West 107th Street about dawn when two or three companies of British light infantry discovered and attacked Knowlton's rangers, a force of about one hundred and twenty New England volunteers whom GW had sent out to obtain intelligence about the dispositions of Howe's army.

After firing eight or nine rounds and suffering ten casualties, Knowlton's men retreated north about two-and-a-half miles to the American advanced posts on the heights overlooking the "Hollow Way," where GW had positioned himself (see letter attributed to Capt. Stephen Brown, 21 Sept., ibid., 154–55; Oliver Burnham's recollections, ibid., 178–80; William Howe to George Germain, 21 Sept., in Davies, *Documents of the American Revolution*, 12:227–29; Tatum, *Serle's Journal*, 107–8; Mackenzie, *Diary*, 1:51; *Kemble Papers*, 1:89; and Lydenberg, *Robertson Diaries*, 99).

The American counterattack was launched about eleven o'clock across the "Hollow Way" from the American-held heights on the valley's north side toward Vandewater's (now Morningside) Heights on its south side, where British troops had taken up positions a short time earlier. Leitch and Knowlton fell as the Americans fought their way up Vandewater's Heights. The British made a stand at the top of the heights in a buckwheat field near present-day 120th Street where the heaviest fighting of the day occurred from about noon to about one o'clock.

Leitch's detachment consisted of captains Charles West's, John Thornton's, and John Ashby's companies. The decoying force that drew the British troops down from Vandewater's Heights included the rest of Weedon's regiment, a detachment of one hundred and fifty volunteers commanded by Lt. Col. Archibald Crary from Gen. John Nixon's brigade, and some Maryland troops, probably Maj. Thomas Price's three companies (see John Chilton to an unknown correspondent, 17 Sept., in "Old Virginia Line," 92–94, and John Gooch to Thomas Fayerweather, 23 Sept., in "Revolutionary Actors," 334–35).

2. The British retreated to their advanced posts near present-day 106th Street, where the Americans broke off the engagement. GW sent Tench Tilghman to recall the troops, who, Tilghman says, "gave a Hurra and left the Field in good Order" (Tench Tilghman to James Tilghman, Sr., 19 Sept., in Tilghman, *Memoir*, 138–39; see also Joseph Reed to Esther De Berdt Reed, 17 and 22 Sept., in Johnston, *Harlem Heights*, 134–39).

The Maryland flying camp troops that GW sent forward included three companies commanded by Maj. Peter Mantz from Col. Charles Greenberry Griffith's 1st Regiment and apparently three companies commanded by Maj. James Eden from Col. Thomas Ewing's 3d Regiment (see Extract of a Letter to a Gentleman in Annapolis, 17 Sept., in Force, *American Archives*, 5th ser., 2:370–71; William Beatty, Jr., to William Beatty, Sr., 18 Sept., in the *Historical Magazine*, 2d ser., 1 [1867], 147; and Johnston, *Harlem Heights*, 82, and note 1). There is no evidence that any troops from Col. William Richardson's 4th Regiment fought on 16 September. The New England reinforcements included the remainder of Nixon's brigade and Col. William Douglas's and Col. Paul Dudley Sargent's regiments (see John Gooch to Thomas Fayerweather, 23 Sept., in "Revolutionary Actors," 334–35; Joseph Hodgkins to Sarah Perkins Hodgkins, 30 Sept., in Wade and Lively, *This Glorious Cause*, 221–23; Martin, *Private Yankee Doodle*, 42–43; and the returns of Nixon's, Sargent's, and Douglas's brigades, in Force, *American Archives*, 5th ser., 3:721–28).

William Richardson (1735–1825), a merchant from Caroline County, Md., was a member of the general assembly from 1771 to 1774 and the convention from 1774 to 17 Aug. 1776 when he was named colonel of the 4th Regiment of the state's flying camp troops. Richardson did not arrive at Harlem Heights until sometime after 5 Oct. (see returns of officers of the Maryland flying camp, that date, in Force, *American Archives*, 5th ser., 2:897, 900). He became colonel of the 5th Maryland Regiment in December and served until 22 Oct. 1779 when he resigned his commission.

3. American losses on 16 Sept. included at least thirty-five officers and men killed, sixteen men missing, and five officers and men captured (see the casualty returns for Nixon's, Sargent's, Fellows's, and Douglas's brigades, and the 10th, 14th, 19th, and 23d Continental regiments, 18–23 Nov. 1776, in Force, *American Archives*, 5th ser., 3:719–30; Extract of a Letter to a Gentleman in Annapolis, 17 Sept., ibid., 2:370–71; and Gustavus B. Wallace to his brother, 18 Sept., in "Old Virginia Line," 94–95). The number of American wounded probably was about one hundred (see Johnston, *Harlem Heights*, 87–88).

British losses in the engagement, General Howe says, were fourteen men killed and eight officers and about seventy men wounded (Howe to George Germain, 21 Sept., in Davies, *Documents of the American Revolution*, 12:227–29). Col. Stephen Kemble agrees that fourteen British soldiers were killed, but says that eleven officers and 146 men were wounded (*Kemble Papers*, 1:89). Hessian Captain Baurmeister says that twenty British were killed and 210 British and five Hessians were wounded (Baurmeister, *Revolution in America*, 50). Gen. George Clinton, who sent out parties to bury the American dead on the morning of 17 Sept., wrote his brother-in-law, Dr. Peter Tappen, on 21 Sept. that "the Enemy removed theirs in the Night[.] we found above 60 Places where dead Men had lay from Pudles of Blood & other appearances & at other Places fragments of Bandages & Lint" (Johnston, *Harlem Heights*, 142–45).

Alexander Leslie (1731–1794), who had served as lieutenant colonel of the 64th Regiment at Boston for several years before the war and during the siege of 1775–76, was brevetted a brigadier general in America by General Howe on 3 April 1776 and commanded the light infantry brigade during the New York and New Jersey campaigns. Leslie became a major general in the spring of 1779, and in October 1780 he led an expedition to Virginia before joining Cornwallis in South Carolina in December. Leslie was promoted to lieutenant general in July 1781, and that fall he succeeded Cornwallis as commander of the southern theater.

4. The main lines of Howe's army ran from Horn's Hook on the East River at present-day East 89th Street to the Hudson River near Bloomingdale with advanced posts a short distance north between McGown's Pass near the northeast corner of present-day Central Park and the Hudson in the vicinity of present-day West 106th Street (see William Howe to George Germain, 21 Sept., in Davies, *Documents of the American Revolution*, 12:227–29, and Mackenzie, *Diary*, 1:56–57). After the landing at Kip's Bay on 15 Sept., Frederick Mackenzie says Howe "took up his quarters at Mr Elliott's house, about 2 miles from New York" (ibid., 50). By 23 Sept. Howe's headquarters was about four miles from the city "at Lt. Col. James Beekman's House on the East River near Turtle Bay" (Letter from New York, 23 Sept., in Johnston, *Harlem Heights*, 210). Apthorp's mansion at Bloomingdale near the present-day intersection

of 91st Street and 10th Avenue probably was Gen. Henry Clinton's headquarters (see ibid., 51–52). Charles Ward Apthorp (d. 1797), a member of the king's council for New York, fled to Governor Tryon's ship, the *Dutchess of Gordon*, in June 1776 when he was summoned to appear before the provincial congress as a suspected Loyalist. In 1779 Apthorp was indicted for treason, and the following year his Bloomingdale estate was confiscated and offered for sale. He returned to New York after the war, however, and was acquitted of the charges against him.

From Major General William Heath

Dear General.   Kingsbridge Sept. 18th 1776

Upon the receipt of yours on Yesterday I immediately sent an Express to West-Chester, with the Letter directed to Col. Williams, & a Line from myself for his immediate march to Mount Washington—The Express informs that Col. Williams with his Regiment was not arriv'd, but hourly expected—The Major of the Regiment is at West-Chester, and will as soon as the Regiment reaches that place deliver the Letters, & quicken their March (Suppose the Rain Yesterday morning retarded their March).[1]

The Ship which lies off Morrissania is continually annoying our Guards at that post—She is a 36 Gun Frigate—Her Shot are 12 & 18 prs—Her Distance from the Shore supposed to be ¾ of a mile[2]—In addition to the ship, Two one Gun Batteries are opened, at a Distance the one from the other which make a Cross Fire—As Col. Knox is with your Excellency I should be Glad to know your Excellency's Opinion, whether it would be best to send Down a Howtzier, & a Piece or Two of Cannon to return their Compliments—The House on Montrosure's Island is undoubtedly filled with Officers, & a very large Barn with Soldiers, we have avoided Cannonading of them lest they should make us uncomfortable at General Morrisses & Mrs Morrisses Houses—But as they have begun, & already fired several Shot thro' the Out Houses, we are desirous to make them equally uneasy, if your Excellency should think it adviseable—Mrs Morris continues still at her House, & whether the preserving of those Houses, which will doubtless be more damaged in Consequence of our Batteries, which must be opened close to them, should forbid it or not Your Excellency will please to determine.

The Condition of the Sick & wounded scattered all along the Road, makes it my Duty to acquaint your Excellency therewith—Some of the wounded were with their wounds undressed Yesterday Afternoon as I was well informed—The Sick are without Physicians actually many of them dying—And where there are Physicians, they are destitute of Medicine, and no Director to be found—Such Scenes are enough to shock every feeling of Humanity, & Regularity, & unless speedily rectify'd will be an eternal Bar to the raising of Troops in future—Your Excellency will excuse me in the mention of the Sick, as Duty constrains me to do—and your Excellency can form no Idea of their Sufferings, unless you were to see them. I have the honor to be With great Respect Your Excellency's Most humbe Servt

W. Heath

ADfS, MHi: Heath Papers.

1. Jeremiah Mason (1730–1813) of Lebanon was the major of Col. William Williams's 12th Regiment of Connecticut militia at this time. During the previous winter Mason had served at Cambridge as a captain in Col. James Wadsworth's Connecticut state regiment, and in December 1776 the general assembly appointed Mason colonel of the 12th Regiment of militia.

2. Heath is referring to the thirty-two-gun British frigate *Brune* (see Robert Hanson Harrison to Hancock, 12 Sept.).

To Major General William Heath

Sir.   Head Quarters. Col. Morriss's Sept. 18th 1776.

I have now your letter of Sept. 18th before me; and cannot say that I, by any means approve of your proposal of sending artillery to annoy the frigate, and the Enemy's batteries on Montrasure's Island; in my opinion, it would only endanger the loss of our cannon, & waste our ammunition, without answering any one good or salutory purpose.

With respect to the sick, I am as much afflicted at their situation as you or any other person can possibly be, and have taken every step in my power to prevent it; I have furnish'd money to officers chosen by the commanders of different regiments, for the purpose of providing suitable & proper accomodations for the convalescents, and as to the others I have this morning spoke to Doctor Mcknight on the subject and have recommended in the strongest manner to him to fall upon every method the nature of the case will admit of for their relief; and I request you will give him every assistance in your power towards effecting this salutary end.[1]

I have ordered over to you, Parsons's Scott's and Sergents brigades, to which will be added Col. Ward's regiment, and Haslett's Shee's, McGaw's & Atlee's battalions are to come to this place; you will post these brigades in the most advantageous manner; for the present I do not concieve you are in any great danger of being attacked on that quarter, as I have recieved intelligence that the enemy have drawn over their principal force to this Island. I am Sir Yr hhble Servt

Go: Washington

LS, in William Grayson's writing, MHi: Heath Papers.

1. Charles McKnight, Jr. (1750–1791), who was surgeon for the Pennsylvania flying camp troops, wrote Adj. Gen. Joseph Reed on 21 Sept. about his inability to find any bark, which "is so very necessary for many of the wounded in their present Condition, Wine may be the best Substitute we can prescribe to support the Strength of the Patient sinking under too profuse a Suppuretion. There are two Pipes near by us, the Property of Montizeiur, & should you think prope⟨r⟩ to grant an Order for it, We can immediately appropriate it for the Use of the Wounded." On the reverse of that letter, GW on the same day signed an order directing Commissary Gen. Joseph Trumbull to procure the wine for the use of the hospital, and below that order appears a copy of Trumbull's receipt of 23 Sept. for two pipes of Madeira, "said to be the property of Colo. [John] Montresor," received from Sarah Morris at Morrisania (Ct: Joseph Trumbull Papers). McKnight became senior surgeon of the flying hospital in the middle department in April 1777. Congress named him surgeon general of that department in February 1778, and in October 1780 it appointed him a chief hospital physician, an office that he held until Congress reduced the hospital department in January 1782.

From Brigadier General Hugh Mercer

Sir,   Perth Amboy [N.J.] 18 Sept. 1776

At the same time that I ordered a Reinforcement to Powlis Hook I wrote to Col. Derkee to know the State of that Post as to force[1]—For tho Col. Humpton had been but a few days ago on that Spot to bring me an exact Return—such is the ever fluctuating State of our Melitia and infamous Desertion—that we are not at any one Post two days in the same State as to Numbers—Your Excellencys Letter was deliverd late last night[2]—I shall regulate the force sent to Powlis Hook agreable to what I hear from Col. Derkee—I expect a Return to my Letter every moment. I have the honour to be Sir Your Excellencys most obedt Servt

Hugh Mercer

ALS, PHi: Gratz Collection.
1. For the reinforcement of Paulus Hook, see Mercer to GW, 17 September.
2. This letter has not been identified.

Letter not found: from Lund Washington, 18 Sept. 1776. On 30 Sept. GW wrote Lund Washington: "Your letter of the 18th . . . now lies before me."

General Orders

Head Quarters, Harlem Heights, Sept: 19th 1776.
Parole Hancock.   Countersign Warren.
    The Companies from Maryland, under the Command of Major Price, are to join Col. Smallwood's Battalion, and Genl McDougall's Brigade; and it is expected that the commanding Officer of every Corps will, together with all the officers therein, exert themselves in seeing good Order & Disipline observed: They are to consider that it is the duty of a good Officer to see, or at least to know that Orders are executed, and not to content themselves with being the mere Vehicles thro' which they are conveyed to the men—We are now arrived at an important Crisis, which calls loudly for the Zeal and Activity of the best of Officers—We see, We know that the Enemy are exerting every Nerve, not only by force of Arms, but the practices of every Art, to accomplish their purposes; And that among other peices of Policy which is also founded on Justice, We find them exceeding careful to restrain every kind of abuse of private Property, whilst the abandoned and profligate part of our own Army, countenanced by a few officers, who are lost to every Sense of Honor and Virtue, as well as their Country's Good, are by Rapine and Plunder, spreading Ruin and Terror wherever they go; thereby making themselves infinitely more to be dreaded than the common Enemy they are come to oppose; at the same time that it

exposes Men who are strolling about after plunder to be sur-priz'd and taken. The General therefore hopes it will be unnec-essary, on any future Occasion, for him to repeat the Orders of yesterday, with respect to this matter, as he is determined to shew no Favor to officer, or soldier, who shall offend herein, but punish without exception, every person who shall be found guilty of this most abominable practice, which if continued, must prove the destruction of any Army on earth.

That the men may be acquainted with the Orders relative to plundering, as well as others; the Neglect of which will incur Blame or Punishment, the General directs and positively orders, that every commanding Officer of a Corps, takes special Care, that the Orders are regularly read to the men every day.

Genl Nixon, with his Brigade, is to remove over to the Jersey, and will receive his orders from Genl Green, with respect to his encamping &c.—such men of his Brigade as are now on duty must be relieved.

The Picquet Guards which are to occupy the Out Posts most advanced to the enemy, are to consist of *800* Men officer'd with 2 Cols:, 2 L. Cols:, 2 Majors, and Captains and Subalterns in proportion—they are to be furnished by Detachment from the several Brigades below Kingsbridge, and so every day 'till fur-ther orders.[1]

Varick transcript, DLC:GW; Df, in Joseph Reed's writing, DNA: RG 93, Or-derly Books, vol. 15. The two passwords in the draft are not in Reed's writing.

1. The draft includes these additional orders at the end: "The above Party to parade this Afternoon at 4 oClock precisely—at. Gen. Wadsworth Brigadier of the Day will shew them the Ground & post them" (see also "Williams' Diary," 48:344).

To John Hancock

Head Qrs at Colo. Roger Morris's House
Sir   Septr 19th 1776

Since I had the honor of addressing you Yesterday, Nothing material has occurred, However It is probable in a little time, the Enemy will attempt to force us from hence, as we are in-formed they are bringing many of their Heavy Cannon towards the Heights and the Works we have thrown up. they have also

Eight or Nine Ships of War in the North River, which It is said, are to Canonade our right Flank when they open their Batteries against our Front. Every disposition is making on our part for defence, and Congress may be assured that I shall do every thing in my power[1] to maintain the post so long as It shall appear practicable and conducive to the General good. I have the Honor to be Sir Your Most Obedt Sert

Go: Washington

LS, in Robert Hanson Harrison's writing, DNA:PCC, item 152; LB, DLC:GW; copy, DNA:PCC, item 169; Varick transcript, DLC:GW.

    1. The LB reads "all in my power."

From Major General William Heath

Dear General   Kingsbridge Sept. 19th 1776

Three Troops of Light Horse, making about 90 Men in the whole, have already got in, & others are nearby—Col. Douglas & Col. Stores's Regiments of Militia are at West Chester—Col. Williams's have not reached this as yet, but will move forward as soon as they come in—Col. Stores acquaints me that about 4000 Militia may be expected soon;[1] what will be done with them I cannot tell—They have neither Covering or Camp Utensils, and almost all the houses & Barns for many miles back, as the Officers inform me are filled with the Sick of the different Brigades of the Army—The Militia are also destitute of Ammunition, owing to the badness of a Quantity of Gunpowder lately made in that State, & on which they depended for a Supply—I shou'd be glad to know your Excellency's Pleasure, if they are to be Supplied & with how much.

This morning about Ten O'Clock I was informed that one of Col. Broadhead's Battalions of Riflemen had drawn up, & were determined to march home—I immediately ordered several Regiments under Arms, & then rode to them—They were partly dispersed before I came to them (about one Company remained) I demanded the Reasons of their Mutinous Behavior; they replied the want of money & Blankets, & the Severe Duty of the Camp; that they were Volunteers &c. I ordered them immediately to repair to their Tents (or the Severest punishment shou'd be inflicted) which they did in an orderly manner[.] I am since informed, that a number of them previous to this had gone off, Six or Seven of whom, are taken & committed to the main Guard, & others I am told are taken between this & Dobbs's Ferry—I am just informed that the other Rifle Battalion of Pensylvanians are extremely uneasy, & talk of going home in a Body, I hope they will be removed this night to the Island—They are retarded this Day by the Waggons being employed in fetching hay &c. from Morrissania, & the Horses engaged in moving the Heavy Cannon And the Boats being ordered to Burditt's Ferry, to ferry over Waggons &c. by means of which they cannot get over their Baggage.[2]

ADf, MHi: Heath Papers.

1. The militia reinforcements that the Connecticut council of safety recently had ordered to rendezvous at Westchester included the 2d and 4th regiments of light horse, Col. John Douglas's 21st Regiment, and Col. Jedediah Elderkin's 5th Regiment commanded by Lt. Col. Experience Storrs.

2. After the Battle of Long Island, Lt. Col. Daniel Brodhead took command of the remnants of Col. Samuel Miles's two Pennsylvania rifle battalions and Col. Samuel John Atlee's Pennsylvania musket battalion. On this date about two hundred men deserted from those battalions, and about thirty more men led by a corporal were stopped from leaving camp by force. Fifty-eight of the soldiers who returned home subsequently petitioned the Pennsylvania committee of safety for redress of their complaints, saying that they "did not leave New York for Cowardice but for bad usage" (*Pa. Archives*, 5th ser., 2:253–55).

To Major General William Howe

Sir   Head Quarters [Harlem Heights] 19 Sepr 1776

I have the honor to advise you, that in Consequence of Genl Sullivan's Information, first by Letter and afterwards verbally, that you were willing to exchange him for Maj. Genl Prescot, and Brig. Genl Lord Stirling for any Brigadier of yours in our possession; I wrote to Congress to send Genl prescot to some convenient place from whence the proposed Exchange might be made.[1] And supposing that it would be agreeable[2] to exchange Lord Stirling for Brig. Genl McDonald, he is also come forward with Genl prescot—Both those Gentlemen are now at Elizabeth Town and I only wait your Answer to this, in which you will please to fix the time and place when and where the Exchanges may be effected. I am Sir with due Respect.

LB, in Tench Tilghman's writing, DLC:GW; two copies, P.R.O., 30/55, Carleton Papers; Varick transcript, DLC:GW.

1. See GW to Hancock, 6 September.
2. Both copies in the Carleton Papers read "agreeable to you."

To the Massachusetts General Court

Gentn   Head Qrs at Colo. Rogr Morris's House
                      10 Miles from New York Septr 19th 1776

I was honored the night before last with your favor of the 13th Inst. and at the same time that I conceive your anxiety to have been great by reason of the vague & uncertain accounts you received respecting the attack on Long Island, give me leave to assure you that the situation of our Affairs and the Important concerns which have surrounded me & which are daily pressing on me, have prevented me from transmitting in many Instances the Intelligence I otherwise should have conveyed.

In respect to the attack and retreat from Long Island, the public papers would furnish you with accounts nearly true—I shall only add, that in the former, we lost about Eight Hundred Men, more than three fourth's of which were taken prisoners. This misfortune happened in a great measure, by Two detachments of our people who were posted in Two Roads leading thro a Wood, in order to Intercept the Enemy in their March, suffering a Surprize and making a precipitate retreat, which enabled the Enemy to lead a great part of their force against the Troops commanded by Lord Stirling which formed a third detachment, who behaved with great bravery and resolution charging the Enemy & maintaining their posts from about Seven or Eight OClock in the Morning till Two in the Afternoon, when they were obliged to attempt a retreat, being Surrounded and overpowered by Numbers on all sides, & in which many of them were taken—One Battallion—Smallwoods of Maryland, lost Two hundred & Fifty Nine men and the General damage fell upon the Regiments from Pensylvania, Delaware & Maryland and Colo. Huntington's of Connecticut. As to the retreat from the Island, It was effected without loss of Men and with but a very little baggage. A few Heavy Cannon were left, not being moveable on account of the Grounds being soft & miry through the Rains that had fallen. The Enemy's Loss in killed, we could never ascertain, but we have many reasons to beleive that It was pretty considerable and exceeded ours a good deal—The Retreat from thence was absolutely necessary, the Enemy having landed the Main body of their Army there to attack us in front, while their Ships of War were to cut off all communication with the City from whence Resources of Men, provisions &c. were to be drawn.

Having made this Retreat, not long after, we discovered by their Movements and the Information we received from Deserters and Others, that they declined attacking our Lines in the City and were forming a plan to get in our rear with their Land Army by crossing the Sound above us, and thereby cut off all Intercourse with the Country and every necessary Supply. The Ships of War were to cooperate, possess the North River, and prevent Succours from the Jersey's &c. This plan appearing probable and but too practicable in Its execution, It became necessary to guard against the fatal consequences that must follow If their Scheme was effected for which purpose I caused a removal of a part of our Stores, Troops &c. from the City, and a Council of Genl Officers determined on Thursday last that It must be entirely abandoned, holding up however every shew and Appearance of defence, till Our sick and All our Stores could be brought away.[1] The Evacuation being resolved on every exertion in our power was made to baffle their designs and effect our Own. The Sick were Numerous and an Object of great Importance—happily we got them away, but before we could bring off all our Stores, On Sunday Morning Six or Seven Ships of War which had gone up the East River above the City some few days before, began a most severe & Heavy Cannonade to Scour the Grounds and effect a Landing of their Troops. Three Ships of War also ran up the North River that Morning above the City to prevent our Boats and small Craft carrying away our Baggage &c.—I had gone the Evening before to the Main body of our Army which was posted about the Heights & plains of Harlem where It seemed probable from the Movements & dispositions of the Enemy they meant to land & make an Attack the next morning. However the Event did not happen. I immediately on hearing the Canonade rode with all possible expedition towards the place of landing and where Breast Works had been thrown up to secure our Men, & found the Troops that had

been posted there to my great surprize and Mortification retreating with the utmost precipitation, & those ordered to their
support, (Parson's & Fellows's Brigades,) notwithstanding the
exertions of their Generals to form 'em, running away in the
most shamefull and disgracefull manner. I used every possible
effort to rally them but to no purpose, & on the appearance of
a small part of the Enemy (not more than Sixty or Seventy in
Number) they ran off without firing a Single Shot. Many of our
Heavy Cannon would have inevitably fallen into the Enemy's
Hands as they landed so soon, but this scandalous conduct occasioned a loss of many Tents, Baggage & Camp Equipage which
would have been easily secured, had they made the least Opposition. The retreat was effected without any or but with the loss
of three or Four Men at most.[2] We Encamped & still are on the
Heights of Harlem which are well calculated for defence against
their Approaches. On Monday Morning they advanced in sight
in Several large bodies, but Attempted nothing of a Genl nature.
Tho there were Smart Skirmishes between their advanced parties and some detachments from our Lines which I sent out. In
these Our Troops behaved with great resolution and bravery
putting them to flight in open Ground & forcing them from
posts they had Seized Two or three Times. A Serjeant who deserted from them says the report was they had Eighty nine missing & wounded & Eight killed, in the last Instance his Account
is too small because our people have buried more than Twice as
many. In number our Loss was very inconsiderable, but in the
fall of Lt Colo. Knolton of Connecticut, I consider It as great,
being a brave and good Officer. Major Leitch who commanded a
detachment from the Virginia Regiment unfortunately received
Three Balls thro his side. he still supports his Spirits and seems
as If he would do well; Col. Knolton was Interred with every
Honor due to his Merit & that the Situation of things would
admit of.[3] Since this Affair Nothing has happened—The Enemy
It is said are bringing forward several Heavy Cannon to force
us from the Heights. At the same time that they open their Batteries in Front their Ships of War, Seven or Eight of which are
in the North River, are to Canonade our Right Flank—Thus
have I run over in a cursory, rough way an Account of the most
material Events from the Battle on Long Island to the present
moment, I have not time to study order or Elegance—This

However I do not so much mind, and only wish my Narrative was more agreable—but we must set down things as they are—I hope they will be better, nothing on my part shall be wanting to bring about the most favourable Events.

I am now to make my most gratefull acknowledgements to your Honorable body for the Succour they mean to afford me in the Militia lately ordered[4] and have only to lament that they should be so unprovided with Tents and other Camp necessaries—Our distresses in these Instances are extremely great, having by no means a sufficiency for the Troops already here, nor do I know, how they can be procured. I am at a loss for the Officers Names who command this Reinforcement, as they are not mentioned—However I have wrote by Fessendon that they should lead the Men on as fast as possible, sending before them when they get within Two or three days March of Kingsbridge an Officer to receive Orders from me, how they are to be disposed of.[5] Instructions given now might become improper by the Intervention of a variety of Circumstances. I have the Honor to be with unfeigned esteem & respect Gentn Your Most Obedt Servt

Go: Washington

LS, in Robert Hanson Harrison's writing, M-Ar: Revolution Letters; LB, DLC:GW; copy, MHi: Ward Papers; Varick transcript, DLC:GW.

1. GW is referring to the council of war held on 12 September.

2. The LB reads: "The Retreat was effected with the Loss of three or four Men only."

3. Knowlton was buried on 17 Sept. (see Extract of a Letter to a Gentleman in Annapolis, 17 Sept., in Force, *American Archives*, 5th ser., 2:370–71).

4. The LB reads "lately ordered to March."

5. This letter, which GW wrote on this date, is addressed: "To The Commanding Officer of the 1st Division of the Massachusets Militia marching towards Kingsbridge" (see the LB and Varick transcript in DLC:GW). It apparently was delivered to Benjamin Lincoln, whom the General Court recently had named to command those reinforcements.

General Orders

Head Quarters, Harlem Heights, Septr 20th 1776.
Parole Spain.   Countersign France.

As many of the Regiments that came last from New York have lost their Tents and cooking Utensils (not from any default of their own, but want of teams, and vessels, to bring them of in time) by which means one part of the Army are greatly distressed, whilst the other part are comfortably supplied; the General earnestly advises and directs the Colonels and commanding Officers of such Corps as have not suffered, to store their men thicker in their tents, and lend all they can spare,[1] to their suffering fellow-soldiers, 'till such time as others can be provided—The tents &c. are to be sent to Genl Spencer's, at Mr Kartright's house, who will cause them to be delivered to the regiments standing most in need of them, which regiments are to be answerable for them when called for.

The General hopes, that soldiers fighting in such a cause as ours, will not be discouraged by any difficulties that may offer; and informs them that the Grounds he now possesses are to be defended at all events; Any Officer, or Soldier therefore, who (upon the Approach, or Attack of the Enemy's Forces, by land or water) presumes to turn his back and flee, shall be instantly Shot down, and all good officers are hereby authorized and required to see this done, that the brave and gallant part of the Army may not fall a sacrifice to the base and cowardly part, or share their disgrace in a cowardly and unmanly Retreat. The Heights we are now upon may be defended against double the force we have to contend with, and the whole Continent expects it of us: But that we may assist the natural strength of the ground, as much as possible, and make our Posts more secure, the General most earnestly recommends it to the commanding Officers of every Brigade, and Regiment, to turn out every man they have off duty, for fatigue, and apply to Col. Putnam for tools, and directions where and how to work—This Measure is also earnestly recommended to the men, as it will tend greatly to their own security & ease, as the Guards will be lessened in proportion as the grounds get strengthened.

Genl Green is to appoint some careful officer at Burdett's ferry to examine passengers, and see that none come over but such as have proper passes—Genl Mifflin is to do the same on this side, to prevent disaffected, or suspected persons, from passing—If Capt: Johnson, and the other Gentlemen who were employed in this business, at New-York, incline to engage in it again, they are to have the preference given them.

The Colonels, or commanding officers of the Militia regiments, now in the service, may make out their Pay-Abstracts in order to receive payment—they will be particularly attentive in doing it, as the disorderly manner, in which many of those men, have left the service, will require the utmost care, to prevent impositions on the public; And the Congress having resolv'd, that all Continental Troops and the Militia going home from service shall restore all Continental Arms, and other property; and also all Ammunition remaining in their possesion, at the time of their being about to return, or to have the value of it deducted.[2]

The Guards will be relieved at four O'Clock this Afternoon, after which they are to be relieved constantly and regularly at Nine O'Clock every day.

The General desires that the Brigade Majors may attend him precisely at seven O'Clock to morrow morning, and account for the remissiness in their several departments, as he is determined to put up with no more negligence in office—He expects the punctual attendance of the whole.

Genl Wadsworth must look out a good person to do the duty of his brigade.

Commanding and other Officers of regiments, are to collect the horses straying about their Encampments, and send them to the Quarter-Master General or one of his Deputies—the Uses these horses may answer when properly employed, will be an inducement to every officer to exert himself.[3]

The officers of the Guard at Kingsbridge to be careful, that no Soldiers take horses over the Bridge, tho' such soldier should have a common pass. Every person riding without a saddle, is to be immediately taken up, and the horse sent to the Quarter Master 'till released by further Orders.

The scarcity of Fodder makes it necessary that no horses should come into Camp, but what belong to the Army; All Visitants therefore are to leave their horses beyond the Bridge, unless they obtain a special Order from some General Officer, or Commandant of a Brigade.

Genl Bell, Brigadier of the day, to meet the Guards at four O'Clock, on the parade, and report immediately, what Brigade Major fails of bringing his proportion of Guards, at the time.

Varick transcript, DLC:GW; Df, DNA: RG 93, Orderly Books, vol. 15. In the draft the last four paragraphs of the general orders are in Joseph Reed's writing.

1. The draft reads: "and lend all they can, together with such pots and pans as they possibly can spare."

2. For this resolution of 14 Sept., see Hancock to GW, 16 Sept., n.1.

3. The draft reads: "the Use these Horses when properly employed will be of to the Army it is hoped will be an Inducement to every Offi⟨cer⟩ to exert himself."

From Colonel William Crawford

Sir   Williamsburgh Sepr the 20th 1776
    I Should have bin Glad to have the honour of being with you at new York, but I am Doutfull we Shall be envolved in an Endien War to the Westward, as the Shawnees and Dallowas Seem in Dout and from the Last Acounts from Fortpitt had not meet our people (Do[c]ter Walker and the Comisioners) [w]ho was Sent to treet with them from this Goverment.[1]
    I Should have com to new York with those Reget ordred their but the Regt I belong to is Ordred to this place.[2]
    If a War With the Westerly Endiens hapen I am to go there.
    I this Spring before I com from over the mountain calld at Simpsons to See your Mill go for the first tim of its Runing and can Ashure you I think it the best Mill I ever saw any where tho I think one of a less Value would have don as well. If you Remember you Saw Som Rocks at the Mill Seet Those are as fine Millston Greet as any in Ameraca, the Millright told me the Stones he got for your Mill there was Equil to Inglish Burrs, Your Land on Shurtees Creek is well Cultiveted Redy to your hand, the men on it thinking you have no patent for that Land or that if you have that you will Lease them the Land on Reasonable tearms.[3]
    at our Last Convention I Mentiond the State of Lands and the Stat of the Claiments in Genaral and a mongest other Surcomstances Mentiond the Expense you had bin at in haveing the first improvements on that Land And then Laying a warrent on them and notwithstanding those person would take it at any rate upon which an Ordenance passd that all Equitable Claims Should take place[4] Som I understand has since bin trying to Sell there right of your Land but I have had Som Advertizements

Printed and Sent up for warning any Person to Purchess those Land Seting forth your title.

I have Laid the ballance of your warrent on Som Land on the river that I think will Sute but has not got it run out to my Mind as there is som Disput and I believe I shall by them out If I can reasonable.

Excuse the Lenth of this Letter I Shall only ad that I wish you to Injoy Life health and overcom all Enemies and Should be hapy to See you once more injoy your self in Pleashure at Mountvernon. I am Sir your most Hume Sorvont

W. Crawford

ALS, DLC:GW.

1. The Indian commissioners for the middle department were Dr. Thomas Walker and John Harvie of Virginia and Jasper Yeates and John Montgomery of Pennsylvania (see *JCC*, 4:348, 5:517). For the commissioners' recent activities, see their letter to Congress's Indian affairs committee, 25 Sept., DNA:PCC, item 78. A conference with the Shawnee and Delaware was held at Fort Pitt sometime later this fall, and in December representatives of the tribes addressed Congress in Philadelphia (see *JCC*, 6:1003, 1006, 1010–11, 1013, and Benjamin Rush's notes, c.5 Dec. 1776, in Smith, *Letters of Delegates*, 5:577–78).

2. Crawford was colonel of the 7th Virginia Regiment from 14 Aug. 1776 to 4 Mar. 1777. His regiment arrived at Williamsburg on 6 Sept. to replace the 5th Virginia Regiment, which had been ordered to New York (see Dixon and Hunter's *Virginia Gazette* [Williamsburg], 21 Sept.).

3. For Gilbert Simpson's efforts to erect a mill at Washington's Bottom, GW's tract of land on the Youghiogheny River in western Pennsylvania, see GW to Lund Washington, 20 Aug. 1775, and *Diaries*, 4:1, 20–21. For GW's land on Millers Run, a branch of Chartiers Creek near present-day Canonsburg, Pa., see ibid., 2:295, 4:22–23.

4. For the resolution regarding western land claims that the fifth Virginia convention passed on 24 June 1776, see Scribner and Tarter, *Revolutionary Virginia*, 7:593.

To John Hancock

Sir   Head Qrs Heights of Harlem Sepr 20th[–21] 1776

I have been honored with your favor of the 16th with Its Inclosures. to prevent the Injury and abuses which would arise from the Militia and Other Troops carrying away Ammunition and Continental property, I have published the substance of the Resolves upon the Subject in General Orders.[1]

Since my Letter of Yesterday Nothing of Importance has cast up. The Enemy are forming a large and extensive Encampment in the plains mentioned in my last and are busily employed in transporting their Cannon & Stores from Long Island. As they advance them this way, we may reasonably expect their Operations will not long be deferred.

Inclosed are Sundry Letters &c. to which Congress will be pleased to pay such regard as they may think them deserving of. The Letter from Monsr Devourony came open under cover of One to me. Those from Colo. Hand & Colo. Ward contain a List of Vacancies in their Regiments and of the persons they esteem proper to fill them. The former I beleive returned no List before, the Latter says he never got any Commissions. Genls Howe & Erskin's proclamations shew the Measures that have been pursued to force & seduce the Inhabitants of Long Island from their Allegiance to the States and to assist in their destruction.[2]

As the period will soon arrive when the Troops composing the present Army (a few excepted) will be disbanded according to the tenor of their Inlistments, and the most fatal consequences may ensue, If a suitable and and timely provision is not made in this Instance, I take the liberty of suggesting to Congress, not only the expediency but the absolute necessity there is, that their earliest attention should be had to this Subject. In respect to the Time that Troops should be engaged for, I have frequently given my Sentiments—nor have I omitted to express my opinion of the difficulties that will attend raising them, nor of the Impracticability of effecting It without the allowance of a large and extraordinary bounty—It is a melancholy and painfull consideration to those who are concerned in the Work and have the command, to be forming Armies constantly and to be left by Troops just when they begin to deserve the Name, or perhaps at a Moment when an Important blow is expected. This I am Informed will be the case at Ticonderoga with part of the Troops there, unless some System is Immediately come into by which they can be Induced to Stay—Genl Schuyler tells me in a Letter received Yesterday, That DeHaas, Maxwells & Winds Regimts stand engaged only till the Beginning of next Month, and that the Men he is fearfull will not remain longer than the Time of their Inlistments.[3]

I would also beg leave to mention to Congress, that the Season is fast approaching When Cloaths of every kind will be wanted for the Army—Their distress is already great and will be encreased as the Weather becomes more severe—Our situation is now bad, but is much better than the Militia that are coming to Join us from the States of the Massachusetts Bay & Connecticut in consequence of the requisition of Congress—They I am informed, have not a Single Tent or a necessary of any kind, nor can I conceive how It will be possible to support them. These circumstances are extremely alarming, and oblige me to wish Congress to have All the Tents, Cloathing of every kind, and Camp necessaries provided and forwarded that are to be procured. These Eastern reinforcements have not a single Necessary not a pan or a Kettle, in which we are now greatly deficient. It is with reluctance that I trouble Congress with these matters, but to whom can I resort for releif unless to them? The necessity therefore which urges the application will excuse It, I am persuaded.

I have not been able to transmit Congress a Genl return of the Army this Week owing to the peculiar situation of our Affairs and the great Shifting and Changing among the Troops. As soon as I can procure One a Copy shall be forwarded to Congress. I have the Honor to be with every Sentiment of respect Sir Your Most Obedt Sert

Go: Washington

P.S: Septr 21st 1776. Things with us remain in the situation they were Yesterday.

LS, in Robert Hanson Harrison's writing, DNA:PCC, item 152; LB, DLC:GW; copy, DNA:PCC, item 169; Varick transcript, DLC:GW. Congress read this letter on 23 Sept. and referred it to the Board of War (*JCC*, 5:808–9).

1. See General Orders, 20 September.

2. Chevalier de Berruyer du Maurony says in the letter that he wrote to GW on 9 Sept. at Boston that he is a 36–year-old French officer who had sailed sometime earlier from Saint-Domingue to New England to establish his health, and having done so, he wishes permission to sail to France (DLC:GW). Berruyer's enclosed letter to Congress asking for that permission has not been identified.

Col. Edward Hand requests in his letter to GW of 14 Aug. that Congress fill the position of major for his 1st Continental Regiment by promoting one of the regiment's nine captains, and in an undated return addressed to GW, Col. Jonathan Ward recommends fifteen officers to fill various vacancies in his 21st Continental Regiment (both documents are in DNA:PCC, item 152).

For Gen. William Howe's proclamation of 23 Aug. and Gen. William Erskine's proclamation of 29 Aug., see Henry Beekman Livingston to GW, 11 Sept., n.6.

3. See Schuyler to GW, 16 September.

From Patrick Henry

Dear Sir.   Williamsburgh Sept. 20th 1776

After a long & Severe Illness, I am now but just able to come hither in Order to discharge as I may be able, the Dutys of my public Station. Will you pardon me for asking the Favor of a Correspondence with you? Besides the pleasure it will give me, I shall be taught by your Ideas, to form more correct Opinions, of those Movements that may be proposed for the general Defence in this Quarter. It is conjectured by Some, that the Enemys Cruisers will come to the South at the End of the Campaign. In the mean Time the Navigation is open. I wish that Circumstance may be well improved.

We have beat the Cherokees in some hot Skirmishes with inferiour Numbers.[1] Colo. Christian marches very shortly with abt 1750 men agt the overhill Towns at which the whole Nation is or must shortly be collected. I doubted whether there were men enough ordered for the Service; but the Colo. thot the Number Sufficient.[2] I hear from good Authority that the Creeks observe a Neutrality & refuse to assist our Enemys, So that I think they will stand the Brunt alone except the Assistance of a few Renegade Shawanese Mingo's &c. The Eastern Towns of the Cherokees are destroyed & 1800 men from S. Carolina (as I'm this day told by a Capt. in Gadsden's Regiment) were marching agt the middle Settlements, but did not propose going to the overhill Towns.[3]

We have heard of the Affair at Long Island. I trust every virtuous man will be stimulated by it to fresh Exertions. My poor friend Sullivan I hear is a prisoner, & Report says at Congress to offer Terms of peace. I should not think he would be the Bearer of disadvantageous Offers.

I can readily guess the infinite Variety of Affairs with which you are worried. God grant you may end the glorious Work in which you are so nobly engaged, & be crown'd with Success.

With Sentiments of the most perfect Esteem I am Dear sir yr most obt Servt

P. Henry Jr.

ALS, MH: Sparks Collection.

1. Henry is referring to the Cherokee raids on the Holston and Watagua river settlements in July, which were repulsed by frontier militia from Virginia and North Carolina (see O'Donnell, *Southern Indians,* 40–43).

2. William Christian (1743–1786) of Fincastle County, one of the most prominent men in western Virginia and a brother-in-law of Henry, served under Henry as lieutenant colonel of the 1st Virginia Regiment from August 1775 to March 1776, when Congress named him to succeed Henry as the regiment's colonel (see *JCC,* 4:211). Christian resigned that commission in August, however, to accept appointment by the Virginia council as colonel of the 1st battalion and commander in chief of all the forces raised for an expedition against the upper or overhill towns of the Cherokee in present-day eastern Tennessee (see *Journals of the Council of State of Virginia,* 1:82, 103). When Christian's troops reached the overhill towns in October, the Cherokee fled without giving battle, and a majority of them subsequently capitulated to Christian (see O'Donnell, *Southern Indians,* 47–49). In January 1777 Henry appointed Christian to the Indian commission that negotiated a preliminary peace treaty with the Cherokee the following April. Christian, who had represented Fincastle County in the House of Burgesses from 1772 to 1776 and the first three conventions, served in the state senate in 1776 and from 1780 to 1783, and he was one of the commissioners who negotiated the Cherokee treaty of 1781. In 1785 Christian moved to Kentucky.

3. In August a force of 1,120 South Carolinians commanded by Col. Andrew Williamson burned the lower Cherokee towns, and during September and early October Williamson's troops joined a force of 2,500 North Carolinians under Gen. Griffith Rutherford in destroying the middle Cherokee towns (see ibid., 43–47). Christopher Gadsden (1724–1805), who became colonel of the 1st South Carolina Regiment in June 1775, served in the Continental Congress from 1774 to January 1776, when he returned to South Carolina to command the provincial forces defending Charleston. Congress appointed Gadsden a brigadier general on 16 Sept. 1776. He resigned that commission in August 1777, however, after a bitter dispute over command of the Continental troops in South Carolina with Gen. Robert Howe, whom he fought in a duel the following year. In the spring of 1778 Gadsden was named vice president of the state, and in 1779 he was designated its lieutenant governor. After Charleston fell to the British in 1780, Gadsden was imprisoned, first in Charleston and then at St. Augustine. He was released in July 1781, and in January 1782 he declined election as governor, choosing instead to serve in the state assembly.

To the New York Convention

HEAD-QUARTERS, *Heights of Harlem, Septr. 20th,* 1776.
GENTN.—Having reason to believe the enemy will attempt to gall us with their ships of war from the North river as soon as they are ready to open their batteries against the front of our lines, which we expect them to erect with great industry, I beg leave to mention that I think it may be of immense consequence if your Honourable Body will order down some of your fire ships, which may lay just above the obstructions in the river under cover of the guns of Fort Washington, where they will be ready to act in case the ships should attempt to come up.

Hurried and surrounded with a thousand things, I have only time to add, that I have the honor to be, with great esteem, Gentn. your most obt. st.

GO. WASHINGTON.

N.Y. Prov. Congress Journals, 1:637. The New York convention read this letter on 21 Sept. (ibid.).

To Major General Philip Schuyler

Head Quarters Colo. Roger Morris
Sir   10 Miles from New York. 20th Septr 1776.
I have Your several Favors of the 9th 12th & 16 instants with their Inclosures. I am particularly happy to find by the Copies of General Arnold and Colo. Dayton's Letters, that Your Apprehensions of an Indian War in Your Quarter, have Entirely Vanished, & that You have disbanded the Militia in Consequence.

I clearly see & have severely felt the Ill Effects of short Enlistments, & have repeatedly Given Congress my Sentiments thereon, I believe they are by this Time Convinced, that there is no Opposing a standing well disciplined Army, but by One upon the same Plan, & I hope, if this Campaign does not put an End to this Contest, they will put the Army upon a different Footing, than What it has heretofore been. I shall take Care to remind them, that the Term, for which, Dehaas, Maxwell's & Wind's Regiments enlisted, expires the Beggining of October, but if they have not already thought of taking some Steps to secure them a While longer, it will be too late, Except the Officers will Exert themselves in prevailing on the Men to stay, till their places can be supplied by some Means or Other.[1] If the Officers are spirited and well inclined, they may lead their Men as they please.

I removed my Quarters to this Place on sunday last, It having been previously determined by a Council of General Officers, on the preceeding Thursday, to Evacuate New York.[2] The Reasons, that principally weighed with them, were, that from Every Information, and Every Movement of the Enemy It was clear, that their Attack was not meditated against the City, their Intent Evidently was to throw their Whole Army between Part of Ours in New York and Its Environs, & the Remainder about Kingsbridge, & thereby cut off our Communication with Each Other & with the Country. Indeed their Operations on Sunday last fully justified[3] the Opinion of the Council, & the Steps taken in Consequence, For on that Morning they began their Landing at Turtle Bay, & Continued to throw Over Great Numbers of Men from Long Island, and from Montresors and Buchanans Islands, on which, they had previously lodged them. As We had exerted Ourselves in removing our Sick and Stores of Every Kind, after the Measure of Abandoning had been determined upon, Very few Things & but three or four Men, fell in the Enemy's Hands.

On Monday last We had a pretty Sharp Skirmish, between two Battalions of Light Infantry & Highlanders & three Companies of Hessian Riflemen commanded by Brigr Leslie & Detachments from our Army under the Command of Lieut. Colo: Knolton of Connecticut and Major Leitch of Virginia. The Colo: received a Mortal Wound & the Major three Balls thro' his Body, but he is likely to do well. Their Parties behaved with Great Bravery & being supported with Fresh Troops, beat the Enemy fairly from the Field. Our Loss, Except in that of Colo: Knolton, a Most Valuable & Gallant Officer, is inconsiderable. That of the Enemy, from Accounts, between Eighty and one hundred Wounded & fifteen or twenty killed. This little Advantage has inspired our Troops prodigiously, they find that It only requires Resolution and Good Officers, to make an Enemy, that they stood in too Much dread of, Give Way.

The British Army lays encamped about two Miles below Us, they are busy in bringing over their Cannon & stores from Long Island, and we are putting ourselves in the best Posture of Defence, that Time & Circumstance will admit of.

I inclose You Copies of several Resolutions of Congress respecting the Northern Army &ca not knowing Whether they have been Yet transmitted to You.[4]

I recd Capt. Varick's Resignation, which shall be forwarded to Congress this Day.[5] I am Sir, with Esteem Yr Most Obedt Servt

Go. Washington.

LB, NN: Schuyler Papers; LB, DLC:GW; copy, NHi: Gates Papers; Varick transcript, DLC:GW.

1. See GW to Hancock, 20–21 September.

2. GW is referring to the council of war that met on 12 September.

3. The LB in DLC:GW reads "satisfied."

4. For these resolutions of 12 and 14 Sept., see Hancock to GW, 16 Sept., n.1.

5. Varick, who had been Schuyler's secretary since June 1775, wrote GW on 14 Sept. resigning his captain's commission in the 1st New York Regiment in accordance with Congress's resolution of 11 July prohibiting Continental officers from holding more than one office (DNA:PCC, item 78). Congress read Varick's letter on 23 Sept., the same date that it read GW's letter to Hancock of 20–21 Sept., and on 25 Sept. Congress appointed Varick deputy mustermaster general of the northern army (*JCC,* 5:808, 824).

From Jonathan Trumbull, Sr.

Sir   Lebanon [Conn.] Septemr 20th 1776

Since the receipt of your Favour of the 9th Instant our nine Regiment of Foot under Command of Brigadier General Saltonstall, and Two Regiments of Horse under the Command of Major Backus have begun their March, with Orders to rendezvous at or near West Chester, and there to attend your Orders, and trust that many of them are arrived there, as the rest will soon.

It gives Me great Concern to learn that so many of our Militia have refused to submit to proper Discipline, and that such Numbers have deserted as to reduce those that remain to about two Thousand; tis certain that by their Absence they were great Sufferers in point of Interest, yet this is far from justifying their Desertion, which ought not to pass unnoticed; I must therefore Intreat your Excellency as soon as it can be conveniently done, to order Returns to be made of all such Deserters and Communicate them to Me, that proper Measures may be taken with them either by returning them to their Corps, mulcting them of their Wages or otherwise; if the Militia may Desert with Impunity there is an End of their Usefullness. I am, with Sincere Esteem & Regard Sir Your most Obedient humble Servant

Jonth; Trumbull

ALS, DLC:GW; LB, Ct: Trumbull Papers.

General Orders

Head Quarters, Harlem Heights, Sept: 21st 1776
Parole Lisbon.   Countersign Dover.

If the Quarter Master General has any Sails, or other Covering; he is to deliver them to Genl Spencer's order, who will see that the regiments most in need of it, now under his immediate command, are first supplied.

The General earnestly exhorts the commanding Officers of every Regiment, and Corps, to fall upon the best and most expeditious method of procuring Cloaths and Necessaries for their men before the season gets too far advanced—For this purpose they are hereby authorised to send out one or more officers, as the nature of the case shall require, and the service will admit of, to purchase and provide them.

Generals Putnam and Spencer, together with the several Brigadiers, on this side Kingsbridge, are to look over the Grounds within our lines, and fix upon places to build Barracks, or Huts, for quartering the men in. No time should be lost in making the choice, that covering may be had as soon as possible, for the ease and comfort of the men.

It is earnestly recommended to all Brigadiers & commanding Officers of Corps, to see or know that the Orders relative to their respective Brigades &c. are complied with; and they as well as commanding Officers of Regiments &c., are requested to attend particularly to the state of the men's health, that those that are really Sick, may be supplied in the best manner our situation and circumstances will admit of, whilst such as feign themselves Sick, merely to get excused from duty, meet with no kind of countenance, or favour, as it only tends to throw the burden upon the spirited and willing men, who disdain such scandalous practices. The General would remind all officers, of the indispensible necessity there is of each of them, exerting himself in the Department he acts, and that where this is the case of the advantages resulting from it, as an Army, let it be ever so large, then moves like *Clock-work;* whereas, without it, it is no better than an ungovernable Machine, that serves only to perplex and distract those who attempt to conduct it.

The Brigadier Generals, and the Brigade-Major, of the day, are both to attend the parade, at the hour of mounting Guard; see them brought on and marched off, and so continue near the advanced lines 'till they are relieved the next day, in order that they may be ready in case of an Attack, to command at the lines—When they are relieved, they are to report extraordinaries to the Commander in Chief.

Varick transcript, DLC:GW; Df, DNA: RG 93, Orderly Books, vol. 15.

Letter not found: from Brig. Gen. William Heath, 21 Sept. 1776. On this date William Grayson wrote to Heath: "In answer to your letter of this date, I am commanded by his Excy to inform you that he thinks it expedient that an officer with about twenty five men should be immediately sent to Dobbs ferry; and that the Pensylvany troops under your command should be marched directly for this place; he is of opinion it is adviseable they sho⟨ul⟩d be paid off here" (MHi: Heath Papers).

From Major General William Howe

Sir,   Head Quarters York Island 21st Septemr 1776.
I have the Favor of your Letters of the 6th and 19th Current; in consequence of the latter, Directions are given for Major General Sullivan being conveyed to Elizabeth Town on the earliest Day, and I conclude Major General Prescot will return in the same Boat.

The Exchange you propose of Brigadier General Alexander, commonly called Lord Stirling, for Mr McDonald, cannot take Place, as he has only the Rank of Major by my Commission, but I shall readily send any Major in the enclosed Lists of Prisoners that you will be pleased to name in Exchange for him; and that Lord Stirling may not be detained, I would propose to exchange him for Governor Montfort Brown, altho' the latter is no longer in the military Line.[1]

Enclosed you have a List of Officers belonging to the Army under my Command who are your Prisoners; it is not so correct as I could wish, having received no regular Return of the Officers of the 42nd and 71st Regiments taken this year, but beg Leave to refer you to Lieutenant Colonel Campbell of the 71st to rectify any Omissions that may be, and am to desire you will put opposite to their Names, such of your Officers of equal Rank as you would have in Exchange for them. The Names of the Non Commissioned and Privates Prisoners with you are not sent, being unnecessary, but the Return herewith enclosed specifies the Number, and I shall redeem them by a like Number of those in my Possession; for which Purpose I shall send Mr Joshua Loring, my Commissary, to Elizabeth Town, as a proper Place for the Exchange of Prisoners, on any Day you may appoint, wishing it to be an early one, wherein I presume you will concur, as it is proposed for the more speedy Relief of the distressed.[2]

As it may be some Time before Mr Lovell arrives here from Halifax, tho' I took the first Opportunity of sending for him after your Agreement to exchange him for Governor Skene, I am willing to believe, upon my Assurances of Mr Lovell's being sent to you immediately on his Arrival, that you will not have any Objections to granting the Governor his Liberty without Delay and am induced to make the Proposal for your Compliance, neither of the Persons being connected with military Service.[3]

General Carleton has sent from Canada, a Number of Officers and Privates, as per Return enclosed, to whom he has given Liberty upon their Paroles, and in Pursuance of his Desire, and their Engagements to him, I shall send them to Elizabeth Town on the earliest Day. It is nevertheless the General's Expectation, that the Exchange of Prisoners as settled by Captain Foster in Canada, will be duly complied with, and I presume you are sufficiently sensible of the sacred Regard that is ever paid to Engagements of this Kind, to suffer any Infringement upon the plighted Faith of Colonel Arnold.[4]

It is with much Concern that I cannot close this Letter without representing the ill Treatment, which I am too well informed, the King's Officers now suffer in common Goals throughout the

Province of New England. I apply to your Feelings alone for Redress, having no Idea of committing myself by an Act of Retaliation upon those in my Power.

My Aid de Camp charged with the Delivery of this Letter, will present to you a Ball cut and fixed to the Ends of a Nail, taken from a Number of the same Kind, found in the Encampments quitted by your Troops on the 15th Instant—I do not make any Comment upon such unwarrantable and malicious Practices, being well assured the Contrivance has not come to your Knowledge. I am with due Regard, Sir, your most obedient Servant

W. Howe

LS, DLC:GW; copy, enclosed in GW to Hancock, 25 Sept. 1776 (second letter), DNA:PCC, item 152; two copies, P.R.O., 30/55, Carleton Papers; copy, DNA:PCC, item 169.

1. Donald McDonald received his commission as a brigadier general from the royal governor of North Carolina, Josiah Martin, on 10 Jan. 1776. Montfort Browne, governor of the Bahamas, who was captured during the American raid on New Providence in April 1776, had retired from the 35th Regiment of Foot as a lieutenant on half-pay at the end of the Seven Years' War.

2. The enclosed return of 21 Sept. shows that the Americans held 891 British prisoners of war, including 43 commissioned officers, 49 sergeants, 19 drummers, and 780 rank and file. An accompanying list gives the names of the commissioned officers (both documents are in DLC:GW). Joshua Loring, Jr. (1744–1789), a Loyalist from Dorchester, Mass., who had served as a subaltern in the 15th Regiment of Foot from 1761 to 1768, sailed to Halifax when the British army evacuated Boston in March 1776, and in June he accompanied the army to New York, where following the Battle of Long Island, he began his duties as commissary of prisoners (see Lydenberg, *Robertson Diaries*, 85, and Return of the Prisoners Taken on Long-Island, 27 Aug. 1776, in Force, *American Archives*, 5th ser., 1:1258). Thomas Jones alleges in his *History of N.Y.*, 1:351, that the office of commissary of prisoners was a very lucrative one, and that Loring obtained it because his wife, Elizabeth Lloyd Loring (d. 1831), became Gen. William Howe's mistress. "Joshua made no objections," Jones says. "He fingered the cash, the General enjoyed madam." Although there is no evidence of an open deal or even an unspoken understanding between Loring and Howe, by the spring of 1777 Howe's intimacy with Mrs. Loring apparently was common knowledge among British officers at New York (see Cresswell, *Journal*, 229; see also Gruber, *Howe Brothers*, 190). Mrs. Loring went to England with her children in 1778 about the same time that Howe returned there. Joshua Loring continued serving as commissary of prisoners in America until 1782 when he joined his wife in England and settled in Berkshire.

3. For this agreement, see GW to Howe, 30 July 1776.

4. According to this undated return, which was made by Carleton's commis-

sary of prisoners Richard Murray, the American prisoners who were sent to New York from Canada consisted of 51 commissioned officers and 373 noncommissioned officers and privates. A note at the end of the return reads: "Two Majors, Nine Captains, twenty Subalterns, and Four Hundred Men, were taken at the Cedars by Capt. Foster, and returned upon an Agreement to send as many of our People taken at St John's" (DLC:GW). For the cartel to which the Americans had agreed at the Cedars the previous May, see William Thompson to GW, 30 May 1776.

From Abraham Yates, Jr.

In Convention of the Representatives of the State
Sir   of New York—Fishkill September 21st 1776.
The Convention have received your Excellency's Letter of Septr 20th And have in consequence entered into the inclosed Resolution which I am directed to transmit: we are sorry that it is not in our Power to send down more than two fire Ships as they have no more charged in such a manner as to be depended on.[1] A Committee of Correspondence has been established by the Convention for the purpose of communicating to, and receiving Intelligence from the Army—the Express will receive Orders to call upon your Excellency Daily[2]—and any Commands or Intelligence which your Excellency may think proper to transmit will be thankfully received, and punctually attended to by—Your Excellency's most Obedient Servant

By Order.
Abm Yates Junr President

LS, DLC:GW. The draft of this letter that the New York committee of safety approved earlier on this date is almost identical in wording to the LS (see *N.Y. Prov. Congress Journals*, 1:637–38).

1. The convention on this date ordered "that Gilbert Livingston Esqr. or any other Member of the Committee for obstructing the Navigation of Hudson's River who may now be at Pou[gh]keepsie do immediately dispatch the two fireships prepared and charged by Capt. [John] Hazelwood with proper Persons to navigate them to Fort Washington under cover of the Guns & there deliver them to the Care of such Person as his Excellency General Washington has or shall appoint to take charge of them" (DLC:GW; see also ibid., 637).

2. On 17 Sept. the convention appointed William Allison, Robert R. Livingston, and Henry Wisner, Sr., to be a committee of correspondence authorized to establish post riders between Fishkill and GW's headquarters. William Duer was added to the committee by 22 Sept. (see ibid., 627, and Duer to GW, 22 Sept.).

General Orders

Head Quarters, Harlem Heights, Septr 22nd 1776.
Parole Hampton.   Countersign Newark.

The Court Martial of which Col. Sage was President is dissolved—The Brigade Majors to form a new one immediately—Col. Magaw to preside, to meet to morrow at Head-Quarters, Nine O'Clock—The Brigade Majors to give notice to the officers of their respective brigades.

There is a shameful deficiency of Officers at Guard-Mounting and other duty—The Brigade Majors are to put in Arrest, any officer, who being warned, does not attend his duty, unless excused by the Brigadier General.

The many Complaints that are hourly made of plundering both public and private property, induces the General to direct that every Regiment be paraded at five O'Clock this evening, the Knapsacks and Tents of the whole to be examined under the inspection of the Field Officers, and all Articles, not the proper Baggage and Accoutrements of a Soldier, set apart, and kept by the Colonel, or commanding Officer, 'till Inquiry can be made, how they came possessed of them—A Report is expected from the commanding Officer of the regiment, to Head Quarters, whether any Articles are found, or not—And the General depends upon the Honor of the officers, to inspect carefully, and make a faithful report.

It is with particular pleasure that the General has it in his power to inform the officers and soldiers, who have been wounded in their Country's Cause, and all others whose lot it may be to be disabled, that The Congress have come to the following resolution. (Viz.)

"That Officers and Privates, loosing a Limb in any Engagement, or who shall be so disabled in the service of the United States of America, as to render them incapable of getting a livelihood, shall receive half of their Monthly-Pay, during life, or the continuance of their disability, from the time their pay ceases as officers, or soldiers.

"Also such officers, or soldiers, as are wounded in any Engagement, and rendered incapable of service, tho' not totally disabled from getting a livelihood, shall receive Monthly, such Sums towards their Subsistence, as the Assembly, or Representa-

tive Body of the state, they belong to, or reside in, judge adequate; they producing in the cases above-mentioned, to the
Committee, or Officer appointed to receive the same, in the
State, where they reside, or belong, or to the Assembly, or Legis-
lative Body of such State, a Certificate from the Commanding
Officer, who was in the Engagement, in which they were
wounded, or in case of his death, from some other officer of the
same Corps, and the Surgeon that attended them; of their
names, office, rank, department, regiment & company, the nature of their wounds and in what action or engagement they
were wounded."[1]

The Brigadier of the day, where the Guards mount at the
lines, is to give strict charge to all the officers, not to suffer any
person whatsoever, to go beyond the out-Sentries, without an
Order in writing from himself—All the Sentries are to be informed of this, and if any person whatever presume to disobey
the Orders, they are to fire upon [him][2] in the same manner as
they would do on a common Enemy. Any persons coming in
from the Enemy's lines are to be carried to the Brigadier of the
day immediately for examination, who is to take their information in writing, and send it with the person or persons to the
Commander in Chief—The Brigadier is to see that a chain of
Sentries extend from the North River to Harlem River, beyond
which no Stragglers are to pass.

The officer commanding the Scouts, is to attend at Head
Quarters, at seven O'Clock, every morning, to know if there are
any orders for these Corps.

The commanding Officers of the several regiments, are to be
particularly attentive, in seeing that their men are supplied with
Ammunition, and that they account reguarly for the Cartridges
delivered to them: They are not to suffer any Pieces to be discharged at Retreat-beating, but such as will not fire in an Engagement, & cannot be drawn. The great Waste of Ammunition
is such, that unless the officers will exert themselves to see justice
done to the public, a sufficiency cannot be kept upon hand to
supply them.

Mr Josiah Adams is appointed Paymaster to Col. Little's Regiment, and Mr Elisha Humphreys to Col. Webb's Regiment.

The Court Martial whereof Col. Sage was President having
found Ebenezer Liffenwell of Capt: Clift's Company and Col.

Durkee's Regt guilty of "Cowardice and Misbehaviour before the Enemy on Monday last"—and also of "presenting his Firelock at his superior Officer, when turning him back a second time"; which by the 27th Article of the Rules and Regulations of the Army is *Death*—He is accordingly adjudged to suffer *Death*.[3]

The General approves the sentence, and orders that he be shot at the head of the Army, on the Grand-Parade, near Kartright's house, to morrow morning at eleven O'Clock—The Men of the several Regiments below Kingsbridge, not upon Fatigue or Guard are to march down at that hour—The Provost Marshal to attend. Major Henly, acting Deputy Adjt General, will order twelve Men, out of the Guards paraded for duty, to morrow, to execute the sentence.

The same Court Martial having found Ensign McCumber of Capt: Barns's Company, and Col. Serjeant's Regt guilty of the infamous Crime of "plundering the Inhabitants of Harlem"— and ordered him to be cashiered—The General approves the sentence and orders him to be turned out of the Army immediately as an officer.[4]

Varick transcript, DLC:GW; Df, DNA: RG 93, Orderly Books, vol. 15.

Various parts of the draft are in Joseph Reed's writing, including the dateline, the words "parole" and "countersign," the first three paragraphs, and the last three paragraphs concerning court-martials. The draft also includes at the end of this day's general orders another paragraph in Reed's writing, which does not appear in the Varick transcript. It reads: "The Detachmt of one Captain—2 Subs. 3 Serjeants & 40 Privates from Col. Durkee's Regt brought up by the late Col. Knowlton are to return [to] their Regimt."

1. The wording of this extract differs in minor details from the wording of the resolution that Congress approved on 26 Aug. (see *JCC*, 5:702–5). Congress ordered the resolution to be published, and it appears in the *Pennsylvania Gazette* (Philadelphia) for 4 September.

2. This word appears in the draft.

3. During the Battle of Harlem Heights on 16 Sept., Ebenezer Leffingwell was on detached duty with Lt. Col. Thomas Knowlton's rangers. At Leffingwell's court-martial on 19 Sept., Adj. Gen. Joseph Reed testified that during the American counterattack on Vandewater's Heights, he ordered Maj. Andrew Leitch's detachment to reinforce Knowlton's men and "was going up to where the firing was, when I met the Prisoner [Leffingwell] running away from where the firing was with every Mark of Trepidation & Fear. I followed him & ordered him back after striking him. he promised to return & went on into the Bushes. A little after I saw him running off again, & pursued him with a Determination to mark him, & came up to him & struck him with my

Hanger & wounded him in the Head & Hand. he bid me keep off or he would shoot me. he presented his Peice & I think snapp'd his Peice at me. I found him after this lying in a Ditch, on his seeing me he fell to bellowing out, & I should have shot him, could I have got my Gun off. He has since confess'd to me that he was running away at the Time I met him" (DLC:GW; see also Reed's letter to his wife of 22 Sept. in Johnston, *Harlem Heights*, 136–39; Martin, *Private Yankee Doodle*, 45–46; and "McMichael's Diary," 16:136). For the subsequent pardoning of Leffingwell, see General Orders, 23 September.

Wills Clift, who had served as a second lieutenant in the 3d Connecticut Regiment during 1775, became a captain in the 20th Continental Regiment on 1 Jan. 1776. He joined the new 3d Connecticut Regiment as a captain on 1 Jan. 1777, and he was promoted to major of that regiment in May 1778. On 1 Jan. 1781 Clift transferred to the 1st Connecticut Regiment, with which he served until he retired from the army two years later.

4. Matthew Macomber of Taunton, Mass., who had been a sergeant in Col. Paul Dudley Sargent's Massachusetts regiment during 1775, was commissioned an ensign in Sargent's 13th Continental Regiment on 1 Jan. 1776. His plundering of Harlem occurred on 17 September. For an account of that incident and the court-martial proceedings against Macomber on 19 and 21 Sept., see GW's first letter to Hancock of 25 Sept., and note 2.

From William Duer

Sir.   Fishkill [N.Y.] September 22d 1776
The Convention of this State have established a Committee of Correspondence for the purpose of facilitating the Intercourse of Intelligence betwixt this Place and Head Quarters. I am directed by that Committee (of which I have the Honor of being a Member) to order their Express to wait on Your Excellency daily to know your Commands, and to receive such Accounts of the Operations of our Army as your Excellency's leizure will admit you to inform us of.[1]

Captain Cooke who has been employed in sinking the Vessels opposite to Mount Washington informed me in his way to Poukeepsie, that he is apprehensive the Cheveux de frise which are sunk in the River may not be sufficient for stopping the Enemy's Ships, and he is of Opinion, that it would tend much, to render the Obstructions effectual, to sink five or Six Vessels, to the northward of the Cheveux de frise. In Consequence of this Information, the Convention of this State, ever sollicitous to exert themselves in effecting so important an Object as the Obstruction of the Navigation of the River; have entered into the enclosed Resolutions which I have the Honor to transmit to your Excellency—they have likewise given the necessary directions for supplying you with a quantity of oak Plank, agreable to General Clintons Request in a late Letter.[2] I have the Honor to be, with the greatest Respect Your Excellency's most Obedient humble Servt

Wm Duer.

LS, DLC:GW.

1. For the appointment of this committee, see Abraham Yates, Jr., to GW, 21 Sept., and note 2. On this date Duer wrote Tench Tilghman that the committee was empowered "to employ a Gentleman near Head Quarters for communicating Intelligence, to whom they have engaged to make an adequate Compensation—Mr [Robert R.] Livingston and myself are anxious you should undertake this Task. . . . The Sum Total of your office will be to write a daily Letter which our Express will wait on you for—As you (I conceive) reside at head Quarters a few short notes of the daily interesting occurrences will serve as material for your—*Daily Advertiser*" (NHi: Duer Papers). Tilghman accepted the committee's offer the following day, and he frequently wrote Duer or Livingston at least until 17 Nov., giving accounts of current military events (see Duer to Tilghman, 25 Sept., NHi: Duer Papers, and *N.Y. Prov. Congress Journals,* 1:712).

2. In the enclosed resolutions of 21 Sept., the convention directs the secret committee for obstructing the Hudson to purchase or impress as many as six vessels to complete the obstructions in the river opposite Mount Washington and to send all oak plank in their possession, there "with the utmost dispatch." The convention also requests the superintendent for building Continental frigates at Poughkeepsie "to send as much of their short oak Plank as they possibly can spare to Fort Washington" (DLC:GW; see also ibid., 639). Gen. George Clinton had written the committee of correspondence on 18 Sept.: "We shall want oak plank for [artillery] platforms, and square timber" (Force, *American Archives,* 5th ser., 2:383–84).

To John Hancock

Sir   Camp near Kingsbridge Sept. 22d 1776

I had flattered myself that the Congress would before this Time have forwarded the amended Articles for the Government of the Army.[1] But as they have not I think it my indispensable Duty to lay before them the Necessity, the absolute Necessity of forming an Article against plundering, marauding & burning of Houses—such a Spirit has gone forth in our Army that neither publick or private Property is secure—Every Hour brings the most distressing Complaints of the Ravages of our own Troops who are become infinitely more formidable to the poor Farmers & Inhabitants than the common Enemy. Horses are taken out of the Continental Teams—The Baggage of Officers & the Hospital Stores, even the Quarters of General Officers are not exempt from Rapine.

Some severe & exemplary Punishment to be inflicted in a summary Way must be immediately administered, or the Army will be totally ruined—I must beg the immediate Attention of Congress to this Matter as of the utmost Importance to our Existence as an Army. I am Sir, with due Respect Your most Obed. & very Hbble Servt

Go: Washington

LS, in Joseph Reed's writing, DNA:PCC, item 152; copy, DNA:PCC, item 169. Congress read this letter on 23 Sept. (*JCC*, 5:810).

1. For Congress's revision of the articles of war, see Hancock to GW, 24 September.

To John Hancock

Sir　　　　　　　Head Qrs Heights of Harlem Septr 22d 1776
I have nothing in particular to communicate to Congress respecting the Situation of our Affairs, It is much the same as when I had the honor of addressing you last.

On Friday night, about Eleven or Twelve OClock, a Fire broke out in the City of New York, near the New or St Pauls Church, as It is said, which continued to burn pretty rapidly till after Sun rise the next morning. I have not been Informed how the Accident happened, nor received any certain account of the damage. Report says many of the Houses between the Broadway and the River were consumed.[1] I have the Honor to be with great esteem Sir your Most Obedt Servt

Go: Washington

LS, in Robert Hanson Harrison's writing, DNA:PCC, item 152; LB, DLC:GW; copy, DNA:PCC, item 169; Varick transcript, DLC:GW. Congress read this letter on 23 Sept. (*JCC*, 5:810).

1. Fanned by strong winds, this fire, which began about midnight on 20–21 Sept. near Whitehall Slip at the southern end of Manhattan Island, burned nearly a quarter of the city before it was brought under control about twelve

hours later. All of the houses in the area directly north of the slip were destroyed as were most of the structures west of Broadway as far north as King's College, including Trinity Church and the Lutheran church. St. Paul's Chapel on Broadway near Vesey Street was saved by citizens who climbed to its flat roof and extinguished the burning debris blown there by the wind. The commercial district east of Broadway escaped destruction in large part because the wind, which had been blowing out of the southwest, shifted about two o'clock in the morning to the southeast and pushed the fire northwest toward the Hudson River instead of northeast up the East River. For contemporary descriptions of the fire and its effects, see particularly David Grin's account in Moore, *Diary,* 1:313–14, n.1; Mackenzie, *Diary,* 1:58–61; *Kemble Papers,* 1:89–90; E. G. Shewkirk to Nathaniel Seidel, 2 Dec. 1776, in the *Pennsylvania Magazine of History and Biography,* 13 (1889), 376–80; the *New-York Gazette; and the Weekly Mercury,* 30 Sept. 1776; and the *Pennsylvania Gazette* (Philadelphia), 2 Oct. 1776. Most British and Loyalist observers believed that the fire was the work of American arsonists, and a number of persons were arrested on suspicion of setting or spreading it. William Tryon says in his letter to Lord Germain of 24 Sept. that "many circumstances lead to conjecture that Mr Washington was privy to this villainous act as he sent all the bells of the churches out of town under pretence of casting them into cannon, whereas it is much more probable to prevent the alarm being given by ringing of the bells before the fire should get a head beyond the reach of engines and buckets. Besides, some officers of his army were found concealed in the city supposed for this devilish purpose" (Davies, *Documents of the American Revolution,* 12:230–31; see also William Howe to Germain, 23 Sept., in Force, *American Archives,* 5th ser., 2:380; Lydenberg, *Robertson Diaries,* 99; Tatum, *Serle's Journal,* 110–11; Huth, "Hessian Mercenary," 494–95; and Baurmeister, *Revolution in America,* 51). No one ever was brought to trial for burning the city, however, and no evidence of an official or unofficial American conspiracy for that purpose has been found.

From Major General William Heath

Dear General   Kingsbridge Sept. 22nd 1776
    If your Excellency should be fully Satisfied with the Intelligence Brought by the Two Lads who Swam from the LaBrune, with respect to the number of the Enemy on Montrasures Island, I think they may be taken,[1] I Desired General Clinton to lay this matter before your Excellency this Day, But having thought more of it Since he left me, and apprehending that He may not return Untill late this afternoon, I am Desireous to Know your Excellency's Opinion as Soon as you Please to Signify it, and if an attempt should be thought Advisable this night, a Party well officered shall be ready, I should think that One

Hundred & fifty or Two Hundred men would be Sufficient for the purpose, we have Both Officers and Soldiers who are Desirous to Distinguish themselves—Four or Five Flat Bottomed Boats will be necessary, and Two or three whale Boats, If this meets with your Excellency approbation every thing shall be got ready in Season.[2] I have the Honor to be &[c.]

W. Heath

ADfS, MHi: Heath Papers.

1. Heath here struck out the words "without much Difficulty." For GW's sending of these deserters to Heath earlier this day with instructions to have them escorted to New London, see Tench Tilghman to Heath, this date, MHi: Heath Papers. Heath says in his memoirs that the deserters told him "that the British had then but a few men on the [Montresor's] island, stating the number; that the piece of cannon, which had been put on the island, was taken back again on board the La Brune; that there were a number of officers at the house in which there was a considerable quantity of baggage deposited, &c." (Wilson, *Heath's Memoirs,* 73).

2. Robert Hanson Harrison replied to Heath later this day that GW "has no Objection to your making the Attempt you propose, If you are of opinion that the Intelligence given by the Two Lads is satisfactory & will Warrant It, and of which he says you are as good a Judge as he is. He requests that you will acquaint him in time of the Resolution you come to in this Affair, that he may know how to conduct himself with respect to our Guards—If It is undertaken, they certainly must be apprized of It to prevent an Alarm." In a second letter of this date to Heath, Harrison conveys GW's good wishes for the success of the raid and his request "that no Houses or private property may be destroyd by burning or Otherwise unless there shall be an absolute necessity" (MHi: Heath Papers). For an account of the raid that the Americans attempted to make on Montresor's Island the next day, see General Orders, 24 September.

To John Augustine Washington

Dear Brother, Heights of Harlem Sepr 22—76

My extreame hurry for some time past has rendered it utterly impossible for me to pay that attention to the Letters of my Friends which Inclination, and natural Affection always Inclines me to. I have no doubt therefore of meeting with their excuse, tho' with respect to yourself, I have had no Letter from you since the date of my last saving the one of Septr the 1st.[1]

With respect to the Attack and Retreat from Long Island the public Papers would furnish you with Accts nearly true. I shall only add, that in the former we lost abt 800 Men, more than three fourths of which were taken Prisoners—This misfortune happened in a great measure by two Detachments of our People who were Posted in two Roads leading thrô a Wood in order to intercept the Enemy in their March, suffering a Surprize, and making a precepitate Retreat, which enabled the Enemy to lead a great part of their force against the Troops Commanded by Lord Sterling which formed a third detachment; who behaved with great bravery and resolution.

As to the Retreat from the Island, under the Circumstances we then were, it became absolutely necessary, and was effected without loss of Men, and with but very little baggage. A few heavy Cannon were left, not being movable, on Acct of the Grounds being soft and Miry thro' the heavy & incessant Rains which had fallen. The Enemys loss in killed we could never ascertain, but have many reasons to believe that it was pretty considerable and exceeded ours a good deal—Our Retreat from thence as I said before was absolutely necessary, the Enemy having landed the main body of their Army to Attack us in Front while their Ships of War were to cut off all communication with the City, from whence resources of Men, Provisions &ca were to be drawn.

Having made this Retreat, not long after we discovered by the movements of the Enemy and the information we received from Deserters and others, that they declin'd attacking our Lines in the City, and were forming a plan to get in our Rear with their Land Army, by crossing the Sound above us, and thereby cut of all Intercourse with the Country and every necessary supply. The Ships of War were to cooperate, possess the North River and prevent Succours from the Jerseys &ca. this Plan appearing probable and but too practicable in its execution, it became necessary to guard agt the fatal consequences that must follow if their scheme was affected; for which purpose I caused a removal of a part of our Stores, Troops, &ca from the City, and a Council of General Officers determined on thursday the 12th that it must be entirely abandoned; as we had, with an Army Weaker than theirs, a line of Sixteen or 18 Miles to defend, to keep open our Communication with the Country, besides the defence of the City—We held up however every show and appearance of

defence till our Sick and all our Stores could be brought away—
the evacuation being resolved on every exertion in our power
was made to baffle their designs, and effect our own. the sick
were numerous (amounting to more than the fourth of our
whole Army) and an object of great Importance, happily we got
them away; but before we could bring off all our Stores, on Sunday Morning Six or Seven Ships of War which had gone up the
East River some few days before began a most severe and heavy
Canonade to scour the Ground and effect a Landing of their
Troops—Three Ships of War also ran up the North River that
Morning above the City, to prevent our Boats and Small Craft
carrying away our Baggage &ca.

I had gone the Evening before to the Main body of our Army
which was Posted about these Heights & the Plains of Harlem,
where it seemed probable from the movements, and disposition
of the Enemy they meant to Land & make an Attack the next
Morning. However the Event did not happen. Immediately on
hearing the Cannonade I rode with all possible expedition towards the place of Landing, and where Breast Works had been
thrown up to secure our Men, & found the Troops that had
been posted there to my great surprize & Mortification, and
those ordered to their Support (consisting of Eight Regiments)
notwithstanding the exertions of their Generals to form them,
running away in the most Shameful and disgraceful manner—
I used every possible effort to rally them but to no purpose, &
on the appearance of a small part of the Enemy (not more than
60 or 70) they ran off without firing a Single Gun—Many of our
heavy Cannon wd inevitably have fallen into the Enemy's hands
as they landed so soon, but this scandalous conduct occasioned
a loss of many Tents, Baggage & Camp Equipage, which would
have been easily secured had they made the least opposition.

The Retreat was made with the loss of a few men only—We
Incamp'd, and still are on, the Heights of Harlem which are well
calculated for Defence against their approaches. On Monday
Morning they advanced in sight in several large bodys but attempted nothing of a general Nature tho' there were smart Skirmishes between their advancd parties and some Detachments
from our lines which I sent out—In these our Troops behaved
well, putting the Enemy to flight in open Ground, and forcing

them from Posts they had siezed two or three times—A Sergeant who deserted from them says they had as he was told 89 Wounded and Missing besides Slain, but other Accts make the wounded much greater.

Our loss in killed and Wounded was about 60—but the greatest loss we sustaind was in the death of Lt Colo. Knolton, a brave and Gallant Officer—Majr Leitch of Weedons Regiment had three Balls through his Side, & behaved exceedingly well—he is in a fair way of recovery—Nothing material has happend since this—the Enemy it is said are bringing up their heavy Cannon, so that We are to expect another Attack soon—both by Land & Water, as we are upon the Hudson (or North River) at the place where we have attempted to stop the Navigation by sinking obstructions in the River & erecting Batteries.

The Dependance which the Congress has placed upon the Militia, has already greatly injured—& I fear will totally ruin, our Cause—Being subject to no controul themselves they introduce disorder among the Troops you have attempted to discipline while the change in their living brings on sickness—this makes them Impatient to get home, which spreads universally & introduces abominable Desertions—In short, it is not in the power of Words to describe the task I have to Act. £50,000 Should not induce me again to undergo what I have done—Our Numbers by Sickness, desertion, &ca is greatly reduced—I have been trying these 4 or 5 days to get a return but have not yet succeeded—I am sure however we have not more than 12 or 14,000 Men fit for duty, whilst the Enemy (who it is said are very healthy) cannot have less than near 25,000.[2] My Sincere love to my Sister and the Family & Complimts to any enquiring Friends concludes me Dr Sir Yr most Affecte Brother

Go: Washington

ALS, DLC:GW.

1. John Augustine Washington's letter to GW of 1 Sept. has not been found. The most recent letter from GW to his brother Jack that is known is the one of 22 July.

2. GW received a general return on 24 Sept. (see GW to Hancock, that date).

General Orders

Head Quarters, Harlem Heights, sept: 23rd 1776
Parole Stamford.   Countersign Norwalk.

Ebenezer Liffingwell being convicted of offering Violence to his superior Officer—of Cowardice and Misbehaviour before the Enemy, was ordered to suffer Death this day—The General from his former good Character and upon the intercession of the Adjutant General, against whom he presented his firelock, is pleased to pardon him, but declares that the next offender shall suffer Death without mercy.

Serjt Major Hutton is appointed Adjutant to Col. Mead's Regiment—Col. Silliman's Brigade.[1]

Mr Charles Knowles is appointed Paymaster to Col. Knox's Regiment of Artillery.[2]

Col. Douglass's Brigade Major being ordered in Arrest for "Neglect of duty, in not giving the Parole & Countersign to the Guards," Col. Douglass is to appoint another to do the duty.

Colonels and commanding Officers of Regiments have neglected to make Reports of the examination of their regiments after Plunder, they are now reminded of it, and will be mentioned in Orders, if they neglect it.

A Report is to be made at Head-Quarters, as soon as possible, of the several officers under Arrest, that they may be tried—Colonels and commanding Officers of regiments to attend to it.

Varick transcript, DLC:GW; Df, in Joseph Reed's writing, DNA: RG 93, Orderly Books, vol. 15. In the draft the two passwords and the words "to Col. Knox's Regt of Artillery" at the end of the third paragraph are not in Reed's writing.

1. Christopher Hutton, who had been a volunteer in Col. John Lasher's independent New York militia regiment earlier this year, apparently served as adjutant of Lt. Col. John Mead's 9th Regiment of Connecticut militia for only two days, because that regiment was one of those that were dismissed on 25 Sept. (see General Orders, that date, and GW to Jonathan Trumbull, Sr., 26 Sept.). On 21 Nov. Hutton was commissioned an ensign in the 3d New York Regiment. He became the regimental adjutant in May 1778, and in February 1779 he was promoted to lieutenant. Hutton joined the 2d New York on 1 Jan. 1783 and left the army the following June.

2. Charles Knowles (d. 1796) had been quartermaster of the 2d Connecticut Regiment during 1775. When his appointment as paymaster of Knox's Continental Artillery Regiment expired at the end of 1776, Knowles became paymaster of Col. John Crane's 3d Continental Artillery Regiment. Promoted to

first lieutenant in September 1778 and captain-lieutenant in September 1780, Knowles served until November 1783.

From William Bradford

                                        State of Rhode Island &c. Bristol
Sir,   September 23d 1776
   Having seen in the publick Papers that your Excellency and the British Admiral have agreed upon an Exchange of Prisoners in the naval Department I beg Leave to apply to you in Behalf of a Mate of a Vessel, and Four Seamen, all belonging to Warwick in this State, some of whom are connected with very reputable Families. They were all taken in the Merchant's Service, and are Prisoners on board One of the Ships of War now in the Sound. We have a Mate of a Merchant's Ship, and Four Seamen, who were taken in a Transport with Part of One of the Highland Regiments, to give for them. I request your Excellency's Directions, as soon as may be, whether we shall send the Prisoners directly to you, or how I shall proceed to procure the Exchange, which will very much oblige many worthy People here. I am with great Esteem and Respect Your Excellency's Most obedient and Most humble Servant

                              William Bradford Deputy Governor

LS, DLC:GW; copy, R-Ar.

From Major General Nathanael Greene

Dear Sir   Camp Fort Constitution [N.J.] Sept. 23 1776
   The Enemy are landed at Powleys Hook, they came up this afternoon and began a Cannonade on the Battery; and after Cannonadeing for half an hour or a little more they landed a party from the Ships. General Mercer had orderd off, from the Hook all the Troops except a small Guard who had Orders to Evacuate the place from the first approach of the Enimy. General Mercer mentions no Troops but those Landed from the Ships, but Colo. Bull and many others that were along the River upon the Heights saw twenty Boats go over from York to Powleys Hook. This movement must have happen'd since General

Mercer wrote.[1] I purpose to Visit Burgen to Night, as General Mercer thinks of going to his Post at Amboy tomorrow. I purpose to detain him one day longer. I am with due respect Your Excellencys Obedient Servant

N. Greene

ALS, enclosed in GW to Hancock, 24 Sept. 1776, DNA:PCC, item 152; copy, DNA:PCC, item 169. GW forwarded this letter to Hancock on 24 Sept., and Congress read it the next day (*JCC,* 5:819). A note on the letter's cover sheet reads: "Express the bearer is to be set over the ferry immediately N. Greene M.G."

Having taken command of the American forces on the New Jersey side of the Hudson River about 17 Sept., Greene was stationed at Fort Constitution near Burdett's Ferry, which was renamed Fort Lee on 19 Oct. (see Greene to Nicholas Cooke, 17 Sept., in Showman, *Greene Papers,* 1:300–302).

1. The British had postponed an attempt to attack Paulus Hook the previous day when a strong northwest wind prevented their warships from getting into position to cover the landing. For contemporary accounts of this day's attack, see particularly Mackenzie, *Diary,* 1:62–63; Baurmeister, *Revolution in America,* 52; *Kemble Papers,* 1:90; Tatum, *Serle's Journal,* 112; the journal of Col. Durkee's chaplain (Benjamin Boardman), 22–23 Sept., in the *Connecticut Gazette and the Universal Intelligencer* (New London), 18 Oct. 1776; and the journals of the *Emerald, Roebuck, Tartar,* and *Preston,* this date, in Clark and Morgan, *Naval Documents,* 6:964–65.

Tench Tilghman wrote William Duer on 25 Sept. that "General *Greene* informs that General *Mercer,* seeing the enemy were determined to possess themselves by a stronger force of ships and men than we could oppose, removed all the stores and useful cannon, so that nothing fell into the enemy's hands but the guns that had been rendered unfit for further service" (Force, *American Archives,* 5th ser., 2:523).

Thomas Bull (1744–1837) was lieutenant colonel of Col. William Montgomery's regiment of flying camp troops that had been raised in Chester County, Pennsylvania. Captured at Fort Washington on 16 Nov., Bull remained a prisoner until April 1778 when he was exchanged. He became a lieutenant colonel in the Chester County militia in 1779, and from 1780 to 1781 he served as colonel of the county's 2d Regiment of militia light horse.

To Major General William Howe

Sir   Head Quarters Heights of Harlem Sept. 23rd 1776

I yesterday evening received the favor of your letter of the 21st by your Aid de Camp, Capt. Montresor,[1] in consequence of which I this morning dispatch'd an express to Elizabeth town, with orders that Majr Genl Prescott, should be permitted to return in the boat that carried Genl Sullivan over to that place.[2]

I most readily concur in the proposition, you are pleased to make for the exchange of Brigr Genl Lord Stirling, for Governor Muntford Brown, & have sent for him accordingly; I should hope that Lord Stirling will be immedy set at liberty, on my promise, that Governor Brown shall be sent to you as soon as he arrives; I had no doubt but Mr McDonalds title would have been acknowledged, having understood that he recieved his commission from the hands of Governor Martin; nor can I consent to rank him as a Major, till I have proper authority from Congress, to whom I shall state the matter, upon your representation.[3]

Agreable to your request, I shall transmit to Lieut: Col. Campbell, a copy of the list of officers of the 42nd & 71st regiments, taken by us last spring, that it may be rectified in the instances, in which it may be wrong, & will then place opposite to their names, the officers I would wish in return for them: The exchange of privates, I shall take the earliest oppertunity in my power to carry into execution but they being greatly dispersed through the New England governments, in order to their better accomodation, will prevent it for some time.

Having the fullest confidence in your assurance, that Mr Lovell will be released, when he arrives, from Halifax, I have wrote for Governor Skeene to come to Head Quarters that he may proceed immedy to you.[4]

As to the exchange of prisoners settled between Capt. Foster, and Genl Arnold, I beg leave to inform you, that it was a transaction, in which I had not the smallest concern, nor have I authority to give directions, in any degree respecting the matter.

The information you have recd concerning the ill treatment of your officers, I would fain hope, is not generally well founded; the letters from them, which have passed through my hands, hold forth a different language; in particular instances, 'tis true, there are some who have been restricted to a closer confinement and severer treatment than they otherwise would have been, for breaking or refusing to give their paroles; Such (I am confident) will not be countenanced by your Excellency, & I am perswaded by a closer investigation of the enquiry, you will discover, that there have been no other persons whatever who have experienced the smallest harshness from us; I shall however obtain all the information on the subject in my power, that

every ground of complaint (if any exists) may be entirely remov'd, it being my most earnest wish, that during this unhappy
contest, there be every exercise of humanity, which the nature
of the case will possibly admit of.

Your Aid de Camp, delivered me the ball you mention, which
was the first of the kind I ever saw or heard of; you may depend
the contrivance is highly abhorred by me, and every measure
shall be taken to prevent so wicked & infamous a practice being
adopted in this army. I have the honor to be with due reguard
Yr Most Obed. Servt

G.W.

LB, in William Grayson's writing, DLC:GW; two copies, P.R.O., 30/55, Carleton Papers; copy, enclosed in GW's second letter to Hancock of 25 Sept.,
DNA:PCC, item 152; copy, DNA:PCC, item 169; Varick transcript, DLC:GW.

1. John Montresor, the British army's chief engineer in America, was also
an aide-de-camp to General Howe at this time. Montresor proposed the British landing at Kip's Bay on 15 Sept., and during the Battle of Harlem Heights
the following day, he deployed two brass cannon that helped slow the American counterattack (see Scull, *Montresor Journals*, 116, 121).

2. GW wrote Gen. Hugh Mercer at Elizabethtown on this date informing
him of Howe's agreement to this exchange and directing Mercer "to have Genl
Prescott in readiness at the [Elizabethtown] point, that he may return without
delay in the Boat that brings Genl Sullivan" (LB, in Robert Hanson Harrison's
writing, DLC:GW; Varick transcript, DLC:GW).

3. GW instructed Mercer in his letter to him of this date to order McDonald's "return to Philadelphia with the Escort that is with him, where Congress
will give their direction concerning him" (DLC:GW). See also GW's second
letter to Hancock of 25 September.

4. See GW to Trumbull, this date.

From Major General Philip Schuyler

Dear Sir   Albany Septr 23d 1776

General Gates has requested me to send up twenty Casks of
Shingle Nails he says "the Carpenters are unable to proceed
with the public works for the want of them"—I have wrote to
Congress on the 8th Instant begging that a Quantity might be
sent up, but if your Excellency can spare any, I wish to have
them sent with all possible Dispatch, as we cannot procure any
here and those from philadelphia may probably not arrive in
Time, if at all.[1]

The Committee of the Town of Schenectady have requested me that Barracks should be built there for the Accommodation of any Troops that may be quartered there or pass thro' it—I do not conceive myself authorized to take such a Step without your Excellency's Consent or that of Congress. I am with the greatest Respect & Esteem Your Excellency's obedient humble Servant

Ph: Schuyler

LS, DLC:GW; LB, NN: Schuyler Papers.

Schuyler apparently enclosed with this letter a copy of Gates's general return of the American forces serving in the northern department dated 22 Sept. (DLC:GW; see also Force, *American Archives*, 5th ser., 2:479–80).

1. Gates's letter to Schuyler requesting these nails has not been identified, but see Schuyler's reply to Gates of this date in ibid., 469–70. See also Schuyler to Hancock, 8 and 25 Sept., in DNA:PCC, item 153.

To Jonathan Trumbull, Sr.

Sir　　　　　Head Quarters Heights of Harlem Sepr 23d 1776

General Howe, in a letter received from him Yesterday evening by a Flag, having offered to exchange Brigadier General Lord Stirling for Governor Montfort Brown, and also requested that Govr Skeene may be granted his liberty without delay, assuring me that Mr Lovell shall be immediately enlarged upon his arrival from Halifax, and whose exchange for Govr Skeene has been agreed on,[1] I must take the liberty of requesting your notice[2] to those two gentlemen, and that you will provide them with a proper escort to repair to Head Quarters as soon as they can, with their baggage, that the proposed exchange for Lord Stirling may be effected, and General Howe's request complied with respecting Governor Skeene's being returned—The Gentlemen are to consider themselves under parole till such time as they are sent from Head Quarters to General Howe.

I must beg your excuse for not having wrote you of late upon the situation of our affairs and such events as have cast up in the Military Line. I shall only add that the important concerns which have constantly commanded my closest attention have been the cause, and I am fully persuaded, will furnish me with a sufficient apology.

Of the evacuation of New York on Sunday Sennight and the

retreat to this place you will have heard before now, and of the manner in which it was conducted. I am certain a minute relation of them would only encrease the uneasiness which would naturally arise upon hearing of the events; and therefore, and as I have not time, I shall not enter upon it. The Enemy by their movements having unfolded their plan of operations and discovered, that they declined making a direct attack upon the Town, and that their designs were to land in our rear and cut off all intercourse with the Country, at the same time to prevent any communication with the Jersey and States South of the North River by means of their Ships of War, it became necessary to adopt such measures as seemed best calculated to baffle their schemes and promote the Common Interest. To these ends a Council of Officers determined the evacuation of the city absolutely Necessary;[3] and I have only to wish that it had been made in a way more honorable and with less loss of Baggage, which might have been the case, had the Troops that remained there for the defence of the Lines not be taken themselves to a most precipitate and disagreeable flight contrary to the motions of their General Officers[4] and every effort in my power to prevent and form them, having gone from hence as soon as the Ships began their Cannonade and whither I had come the night before to the main Body of our Army in expectation of an attack that night or the next morning, as the parade by the Enemy and the unusual stir among them strongly indicated one—The next morning several large Columns of them appeared on the Plains at the distance of about two miles and a half below us, and some smart skirmishes ensued between their advanced Parties composed of the second Battalion of Infantry, a Regiment of Royal Highlanders and three Companies of the Hessian Chausars or Riflemen, and the Detachments which I sent out to oppose them—Upon this occasion our men behaved with great spirit and intrepidity, putting the Enemy to flight and forcing them from their Posts two or three times. Our people buried sixteen or eighteen of their dead, as they say; and a Serjeant who has since deserted reports they had eighty nine missing and wounded. Our loss in number was very inconsiderable, but must be considered as great, in the fall of Lieut. Colo. Knowlton of your State who commanded a party of Rangers composed of Volunteers from the several New-England Regiments, and who was a brave and good Officer—Every honor was paid to his merit in his interment that the situation of things would admit of. The Enemy have formed a large Encampment in the Plains (or rather heights) below us, extending across, as it were, from the East to the North River, but have attempted nothing, as yet, of a general nature. We are making every disposition, in our power, for defence, and I should hope from the ground we are on, if they make an attack and our men behave with tolerable resolution and firmness, that they will meet with a repulse, or at least, any advantage they gain will be attended with sorrow and loss.[5] Major Leitch who led on a Detachment of the Virginia Regiment in the affair of monday received three balls through one side. He still retains his spirits and seems as if he would recover.

On Friday night about eleven or twelve oClock a fire broke out in the City of New York, which burning rapidly till after Sunrise next morning, destroyed a great number of Houses— By what means it happened we do not know; but the Gentleman who brought the letter out last night from General Howe, and who was one of his Aid De Camps informed Colo. Reed that several of our Countrymen had been punished with various deaths on account of it. Some by hanging, others by burning & c. alledging that they were apprehended when committing the fact. I have the honor to be with great Esteem Sir Your most obedient Servant

Go: Washington

P.S. I would choose that Govrs Brown and Skeene should be stopped when they come within ten or twelve miles, and detained till one of the Escort can inform me of their coming & receive my directions respecting them.

LB, Ct: Trumbull Papers; LB, DLC:GW; Varick transcript, DLC:GW.

1. See Howe to GW, 21 September.

2. The LB in DLC:GW reads: "requesting the favor of your notice."

3. GW is referring to the council of war held on 12 September.

4. The LB in DLC:GW reads: "a most precipitate and disgracefull flight contrary to the exertions of their Genl Officers."

5. The LB in DLC:GW reads: "with sorrow and a considerable loss."

To Abraham Yates, Jr.

⟨Head Quarters at the Heights of Harlem⟩
⟨Sir⟩ ⟨Sept. 23rd 1776⟩

Your favour of the ⟨21st inst.⟩ inclosing the resolution of the repre⟨sentatives of⟩ the State of New York, has come du⟨ely to hand;⟩ and will be properly attended to; I am ⟨exceeding⟩ly oblig'd by the readiness, you dec⟨lare you⟩ will pay to any commands, which ⟨you⟩ may recieve from me respecting the ⟨great⟩ cause in which we are ingaged.

The maneuvres of the En⟨emy⟩ before their landing on Sunday last, ⟨were⟩ various and perplexing, however ⟨about⟩ eight OClock in the morning they be⟨came⟩ extremely plain and obvious; at that time they began their operations, by sen⟨ding⟩ three ships of war up the North river as ⟨high⟩ as Bloomendahl, which put a stop to the removal of our stores by water, & about ele⟨ven⟩ those in the East river, began a constant ⟨&⟩ heavy canonade, for the purpose of scour⟨ing⟩ the grounds & covering the landing of the⟨ir⟩ troops, where breast works had been thrown up ⟨to⟩ oppose them; as soon as I heard the fir⟨ing,⟩ I immedy repaired to the place of landi⟨ng⟩ when to my extreme astonishment I discovered the troops who were posted on ⟨the⟩ lines retreating in the greatest disord⟨er⟩ and Parsons and Fellows brigades, who ⟨were⟩ directed to support them retreating in ⟨the greatest confusion & without making the slightest opposition, although only a small party of the enemy appeared in view—As I preceived no dependanc⟩e could be rep⟨osed on these troop⟩s and apprehending another ⟨impression⟩ might be made on Harlem plains, by which means our retreat to this place might ⟨be⟩ cut off, I directed the heights to be secured; & ⟨Ou⟩r retreat was effected with little or no loss ⟨of⟩ men, though of a considerable part of the ⟨b⟩aggage; Some of our Heavy cannon & a part ⟨of⟩ our Stores & provisions, which we were about removing, was unavoidably left in the City, though every means (after it had been determined in Council to abandon the post) had been used to prevent it.

On Monday morning last, sevl parties of the enemy appeared on the high grounds opposite to our heights, and some Skirmishing had happened between our troops & those of the enemy; On reconnoitring their situation, I formed the design of cutting off such of them as had or might advance to the extremity of the wood; I accordingly ordered three companies of Virginia rifle men under the command of Major Leitch & Col. Knolton with his rangers, to endeavor to get in their rear, while an apparent disposition was making as if to attack them in front; The Enemy ran down the hill with great eagerness to attack the party in front; but unluckily, from some mistake ⟨or misapprehension, the parties under Maj. Leitch & Col. Knolton began the fire on their flank instead of their rear; the Major⟩ was soon brought ⟨off the field wounded & Colo.⟩ Knolton soon recieved a wou⟨nd of which he is⟩ since dead; Their men h⟨owever behaved⟩ with the greatest resolution; Fin⟨ding that⟩ they wanted assistance, I advan⟨ced part⟩ of Col. Griffiths & Col. Richardsons M⟨aryland⟩ regiments with some detachments of ⟨Eastern⟩ troops, who charged the enemy & drove ⟨them⟩ from the wood to the plain, & were s⟨till pur⟩suing, when I judg'd it prudent to ⟨with⟩draw them, fearing the enemy mig⟨ht be⟩ sending a large reinforcement to ⟨their⟩ troops which were engaged, which was ⟨the⟩ case as I have since understood: A ⟨Seargent⟩ who deserted from the Enemy has inform⟨ed⟩ me their party was greater than I imag⟨ined;⟩ as it consisted of the 2nd battalion of light ⟨Infantry⟩ a battalion of royal Highlanders, & three ⟨Compa⟩nies of Hessian riflemen, under the com⟨mand⟩ of General Leslie; their loss by his report am⟨ounted⟩ to 89 wounded & missing & eight Killed; ⟨in⟩ the latter his account is altogether imperf⟨ect,⟩ as our people discovered and buried doub⟨le⟩ that number; I am in hopes this little success will be productive of salutary consequences, as our army seems to be greatly inspirited by it. I am Sir Yr Most Obedt Servt

Go: Washington

LS, in William Grayson's writing, N: New York Provincial Congress, Revolutionary Papers; transcript, MH: Sparks Collection. The LS was damaged in the New York State Library fire of 1911, and the missing portions of the text are supplied within angle brackets from the Sparks transcript. The New York committee of safety read this letter on 25 Sept. (see *N.Y. Prov. Congress Journals*, 1:642).

General Orders

Head Quarters, Harlem Heights, Septr 24th 1776.
Parole Bristol.   Countersign Salem.

The Qr Mr Genl, and the Chief Engineer, are to mark the grounds, to morrow, on which the Barracks, and Huts, are to be built this side Kingsbridge—They are to call upon the General, previous to their setting out upon this business, for directions.

When the ground is marked out, the Quarter Master General is to cause the materials for building to be laid thereon as quick as possible.

The General is informed that in consequence of his recommendation of the 20th Instant many Regiments have turned out very cheerfully to work, when others have sent few or no men on fatigue. the first he thanks for their Conduct, whilst the others are to be informed that their conduct will be marked—The General would have them recollect that it is for their own safety and self defence, these Works are constructing, and the sooner they are finished the sooner they will be able to erect warm and comfortable Barracks, or Huts for themselves to lodge in.

The Militia which came to the assistance of this Army, under the Command of Genl Walcott are to hold themselves in readiness to return home; before they go, they are to return into the public stores, every thing they drew from thence, such as Ammunition, Camp Kettles &c.

Joseph Jackson appointed Paymaster to Col. Hutchinson's regiment.[1]

Major Henly Aid-de-Camp to Genl Heath, whose Activity and Attention to duty, Courage and every other Quality, which can distinguish a brave and gallant Soldier, must endear him to every Lover of his Country, having fallen in a late Skirmish on Montresor's Island while bravely leading a party on—his Remains will be interr'd this afternoon, at five, OClock, from the quarters of Major David Henly, acting Adjt Genl below the hill where the Redoubt is thrown up on the road.[2]

The General thanks the Colonels, and commanding Officers of Regiments, for their care in examining the Tents, and Knapsacks of the Soldiers, after plunder—he directs that what has been found be sent to the House on the Road below Head Quarters, and that regimental Courts Martial immediately sit, to try every one who cannot prove that he came honestly by what is found in his possession—The Offenders to be punished, as soon as the sentence is approved by the Colonel, or commanding Officer—As a little wholesome severity now may put a stop to such ruinous practices in future, the General hopes a very strict Inquiry will be made, and no Favor shewn—The General does not admit of any pretence for plundering, whether it is Tory property taken beyond the lines, or not, it is equally a breach of Orders, and to be punished in the officer who gives Orders, or the Soldier who goes without.

Such Colonels, or commanding Officers of Regiments, as have not reported will be mentioned by Name in to morrow's Orders, if Reports are not made before.

A working Party of *1000* Men, properly officered, to parade to morrow, opposite Head Quarters, at Seven O'Clock—The Parade will be attended by some General Officers, who will put in Arrest, any officer found deliquent in bringing his men in time.

A Field Officer, of the Regiment posted at Mount Washington, is to visit the Guards there carefully; the distance from the Lines not admitting the General Officer of the day to go up.

Varick transcript, DLC:GW; Df, DNA: RG 93, Orderly Books, vol. 15. The last five paragraphs of the general orders in the draft are in Joseph Reed's writing.

1. Joseph Jackson (1730–1803) of Massachusetts served as paymaster for Israel Hutchinson's 27th Continental Regiment until the end of 1776.

2. The raid that a party of about two hundred and forty men commanded by Lt. Col. Michael Jackson had attempted to make on Montresor's Island shortly before dawn the previous day failed when two of the three boats carrying the troops turned back before landing, obliging Jackson and the men of his boat, who had landed on the island, to beat a hasty retreat. Thomas Henley, who had "importuned" Heath for permission to accompany Jackson on the raid, was a younger brother of David Henley. For accounts of this action and the light but variously reported casualties on each side, see Wilson, *Heath's Memoirs*, 73–76; Tench Tilghman to William Duer, 25 Sept., in Force, *American Archives*, 5th ser., 2:523; Extract of a Letter from an Officer at Harlem, 25 Sept., ibid., 524; List of Men taken at Montressor's Island, 17 Nov. 1776, ibid., 3:717–18; Mackenzie, *Diary*, 1:62–64; Tatum, *Serle's Journal*, 112; Lydenberg, *Robertson Diaries*, 100; and Baurmeister, *Revolution in America*, 52. For the court-martial of two officers for "Cowardice and Misbehaviour" during the raid, see General Orders, 29 September.

From Nathaniel Folsom

Exeter [N.H.] 24 Sept. 1776. Informs that in accordance with a request received on 14 Sept. from the Continental Congress, "this State hath raised one thousand Men who are just beginning their March for New York—They are form'd into two Regiments of five hundred Men each under Coll Thomas Tash, and Coll Nahum Baldwin, who are ordered to march their Regiments forward with all possible speed, & put themselves under Your Direction at New York and continue so until the first of December next."[1]

LS, DLC:GW. Folsom signed this letter as chairman pro tempore of the New Hampshire committee of safety.

1. For Congress's resolution of 3 Sept. requesting additional reinforcements for the army at New York, see *JCC,* 5:734; see also Hancock to Certain States, 3 Sept., in Smith, *Letters of Delegates,* 5:96–97. For the proceedings of the special convention of the New Hampshire council and assembly that convened on 14 Sept. to authorize the raising of these two regiments, see Bouton, *N.H. State Papers,* 8:337–38. Thomas Tash (1722–1809), who had served as a provincial captain during the French and Indian War, represented Newmarket in the assembly before his appointment as colonel of the first regiment of reinforcements on 17 September. In December 1777 he became a member of the assembly representing New Durham, the Gore, and Wolfeborough. Nahum Baldwin, Sr. (1734–1788), of Amherst was also a member of the assembly when he was appointed colonel of the second regiment of reinforcements on 17 September. He had been named treasurer of Hillsborough County in January 1776, and in June he had become mustermaster for all forces raised in New Hampshire. Baldwin was appointed a justice of the peace for Hillsborough County in June 1777.

To John Hancock

Sir   Head Qrs Harlem Heights Septr 24th 1776

The post being about to depart I have only time to add, That no event of importance has taken place on this side Hudson's River since my last of the 22d Instt.

The Inclosed Letter received last night from Genl Greene, who now commands in the Jerseys, will give Congress all the information I have respecting the evacuation of powles Hook and the landing of the Enemy to possess It.[1]

I this minute obtained a Copy of the Genl Return of our

Force, the first I have been able to procure for some time past, which I do myself the honor of transmitting for the satisfaction of Congress.[2] I am Sir with the greatest respect Yr Most Obedt Servt

Go: Washington

P.S. The Thirteen Militia Regiments from Connecticut being reduced to a little more than Seven Hundred Men Rank & file, fit for duty, I have thought proper to discharge the whole, to save the States the immense charge that would arise for Officer's pay[3]—There are too, many Militia that have just come in & on their way from that State, none of which are provided with a Tent or a Single Camp Utensil. This distresses me b[e]yond measure.

LS, in Robert Hanson Harrison's writing, DNA:PCC, item 152; LB, DLC:GW; copy, DNA:PCC, item 169; Varick transcript, DLC:GW. Congress read this letter on 25 Sept. (*JCC*, 5:819).

1. See Greene to GW, 23 September.

2. This general return of American forces "at Kingsbridge & its Dependencies" on 21 Sept. is in DNA: RG 93, Revolutionary War Rolls, 1775–83; see also Force, *American Archives*, 5th ser. 2:449–52. It shows that GW then had under his direct command 1,754 commissioned officers, 273 staff officers, 2,501 noncommissioned officers, and 27,377 rank and file, of whom 15,666 were present and fit for duty, 4,418 present and sick, 3,379 absent and sick, 3,736 on command, and 93 on furlough. An attached return for Knox's artillery regiment shows that it contained a total of 543 officers and men, of whom 357 were present and fit for duty. A note at the end of the return reads: "There is besides the above a Company of Artillery at Powles Hook of which no Return has been made this Week. Col. Durkees Regt is also at Powles Hook & has made no Return this Week."

3. Fourteen regiments of Connecticut militia were discharged the following day. The general return of 21 Sept. fails to identify Col. Samuel Chapman's regiment as militia (DNA: RG 93, Continental Army Returns; see also Jonathan Trumbull, Jr., to GW, 13 Aug. 1776).

From John Hancock

Sir,   Philada Septr 24th 1776.

You will perceive by the enclosed Resolves of Congress, which I have the Honour to forward, that they have come to a Determination to augment our Army, & to engage the Troops to serve during the Continuance of the War. As an Inducement to enlist on these Terms, the Congress have agreed to give, besides a Bounty of twenty Dollars, a Hundred Acres of Land to each Soldier; and in Case he should lose his Life in Battle, they have resolved that his Children or other Representatives shall succeed to such Grant.[1]

It is unnecessary to repeat to you the numberless ill Consequences resulting from the limited Inlistment of Troops. The untimely Death of General Montgomery alone, independent of other Arguments, is a stricking Proof of the Danger and Impropriety of sending Troops into the Field, under any Restriction as to the Time of their Service. The noblest Enterprize may be left unfinished by Soldiers in such a Predicament, or abandoned the very Moment Success must have crowned the Attempt. Your own Experience has long since convinced you, that without a well disciplined Army we cannot rationally expect Success against veteran Troops; and that it is totally impossible we should ever have a well disciplined Army, unless our Troops are engaged to serve during the War. The Congress therefore, impressed with these, & other Reasons, and fully convinced, that our Militia is inadequate to the Duty expected of them have adopted the enclosed Resolves, which I am persuaded will afford you Pleasure, as the only Means left to defend our Country in its present critical Situation. I have wrote to all the States, and forwarded a Copy of the printed Resolves herewith transmitted, and urged them in the most pressing Language to comply in the fullest Manner with the Requisition of Congress.[2]

As the Troops now in Service belonging to the several States will be considered as Part of their Quota in the American Army, it will be necessary to ascertain what Number of the Troops, as well as what Officers will engage to serve during the War. For this Purpose I have wrote to the States, and forwarded blank Commissions for all such Officers, and others whom they shall appoint agreeably to the enclosed Resolves.

The Articles of War as first adopted by Congress being exploded, I send you sundry Copies of those, which they have instituted in their Room.[3]

I enclose you also sundry other Resolves, to which I beg Leave to request your Attention.[4]

As the Committee of Congress will confer with you on the State of the Army, to them I beg Leave to refer you, and am with every Sentiment of Esteem & Respect Sir, your most obedient and very hble Sevt

John Hancock Presidt

LS, DLC:GW; LB, DNA:PCC, item 12A.

1. Hancock enclosed copies of Congress's several resolutions of 16, 18, 19, and 20 Sept. regarding the raising an army of eighty-eight regiments for the duration of the war (DLC:GW; see also *JCC*, 5:762–63, 780–81, 787–88, 807, 6:1125).

2. See Hancock to the States, this date, in Smith, *Letters of Delegates*, 5:228–30.

3. The new version of the articles of war that Congress approved on 20 Sept. was printed by John Dunlap of Philadelphia (see *JCC*, 5:788–807, 6:1125). This version is an "exploded" one in that it is divided into eighteen sections, each of which contains several related articles. For example, five articles concerning mutiny, sedition, and insubordination compose section 2.

4. The enclosed handwritten copy of Congress's resolutions of 16, 18, 19, and 20 Sept. concern various military matters, including several officer appointments, medicines for the northern army, the importance of training and discipline, a reiteration of the prohibition on holding multiple commissions, and the appointment of a committee to go to GW's headquarters and "enquire into the state of the army, and the best means of supplying their wants" (DLC:GW; see also ibid., 5:761, 780–81, 783–85, 808). The committee, which consisted of Roger Sherman, Elbridge Gerry, and Francis Lewis, consulted with GW and his general officers on 26 and 27 Sept. (see GW to Heath, 26 Sept., and GW to Hancock, 27 Sept.).

From Lieutenant Colonel Henry Beekman Livingston

Sir   Say Brook [Conn.] 24th Sepr 1776

since my Last I have made a little excursion upon Long Island and braught off 3,129 Sheep and 400 Head of Horned Cattle from Shenecock Plains about thirty Miles from Sag Harbour[1] there Hearing a Mr Richard Miller and some others were raiseing Companies to aid and Assist General How I dispatched Captain Roe with about thirty Men to Seize their Leaders and hinder the People from Collecting, at the Time of Captain Roe's Arrival at Satauket he found that Mr Millar had inlisted about 40 Men and was on his way to Head his Company, when he fell in with Captain Roe and his Party who lay in wait for him in hopes to make him their Prisoner he was hailed several times and Ordered to Stop but attempting to make his Escape was Shot through the Body, I have thought proper to be thus particular with regaurd to this Transaction lest it Should be misrepresented as the Young Gentleman has Many Freinds, he is said to have been recomended to the Notice of Lord How by Judge Ludlow.[2] Oliver Delancey is a Brigadier General under Lord How as Your Excellency may see by the inclosed Copies of Orders sent to Colonel Finehas Fanning I was permitted a sight of the Originals on Condition they should be again Returned.[3] A Reward of £500 is offerd for my Head by General Delancey I am told, I am in Great hopes of being even with him soon if Your Excellency pleases to Continue Me on this Station, if it was possible for me to Obtain a few More Men I beleive it would be in My Power to make their Quarters very Warm for them at Jamaica as I am informed most of their Army have Crossed the East River however Should this not be a Fact it is Certain that Lord How has Ordered all Grain Hay &c. to be Valued and reserved for the Use of the B[ri]t[is]h Army the defending or destroying this would be advantageous I should Immajine The New England People are very Backward in supplying Vessels to Carry Off Stock Otherwise I Should have removed treble the Quantity Most of those I have[,] have been pressed for that purpose and Given them Certificates on the Conventi⟨on⟩ of New York in payment for The time they were Employed—Any Directions Your Excellency will be pleased to Honour me with Shall be Strictly Complied with. I remain Your Excellencies Mos⟨t⟩ Obt Humble Servt

Henry B. Liv⟨ingston⟩

ALS, enclosed in GW to Hancock, 2 Oct. 1776, DNA:PCC, item 152; copy, DNA:PCC, item 169. The portions of the text within angle brackets are mutilated.

1. Livingston had written GW most recently on 11 September. The low sandy Shinnecock Hills, located about twenty miles west of Sag Harbor, were one of the principal grazing grounds on Long Island.

2. Richard Miller, Jr., a Suffolk County Loyalist who had refused to sign the Brookhaven association in 1775, died from his wounds. Daniel Roe (1740–1820), a member of the Suffolk County committee of safety, commanded a company of minutemen during 1775, and in April 1776 he joined Col. James Clinton's 2d New York Regiment, serving as a captain in Livingston's detachment. Roe became a captain in Livingston's 4th New York Regiment in No-

vember 1776. Setauket is on the north shore of Long Island directly across the sound from Bridgeport, Connecticut.

3. Phineas Fanning, a cousin of Gen. Nathaniel Woodhull and a veteran of the French and Indian War, was appointed by the provincial congress in July 1775 as mustermaster for troops raised in Suffolk County, and in August 1775 he commanded the militia ordered to protect the livestock in eastern Long Island from British foraging parties. The enclosed copies of De Lancey's orders of 1, 2, 5, and 11 Sept. are in DNA:PCC, item 152. The order of 1 Sept. conveys General Howe's willingness to accept the submission of the inhabitants of Suffolk, and the one of 2 Sept. directs Fanning to order the captains in the 3d battalion of the county's militia to assemble their men and command them to lay down their arms and swear allegiance to the king. The order of 5 Sept. concerns the raising of troops in the county for British service. The order of 11 Sept. directs Fanning to drive "all the fat Cattle and Sheep in Suffolk County" to Jamaica (DNA:PCC, item 152). For Livingston's subsequent capture of Fanning and Fanning's success in convincing the New York convention that he was a friend of the American cause, see Livingston to GW, 14 October.

From the Massachusetts General Court

Sir   Watertown September 24th 1776

The Board have received your Favour of the 19th instant, and are much obliged to your Excellency for the particular Account you have favoured us with, relative to the Attack and retreat of the Continental Troops from Long Island as also of their Evacuating the City of New York, We are glad to hear the retreat was Effected with the loss of but three or four Men. We shall have been Well pleased to have heard that in the late Action on the 15th instant the Troops had made a bold and resolute Stand against the Enemy instead of being informed that some of them deserted their Post, in so Shameful and disgraceful a Manner as you have represented notwithstandg the Exertions of their General, and the Attempts your Excellency made to rally them.

At the time we informed you that this State had resolved to draft one fifth part of their Militia to reinforce the Army at New York, there had been no Appointment [of] a General Officer to Command these Troops,[1] We have now to inform you that Since our last, the Hon'ble Benjamin Lincoln Esqr. Major General of the Militia of this State, has been Appointed to this Command who will Soon be able to give you the Necessary Information with respect to the Officers who are to Command the respective regiments of which this reinforcement will Consist.[2]

LB, M-Ar: Revolution Letters; Df, M-Ar: Revolution Letters.

1. The word "of" appears in the draft. For the General Court's earlier action regarding these reinforcements, see its letter to GW of 13 September.

2. The General Court appointed Lincoln to command the reinforcements on 16 Sept. (see "Mass. Council Journal," Mar.–Sept. 1776 sess., 586).

General Orders

Head Quarters, Harlem Heights, Sept: 25th 1776.
Parole Cumberland.   Countersign Pitt.

Col. Sergeant is to send to the Provost Guard the Soldiers, who were with Ensign McCrumber, and charged with plundering at Harlem.

The Brigadiers who are in want of tents for their Brigades, are to meet at the Quarter Master General's this Afternoon, four O'Clock, and divide such as are on hand among them.

Such Regiments of Militia, as have returned, to the Quarter Master General, the Articles belonging to the public they have received; and to their respective Brigadiers, the Ammunition they have drawn, of which they are first to produce Certificates, are discharged, and may return home, as soon as they think proper.

The General hopes the commanding Officers, and all others, of those Regiments, will take care that no other Men mix with them when going off—and that particular Care to be taken, that no Horses be carried away by the men, but what are certainly and properly employed in that service.

Varick transcript, DLC:GW; Df, in Joseph Reed's writing, DNA: RG 93, Orderly Books, vol. 15. The two passwords in the draft are not in Reed's writing. An order not found in the Varick transcript appears as the first paragraph of the draft: "The same Number of Men to parade tomorrow as this Day for a Fatigue Party at the same Time & Place."

To John Hancock

Colo. Morris's on the Heights of Harlem
Sir,   Septr 2[5]th 1776.

From the hours allotted to Sleep, I will borrow a few moments to convey my thoughts on sundry important matters to Congress. I shall offer them with that sincerety which ought to characterize a Man of candour; and with the freedom which may be used in giving useful information, without incurring the imputation of presumption.

We are now as it were, upon the eve of another dissolution of our Army—the remembrance of the difficulties wch happened upon that occasion last year—the consequences which might have followed the change, if proper advantages had been taken by the Enemy—added to a knowledge of the present temper and Situation of the Troops, reflect but a very gloomy prospect upon the appearance of things now and satisfie me, beyond the possibility of doubt, that unless some speedy, and effectual measures are adopted by Congress; our cause will be lost.

It is in vain to expect that any (or more than a trifling) part of this Army will again engage in the Service on the encouragement offered by Congress—When Men find that their Townsmen & Companions are receiving 20, 30, and more Dollars for a few Months Service (which is truely the case) it cannot be expected; without using compulsion; & to force them into the Service would answer no valuable purpose. When Men are irritated, & the Passions inflamed, they fly hastily, and chearfully to Arms, but after the first emotions are over to expect, among such People as compose the bulk of an Army, that they are influenced by any other principles than those of Interest, is to look for what never did, & I fear never will happen; the Congress will deceive themselves therefore if they expect it.

A Soldier reasoned with upon the goodness of the cause he is engaged in and the inestimable rights he is contending for, hears you with patience, & acknowledges the truth of your observations; but adds, that it is of no more Importance to him than others—The Officer makes you the same reply, with this further remark, that his pay will not support him, and he cannot ruin himself and Family to serve his Country, when every member of the community is equally Interested and benefitted by his Labours—The few therefore, who act upon Principles of disinterestedness, are, comparitively speaking—no more than a drop in the Ocean. It becomes evidently clear then, that as this contest is not likely to be the Work of a day—as the War must be carried on systematically—and to do it, you must have good Officers, there are, in my judgment, no other possible means to obtain them but by establishing your Army upon a permanent footing; and giving your Officers good pay. this will induce Gentlemen, and Men of Character to engage; and till the bulk of your Officers are composed of Such persons as are actuated by Principles of honour, and a spirit of enterprize, you have little to expect from them. They ought to have such allowances as will enable them to live like, and support the Characters of Gentlemen; and not be driven by a scanty pittance to the low, & dirty arts which many of them practice to filch the Public of more than the difference of pay would amount to upon an ample allowe—besides, something is due to the Man who puts his life in his hand—hazards his health—& forsakes the Sweets of domestic enjoyments—Why a Captn in the Continental Service should receive no more than 5/. Curry per day for performing the same duties that an Officer of the same Rank in the British Service receives 10/. Sterlg for, I never could conceive; especially when the latter is provided with every necessary he requires upon the best terms, and the former can scarce procure them at any Rate. There is nothing that gives a Man consequence, & renders him fit for Command, like a support that renders him Independant of every body but the State he Serves.

With respect to the Men, nothing but a good bounty can obtain them upon a permanent establishment; and for no shorter time than the continuance of the War, ought they to be engaged; as Facts incontestibly prove, that the difficulty, and Cost of Inlistments, increase with time. When the Army was first raised at Cambridge, I am perswaded the Men might have been got without a bounty for the War—after this, they began to see that the contest was not likely to end so speedily as was immagined, & to feel their consequence, by remarking, that to get the Militia In, in the course of last year, many Towns were induced to give them a bounty—Foreseeing the Evils resulting from this and the destructive consequences which unavoidably would follow short Inlistments, I took the liberty in a long Letter written by myself (date not now recollected, as my Letter Book is not here) to recommend the Inlistments for and during the War, Assigning such Reasons for it, as experience has since convinced me were well founded[1]—At that time Twenty Dollars would, I am perswaded, have engaged the Men for this term. But it will not do to look back, and if the present opportunity is slip'd, I am perswaded that twelve months more will Increase our difficulties four fold—I shall therefore take the freedom of givg it as my opinion, that a good Bounty be immediately offered, aided by the proffer of at least 100 or 150 Acres of Land and a Suit of Cloaths & Blankt to each Non Comd Officer & Soldier, as I have good Authority for saying, that however high the Mens pay may appear, it is barely sufficient in the present scarcity & dearness of all kinds of goods, to keep them in Cloaths, much less afford support to their Families—If this encouragement then is given to the Men, and such Pay allowed the Officers as will induce Gentlemen of Character & liberal Sentiments to engage, and proper care & precaution used in the nomination (having more regard to the Characters of Persons, than the number of Men they can Inlist) we should in a little time have an Army able to cope with any that can be opposed to it; as there are excellent Materials to form one out of: but while the only merit an Officer possesses is his ability to raise Men—while those Men consider, and treat him as an equal; & (in the Character of an Officer) regard him no more than a broomstick, being mixed together as one common herd, no order, nor no discipline can prevail— nor will the Officer ever meet with that respect which is essensially necessary to due subordination.

To place any dependance upon Militia, is, assuredly, resting upon a broken staff. Men just dragged from the tender Scenes of domestick life—unaccustomed to the din of Arms—totally unacquainted with every kind of Military skill, which being followed by a want of Confidence in themselves when opposed to Troops regularly traind—disciplined, and appointed—superior in knowledge, & superior in Arms, makes them timid, and ready to fly from their own Shadows. Besides, the sudden change in their manner of living (particularly in the lodging) brings on sickness in many; impatience in all; & such an unconquerable desire of returning to their respective homes that it not only produces shameful, & scandalous Desertions among themselves, but infuses the like spirit in others—Again, Men accustomed to unbounded freedom, and no controul, cannot brooke the Restraint which is indispensably necessary to the good Order and Government of an Army; without which Licentiousness, & every kind of disorder triumphantly reign. To bring men to a proper degree of Subordination is not the work of a day—a Month—

or even a year—and unhappily for us, and the cause we are Ingaged in, the little discipline I have been labouring to establish in the Army under my immediate Command, is in a manner done away by having such a mixture of Troops as have been called together within these few Months.

Relaxed, and as unfit as our Rules & Regulations of War are for the Government of an Army, the Militia (those properly so called, for of these we have two sorts, the Six Months Men and those sent in as a temporary aid) do not think themselves subject to 'em, and therefore take liberties which the Soldier is punished for—this creates jealousy—jealousy begets dissatisfactions—and these by degrees ripen into Mutiny; keeping the whole Army in a confused, and disordered State; rendering the time of those who wish to see regularity & good Order prevail more unhappy than Words can describe—Besides this, such repeated changes take place, that all arrangement is set at nought, & the constant fluctuation of things deranges every plan, as fast as adopted.

These Sir, Congress may be assured, are but a small part of the Inconveniences which might be enumerated, & attributed to Militia—but there is one that merits particular attention, & that is the expence. Certain I am that it would be cheaper to keep 50 or 100,000 Men in constant pay than to depend upon half the number, and supply the other half occasionally by Militia—The time the latter is in pay before and after they are in Camp, Assembling & Marching—the waste of Ammunition—the consumption of Stores, which in spite of every Resolution, & requisition of Congress they must be furnished with, or sent home—added to other incidental expences consequent upon their coming, and conduct in Camp, surpasses all Idea; and destroys every kind of regularity & œconomy which you could establish amg fixed and Settled Troops; and will in my opinion prove (if the scheme is adhered to) the Ruin of our Cause.

The Jealousies of a standing Army, and the Evils to be apprehended from one, are remote; and in my judgment, situated & circumstanced as we are, not at all to be dreaded; but the consequence of wanting one, according to my Ideas; formed from the present view of things, is certain, and inevitable Ruin; for if I was called upon to declare upon Oath, whether the Militia have been most Serviceable or hurtful upon the whole I should subscribe to the latter. I do not mean by this however to arraign the

Conduct of Congress, in so doing I should equally condemn my
own measures (if I did not my judgment) but experience, which
is the best criterion to work by, so fully, clearly, and decisively
reprobates the practice of trusting to Militia, that no Man who
regards order, regularity, & Œconomy; or who has any regard
for his own honour, character, or peace of Mind, will risk them
upon this Issue.

No less Attention should be paid to the choice of Surgeons
than other Officers of the Army. they should undergo a regular
examination; and if not appointed by the Director Genl & Surgeons of the Hospital, they ought to be subordinate to, and governed by his directions—the Regimental Surgeons I am speaking of—many of whom are very great Rascals, countenancing
the Men in sham Complaints to exempt them from duty, and
often receiving Bribes to Certifie Indispositions with a view to
procure discharges or Furloughs; but independant of these
practices, while they are considered as unconnected with the
Genl Hospital there will be nothing but continual Complaints of
each other—The director of the Hospital charging them with
enormity in their drafts for the Sick; & they him, for denying
such things as are necessary—In short there is a constant bick-
ering among them, which tends greatly to the Injury of the Sick;
and will always subsist till the Regimental Surgeons are made to
look up to the Director Genl of the Hospital as a Superior—
whether this is the case in regular Armies, or not, I cannot undertake to say; but certain I am there is a necessity for it in this,
or the Sick will suffer. the Regimental Surgeons are aiming, I
am perswaded, to break up the Genl Hospital, & have, in numberless Instances, drawn for Medicines—Stores—&ca in the
most profuse and extravagent manner, for private purposes.

Another matter highly worthy of attention, is, that other Rules
and Regulation's may be adopted for the Government of the
Army than those now in existence, otherwise the Army, but for
the name, might as well be disbanded—For the most atrocious
offences (one or two Instances only excepted) a Man receives no
more than 39 Lashes, and these perhaps (thro the collusion of
the Officer who is to see it inflicted) are given in such a manner
as to become rather a matter of sport than punishment; but
when inflicted as they ought, many hardend fellows who have
been the Subjects, have declared that for a bottle of Rum they

would undergo a Second operation—it is evident therefore that this punishment is inadequate to many Crimes it is assigned to—as a proof of it, thirty and 40 Soldiers will desert at a time; and of late, a practice prevails (as you will see by my Letter of the 22d) of the most alarming nature; and which will, if it cannot be checked, prove fatal both to the Country and Army—I mean the infamous practice of Plundering, for under the Idea of Tory property—or property which may fall into the hands of the Enemy, no Man is secure in his effects, & scarcely in his Person; for in order to get at them, we have several Instances of People being frieghtned out of their Houses under pretence of those Houses being ordered to be burnt, & this is done with a view of siezing the Goods; nay, in order that the Villainy may be more effectually concealed, some Houses have actually been burnt to cover the theft.

I have with some others used my utmost endeavours to stop this horrid practice, but under the present lust after plunder, and want of Laws to punish Offenders, I might almost as well attempt to remove Mount Atlas—I have ordered instant corporal Punishment upon every Man who passes our Lines, or is seen with Plunder that the Offender might be punished for disobedience of Orders; and Inclose you the proceedings of a Court Martial held upon an Officer, who with a Party of Men had robbd a House a little beyond our Lines of a number of valuable Goods; among which (to shew that nothing escapes) were four large Peer looking Glasses—Womens Cloaths, and other Articles which one would think, could be of no Earthly use to him—He was met by a Major of Brigade who ordered him to return the Goods as taken contrary to Genl Orders, which he not only peremptorily refused to do, but drew up his Party and swore he would defend them at the hazard of his Life; on which I orderd him to be Arrested, and tryed for Plundering, Disobedience of Orders, and Mutiny; for the Result, I refer to the Proceedings of the Court; whose judgment appeared so exceedingly extraordinary, that I ordered a Reconsideration of the matter, upon which, and with the assistance of a fresh evidence, they made Shift to Cashier him.[2]

I adduce this Instance to give some Idea to Congress of the Currt Sentimts & general run of the Officers which compose the present Army; & to shew how exceedingly necessary it is to be careful in the choice of the New sett even if it should take double the time to compleat the Levies—An Army formed of good Officers moves like Clock work; but there is no Situation upon Earth less enviable, nor more distressing, than that Person's who is at the head of Troops, who are regardless of Order and discipline; and who are unprovided with almost every necessary— In a word, the difficulties which have forever surrounded me since I have been in the Service, and kept my Mind constantly upon the stretch—The Wounds which my Feelings as an Officer have received by a thousand things which have happened, contrary to my expectation and Wishes—the effect of my own conduct, and present appearance of things, so little pleasing to myself, as to render it a matter of no Surprize (to me) if I should stand capitally censured by Congress—added to a consciousness of my inability to govern an Army composed of such discordant parts, and under such a variety of intricate and perplexing circumstances, induces not only a belief, but a thorough conviction in my Mind, that it will be impossible unless there is a thorough change in our Military System for me to conduct matters in such a manner as to give Satisfaction to the Publick, which is all the recompense I aim at, or ever wished for.

Before I conclude I must appologize for the liberties taken in this Letter and for the blots and scratchings therein—not having time to give it more correctly. With truth I can add, that with every Sentiment of respect & esteem I am Yrs & the Congresses Most Obedt & Most H. Servt

Go: Washington

ALS, DNA:PCC, item 152; LB, DLC:GW; copy, DNA:PCC, item 169; Varick transcript, DLC:GW. Although GW dated this letter 24 Sept., he refers to it in his succeeding letter to Hancock of 25 Sept. as having been written "this morning." GW's remark at the beginning of this letter about borrowing time "from the hours allotted to Sleep" indicates that he wrote it very early on the morning of 25 September. Congress read this letter on 27 Sept. and referred it and its enclosures to a committee consisting of George Wythe, Francis Hopkinson, Edward Rutledge, John Adams, and Thomas Stone (*JCC*, 5:830).

1. GW is referring to his first letter to Hancock of 9 Feb. 1776.

2. Ens. Matthew Macomber's principal accuser at his initial trial on 19 Sept. was Brigade Maj. Daniel Box, who testified that two days earlier on Harlem Plains, he met Macomber and "a party of upwards of twenty all loaded with plunder, such as House furniture, Table Linen and Kitchen Utensils, China & Delph Ware. I ordered him to lay it down, or carry it back to the place he took it from, he said he had his Colonels order for what he had done and that he

would defend the plunder as long as he had life." When Box tried to force Macomber to surrender the goods at pistol point, the ensign ordered his men to prepare to fire, and Box wisely withdrew to get reinforcements. A sergeant and three soldiers who were with Box during the incident supported his story, but two soldiers from Macomber's party testified that Macomber had given explicit orders against plundering. The court acquitted Macomber on the charges of plundering and robbery and only convicted him of "offering Violence to and disobeying Major Box his superior Officer." Macomber was sentenced to ask Box's pardon and to be severely reprimanded by his colonel. At the bottom of the enclosed copy of the court-martial proceedings for 19 Sept., GW wrote: "Note, It is to be observed that the Men who were to share the Plunder became the Evidences for the Prisoner[.] G.W." (DNA:PCC, item 152). The court convened again on 21 Sept. to reconsider the case, and after hearing testimony from Capt. Nathaniel Ramsay of Maryland about the confrontation between Box and Macomber, it found Macomber guilty of plundering and mutiny and ordered him to be cashiered (see the copy of the court-martial proceedings for that date in DNA:PCC, item 58, and General Orders, 22 Sept.).

Congress on 30 Sept. directed GW to call on the members of the court-martial who "concurred in the acquittal of Ensign Macumber, to assign their reasons for their first judgment" and send the names of those officers and their reasons to Congress (*JCC*, 5:836). For the officers' refusal to comply with that demand, see GW to Hancock, 8–9 Oct., and note 7.

To John Hancock

Sir   Head Qrs Harlem Heights Septr 25th 1776.

Having wrote you fully on sundry important Subjects this morning, as you will perceive by the Letter which accompanies this, I mean principally now to inclose a Copy of a Letter, received from Genl Howe on Sunday evening with the Lists of the prisoners in his Hands—of those in our possession belonging to the Army immediately under his Command, & of my Answer, which were omitted to be put in the Other.[1]

His Letter will discover to Congress his refusal to exchange Lord Stirling for Mr McDonald, considering the latter, only as a Major. they will be pleased to determine how he is to be ranked in future.[2]

The number of prisoners according to these Returns, is greater than what we expected; However I am inclined to believe, that among those in the List from Long Island, are several Militia of Genl Woodhulls party, who were never arranged in this Army. As to those taken on the 15th they greatly exceed the

Number that I supposed fell into their Hands in the retreat from the City. At the time that I transmitted an Account of that affair, I had not obtained Returns & took the matter upon the Officers Reports.[3] they are difficult to get with certainty at any time. In the skirmish of Monday Sennight, they could not have taken but very few.

Before I conclude, I shall take occasion to mention, that those returns made with such precision, and the difficulty that will attend the proposed exchange on account of the dispersed and scattered state of the prisoners in our Hands, will clearly evince the necessity of appointing Commissarys and proper persons to superintend & conduct in such instances. This I took the liberty of urging more than once, as well on account of the propriety of the measure, and the saving that would have resulted from It, as that the prisoners might be treated with humanity and have their wants particularly attended to.[4]

I would also observe, as I esteem It my duty—that this Army is in want of almost every necessary—Tents—Camp Kettles—Blankets & Cloaths of all kinds; But what is to be done with respect to the Two last Articles I know not, as the term of Inlistment will be nearly expired by the time they can be provided. This may be exhibited as a further proof of the disadvantages attending the levying of an Army upon such a footing, as never to know how to keep them without injuring the public or incommoding the Men. I have directed the Colonel or Commanding Officer of each Corps to use his endeavours to procure such Cloathing as are absolutely necessary, but at the same time I confess, that I do not know how they are to be got.[5] I have the Honor to be with great respect Sir Yr Most Obedt Servt

Go: Washington

LS, in Robert Hanson Harrison's writing, DNA:PCC, item 152; LB, DLC:GW; copy, DNA:PCC, item 169; Varick transcript, DLC:GW. Congress read this letter on 27 Sept. and referred it to a committee (*JCC,* 5:830).

1. See Howe to GW, 21 Sept., and GW to Howe, 23 September.

2. Congress resolved on 30 Sept. that McDonald "be not exchanged for any officer under the rank of brigadier general" (ibid., 836).

3. See GW to Hancock, 16 September.

4. See GW to Hancock, 8 Nov. 1775, 9 Feb. (third letter), 14 Feb., and 11 May 1776.

5. See General Orders, 21 September.

From Major General Philip Schuyler

Dear Sir   Albany September 25th 1776

I am honored with your Excellency's Favor of the 20th Instant—Your Situation at New York has been truly alarming and it is probable that had you not so judiciously retreated, & with such good Order and Dispatch you would have been involved in almost inextricable Difficulties—I hope the Enemy have got all they will get this Campaign, and that we shall be better able to cope with them in another.

I thank your Excellency for the Copy of the Resolves of Congress, inclosed in yours—They had not been transmitted me from philadelphia—Indeed, I have not been honored with a Line from Congress, for a very long Time past: a Neglect, which I do not think I have deserved, and which I therefore feel the more sensibly. I shall hope that one of their Resolutions of the 14th Instant was not meant to insult me: It was certainly improper to resolve that the Military Stores should be immediately sent to General Gates *for the Use of the Northern Department,* as Congress had not then received my Resignation.[1]

I have taken Measures to have all the Boards in the Country brought to this place and to the Banks of Hudson's River below it, and shall have them forwarded to you as fast as they arrive and give me Leave to assure you that altho' I shall soon be out of the Army I shall with as great Chearfulness obey any Commands that you may honor me with when I am a private Citizen, as I have always done, those which I received from you as my superior officer. I am Dr Sir with every Sentiment of Esteem & Affection Your Excellency's most obedient hble Servant

Ph: Schuyler

LS, DLC:GW; LB, NN: Schuyler Papers.

1. Schuyler complained about this resolution in his letter to Hancock of this date (DNA:PCC, item 153). For the resolution of 14 Sept., see *JCC,* 5:758.

Letter not found: from Lund Washington, 25 Sept. 1776. On 6 Oct. GW wrote to his cousin Lund: "Your Letter of the 25th Ulto has reached my hands."

General Orders

Head Quarters, Harlem Heights, Sept: 26th 1776.
Parole Halifax.   Countersign Georgia.

The Court Martial of which Col. Magaw is President, having found that Lieut: Stewart, struck Serjeant Philips, but that he was provoked so to do by the latter, and acquitted him of "threatning the life of Col. Silliman."[1]

The General approves the sentence, and orders Lieut: Stewart to be discharged from his arrest.

The same Court Martial having tried and convicted Lieut: Danl Pelton, of Col. Ritzema's Regiment, of leaving Camp, two days, and being absent without leave, the Court orders him to be mulcted of one Months pay—The General approves the Sentence, and directs that care be taken accordingly in the next Pay-Abstract.[2]

Serjt Philips of Capt: Hubbels Company, and Col. Silliman's Regiment, tried by the same Court Martial for "Cowardice & leaving his party on the 17th Instant," was acquitted; The General approves the sentence and orders him discharged.[3]

The Regiments of Militia which composed the Brigades commanded by Cols. Douglass & Silliman, being dismissed; those regiments are to join their former brigades.

Courts-Martial for the trial of Desertion, and other Crimes, not capital, are immediately to be formed in the several Brigades, and the sentences, when approved by the Brigadier, immediately executed.

Col. Magaw being necessarily detained from the Court Martial, Col. Ewing is to preside during his absence.

The General expects, and insists, that all the plunder, and other things, found in consequence of the examination lately made, be sent immediately to the White-House, on the Road near Head Quarters, delivered to the Captain of the Guard to be deposited there, 'till farther Orders—Colonels, & commanding Officers of regiments are to see that it is done immediately.

The officer commanding the Rangers may give passes to any of his own parties, but to none others.

Upon any Alarm, or Approach of the Enemy towards our lines, Genl Mifflin, with his Brigade, is to possess our left-flank, from the hollow-way, by Col. Sergeant's late Encampment, to the point of Rocks, on the left-front of our lines;[4] and 'till the Regiment commanded by Col. Wedon is brigaded, is to be joined by the same—Genl McDougall's Brigade is to repair to the plains back of Genl Mifflin, and be ready to support him or the picquet in the front as occasion may require—Genl Bell's Brigade is to repair to the lines which cross the road by Col. Moylan's lodging, and to extend their right-flank to the middle Redoubt by Mr Kortright's house, occupying the same—Genl Wadsworth and Fellows are to take the remaining part of these lines, with the Redoubt therein on the North River—These three Brigades to defend these lines, or wait there for Orders—Genl Heard's is to parade, and be ready to march wherever ordered—Genl Putnam is to command in front of the lines by Mr Kortright's—Genl Spencer in the rear of them.

Varick transcript, DLC:GW; Df, DNA: RG 93, Orderly Books, vol. 15. The draft is in Joseph Reed's writing except for the two passwords and the last two paragraphs of the general orders.

1. The altercation between John Steward (Stewart; d. 1782), who was the first lieutenant of Capt. John Allen Thomas's 5th Independent Maryland Company in Col. William Smallwood's regiment, and William Phelps (c.1730–1826), a sergeant or ensign in Capt. William Gaylord Hubbell's company in Col. Gold Selleck Silliman's regiment of Connecticut militia levies, occurred on the morning of 18 Sept. when Steward accused Phelps of cowardly behavior while scouting with him the previous day. A copy of the proceedings of the court-martial that tried Steward on 23 Sept. is in DLC:GW. Steward became a captain in the 2d Maryland Regiment in December 1776, and the following April he was promoted to major of that regiment. Captured on 22 Aug. 1777 during Sullivan's raid on Staten Island, Steward escaped from a British prison ship in December 1777, and during the next two years he spent much time on detached duty with the Continental light infantry (see General Orders, 8 Aug. 1778 and 15 June 1779). On 26 July 1779 Congress resolved to present Steward a silver medal for his role in the successful storming of Stony Point ten days earlier (*JCC*, 14:890). Steward became lieutenant colonel of the 1st Maryland Regiment in February 1781. He died in late 1782 apparently from injuries sustained in a fall from a horse near Charleston, S.C., where he was serving with Gen. Nathanael Greene's forces. William Phelps, a native of Fairfield, Conn., is called both a sergeant and an ensign in the court-martial proceedings of 23 Sept. (DLC:GW). Phelps had served as a sergeant under Captain Hubbell in the 7th Connecticut Regiment during 1775, and he appears as an ensign in Hubbell's company of the 16th Regiment of Connecticut militia in 1779.

2. Daniel Pelton, who had been a drum maker in New York City before becoming a lieutenant in Col. Rudolphus Ritzema's 3d New York Regiment earlier this year, pleaded guilty to this charge at his court-martial on 23 Sept.

(see the *New York Journal; or, the General Advertiser,* 5 Oct. 1775, and Force, *American Archives,* 5th ser., 2:468).

3. For the proceedings of Phelps's court-martial on 23 Sept., see ibid., 468–69. William Gaylord Hubbell (1736–1779) of Fairfield, Conn., who had been a captain in the 16th Connecticut militia regiment since October 1772, served as a captain in the 7th Connecticut Regiment from July to December 1775 and in Colonel Silliman's regiment of Connecticut militia levies from June to December 1776.

4. The Point of Rocks was a high promontory overlooking the "Hollow Way" and the post road at the southeastern corner of the American positions on Harlem Heights (see Johnston, *Harlem Heights,* map facing page 70).

To Major General William Heath

Dear Sir,   Colo. Morris's at Harlem Septr 26th 1776.

I should be glad if you would order Genl Saltenstall to draw as much Powder as will compleat his Militia to about fifteen or 18. Rounds a Man; as also Lead if they have it not, and Cartridge Paper that they may make their own Cartridges. At the sametime let him know, & desire him to Impress it strongly upon the Minds of his Men, that they must Acct for every Load which is not used in Action.

Be so good as to request in my name, General Clinton's attendance at Head Quarters with you at Nine Oclock this forenoon on the business I mentioned to you yesterday.[1] I Am Sir Yr Most Obedt

Go: Washington

ALS, MHi: Heath Papers.

1. Heath and George Clinton attended the council of general officers that met with the committee of Congress at GW's headquarters on this and the following day (see Wilson, *Heath's Memoirs,* 76, and GW to Hancock, 27 Sept.).

To Brigadier General Hugh Mercer

Dear Sir   Colo. Morris's at Harlem 26 sept. 1776

If the Troops at this Post can be prevailed upon to defend it as they should do, it must cost General Howe a great many men to carry it if he succeeds at all—If this should happen to be *his* Opinion there is scarce a Doubt but that he will turn his thoughts another way, as inactivity is not to be expected from him—Whither his operations may be directed is uncertain—perhaps an irruption into the Jerseys—possibly he may bend his course towards Philadela (for I conceive that 2000 men with the Assistance of their shipping will effectually preserve New York against our whole Strength)—Or which in my judgment is exceedingly probable, knowing that the Troops are drawn off from the Southern Colonies, he may detach a part of the Army to the Southward for a Winters Campaign, as was recommended to him last Fall by Lord Dunmore.[1]

In either of these Cases it behoves us to keep the best look out, & to obtain the earliest intelligence possible of the Enemy's motions and as it is now the current Opinion that the shipping are greatly thinned I earnestly recommend to you the necessity of having sensible & judicious Persons in different places to observe the movements of the Shipping, among others at the Neversinks,[2] for if they should send out a fleet without our giving notice of it to Congress we shall be thought exceedingly remiss—In short I intreat you to exert your best endeavours to obtain every useful Intelligence you possibly can of the Enemy's motions by Sea and Land—in doing this Money may be required, and do not spare it.

Communicate every thing of Importance to me with dispatch and be assured that I am Dr sir Your most Obedt Servt

G.W.

LB, in Tench Tilghman's writing, DLC:GW; Varick transcript, DLC:GW.

1. For Dunmore's desire to transplant the war to the southern states, see GW to Hancock, 18 Dec. 1775, and GW to Richard Henry Lee, 26 Dec. 1775.

2. Because the Highlands of Navesink in Monmouth County, N.J., afford a panoramic view of New York Harbor and its approaches, the Americans frequently stationed observers there to watch the British fleet.

From Colonel Rufus Putnam

Sir   Sept. 26th 1776

I Hope the Importence of the Subject will be a Sufficient appollogie for the Freedom I take in adressing your Exelency at this time. I have long Wondered that no Corps of Engeneers was yet Established. the Number of Works to be Executed; the Nesesity of Dispatch in them; the Imposability for a Common hand to be made at once to Comprehend what they ought to

do. with out a Core of Engeneers is Established the Works Never
will be properly Executed nor don in a Reasonable time. and I
Cannot give my Ideas of Such a Core and there duty Better then
In the Words of Mr Maigrets Speaking of there Subordinary
Disepline. he Sais "the first part of this Disepline Consists of the
divition of one Corps Into Several. and the Subdivition of the
Latter into Still less.["] again "in the Construction of places that
Corps of Workmen are Devided into Several others Who are
Called Bands. the officers of Each of those Companys Should be
Engeneers. and tis a Leading Circumstance to the Success of any
action that the Soldiers and there officers Should be acquainted
with Each other Before hand. and tis from the Engeneers that
the former are to Recive ordors for the Works of attack; defence;
and Construction of places. tis Evedent that the latter ought to
be Charged With the Conduct and Command of them. Engineers are the Natural officers of Workmen. ancient and Con-
stent Useage has Confirmed the practice.["] again "if teachers
Ware appointed to Each of these principle Corps Such a Number of Hopefull youth might be formed as would be a grate Benifit to the Service. these Work men are properly Speeking Soldiers or Rather Both one and tother. there Business Being
Either Fighting or Working as ocation Requiers. the first Excer-
size to be taught them is the use of there arms; the Next is to
keep them to there Business. the third kind of Exercise is the
Instructing them in the Several forms Dementions and Proper-
ties of Works.["] again "all Workmen Imployed in Buildings of
any kind may Serve Very well for Works of Fortification.["] again
"by this means you may have good Miners and Sappers in abun-
dence who in time of Seages may Ease the Engineers and Even
Supply the Want of them up on ocation.["][1] two years Experance
has fully Convinced me Sir that till the Engineers are Rendered
Intepident of any other Department for there Artificers till
they have Miners and Sappers or persons Seperate from the
Common Feteague men to take Care of Sinking the Ditch properly laying the turf well And to Build the parrapet with its
propper Talus.[2] I Say till this is don No Engineer will be able to
Execute his Works Well nor do them in a Reasonable time[.] the
Service has already Suffered much and will Continu So to do till
Some Such Corps as What I have mentioned is Established and

to Convince your Exeleny that I have no Intristed motives but
the Common good in this adress; I Beg leave to Quit the Department Sence the army are or may be So well Suplyed with Re-
guler Bread Engineers.[3] I am Sir your Exelencys Most obedient
devoted Humbl. Servnt

Rufus Putnam

ALS, DLC:GW. Putnam's liberal and apparently random use of semicolons
throughout the manuscript has been ignored. Only the few that serve some
grammatical function have been retained.

1. Putnam apparently is quoting from J. Heath's 1747 English translation
of Maigret's *Traité de la sureté et conservation des états, par le moyen des forteresses* (A
treatise on the safety and maintenance of states, by the means of fortresses),
published in Paris in 1725.

2. The talus of a rampart is its rearward slope.

3. On 3 Oct. Putnam sent GW a plan for the establishment of a corps of
engineers.

From Major General Philip Schuyler

Albany [26] September 1776. "Since my last of Yesterday, I have
received sundry papers from General Gates, Copies of all
which I do myself the Honor to inclose—I have mentioned to
Congress that I had sent them to your Excellency."[1]

LS, DLC:GW; LB, NN: Schuyler Papers. Although the LS is dated 20 Sept.
and the LB is dated 25 Sept., the context of this letter indicates that it was
written on 26 Sept. (see note 1). In Schuyler's letter book this letter immediately follows his letter to GW of 25 September.

1. Schuyler wrote Hancock on 26 Sept.: "Yesterday I received sundry Letters & papers from General Gates and General Arnold, Copies whereof I have
transmitted to the Commander in Chief, and which his Excellency will prob-
ably forward to Congress by this Conveyance" (DNA:PCC, item 153; see also
Schuyler to Gates, 26 Sept., in Force, *American Archives*, 5th ser., 2:555). The
enclosures that Schuyler sent to GW include copies of Gates's letters to
Schuyler of 22 and 23 Sept., Arnold's letters to Gates of 15, 16, and 18 Sept.,
Sgt. Thomas Day's deposition of 12 Sept., Sgt. Eli Stiles's deposition of 16
Sept., and Antoine Girard's deposition of 20 Sept., all of which are in
DNA:PCC, item 153. GW forwarded these documents to Congress with his
letter to Hancock of 2–3 October. Most of them concern Arnold's efforts to
defend Lake Champlain with his fleet or intelligence about British strength
in Canada.

To Jonathan Trumbull, Sr.

Sir   Harlem Heights Septemr 26th 1776

Your favor of the 20th instant is Duly received. The several Regiments of Militia from Connecticut lately commanded by General Wolcott being reduced to almost nothing, one having returned under twenty and another short of Thirty effective men—they were yesterday discharged. I am full in opinion with you that some severe examples ought to be made of the late deserters. For a return of their names I must refer you to the several Commanding Officers of the different Regiments. I hope those under Brigadier Saltonstall may have a better spirit.

A proposal for an immediate exchange of Prisoners has been made by General Howe agreeable to the resolves of Congress. I am to request a return as soon as possible of all those in Connecticut, mentioning the names and ranks of all Commissioned Officers, and distinguishing particularly between those of the Army and Navy, as well Privates as Officers.[1]

It appears to me their being marched to some convenient Port, and coming by water, will be most convenient, at least it must save expence, and will prevent their having a view of the different Towns and their Situations on the Sea Coast. Your sentiments on the subject, together with the return of Prisoners as early as possible will much oblige me. I am with Esteem Sir Your most obedient and very humble Servant

                                        Go: Washington

LB, Ct: Trumbull Papers; LB, DLC:GW; Varick transcript, DLC:GW.

1. Trumbull enclosed a return of British prisoners held in Connecticut in his letter to GW of 6 Oct., which has not been found (see GW to Trumbull, 15 Oct.; see also Trumbull to GW, 2 Oct., and GW to Trumbull, 8 Oct.).

From Major General Artemas Ward

Sir   Boston 26 Sept. 1776

The State of New Hampshire applied to me to furnish a thousand men who are soon to march for Newyork from that State, with ammunition, and as they were likely to march without ammunition, unless furnished out of the Continental Store, and as the public Cause might suffer by their not being supplyed, I therefore supplied them with 500 lb. powder & 1000 lb. ball, hoping this quantity by might serve until they could be otherways supplied.[1] I am &c.

Artemas Ward

LB, MHi: Ward Papers.

1. Ward on this date sent this ammunition to the Hartford committee of correspondence, instructing the committee to deliver it to the "two Small Regiments now on their march to reinforce our Army at N. York" as they passed through Hartford (MHi: Artemas Ward Papers).

Letter not found: from Samuel Washington, 26 Sept. 1776. On 18 Oct. GW wrote to his brother Samuel: "Your Letter of the 26th Ulto . . . was delivered to me."

General Orders

Head Quarters, Harlem-Heights, Sept: 27th 1776.
Parole Hampton.   Countersign Walton.

Lieut: Drake of Col. Philips's Regt, tried by a Court Martial, whereof Col. Ewing was President for "Leaving the regiment without permission of his commanding Officer, and being absent twenty days"—was acquitted.[1]

The General approves the Sentence and orders him to be discharged.

The Returns are expected to morrow at Orderly time, which the Brigade Majors & Adjutants would do well to attend to.[2]

The General is not more surprised than vexed, to find, that in spite of all his care to prevent unnecessary firing, and waste of Ammunition, that every afternoon produces fresh instances of the shameful discharge of Muskets, when there has been no rain to wet, or otherwise injure the loads—He now positively orders that there shall be no firing, without leave from the Brigadier of the Brigade, the men belong to; who are to inqure minutely into the necessity of the case, and whether the Pieces cannot be drawn without—The General also directs, that none but the Out-Sentries, shall ever have their Musquets loaded; and if those would be watchful, and vigilant on their posts, they need not load till occasion should require it.

Varick transcript, DLC:GW; Df, DNA: RG 93, Orderly Books, vol. 15. The draft is in Joseph Reed's writing except for the two passwords and the last paragraph of the general orders.

1. Henry Drake of Capt. Joel Houghton's company of New Jersey militia levies said at his court-martial trial on 26 Sept. "that he was only a Volunteer, that he has no Commission, & that when he came into the Service he publickly declared that he would serve only for 2 Months, that he has never received, but refused to accept either Pay or Rations, & that he has tarried his two Months & now considers himself at Liberty to return home" (see the copy of the court-martial proceedings for that date in DLC:GW).

Joseph Phillips (1718–1788) was commissioned on 14 June 1776 as major of the regiment of militia levies to be raised in Hunterdon and Somerset counties, New Jersey. He was promoted to lieutenant colonel on 1 Aug., and following the death of the regiment's commander, Col. Philip Johnston, at the Battle of Long Island, Phillips succeeded him as colonel. Phillips returned home with his men on 1 Dec., and on 15 Mar. 1777 he became colonel of the 1st Regiment of Hunterdon County militia.

2. The general return of the army for 28 Sept. is in DNA: RG 93, Revolutionary War Rolls.

To John Hancock

Sir   Head Qrs Heights of Harlem 27th Septr 1776

I have nothing in particular to communicate to Congress by this days post, as Our situation is the same as when I last wrote.

We are now sitting on the business, the Committee came upon, which it is probable will be finished this Evening. the result they will duly report upon their return.[1]

I received Yesterday, the Inclosed Declarn by a Gentleman from Eliza. Town, who told me, many Copies were found in the possession of the Soldiers from Canada that were landed there a day or Two ago by Genl How's permission. I shall not comment upon it, It seems to be founded on the plan that has been artfully pursued for sometime past.[2] I have the Honor to be Sir Your Most Obedt Servt

Go: Washington

P.S. The Account of the Troops &c. in Canada, comes from a person who is among the prisoners sent from Canada—It was Anonymous, nor do I know the Intelligencer: according to him, the Enemy in that Quarter are stronger than we supposed &

their Naval force much greater on the Lakes than we had any Ideas of. I trust he has taken the matter up on the Enemy's report.[3]

LS, in Robert Hanson Harrison's writing, DNA:PCC, item 152; LB, DLC:GW; copy, DNA:PCC, item 169; Varick transcript, DLC:GW. Congress read this letter on 30 Sept. (*JCC*, 5:834).

1. For Congress's sending of this committee to the army, see Hancock to GW, 24 Sept., and note 4.

2. The Howe brothers' printed broadside of 19 Sept. criticizes Congress for having "disavowed every Purpose of Reconciliation, not consonant with their extravagant and inadmissable Claim of Independency" and declares the peace commissioners' desire "to confer with His MAJESTY's well-affected Subjects, upon the Means of restoring the public Tranquillity, and establishing a permanent Union with every Colony, as a part of the B[RITISH] Empire." The king, they say, is "most graciously disposed to direct a Revision of such of His Royal Instructions as may be construed to lay an improper Restraint upon the Freedom of Legislation, in any of His Colonies, and to concur in the Revisal of all Acts by which His Subjects there may think themselves aggrieved" (DNA:PCC, item 152).

3. This anonymous and undated report reads: "The force of the Enemy in Canada and on the Lake is from the best Intelligence as follows. 10,000 men landed in Canada from Europe &c., 8,000 of which with many Canadians are to go against Tyconderoga &c., all Effective men and in good Order and appearance—It is without doubt General Carleton intends to command in Person, with Burgoyne, Frazier [Simon Fraser], [Valentine] Jones & Nesbit [William Nesbitt] &c. Their Naval Force is A ship built in England taken to pieces & brought out on Board the Fleet, she is put up at St Johns & launched there, has 18 Guns, 24 pounders, Swivels &c. 2 Brigs about 10 Guns each 3 schooners about 8 Ditto Swivels &c. 20 Gondolas two Guns each, from 9 to 12 pounders. 250 Batteaus all with Swivells, & many of them with Guns in their Bows. A very fine Train of Artillery of Six Companies, & at least 100 Pieces of Cannon, thought to be the finest ever sent from England—A General Officer commands it—General [William] Phillips. Every Sailor & Marine that could possibly be spared is sent to man their Fleet. Their determined Intention is, if possible, to form a Junction of their Army with General Howe, in which Case Genl Carleton will command the whole. Sr John Johnson is gone round by Oswego with near 800 Indians, McCleans [Allen Maclean's Royal Highland] Emigrants & some Canadians & Scotch Volunteers—There is some doubt he may come in by Fort George, & cut off our communication with Tycondaroga—He is sanguine in his Expectation of taking Fort George, & getting the Command of the Lake" (DNA:PCC, item 152).

From a Secret Committee of the New York Convention

Sir.   Poughkeepsie, Sepr 27. 1776.

The Committee which the Convention of this State appointed for devising ways and means to obstruct the Navigation on Hudsons river, have lately received directions from the Convention to purchase vessels to be sunk near fort Washington. To effect this, we immediately proceeded up to this place, with Capt. Grennal, whose assistance, by reason of his naval experience, the Convention conceived might be useful to the Committee.[1]

The Committee upon their arrival here, sent down an old Sloop which we had purchased some time before, and directed that another Sloop lying in the highlands should also be sent down: both are intended to be sunk; and we make no doubt but, by this time, they are at the Bridge, as also the fire ship charged by Capt. Hazelwood, he having charged but one here, for want of Materials.[2]

The Committee have also impressed and now send down two large ships and two Brigs—And in order to ascertain their respective values, have appointed persons of unexceptionable characters and great experience to appraize the same on oath, for the purpose that the Owners thereof may receive from the Public a Recompence—The said appraisement stands as follows.

The Brig of Lowthrop & others	£ 400	00	0
The Brig of Malcom & others	760	00	0
The new Ship of John Franklin	3429	00	0
The new Ship of Samuel Franklin	2800	00	0
	7389	00	0
The fire sloop was purchased for	£ 200	00	0
The sloop sent from Poughkeepsie	125	00	0
The sloop in the Highlands	130	00	0
	455	00	0
total amot	£7844	00	0

We found in the Brig owned by Mr Lowthrop, a quantity of Boards, and knowing that they were much wanted at the Bridge, we concluded to send them down, and have requested

Capt. North to deliver them to such officer as may be appointed to receive and purchase the same, and at the price usually paid, with power to receive the money.[3]

The two ships have never been out at Sea, and by the Report of Masters of vessels and ship Carpenters they are exceedingly well built, and of the very best materials—It would therefore become a matter of Concern to sink those vessels, if the interest of the public should not render the measure absolutely necessary and unavoidable.

In order to afford Capt. Cook all proper assistance in procuring plank, we directed Capt. Casewell of the Sloop of War Cambden, equipped by this State to carry down all the spare plank in the ship Yards here. We have also purchased upwards of 6,000 feet and sent them down by Capt. Donaldson; and as those sloops proceeded down with a fair wind on Tuesday last,[4] we make no doubt but they are safely arrived. We have the honour to be with great respect Your Excellency's most obedient and very humle servants

By order of the Committee
Robert Yates Chairman

LS, DLC:GW; Df, NNebgGW.

1. This secret committee, which had been appointed on 16 July, was directed on 21 Sept. to purchase up to six vessels and "to request the services of Capt. Thomas Greenell in ballasting and navigating, and delivering those vessels to Capt. Cook at Fort Washington" (*N.Y. Prov. Congress Journals*, 1:639; see also a Secret Committee of the New York Convention to GW, 17 July, and William Duer to GW, 22 Sept., and note 2). Thomas Grenell, who had been one of the commissioners for fortifying the Hudson highlands during the fall of 1775, was appointed by the Continental Congress on 15 June 1776 to command the frigate *Montgomery* at New York, and by August he was designated captain of the new frigate *Congress* at Poughkeepsie (see ibid., 139; *JCC*, 5:444; 6:861; and Francis Lewis to Grenell, 22 Aug. 1776, in Smith, *Letters of Delgates*, 5:47, n.2).

2. The old sloop was the *Clinton* (see Robert Yates to the convention, 25 Sept., in *N.Y. Prov. Congress Journals*, 1:650). For the convention's resolution of 21 Sept. ordering fireships to Fort Washington, see Abraham Yates, Jr., to GW, 21 Sept., n.1. The "Bridge" is King's Bridge.

3. One of the brigs, Robert Yates wrote the convention on 25 Sept., "belongs to Malcom, Kip and Lott, the other is a New-England vessel, about 120 tons burthen, loaded with wheat, staves, and a considerable quantity of inch boards; the wheat and staves we have ordered to be stored, but send down the boards for public use" (ibid.).

4. The previous Tuesday was 24 September. The sloop *Camden*, which had

been fitted out by order of the secret committee, was commanded by Capt. Robert Castle (see ibid., 771; see also Robert Yates to the convention, 25 Sept., in ibid., 650).

To Major General Philip Schuyler

Dear Sir   Head Qurs Harlem Septr 27th 1776.
I yesterday received Your Favor of the 23d instt. The Nails wanted by General Gates, cannot be sent from hence, our own Demands being Great & pressing & supplies but small.

In Respect to building Barracks in the Town of Schenectady, if they are necessary, I suppose It must be done. However I do not apprehend, I have any Power to give Directions in the Case, Nor do I mean to do It, You had better Mention the Matter to Congress & have their Opinion and Determination upon It.

A paper, of Which the enclosed is a Copy, came to my Hands Yesterday Morning. This Account makes the Enemy's force in Canada Greater than What We supposed It to be, their Naval Force on the Lakes, to surpass any Thing We had an Idea of, The Person Who Communicated It is not known. He however, I beleive is among those sent from Canada, by General Carlton, and who have lately arrived at New York. I am in Hopes It is a Good Deal exaggerated.[1] I am, Dr Sir, Your Most Obedt Servt
                                                Go: Washington.

LB, NN: Schuyler Papers; LB, DLC:GW; copy, NHi: Gates Papers; Varick transcript, DLC:GW.
1. For this anonymous undated intelligence report, see GW to Hancock, this date, n.3. Schuyler forwarded this intelligence to Gates on 1 Oct. (see Force, *American Archives*, 5th ser., 2:833).

From Jonathan Trumbull, Sr.

Sir   Lebanon [Conn.] Septemr 27th 1776
I am now to acknowlege the receipt of your favour of the 23d Instant.

I have given Orders that Governor Skeene be set at Liberty, and that he and Governor Browne sett out on Tuesday next for Head Quarters under an Escort of Ten Men commanded by Capt. John Skinner, who has Orders to detain them ten or twelve Miles on this Side Head Quarters, and send one of the Escorts to receive your Directions concerning them.[1]

I have likewise given Notice to them, agreable to your request, and appointed as early a Day for them to begin their Journey as the Necessary Preparation for it will admit of. I am, Sir, with the greatest Respect and Esteem your obedient humble Servant

Jonth; Trumbull

ALS, DLC:GW; LB, Ct: Trumbull Papers.

1. The following Tuesday was 1 October. John Skinner (1734–1819) of Hartford had served as a lieutenant in Col. James Wadsworth's 1st Regiment of Connecticut militia during the previous winter when the Connecticut militia temporarily reinforced the Continental army at Cambridge, and he was at this time a captain in that regiment.

From Jonathan Trumbull, Sr.

Sir   Lebanon [Conn.] September 27th 1776

I have your favour of the 23d Instant, and have given the necessary Orders respecting the Governors Browne and Skeene.

The Evacuation of New York, in the Situation You were, appears to me a very Prudent and Necessary Measure, however we could wish the Post had been tenable; the Panic and Flight of our Troops, and Confusion of the retreat I have heard from many Persons with Concern and Anxiety; I flatter myself they will be sensible of the Danger and Dishonour of such Conduct, and avoid it in future, and would consider their spirited and brave Conduct on Monday as a prelude that their future Behaviour will atone for the past.[1]

Can your Excellency spare our Two Gallies from further Continental Service? the Men and their Arms may be used to great Advantage on board our Ship and Brigantine in the Enterprize formerly mentioned to You in which I have the promise of Admiral Hopkins' Concurrence;[2] your Advice on this Head is wanted, as we are not so well acquainted what alteration your present Situation may make in regard to it. An early Answer will be necessary if the Gallies can be spared, and the intended naval Expedition is yet prudent and practicable. I am, Sir, with great Truth and Esteem your obedient humble servant

Jonth; Trumbull

P.S. if the Gallies cannot be conveniently spared or come, cannot a part of the Men and Arms especially Pistols and Cutlasses?

ALS, DLC:GW; LB, Ct: Trumbull Papers.

1. Trumbull is referring to the Battle of Harlem Heights on Monday, 16 September.

2. For this plan to clear Long Island Sound of British warships, see Trumbull to GW, 5 Sept., and GW to Trumbull, 9 September. For Commodore Esek Hopkins's approval of it, see his letter to Trumbull, 22 Sept., in Clark and Morgan, *Naval Documents*, 6:948; see also Hopkins to the Continental marine committee, 22 Sept., ibid., 948–49. The Connecticut naval vessels were the ship *Oliver Cromwell* and the brig *Defence*.

General Orders

Head Quarters, Harlem Heights, Sept. 28th 1776.
Parole Stamford.   Countersign Rye.

Mr Finn Wadsworth is appointed Major of Brigade to Genl Wadsworth.[1]

William Higgins of Capt: Hamilton's Company of the Artillery convicted by a General Court Martial whereof Col. Weedon is President of "plundering and stealing"—ordered to be whipped Thirty-nine lashes.[2]

The General approves the sentence, and orders it to be executed to morrow morning at the usual time and place.

A number of the new Rules and Regulations of the Army having come to hand, the several Brigades Major are to receive their proportion, and deliver them to commanding Officers of the several Regiments, who are immediately to cause them to be read to their regiments, and made known to both Officers and Men so that there may be no pretence of ignorance.

It is with great Concern the General finds, that so many excuses are made by Field Officers, and others, when ordered on duty, especially on Picquet—By this means, active and willing Officers are discouraged—He hopes triffling Reasons and slight Complaints will not be urged to avoid duty when the utmost Vigilance and Care is necessary.

The General has also, in riding thro' the Camps, observed, a shameful waste of provision; large peices of fine Beef not only thrown away, but left above ground to putrify—While such practices continue, troops will be sickly—The Colonels or commanding Officers of regiments, who have not done it, are immediately to appoint Camp-Colour-Men; and Officers who have spirit and zeal will see that all such Nuisances are removed— Some of the Camps nearest to Head Quarters are very faulty in this respect and will be pointed out in General Orders, if there is not a reformation.

Stephen Moylan Esqr: having resigned his office of Quarter Master General—Brigadier General Mifflin is appointed thereto 'till the pleasure of Congress is known.[3]

The Quarter Master General will deliver to Genl Spencer's order, such tents as are wanting for the Regiments in Wadsworth's and Fellows's Brigades.

That the approach of the Enemy to the front of our lines may be communicated as speedily as possible—Two Field Pieces are to be fired by Order of the Brigadier of the day, at the Redoubt on the road by Col. Moylan's—This to be repeated by two others at Head Quarters, and the like number at Mount-Washington.

Col. Shee is to take charge of Genl Mifflin's Brigade till further Orders.

Genl Soltanstall is to order in four of the Militia Regiments, under his command, who are to encamp on the hill opposite to Fort-Washington, towards the point opposite to the Encampment on the other side Harlem river.

The General desires that the several Works, in which we are now engaged may be advanced as fast as possible, as it is essentially necessary.

In future, when an Officer is ordered on duty, and through Illness, or any other private reason, cannot attend, he is to procure one of equal Rank, to do the duty for him, unless some extraordinary reason, should occasion an application to Head Quarters; otherwise a regular Roster can never be kept.

The Brigade Majors are to furnish the Chief-Engineer, with a detail of the men, from their respective Brigades, ordered for fatigue—this is to be left at his Office near Head-Quarters, and when any alteration is made, they are to give him a new detail.

Major Bicker is ordered to attend the Works & be excused from other duty.[4]

Any Soldier detected in cutting any Abbatis, without orders from the Chief Engineer, is to be sent to the Provost-Guard, and tried by a General Court Martial. Officers are desired to put a Stop to so dangerous a practice immediately.

Fatigue Men are to breakfast before they go to Parade, No man to be allowed to return hereafter to his Tent or Quarters on this account.

The building up Tents with Boards, is a practice peculiar to this Army, and in our present situation cannot be indulged, without the greatest Injury to the service—The Boards brought into Camp are for Floors to the Tents, and officers will do well, immediately to prevent their being applied to any other use.

Varick transcript, DLC:GW; Df, DNA: RG 93, Orderly Books, vol. 15. The draft is in Joseph Reed's writing except for the two passwords and the seventh through twelfth paragraphs of the general orders.

1. Fenn Wadsworth (1752–1785), of New York City and later Hartford, a distant relation of Gen. James Wadsworth, apparently held this office only a short time, because another brigade major was appointed for Wadsworth's brigade on 11 Oct. (see General Orders, that date).

2. Higgins had been convicted the previous day of "breaking open a Chest & stealing a Number of Articles out of it in a Room of the Provost Guard" (see the proceedings of the court-martial, 27 Sept., in DLC:GW).

3. Moylan wrote Hancock on 27 Sept. that "the Field Deputies from Congress Conferd with me this day on the business of the Quarter Master Generals department, they told me that they found a disatisfaction prevail[ing] in the army, by its not being Supplied Sufficiently with the necessaries in that department—that it was their wish, to reconcile a body of men So very necessary for the defence, of the glorious Cause we are all engaged in, and proposed that General Mifflin Shoud resume that department as it appeard to them an effectual method, of giveing Satisfaction to the Army, and bringing the department into more regularity. . . . these Gentlemen urged the necessity of this plan, which they had adopted, So forceably, and at the Same time, in So delicate a manner, that I did not hesitate, in telling them, that as a Servant to the publick, I woud very willingly resign my office" (DNA:PCC, item 78). Moylan declined the committee's offer to command a regiment. Congress confirmed Mifflin's appointment on 1 Oct. (see *JCC*, 5:838).

4. Henry Bicker (1723–1801), major of Col. John Shee's 3d Pennsylvania Regiment, served during the French and Indian War as a captain in Col. Peter Schuyler's New Jersey regiment on the Niagara expedition of 1756 and subsequently as quartermaster of the regiment of provincial light infantry that Gen. Thomas Gage raised in 1758. Although Bicker was a royal customs officer in Philadelphia at the beginning of the Revolutionary War, he helped train American soldiers during 1775, and he accepted appointment as major of Shee's regiment on 4 Jan. 1776. Bicker transferred to the 10th Pennsylvania Regiment on 25 Oct. 1776, and in December he became lieutenant colonel of the state's 6th Regiment. After his promotion to colonel in June 1777, Bicker commanded the 2d Pennsylvania Regiment until he retired from the army on 1 July 1778.

To John Hancock

Sir   Head Quarters, Heights of Harlem Septr 28th 1776

Being about to cross the North River this morning in order to view the post opposite[1] and the Grounds between that and powles Hook, I shall not add much more than that I have been honored with your favor of the 24th and Its several inclosures, and that since my Letter of Yesterday no Important event has taken place.

As Colo. Hugh Stephenson of the Rifle Regiment ordered lately to be raised, is dead, according to the information I have received,[2] I would beg leave to recommend to the particular notice of Congress, Captn Daniel Morgan just returned among the prisoners from Canada as a fit and proper person to succeed to the vacancy occasioned by his death. The present feild Officers of the Regiment cannot claim any right in preference to him, because he ranked above them and as a Captain when he first entered the service. His conduct as an Officer on the expedition with Genl Arnold last fall; his intrepid behavior in the Assault upon Quebec when the brave Montgomery fell—the inflexible attachment he professed to our cause during his imprisonment and which he perserveres in; added to these his residence in the place Colo. Stevenson came from & his interest and influence in the same circle and with such Men as are to compose such a Regiment, all in my opinion, entitle him to the favor of Congress and lead me to beleive that in his promotion, the States will gain a good and valuable officer for the sort of Troops he is particularly recommended to command.

Should Congress be pleased to appoint Captn Morgan in the instance I have mentioned, I would still beg leave to suggest the propriety and necessity of keeping the matter close and not suffering It to transpire untill he is exonerated from the parole he is under. His acceptance of a Commission under his present circumstances might be construed a violation of his Engagement, and if not, the difficulty attending his exchange might be encreased; the Enemy perhaps would consider him as a Feild Officer, of which we have but very few in our hands and none that I recollect of that rank. I have the Honor to be with great esteem Sir Your Most Obedt Sert

Go: Washington

LS, in Robert Hanson Harrison's writing, DNA:PCC, item 152; LB, DLC:GW; copy, DNA:PCC, item 169; Varick transcript, DLC:GW. Congress read this letter on 30 Sept. (*JCC*, 5:834).

1. The LB reads "the post opposite Mt Washington." GW is referring to Fort Constitution (soon to be renamed Fort Lee) in New Jersey.

2. Stephenson, who recently had returned to Virginia to recruit his new regiment, apparently "was taken ill, with a return of camp fever, and died at his home on the Bullskin" in Berkeley County (Dandridge, *Shepherdstown*, 349). His will, which includes a codicil of 3 Mar. 1776 executed at "Roxbury Camp, New England," was probated on 20 Nov. (see Aler, *History of Martinsburg and Berkeley County*, 141).

From Major General Benjamin Lincoln

Fairfeild Sept. 28th 1776

The Militia from the State of Massachusetts Bay were directed by the General Court to receive their Amunition at this place and the Court Ordered out a quantity of Powder for that purpose which has not yet arrived[1]—The Troops are Collecting here and finding it dificult to git supplies and detaining them till the Powder shall come in will greatly incommode those who are following and being informed that there was a large Continental magazine of Powder at Stamford I ordered the Companies now here to march to that Town immediately hopeing that the men can be supplied there[.] if so I can replace the powder by Ordering forward some Sent from the state of Mass. Bay[.] I supposed the orders for marching the men were necessary even if they could not be supplied at Stamford as it would be dispersing them in such Division as would facilitate their being Billetted by the inhabitants: As I have missed your Excellency['s] Orders sent forward I hope to receive them on the Road by the bearer hereof Major Turner who will wait your direction.[2] I am with perfect regard & Esteem, Sir, your most devoted Hum. Servant.

ADf, MHi: Lincoln Papers.

1. For the General Court's resolution of 13 Sept. ordering arms and ammunition for the militia reinforcements to be sent to Fairfield, see "Mass. Council Journal," Mar.–Sept. 1776 sess., 570.

2. William Turner (1747–1808) of Scituate, Mass., who kept the town's Latin school, commanded a company of minutemen called the Scituate Rangers in 1775, and in January 1776 he became major of Col. Simeon Carey's regiment of militia levies. On 27 Oct. GW appointed Turner an aide-de-camp to Lincoln (see General Orders, that date). Turner served in the Massachusetts house

of representatives in 1777 and apparently became a militia colonel later in the war.

From the Massachusetts Council

sir   Watertown Council Chamber Septr 28, 1776

Your Excellency in your Letter of the 19th Instant to the General Assembly of this State, having Mentioned that the Army under your Command were much in want of Camp Utensells, and that you knew not how to procure a Sufficiency, The Council have directed the Commissary General of this State to forward to your Excellency, Two Loads of Iron Potts, which he had in his Store for the Use of the Continental Army which we hope will be agreeable to your Excellency: In case you should have occasion for any more, if you will please to signify it, we will endeavor to procure, and forward them.

We should have sent Tin Kittles, but Tin was not to be obtained. I am with great respect, In the name & behalf of the Council Your Most Humble servant

Walter Spooner

LS, DLC:GW; LB, M-Ar: Revolution Letters; Df, M-Ar: Revolution Letters.

From Jonathan Trumbull, Sr.

Sir   Lebanon [Conn.] 28th Septr 1776

The 25th instant the enclosed Petition was delivered me by two of the Subscribers Messrs Kissam and Nicoll, the principal matter they plead, is contained in the Second Paragraph.[1] It was observed to them the Events therein intended is not over, although Long-Island is evacuated by our Troops, yet the reason of their being sent here continues—That their desire to return is an Evidence of their inimical character, for they are sensible if they return, they must take an Oath of Allegiance to King George the third, and submit to such Orders as General Howe pleases to give. Moreover, They having been in this State, puts it in their power to give important intelligence to the Enemy. They answered That nothing had ever appeared, Wherefore they should be sent from their Families—That Adjutant General

Read, gave them encouragement that they should return as soon as that Affair was determined. If never before, doth not their Motion to return to the Island shew them to be really inimical? I told them, I was not privy to Adjutant General Read's discourse; but if they were desirous of it, I would transmit their Petition to your Excellency for your Consideration and Advice— Which is my only Apolo[g]y for this Trouble.

Pray God to give you Wisdom, to guide your Counsels, and to crown your Arduous Labours with Success. I am, with great Esteem and Respect Sir, Your most Obedient humble Servant

Jonth; Trumbull

ALS, DLC:GW; LB, Ct: Trumbull Papers.

1. This petition to Trumbull of 17 Sept. is signed by sixteen suspected Long Island Loyalists who were sent to Norwich, Conn., as a temporary security measure when the British landed on the island in late August. The signers include Charles Nicoll (d. 1780), a New York City wine merchant, and Daniel Kissam, Jr., a son of Justice Daniel Kissam, who was a prominent Queens County Loyalist from Cow Neck. The second paragraph of the petition reads: "Conscious of no Crime, and solicitous of knowing the charge against them, they were informed by Adjutant General Joseph Reid, that there were no particular Matters with which they stood charged, But that the only Occasion of their being removed, was that an Attack on Long Island was hourly expected, and that it was thought expedient to remove them from the Place of Action until that Event was over, They therefore flatter'd themselves that as soon as that Affair was determined they should have been discharged" (DLC:GW). All of the petitioners apparently were released on parole by the end of the year.

General Orders

Head Quarters, Harlem Heights, Sept: 29th 1776.
Parole Fairfield. Countersign Leyden.

Ensigns Fosdick and Chipman, of Col. Webb's Regiment but lately in a Detachment of Rangers under Capt. Holmes, having been tried by a General Court Martial whereof Col: Weedon was President for "Abusive language to their officers—Mutiny and Disobedience of orders"—They are convicted of giving abusive language to their Officers, and ordered to be reprimanded for their Conduct, before the officers of Col. Webb's Regiment.[1]

The General approves the sentence and orders them to join their regiment, that it may be carried into execution.

As there is the greatest appearance of bad Weather, the General directs and begs, that the Officers would have a special Care of the Arms and Ammunition, wherever their is a convenient Cover for either—Bell-Tents, or painted Tents to have the Arms & Ammunition put into them.

He also directs that the several Brigades as soon as the Weather admits, be marched down to their Alarm Posts, as fixed in the Orders of the 26th that the troops may know how to repair to them and defend them to the best advantage—And that this be repeated, until both Officers and Men, are well acquainted with the ground and the posts.

From some discoveries made yesterday, there is reason to think, the Enemy meditate a speedy and general Attack; it is therefore of great consequence, that we should be well prepar'd in all respects to meet it.

A Court Martial consisting of the following Members, are to meet to morrow at ten O'Clock, at the White House near Head Quarters, for the Trial of Capt: Weisner & Capt. Scott for "Cowardice and Misbehaviour in the Attack made upon Montresor's Island on the morning of the 23rd Instant"—Brigadier Genl Bell President[.] Col. Magaw. Col. Holman. Col. Newcomb. Lt Col. Cadwallader. Lt Col. Brodhead. Lt Col. Russell. Major Putnam. Major Hopewell. Major Mott. Capt. Beatty. Capt. Winship. Capt: Gillet. Members. All Evidences are directed to be punctual in their attendance.[2]

Varick transcript, DLC:GW; Df, in Joseph Reed's writing, DNA: RG 93, Orderly Books, vol. 15. The two passwords in the draft are not in Reed's writing.

1. Thomas Updike Fosdick and Benoni Shipman had been tried the previous day, when Lt. Ephraim Cleveland testified that on the night of 26 Sept.: "I went home to the house where all of us who are officers in the Ranging service quarter, and, sitting at supper, a dispute soon arose between some of the officers, when Ensigns *Fosdick* and *Chipman* were very abusive to Lieutenant *Holmes,* and *Chipman* damned them, told them they would not obey their commands, and said they would turn out their company against the rest of the party, and immediately went in, and came out of their room with their guns. We disarmed them and confined them to their room." That account was supported by Lt. Lemuel Holmes and three other officers (see the court-martial proceedings, 28 Sept., in Force, *American Archives,* 5th ser., 2:589–90; an incomplete copy of those proceedings is in DLC:GW).

Thomas Updike Fosdick (1754–1811) of Hartford joined Col. Charles Webb's 19th Continental Regiment as a sergeant on 1 Jan. 1776 and became an ensign on 11 July. Benoni Shipman (d. 1820) of New Haven, who had served as a private in the 3d Connecticut Regiment during 1775, became sergeant major of Webb's regiment on 1 Jan. 1776 and was commissioned an ensign on 11 August. Lemuel Holmes (1737–1822) of Surry, N.H., was a first lieutenant in Col. Paul Dudley Sargent's Massachusetts regiment during 1775 and continued as lieutenant after 1 Jan. 1776 in Sargent's 16th Continental Regiment. Although Holmes was acting as captain of the rangers at this time, he apparently was not promoted to that rank until 15 October. Fosdick and Holmes were captured at Fort Washington on 16 November. Shipman became a second lieutenant in Webb's new 2d Connecticut Regiment on 1 Jan. 1777. He was promoted to first lieutenant in May 1777 and captain-lieutenant in June 1778 and served until 1 Jan. 1781.

2. The members of this court-martial were Brig. Gen. Rezin Beall, Col. Robert Magaw, Col. Jonathan Holman, Col. Silas Newcomb, Lt. Col. Lambert Cadwalader (1743–1823) of the 3d Pennsylvania Regiment, Lt. Col. Daniel Brodhead, Lt. Col. Giles Russell (1729–1779) of Col. Comfort Sage's regiment of Connecticut militia levies, Maj. Ezra Putnam (1729–1811) of the 27th Continental Regiment, Maj. William Hopewell of the 4th Maryland Regiment of flying camp troops, Maj. Edward Mott (c.1735–p.1790) of Col. Fisher Gay's regiment of Connecticut militia levies, Capt. John Beatty (1749–1826) of the 5th Pennsylvania Regiment, Capt. Ebenezer Winship, and Capt. Jonah Gillet, Jr., of Colonel Gay's regiment. Captains Alexander Graydon of the 3d Pennsylvania Regiment and Christopher Stuart of the 4th Pennsylvania Regiment replaced Brodhead and Gillet when the court-martial convened on 30 Sept., and Colonel Holman did not attend.

John Wisner, a captain in Col. Isaac Nicoll's regiment in the New York militia levies, and John Budd Scott, a captain in the 2d New Jersey Regiment, each commanded a boat loaded with troops that failed to land on Montresor's Island during the attack, leaving Lt. Michael Jackson and the men of his boat unsupported on the beach (see General Orders, 24 Sept., and note 2).

At Wisner's trial, which lasted two days from 30 Sept. to 1 Oct., Adj. George Marsden of the 7th Continental Regiment, who had been in Wisner's boat on 23 Sept., testified that "we had got about a Mile from the Place we set off at, when Capt. Wisner observed that he was certain from Information that there was five Times the Number of the Enemy on the Island that we thought for, & that we were led into a plaguy Scrape; That a Ship lay near the Island which would rake us with Grape Shot, some of the men heard this & it was soon known throughout the Boat." When "a scattering fire began from the Enemy," Marsden says, Wisner "immediately squatted down in the bottom of the Boat, the firing increasing the Prisoner [Wisner] said the Enemy had A Number of Boats & that we should be cut off & beg'd for God's sake that we would land on a Point of Land on Morisania Side. This was said loud & must have been heard by the Men. The Boats soon run foul of each other, & so much Confusion ensued that we were obliged to land at Morisania." By that time Jackson's boat was out of sight, and the men in Wisner's boat could not be persuaded to proceed. Capt. James Eldridge, a sergeant, a corporal, and two privates supported Marsden's account. The testimony that seven privates, including four from Wisner's company, gave for the defense was weak and inconclusive (see the court-martial proceedings for 30 Sept.–1 Oct. in DLC:GW).

On 1 Oct. the court convicted Wisner of the charges and sentenced him to be cashiered. GW thought, however, that Wisner should have been sentenced to death, and on 5 Oct. Joseph Reed wrote Beall on behalf of GW requesting that the court reconsider Wisner's case. GW, Reed writes, "has directed me . . . to remark that the discretionary power of the Court seems to have been exercised rather from some motive of compassion than any circumstance appearing on the face of the proceedings. He would therefore wish the Court to point out the circumstances which have induced them to mitigate a sentence which seems to have been generally expected by the army. Had the Court, upon the contrariety of evidence, acquitted the prisoner, the General apprehends the same consequences would not have remitted to the publick, and he should have acquiesced in the opinion, though it differed from his own. But to convict an officer of the crime of cowardice, and in a case where the enterprise failed on that account, where several brave men fell because they were unsupported, and to impose a less punishment than death, he is very apprehensive will discourage both officers and men, and render it, hereafter, difficult, if not impossible, to make an exemplary punishment, and especially in the case of a common soldier, who will suppose distinctions are made by officers in the case of an officer" (Force, *American Archives*, 5th ser., 2:895).

Beall and the other members of the court replied to Reed on 6 Oct.: "As no new Testimony is mentioned to be offered to the Court, they conceive the Judgment they have given in the Case, consistant with their Duty as Officers and the Rules for the Government of the Army.

"You, Sir, must be sensible of the very great Diversity between written Evidence, and that given viva Voce—The Manner, the Behaviour and a Number of Circumstances in the Conduct of a Witness, which may enforce Credit, Doubt or Discredit before a Court, cannot possibly be reduced to Writing, so as to enable a Reader to judge with any Degree of Certainty or Precision; upon those Principles we contend we are the best, the sole Judges.

"If his Excellency is of Opinion from the written Testimony that the Miscarriage of that unfortunate Enterprize was owing principally to Captain Weisner's Misbehaviour before the Enemy, it far exceeds the Amount of the Evidence in the Minds of the Court.

"The only Evidence which stands uncontradicted, is that relative to the Prisoner's Conduct before the Firing from the Enemy began, and even here the Testimony of some of the Witnesses suffered much in Point of Credibility by their after Testimony—on this Ground the Court proceeded in finding the Prisoner guilty under the 17th of the Articles of War, where a Species of Cowardice is plainly implied, different from that in the 27th—his Life was in Question on this Article—The Testimony was contradictory—on the Part of the States, the Witnesses produced were considered interested—their Lives in some Measure were at Stake—throwing the Fault on some one or more Persons might be essential to their own Justification and Preservation" (DLC:GW).

Not until 31 Oct. did GW approve the sentence cashiering Wisner (see General Orders, that date). No record of John Budd Scott's trial has been found.

Heitman, *Register,* 485, says that he was cashiered on 2 Nov. and "joined the enemy." Heath writes in his memoirs, however, that only one captain was cashiered for misbehavior in the attack on Montresor's Island (see Wilson, *Heath's Memoirs,* 76).

To William Bradford

Sir　　　　　　　Head Qurs Heights of Harlem Septr 29th 1776

I have been honoured with your Two favors of the 14th & 23d Instt and am to return you my thanks for the measures you have taken to forward the Two Continental Batallions from your State.

In respect to the exchange of the persons you mention, I apprehend it cannot be effected, till a General one takes place. This I am trying to carry into execution as well in the Naval as the Land service and therefore must request the favor of your State to make out and transmit me a Return as soon as possible of all Continental prisoners in their Hands, distinguishing the Names & Ranks of the Commissioned and Staff Officers & the Corps to which they belong & the number of Non Commiss[i]oned & privates, observing the same rule in regard to those in the Sea service. It will be well to have the whole Collected at One or two Convenient places in order that they may be sent forward as soon as the plan is properly digested, of which I shall advise you as soon as I obtain the Return.

I have wrote to the Other Eastern States upon the same subject, and to me it appears that the prisoners with you had better Join those in Connecticut that they may come together.[1] I would recommend your writing to Governr Trumbul for information where their prisoners are to be assembled and for his sentiments in this instance. It also seems adviseable that they should come by Water rather than by Land; But of this you will have due notice as I mean to settle upon some regular mode with the Admiral & Genl Howe against the time I am furnished with the Returns by the States. I have the Honor to be with great respect Sir Your Most Obed. Sevt

　　　　　　　　　　　　　　　　Go: Washington

LS, in Robert Hanson Harrison's writing, R-Ar; LB, DLC:GW; Varick transcript, DLC:GW.

1. See GW to Jonathan Trumbull, Sr., 26 Sept., and GW to the Massachusetts General Court, this date.

From Major General William Heath

Dear General   Kingsbridge Sept. 29th 1776

Inclosed I send your Excellency the report of the Court Martial, which I laid before you the Last Evening, with the addition of another report Given in this morning, I have Passed upon all the Sentences in the first report Except that of McCormick and on all in the Second Report, Except the Lieutenants, I Should be Happy to Know your Excellency's Opinion, not only with respect to the Present, But also future Tryalls of offenders in this Division, which I should be glad to Know as Soon as is agreable to your Excellency, as there are many Prisoners yet untried.[1] I have the Honor to be with great respect &c.

W. Heath

ADfS, MHi: Heath Papers.

1. The two enclosed reports contain proceedings of the court-martial over which Col. John Lasher presided at King's Bridge on 26, 27, and 28 September. The first report, which covers 26–27 Sept., is in DLC:GW, and the second one, covering 28 Sept., is in MHi: Heath Papers. Adj. Gen. Joseph Reed returned the second report to Heath on 1 Oct. (see Reed to Heath, that date, in Force, *American Archives*, 5th ser., 2:827–28). James McCormick, a soldier in the 16th Continental Regiment who had been convicted of desertion in early August, was found guilty on 26 Sept. of mutiny and attempted desertion during the retreat from Horn's Hook several days earlier, and he was sentenced to die (see report for 26–27 Sept., DLC:GW, and General Orders, 6 Aug. and 1 Oct.). GW approved that sentence in an undated statement that he wrote and signed on the report following the part concerning McCormick. Lt. Thomas Younkman of Col. Henry Haller's 2d Pennsylvania Flying Camp Regiment and Lt. Oliver Mildeberger of Col. Lasher's regiment of New York levies were sentenced on 28 Sept. to be cashiered for being absent from their regiments without leave. Mildeberger also was fined one month's pay (see report for 28 Sept., MHi: Heath Papers). GW's aide-de-camp William Grayson informed Heath in a letter of 1 Oct. that GW had approved McCormick's and the two officers' sentences. "I have it further in command," Grayson wrote, "to acquaint you, that whenever any prisoners in your division are charged with capital offenses, that it will be adviseable to send them here [GW's headquarters] for tryal; in other instances you are to proceed as heretofore" (MHi: Heath Papers).

To the Massachusetts General Court

Gentn   Head Quarters Harlem Heights 29th Sepr 1776

Genl Howe having signifyed to me, a desire of making a General Exchange of Prisoners both Officers, and privates, it becomes necessary to have an exact Return of the Numbers in our possession.[1]

You will therefore be pleased to have all the Continental prisoners of War, (belonging to the Land Service) in the different Towns in your State, collected and brought together to some convenient place, from whence they may be removed hither when a Cartel is fully settled—When they are collected you will please to have made out, and transmit to me, an exact Return of the Names of the Commissioned and Staff Officers, their Ranks and the Corps to which they belong; The Names of the non commissioned and privates need not be mentioned their Numbers will be sufficient.

As it will be more convenient to send them by Water than by land, which may always be safely effected by Means of a Flag; I think you had better order the prisoners to some place contiguous to a port, there to remain till you hear farther from me.

As I apprehend the Number of prisoners in the State of New Hampshire to be too small to make up a Freight for a Vessel, I have directed, if that should be the Case, that they should be sent to your State, that they may come forward with your prisoners.

You will be pleased to forward the enclosed to Lieut. Colo. Campbell of the 71st Regt. I am not certain where he is stationed but think it is at Reading.[2] I have the Honor to be Gentn Yr most obt Servt

Go: Washington

P.S. Be pleased also to make a Return of the prisoners belonging to the British Navy with the Names & Ranks of the Officers. Inclosed you have a Letter from Capt. Campbell of the 71st Regt to me: As he seems to acknowledge his Error and promise[s] a more circumspect Behavior in future, I could wish you would consider his Case and if you think proper admit him again to his Parole.[3]

LS, in Tench Tilghman's writing, M-Ar: Revolution Letters; LB, DLC:GW; Varick transcript, DLC:GW. A note on the LS indicates that on 10 and 11 Oct. the Massachusetts General Court appointed a committee to consider this letter.

The main body of the letter that GW wrote to the New Hampshire General Court on this date consists of an almost identical copy of the text of the first three paragraphs of this letter followed by a paragraph that reads: "But if the Number should be too small to make up a Freight for a Vessel, I think you had better send them to the State of Massachusetts Bay, that they may come forward with the prisoners from thence." The postscript to the New Hampshire letter includes only the first sentence regarding the naval return (L[S], in Tench Tilghman's writing, Nh-Ar; LB, DLC:GW; Varick transcript, DLC:GW; the signature has been clipped from the LS).

1. See Howe to GW, 21 September.

2. In the letter that GW wrote to Lt. Col. Archibald Campbell on this date, he enclosed the list of officers and privates of the 42d and 71st regiments that Howe had sent with his letter to GW of 21 Sept., and after quoting the part of Howe's letter regarding the incorrectness of that list, GW asks Campbell to "make the proper Additions or Alterations and return the same to me" (LB, in Tench Tilghman's writing, DLC:GW; Varick transcript, DLC:GW).

3. This letter has not been found. The undated list of the names of captured British officers that Howe enclosed in his letter to GW of 21 Sept. shows four Captain Campbells from the 71st Regiment who were held prisoner by the Americans: J. Campbell, L. R. Campbell, C. Campbell, and A. Campbell (DLC:GW).

From Major General Artemas Ward

Boston, 29 September 1776. "Having been informed that the Army was in great want of cooking utensils, and there being fifty five Copper Camp kettles and twenty nine Iron Pots and Kettles in the Store here, I have this day sent them forward with directions to the Waggoner to make the utmost expedition in going to the Army and to deliver them to Your Order as soon as he arrives."[1]

LS, DLC:GW; LB, MHi: Ward Papers.

1. Samuel Blachley Webb wrote Ward on 6 Oct. that this letter had arrived the previous day and GW "is obliged for your care in forwarding the camp Kettles which are much wanted" (MHi: Ward Papers).

General Orders

Head Quarters, Harlem Heights, Sept. 30th 1776
Parole Norfolk.   Countersign York.

The movements of the Enemy indicating a speedy Attack, the officers of the several Regiments, of all Ranks, are to be very attentive to the state of the Arms and Ammunition of their respective regiments, and to be particularly alert in Case of Alarm.[1]

The Order of yesterday, with respect to the Troops marching to their Alarm Posts, and making themselves acquainted with the Guard, is to be carried into execution immediately.

Ammunition Boxes in each regiment, not having Ammunition in them, are to be collected that they may be filled—Commanding Officers of Regiments will send them to their respective Brigadier's Quarters immediately.

All the Troops are every Morning to be *under Arms* a little before break of day—and continue 'till sun-rise, when they may be dismissed—As the preservation of our Country may depend very much on a strict obedience to this Order, it is hoped that commanding Officers of Brigades & Regiments will pay a special attention to it.

A working party of 1200 Men, exclusive of those at Mount Washington, to parade at the usual place, at seven OClock in the morning, properly officered, for the Engineer's department—Fellows's and Wadsworth's Brigades to take their tools at Quarter Master Stone's quarters, nigh to Genl Spencer's quarters. Major Clift and Capt: Parsons will attend them. Col. Weedon's Regt will take their Orders from Lt Col. Marshall.[2] The Overseers of the works will attend at the Engineer's Office, every morning, to receive their Orders and parties. The number of fatigue men not to be lessened till further orders. The Engineer must have a list of the several Brigades and the number of men they furnish for the works, or he never can proportion the men to the works in a proper manner.

Varick transcript, DLC:GW; Df, DNA: RG 93, Orderly Books, vol. 15. The draft is in Joseph Reed's writing except for the two passwords and the last paragraph of the general orders.

1. Sgt. James McMichael of Col. Samuel Miles's Pennsylvania rifle regiment writes in his diary for this date that "we received intelligence at midnight, that

the enemy were advancing. We all paraded immediately and man'd the lines. The alarm proved false and at daybreak we returned to our encampment" ("McMichael's Diary," 16:136).

2. Waterman Clift (1741–1828), who had been a captain in the 6th Connecticut Regiment during 1775, served as a major of Col. Samuel Selden's regiment of Connecticut militia levies from 2 July to 25 Dec. 1776. Hezekiah Parsons, Sr. (1728–1813), of Hartford County, served as a captain in the 4th Connecticut Regiment during 1775 and in Col. Comfort Sage's Connecticut state regiment from 20 June to 25 Dec. 1776. Thomas Marshall (1730–1802) of Oak Hill in Fauquier County, the father of Chief Justice John Marshall, was commissioned major of the 3d Virginia Regiment by the Virginia convention on 12 Jan. 1776, and on 13 Aug. the Continental Congress promoted him to lieutenant colonel of the regiment. A former member of the House of Burgesses and the first three Virginia conventions, Marshall had dined at Mount Vernon in February 1775 when he offered GW command of the Fauquier County Independent Company (see *Diaries*, 3:309). In February 1777 Marshall became colonel of the 3d Virginia Regiment. He resigned his commission on 4 Dec. 1777 to take command of the 1st Virginia Artillery Regiment, and in November 1780 the state's house of delegates sent him to Kentucky to arrange the surveying of bounty lands for Virginia soldiers.

Orders to Brigadier General George Clinton

Sir   [Headquarters, Harlem Heights, 30 September 1776]

Take with you Lieut. Colo. [   ] and proceed immediately to Fairfield and there in Consultation with General Lincoln of the Massachusets Bay, Mr Hobart of this State and Lieut. Colo. Livingston if you can meet with him, concert an Expedition to Long Island for the purpose of aiding the Inhabitants removing or destroying the Stock, Grain, &ca which must otherwise fall into the Hands of the Enemy.[1]

This Expedition is to be performed under the Command of such Officers as Genl Lincoln and yourself may fix upon and by the Troops from Massachusets Bay, aided by the three Continental Companies commanded by Colo. Livingston.

If there is a possibility of your seeing Govr Trumbull without too great a delay of time, I shall much approve of your consulting him upon this Occasion previous to your concerting any plan; but if this cannot be done conveniently, you will forward my Letter[2] with your Reasons for not doing so, and a Request of such Assistance from the State of Connecticut as you shall find necessary to apply for.

Dispatch is essentially necessary to the Success of such an Enterprise and Secrecy in obtaining Craft for the Transportation of the Troops across the Sound will contribute not a little towards it—Circumstances and Information must direct you to the Number of Men necessary for such an Expedition as this, and therefore I shall not biass your Judgments by any Order or Opinion of mine upon the Occasion but leave the Matter wholely to yourselves, with earnest and best Wishes for Success. Given under my Hand at Head Quarters on Harlem Heights Colo. Morris's this 30th day of Sepr 1776.

G.W.

LB, in Tench Tilghman's writing, DLC:GW; Varick transcript, DLC:GW.

1. The name of the lieutenant colonel was left blank in both the LB and the Varick transcript, but at a later date someone wrote "Hurlbut" in the blank on the LB. Lt. Col. John Hulbert's expense account for 1–6 Oct. shows that he, Clinton, Lincoln, and John Sloss Hobart met at Isaac Beers's Tavern in New Haven from 2 to 5 Oct. to make preparations for the expedition, which was canceled just before it began (see Hastings, *Clinton Papers,* 1:371–73; GW to Col. William McIntosh, 21 Oct.; and Lt. Col. Henry Beekman Livingston to GW, 28 Oct.). John Hulbert (1741–1829) of Sag Harbor, Long Island, who had served as a captain in the 3d New York Regiment from late June 1775 to 5 Jan. 1776, became lieutenant colonel of Col. Josiah Smith's regiment of Suffolk County minutemen in February, and on 10 June he was made lieutenant colonel of Col. Samuel Drake's regiment of New York militia levies. Hulbert's service with the Continental army ended on 30 Nov., and he subsequently was active in outfitting privateers.

2. See GW to Trumbull, this date.

To John Hancock

Sir   Head Qrs Heights of Harlem Septr 30th 1776

Since I had the honor of addressing you last nothing of importance has transpired,[1] tho from some movements yesterday on the part of the Enemy it would seem as if something was Intended.

The inclosed memorial from Lieut. Colo. Sheppard of the 4th Regiment,[2] I beg leave to submit to the consideration of Congress, and shall only add that I could wish they would promote him to the Command of the Regiment and send him a Commission, being a good and valuable Officer and especially as the vacancy is of a pretty long standing and I have [not]³ had nor has he, any Intelligence from Colo. Learned himself who had the command and who obtained a discharge on account of his indisposition, of his designs to return.⁴ I have also inclosed a Letter from Captn Ballard which Congress will please to determine on, the Subject being new and not within my authority.⁵ I have the Honor to be Sir Your Most Obedt St

Go: Washington

P.S. A Commission was sent for Colo. Learned, which is now in my Hands, having received no application or heard from him since It came.

LS, in Robert Hanson Harrison's writing, DNA:PCC, item 152; LB, DLC:GW; copy, DNA:PCC, item 169; Varick transcript, DLC:GW. Congress read this letter and its enclosures on 2 Oct. (*JCC*, 5:838).

1. See GW to Hancock, 28 September.

2. GW means the 3d Continental Regiment.

3. The word "not" is inserted above the line at this place in the text in both the LB and Varick transcript by some person or persons other than the copyists who wrote those documents.

4. Lt. Col. William Shepard in his petition to GW of 28 Sept. asks permission to resign his commission, because, he says, "when he views the Regiment to which he belongs, which has been destitute of a Chief Col. for almost six months and not filled, and other Regiments, vacant, but a few hours before they are filled by advancements from their own Corps, Your Petitioner is convinced, that he is judged by the wise and prudent Rulers of the States (whom he will honour and esteem) not to be an Officer worthy of promotion, or the most flagrant injustice is done him" (DNA:PCC, item 152). Congress on 2 Oct. promoted Shepard to colonel of the 3d Continental Regiment ranking from 4 May 1776 when it was calculated that Col. Ebenezer Learned's command of the regiment ceased (ibid., 839; see also Hancock to GW, 4 Oct.).

5. Robert Ballard (d. 1793), who resigned as clerk of Mecklenburg County, Va., in 1775 to command a company in the 1st Virginia Regiment, wrote GW on 26 Sept. from Fort Constitution (Fort Lee), N.J., asking permission to sell his commission to Lt. John Pettrus in order to pursue "a Captaincy of Marines in an armed Vessell that is now fitting out in Virginia." The reason for his request, he says, "is not from any dislike to the service, or for want of zeal to the glorious cause, but from experience [I] find that I cannot afford to stay in the Service, being naturally of an extravagant turn & not fortune sufficient to support that Dignity that is observ'd in our Camp" (DNA:PCC, item 152). Congress took no action on Ballard's request, and on 22 Mar. 1777 he was promoted to major of the 1st Virginia Regiment (see General Orders, that date, DLC:GW). In October 1777 Ballard became the regiment's lieutenant colonel and commanded a garrison on the Delaware River (see GW to Ballard,

25 Oct. 1777, DLC:GW). Ballard transferred to the 4th Virginia Regiment in September 1778, and he resigned his commission the following July. In August 1789 GW named Ballard surveyor of the port of Baltimore, and in 1791 Ballard also obtained the office of inspector of that port.

From Major General William Heath

Dear General   Kingsbridge Sept. 30th 1776

By a Letter Just received from Colo. Harrison, I am Informed that it is your Excellency's Pleasure, That Such of the militia belonging to General Saltonstalls Brigade as have not been ordered to move Forward, should now march and take Post opposite to Head Quarters on the Morrisania Side of Harlem River & c.[1] I beg leave Just to represent to your Excellency, That this Brigade Consists of nine Regiments One of which is on the Jersey side, Two orderd to Newyork Island, Four to Joyn Colo. Chester, and the Other Two Posted from East Chester to the Saw Pitts, Where as I am Informed by Colonel Trumbull, That He is Collecting Large Quantitys of Stores, in Places Easy of access to the Enemy, and Surrounded by those Unfriendly to our Cause,[2] I think the greater Part if not the whole of the Two Regiments are wanted there, However I Submitt it to your Excellency's better Judgment If it should be thought best to Continue those Regiments at their Present Posts, and that Two, of the Four ordered to Joyn Colo. Chester should Take Post on Harlem River, as Soon as your Excellency's Pleasure is Known it shall be Done. I have the Honor to be &c

W. Heath

If I should hear nothing further I shall order the whole to march forward.[3]

ADfS, MHi: Heath Papers. The receiver's copy of this letter, which has not been found, apparently included some additional text, because GW's aide-de-camp William Grayson wrote Heath on 3 Oct. that "on looking over your letter of the 30th of Sepr he [GW] has discovered a passage respecting Col. Trumbull, which he thinks has nor [not] yet been answered; He has no objection to Col. Trumbuls inlisting the number of men out of the Militia which you have mentioned; indeed he looks upon it as a proper step" (MHi: Heath Papers).

1. See Robert Hanson Harrison to Heath, this date, MHi: Heath Papers. These militiamen, Harrison writes, were to be instructed to build huts for themselves "with Straw, Rails & Sod . . . on this side the Heights facing Harlem

River, that they may not be in the way of such Works & Lines as may be judged necessary to be thrown up on them."

2. Saw Pit, now called Port Chester, was a small village near the mouth of the Byram River in Westchester County. Its name derived from the building of boats there.

3. William Grayson writes in a postscript to his letter to Heath of 3 Oct. that GW "cannot imagine what has been the reason why the Regiment ordered to the heights opposite to this, are not yet arrived there; he desires you may forward it with all possible dispatch; they may be furnished with tents from the Quarter Master here" (MHi: Heath Papers).

To Major General Benjamin Lincoln

Sir　　　　　Hd Qrs Heights of Harlem 30th Sept. [1776]
Your letter of the 28th Instt noticeing Me the forwardness of the Troops under your Command was this day handed Me by Majr Turner, on Receipt of this you'll please to Halt your Men till a Conference with General Clinton who waits on to advise with You, and determine on a Secret Expedition to Long-Island—which if properly conducted I have no doubt will be attended with Success and be exceedingly beneficial to the United States, to carry into Execution the proposed Plan I must request a Sufficient number of the Militia from your State makeing choice of (both Officers & Men) those which may be depended on. I am wishing Success, Sir Yours &c.

G.W.

P.S. You'll be pleased to return to Fairfield wt. General Clinton to consult on the above Subject.

LB, in Samuel Blachley Webb's writing, DLC:GW; Varick transcript, DLC:GW. The LB is addressed: "To Majr Genll Lincoln att Stamford or Fariefield in Connecticut."

To Major General Philip Schuyler

Dear Sir　　　　Head Qrs Harlem Heights Septr 30th 1776.
Your Favors of the 20th[1] & 25th with their several Inclosures I received this Morning. The Letters for Congress with the Rest of the Papers I shall transmit them by the Earliest Opportunity.[2]
I cannot conceive That their Resolution of the 14th was Calculated or designed in the smallest Degree to give You Offence.

The Application for Stores had been made, as a Requisition from General Gates, which I presume occasioned the Resolve Ordering 'em to be sent to him. As to the Words, "for the Use of the Northern Army," Nothing is to be inferred from them, Whenever stores are sent to any Department, It is always said, for the Use of the Army there.

I am greatly Obliged by the Measures You have taken to provide us with Boards, as they are so material and so difficult to procure. Your Assurances to execute any Commands I may have Occasion to impose on You when out of the Military Line call for a Return of my warmest Acknowledgements; These I tender You, & of these I beg Your Acceptance.

Since my Letter of the 27th Nothing of Importance has occurred; Things remain Nearly in the Situation they then were. There were some small Movements Yesterday on the Part of the Enemy, But as Yet, they have Attempted Nothing, Nor have I been able to find out their Design. A little Time I suppose must shew what Plans they Mean to pursue for the Remainder of the Campaign. I am, My Dr Sir, With sentiments of the Greatest Esteem, Your Most Obedt Servt

Go: Washington

LB, NN: Schuyler Papers; LB, DLC:GW; Varick transcript, DLC:GW.

1. GW is referring to Schuyler's letter to him of 26 Sept., which Schuyler inadvertently dated 20 September.

2. See GW to Hancock, 2–3 October.

From Major General Philip Schuyler

Dear Sir   Albany September 30th 1776

I have the Honor to acknowlege your Excellency's Favor of the 27th Instant, with the paper inclosed, which I shall immediately transmit to General Gates.

The Resolution of Congress of the 14th Instant received since I wrote your Excellency on the Subject of Barracks, has empowered the Commander in this Department, to build Barracks where he may think Proper;[1] but no Nails can as yet be procured.

Major William Edmenston of the British 48th Regiment, who

is now a prisoner sent down by the Committee of Tryon County, has requested my Leave to wait on you, in Order to get exchanged, which I have refused until I should receive Orders thereon.[2]

We have Intelligence from Oswego, since the 20th Instant— No Enemy then there. I am Dr Sir with great Respect Your Excellency's most obedient humble Servant

Ph: Schuyler

LS, DLC:GW; LB, NN: Schuyler Papers.

1. Schuyler proposed building barracks at Schenectady in his letter to GW of 23 September. For Congress's resolution of 14 Sept., see *JCC*, 5:757.

2. William Edmeston (Edmestone), who immigrated to New York from England in 1755, lived on a 10,272–acre plantation called Mount Edmeston in Tryon County about ninety miles west of Albany. A brevet major and captain in the 48th Regiment, Edmeston expected "to serve as an officer when General Sir William Howe came into the district" (Palmer, *Biographical Sketches of Loyalists*, 249). On 18 Oct. 1776 the Albany committee of correspondence ordered Edmeston to be sent to nearby Berkshire County, Mass., and on 21 Jan. 1777 it sent him to Boston (*Minutes of the Albany and Schenectady Committees*, 1:580–81, 662). After being exchanged sometime in 1777, Edmeston became a lieutenant colonel of the 48th Regiment. He was captured by a French privateer in 1779, but he made his way to England the following year and spent the remainder of the war in Europe, serving as a lieutenant colonel of the 48th Regiment until 1782 and of the 50th Regiment from 1782 to 1783.

To Jonathan Trumbull, Sr.

Sir   Head Quarters Heights of Harlem [30] Sepr 1776

Having received authentic advice from Long Island, that the Enemy are recruiting a great number of men with much success, and collecting large quantities of Stock, throughout the Island, for their support, I have directed Brigadier General Clinton forthwith to repair to Fairfield to meet Genl Lincoln on his march hither with a part of the Troops lately voted by the Massachusetts State to reinforce this Army, in order to concert with him an expedition to the Island; to check and suppress, if possible, a practice so injurious and detrimental to our cause— Those Gentlemen will wait on you for your advice in the matter, if time and the situation of things will admit of it, and with a view of obtaining such aid as you and they may judge necessary to facilitate the enterprize—However, if it should not be in their power personally to attend you, I must take the liberty of requesting your good offices upon the occasion, and that you will afford them every assistance that you conveniently can and which they require, either in men, Vessels, &c. for carrying their scheme into execution. It is absolutely necessary that the measures of the Enemy should be effectually counteracted in this instance, or in a little time they will levy no inconsiderable Army of our own people—The influence of their money, and their artifices have already passed the Sound and several have been detected of late who had enlisted to serve under their Banner and the particular command of Majr Rogers.[1]

Being in haste I have not time to add more, than that I have the fullest confidence that your favor will not be wanting in this instance and that I have the honor to be with Regard and Esteem

Go. Washington

LB, Ct: Trumbull Papers; LB, DLC:GW; Varick transcript, DLC:GW.

1. William Duer wrote Tench Tilghman on 28 Sept. from Fishkill, N.Y., that "a Discovery was made sometime ago of a Battalion of Rangers, which was raising in Westchester County to be commanded by Major Rogers, who is for that Purpose commissioned by Lord Howe—I have little or no Doubt, but it is intended for the Purpose of acting as Partisans to the army in that Quarter as the Inhabitants must be the best acquainted with the Grounds, Bye ways &c. There are several other Circumstances, wh. have occurr'd in the Examination of Tories that tend to confirm this matter—I trust that you will exert yourself so as [to] put our army on their Guard. . . . We have this day made a Discovery of a Company enlisting in the service of the Enemy in this [Dutchess] County—The muster Roll contains no less than Fifty seven names, Twenty five of whom we have already apprehended—I am in hopes we shall secure the Remainder" (NHi: Duer Papers).

To Lund Washington

COL. MORRIS'S, ON THE HEIGHTS OF HARLEM,

DEAR LUND,   30 September, 1776.

Your letter of the 18th, which is the only one received and unanswered, now lies before me.[1] The amazement which you seem to be in at the unaccountable measures which have been adopted by ——[2] would be a good deal increased if I had time to unfold the whole system of their management since this time

twelve months. I do not know how to account for the unfortunate steps which have been taken but from that fatal idea of con-
ciliation which prevailed so long—fatal, I call it, because from
my soul I wish it may prove so, though my fears lead me to think
there is too much danger of it. This time last year I pointed
out the evil consequences of short enlistments, the expenses of
militia, and the little dependence that was placed in them. I assured [Congress] that the longer they delayed raising a standing
army, the more difficult and chargeable would they find it to get
one, and that, at the same time that the militia would answer
no valuable purpose, the frequent calling them in would be attended with an expense, that they could have no conception of.
Whether, as I have said before, the unfortunate hope of reconciliation was the cause, or the fear of a standing army prevailed,
I will not undertake to say; but the policy was to engage men for
twelve months only. The consequence of which, you have had
great bodies of militia in pay that never were in camp; you have
had immense quantities of provisions drawn by men that never
rendered you one hour's service (at least usefully), and this in
the most profuse and wasteful way. Your stores have been expended, and every kind of military [discipline?] destroyed by
them; your numbers fluctuating, uncertain, and forever far
short of report—at no one time, I believe, equal to twenty thousand men fit for duty. At present our numbers fit for duty (by
this day's report) amount to 14,759, besides 3,427 on command,
and the enemy within stone's throw of us.[3] It is true a body of
militia are again ordered out, but they come without any conveniences and soon return. I discharged a regiment the other day
that had in it fourteen rank and file fit for duty only, and several
that had less than fifty.[4] In short, such is my situation that if I
were to wish the bitterest curse to an enemy on this side of the
grave, I should put him in my stead with my feelings; and yet I
do not know what plan of conduct to pursue. I see the impossi-
bility of serving with reputation, or doing any essential service
to the cause by continuing in command, and yet I am told that
if I quit the command inevitable ruin will follow from the dis-
traction that will ensue. In confidence I tell you that I never was
in such an unhappy, divided state since I was born. To lose all
comfort and happiness on the one hand, whilst I am fully persuaded that under such a system of management as has been

adopted, I cannot have the least chance for reputation, nor those allowances made which the nature of the case requires; and to be told, on the other, that if I leave the service all will be lost, is, at the same time that I am bereft of every peaceful moment, distressing to a degree.[5] But I will be done with the subject, with the precaution to you that it is not a fit one to be publicly known or discussed. If I fall, it may not be amiss that these circumstances be known, and declaration made in credit to the justice of my character. And if the men will stand by me (which by the by I despair of), I am resolved not to be forced from this ground while I have life; and a few days will determine the point, if the enemy should not change their plan of operations; for they certainly will not—I am sure they ought not—to waste the season that is now fast advancing, and must be precious to them. I thought to have given you a more explicit account of my situation, expectation, and feelings, but I have not time. I am wearied to death all day with a variety of perplexing circumstances—disturbed at the conduct of the militia, whose behavior and want of discipline has done great injury to the other troops, who never had officers, except in a few instances, worth the bread they eat. My time, in short, is so much engrossed that I have not leisure for corresponding, unless it is on mere matters of public business.

I therefore in answer to your last Letter of the 18th shall say

With respect to the chimney, I would not have you for the sake of a little work spoil the look of the fireplaces, tho' that in the parlor must, I should think, stand as it does; not so much on account of the wainscotting, which I think must be altered (on account of the door leading into the new building,) as on account of the chimney piece and the manner of its fronting into the room. The chimney in the room above ought, if it could be so contrived, to be an angle chimney as the others are: but I would not have this attempted at the expence of pulling down the partition.—The chimney in the new room should be exactly in the middle of it—the doors and every thing else to be exactly answerable and uniform—in short I would have the whole executed in a masterly manner.

You ought surely to have a window in the gable end of the new cellar (either under the Venitian window, or one on each side of it).

Let Mr. Herbert know that I shall be very happy in getting his brother exchanged as soon as possible, but as the enemy have more of our officers than we of theirs, and some of ours have been long confined (and claim ye right of being first exchanged,) I do not know how far it may be in my power at this time, to comply with his desires.[6]

Remember me to all our neighbors and friends, particularly to Colo. Mason, to whom I would write if I had time to do it fully and satisfactorily. Without this, I think the correspondence on my part would be unavailing—I am with truth and sincerity, Dr Lund yr affect'e friend.

Ford, *Writings*, 4:456–60.

1. This letter has not been found.

2. The omitted word is "Congress" (see ibid., 456, n.2).

3. The return of brigades under GW's immediate command for this date shows 14,759 rank and file present and fit for duty and 3,479 rank and file on command (DNA: RG 93, Revolutionary War Rolls, 1775–83; see also Force, *American Archives*, 5th ser., 2:607–8).

4. GW is referring to the Connecticut militia regiments that were dismissed on 25 Sept. (see GW to Jonathan Trumbull, Sr., 26 Sept.).

5. Charles Lee, who arrived at New York from the southern department on 14 Oct., wrote Horatio Gates on that date: "*Inter nos* the Congress seem to stumble every step—I do not mean one or two of the Cattle, but the whole Stable—I have been very free in delivering my opinion to 'em—in my opinion General Washington is much to blame in not menacing 'em with resignation unless they refrain from unhinging the army by their absurd interference" (*Lee Papers*, 2:261–62).

6. William Herbert (1743–1818), who emigrated from Ireland to America about 1770 and became a prominent merchant in Alexandria, was a frequent visitor at Mount Vernon during the years immediately preceding the Revolutionary War. His brother, Thomas Herbert, became a captain in Col. Samuel John Atlee's Pennsylvania rifle regiment on 15 Mar. 1776 and was captured at the Battle of Long Island on 27 August. Exchanged sometime in November, Thomas Herbert was appointed a captain in the 10th Pennsylvania Regiment on 4 Dec., but he resigned his commission on 12 Feb. 1777 and subsequently moved to Alexandria.

General Orders

Head Quarters, Harlem Heights, October 1st 1776.
Parole Spotswood.   Countersign Gates.
The Picquet duty being too severe on the few Brigadiers who are now here; after this day, the Brigadier General of the day is

not expected to lay out on picquet—He will attend on the parade, march off the Guards; see them properly posted; visit them twice in the day, and at day-break in the morning, The Colonel being the immediate commanding officer of the picquet, will be very vigilant to prevent surprise; give immediate Notice to the Brigadier, of any approach of the enemy, or other extraordinary occurrences.

James McCormick of Capt: Farrington's Company, Col. Sergeant's Regiment, having been tried and convicted by a Court Martial whereof Col. Lasher was President of "Desertion and Mutiny"—is ordered to suffer Death, on the 8th and 5th Articles of War—The General approves the sentence, and orders him to be hang'd to morrow at 11 O'Clock—The troops off duty are to be paraded on the Grand Parade at that time.[1]

Capt. Marony, late Provost Marshal, having absented himself from Camp without leave, is suspended, and Thomas Bryan appointed in his stead—He is to be obeyed and respected accordingly.[2]

No Officer is on any pretence to leave the Camp, without permission in writing from the Commander in Chief; one of the Major Generals, through their respective Brigadiers, or commanding officers.

The General also thinks it proper to acquaint the officers and soldiers, who have stayed and faithfully attended to their duty, that he has wrote to the respective States, to order back all officers, and soldiers, who have absented themselves with, or without leave; and that he will take the most effectual measures for the purpose. From the movements of the Enemy, and other corroborating Circumstances, to say nothing of the advanced season, and the necessity which must induce them to bring on a decisive Engagement; the General has abundant reason to believe, that an Attack may be hourly expected—He exhorts every commanding Officer therefore of Corps, to pay particular attention to the state of the Arms and Ammunition of their men; that nothing may be amiss whenever we are called upon, however sudden it may happen—At the same time he once more recommends, to every officer and soldier, the importance of the cause they are engaged in, and the necessity there is of their behaving like men, who are contending for every thing that freemen should value—He assures the whole, that it is his fixt determination to defend, the Posts we now hold, to the last extremity; and nothing but unpararelled Cowardice can occasion the loss of them, as we are superior in number, and have a better Cause to contend in, than the enemy have. He further declares, that any spirited behaviour, in Officers, or Soldiers, shall meet with its reward, at the same time that Misbehaviour and Cowardice, shall find exemplary punishment.

Every Brigadier, or Officer commanding Brigade, is hereby enjoined and ordered, to select some good officers to be in the rear of their Battalions, and these Officers are positively ordered to shoot any Officer, or Soldier, who shall presume to quit his Ranks, or retreat, unless the Retreat is ordered by proper Authority; And to prevent the confusion which is occasioned by every person's undertaking to give, or carry Orders, none are to be looked upon as valid, that are not delivered in the manner mentioned in the Orders of the 17th Ultimo.

The Militia if they have not already done it, are to get completed with as much Powder, Ball and Cartridge Paper, as will make 20 Rounds of Cartridges.

That no man, either officer or soldier, may plead ignorance of these Orders, the Colonels, or commanding Officers of Corps are to take especial care that they be read to the whole, as they will answer the contrary: The Adjutant General is to transmit Copies thereof to Major Genl Heath and Greene, that the whole Army may be apprised thereof; the General being determined to punish Cowardice, the instant it happens, for the sake of example.

Major Colbourne is appointed to command the Rangers, lately under Col. Knowlton—he is to take Orders from General Putnam, to whom they are to make daily reports.[3]

After Orders. The following troops to parade at 5. O'Clock,[4] on the Grand Parade, and there receive Orders from Genl Putnam.

Light Infantry of the Pennsylvania Battalions.

Genl Mifflin's Brigade to furnish a Lieut: Colonel and 300 Men.

Genl Wadsworth's Brigade to furnish 200 Men; to be commanded by Col. Silliman.

Genl McDougall's Brigade to furnish a Lieut: Colonel and 200 Men.

Genl Fellow's Brigade to furnish a Major & 150 Men.

Varick transcript, DLC:GW; Df, DNA: RG 93, Orderly Books, vol. 15; copy (incomplete), MHi: Heath Papers. Except for the two passwords, the first part of the draft through the first sentence in the fifth paragraph is in Joseph Reed's writing as is the order regarding Colburn near the end of the document. The copy in the Heath Papers begins with the second sentence in the fifth paragraph and continues to the end of the eighth paragraph.

1. For McCormick's conviction on these charges on 26 Sept., see Heath to GW, 29 Sept., and note 1. GW's aide-de-camp William Grayson wrote Heath on this date, directing him to set the time and place for McCormick's execution and acquaint GW "therewith that he may have an oppertunity of putting it into general orders." In a postscript, however, Grayson writes: "His Excy upon considering farther on the Subject of McCarmick, thinks it will be best to order him here [GW's headquarters] for execution, you will therefore be pleased to have this done; You will please to ⟨let⟩ the prisoner know he is certainly to dye & direct that a Clergyma⟨n⟩ may attend him" (MHi: Heath Papers). Adj. Gen. Joseph Reed also wrote Heath twice on this date, requesting that McCormick be sent to headquarters without delay (MHi: Heath Papers). For McCormick's accidental release this morning by the captain of the main guard at King's Bridge, see Heath to GW, 3 Oct. and 10 Oct. (first letter) and note 2.

2. On 10 Oct. GW granted William Marony a warrant for "2 Months & 20 day's pay to 20 Septr." Thomas Bryan served as provost marshal until the end of 1776, receiving pay warrants on 4 Nov. 1776 and 13 Jan. 1777 (see Warrant Book no. 2, DLC:GW; see also General Orders, 14 Jan. 1777).

3. Andrew Colburn (d. 1777) of Marlborough, N.H., served as adjutant of the New Hampshire brigade at the siege of Boston during 1775 and became major of Col. John Nixon's 4th Continental Regiment on 1 Jan. 1776. Wounded at the Battle of White Plains on 27 Oct., Colburn soon recovered, and on 10 Dec. 1776 the New Hampshire assembly appointed him lieutenant colonel of the 3d New Hampshire Regiment. Colburn was killed at the Battle of Stillwater on 19 Sept. 1777.

4. The draft reads "tomorrow morning at 5 oClock."

From Brigadier General James Clinton

Fort Montgomery [N.Y.]

May it Please Your Ex[c]ellency   Octr 1st 1776

Inclos'd you have a Copy of a Letter and a Deposition sent to Me By the Chairman of the Committee of New-Windsor[.][1] the Prisoners Mention'd in the Deposition are both Confined in the Guard-House at fort Constitution And their Butter put in the Commissary's Store & I have ordered an Exact account of the Quantity of Butter taken to be sent to me, But I have not yet receiv'd it. I Understand there is between 50 And 60 Firkins And Pails[.] it Appears that the said Connor has a Quantity of Flower in Collo. Ellison's store, at New Windsor.[2] But I have not heard how much. their Conduct has been very Suspicious ever since they Came in the Country tho' the Evidence given against Connor is only what Montgomery inform'd the said Lightbody, if I were Convinc'd or had reason to beleive that the Butter &c. Was intended for Our Army at Kingsbridge I would be very unwilling to stop it. tho' in my opinion it was intended for our Enemy's I intend to keep them and the Butter untill I receive your Excellencys Directions about the Matter. Coll Snider who was appointed Coll of the New Recruits to assist in fortifying and Defending these Posts is lately Arriv'd here with part of three Company's which Consists of about an Hundred Men including officers[.] there is part of Two Companys of the same Regiment at Fort-Constitution but I have no return of their Number as yet[3]—We have not a Sufficient number of entrenching Tools for to Carry on our Work[.] I have apply'd to Congress for them but I am not yet Supply'd. I am your Excellencys Most Obt Humble Servt

James Clinton Brigdr Gen.

ALS, DLC:GW.

1. The enclosed deposition, which was made before the New Windsor committee of safety on 23 Sept., has not been identified. The committee's covering letter of that date, which is addressed to GW and signed by Samuel Brewester as chairman, is in DLC:GW. The committee writes that it had decided to send GW "the Culprits with their property in order to be dispos'd of as you may Judge Proper. Mr Connor Alledges in his Favour that he hath for some time Past sold necessaries to our army in New York, And that he intented what he now possesses should be dispos'd of in the same way. But as Mr Connor purchas'd the Butter after he heard that our People evacuated the Town, And the ships of War hath proceeded some way up the North River the Committee was of opinion that he might design it for the enemy, as he Confess'd that he did design to stay in Town till the Regulars was on his back. It farther appear'd to the Committe that Montgomery sold a Quantity of Butter to Connor after he had heard said Connor Make the declarition as recited in the above Affadavit. By which the Committee are of opinion that Montgomery is Highly Culpable. . . . P.S. Since the Committee determin'd on the above, They receiv'd information that Connor hath a Qty of Flower in Coll Ellisons Store which they have not determin'd Concerning at present."

2. This store apparently was owned by Thomas Ellison of New Windsor, who had been colonel of the 2d Regiment of Ulster County militia during the French and Indian War. Although Ellison was reported in September 1779 to be "dangerously ill" and about to die, he apparently recovered (see Margaret Crooke to George Clinton, 15 Sept., and Clinton to Crooke, 24 Sept. 1779, in Hastings, *Clinton Papers,* 5:280–81).

3. Johannes Snyder (1720–1794) of Ulster County was appointed by the New York convention on 7 Sept. to be colonel of the 600 militia levies that were to be raised in Ulster, Orange, Albany, and Dutchess counties to reinforce forts Constitution and Montgomery for two months (see *N.Y. Prov. Congress Journals,* 1:613–14). Commissioned major of the 1st Regiment of Ulster County militia in October 1775, Snyder was promoted to lieutenant colonel of that regiment in February 1776 and became its colonel in May 1776. During May he also was named a delegate to the provincial congress, and in 1777 he became a member of the state council of safety and the general assembly. Snyder served in the assembly until 1779 and as a militia colonel until the end of the war.

From Major General William Heath

Dear General   Kingsbridge Octr 1st 1776.

Yesterday at Ten oClock A:M. a Sloop or Frigate Came through Hell Gate and Came to Anchor near L[a] Brune where she remained untill about Twelve when She Came to Sail and Stood to the Eastward, and was Soon out of Sight Just at night another Ship Came through Hell Gate, and this morning is at Anchor in Harlem River, not far from Montizure's Island— These movements seem to indicate an Intention in the Enemy I think to land where I have ever supposed they would if they act like masters of their business viz at Morrissania. I have the honor to be With great respect Your Excellency's most Humble Servt

W. Heath

ADfS, MHi: Heath Papers.

From Major General Philip Schuyler

Dear Sir   Albany October 1st 1776.

Two Sachems of the Cayugas, who have been with me on some Buisiness, expressed an Inclination to visit Your Excellency, which I greedily embraced, As their Report, when they return, will I hope, eradicate the various Accounts, which prevail amongst the savages to our Disadvantage, they go down under the Care of Mr Deane the Interpreter to this Department. I wish, if convenient, that they might be shewn as much of our Force as possible, & to have some Presents made them, they do not wish to remain above a Day or two, with You. I am Dr Sir Most respectfully Your Excellency's Most Obedt Humble servt

Ph: Schuyler

LS, DLC:GW; LB, NN: Schuyler Papers.

From Nathaniel Shaw, Jr.

Sir   New London October 1st 1776

The 29th Ulto I shipt by Capt. Webster Seventy Two Tents which was Sent me by Daniel Tillinghast Esqr. of Providence and hope they will git Safe to hand—I now by Capt. Thos King Send you Nine Marque and Ninety Seven Common Tents which I hope will also Come Safe[1]—In Case any of the Brittish Ships Should come down this way, I think we Should have the Earliest Notice of it, as we are Daly Shiping Goods up the Sound for the Army. I am Sir Your very huml. Servt

Nathl Shaw Junr

ALS, DLC:GW.

1. Daniel Tillinghast, the Continental agent at Providence, wrote GW on 26 Sept. that "agreeable to a Resolve of Congress," he was sending him seventy-two tents through Shaw, the agent at New London, and in a letter of the next day, Tillinghast informed GW that nine marquees and ninety-seven tents were coming by the same way. "I shall," Tillinghast says in the second letter, "forward a number more as soon as finish'd" (both letters are in DLC:GW; for Congress's resolutions regarding tents from Rhode Island, see *JCC,* 5:718, 735). On 29 Sept. Shaw directed Nicholas Webster, master of the sloop *John Wilkes,* to deliver Tillinghast's seventy-two tents to GW's order "as farr up the [Long Island] Sound as you think you can with safety." Webster also was instructed to unload at Fairfield ninety tents, fifteen marquees, and other camp equipment aboard his vessel belonging to Col. Christopher Lippitt's Connecticut state regiment, which was marching to New York. If Lippitt's regiment had proceeded to New York before Webster arrived at Fairfield, he was to sail to Stamford, if safe to do so, and consult Lippitt (Clark and Morgan, *Naval Documents,* 6:1045; see also Metcalf Bowler to Shaw, 29 Sept., in ibid., 1044). Thomas King, master of the sloop *Susannah,* on this date signed a receipt for Tillinghast's nine marquees and ninety-seven tents, which he promised, "the

Danger of the Seas Excepted[,] to Deliver as farr up the Sound as the Sd Vessell Can Procede with Safety . . . to General Washington or his order" (DLC:GW). A resident of Groton, Conn., King became captain of the privateer *Defiance* in September 1779 and subsequently captured three British vessels. In January 1782 another vessel under King's command was wrecked in the West Indies during a storm, and he and his crew were captured by the British and taken to Antigua.

To Jonathan Trumbull, Sr.

Sir   Head Quarters on Harlem Heights Octor 1st[–3] 1776
   I have the honor of your favor of the 27th ulto and note the contents.[1] The Row Galleys belonging to your State together with those the property of the United States and all other vessels, on the approach of the Men of War, ran up the North River under cover of the Battery on Mount Washington, from whence tis now impossable to remove them. As they are now posted they are serviceable to us, by preventing a communication with the Ships, and keeping out Row Guards by night, to give us timely notice of the approach, or any movements of the Enemy. To take from them their Crew would be rendering them entirely useless, and to rob them of their weapons would dispirit the men. However, if it should be thought advisable, after weighing the above circumstances, to have the Crew ordered to Connecticut or any of the Arms or other weapons on board to be sent there, your orders shall be attended to. The situation of the Enemy's Ships is very different at this time from what it was before the evacuation of New York. We then had the command of a narrow pass communicating from the Sound to the East River, commonly called Hell-Gate, which is now in their possession—Two of their Ships came through yesterday, one I think a Transport, the other a Frigate mounting 24 Guns.
   October 3d 1776. Since the above I am honored with yours of the 28th inclosing the Petition from the Gentlemen sent from this State on Parole to Connecticut. They were looked upon as favorers to Governor Tryon and the British Troops, and were removed to prevent giving any intelligence or otherways aiding the Enemies of our Country—It was intended that when the Theatre of action was removed they might return; but that, at present, is not the case, nor do I think it prudent they should

be permitted to return during our present situation, as undoubtedly they may have it in their power to give information concerning your State &c., which might be prejudicial to the general good. They particularly mention in their Petition "That they were removed from Long Island into Connecticut untill such time as the situation and state of affairs there should admit of their return to their respective Families again"—You will be pleased to inform them I agree with you in sentiment, that that period is not yet arrived—There is no material difference in our situation since I last wrote you.[2] The Enemy have nearly compleated their works from the North to the East River—As the Season is far advanced we cannot reasonably expect a state of inactivity: but should they attempt to dislodge us from our present Quarters I am in hopes to defeat their designs and give a favorable account to the Public of the conduct of the Troops under my Command. I have the Honor to be Sir Your most humble Servant

Go: Washington

LB, Ct: Trumbull Papers; LB, DLC:GW; Varick transcript, DLC:GW.

1. GW is referring to Trumbull's second letter to him of 27 September.
2. See GW to Trumbull, 30 September.

General Orders

Head Quarters, Harlem Heights, October 2nd 1776.
Parole Hartford.   Countersign Harlem.[1]

Jonathan Pollard Esqr. is appointed Aid-de-Camp to Genl Heath, and is to be obeyed and respected accordingly.[2]

It is with much Concern the General is informed, that tho' the new Rules for the Government of the Army have been out sometime, they have not been generally read to the soldiers—Surely Gentlemen do not reflect what prejudice it is to the service, to omit so material a point of duty.

It is once more repeated, that every Soldier is to be completed with Ammunition to 24 Rounds a Man; and it is the duty of Officers to see that they have it[3]—Some of the troops who went out on the covering party this morning, had not their Complement, nor had their Officers examined their Arms and Ammunition, before they marched them on the Grand Parade—This

Conduct if not amended will be fatal to the Army and the Country—Where the Cartridge-Boxes will not hold the full Complement, application is to be made for Pouches, which may be had at the Commissary's Store.

Varick transcript, DLC:GW; Df, in Joseph Reed's writing, DNA: RG 93, Orderly Books, vol. 15. The two passwords in the draft are not in Reed's writing.

1. "Williams' Diary," 49:45, gives the parole for this date as "Glocester" and the countersign as "Falmouth." In the draft they are the same as in the Varick transcript.

2. Jonathan Pollard of Massachusetts, who had been quartermaster of Knox's artillery regiment since April 1776, served as one of Heath's aides with the rank of major until May 1778 when Heath named him deputy adjutant general of the eastern department with the rank of lieutenant colonel (see Heath to GW, 23 May 1778, DLC:GW; Heath to Pollard, 18 June 1778, DNA:PCC, item 57; and GW to Heath, 17 June 1778, MHi: Heath Papers).

3. This order was issued originally in the general orders for 19 May 1776.

To John Hancock

Sir   Head Qrs Harlem Heights Octobr 2d 1776

I do myself the Honor of transmitting to you the inclosed Letter from Lt Colo. Livingston with Sundry Copies of Genl Delancey's Orders, which discover the measures the Enemy are pursuing on Long Island for raising Recruits and obtaining supplies of provisions;[1] in consequence of the intelligence they contain and authentic advices thro other Channels respecting these matters, I have sent Brigadr Genl Geo. Clinton to meet Genl Lincoln who has got as far as Fairfield with part of the Troops lately ordered by the Massachusets Assembly, to concert with him and Others, an Expedition across the Sound with these Troops—three Companies under Colo. Livingston and such further aid as Governor Trumbull can afford, in order to prevent, if possible, their effecting these important Objects, and to assist the Inhabitants in the removal of their Stock, Grain &c. or in destroying them, that the Enemy may not derive any advantage or benefit from 'em. The recruiting Scheme they are prosecuting with uncommon industry, nor is it confined to Long Island alone, having just now received a Letter from the Committee of Westchester County, advising, that there are several Companies of Men in that & Dutchess County preparing to go off and join the King's Army.[2] I have given directions to our

Guard Boats and the sentries at our Works at Mount Washington to keep a strict look out in case they attempt to come down
the North River, also to Genl Heath at Kingsbridge, that the
utmost vigilance may be observed by the Regimts and troops
stationed above there, and down towards the East River, that
they may intercept them, should they take that Route with a
view of crossing to Long Island.[3] I will use every precaution in
my power to prevent these parricides from accomplishing their
designs, but I have but little hopes of success, as it will be no
difficult matter for 'em to procure a passage over some part or
other of the Sound.

I have been applied to lately by Colo. Weedon of Virginia for
permission to recruit the deficiency of Men in his Regiment out
of the Troops composing the flying Camp, informing me at the
same time, that some of those from Maryland had offered to
engage; Colo. Hand of the Rifle Batallion made a similar application to day: If the Inlistments could be made, they would have
this good consequence, the securing of so many in the Service;
However as the measure might occasion some uneasiness in
their own Corps and be considered as a Hardship by the States
to which they belong, & the means of their furnishing more than
the Quota exacted from them in the General arrangement, and
would make it more difficult for 'em to compleat their own Levies, I did not conceive myself at liberty to authorize It without
Submitting the propriety of it to the consideration of Congress
and obtaining their opinion, whether It should be allowed or
not.[4]

I have inclosed a List of Warrants granted from the 2d to the
30th Ulto inclusive, the only return of the sort, that I have been
able to make since the Resolution for that purpose, owing to the
unsettled state of our Affairs and my having sent my papers
away: You will also receive Sundry Letters &c. from Genl
Schuyler, which came under cover to me and which I have the
honor of forwarding.[5]

By a Letter just received from the Committee of Safety of the
State of New Hampshire, I find a Thousand of their Militia were
about to march on the 24th Ulto to reinforce this Army in consequence of the requisition of Congress. previous to their march
Gen. Ward writes me, he was obliged to furnish them with 500
lb. of powder and 1000 lb. of Musket Ball,[6] and I have little

reason to expect that they are better provided with other Articles, than they were with ammunition; in such case they will only add to our present distress, which is already far too great & become disgusted with the service tho' the time they are engaged for is only till the first of Decemr—This will injure their inlisting for a longer Term, if not wholly prevent it.

From three Deserters who came from the Galatea Man of War about Five days ago, we are informed, that Several Transports had sailed before they left her for England as it was generally reported, in order to return with a supply of provisions, of which they say there is a want. Genl Mercer in a Letter informed me, that Genl Thompson said he had heard they were going to dismiss about a Hundred of the Ships from the service. I am also advised by a Letter, from Mr Derby at Boston of the 26th Ulto that the day before, a Transport Snow had been taken & sent into Piscatawa by a privateer in her passage from N. York to the West Indies—she sailed with Five more under the Convoy of a Man of War in order to bring from thence the Troops that are there to Join Genl Howe—they were all victualled for four months. From this intelligence it would seem, as if they did not apprehend any thing to be meditating against them by the Court of France.[7]

Octor the 3d. I have nothing in particular to communicate respecting our situation, It being much the same as when I wrote last. We had an Alarm this morning a little before Four OClock from some of our Out Sentries who reported that a large body of the Enemy was advancing towards our Lines—this put us in motion, However turned out entirely premature—or at least we saw nothing of them. I have the Honor to be with every Sentiment of respect Sir Your Most Obedt Servt

Go: Washington

LS, in Robert Hanson Harrison's writing, DNA:PCC, item 152; LB, DLC:GW; copy, DNA:PCC, item 169; Varick transcript, DLC:GW. Congress read this letter on 4 Oct. and referred it to the Board of War the next day (*JCC*, 5:847–48).

1. See Henry Beekman Livingston to GW, 24 September.

2. This intelligence is contained in the letter that the Westchester committee of safety wrote to the commanding officer at Mount Washington on 1 Oct. and which was forwarded to GW that evening. "We are taking all possible pains to detect and apprehend them [the recruits] by raising and sending off Guards," the committee writes. "We beg, as they may go down the North river this

evening or perhaps in a night or two, that you'll keep a strict watch at your Fort by the water side—They may likewise endeavour to pass over the East river to Long Island, and we think they will meet with no difficulty in effecting their scheme that way, as the Connecticut Militia keep so indifferent a Guard along that shore" (DLC:GW).

3. GW's aide-de-camp Samuel Blachley Webb conveyed these instructions to Heath in the letter that he wrote him at 10:00 P.M. on 1 Oct. (MHi: Heath Papers). For Heath's implementation of GW's orders, see his letter to Maj. Ebenezer Backus of 2 Oct. in MHi: Heath Papers.

4. For Hand's subsequent recruiting of Pennsylvania troops from the flying camp, see Recruiting Instructions for Colonel Hand, 11 Oct., and the Pennsylvania Commissioners of Arrangement to GW, 23 October.

5. The enclosed list of warrants has not been identified. Congress resolved on 2 Aug. that each departmental commander should submit monthly returns of drafts made on the paymaster (*JCC*, 5:628). For GW's sending of his papers to Congress for safekeeping, see GW to Hancock, 13 August. For the documents sent by Schuyler, see Schuyler to GW, 26 Sept., and note 1.

6. See Nathaniel Folsom to GW, 24 Sept., and Artemas Ward to GW, 26 September.

7. The British warship *Galatea* arrived at New York from Plymouth, England, on 13 Sept. and left several days later to cruise off Bermuda. The letters from Hugh Mercer and Richard Derby, Jr., have not been found. Tench Tilghman communicates Derby's intelligence to William Duer in a letter of 3 Oct. and says: "Does not this look as if Genl Howes Army was not so strong as we have apprehended? or would he drain the Islands of their weak Garrisons considering how matters stand affected in the french Islands. They have already insulted the British Flag by affording an Asylum to Capt. Weeks [Lambert Wickes] in a Continental ship of war and refusing to give her up to the Pomona Frigate" (NHi: Duer Papers).

From John Hancock

Philadelphia, 2 October 1776. "The Bearer Major Ross calling on Me previous to his setting out for Head Quarters, I have only Time to enclose you sundry Resolves, and to inform you, that I shall write you fully by General Mifflin."[1]

LS, DLC:GW.

1. The enclosed resolutions of 25, 26, 27, 30 Sept. and 1 Oct. concern Congress's actions on a variety of matters affecting the army, including James Ross's promotion to major of Col. Edward Hand's 1st Continental Regiment on 25 Sept. and Thomas Mifflin's appointment as quartermaster general on 1 Oct. (DLC:GW; see also *JCC*, 5:819–25, 829–32, 836–38, and General Orders, 5 Oct.).

From Jonathan Trumbull, Sr.

Sir   Lebanon [Conn.] Octobr 2nd 1776

I recievd Your favour of the 26th Ultmo in which you Informed me of the Discharge of the Militia Under the Command of Genll Woolcott, who were much Reduced by Desertions &c.; I flattered myself that those Under Genll Saltonstal, seeing their error & the dishonour they have brot on the state to which they belong'd, would have Manifested a different Temper: but with most sensible pain have heard that Numbers of those have also deserted the Army. I hope and trust this state will in a proper manner discover their resentments against such Vile and Scandalous Behaviour, And that those who still remain will faithfully Abide & discharge their Duty 'till regularly dismissed.

Your request of a Return of the Names of the Prisoners in this State shall be Comply'd with as soon as possible & have given Orders to the several Comtees Immediately to furnish me therewith; those in the Countys of Hertford & Windham will, when I recieve your Excellencys directions be sent by Water down Connecticutt River & through the Sound as far as Norwalk or Stanford, those in the County of Litchfield must be sent down through the Country to one or both of those Towns; should be glad to be Informed whether such of the Privates as are Mechanicks, & some Others who have a strong Inclination to Abide & remain in the Country, must be forced & Oblidged to return & be exchanged, Unless there should be a deficiency to redeem those of our people in the hands of the Enemy; & whether it is expected that the Charge & expence Attending the keeping the prisoners be forwarded to your Excellency with them.

I have recieved from the Honble Congress of the United States, their Resolution of Enlisting a New Army of 88 Battalions to serve during the present War, with the bounty of Money and Land therein Offered; that the appointment of all Officers & filling up Vacancies (except General Officers) be left to the Governments of the Several States; the Quota Assigned this State is Eight Battallions[1]—The appointment of suitable Officers is a Matter of the greatest Consequence to the States and Armies; Wish to have such persons appointed as may serve with courage, good Conduct, & Honor; And Ask the favour of your Excellency to take some sutable Steps (Consulting our General Officers if

Agreable) & furnish me with Intelligence of such in the Army who are willing to Undertake, And fit for the service; And give me your Sentiments on the Affair, that appointments may properly be made. Shall request the same favour from General Gates at Tyconderoga for the three Battallions in that quarter, where will probably be enough to make one Battalion or more.[2] I shall meet the Assembly at New Haven the 11th Instant, and your Information as soon as Convenient will be very Acceptable. I am with great Esteem & regard Sir Your Obedient, Humble Servant

Jonth; Trumbull

P.S. when the Field Officers are agreed upon, will not they be able to point out the best Captains, & Subalterns for the several Companies, in their respective Regiments, Subject to your Excellencies Correction.

LS, DLC:GW; LB, Ct: Trumbull Papers.
    1. For this resolution of 16 Sept., see *JCC*, 5:762–63; see also Hancock to the States, 24 Sept., in Smith, *Letters of Delegates*, 5:228–30.
    2. See Trumbull to Gates, 5 Oct., in Force, *American Archives*, 5th ser., 2:912.

General Orders

Head Quarters, Harlem Heights, Octobr 3rd 1776.
Parole Ireland.   Countersign Florida.
    Genl Putnam will please to point out proper places for Huts, to shelter the Picquet-Guard (in front of our lines) and direct the officers who command these Guards, to see that the Men are employed every day at work thereon 'till they are completed; and this, for the sake of their own Health and Convenience, it is hoped they will do as soon as possible, as the weather will soon grow too uncomfortable to lay without shelter.
    As the new Articles for the Government of the Army, are to take place on Monday next,[1] it is expected that the officers will make their men acquainted with them as soon as possible, that Crimes may not pass unpunished on any pretence of ignorance.
    The several Brigadiers are immediately to return a List, to Head Quarters, of the Field Officers of their respective Brigades, who are absent, and on what account; noting such (if any) as have absented themselves without leave, or stayed beyond their limited time. Colonels & commanding Officers of Regiments are to do the same in their regiments respectively—This

Return to be made on Saturday at 12 O'Clock. When the Brigadier is absent, the eldest officer of the Brigade to make the return.[2]

Capt: Fitzgerald is appointed to act as Major to Col. Weedon's regiment, 'till further orders, instead of the brave Major Leech who is dead of his wounds.[3]

An exact Return of the Officer's Names, *fit for duty* in Camp, and *unfit;* is to be made seperate from the General Return.[4]

The Brigades which send their Detachments first on the parade, are to take the right, as has been the usage for a long time.

No Officer is on any pretence to take off any Soldier, who is employed either as Waggoner, Butcher, Tallow-Chandler,[5] or other Business under the Qr Mr General or Commissary General, without first applying to the Head of the department; and in case of dificulty or difference on the occasion, to apply to Head Quarters, and in the meantime the Soldier to continue on the Command.

Varick transcript, DLC:GW; Df, in Joseph Reed's writing, DNA: RG 93, Orderly Books, vol. 15. The two passwords in the draft are not in Reed's writing.

1. The following Monday was 7 October.

2. The following Saturday was 5 October. Many of these returns are printed in Force, *American Archives,* 5th ser., 2:870–81, 897–906, 1060–61.

3. John Fitzgerald (d. 1799), an Alexandria merchant who came to America from Ireland in 1769, was commissioned a captain in the 3d Virginia Regiment in February 1776. He was well acquainted with GW, having lodged at Mount Vernon several times before the war, and in November 1776 GW made him one of his aides-de-camp with the rank of lieutenant colonel. Fitzgerald was one of two GW aides who were slightly wounded at the Battle of Monmouth on 28 June 1778 (see Alexander Hamilton to Elias Boudinot, 5 July 1778, in Syrett, *Hamilton Papers,* 1:510–14). Soon after that battle, Fitzgerald resigned from the army and returned to Alexandria where he served as mayor from 1792 to 1794. He was named director of the Potomac Company in 1785 and eventually became its president.

4. These returns in most cases are combined with those of absent officers requested in this day's orders. See note 2.

5. "Williams' Diary," 49:47, includes "baker" in these occupations.

From Major General William Heath

Dear General   Kingsbridge Octr 3d 1776

I have just received by a Letter from Col. Grayson, the Signification of your Excellency's Pleasure, that the Officers of my Division should get thoroughly acquainted, with the Grounds between this post & Morrissania[1]—This I have been daily inculcating already, & shall now press, in consequence of your Excellency's Direction.

In my Orders on Yesterday I endeavoured to rouse the Officers & Soldiers to compleat the Works, especially the Former (at this critical moment to exert themselves) and that I was determined to work myself I have the Pleasure to acquaint your Excellency, that it has had a most desirable Effect I have not seen the Officers or Men, so disposed to work as I find them this morning—and several new works are executing—Two Regiments of Genl Saltonstall's Militia have marched on to the Island; Two will this day take post opposite to Head Quarters Two are near Col. Chester; Two are still on the Sea Coast—I had ordered one of them forward but find them, so small that it cannot be done, unless 4 or 5 Miles of Sea Coast should be left unguarded, & in dangerous places also—I have therefore tho't it my duty to let them remain, until Your Excellency was informed of the Situation that matters would be in, if both Regiments were removed, & hope that my Conduct in this particular will meet with your Excellency's Approbation.

I have now all the Commanders of Brigades in my Division (except General Clinton) together, in order to form a proper plan of defence in case we should be attacked.[2]

Capt. Dewit who had the Charge of McCormick, was arrested on Yesterday, & will be brought to Tryall to morrow.[3]

One Justice Palmer of Frog's Neck—Read an Attorney at Law, living near this place, & one Underhill, have just been brought here, charged with being unfriendly to our Cause & dangerous Persons, As I know Your Excellency is crowded with Business, I shall send them to the Convention of this State.[4] I have the honor to be With great respect Your Excellency's Most humble Servt

                                                            W. Heath

ADfS, MHi: Heath Papers.

1. William Grayson wrote Heath twice on this date informing him of GW's desire to have the officers of his division reconnoiter the terrain between their several posts and all possible British landing places such as Morrisania (both letters are in MHi: Heath Papers).

2. Grayson wrote in his second letter to Heath of this date that "it is the opinion of the Genl [GW] that you should form and digest proper dispositions for your troops to take effect eventually on their [the British] landing at this or that place, as the case may happen to be; he imagines it will be too late, after the Enemy have actually landed to consider of and digest, a proper disposition, for your forces" (MHi: Heath Papers). For Heath's plan of defense, see his letter to GW of 7 October.

3. For James McCormick's court-martial and death sentence, see Heath to GW, 29 Sept., and note 1. The arrested officer, who was accused of releasing McCormick from the main guard at King's Bridge on 1 Oct., belonged to Col. Cornelius Humphrey's regiment of New York levies. He was probably John (Jan) L. De Witt (1731–1803), a captain in the Ulster County militia, who was reported in August to be stationed at New York with Brig. Gen. John Morin Scott's brigade of New York levies (see Johannes Snyder to George Clinton, 9 Aug. 1776, in Hastings, *Clinton Papers,* 1:299–300). For De Witt's court martial on 8 Oct., see Heath's first letter to GW of 10 October.

4. Philip Palmer, Israel Underhill, and Joseph Read, all of Westchester County, were escorted to the New York convention at Fishkill by a detachment under the command of Capt. William Stewart, and on 7 Oct. the convention referred them to its committee for detecting and defeating conspiracies (see *N.Y. Prov. Congress Journals,* 1:665, and Heath to Stewart, 4 Oct., MHi: Heath Papers).

From the Massachusetts Council

Council Chamber, Watertown, 3 October 1776. Transmits a copy of a letter just received from Richard Derby "containing some Intelligence Which the Board Apprehend your Excellency ought to be made acquainted with."[1] The council asks to be informed of the posts and commanding officers of the state's regiments.

Df, M-Ar; LB, M-Ar.

1. Richard Derby, Jr., of Salem informs the council in his letter of this date that the state brigantine *Massachusetts,* commanded by Capt. Daniel Souther, recently had captured a British transport carrying the chaplain, "a Capt: & about 20 Privates, of the 16th Regt of Dragoons, with their Horses & Acoutremts." The captured transport was the brig *Henry and Ann,* John Farrah, master. It had sailed to America from Falmouth, England, on 27 July in convoy with twelve other transports, all of which, Derby writes, "had the same kind of

Cargo, makeing in the whole two Hundred & thirty Horses, a Fleet of about Seventy Sail Sailed About Three Days before them, Under a Strong Convoy, having on Board the Remainder of the 16th Regt of Dragoons, and the last Division of Hanoverians . . . About 5,000 Men bound for New York. . . . I think You may Depend on the Account . . . of the Sailing of the Fleets, & that they are now near if not Arrived at York" (DLC:GW).

From Colonel Rufus Putnam

May it Please your Exelency october 3d 1776
   the following Establishement of artificers &c. are in propotion to the 88 Battallions of Infentry as one Compeny to 5½ Battallions which I think is as Small a propotion as will answer the Ends proposed[1] the Battallions in general may give 50 Each for the Works the Miners and Sappers are in propotion to these nearly as 1 to 10—the Carpinters Will not Exceed if we are to Consider they have in Charg the makeing of Platforms—Cheveaux-De-Frize gates guard Houses ordinance Stoars & Barracks with in the fortifications or Necessary for the Garison of Each place and many other things in the Engineer Department. I have had no Reguard to Carrages beads [beds,] Boxes and other matters Belonging to the Artillery. Nor Waggons or other Carrages Belonging to the Quarter Masters Department or Barracks for the Quartering of Troops in general Nor any Stoars for the Commesary (Except for the Different Fortress these only Come with in the Engineers Department) However if the Carpinters are thought to Exceed there may be a part of them attached to the artillery and the Same with Reguard to Smiths and they may also be Imployed in any other Department when the Fortifications do not Requier there Labour—For my own part I Should Rather Chuse to Increase there Number then Lessen them Sence if the Service do not Requier there Labour they are not to be paid more then other Troops and Subject to like duty. I am Sir your Excelencys Most obedient Humble Servent

Rufus Putnam

ADS, enclosed in GW to Hancock, 5 Oct. 1776, DNA:PCC, item 152.
   1. Putnam enclosed an undated document entitled: "An Establishment for a Corps of Engineer[s] artificer[s] &c. To Consist of 2 Battallions of 8 Companys Each 100 men In a Company Including officers" (DNA:PCC, item 152).

Each battalion was to have 10 field and staff officers, and each company was to consist of 4 commissioned officers, 10 noncommissioned officers, 30 carpenters or wheelwrights, 5 smiths, 6 masons, 25 miners and sappers, and 20 laborers.

From Major General Artemas Ward

Sir   Boston 3 October 1776.

Several Persons who were employed to purchase Arms for the Continent, and received money for that purpose, have applied to me to settle their accounts, but as I was not possessed of the Receipts which they gave for the money they received I could not settle with them. If your Excellency inclines that I should settle those accounts you will be pleased to forward copies of those Receipts which are necessary for that purpose. I am Your Excellency's Obedient Humble Servant

Artemas Ward

LS, DLC:GW; LB, MHi: Ward Papers.

General Orders

                     Head Quarters, Harlem Heights, Octob: 4th 1776
Parole Holland.   Countersign Boston.

The shameful Inattention in some of the Camps to decency and cleanliness, in providing Necessaries, and picking up the Offal and Filth of the Camp, having been taken Notice of before in general, After this time particular Regiments will be pointed out by Name when such practices prevail.

The Court Martial whereof Col. Magaw was President is dissolved—The Brigade Majors are immediately to settle a new one, Col. Weedon to preside.

As there are many Officers in Camp, whose Health will not admit their going on Picquet, but can attend Court Martial, the Brigade Majors are to attend to this Circumstance in forming the Court, by which means the duty will be easier to the whole.

Varick transcript, DLC:GW; Df, in Joseph Reed's writing, DNA: RG 93, Orderly Books, vol. 15. The two passwords in the draft are not in Reed's writing.

The draft includes the following orders at the beginning: "300 Men properly officer'd to parade at 1 oClock on the Road opposite to Head Quarters for special Duty this Afternoon without Arms—General Puttnam will give them Orders. Major Leech's Funeral will be attended this Afternoon at 4 oClock from Col. Weden's Tent."

To John Hancock

Sir,   Haerlem October 4th 1776.

Before I knew of the late resolutions of Congress which you did me the honour to Inclose in your Letter of the 24th, and before I was favour'd with the visit of your Comee, I took the liberty of giving you my Sentimts on several points which seem'd to be of Importance.[1]

I have no doubt but that the Comee will make such report of the State & Condition of the Army as will induce Congress to believe, that nothing but the most vigorous exertions can put matters upon such a footing as to give this Continent a fair prospect of success—Give me leave to say Sir—I say it with due deference and respect, (and my knowledge of the Facts, added to the importance of the Cause, & the stake I hold in it, must justify the freedom) that your Affairs are in a more unpromising way than you seem to apprehend.

Your Army, as I mentioned in my last, is upon the eve of its political dissolution[2]—True it is you have voted a larger one in lieu of it, but the Season is late, and there is a material difference between voting of Battalions and raising of Men. In the latter, there are more difficulties than Congress are aware of; which makes it my duty (as I have been informed of the prevailing Sentiment of this Army) to inform them, that unless the pay of the Officers (especially that of the Field Officers) is raised, the chief part of those that are worth retaining will leave the Service at the expiration of the present term; as the Soldiers will also, if some greater Incouragement is not offered them than Twenty Dollars, & one hundred Acres of Land.

Nothing less in my opinion, than a suit of Cloaths annually given to each Non-commissioned Officer & Soldier, in addition to the pay and bounty, will avail, and I question whether that will do, as the Enemy from the Information of one John Mash, who with Six others were taken by our Guards, are giving Ten pounds bounty for Recruits; and have got a Battalion under Majr Rogers nearly compleated upon Long Island.[3]

Nor will less pay according to my judgment than I have taken the liberty of mentioning in the Inclosed estimate retain such Officers as we could wish to have continued.[4] the difference pr Month in each Battalion will amount to better than one hundred pounds—to this may be added the pay of the Staff Officers, for it is presumable they will also require an augmentation; but being few in number, the Sum will not be greatly Increased by them, & consequently is a matter of no great moment; but it is a matter of no small Importance to make the several Offices desirable—When the pay & establishment of an Officer once become objects of Interested Attention, the Sloth, negligence, and even disobedience of Orders which at this time but too generally prevails, will be purged off—but while the Service is viewed with Indifference—while the Officer conceives that he is rather confering than receiving an obligation, there will be a total relaxation of all order and Discipline, and every thing will move heavily on, to the great detriment of the Service, and inexpressible trouble & vexation of the General.

The critical Situation of our Affairs at this time will justify my saying, that no time is to be lost in making of fruitless experiments—an unavailing tryal of a Month to get an Army upon the terms proposed, may render it impracticable to do it at all; and prove fatal to our cause; as I am not sure whether any rubs in the way of our Inlistments, or unfavourable turn in our Affairs, may not prove the Means of the Enemy Recruiting Men faster than we do—to this may be added the inextricable difficulty of forming one Corps out of another, and arranging matters with any degree of Order in the face of an Enemy, who are watching for advantages.

At Cambridge last year, where the Officers (and more than a sufficiency of them) were all upon the spot, we found it a work of such extreame difficulty to know their Sentiments (each having some terms to propose) that I despair'd once of getting the arrangemts compleated; and do suppose that at least a hundred alterations took place before matters were finally adjusted; what must it be then under the present regulation, where the Officer is to negociate this matter with the State he comes from, distant perhaps two or three hundred Miles—some of whom, without leave or license from me set out to make personal application the moment the resolve got to their hands—what kind of Officers these are, I leave Congress to judge.

If an Officer of reputation (for none others should be applied to) is ask'd to stay what answer can he give, but in the first place, that he does not know whether it is at his option to do so—no provision being made in the Resolution of Congress even recommendatory of this Measure; consequently, that it rests with the State he comes from (surrounded perhaps with a variety of applications, and influenced probably by local Attachments) to determine whether he can be provided for or not. In the next place, if he is an Officer of Merit, and knows that the State he comes from is to furnish more Battalions than it at present has in the Service, he will scarcely, after two years faithful Services, think of continuing in the Rank he now bears when new Creations are to be made, and Men appointed to Offices (no ways superior in merit, and ignorant perhaps of Service) over his head.[5] A Committee sent to the Army from each State may, upon the Spot, fix things with a degree of propriety & certainty; and is the only method I can see, of bringing matters to a decision with respect to the Officers of the Army; but what can be done in the meanwhile, towards the arrangement in the Country I know not—In the one case, you run the hazard of loosing yr Officers—in the other, of encountering delay, unless some method could be devised of forwarding both at the same Instant.

Upon the present Plan, I plainly forsee an intervention of time between the old & New Army, which must be filled with Militia (if to be had) with whom no Man, who has any regard for his own reputation can undertake to be answerable for Consequences—I shall also be mistaken in my conjectures, if we do not loose the most valuable Officers in this Army under the present mode of appointing them; consequently, if we have an Army at all, it will be composed of Materials not only entirely raw, but if uncommon pains is not taken, entirely unfit—and I see such a distrust & jealousy of Military power, that the Commander in chief has not an oppertunity even by recommendation, to give the least assurances of reward for the most essential Services. In a word such a cloud of perplexing Circumstances appear before me without one flattering hope, that I am thoroughly convinced unless the most vigorous and decisive exertions are immediately adopted to remedy these Evils, that the certain and absolute loss of our Liberties will be the inevitable consequence, as one unhappy stroke will throw a powerful weight into the Scale against us, enabling Genl Howe to recruit his Army as fast as we shall ours, numbers being disposed, and many actually doing so already. Some of the most probable remedies, and such as experience has brought to my more intimate knowledge, I have taken the liberty to point out—the rest I beg leave to submit to the consideration of Congress.

I ask pardon for taking up so much of their time with my opinions, but I should betray that trust which they and my Country have reposed in me, were I to be silent upon a matter so extremely Interesting. with the most perfect esteem I have the honour to be their, and Yr Most Obedt & Most Hble Servt

Go: Washington

ALS, DNA:PCC, item 152; LB, DLC:GW; copy, DNA:PCC, item 169; Varick transcript, DLC:GW. Congress read this letter on 8 Oct. and ordered it to lie on the table (*JCC*, 5:854).

1. See GW's first letter to Hancock of 25 September.

2. GW is referring again to his first letter to Hancock of 25 September.

3. John Marsh, a 20-year-old inhabitant of Philipse's Patent in Westchester County, says in a deposition dated 3 Oct. that he enlisted in the British service about two weeks earlier for a bounty of £10 and was captured with six other Loyalist recruits from Westchester County on the night of 25 Sept. while attempting to cross to Long Island from Pell's Point (DLC:GW; for the examinations on 29 Sept. of four of Marsh's fellow prisoners who denied enlisting in the British service, see Force, *American Archives*, 5th ser., 2:597–98).

4. See the enclosure printed below.

5. The LB includes here a deleted paragraph that reads: "How these difficulties are to be got over without much time elapsing, I know not; and with respect to those States that are called upon for a less number of Batallions then they now furnish (New York for Instance) their Officers must in part be disbanded let their Qualifications be never so great—in the mean while, all recruiting in the Army is at a stand, for strange as it may seem, it is a fact nevertheless true, that the men will know something of their Officers before they engage, and who can inform them till the appointments are made by the respective States or who is to recruit?"

Enclosure

[c.4 October 1776]

Table of Proposed Pay Increases for Officers

	Present Pay		Suppose intended		Difference
1 Colonel		£15		£ 25	£ 10
1 Lieut. Colo.		12		20	8
1 Major		10		15	5
8 Capts.	@ £8	64	£10	80	16
16 Lieuts.	5.8	86.8	7.10	120	33.12
8 Ensigns	4	32	6	48	16
1 Chaplain		10		15	5
1 Adjutant		5.10		10	4.10
1 Qr Master		5.10		10	4.10
1 Surgeon		10		15	5
Mate		4		7.10	3.10
					£111. 2.0

D, in Tench Tilghman's writing, DNA:PCC, item 152; copy, DNA: PCC, item 169. Congress's secretary, Charles Thomson, mistakenly docketed this document: "Enclosed in his [GW's] letter of the 25 Sept. 1776."

From John Hancock

Sir,   Philada Octr 4th 1776.

The enclosed Resolves will inform you of the Steps the Congress are taking to provide for the Army[1]—they are so explicit that[2] I need only refer your Attention to them—and indeed this is all I have Time to do at present. By General Mifflin who will set out tomorrow or next Day, I shall do myself the Pleasure to write you fully. I have the Honour to be with the greatest Esteem, Sir your most obed. & very hble Sert

John Hancock Presidt

Inclos'd you have Col. Shepard's Commissn.[3] The Vacancy of Col. in room of the late Col. Stephenson is order'd to be kept for Mr Morgan, agreeable to yor Recommendation.[4]

LS, DLC:GW; LB, DNA:PCC, item 12A. The postscript of the LS is in Hancock's writing.

1. These resolutions of 2 Oct. concern the procurement of various supplies for the army including wagons, horses, oxen, forage, lumber, nails, tools,

knapsacks, kettles, and tents; the authorization of a wagonmaster, a deputy, and twenty wagon conductors; the sending of blacksmiths, harness makers, and wheelwrights to camp; William Shepard's promotion to colonel; and the denial of Schuyler's request to resign his commission (DLC:GW; see also *JCC*, 5:839–41).

2. The clerk inadvertently wrote "than" on the manuscript.

3. GW forwarded this commission to Shepard with a brief covering letter to him of 6 Oct. (ALS, MWeAt).

4. For GW's recommendation of Daniel Morgan for the vacant colonelcy of the Virginia and Maryland rifle regiment, see GW to Hancock, 28 September. Morgan became colonel of the 11th Virginia Regiment in November.

From Major General William Howe

Sir,   Head Quarters York Island 4th Octor 1776.

Having heard by Report of Governor Brown's Vicinity in Connecticut, I have been in daily Expectation of his Arrival for the Exchange of Lord Stirling; but as the Governor is not in the military Line, and as I proposed the Ex[c]hange to gratify your Desire for the Return of Lord Stirling, whose Services would take Place with you some Days sooner, were I to comply with your Request for his immediate Dismission, you will excuse my detaining his Lordship until the Arrival of Governor Brown.

With Relation to the Non Performance on your Part of the Agreement between Captain Forster and General Arnold, that General being immediately under your Command, from your Situation made known to me by your own Subscription, it rests with you to see them fulfilled, agreeable to the plighted Faith of the General, which no doubt, to save his Honor, he has a Right to expect, or that you will return the Prisoners given up by Captain Forster—In the mean while I trust, from the Declaration in your Letter of the 23rd last past, that you will not allow of any Delay in the Exchange of the Officers and Soldiers in your Possession belonging to His Majesty's Troops.

Brigadier General Woodhull was yesterday reported to me to have died of his Wounds.

The enclosed Note from Mrs De Lancey I have taken the Liberty of sending for your Determination upon the Contents.[1] I am with due Regard, Sir, your most obedient Servant

W. Howe

LS, DLC:GW; copy, enclosed in GW to Hancock, 5 Oct. 1776, DNA:PCC, item 152; two copies, P.R.O. 30/55, Carleton Papers; copy, DNA:PCC, item 169. The LS is addressed to "General Washington, &ca, &ca."

1. Elizabeth Colden De Lancey (1720–1784), daughter of Lt. Gov. Cadwallader Colden and wife of Peter De Lancey, wrote GW on 1 Oct. asking permission to return with her daughter to Westchester County from Spring Hill, the Colden family estate near Flushing, Long Island, where she had cared for her terminally ill father until his death on 28 September. "If this cannot be," she writes, "may she not hope that he [GW] will take some method to prevent the destruction of her Property" in Westchester County (AD, DLC:GW).

To Major General Philip Schuyler

Dear Sir   Head Qrs Harlem Heights Octor 4th 1776.

I last Night received the Favor of Your Letter of the 30th Ulto and am happy that You have Got the Directions of Congress upon the subject of Barracks, as It is high Time they should be begun where they are wanted. The Nails that are necessary I cannot supply.

In Respect to Major Edminston's Request, I cannot consent to his coming here. You may inform him that a General Exchange of Prisoners is now in Agitation & When It is ready to be executed, he No Doubt will have proper Notice of It.

I am [in]¹ Hopes That the Expedition by Way of Oswego, that was talked of, is Not intended as the Season begins to Grow late.

The Situation of our Affairs here is Much the Same, as When I last wrote,² Which leaves Me only to Add, That I am Dr Sir, with Great Esteem, Your most Obedt Servt

Go: Washington

LB, NN: Schuyler Papers; LB, DLC:GW; Varick transcript, DLC:GW.
1. This word appears in the LB in DLC:GW and the Varick transcript.
2. See GW to Schuyler, 30 September.

General Orders

Head Quarters, Harlem Heights, Octobr 5th 1776

Parole   Countersign¹

The General conceiving it to be his indispensible duty to lay before the Congress the proceedings of the General Court Martial, on the trial of Ensign McCumber, has received the following Orders from them, which he desires those Members, who were favourers of the first judgement would immediately comply with.

"In Congress, Septr 30th 1776. Resolved. That General Washington be directed to call upon such of the Members, of the Court Martial, as sat in the trial and concur'd in the acquital, of Ensign McCumber; to assign the reasons for their first judgement, together with the Names of such of the said Members, who were for the acquital; to be returned to Congress."[2]

For the greater ease and convenience of doing the duty the General directs, that the two Virginia Regiments be formed into a Brigade, and for the present be under the Command of the eldest Colonel thereof:[3] Also that the regiments lately from Rhode Island, and the Militia regiments from Connecticut, under the Command of Lieut. Col. Storrs and Major Graves, be formed into another Brigade, and at present be under the command of Col. Lippet[4]—Proper persons to do the duty of Brigade Majors, to be recommended by the Colonel who commands them, who will be paid during the time of their acting in that office: It is expected that Gentlemen capable of doing the duty, will be recommended, and none others; as it is a melancholy thing, to have the business of the Army, conducted with irregularity and sloth; when every thing should put on the face of activity and life.

After Monday, no Adjutant on the East-side of Hudson's river, will be allowed to take orders at Head Quarters, but they must attend their Brigade Majors, and receive 'em from them[5]—If any Brigade Major is sick, or otherwise unable to attend, the Brigadier, or Colonel commanding, is to signify it to the Adjutant General, and recommend some suitable person to act in his stead.

Varick transcript, DLC:GW.

1. "Williams' Diary," 49:48, gives the parole for this date as "Glocester" and the countersign as "Green."

2. This resolution was among those enclosed in Hancock to GW, 2 Oct. (see also *JCC*, 5:836). For Matthew Macomber's court-martial, see General Orders, 22 Sept., and GW to Hancock, 25 Sept. (first letter). For the response of the members of the court to this request, see GW to Hancock, 8–9 October.

3. Col. George Weedon commanded this brigade, which consisted of Col. Isaac Read's 1st Virginia Regiment and Weedon's 3d Virginia Regiment.

4. Sylvanus Graves (1729–1801) of Killingsworth, Conn., became major of the 7th Regiment of Connecticut militia in March 1775, and during the spring of 1776 he served temporarily as major of a regiment of militia levies that reinforced New York. Graves's 7th Regiment and Lt. Col. Experience Storrs's 5th Regiment were among the militia regiments that the Connecticut council of safety on 6 Sept. 1776 ordered to march toward New York (see Hinman, *Historical Collection*, 163, 350, 384–85, 398). By April 1778 Graves was promoted to lieutenant colonel and was in service at Peekskill, New York. Christopher Lippitt (1744–1824) of Cranston, R.I., was appointed lieutenant colonel of Col. Henry Babcock's Rhode Island state garrison regiment in January 1776 and succeeded him as its colonel in May. Although the regiment was taken into Continental pay on 11 May, Lippitt did not receive a Continental commission until 7 Sept., and the regiment remained in Rhode Island until 14 Sept. when, under orders from Congress to reinforce GW's army, it began its march to New York (see *JCC*, 4:347, 5:734, 742, and Lippitt's regimental orders in Force, *American Archives*, 5th ser., 2:338). Lippitt's regiment served with the Continental army until it was disbanded at Morristown on 18 Jan. 1777. He was a member of the general assembly from 1777 to 1779 and became a brigadier general of the state militia by 1780.

5. The following Monday was 7 October.

To Brigadier General James Clinton

Sir: Hd Qrs on Harlem Heights. Octor 5th 1776

Your Lettr of the 1st Inst. enclosing one from the Committee of New Windsor and a Deposition against Mr Conner is duly Recieved, they say the Butter was intended for this Army I would therefore advise its being immediately sent to Colo. Trumbull Commissary General who will pay the Current Price, this Step cannot but be agreeable to Mr Conner if he is Innocent of the Charge if otherways will be secured from going to the Enemy.

The Committee should take upon them the further Examination of Conner & Montgomery and deal with them according to their Crimes, if found Guilty the same steps ought to be taken in regard to the Flour you mention to be in Store at New-Windsor, In respect to Intrenching Tools much time elapses in sending them from here, besides we have not more than are wanted for present use—you must apply to the several Committees in the Country or send an Officer to pick up such a number as may be necessary, for the Amount you may draw on the Quarter Mastr General. I am sir &c.

G.W.

LB, in Samuel Blachley Webb's writing, DLC:GW; Varick transcript, DLC:GW.

From Nicholas Cooke

Sir,   Providence October 5th 1776.

Your Excellency's Letter of the 17th instant by the Committee of this State hath been received.[1]

Deputy-Governor Bradford informed you that it had been recommended to Colo. Richmond to march with his Battalion to join your Army;[2] since which Mr Hopkins a Member from this State of the Continental Congress arrived here; by whose advice it was concluded to stop their March and to permit such of the Men, as should incline to inlist into the Continental Navy.[3] The Reasons that induced the Committee to alter their first Intention were these. Eight Companies of the Twelve of which that Battalion consists were inlisted about the middle of November last for a year. But Part of the Regiment of Militia from the Massachusetts is yet arrived, and it will be some Time longer before the Remainder will arrive, so that by the Time Col. Richmonds Battalion could be got under proper Regulations in Camp their Inlistments would expire, and it might be expected they would return Home to the great Discouragement of the Troops left behind. In that Battalion are a considerable Number of Seamen who it is thought will enter in the Navy, and in the present scarcity of Seamen in this State, upwards of Twelve Hundred being at Sea in the different Privateers, it is absolutely impossible to supply them with Men in any other Way.

After the Committee had taken the last mentioned Resolution Mr Burr a Gentleman of Character arrived here from Governor Trumbull with a Plan of landing a Body of Men upon the East End of Long Island and collecting a considerable naval Force in the Sound.[4] Upon Conference with him and Commodore Hopkins, the Committee determined to recommend it to Col. Richmond to proceed with such Part of his Battalion as should not enter into the Sea-Service to New-London, there to receive Orders from such General Officer as you should appoint to command in that Expedition. The Two Row-Gallies of this State with about Sixty Whaleboats from the Massachusetts, and between Twenty and Thirty belonging to us will proceed to New-London with the Battalion and their Baggage; The Gallies and Whaleboats will be under the Direction of Commodore Hopkins to assist in the Expedition.

I last Night received the Resolutions of Congress for inlisting Eighty-eight Battalions in the Continental Service during the War: Copies of which without Doubt have been transmitted to your Excellency. By them a Requisition is made of Two Battalions from this State. At the same Time we are informed by Mr President Hancock that the Troops now in Service belonging to the several States who shall inlist for the War will be considered as Part of their Quota in the American Army.[5] There are Four Battalions in Continental Pay which were originally raised by this State viz: Col. Varnum's Col. Hitchocks, and Col. Lippitts who are now in the Army under your immediate Command and Col. Richmonds which is under Orders for New-London. I write by this Opportunity to the Three former to make Report to me of the Officers in their several Battalions who will engage to serve during the War: And by the Advice of the Committee I request your Excellency to transmit to me to be laid before the General Assembly at their Session on the 28th instant the Names of such of them as you shall think merit Promotion. I beg Leave to assure your Excellency that this State will give all possible Efficacy and Dispatch to those important Resolutions; and that I am with great Sincerity and Esteem, Sir Your most obedient and most humble Servant

Nichs Cooke

P.S. This Letter will be delivered to your Excellency by Mr Jonathan Hazard who is a Member of the General Assembly of this State, and who I beg Leave to recommend to your Attention.[6]

LS, DLC:GW; Df, R-Ar.

1. Cooke is referring to GW's letter to him of 17 September.

2. See William Bradford to GW, 14 September.

3. Stephen Hopkins (1707–1785), a Providence merchant who was chief justice of the Rhode Island superior court from 1751 to 1755 and 1773 to 1776 and governor of the colony for several terms between 1755 and 1767, attended the first Continental Congress in 1774 and 1775 and the second Continental Congress from 13 Sept. 1775 to 7 Sept. 1776, when he returned to Providence. Although Hopkins was reelected a member of Congress each of the next three years, he remained in Rhode Island and served on the state council of war, to which he was named in December 1776.

4. The bearer probably was Thaddeus Burr of Fairfield, Connecticut. For Cooke's response, see his letters to Trumbull and William Richmond of this date in "R.I. Revolutionary Correspondence," 172–74.

5. See Hancock to the States, 24 Sept., in Smith, *Letters of Delegates,* 5:228–30. A copy of this resolution of 16 Sept. was enclosed in Hancock to GW, 24 Sept. (see also *JCC,* 5:762–63).

6. Jonathan J. Hazard (born c.1744) represented Charlestown in the session of the Rhode Island general assembly that began in May 1776. He was named paymaster of the 1st Rhode Island Regiment in late October 1776 and served in that capacity during the following year. In May 1778 Hazard returned to the assembly, where he held a seat with occasional interruptions until 1805. In October 1778 and October 1779 Hazard was appointed to the state council of war, and in 1787 and the two following years he was elected a delegate to the Continental Congress. Hazard attended Congress only from June to August 1788, however.

Letter not found: to William Fitzhugh, 5 Oct. 1776. On 13 Oct. Fitzhugh wrote to GW: "I had the Honor to recieve your favr of the 5th Inst."

To John Hancock

Sir   Head Qrs Harlem Heights Octobr 5th 1776

I was last night honoured with your favor of the 2d, with sundry Resolutions of Congress. The Officers that concurred in the Acquittal of Ensign Macumber shall be called upon, to assign their reasons for their first judgement which shall be sent as soon as they are collected.[1]

In respect to the Exchange of prisoners, I fear it will be a work of great difficulty owing to their dispersed and scattered situation thro out the States; in order to effect it, I have wrote to the Eastern Governments to have them collected and to transmit me an Account of their number, distinguishing the Names and Ranks of the Feild & Commissioned Officers, and the Corps they belong to; I have also wrote to Govr Livingston of the Jersey's upon the Subject,[2] and must take the liberty of requesting Congress to give directions that a similar return may be made of those in pensylvania and Maryland, and for their being brought to Brunswick that they may be ready to be exchanged for an equal number and those of the same Rank. I observe by the Resolve of the 26th Ulto that the Exchange is particularly directed to be made of the Officers and Soldiers taken on Long

Island, but should not that follow the exchange of those Officers and Men who have lately returned from Quebec, whose imprisonment has been much longer, and whose service has not been less severe and in many instances conducted with great Intrepidity; I have had many applications since their arrival, by which they claim a kind of preference, as far as their Number and the circumstances of their Rank will allow, and which I thought it my duty to mention that I may obtain some direction upon the subject.[3]

You will observe by a paragraph of a Letter received yesterday from Genl Howe, a Copy of which you have at length that the Nonperformance of the Agreement between Captn Forster and Genl Arnold, by which the latter stipulated for the return of an equal number of Officers and prisoners in our Hands for those delivered him, is considered in an unfavourable light and entirely imputed to me, as having the Cheif command of the Armies of the States, and a controlling power over Genl Arnold.[4] The pointed manner in which Mr Howe is pleased to express himself could not personally affect me, supposing there had been no good grounds for the Treaty not being ratified, having been nothing more than an instrument of conveying to him the Resolutions formed upon the Subject; but as there were but too just reasons, his Censure could have no weight was it not directed against me; However I would beg leave to observe, from the Letters from the Hostages; from what has been reported by Others, respecting Captn Forster's having used his endeavours to restrain the Savages from exercising their wonted barbarities (tho' in some instances they did)—his purchasing some of the prisoners for a pretty considerable premium—but above all, from the delicate nature of such Treaties, and because the Non observance of them, must damp the Spirits of the Officers, who make them, and add affliction to the misfortunes of those whom necessity and the nature of the case, force into Captivity to give them a sanction, by a long and irksome confinement—For these reasons and many more that will readily occur that I could wish Congress to reconsider the matter, and to carry it into execution. I am sensible the wrong was originally in their employing Savages and that whatever cruelties were committed by them, should be esteemed their own Acts—Yet perhaps in point of policy, it may not be improper to overlook these infractions, on their part and to pursue that Mode which will be the most likely to render the hardships incident to War most tolerable, and the greatest benefits to the State. I have ventured to say thus much upon the Subject from a regard to the service, and because such Gentlemen of the Army as I have heard mention it, seem to wish the Treaty had been ratified rather than disallowed.

Inclosed is a List of Vacancies in the Third Regiment of Virginia Troops in part occasioned by the death of Major Leitch, who died of his Wounds on Tuesday morning, and of the Gentlemen who stand next in Regimental order and who are recommended to succeed to 'em; you will observe that Captn John Fitzgerald is said to be appointed to the duty of Major; this I have done in Orders, being the eldest Captain in the Regiment and I beleive an Officer of unexceptionable merit, and as It was highly necessary at this time, to have the Corps as well and fully Officered as possible;[5] There is also a Vacancy in the 1st Continental Battallion by the promotion of Lieut. Clark to a Majority in the Flying Camp to which Colo. Hand has recommended William Patten to succeed, as you will perceive by his Letter inclosed.[6]

I have taken the liberty to transmit a plan for establishing a Corps of Engineers, Artificers &c. sketched out by Colo. Putnam, and which is proposed for the consideration of Congress.[7] How far they may incline to adopt It, or whether they may chuse to proceed upon such an extensive scale, they will be pleased to determine; However I conceive it, a matter well worthy of their consideration, being convinced from experience and from the reasons suggested by Colo. Putnam, who has acted with great diligence and reputation, in the business, that some establishment of the sort is highly necessary and will be productive of the most beneficial consequences. If the proposition is approved by Congress, I am informed by good authority, that there is a Gentleman in Virginia in the Colony service John Stadler Esqr., a Native of Germany, whose abilities in this way are by no means inconsiderable. I am told he was an Engineer in the Army under Genl Stanwix, and is reputed to be of skill and ingenuity in the profession. In this capacity I do not know him myself, but am intimately acquainted with him in his private character, as a man of understanding and of good behaviour. I would submit his merit to the inquiry of Congress, and if he shall answer the report I have had of him, I make no doubt but he will be suitably provided for.[8]

The Convention of this State have lately Seized & had appraised Two New Ships, valued at 6229£ Y[ork] Curry, which they have sent down for the purpose of sinking and obstructing the Channel opposite Mount Washington. The price being high and Opinions various as to the necessity of the measure, some conceiving the obstruction nearly sufficient already, and Others, that they would render it secure, I would wish to have the direction of Congress upon the Subject by the earliest opportunity, thinking myself that if the Enemy should attempt to come up that they should be used sooner than to hazard their passing. I must be governed by circumstances, yet hope for their Sentiments before any thing is necessary to be done.[9]

Sundry disputes having arisen of late between Officers of different Regiments and of the same rank, respecting the right of succession to such vacancies as happen from death or other causes, some suggesting that it should be in a Colonial line and governed by the priority of their Commissions, Others that it should be Regimentally, and there being an instance now before me between the Officers of the Virginia Regiments, occasioned by the death of Major Leitch, It has become absolutely necessary that Congress should determine the mode by which promotions are to be regulated, Whether Colonially & by priority of Commissions, or Regimentally, reserving a right out of the General rule they adopt, to reward for particular merit, or of witholding from Office such as may not be worthy to succeed. I have only proposed Two modes for their consideration, being satisfied that promotions thro' the line as they are called can never take place without producing discord, jealousy, distrust and the most fatal consequences. In some of my Letters upon the subject of promotions and one which I had the Honor of addressing the Board of War on the 30th Ulto, I advised that the mode should be rather practised than resolved on,[10] but I am fully convinced now of the necessity there is of settling it, in one of the two ways I have taken the liberty to point out and under the restrictions I have mentioned, or the disputes and applications will be endless and attended with great inconveniences. I have the Honor to be with great esteem Sir Your Most Obedt Servt

Go: Washington

LS, in Robert Hanson Harrison's writing, DNA:PCC, item 152; LB, DLC:GW; copy, DNA:PCC, item 169; Varick transcript, DLC:GW. Congress read this letter and ordered it to lie on the table on 8 Oct. (*JCC*, 5:854).

1. See General Orders, this date.

2. See GW's letters to Jonathan Trumbull, Sr., of 26 Sept., William Bradford of 29 Sept., the Massachusetts General Court of 29 Sept., and William Livingston of this date.

3. On 10 Oct. Congress resolved that GW "be directed to negotiate with General Howe, an exchange of the officers returned from Canada, and that they have a preference to the officers taken on New York and Long Island" (ibid., 6:862). For Congress's resolution of 26 Sept. regarding the prisoners captured on Long Island, see ibid., 5:829–30.

4. See Howe to GW, 4 October.

5. The previous Tuesday was 1 October. The enclosed list of vacancies has not been identified. For John Fitzgerald's temporary appointment as major, see General Orders, 3 October. Congress on 10 Oct. named William Taliaferro major of the 3d Virginia Regiment and granted commissions to two captains and several subalterns in the regiment (see ibid., 6:864).

6. Col. Edward Hand's undated letter to GW recommending William Patton to succeed John Clark as a lieutenant in his regiment is in DNA:PCC, item 152. John Clark, Jr. (1751–1819), who had been a first lieutenant in the 1st Continental Regiment since January, resigned that commission in a letter to GW of 16 Sept. (DNA:PCC, item 152) and accepted one as major of the 2d Regiment of the Pennsylvania flying camp troops dated 14 September. William Patton (d. 1777) was commissioned a third lieutenant in Hand's regiment by Congress on 10 Oct. 1776 (see ibid., 862). Patton became a second lieutenant in Col. John Patton's Additional Continental Regiment on 15 Jan. 1777 and was killed at the Battle of Germantown on 4 Oct. 1777.

7. See Rufus Putnam to GW, 3 October.

8. John Stadler was one of two engineers that Congress had appointed for the southern department on 30 Mar. 1776 (see ibid., 241). John Stanwix (c.1690–1766), a British general in the French and Indian War, supervised the building of Fort Stanwix in western New York during 1758 and the reconstruction of Fort Duquesne, which was renamed Fort Pitt, during 1759.

9. For purchase of these ships, see a Secret Committee of the New York Convention to GW, 27 September. William Duer wrote Tench Tilghman on 1 Oct. regarding the two ships: "Dont let their *Youth* or their *Beauty* plead for them, if there is the least Probability of their rendering the obstructions in that Part of Hudson's River more effectual, I am convinced upon the maturest Reflection that a million of money would be a trifling Compensation for the Loss of the Navigation of Hudson's River" (NHi: Duer Papers). Tilghman replied to Duer on 3 Oct.: "If the new Ships should be found necessary to our Salvation you need not fear their being sacrificed, but our public Money goes fast enough without using it wantonly" (NHi: Duer Papers). Congress on 10 Oct. directed GW "if he shall judge it necessary, to sink the new ships mentioned in his letter of the 5th instant" (ibid., 6:862). On 11 Oct., two days after British warships had passed the obstructions in the Hudson below Fort Washington, William Grayson wrote Thomas Mifflin that GW wished him to

appoint someone "to take charge of the two Ships & two brigs that were sent down to be sunk," and Mifflin later that day committed them to the care of Captain Cook who had supervised the effort to obstruct the river at Fort Washington (NNebgGW).

10. For this letter and the petitions that GW received during September from the second lieutenants of the 1st Virginia Regiment and the first lieutenants of the 3d Virginia Regiment disputing the method of promotion, see Richard Peters to GW, 16 Sept., and note 1.

To Patrick Henry

Dr Sir   Head Quarters Heights of Harlem Octor 5th 1776

Your Obliging favor of the 20th Ulto came duly to hand, and demands my best acknowledgments. I congratulate You Sir most cordially upon your appointment to the Government & with no less sincerity on your late recovery—Your Correspondence will confer honor and satisfaction, and whenever it is in my power I shall write to you with pleasure—Our retreat from Long Island under the peculiar Circumstances we then labored became an Act of Prudence and necessity, and the Evacuation of New York was a consequence resulting from the other—Indeed after we discovered the Enemy, instead of making an Attack upon the City, were endeavouring (by means of their Ships and a superior Land Force) either to intercept our retreat by getting in our Rear, or else by landing their *forces* between our Divisions at Kingsbridge & those in the Town to seperate the one from the other, it became a matter of the last importance to alter the disposition of the Army.

These measures however (although of the most evident utility) have been productive of some inconveniences, the troops having become in some measure dispirited by these successive retreats, & which I presume has also been the case among several of our Friends in the Country—In order to recover that military Ardor which is of the utmost moment to an Army, almost immediately on my arrival at this place, I formed a design of cutting off some of the Enemy's light troops (who encouraged by their Successes) had advanced to the extremity of the High Ground, opposite to our present incampment—to effect this salutary purpose Colo. Knolton & Majr Leitch were detached with parties of Riflemen and rangers to get in their rear, while a disposition was made as if to attack them in front—By some unhappy mistake the fire was commenced from that quarter, rather on their flank than in the Rear, by which means though the Enemy were defeated & pushed off the Ground, yet they had an opportunity of retreating to their Main Body—This piece of success (though it tended greatly to inspire our troops with confidence) has been in some measure imbittered by the loss of those two brave Officers, who are dead of the Wounds they received in the Action—Since this Skirmish, excepting the Affair at Montresors Island, where Major Henley another of our best Officers was slain, there has been nothing of any material Consequence—Indeed the advantage obtained over the Enemys light troops, might have been improved perhaps to a considerable extent had we been in a proper situation to have made use of this favorable Crisis; but a want of confidence in the generality of the Troops has prevented me from availing myself of that and almost every other opportunity which has presented itself.

I own my fears, that this must ever be the case, when our dependence is placed on men inlisted for a few months, commanded by such Officers as Party or Accident may have furnished, and on Militia who as soon as they are fairly fixed in the Camp are impatient to return to their own Homes; & who from an utter disregard of all discipline and restraint among themselves are but too apt to infuse the like Spirit into others.

The Evils of Short Inlistments, and of employing Militia to oppose against regular and well appointed troops I strongly urged to Congress before the last Army was engaged—indeed my own Situation at Cambridge about the close of the last Campaign, furnished the most striking example of the fatal tendency of such measures—I then clearly foresaw that such an Armament as we had good reason to expect would be sent against us could be opposed only by troops inlisted during the War & where every Action would add to their experience & improvement; and of whom (if they were unsuccessfull in the beginning) a reasonable Hope might be entertained that in time they would become as well acquainted with their Business as their Enemies—This method I am convinced would have been attended with every good Consequence, for beside the Militia's being altogether unfit for the Service, when called into the Field, we have discovered from experience they are much more expensive than any other kind of Troops, and that the war could have been conducted on more moderate Terms, by establishing a permanent Body of Forces who were equal to every contingency, than by calling in the Militia on imminent & pressing Occasions.

I would not wish to influence your Judgment with respect to Militia in the management of Indian Affairs; as I am fully persuaded the inhabitants of the frontier Counties in your Colony are from inclination as well as ability peculiarly adapted for that kind of Warfare—At the same time I should think it would be highly adviseable, in case you should conceive yourselves to be in danger from any detachment of the British Army or from their Marines, not to depend on any troops but such as are well officered and inlisted during the War.

I make no doubt but your State have turned their views towards forming some Obstacles against the Enemies ships and Tenders who may go up your Rivers in quest of provisions or for the purpose of destroying your Towns—If they have depended on Batteries to prevent them without any other Obstruction, a tryal of the matter has taught us to believe it will be altogether ineffectual, as when under Sail with Wind and Tide in their favor any damage they may receive from a Battery will be of very little consequence. At the same time I must Observe that this kind of Opposition is exceedingly proper for the defence of a Town or in any Case where it is necessary the Ships should come to anchor before the Batteries for the purpose of silencing them—In the first instance I would strongly recommend row Gallies, which if Officered with brave & determined Men, & conducted with Prudence would in my Opinion be productive of the greatest advantage, and be the most likely means (in your Situation) of securing your Towns & Houses on the navigable Waters from any impression of the Shipping.

I imagine before this, Congress has made you acquainted with their Resolutions for raising the new Army and that your Colony is to furnish fifteen Battalions, to be inlisted during the War[1]— As this will occasion the choosing a number of new Officers, I would in the most urgent manner recommend the Utmost Care & Circumspection in your several appointments—I do not expect that there are many experienced Gentlemen now left with you, as from what I have understood, those who have served in the last War are chiefly promoted; however I am satisfied that the military Spirit runs so high in your Colony, and that the number of applicants will be so considerable that a very proper choice may be made—Indeed the Army's being put upon such a permanent footing will be a strong inducement for them to step forth on the present interesting occasion—One Circumstance in this important Business ought to be cautiously guarded against, and that is the Soldier & Officer being too nearly on a level—Discipline & subordination add Life & Vigor to military movements—the Person commanded yields but a reluctant obedience to those he conceives are undeservedly made his Superiors—the Degrees of Rank are frequently transferred from civil Life into the Departments of the Army—the true Criterion to judge by (when past services do not enter into the Competition) is to consider whether the Candidate for Office has a just pretension to the character of a Gentleman, a proper Sense of Honor, & some Reputation to loo[s]e.

Perhaps Sir you may be surprised at my pressing this Advice so strongly as I have done in this Letter—but I have felt the inconveniences resulting from a contrary principle in so sensible a manner, and this Army has been so greatly enfeebled by a different line of Conduct, that I hope you will readily excuse Me. I am sir with Sincere Regard Yr Affect. Hum. Servt

G.W.

LB, in Tench Tilghman's writing, DLC:GW; Varick transcript, DLC:GW.
　1. For these resolutions of 16 Sept., see *JCC*, 5:762–63.

To William Livingston

Sir　　　　　　　　Head Quarters Harlem Heights Oct. 5. 1776
　The Congress having directed me, by a Resolve of the 26th Septemr to procure as soon as possible, an Exchange of the Officers and Soldiers taken on Long Island for the same Number of British Officers and privates, now prisoners in the united States, it becomes necessary for me to be informed of the Number and Ranks of the prisoners in the different States, in order to carry the same into Execution—You will therefore oblige me, by having made out and transmitted to me, an exact Return of the Number of Officers in New Jersey, their Ranks, Names and the Corps to which they belong. The Numbers of the non commissioned Officers and privates without their Names will be sufficient: They should also be collected from the different places

where they are stationed and brought together to some convenient place (Brunswick I should think) from whence they may be sent to Genl Howe when the Cartel is fully settled.[1] I am Sir Yr most obt Servt.

LB, in Tench Tilghman's writing, DLC:GW; Varick transcript, DLC:GW.

1. On 8 Oct. Livingston ordered Capt. Rowland Chambers of the Somerset militia to begin collecting prisoners for the exchange (see Chambers to Livingston, 14 Oct., in Prince, *Livingston Papers*, 1:165–67). Livingston enclosed a return of British prisoners in his letter to GW of 9 November.

From the Massachusetts Council

Sir   Council Chamber, Watertown, Octor 5. 1776

In consequence of the measures taken by this Government to Engage a number of Indians of the Penobscott, St Johns and Mickmac Tribes in the Service of the united States of America agreable to the desire of your Excellency, Seven of the Penobscott Tribe have Inlisted for the Term of one Year, and have arrived here on their way to New York. As they were very poorly Cloathed, and would not proceed without some supply; We have furnished them with a few necessary Articles, amounting to twenty pounds, four shillings & 4d., Lawful Money, which must be stopped out of their Wages. And their Subsistance while here amounts to Fifteen pounds, sixteen shillings & 5d., And We have advanced Mr Andrew Gilman, who has the care of them Twenty pounds, Lawful M[one]y in order to subsist them in their way to New york.[1] These were all that could be obtained from that Tribe, and whether you can depend upon any from the St Johns, or the Mickmac Tribes, we have not as yet any certain Intelligence. In the Name and behalf of the Council I am with great respect Your Humble Servant

John Winthrop Presidt

LS, DLC:GW; Df, M-Ar; LB, M-Ar.

1. In a letter to the Massachusetts General Court that apparently was written sometime later this month, GW says: "This will be delivered you by Mr [Andrew] Gilman who conducted 7 Penobscot Indians into this Camp & expects to meet a larger number on his Return, as he desired my Instructions with Respect to the latter I have given them founded on the Advancement of the Season, & the little Probability of deriveing any essential Benefit from them at this Time, when both Armies are most probably retireing into Winter Quarters, My Directions to him are not to have them advanced farther at present

but to return with them and take such further Orders from You with Respect to their future Destination as you from your Knowledge of their Circumstances & Situation shall think best. Whatever Expence has or may accrue on their Account will certainly be brought into the Continental Account, & I make no doubt but such gratueties will be also allowed as you may think proper & necessary, should there be any other Disposition of them ariseing from Circumstances not now known I must beg leave to observe to you that this Army is so unprovided with all kinds of Woollens, that I have not the most distant prospect of supplying them with those Necessaries here, & it is much to be feared that any Disappointment would make the most unfavorable Impressions on their Minds, Should they therefore proceed to this Camp I flatter myself they will be furnished with the Articles necessary for the Season before they proceed hither.

"If they are to be put into service the next Season in Consequence of any Engagements already entered into or which may be done I would suggest the propriety of keeping them collected together in some proper place rather than suffering them to disperse into their several Towns from which it may be difficult to gather them when wanted" (DfS, in Samuel Blachley Webb's writing, CtY: Webb Family Collection).

From Brigadier General William Thompson

Sir. Phila. Oc. 5th 1776

The wants of the Prisoners being many, I procured them Credit with Mr Freeman at Quebec for £630.9.8½ Halifax; equal to £945.14.6¾ Pennsylvania Currency, For which I have reced the following Bills and Cash viz.

Col. Greens's Bill for	£335. 2. 6¾ Halifax
Capn Morgan's do for	105. 6. 9¼
Cap. Lam[b]'s do for	57. 6. ½
Messrs Nichol's[1] & Steel's do for	40. 0. 1
Dr McKenzie Cash	12. 3. 4
Mr Duncan Cash[2]	8.13. 9
Col. Green for the Sick (still Dr.)	63. 3.10½
Captn McClean Cash[3]	8.13. 3
	£630. 9. 8 Halifax

Col. Green took up for the use of the Sick Soldiers belonging to the New-England Colonies, sundry Articles amounting to £63.3.10½ Halifax which he has not Included in his Bill—Your

Excellency will please to direct whether It is to be charged to the poor Soldiers or the Publick.

I have also drawn five months Pay, for the Officers & three Months Pay for the Soldiers, belonging to the Pennsylvania & Jersey Regiments, who have return'd with me from Canada. I enlcose the account that Stoppages may be made in the Regimts to which they belong.

I have made myself liable for the Goods supply'd by Mr Freeman, to Messrs Meredith[4] & Clymer of this City, and must request that you will order the Bills to be Paid, that I may be released From that obligation. I have the Honor to be Yr Excellency's Most obt Hble Servant

Wm Thompson

ALS, DLC:GW. The cover of this letter is addressed: "To His Excellency General Washington King's-Bridge." The docket in Robert Hanson Harrison's writing reads: "Genl Thompson's Letter 5 Octo. 1776 received not before 8 July 1777. Ansd 17." For GW's reply, see his letter to Thompson of 17 July 1777 (DLC:GW).

1. Francis Nichols (1737–1812) of Pottstown, Pa., was a second lieutenant in Capt. William Hendricks's company of Thompson's Pennsylvania rifle regiment when he was captured at Quebec on 31 Dec. 1775. Named a captain in the 9th Pennsylvania Regiment in December 1776, Nichols became major of that regiment the following February and served until he resigned in May 1779. Nichols later became brigadier general of the Montgomery County militia.

2. Matthew Duncan of Philadelphia went to Cambridge, Mass., in the summer of 1775 as a gentleman volunteer with the Pennsylvania riflemen, and that fall he served as a volunteer on Arnold's expedition to Quebec, where he was captured on 31 December. Soon after his return from Canada, Duncan joined the 5th Pennsylvania Regiment, in which he had been commissioned a captain on 5 Jan. 1776, and he was taken prisoner with that regiment at Fort Washington on 16 November.

3. Moses McClean (1737–1810) of York County, Pa., who was commissioned a captain in the 6th Pennsylvania Regiment on 9 Jan. 1776, was captured while fishing with several members of his regiment near Île aux Noix in June 1776. McClean was exchanged in March 1777 and subsequently became lieutenant colonel of the second battalion of the York County militia.

4. Samuel Meredith (1741–1817), a Philadelphia merchant, was appointed major of the 3d Battalion of the Philadelphia associators in 1775, and in April 1777 he became a brigadier general of the state militia. Meredith served in the Pennsylvania legislature from 1778 to 1779 and from 1781 to 1783, and during 1787 and 1788 he was a member of the Continental Congress. He served as United States treasurer from 1789 to 1801.

To Samuel Washington

Dear Brother,   Heights of Harlem 5th Oct. 1776.

Altho the multiplicity of Ingagements which employ all my waking hours, will not allow me to corrispond with my Friends with that freedom and punctuality I could wish, they may nevertheless be assured that neither time—distance—or change of Circumstances have, in the smallest degree altered the Affection I have ever entertained for them.

Your favour of the 16th of last Month came safe to hand by Captn Shepherd, and gave me the pleasure of hearing that yourself, and family were well.[1] the Acct given you by Doctr Walker, of the unfriendly disposition of the Western Indian's is really alarming; but if our success against the Cherokees is equal to report, I am in hopes it will bring the Western gentry to their Second thoughts before they strike. Your Acct of the want of Arms among the People of the Frontiers is also alarming; but I hope the difficiency will, by one means or other, soon be repaird. Poor Stephenson! I sincerely lament his loss; he was a brave & a good Officer.

Mr Pendleton obtaind my Deed; or a Bond, or something obligatory upon me, and my heirs, to make him a title to the Land he had of me, & sold you, upon the purchase Money being paid; not one farthing of which has yet been done—even the last years Rent, if I remember right, which he took upon himself to pay, is yet behind—However, so soon as I can get Evidences, I will send a power of Attorney to Lund Washington to make a legal conveyance of the Land, to you. In the meanwhile the Instrument of writing I passed to Mr Pendleton will always be good against my Heirs, upon the Condition's of it being complied with.[2]

Matters in this Quarter, have by no means worn that favourable aspect you have been taught to believe from the publications in the Gazettes—The pompous Acct of the Marches, & Counter Marches of the Militia, thoˆ true so far as relates to the Expence, is false with respect to the Service, for you could neither get them to stay In Camp or fight when they were there— in short, it may truely be said they were eternally coming and going without rendering the least Earthly Service, althoˆ the expence of them surpasses all description.

At no one time since General Howe's arrival at Staten Island has my Force been equal (in Men fit for duty) to his; and yet, people at a distance, as I have understood by Letters, have conceivd that they were scarce a mouthful for us. To this cause—the number of Posts we were obliged to occupy in order to secure our Communication with the Country—& the intended mode of Attack is to be attributed our Retreat from Long Island, and the Evacuation of New York.

We found that General Howe had no Inclination to make an Attack upon our Lines at the last mentioned place—We discovered at the sametime by their movements, and our Intelligence, that with the assistance of their Ships they intended to draw a Line round us, and cut of all communication, between the City and Country; thereby reducing us to the necessity of fighting our way out under every disadvantage—surrendering at discretion—or Starving—That they might have accomplished one or the other of these, if we had stayed at New York, is certain; because the City, as I presume you know, stands upon the point of a narrow Neck of Land laying between the East & North Rivers; & not more than a Mile Wide for Six or Seven Miles back; both Rivers having sufficient depth of Water for Ships of any burthen; and because they were not only Superior in Numbers, but could bring their whole force to any one point, whereas we, to keep open the communication were obliged to have an extended Line, or rather a chain of Posts, for near 18 Miles.

It may be asked how we come to take possession of, and continue so long in a place thus Circumstanced—to the first I answer, that the Post was taken, and the Works advanced, before I left Boston—& to the Second, that if our strength had been equal to the determinations of Congress we should have had Men enough to defend the City & Secured the Communication if their behaviour had been good.

Our retreat from Long Island was made without any loss—so might that have been from New York, but for a defect in the department of the Quarter Master Genls not providing Teams enough; and for the dastardly behaviour of part of our Troops, two Brigades of which run away from a small party of the Enemy, and left me in the Field with only my Aid de Camps, The day after our Retreat from New York (which happend on the 15th Ulto) we had a pretty smart skirmish with the Enemy, in which about 60 of our Men were killed and Wounded, and by the Smallest 100. and by most other Accts two hundred of the Enemys—In this Ingagement poor Majr Leitch of Weedon's Regiment received three Wounds through his Side, of which he died on Wednesday last, after we thought him almost Well.[3] Since that nothing extraordinary has happen'd, tho⌃ an Attack from the Enemy has been, & now is, daily expected—We are strengthning our Post, as the Enemy also are theirs.

My love to, & best wishes attends my Sister & the Family, as also our Friends at Fairfield—to these please to add my Compliments to Mr Booth, & all other Friends,[4] & be assured that with the sincerest love and regard I am Dr Sir Yr Most Affecte Bro.

Go: Washington

ALS, PHi: Gratz Collection.

1. This letter has not been found. Abraham Shepherd (1754–1822) of Shepherdstown, Va. (now W.Va.), who had joined Hugh Stephenson's Virginia rifle company as a lieutenant in July 1775, was appointed a captain in Stephenson's Maryland and Virginia rifle regiment by Congress on 9 July 1776 (see *JCC,* 5:529), and he now was returning to the army after spending some time in Virginia recruiting for the new regiment. Captured at Fort Washington on 16 Nov., Shepherd was not exchanged until August 1778, when, citing poor health, he declined a commission as a captain in the 11th Virginia Regiment.

2. Philip Pendleton (1752–1802) agreed with GW in June 1771 to buy 180 acres of GW's Bullskin plantation "for £400 the Money to be paid in two years with Int[eres]t from the 25th. of next Decr." (*Diaries,* 3:37). A contract was signed that December, but Pendleton did not make any payments on either the principal or the interest, and in early 1773 he transferred his right to purchase the property to Samuel Washington, who also failed to pay for it (see ibid., 74, 155). The land was left encumbered in Samuel Washington's estate when he died in 1781 (see GW to David Stuart, 21 Sept. 1794, PHi: Dreer Collection).

3. The previous Wednesday was 2 October. GW says in his letter to Hancock of this date that Leitch died on Tuesday.

4. GW's sister-in-law was Anne Steptoe Washington. Fairfield, located near Samuel Washington's house in Berkeley County, Va., was the home of Warner Washington, Sr. Col. William Booth, who had lived previously on Nomini Creek in Westmoreland County, Va., settled in 1774 on upper Buck Marsh Run in Frederick County, Va., about two miles southwest of Fairfield (see ibid., 2:62–63, 3:293). Booth's wife, Elizabeth Aylett Booth, was the sister of Anne Aylett Washington, the wife of GW's half brother Augustine Washington.

General Orders

Head Quarters, Harlem Heights, Octob: 6th 1776.
Parole.   Countersign

Forty men, one Capt: two sub's to be furnished by the regiments at Mount Washington, to assist in ballasting the Vessels: They are to take Orders from Andrew Ober on board the sloop Nightingale—This party to be continued 'till the business is done; Besides, the above regiments stationed at Mount Washington, are to furnish Men in proportion to their strenght for the works there. Col. Lippet's Brigade is to furnish men for the Works opposite Mount Washington, to be laid out by Col. Putnam, from whom they are to take Orders.

Varick transcript, DLC:GW.

To Major General William Howe

Sir   Head Qrs Harlem Heights Octr 6th 1776

I beg leave to inform you that in consequence of my directions founded on your favor of the 21st Ulto, Governors Browne & Skeene are arrived within the Neighbourhood of this place and will be conveyed to morrow between the Hours of One & two to one of the ships of War in the North river, when it is hoped that my Lord Stirling will be permitted to return, as also Mr Lovell if he has come from Halifax.[1]

The particular manner in which you rest upon me, by your Letter of the 4th Instt, a performance of the Agreement between Genl Arnold and Captn Foster, was entirely unexpected, as I inclosed you some time ago the Resolutions of Congress upon the Subject, by which you would perceive that they, to whom I am amenable, had taken upon themselves the consideration of the matter;[2] As to the prisoners mentioned in my [letter] of the 23d[3] their Exchange shall be effected as soon as the circumstances I made you acquainted with will admit of.

The enclosed Note for Mrs Delancey you will be pleased to have conveyed by the earliest opporty.[4] I am Sir with great respect &c.

LB, in Robert Hanson Harrison's writing, DLC:GW; two copies, P.R.O. 30/55, Carleton Papers; Varick transcript, DLC:GW.

1. Joseph Reed conveyed GW's instructions regarding the implementation of this exchange to an unidentified correspondent in a letter of 7 October. "The General," Reed writes, "Desires you would Just before you get to Spiking Devil Creek draw the Curtains close & keep them so till you get near the Shiping—then you will wait for Ld Stirling—The Genl Desires his Compliments to the Governor [Browne] & that He should have been happy to have Received them here if the usual Restraints to which they must Submit in passing this a fortified Camp would not prove more inconvenient than any Pleasure or Convenience which they could derive from it" (owned [1993] by Mr. Richard Maass, White Plains, N.Y.).

2. See GW to Howe and Burgoyne, 15 July 1776.

3. The copies in P.R.O. both read "my Letter."

4. This reply to Elizabeth Colden De Lancey has not been found. Howe forwarded the note to her with a cover letter of 7 Oct. that reads: "General Howe presents his Compliments to Mrs D'Lancey, & has the honor of Enclosing General Washingtons answer to her Note, in which he shoud have had more pleasure had it been correspondent to her wishes" (DRC).

From Colonels Henry Knox and Rufus Putnam

Camp below Kings bridge,
May it please your Excy   Octobr 6th 1776.

Agreable to your directions, we view'd the hill, East of Mount Washington, & the camp in general, & beg leave to make the following report Viz.

That the highest part of said hill, be secured by a fort, principally made of the timber now standing there, strengthened with a good abattis, form'd of the tops of the trees, which are to be cut down; And that on the North part of the hill, a redoubt be form'd, to scour the roads, & river adjacent.[1]

That at the three trees, on the East side Harlem river, a considerable work be form'd, which shall constitute the right of the camp, on the heights of West Chester; And that the ridge of hills stretching from this on the East side of Harlem river towards Morissania, be fortify'd with Redoubts.

That on Valentine's Hill near to Williams's brook, a strong capacious work, be made, which shall form the left of the works of the West Chester camp,[2] & that from this, to the three trees upon the right, every advantage to be taken of the ground, by throwing up redoubts, lines & abattis, to render the line complete from right to left.

All the roads, passes, & woods in front, of this line towards

Hunts and Wyllet's points,[3] & the point of Morissania be secured, with Fleches, Redoubts, Abattis & every other obstruction, to retard the progress of the Enemy.

That a chain of Redoubts, be completed from Fort Washington to the lower lines towards Haerlem Cove on Hudson's river.[4] We are respectfully yr Excys Most Obedt hhble Servts

Signed—Henry Knox Col. Ary
Rufus Putnam Engr

Copy, MHi: Heath Papers. GW enclosed this document with his first letter to Heath of 9 October.

1. Laurel Hill, located on the west bank of the Harlem River at present-day 192d Street and Audubon Avenue, was fortified with two small redoubts during the next few weeks. Defended by Col. William Baxter's Pennsylvania flying camp troops, those works were overrun on 16 Nov. by the Black Watch Regiment during the British attack on Fort Washington. The British subsequently fortified the hill with a more substantial work that they named Fort George.

2. Knox and Putnam are referring to Valentine's Hill on the Boston post road about two miles east of King's Bridge and about a mile west of the place where Williams's Bridge crossed the Bronx River. Isaac Valentine lived near the hill bearing his name in a house that stands in the present-day Bronx at Bainbridge Avenue and East 208th Street.

3. Willett's Point, now called Clason Point, is on the north side of the East River about three miles west of Throg's Neck and about a mile and a half east of Hunt's Point.

4. Harlem Cove, or Manhattanville, is on the Hudson near present-day 130th Street.

From Major General Philip Schuyler

Dear Sir   Albany October 6th 1776

By Mr Bennet, who arrived Yesterday, I was honored with your Excellency's very obliging Favor of the 30th Ultimo.

I should have been much happier than I am if the Resolutions of Congress of the 25th Ultimo had not put it out of my power to be in Sentiment with you on the Resolution of the 14th of the same Month. Without advising me that I am no longer in Command, they resolve that "Mr Stockden and Mr Clymer" are "appointed a Committee to proceed to Tyonderoga to confer with General Gates with Respect to the Army under his Command."[1]

I believe I shall be able to collect about forty thousand Boards, part of them are already gone from hence, together with a considerable Number of Rafters—I believe the Committee of this place will be able to procure about 20,000 Boards & they have employed people to procure the Timber Mr Ayres requested of them.[2]

Be so good as to order the Quarter Master General to send me about two thousand pounds on Account or if it makes no Difference, I will draw on the Military Chest here.

I am in great Hopes that you have so embarrassed the Enemy by your Movement from New York that they will find it impossible to form and execute any plan that will materially distress you in the Remainder of this Campaign.

The Army in this Quarter is well supplied with provision and I trust will continue to be so—The three Row Gallies are gone to join the Fleet and a fourth will be very soon equipped—I do not apprehend that the Enemy will be able to do any Thing of Consequence to the Northward, unless they should suspend their Operations until the Term of Inlistment of our Troops expires. I confess, my Hopes of seeing an Army speedily raised on the new Establishment are not very sanguine; that the Soldiers are to pay for their Cloathing will be a great Obstacle, as the price of every Necessary is so extremely high—perhaps it would have been as well if Congress had enumerated the Articles each Soldier should be furnished with, and determined the Stoppage that should be made for it. I am dear Sir with every friendly Wish & every respectful Sentiment Your Excellency's most obedient humble Servt

Ph: Schuyler

LS, DLC:GW; LB, NN: Schuyler Papers.

1. Congress created this committee on 25 Sept., and the next day it elected Richard Stockton (1730–1781) of New Jersey and George Clymer of Pennsylvania as its members (see *JCC*, 5:822–23, 828).

2. On the orders of former Q.M. Gen. Stephen Moylan, Benjamin George Eyre appeared before the Albany committee of correspondence on 21 Sept. to request its aid in procuring boards and other materials to build barracks for twenty thousand men (see *Minutes of the Albany and Schenectady Committees,* 1:560–61, and Moylan's certificate for Eyre, 27 Sept. 1776, DNA:PCC, item 41).

Letter not found: from Jonathan Trumbull, Sr., 6 Oct. 1776. On 15 Oct. GW wrote to Trumbull: "I was last night favored with your letter of the 6th instant."

From Major General Artemas Ward

Sir   Boston 6 October 1776.

Yesterday I received from Mr Glover, Agent at Marblehead, a Box of broad Swords, which he lately found in the Scotch Ship Ann, that was taken some time since.[1] Also received from Mr Bradford, Agent for Continental prizes, the inclosed Invoice, of articles which he has in his hands. The reason he gave for delaying it so long, was, the plaids were infected with the small pox, and he thought it necessary to cleanse and air them considerable time before they were used.[2] I am Your Excellency's Obedient Humble Servant

                                                    Artemas Ward

LS, DLC:GW; LB, MHi: Ward Papers.

1. For the capture of the British transport *Anne*, see Ward to GW, 9 June, and note 2. Continental Prize Agent Jonathan Glover previously had given most of the arms from the *Anne* to his brother, Col. John Glover, for the use of his regiment (see Ward to GW, 29 July).

2. John Bradford's invoice of this date lists not only plaid cloth but also camp kettles, canteens, candlesticks, tablespoons, rugs, and blankets (DLC:GW).

Letter not found: from John Augustine Washington, 6 Oct. 1776. In a letter dated 6–19 Nov. GW wrote to his brother John: "I have had the pleasure to receive your Letter of the 6th Ulto."

To Lund Washington

Dear Lund,   Heights of Haerlem Octr 6th 1776

Your Letter of the 25th Ulto has reached my hands since the date of my last about this day Week.[1] nothing material has happened since that time—We are strengthning ourselves in this Post, as the Enemy also are in theirs. They have moved some of their Ships up the North River opposite to their own Lines, & a little below ours; whether with a view to cover their own Flanks, or at a proper time to aid in their Attack upon our present Post, time only can discover. We have been in daily expectation of having our Quarters beat up, but as yet nothing of the Kind has been attempted—On Wednesday last I expected to have had some pretty warm work, but it turnd out otherwise—It arose

from this—I sent a Party of 1000 Men to cover some Waggons
in bringing of Grain from a Place where I expected opposition
from them. this occasioned them to strike their Tents, & put
their whole Line in Motion, & of course brought all our Men
under Arms; but nothing more came of it, except that we went
on, & brought of all the Grain.[2]

Had I been left to the dictates of my own judgment, New York
should have been laid in Ashes before I quitted it—to this end
I applied to Congress, but was absolutely forbid[3]—that they will
have cause to repent the Order, I have not a moments doubt of,
nor never had, as it was obvious to me (covered as it may be by
their Ships) that it will be next to impossible for us to dispossess
them of it again as all their Supplies come by Water, whilst ours
were derived by Land; besides this, by leaving it standing, the
Enemy are furnished with warm & comfortable Barracks, in
which their whole Force may be concentred—the place secured
by a small garrison (if they chuse it) having their Ships round
it, & only a narrow Neck of Land to defend—and their principal
force left at large to act against us, or to remove to any other
place for the purpose of harrassing us. this in my judgment may
be set down amg one of the capitol errors of Congress.

Their Motives for sending Deputies to hear Lord Howes proposals were, in my opinion, tolerably well founded—they had
no Idea of treating with him otherwise than as Independant
States—they declared so, previous to the appointing of their
Commissioners—But as Lord Howe, a thorough paced Court-
ier, had taken uncommon pains to signify at all times, and upon
all occasions, that he was vested with full powers to accomodate
matters upon better terms than the Americans ever had askd,
and became more importunate, as our Indifference Increased,
it had the effect intended by him, on three classes of People.
Our open and avowed Enemys, together with the Officers and
Soldiers of their Army, were exasperated at it, from a conviction
that our Aim, at the beginning, was Independance; the Neutrals
had this doctrine so strongly inculcated into them by the Tories,
that they began to adopt the same Sentiments & wonderd that
we would not accept of more than we asked—whilst it remaind
necessary to convince the third class who were really friendly,
but great sticklers for the powers of, and the advantages to be
derived from the long expected Commissioners, that the whole

was a falacy, calculated to deceive, as I suppose they now are; since it evidently appears that Lord Howe had nothing more to propose than that, if we would Submit, his Majesty would consider whether we should be hung or not. If this meeting shd have a bad effect with foreign Powers, who may be unacquainted with the inducements to it, it will be unlucky.

In speaking of New York, I had forgot to mention that Providence—or some good honest Fellow, has done more for us than we were disposed to do for ourselves, as near One fourth of the City is supposed to be consumed. however enough of it remains to answer their purposes.

I have got Harry Young here, & do not know what to do with him—he made his escape from the Roebuck and came to me at New York—I am affraid to entrust him to go home by himself & here he is useless to me.[4] remember me to all friends—give the Inclosed Letter to my Brother a safe passage if it should even be delayed by it.[5] I am with sincere regard Dr Lund Yr Affecte friend

Go: Washington

ALS (photocopy), CtY: Washington Family Papers.

1. Lund Washington's letter of 25 Sept. has not been found. GW's most recent letter to him was the one of 30 September.

2. Maj. Stephen Kemble of the British 60th Regiment says in his diary entry for Wednesday, 2 Oct.: "The Rebels made a Movement from Morris's House and marched about 2,000 Men into Harlem plains, supposed to take off the Forage" (*Kemble Papers*, 1:91).

3. See GW to Hancock, 2 Sept., and Hancock to GW, 3 Sept., and note 1.

4. Henry Young, an indentured stonemason whom GW had purchased in 1773, apparently was one of the three servants belonging to GW who were taken aboard the British warship *Roebuck* on 24 July when the *Roebuck* was anchored in Potomac River near the mouth of Aquia Creek in Stafford County (see John Parke Custis to GW, 8 Aug. 1776, and note 4). The *Roebuck* arrived in New York Harbor by 14 Aug. (see Tatum, *Serle's Journal*, 63), and it subsequently participated in the British operations against GW's army. Young eventually returned to Mount Vernon. He worked for GW for wages from 1778 to 1781, and in 1781 he made repairs to Mount Vernon.

5. GW apparently is referring to his letter to Samuel Washington of 5 October.

General Orders

Head Quarters, Harlem Heights, Octob: 7th 1776
Parole   Countersign[1]

Capt: William McWilliams, of the 3rd Virginia Regiment is to do the duty of Brigade Major in Col. Weedon's Brigade, 'till further orders.[2]

Representation having been made to the General, that numbers of the Picquet Guard are absent from their Posts, under pretence of fetching provisions, and water; He positively orders, that every man (as well Officers, as Soldiers) shall carry provisions with, or have it brought to them at their posts, by their Messmates; as the safety of the Army depends too much on their diligence and attention, to admit of such practices—It is moreover expected of the Officer commanding the Picquet, that he does not, under any pretence whatever, suffer the men to straggle from their respective Posts, without they are sent upon scouting parties by himself; But always to have them in readiness to give such effectual opposition, as to allow time to the line to turn out; which being the end and design of Guards, is defeated if the men, who mount, are not in a posture to give instant opposition.

The Quarter Master General is immediately to provide twenty Wood-Axes, for the Picquet Guards, in front of our lines; When provided, he is to deliver them to the Officer commanding the Picquet, who is to see that they are delivered over to the officer relieving, and so from one to the other—the Officer failing will be answerble—These Axes are intended for the purpose of providing Wood, and erecting Hutts for the Guards, which last ought not to be delayed.

The Brigadiers, and Officers commanding Regiments, are to prevent the irregular and promiscuous placing of Hutts, and to see that they are built in such a manner, as to stand the weather and weight of Snow, which may lodge on them, that no accident may befal the men.

Serjt George Douglass of Capt: Fosters Company, late McDougall's Regiment, being convicted by a General Court Martial whereof Col. Weedon is president of "Embezelling and selling provisions, belonging to the Company"—is sentenced to be reduced to the Ranks, and whipped 39 Lashes—to be continued under Provost-Guard for "Mutinous Speeches and disrespectful language of the Commander in Chief"[3]—George Harris of Capt: Howell's Company, Col. Wind's Regiment tried by the same Court Martial, and convicted of "Desertion"—is ordered to be whipped 39 Lashes.[4]

The General approves the above sentences, and the Provost Marshall is to see the sentence on Harris, executed to morrow morning at Guard mounting.

Varick transcript, DLC:GW.

1. "Williams' Diary," 49:50, gives the parole for this date as "Chester" and the countersign as "Newtown."

2. William McWilliams (1751–1799) of Spotsylvania County, Va., had been commissioned a captain in the 3d Virginia Regiment in February 1776, and prior to this day's appointment, he had served as regimental adjutant. McWilliams was an aide-de-camp to Lord Stirling from October 1777 to May 1778 when he resigned from the army (see General Orders, 7 May 1778). In July 1780 McWilliams became a major in the Spotsylvania County militia, and in August 1781 he was promoted to lieutenant colonel.

3. Douglass, who had been acquitted of mutiny and sedition in July (see General Orders, 7 July 1776), was convicted on 6 Oct. of stealing and selling flour drawn for some of the men of his company (see the proceedings of the general court-martial, that date, DLC:GW). For Douglass's trial on the second charge against him, see General Orders, 8 October. Douglass's company was commanded by William A. Forbes, who entered Col. Alexander McDougall's 1st New York Regiment as a captain-lieutenant and was promoted to captain on 10 Aug. 1776.

4. George Harris, a private in the 1st New Jersey Regiment, confessed at his trial on this day "that he deserted from the Regiment last May when the Regiment was at Albany, & about three Weeks ago was taken up at Brunswick & sent a Prisoner to the Camp at Haerlem" (proceedings of the general court-martial, 7 Oct., DLC:GW). Silas Howell (1746–1812) of Sussex County, N.J., served as captain of the 1st New Jersey Regiment from 14 Nov. 1775 until his resignation on 26 Sept. 1780.

To Comte d'Ennery

Head Quarters Harlem Heights
Sir   10 Miles from New York 7th Octobr 1776

I yesterday had the honor of receiving your Letter of the 4th Augt and I take the earliest Opportunity of testifying[1] the pleasure I have in complying with your request, by immediately ordering the Release of Monsr Dechambault. He shall be accommodated with a Passage in the first Vessel that sails from

Philadelphia to the French Colonies in the West Indies. Had it not been for your Interposition Monr Dechambault must have remained a prisoner till released by a Cartel, but I could not hesitate to comply with a Request made by a Nobleman who by his public Countenance of our Cause has rendered such essential Services to the thirteen united independent States of America, whose Armies I have the honor to command. I have the honor to be Sir with the highest Esteem yr most obt Sert.

LB, in Tench Tilghman's writing, DLC:GW; copy, DLC:GW; Varick transcript, DLC:GW. The LB is addressed: "To Monsr L'Compte D'Emery Govr Genl of the French part of St Domingo." The receiver's copy of this letter, which GW forwarded to Congress with his first letter to Hancock of this date, has not been found.

1. Tilghman inadvertently wrote "testitying" on the manuscript.

To John Hancock

Sir   Head Qrs Heights of Harlem Octor the 7th 1776
I do myself the honor of transmitting to you, a Copy of a Letter from the Compte D'Emery, Govr Genl of the French part of St Domingo, which I received Yesterday, and also my Answer, which I have enclosed and left open for the consideration of Congress, wishing that it may be sealed, if they approve of the Seiur De Chambeau's releasment, and which I think may be attended with many valuable consequences. If Congress concur in sentiment with me, they will be pleased to give direction for his passage by the first Opportunity to the French Islands; if they do not, I shall be obliged by your returning my Letter.[1]

I have also the pleasure of inclosing a Copy of a Letter from Monsr P. Pennet which came to hand last night and which contains intelligence of an agreable and interesting nature, for which I beg leave to refer you to the Copy.

The polite manner in which Monsr Pennet has requested to be One of my Aid de Camps, demands my acknowledgements. As the Appointment will not be attended with any expence and will shew a proper regard for his complaisance and the Attachment he is pleased to express for the service of the American States, I shall take the liberty of complying with his requisition and transmit him a Brevet Commission, provided the same shall agreable to Congress. their sentiments upon the subject you will be kind enough to favor me with, by the first Opportunity.[2]

The Enclosed Letter for the Seignr De Chambeau you will please to forward to him if he is to be enlarged after closing It.[3]

Before I conclude I must take the liberty to observe that I am under no small difficulties on account of the French Gentlemen that are here in consequence of the Commissions they have received, having no means to employ them or to afford them an Opportunity of rendering that service, they themselves wish to give, or which perhaps is expected by the public.[4] Their want of our language is an objection to their being joined to any of the Regiments here at this time, were there vacancies, and not other Obstacles. These considerations induce me to wish, that Congr⟨ess⟩ will adopt and point out some particular ⟨m⟩ode to be observed respecting them—What it should be, they will be best able to determine—But to me it appears, that their being here now, can be attended with no valuable consequences, and that as the power of appointing Officers for the New Army is vested in the Conventions &c. of the Several States, it will be necessary for Congress to direct them to be provided for in the Regiments to be raised according to the Ranks they would wish 'em to bear, or I am convinced, they will never be taken in, let their merit be what it may, or to form them into a distinct Corps, which may be encreased in time. they seem to be Genteel, sensible Men, and I have no doubt of their making good Officers as soon as they can learn as much of our language as to make themselves well understood, but unless Congress interfere with their particular directions to the States, they will never be incorporated in any of the Regiments to be raised and without they are, they will be entirely at a loss and in the most irksome situation for some thing to do as they now are. I have the Honor to be Sir your Most H. Servt

Go: Washington

LS, in Robert Hanson Harrison's writing, DNA:PCC, item 152; LB, DLC:GW; copy, DNA:PCC, item 169; Varick transcript, DLC:GW. Congress read this letter on 11 Oct. and referred it to the Board of War (*JCC*, 6:866).

1. See Comte d'Ennery to GW, 4 Aug., and GW to d'Ennery, 7 October. Congress on 11 Oct. agreed to the release of Chambault (see ibid.).

2. See Pierre Penet to GW, 3 August. Congress on 14 Oct. approved of Penet's appointment as a brevet aide-de-camp to GW (ibid., 869–70).

3. This letter has not been identified.

4. GW is referring to the four French officers from Martinique who received Continental commissions from Congress on 19 Sept. (ibid., 5:783–84) and who were introduced to GW in a brief letter that Richard Peters, secretary of the Board of War, wrote to him on 20 Sept. (ALS, DLC:GW). Christian de Colerus and the marquis de Malmedy were majors by brevet; Jean Louis de Vernejout was a captain by brevet; and Jean Louis Imbert was an engineer without particular appointment. On 4 Nov. Robert Hanson Harrison wrote the Board of War: "Agreable to your request his Excellency [GW] has consulted with Genl Lee upon the best mode for employing the French Gentlemen and of making them serviceable. The result is, that they should be appointed to Regiments by Congress according to the Ranks they have been pleased to give 'em, and with the same pay as is allowed other Officers in such cases. their want of our Language is rather an objection, but it is hoped they will attain a sufficient knowledge of it, 'ere it be long, to be of great service, and that in the Interim their advice & assistance in directing of works may be of use where they may be stationed" (DNA:PCC, item 152).

To John Hancock

Sir.   Head Quarters Heights of Haerlem Octobr 7th 1776.
Dr Skinner having been very urgent and pressing to go to Philadelphia, in order to procure medicine for the sick of his regiment, I could by no means refuse my assent to his proposition; By him I beg leave to inform you, that the applications of the Regimental Surgeons, are very frequent and importunate; & it is not in my power to satisfy their demands; their situation will be fully made known by Doctr Morgan's letter to one of my Aid de Camps, in answer to one wrote to him on that subject, which I have inclos'd to you, for yr consideration.[1] I have the honor to be Yr Most Obedt Servt

Go: Washington

LS, in William Grayson's writing, PPL; LB, DLC:GW; Varick transcript, DLC:GW. Congress read this letter on 14 Oct. (*JCC*, 6:869).
1. John Morgan's letter, which has not been identified, was referred by Congress on 14 Oct. to the medical committee (ibid.).

From Major General William Heath

Dear General   Kingsbridge Octr 7th 1776
Inclosed is the Disposition which I have made of the Troops of this Division which is to be observed in Case of attack[1]—Colo.

Knox has a map of new York & its vicinity by which your Excellency may Determine if the Disposition is properly made[.] I did not See the map untill the Disposition was Compleated—I have this Day ordered a party to the Heighth on Harlem River who are to throw up a work there as the Massachusetts militia are nearby[.] I hope your Excellency will order Some of them to this Post where I am Sure they might be well Employed in Fortifying the Post[.] This However I humbly Submit to your Excellencys Determination. I am &c.

W. Heath

ADfS, MHi: Heath Papers.
    1. A copy of this long, detailed disposition dated 3 Oct. and addressed to Col. John Chester is in MHi: Heath Papers; see also Force, *American Archives*, 5th ser., 2:855–56.
    Samuel Blachley Webb had written Heath the previous day at GW's direction to inform him "that in the night about twelve oClock our Men distinctly heard the Enemy throwing tools into Boats from Montrasors & Blackwells Islands—and that Boats were moveing up [the] Sound most of the Night. abt day light Twenty Boat Load of Men—row'd up & Landed on one of the Islands call'd the two Brothers. The General [GW] thinks the above Manoevre should not in the least draw your Attention from Morrissea [Morrisania], tho: a good look out should be keep [kept] on all their Movements—& at the same time bids Me add 'that no time should be lost in takeing possession of the Hill['] you yesterday mentioned to him—below the Gut" (MHi: Heath Papers). North Brother and South Brother islands are in the East River a short distance east of Montresor's (now Randall's) and Blackwell's (now Ward's) islands.

Orders to Major General Benjamin Lincoln

Sir.   [Headquarters, Harlem Heights, 7 October 1776]
    As I am credibly inform'd that the inhabitants along the Sound carry on a frequent communication with the Enemy on Long Island, you are hereby instructed to collect all the boats, & other small craft on the sound, from Horse Neck downwards to any extent you shall think proper, & convey them to any place you shall concieve to be most convenient. Givn under my hand at Head Quarters this 7th Octob. 1776.

Go: Washington

LS, in William Grayson's writing, MHi: Waterston Papers.

From Major General Philip Schuyler

Dear Sir   Albany October 7th 1776

I am to acknowlege the Honor of your Excellency's Favor of the 4th Instant.

I have long since written to Congress for a Supply of Nails, all I can procure in this Quarter are insufficient for the Works at Tyonderoga, so that I fear no Barracks will be built in this Quarter, unless a speedy Supply arrives from Philadelphia—We have Nothing new in this Quarter worthy communicating. I am Dr Sir most unfeignedly and sincerely Your Excellency's most obedient humble Servant

Ph: Schuyler

LS, DLC:GW; LB, NN: Schuyler Papers.

General Orders

Head Quarters, Harlem Heights, Octobr 8th 1776.

Parole   Countersign[1]

The late Serjeant Douglass of Capt. Foster's Company, late McDougall's Regiment, being convicted by a General Court Martial, whereof Col. Weedon was President of "Mutinous Speeches and speaking disrespectfully of the Commander in Chief" and sentenced to receive 39 Lashes—The General approves the sentence, and orders it to be executed at the usual time and place—This Offender being a very bad character, is to be continued in the Provost Guard 'till further Orders.[2]

The Commanding Officer of the Rangers having represented, that Soldiers are continually straggling down to Harlem, and other Places; frequently without Arms—and that when he has apprehended, and sent them to their regiments, no farther notice has been taken of them; As this is a plain breach of General Orders, the General hopes there is some mistake in the matter; however to prevent it in future, he now orders that no officer or soldier (Rangers excepted) go on any pretence beyond the lines, without leave from himself, a Major General, the Brigadier of the day, or the Adjutant General, in writing; unless either of those officers are with them in person: And in order to distinguish the Rangers,[3] they are to wear something *white* round their Arms. If any such Straggler is found hereafter, he is to be sent to the quarter-guard of the regiment, tried by a Regimental Court Martial, and receive ten Lashes immediately.

There is now an issuing Store for Ammunition, near Genl Spencer's quarters, the Officers of every regiment will be responsible if there is any deficiency in their regiments, as they may now receive a full supply by making a Return of the State of their Ammunition, and getting an Order from the Adjutant General.

The Brigade lately commanded by Genl Mifflin is to be under the care of Lord Stirling who is just returned from his Captivity.

The General desires the commanding Officers of each Regiment, or Corps, will give in a list of the names of the Officers & Men,[4] who were killed, taken, or missing in the Action of the 27th of August on Long Island, and since that period: He desires the Returns may be correct, and that any persons who have it in their power, will give in the Returns of this kind in behalf of any Militia Regiments which are discharged.[5]

The General, to prevent any plea of ignorance, again repeats his order against all kinds of Gaming, as destructive and pernicious to the service: He hopes the officers will set no examples of this kind, and that they will punish it among the men.

The General is surprised to find that manning the lines every morning, is discontinued—He desires that the practice of doing it, for the future, may not be omitted, unless contradicted by General Orders.

The Quarter-Master General is to use the greatest diligence, in providing straw for the accomodation of the troops.

Lieut. Kidd of Col. Smallwood's regiment, convicted by a Court Martial whereof Col. Ware was President of a breach of General Orders, in "Taking fatigue-men from their duty"—is sentenced to be dismisd the service—Ensign Fairly of the regiment late McDougall's, tried by the same Court Martial, for the same, is acquitted and discharged from Arrest. Capt. Hardenburgh of Col. Ritzema's Regiment, convicted by the same Court Martial of "Defrauding his men"—is sentenced to be cashiered, and his name, place of abode, and offence, published agreeable to the 2nd & 4th late additional Articles of war.[6]

The General approves each of the above sentences, and orders to be executed.

Varick transcript, DLC:GW.

1. "Williams' Diary," 49:50, gives the parole for this date as "France" and the countersign as "Spain."

2. At George Douglass's trial on this charge the previous day, Ensign Bonner testified that he heard Douglass, while confined for disobeying orders, say "that the Generals had sold the Troops upon Long Island, & had brought the Army up to Haarlem to sell them there." Douglass's company commander, Capt. William A. Forbes, testified that he heard Douglass sing "*God Save the King*" and then say: "*He* was his King. & he would have no other King which we should soon see" (see the proceedings of the general court-martial, 7 Oct., DLC:GW). For Douglass's previous conviction on another charge, see General Orders, 7 October.

3. "Williams' Diary," 49:50, says: "to distinguish the rangers from the rest of the army."

4. "Williams' Diary," 49:50, says: "of officers & men respectively belonging to them."

5. These returns, which GW wanted in order to verify that the prisoners being offered for exchange by the British actually had been in American service, apparently were not submitted until the following month. A number of them variously dated between 17 and 23 Nov. are printed in Force, *American Archives*, 5th ser., 3:715–30. See also GW to William Heath and Charles Lee, 14 Nov., DLC:GW.

6. The undated proceedings of the court-martial that tried these three officers are in DLC:GW. John Kidd (1753–1826) of Harford County, Md., who had been commissioned a second lieutenant in Col. William Smallwood's Maryland regiment on 2 Jan. 1776 and was promoted to first lieutenant on 9 July, pleaded guilty to the charge against him but said that "he was not acquai[n]ted with the Orders." Lt. Marcus Cole, an engineer at the fortifications on which Kidd's men were assigned to work, testified that "as soon as Lieut. Kidd had marched his Men to the Fort, he drew an Order for the Rum and paraded them to march Home." Although Cole informed Kidd that "'twas contrary to general Orders to go home to Breakfast," Kidd left with his detachment and did not return until after 11:00 A.M. Before noon Kidd attempted to turn in his men's tools because it was raining, but his party immediately was ordered back to work by Capt. Thomas Woolford of Maryland, who testified that he told Kidd that "the Rain was very trifeling." Woolford dismissed the party for dinner at 1:00 P.M., and Kidd did not return that day. Kidd testified in his defense "that he was sick and unable to go in the Afternoon."

James Fairlie (1757–1830), who had been appointed an ensign in the 1st New York Regiment on 24 Feb. 1776, confessed "that he marched the fatigue Men off contrary to general Orders, but that it was the next Morning after the Orders were issued, and he had not heard them, And that he was under the Command of Lieut. Kidd, and it was by his Order that the Men marched off." Arendt Van Hook, adjutant of the 1st New York Regiment, testified "that he did not that Evening read the Orders to the Regt as they came very late, the next Morning, he says he mentioned the Orders to the Men, but does not know that Ensn Fairly was present." Fairlie became a second lieutenant in the

2d New York Regiment on 21 Nov. 1776, and from July 1778 to the end of the war he was an aide-de-camp to Baron von Steuben with the rank of major.

Cornelius Hardenbergh was convicted on the testimony of two lieutenants, Edward Lounsberry and Charles Newkirk, who said that Hardenbergh had not paid his men all of their wages and subsistence at Kingston, N.Y., in April and that although he had promised to rectify matters when the company went to New York, he had not done so.

Francis Ware, Sr., of Port Tobacco, Md., who had served in the Maryland assembly before the war and in the provincial convention during 1774 and 1775, was appointed lieutenant colonel of Smallwood's regiment on 2 Jan. 1776. Ware was named colonel of the 1st Maryland Regiment in December 1776, but he resigned his commission the following February. During the summer of 1777, the Maryland council appointed him county lieutenant of Charles County.

To John Hancock

Head Qurs Heights of Harlem

Sir   Octobr 8[–9]th 1776

Since I had the honor of writing you Yesterday, I have been favoured with a Letter from the Honble Council of Massachusetts bay, covering One from Richard Derby Esqr., a Copy of which is herewith transmitted, as it contains intelligence of an important and interesting nature.[1]

As an Exchange of prisoners is about to take place, I am induced from a Question stated in a Letter I received from Govr Trumbull this morning,[2] to ask the Opinion of Congress in what manner the States that have had the care of them, are to [be][3] reimbursed the Expences incurred on their Account. My want of information in this instance or whether any account is to be sent in with the prisoners, would not allow me to give him an Answer, as nothing that I recollect has ever been said upon the Subject. he also mentions another matter Viz. Whether such privates as are Mechanicks & Others who may desire to remain with us, should be obliged to return; In respect to the latter, I conceive there can be no doubt of our being under a necessity of returning the whole, a proposition having been made on our part for a Genl exchange and that agreed to;[4] Besides the ballance of prisoners is greatly against us & I am informed it was particularly stipulated by Genl Montgomery, that all those that were taken in Canada, should be exchanged when ever a Cartel was settled for the purpose. Under these circumstances, I should suppose the Several Committees having the care of them, should be instructed to make the most exact returns of the whole, however willing a part should be to continue with us; At the same time I should think it not improper to inform them of the reasons leading to the measure, and that they should be invited to escape afterwards, which in all probability they may effect without much difficulty[5] if they are attached to us, extending their influence to many more & bringing them away also.

The situation of our Affairs, and the present establishment of the Army, requiring our most vigorous exertions to ingage a New One, I presume it will be necessary to furnish the paymaster General, as early as possible, with Money to pay the bounty lately resolved on to such Men as will inlist. prompt pay perhaps may have a happy effect and induce the continuance of some who are here, but without it, I am certain that nothing can be done—nor have we time to lose in making the Experiment. but then it may be asked, who is to recruit—or who can consider themselves as Officers for that purpose till the Conventions of the different States have made the appointments.

Yesterday afternoon the exchange between Lord Stirling and Govr Browne was carried into execution and his Lordship is now here; he confirms the intelligence mentioned by Captn Souther about the Transports he met, by the arrival of the Daphne Man of War (a Twenty Gun Ship) a few days ago with Twelve Ships under her Convoy having light Horse on board.[6] they sailed with about Twenty in each and lost about Eighty in their passage besides those in the Vessel taken by Captn Souther. he further adds, that he had heard it acknowledged more than Once, that in the Action of the 16th Ulto the Enemy had a Hundred men killed, about Sixty Highlanders of the 42d Regiment and Forty of the light infantry—This confession coming from themselves, we may reasonably conclude did not exaggerate the Number.

In pursuance of the Resolve which you were pleased to transmit me, I called upon the Members who concurred in the acquittal of McCumber to assign their reasons. Inclosed you have their Answer, by which you will perceive the direction has given them great uneasiness, and from the information I have received, it has become a matter of much more general concern, than could have been expected, in so much that I will take the liberty to advise that it may rest where it is, having heard that most of the Officers have become party to it and consider that the Resolve materially affects the whole.[7]

Octobr the 9th. About 8 OClock this Morning, Two Ships of 44 Guns each, supposed to be the Roebuck & Phenix and a Frigate of 20 Guns with Three or four Tenders got under way from about Bloomingdale where they had been laying some time and stood with an easy southerly breeze towards our Chevaux de Frise, which we hoped would have interrupted their passage while our Batteries played upon them, But to our surprize and mortification, they ran thro without the least difficulty and without receiving any apparent damage from our Forts tho they kept up a heavy Fire from both sides of the River. their destination or views cannot be known with certainty, but most probably they are sent to stop the Navigation and cut off the supplies of boards &c. which we should have received and of which we are in great need.[8] they are standing up, and I have dispatched an Express to the Convention of this State, that notice may be immediately communicated to Genl Clinton at the Highland Fortifications to put him on his guard in case they should have any designs against them and that precautions may be taken to prevent the Craft belonging to the River falling into their Hands.[9] I have the honor to be with great esteem Sir Yr Most Obedt Servt

Go: Washington

LS, in Robert Hanson Harrison's writing, DNA:PCC, item 152; LB, DLC:GW; copy, DNA:PCC, item 169; Varick transcript, DLC:GW. Congress read this letter on 11 Oct. and referred it to the Board of War (*JCC*, 6:866).

1. See the Massachusetts Council to GW, 3 October.

2. See Jonathan Trumbull, Sr., to GW, 2 October.

3. This word appears in the LB.

4. The LB, which is also in Harrison's writing, contains a draft version of the first part of this paragraph which has been struck out. It reads: "In consequence of a Letter which came to hand this morning from Govr Trumbull in part on the Subject of an Exchange of prisoners, I would beg leave to lay before Congress, with a view of obtaining their Opinion as soon as possible, the substance of Two Questions contained therein, Viz. Whether such privates as are Mechanics & Others who wish to remain in the Country shall be obliged

to return; and in what manner the expences and charges incurred on account of the prisoners are to be defrayed[.] In respect to the first, it appears to me."

5. The LB reads "they may easily effect."

6. For Capt. Daniel Souther's intelligence, see the Massachusetts Council to GW, 3 October. The *Daphne* and its convoy arrived at New York on 3 Oct. (see Tatum, *Serle's Journal,* 118). Tench Tilghman says in his letter to William Duer of 8 Oct. that because Stirling "was on b[o]ard Ship the whole time of his captivity he can Say very little of the Situation or intentions of the enemy— He apprehends they are not so strong as they give out as he often heard them mention the want of their reinforcement, he confirms the account of the bad blood between the English & Hessian Troops[.] the latter plunder whig & tory indiscriminately & without punishment while the former are under the severest restrictions" (MHi: Sparks transcripts).

7. For Congress's resolve of 30 Sept. regarding the court-martial of Ens. Matthew Macomber, see General Orders, 5 October. In the enclosed unaddressed document dated 7 Oct., the nine officers who sat on the court, including both those who found Macomber guilty of plundering and those who acquitted him of the charge, unanimously refused to give reasons for the court's verdict. "It has ever been an established Maxim," they say, "that Judges should be free from all Influence, that their Opinions should proceed from the Dictates of an honest & upright Mind, and that no bias to any particular party or fear of Censure should have Weight in their Judgements—Should we Consent to assign reasons for our Verdict on Mcumbers trial, we think it would be establishing a Precedent of the most dangerous Consequence. Whenever the Sentence of a Court Martial is disagreeable to a Commander in chief, or any other Power, the Members who do not Concur in Opinion with them are expos'd to their Resentment. This certainly must influence some persons, & be of dangerous tendency—Men of Spirit will not attend the Courts, and Servile Cringing Men should not be entrusted with the lives of their Fellows.

"We do not mean absolutely to refuse complying with the Order of Congress: Let us be convinc'd that we ought to do it, and reasons shall be given. We are Young & inexperienced in these matters, and are only guided by the natural impropriety of the thing. Have not the Congress thought it improper? They have. By the last Articles of War every Member is to be Sworn not to disclose the Opinion of any particular Member. Are laws to be made which are not binding on Legislators?" (DNA:PCC, item 152).

8. The *Roebuck* and *Phoenix* were accompanied through the obstructions at Fort Washington by the frigate *Tartar,* the armed vessel *Tryal,* and two tenders. The Americans, Capt. Andrew Snape Hamond of the *Roebuck* says in his account of events, "had taken a great deal of pains to throw a Boom a cross [the Hudson], by sinking Vessels & frames of Timber, to prevent our ships from passing up. They had placed these obstructions in the narrowest part, where the River is about 12 hundred Yards wide, between two High Lands, having Fort Washington on the Right, and Fort Constitution [Fort Lee] on the left, each containing several batterys of heavy cannon, placed at some distance along the shore, and six row Galleys with each a large Gun in their prow guarded the boom in front; so that, we understood, they looked upon it to be

perfectly secure: and it is possible, from seeing the great preparation they had made, we might also have thought so, if a deserter had not informed the Admiral [Howe] that there was a passage open between two of the sunken Vessels (which his Brother the Ferry Man had given him marks for) and offered himself as a Pilot. This intelligence was exceedingly agreable to both the General & Admiral, concieving, that if ships could be got up the North [Hudson] River, the Rebel's supplys would not only be cut off from Albany & that country, but even their Communication with the Jerseys would become very uncertain & unsafe which could not fail of distressing them, and would very much assist in the intended opperation of surrounding their Army as soon as the Hessians should arrive."

As the ships approached the obstructions, however, the pilot told Capt. Hyde Parker of the *Phoenix* "that the marks which then appeared were not those that had been described to him, and he was totally at a loss." Parker decided "to take his chance where he knew the deepest water to be, which was Close to the eastern Shore, and which was the passage he came through when he passed down, before the obstruction of the Channel were said to be completed" (Hamond's narrative, 3–9 Oct., in Clark and Morgan, *Naval Documents*, 6:1182–84).

In passing the American batteries, the *Phoenix* and *Tartar* suffered much damage to their masts, sails, and rigging. The *Phoenix* received four shot through its hull, and the *Tartar* was hulled several times (see the journals of the *Phoenix, Roebuck,* and *Tartar,* 9 Oct., ibid., 1178–81). A total of nine men aboard the British ships were killed, and eighteen men were wounded (see Captain Parker's return of casualties, 23 Nov., ibid., 1182).

After reading this letter on 11 Oct., Congress resolved that GW "be desired, if it be practicable, by every art, and whatever expence, to obstruct effectually the navigation of the North river, between Fort Washington and Mount Constitution, as well to prevent the regress of the enemies' frigates lately gone up, as to hinder them from receiving succours" (*JCC,* 6:866).

9. See Tench Tilghman to the New York committee of correspondence, 9 Oct., in MH: Sparks transcripts. For the letter to Gen. James Clinton that the convention drafted on 10 Oct. after reading Tilghman's letter, see *N.Y. Prov. Congress Journals,* 1:669–70. In a second letter to the committee of correspondence of 9 Oct., Tilghman writes: "Mr Weisner [Henry Wisner, Jr.] came here and informed the General [GW] that there were ten Tons of Powder at New Windsor[,] five from his Mill and five from Philadelphia, it would be well to send immediately over and have it secured" (NHi: Duer Papers).

The New York committee of safety read Tilghman's second letter on 12 Oct. and appointed a committee of three members to secure the gunpowder mentioned by him and move it to some safe place (see ibid., 672). Two days later that committee reported "that there is not any quantity of gunpowder belonging to the public now at that [the New Windsor] landing. That they are informed that the 5 tons of gunpowder which arrived at New-Windsor from Philadelphia, was immediately carried down to Fort Constitution, and there lodged, from whence part of it, by order of the commanding officer, has been taken to Fort Independence [near Peekskill], and placed in such a manner as to supply the troops or militia there. That the powder brought from the mill of Messrs. Wisner and Phillipse to New-Windsor, was immediately put on board of a proper vessel for the purpose, to be transported to Spytden-Duyvel creek. Mr. Phillips, one of the manufacturers, proceeded with the vessel with the powder. The enemy's ships having got up the river before the vessel with the powder could reach her destination. Information is received that Mr. Phillips, who was at Peekskill with the powder, intended to land it there, and proceed by land. That a letter has been sent by Mr. [John] McKesson, one of the Secretaries, to the owners of the two powder mills near Goshen, requesting them not to send any gunpowder to the river side until further order" (ibid., 673).

The committee of safety on that same date ordered a copy of the report to be sent immediately to GW (ibid.). On 20 Oct. Tilghman wrote William Duer: "The General [GW] desires that Mr Philipse would not send down the powder from his *Mill* but Keep it in some secure place untill further orders—This is in answer to Mr McKessons Letter of the 14th Our hurry will excuse my not writing him particularly" (MH: Sparks transcripts). McKesson's letter has not been identified.

From Major General William Heath

Dear General   Kingsbridge Octr 8th 1776
Being Posted at Some Distance from The other General Officers of the State of Massachusetts Bay, I have found it very difficult to Obtain their Opinion of the Field Officers Proper to be Recommended, to that State, to Serve in the Army in future, General Nixon was at my Quarters on Yesterday, General Fellows was on Duty and Could not attend. I did with General Nixon arrainge The Officers for 12 Regiments whose Names are in the Inclos'd List[1]—I shew the List this morning to General Lincoln, who Joyns with us in Sentiment and Desired that Lieut. Colo. Seth Read of Colo. Patersons Regiment might be Added for a Regiment, I think He is worthy of one, We have put Colo. Prescott on the List—our motive was his past Heroic Conduct— I think He will not Serve after the Present Campaign, and I submit it to your Excellency's better Judgment, whether it be best to put him on the List or not, Parks, Fuller, Hamblin, Peters, and Thompson are at Present Captains,[2] I wish to Know your Excellency Opinion of this List, And whether it be your Pleasure, That we should proceed to Communicate it, to such of the Field officers as we Can, and Obtain from them a Recommendation of Capts. and Subalterns most proper to Serve in the New Army, we Also beg leave to propose an alteration in the List, (if

it should appear to be for the Interest of the Service) this Day or tomorrow, as a more Particular Enquiry is makeing with respect to Several of the Officers, whose Conduct Since in the army, is better Known to Some other General officers.

I also take the Liberty to Inclose to your Excellency, The Sentence of a General Court Martial, upon Two Subaltern Officers and beg leave to Suggest to your Excellency (In Case your Excellency should approve the Sentences) if it might not be as well, to remitt the mulcts—Especially in the Case of Smedes.[3] I have the Honor to be &c.

W. Heath

ADfS, MHi: Heath Papers.

1. This list has not been identified.

2. Col. William Prescott left the army at the end of 1776. The captains mentioned here are Warham Parks, Nathan Fuller, Eleazer Hamlin, Andrew or Nathan Peters, and Joseph Thompson.

3. The court-martial proceedings of 7 Oct. against lieutenants John Hulbert of Col. John Chester's Connecticut State Regiment and Abraham Smedes of Lt. Col. Johannes Hardenbergh's regiment of New York militia levies are in MHi: Heath Papers. Hulbert was charged with "having deserted the Camp in Time of Danger and being absent 26 Days without Leave." Following the retreat from Long Island, he had been ordered to escort the regiment's baggage to a safe place two or three miles north of New York City, but instead of stopping there, he had proceeded to his home 126 miles away. Hulbert was found guilty only of absence without leave, and he was sentenced to be cashiered and was mulcted (fined) one month's pay. Smedes, who was tried "for spreading a false and malicious Report concerning Col: Hardenburgh's Conduct on the Day of the Retreat from New York" and "for absenting himself from the Regt without Leave," was found guilty of both charges. Smedes was sentenced on the first charge to "beg the Col.'s pardon at the Head of the Regt and confess that the whole was a scandalous, malicious Lie without the least Foundation, & that this Confession be inserted in the public papers." On the second charge he was sentenced to be cashiered and mulcted one month's pay. At the end of the enclosed copy of these court-martial proceedings, GW wrote: "Both of the foregoing Judgments are approvd by Go: Washington." The document was returned to Heath with GW's first letter to him of 9 October.

To Jonathan Trumbull, Sr.

Sir　　　　　Head Quarters Heights of Harlem Octor 8th 1776

I was this morning honored with your favor of the 2d instant and beg leave to return you my thanks for the measures you have adopted upon my request for obtaining an account of the prisoners in your State, and for your assurance that I shall be furnished with a return, as soon as it is procured, in order that I may give further directions about them.

The proposition respecting the Prisoners that wish to remain with us, and about the expence that has been incurred for the maintenance of the whole that have been in your State I shall lay before Congress by the earliest opportunity, and will transmit you the result of their opinion. However, it appears to me that there will be a necessity for returning the whole of their Prisoners, not only because the balance is against us, but because I am informed it was particularly stipulated on the part of General Montgomery for those that were taken in Canada. The case will be hard upon those that want to remain and who have become attached to us,[1] and should Congress determine on their being returned, it will be but right, that some pains should be used to inform them of the reasons leading to the measure, and I doubt not, if they act with proper caution, that they may afterwards effect their escape to which they should be encouraged— Indeed I think, if they are heartily disposed towards us, that their exchange may be productive of many good consequences. They may extend their influence to many others, and who, perhaps, will be induced to desert.

I hope the resentment which your State mean to express against those who have scandalously deserted from the defence of our Cause will have a happy effect, and prevent a like conduct in future. Nothing can be too severe for them.

Before the receipt of your favor I had desired the General Officers to make out a list of such Field and other Officers as are esteemed worthy of command and entitled to Commissions in the Service—This is a consideration of exceeding importance, for without good officers we can never have Troops that will be worthy of the name, and with them we may, in time, have an Army equal to any. We have good materials to work upon. As soon as the list is obtained I will forward it by the first conveyance that may offer. I have strongly inculcated on the Generals the impropriety of giving in or recommending any but those who are fit for service; and you may rest assured Sir, as you have been pleased to honor me with your confidence upon this occasion, that as far as it shall be in my power, I will only return those that are well spoken of, and who, from report, will answer what you have ever had in view, the advancement of our Common Rights and the happiness of the United States. I am Sir with sentiments of great respect Your most obedient Servant

Go: Washington

P.S. The following payments have been made to the Militia of your State lately here. 28th Sepr 1776. Major Nathl Terry for his regiment 5185⁹/₇₂. 30th. To Capt. Amos Barnes for his regiment 5211³⁸/₇₂.[2]

LB, Ct: Trumbull Papers; LB, DLC:GW; Varick transcript, DLC:GW.

1. The LB in DLC:GW reads: "and who have all become attachd to us."

2. The LB in DLC:GW reads "30. Capn Amos Barnes. 15th Regt commd by Majr Shaw 5211³⁸/₇₂." GW's warrant book no. 2 says that Capt. Amos Barnes received a warrant for $5,211³⁸/₇₂ on 30 Sept. "for the 15th Regt Connectt Militia commd by Majr Strong" (DLC:GW). Simeon Strong was the major of the 15th Regiment of Connecticut militia (see Hinman, *Historical Collection,* 163). Nathaniel Terry (1730–1792) of Enfield, Conn., a member of the general assembly, was major of the 19th Regiment of Connecticut militia. Promoted to colonel of militia in 1777, Terry apparently served again with the Continental army at Peekskill in 1777 and 1778. Amos Barnes (1732–1814) served as a captain in Maj. Judah Woodruff's regiment of Connecticut volunteers from 13 Oct. 1776 to 22 Oct. 1777 and the 17th Regiment of militia in 1778.

To Joseph Trumbull

Sir. Head Quarters Octob. 8. 1776.

I have reciev'd your letter, requesting information, relative to the persons who are to draw the rations of the sick;[1] 'Tis true, there was a general order, directing a payment of the rations, to the Director Genl, for those sick, who were lodg'd in the General hospital but the inconveniences, resulting to the sick, from this piece of duty being disputed and unsettled between the General and Regimental Surgeons being so great; I did, (to relieve their sufferings and to render their situation more comfortable) issue out special directions, for the Col. of each regiment, to chuse a proper person to carry the sick into the country, & provide proper necessaries and accommodations for them out of the ration mon⟨ey.⟩[2] I did not think it proper or adviseable to make this a general order, lest it should have been establish'd as a precedent, and become a color for some imposition, after the present necessity for the measure shall have subsided; though I must observe to you, that in the settlement of your accounts, there will be the same attenti⟨on⟩ paid to a special as to general order; I should therefore concieve it will be productive of no inconvenience whatever, to pay the ration money to the person appointed as before mentioned, by the Col. when he furnishes you a proper certificate specifying the numb⟨er⟩ of men, the name of the regiment, & also th⟨e⟩ length of time his officer has had them under his care. I am Sir Yr hhble Servt

Go: Washington

LS, in William Grayson's writing, Ct: Trumbull Papers. The material in angle brackets is mutilated.

1. This letter has not been identified.

2. For GW's previous orders and directions regarding provisions for sick soldiers, see General Orders, 28 July and 12, 13 September.

General Orders

Head Quarters, Harlem Heights, Octobr 9th 1776

Parole. Countersign.[1]

The General positively forbids covering the bottoms of Tents with Earth, as in a few days that situation, must render them totally unfit for service—The commanding Officer of each Corps, will take care to see that this Order is strictly complied with in his own Encampment—In Order that the regiments may get out of Tents as soon as possible, the Brigadiers may apply to the Qr Mr General for Boards, and under his direction, employ the spare time of their men in building Barracks, or Hutts, fit for Winter use. These Hutts, or Barracks, are to be built with regularity. The Works of defence are not to be retarded by these buildings; they are to be advanced by the men off duty, if tools are to be had for them to work.

The respective Brigadiers are to inquire into the state of the Ammunition of their Brigades, and every Colonel is to have a Box of spare Cartridges, to supply occasional deficiencies.

Edward Sherburne Esqr. is appointed Aide-De-Camp to General Sullivan, and is to be obeyed and respected accordingly.[2]

David Dexter Esqr. is appointed to act as Brigade Major to the Brigade under Col. Lippet.[3]

Varick transcript, DLC:GW.

1. "Williams' Diary," 49:50, gives the parole for this date as "Billoa" and the countersign as "Lisbon."

2. Edward Sherburne (d. 1777) of New Hampshire served as one of Sullivan's aides-de-camp with the rank of major until he was wounded fatally at the Battle of Germantown on 4 Oct. 1777. He died the following day.

3. David Dexter of Cumberland, R.I., who had been an ensign in the 2d Rhode Island Regiment during 1775, became in January 1776 a captain in the state regiment that Col. Christopher Lippitt now commanded. In February 1777 Dexter was appointed a captain in the new 2d Rhode Island Regiment, and he served with that regiment until he was dismissed in January 1779.

From John Hancock

Sir,   Philada Octr 9th 1776.

The enclosed Resolves, which I do myself the Honour to forward, will inform you of the ample Provision the Congress have made for the Support of both Officer and Soldier who shall enter into the Service during the War. The Pay of the former is considerably increased, and the latter is to receive annually a compleat Suit of Cloaths, or in Lieu thereof, the Sum of twenty Dollars, should he provide the Suit for himself.[1] This additional Encouragement, besides the twenty Dollars Bounty and fifty Acres of Land formerly granted, the Congress expect, will be the Means, (if any Thing can) of engaging the Troops during the War.

The Importance, and indeed the absolute Necessity of filling up the Army, of providing for the Troops, and engaging them during the War, having induced Congress to come to the enclosed Resolves, in Obedience to their Commands, I am preparing to forward them with all possible Expedition to the several States.[2]

Your Letters to the 5th of October have been duely received and laid before Congress. I shall immediately transmit all such Resolves which may hereafter be passed, and Ways relative to your Department, or necessary for your Information. I have the Honour to be, with every Sentiment of Respect, & Esteem Sir, your most obed. & very hble Servt

John Hancock Presidt

The several Resolves go to the States this day by Express.

LS, DLC:GW; LB, DNA: RG 12A. The postscript of the LS is in Hancock's writing.

1. Although the enclosed copy of these resolutions of 7 and 8 Oct. has not been identified, they are in *JCC*, 5:853–56. The new monthly pay rates for officers were: "a colonel, 75 dollars; lieutenant colonel, 60; major, 50; captain, 40; lieutenant, 27; ensign, 20; quarter master, 27½; adjutant, 40 dollars." Each soldier's "suit of cloaths" was to consist "of two linen hunting shirts, two pair of overalls, a leathern or woollen waistcoat with sleeves, one pair of breeches, a hat or leathern cap, two shirts, two pair of hose, and two pair of shoes." Congress on 8 Oct. also recommended to the states that had regiments in Continental service "at New York, Ticonderoga, or New Jersey, that they forthwith appoint committees to proceed to those places, with full powers to appoint all the officers of the regiments to be raised by their states under the new establishment, that such officers may proceed immediately to inlist such men as are now in the service, and incline to re-inlist during the war, and that such committees be instructed to advise with the general officers, and promote such officers as have distinguished themselves for their abilities, activity, and vigilance in the service, and especially for their attention to military discipline."

2. See Hancock to Certain States, this date, in Smith, *Letters to Delegates*, 5:324–25.

To Major General William Heath

Dr Sir,   Harlem Heights 9th Octr 1776.

Your Letter of yesterday is before me with the list Inclosed; but this is doing the matter by halves only, and the delay must inevitably defeat the end; as it is impossible from the nature of things that the different Governments can withhold the nomination of Officers much longer—I therefore entreat you to delay not a moments time in summoning the Officers (under Sanction from me) to consider of this matter, that the Lists may be forwarded. the Committee of Congress directed this—Genl Lincoln earnestly recommended it. Governor Trumbull has requested it in precise terms[1]—In short the good of the Service, & our Duty, renders it necessary; let it be received in never So unfavourable a light (which by the by I do not conceive to be the case) by the states they are sent to. I think you would do well to consult the Field Officers with respect to the Captns &ca—I beseech you once more to delay no time—& I beseech you to exhort the Officers you consult to lay aside all local prejudices & Attachments in their choice. the Salvation of their Country, & all we are contending for depends (under Providence) upon a good choice of Officers to make this Army formidable to the Enemy, and Servicable to the cause we are endeavouring to Support. Men who have endeavourd to support the Character of Officers & who have not placed themselves upon a level with the common Soldiery, are fit to be prefered—Officers of the latter class will never—in short they cannot—conduct matters with propriety; but I need not point out the qualification's necessary to constitute a good Officer; your own observations and good judgments will readily point out who are, and who are not fit for the new appointment. I would have you confine yourself to the Massachusets bay Officers.

Inclosed you have some Lists han⟨d⟩ed into me by General Green which may be attended to with the rest.[2] Inclosed also, you will receive the opinion, and report of Colo. Knox & Colo. Putnam respecting our Works of defence,[3] which so far as relates to your Department I shall have no objection to the Execution of with all possible dispatch. those on the Island we will attend to.

I have approvd the Sentences of the Court & desire you will order them to be executed.[4] I am with respect &ca Yr Most Obedt Servt

Go: Washington

ALS, MHi: Heath Papers. The cover is addressed in GW's writing: "To Majr Genel Heath. Kings Bridge." Robert Hanson Harrison wrote and signed a note on the cover that reads: "Permit the Bearer to pass Kings bridge."

1. See Trumbull to GW, 2 October.

2. These lists have not been identified.

3. See Henry Knox and Rufus Putnam to GW, 6 October.

4. For GW's approval of these court-martial sentences, see Heath to GW, 8 Oct., n.3.

To Major General William Heath

Sir   Head Quarters 9th October 1776

I have this Moment yours of this Evening.[1] The Party of 100 Men were ordered up to assist a Detachment of Artillery in covering the two New Ships, should the Enemy attempt to cut them out or destroy them. Soon after I got home from Fort Washington I recd a Report that the Enemy had passed the new Ships and were landing at Dobb's Ferry, I then directed Colo. Read to desire you, if that should be the Case to send the Feild Peices and Howitzers forward if it should be judged necessary, and as Genl Clinton best knew the Ground to consult him upon the Necessity of sending on the Artillery, and if it was sent, that a strong covering Party should go with it.[2] Till I recd yours I heard no more of the Matter. I am sorry you have been misinformed as to the Movement of the other Ships below, they have never stirred from their Moorings. You will therefore be pleased to order Capt. Benson to be as expeditious as possible in getting the new Ships afloat and bringing them down to where they may be conveniently ballasted.[3] I will take proper Care of the prisoners you are sending down.

L, in Tench Tilghman's writing, MHi: Heath Papers. Tilghman added a concluding paragraph that reads: "While I was writing the above by his Excellency's Direction he went to Bed. I thought it a pity to disturb him to sign it. I therefore have the Honor to subscribe myself Yr most obt Servt Tench Tilghman."

1. This letter has not been found.

2. The report that the British warships that went up the Hudson River on this date were landing men at Dobbs Ferry proved to be false (see Heath's first letter to GW of 10 Oct.). On 10 Oct. Heath wrote Capt. Jotham Horton: "You will remain with the Cannon and Howtzer which were Ordered up with you, at the Place which you were directed to take Post, by the General [GW], which I Suppose is to Cover our Ships and prevent the Enemy Burning them or Cuting them out, If there is not a Sufficient number of men there to Cover them, upon your Signification of it they shall be Sent to you[.] as Soon as the Ships are got off you will return with the Cannon &c. Major [Edward] Crafts will return with his Howtzer Immediately" (MHi: Heath Papers).

3. See Heath's orders to Capt. Henry Benson of 10 Oct. in MHi: Heath Papers.

From Lieutenants Jeremiah Putnam and Nathaniel Cleaves

Sir   North Rever October the 9th 1776
    this is a Coppey of the precedin⟨gs⟩ On Bord the Galley Independance On the 8th Coll Tupper sent Orders On Bord for Capt. Baker to prosceed On shore and that there Was no further Buisness for him On Bord[1] On the 9th at about 7 A.M. We Observed the ships Below to Be moving We Imeadetly Cauld all Hands, after seeing the Other Galley Under way We hove Up

and stood Up the river after them and When We got Above the Chevux De' free, spoke With Cook and askt what he Intended to Doo He answerd that he Did not know But stood Up the river and said there Was Not Warter Enough to Goo in to the Creek the Wind Being Morderate we gained a head of them wich gave Us Encoregment to keep along it soon after Breessd Up & the ships Gaind Upon Us fast: and at a bout 11 A.M., the[y] Began to fire Upon Us With theire Bow Chases[2] at A bout twelf they Over reacht Us wich Causd Us to Bare in shore and at ½ P.M. We run her On shore Just Above Dobsey Ferry Where We had not time Enough to Git Our people and things On shore in the Boats: and the shiping Began the fire Wich Oblig'd Us to Swim On shore. But no Livs Lost But, part of theire Guns and Cheif of theire Baggage, And I Observed the Enemy to hawl Up thire Boats And man them, Wich, they Emeadetly Dropt On stern and fired a Brad side of Grape shot as We Ley in the Bushes and Emeadetly sent theire Boat On Bord With a Warp and hove her a long side,[3] from your Most Obedt Serts

Jeremh Putnam Lt
Nathaniel Cleaves Liut.

LS, in Cleaves's writing, DLC:GW.

Although Jeremiah Putnam (1737–1797) signs this letter as a lieutenant, Col. Israel Hutchinson's return of the 27th Continental Regiment for 5 Oct., lists him as an ensign "on command on board the galley" (Force, *American Archives*, 5th ser., 2:901–2). A native of Massachusetts who had served as a sergeant in the Lexington alarm, Putnam joined Col. John Mansfield's Massachusetts regiment as a sergeant in May 1775, and on 1 Jan. 1776 he was commissioned an ensign in Hutchinson's 27th Continental Regiment. Putnam left the Continental army at the end of 1776 and served the remainder of the war as a captain in the Massachusetts militia. Nathaniel Cleaves of Massachusetts, who had been wounded while serving as a lieutenant in the Lexington alarm, was a first lieutenant in Mansfield's Massachusetts regiment from May to December 1775 and in the 27th Continental Regiment during 1776. Taken prisoner at Fort Washington on 16 Nov., Cleaves was not exchanged until March 1780.

1. John Baker, Jr., of Massachusetts, a captain in the 27th Continental Regiment, commanded the Continental row galley *Independence* until Lt. Col. Benjamin Tupper relieved him on 8 Oct. (see ibid.).

2. Bow chasers are guns mounted in the forward part of vessels for use when pursuing other vessels.

3. The British warships that passed through the obstructions at Fort Washington pursued the American row galleys up the Hudson, and near Dobbs Ferry they ran ashore the galleys *Independence* and *Crane*, two sloops, and a

schooner, all of which were subsequently refloated by the British and taken as prizes (see the journals of the *Phoenix, Roebuck,* and *Tartar,* 9 Oct., in Clark and Morgan, *Naval Documents,* 6:1178–81). Capt. Andrew Snape Hamond of the British warship *Roebuck* says in his account of events that the capture of the two American row galleys "was a great acquisition to us, as they [the Americans] never after dared to shew us their Galleys again" (Hamond's narrative, 3–9 Oct., ibid., 1183).

To Jonathan Trumbull, Sr.

Sir   Head Quarters Harlem Heights Octo. 9[–10]th 1776
   Agreeable to your request and the promise contained in my letter of yesterday I beg leave to transmit you the enclosed list comprehending the names of such Gentlemen as are recommended by the General Officers from your State, as proper Persons to be promoted in the Regiments you are about to raise, with the ranks which they conceive they ought to hold.[1] Sensible that the very existence, that the well doing of every Army depend upon good Officers[,] I urged, I pressed the Gentlemen to whom the business was confided and whose situation has given them an opportunity of being better acquainted through the different Corps than I am, to pay their most serious attention to the matter, and to return such, and only such, as will, in their estimation, by their fidelity, attachment and good conduct, promote the great end we have in view, the establishment of our Rights and the happiness of our Country, by that mode which sad necessity has obliged us to pursue. This I hope they have done. They have taken no notice of any Officer in the Northern Army, or of those of the 17th Regiment (Huntingdon's) who were taken on Long Island, whose imprisonment I should suppose, if they have merit, should be no objection to their having promotion; nor do they mean, by the list they have given in, to preclude others of greater merit than those they have mentioned, if they are to be found. Congress, by a late Resolution have allowed a Paymaster to each Regiment,[2] in the appointment of whom, I would recommend, that particular care be had to the choosing of men intimately acquainted with and well versed in accounts; and who will be able to keep them in a fair and distinct manner, as they will have not only to receive the

Regiments pay, but to keep accounts of every transaction incident to them, such as respect their Cloaths &c. In some appointments lately made by the Field Officers to whom I submitted the
matter they nominated men who could not write their names
legibly. They receive Captns Pay.

As our present Army is upon the eve of their dissolution it
behoves us to exert every nerve to enlist immediately for the
new one. Without, I am convinced we shall have none to oppose
the Enemy, and who will have it in their power to spread havock
and devastation wherever they will. I would therefore submit it
to your consideration, whether it may not be proper, as soon as
you have made choice of your officers (and which I think should
be effected as early as possible) to appoint a Committee with
power to repair to this place and make such arrangements as
may be necessary with respect to those who are now in the service, in order that they may begin to recruit out of the present
Corps without any loss of time.

I perceive the Generals in the list they have made have set
down the Commissary for a Regiment.[3] In this I think they have
done exceedingly right, and that it is nothing more than a reward justly due his merit, in case he should quit his present department. However, I hope that the apprehensions which have
given rise to this step will never become malicious,[4] and that he
will still continue in his present Office and upon such terms as
may be agreeable to him, but least he should decline the provision they have made is extremely proper.

I this minute saw Genl Spencer who informed me, that they
had never taken the Officers, Prisoners upon Long Island, into
consideration, making out[5] their arrangement not knowing
whether they could be noticed in their present situation. I have
made out a list of them,[6] and as I have before observed, if they
are men of merit, their imprisonment most certainly should not
operate to their prejudice, if it can be avoided. If a principle of
that sort was adopted it would give the greatest discouragement
and have a tendency[7] to suppress every brave and manly enterprize which might be attended with captivity.

I would also mention Major Sherman Son of Mr Sherman of
the Congress, a young gentleman who appears to me, and who
is generally esteemed an active and valuable Officer, whom the

General Officers have omitted to set down in their list, expecting, I suppose, (if they thought of him at all) that he would be provided for in the Massachusetts Regiments because he is in one at this time—But as it is probable promotions in that State will be confined to their own People, I should apprehend that he should be properly noticed in your appointments, lest we should lose an Officer who, so far as I can judge, promises good services to his Country.[8]

On yesterday morning three Ships of War, two of 44 and the other of 20 Guns, with two or three Tenders passed up the North-River without meeting any interception[9] from the Chevaux de frize or receiving any material damage from our Batteries, though they kept a heavy fire at them from both sides of the River—Their views most probably are to cut off all supplies of boards &c. which might come down the River and of which we shall have great need—I have given directions to proceed as fast as possible in carrying on the obstructions and I would feign hope,[10] if they allow us a little more time, that they will be so far compleated as to render the passage dangerous if not altogether insecure.[11] I have the honor to be with great Respect Sir Your most obedient Servant

Go: Washington

P.S. In respect to the appointment of Officers I would beg leave to add, that the merit of the Officers who went through the Canada Expedition with General Arnold should, in my opinion, be particularly noticed, though they are upon their parole and cannot act, nor would I have them commissioned yet. Should not suitable provision be made for them against their releasment which, I should suppose, ought to be among the first.

LB, Ct: Trumbull Papers; LB, DLC:GW; Varick transcript, DLC:GW. Although this letter was begun on 9 Oct., it apparently was not completed until 10 Oct. (see note 11).

1. The LB in DLC:GW reads "ought to bear." For the 9 Oct. list of Connecticut officers recommended by generals Putnam, Spencer, Parsons, and Wadsworth for appointment in the new army, see Force, *American Archives*, 5th ser., 2:959–61.

2. For this resolution of 16 July, see *JCC*, 5:564.

3. GW is referring to Trumbull's son, Commissary Gen. Joseph Trumbull, who continued to hold that office until July 1777.

4. The LB in DLC:GW reads "will never become realities."

5. The LB in DLC:GW reads "in making out."

6. This list has not been identified.

7. The LB in DLC:GW reads "have a direct tendency."

8. Isaac Sherman (1753–1819) of New Haven, the third son of Continental Congress delegate Roger Sherman, joined Col. Samuel Gerrish's Massachusetts regiment as a captain in May 1775, and on 1 Jan. 1776 he became a captain in Col. Loammi Baldwin's 26th Continental Regiment, which was formed principally out of Gerrish's regiment. Sherman was promoted to major of the 26th Continental Regiment in March. Thanks in part at least to GW's support, he was commissioned lieutenant colonel of the 2d Connecticut Regiment on 1 Jan. 1777. In October 1779 Sherman became lieutenant colonel commandant of the 8th Connecticut Regiment. He transferred to the 5th Connecticut Regiment on 1 Jan. 1781 and retired on 1 Jan. 1783. In 1785 Congress appointed him an assistant surveyor for western lands.

9. The LB in DLC:GW reads "without meeting any interruption."

10. The LB in DLC:GW reads "I would fain hope."

11. GW must have written this paragraph sometime on 10 Oct., because the British warships passed the American obstructions at Fort Washington on the morning of 9 October. See GW to Hancock, 8–9 Oct., and Jeremiah Putnam and Nathaniel Cleaves to GW, 9 October.

General Orders

Head Quarters, Harlem Heights, Octob: 10th 1776

Parole. Countersign.

If the weather is favourable to morrow morning, the General purposes to visit the troops at their Alarm-posts. Commanding Officers of regiments, and others, are desired to make themselves well acquainted with their Alarm Posts, and the best ways to them; And also with the Ground in general, upon which they may be called to act, so as to avail themselves of every advantage. If Officers do not acquire this knowledge, they will miss the best opportunity of distinguishing themselves, and serving their Country.

If there should be any bad weather, the greatest care is to be taken of the Arms, and Ammunition; and Officers must attend to it themselves, or, from experience we know, there will be great danger of their being unfit for action.

Whenever any Field Officer is sick, leaves the Camp, or by any other means becomes incapable of duty, his Brigade Major is desired to signify it to the Adjutant General, otherwise it is impossible to have the duty regularly done.

Daniel Murphey of Capt. Edward's Company, 3rd Pennsylvania Battalion; Thomas Dickens of Capt: Hobby's Company Col. Ritzema's regiment—John Stone of Capt. Grubb's Company, Col. Brodhead's Battalion—All having been tried by a Court Martial whereof Col. Weedon is President, and convicted of "Desertion"—are sentenced to receive 39 Lashes each—the above Daniel Murphey having been convicted by the same Court Martial of "Inlisting into another regiment"—is sentenced to receive 39 Lashes for that offence.[1]

The General approves the above sentences, and orders them to be executed at the usual time and place.

Varick transcript, DLC:GW.

1. These three enlisted men pleaded guilty to the charges against them at their trials on this date (see the court-martial proceedings, 10 Oct., DLC:GW). Evan Edwards (1752–1798) of Delaware County, Pa., who had been a lieutenant in the 1st Pennsylvania Regiment during 1775, became a lieutenant in the 3d Pennsylvania Regiment on 6 Jan. 1776, and he was promoted to captain on 23 March. Although Edwards was commissioned a captain in Col. Thomas Hartley's Additional Continental Regiment on 1 Jan. 1777, he apparently served as an aide-de-camp to Gen. Charles Lee with the rank of major during much of 1777 and 1778, and in December 1778 he was Lee's second in a duel with Lt. Col. John Laurens. When the "new" 11th Pennsylvania Regiment was formed from Hartley's and Col. John Patton's additional regiments in December 1778 and January 1779, Edwards became its major. He transferred to the 4th Pennsylvania Regiment in 1781 and retired on 1 Jan. 1783. Peter Grubb, Jr. (1740–1786), of Lancaster County, Pa., served as a third lieutenant in Col. William Thompson's rifle regiment during the summer of 1775, and in March 1776 he became a captain in Col. Samuel Miles's rifle regiment. Grubb joined the 10th Pennsylvania Regiment as a captain in November 1776, and in January 1777 he transferred to Col. John Patton's Additional Continental Regiment. Grubb resigned his commission in July 1778.

From William Bartlett

Honr Sir   Beverly [Mass.] 10th Octor 1776.

I once more take the Liberty to write your Exelly which at this time when you are so deeply ingaged against Our unatural Enemies would Gladly Omitt did I not think it my duty therefore beg you'll Excuse it.

I wrote your Excelly some time Sence Concerning those Prizes taken by Commo. Manly Viz. the Ordinance Brigr Nancey Ship

Concord & Ship Jenny[1] Genr. Miffilin having Recd a Part of Each Cargo Agreeable to your Order without any Prise being Stipulated prevents their being Settl'd and the poor Captors are kept Out of their Money Some of which being in the Army while their famileys are here Almost Suffering for want off the Necesaries of Life Your Exelly Answer I Reced with the Gratest pleasure in which you informed me you would Order Genl Mifflin to have a Valuation made upon those Goods and Transmitted me in Order for Settlement[2] but have not as Yet Received it Beg your Excelly will Excuse me and not Receive this as dictating, as I well know your Exelly to be full of humanity am Well Assured it would have ben done Long sence had not your time ben taken up in Matters of more and Grater importance.

If your Excelly will please to Order me to Charge the United States for the Coals out of Ship Jenny at the Same Rate the Remainder was Sold for being about Eleven dollors ℔ Chaldron that Ship may be Settled.

Your Exelly was Pleas'd to Appoint or have Appointed a Committe to Apprize the Ordinance Stores they have presented their Bill to me for payment Butt have put it off untill I should Receive your Excelly orders they having Charg'd One hundred pounds L[awful] Money for their Trouble.[3]

When Your Exelly finds it Convenient to have Transmitted me the Value Reced out of Ship Concord and the Valuation of the Ordinance Stores with Orders for Settlement Beg you'll Give me Orders to draw for what money I may want togeather with what Remains in my hand to be Sufficient to pay the Captors.

Your Excelly may Rely on my fidelity in not drawing for any more then will be Suffecient for that purpose.

Capn Bradford of Boston who his [has] Superceeded me in my Agencey Says he has Orders to Settle with all the Old Agents beg your Exelly Orders with Respect to it.

I shall forever acknoledge with Gratitude to your Exelly that Honour you was pleas'd to Confer on me in appointing me Agent for this department and hope have transacted the Bussiness to your Exellys Satisfaction.

The Reflection join'd to the impeachment which is Generally implied or at least understood by a dismission from any Office under Government his [has] I confess given me Very Sensible pain.

If your Excelly thinks me Capable or Worthy off being Reinstated in the Office of agencey for this department hope Shall do honour in my Station and shall Ever acknoledge the favour with the Gratest Gratitude.

Hope that being who Governs all things both in heaven and in Earth will preserve & Protect you from falling into the hands of those Unatural Enemise and that you may be the means Under him of driving them Back to their Native Land Asham'd. Wishing your Excellency all that Happiness that can be injoy'd in this Life Beg Leave to Subscribe my Self Your Exellencys Most Obedt Humbl. Servt

William Bartlett

ALS, DLC:GW.
    1. See Bartlett to GW, 11 June 1776.
    2. This answer has not been identified.
    3. See GW to Henry Bromfield and John Manley, 24 June 1776, and Bromfield to GW, 13 Aug., and note 1.

From Major General William Heath

Dear General   Kingsbridge Octr 10th 1776
    Upon being Informed yesterday in the afternoon that a party of the Enemy had Landed at Dobbs's Ferry, and had Posted Sentries in the Road, I Ordered Colo. Sargent with 500 men and 40 of the Light Horse to march and Dislodge them, at Two oClock this morning he Sent an Express Informing me, that he had reach'd The Ferry, & that there was no Enemy Landed, at that Time, and that the Ships were about three miles above that Place—I have Ordered him to leave about 100 men and a few of the Light Horse for Expresses, and to return with the remainder of the Detachment.[1]

I every moment Expect further Intellegance, of our Gallies, The Ships which are a Shore &c. which shall without Delay be Transmitted to your Excellency.

Inclosed is the Judgment of the Court Martial on Capt. DeWitt.[2]

I have Desired Generals Nixon and Fellows to be at my Quarters this Day and if Possible the List of Officers shall be Compleated. I have the Honor to be &c.

W. Heath

ADfS, MHi: Heath Papers.

1. See Heath to Paul Dudley Sargent, 9, 10 Oct., and Sargent to Heath, 10 Oct., MHi: Heath Papers; see also Wilson, *Heath's Memoirs*, 79–80.

2. John L. De Witt (1731–1803) of Dutchess County, who was a captain in Col. Cornelius Humphrey's regiment of New York militia levies, was tried on 8 Oct. for releasing James McCormick, a soldier under sentence of death, from the main guard on 1 Oct. (see Heath to GW, 29 Sept., and note 1). The court acquitted De Witt on the grounds that he knew of no crime alleged against McCormick and "none appear in the Return of the Prisoners &c." (see the court-martial proceedings for 8 Oct. in MHi: Heath Papers). "The General," GW's aide-de-camp Richard Cary wrote Heath later this day, "has ordered the proceedings of the Court Martial to be returned, & says, he leaves the mater intirely with you, tho' the conduct of the Capt. in releasing the prisoner appears extraordinary" (MHi: Heath Papers).

From Major General William Heath

Dear General   Kingsbridge 10th Octr 1776

Col. Sargent has just return'd from Dobbs's Ferry—he informs that the Enemy's Ships, took Two of our Gallies on Yesterday near that place which were run on shore—our men got out the small Arms & Baggage—That the Enemy sent Four Boats from their Ships, three to the Gallies & one on Shore, the men in the latter landed & broke open a Store, & plunder'd many Articles, & Stove the Remainder, & set fire to the Store, which was extinguish'd by our people—After this their Ships weighed Anchor, & with the Gallies which they had taken, stood up the River to Taupan Bay, where they all lie at Anchor—They also took a Schooner loaded with Rum Wine Brandy &c.[1]

Col. Sargent has left about 180 men at Tarrytown, & ordered a Chain of Sentries for a number of Miles, I hope these will soon be relieved by Genl Lincoln's Militia.[2]

The Machine designed for the blowing up the Enemy's Ships happened to be on board a Sloop which had the misfortune to be sunk by the Enemy[3]—A Contrast this to blowing of them up—One of the Ships, suppos'd to be the Roebuck was on Careen for several hours this morning—Suppos'd to be stopping her leaks—I have the pleasure to inform your Excellency that one of the Ships is got off & hope the other will be the next Tide—I have ordered 100 Men to assist in ballasting of the Hulks[4]—Capt. Horton remains with the Two Twelve pounders near the Ship which is still on Shore.[5] I have the honor to be &c.

W. Heath

ADfS, MHi: Heath Papers.

1. For the capture of these row galleys, see Jeremiah Putnam and Nathaniel Cleaves to GW, 9 October.

2. GW's aide-de-camp Richard Cary wrote Heath later on this date that GW "wishes you to be well informed on every occasion, & in the speediest manner of the movements of the Enemy up the North River, in order to frustrate any designs they may have in view—As Genl Clinton is supposed to be perfectly well acquainted with the Situation of the Ground, & the most advantageous Posts &c., adjacent to Dobbs's Ferry, or where ever the Enemy may intend a Diversion, General Lincoln is therefore referred to him for Advice & direction, respecting the number, & in what manner to post his Men, so as to harrass the Enemy, & effectually prevent any communication between them & the inhabitants in the Country. . . . [P.S.] You will please to communicate to the General as early as possible, such Intelligence as you may from time to time receive relative to the motions of the Enemy" (MHi: Heath Papers).

3. David Bushnell says in a document that he sent to Thomas Jefferson on 13 Oct. 1787 that his experiments with the submarine *Turtle* in the Hudson River during the New York campaign ended when "the Enemy went up the river, and pursued the boat, which had the submarine Vessel on board, and sunk it, with their shot. After I recovered the Vessel, I found it impossible, at that time to prosecute the design any farther" (Clark and Morgan, *Naval Documents*, 6:1500–1507; see also Wilson, *Heath's Memoirs*, 79).

4. Joseph Reed had written Heath the previous day: "Besides the Men ordered on the Duty in bringing down the [two new] Ships—the General [GW] desires you would order 100 Men from the Regiments of your Division nearest Kingsbridge immediately to be employed in ballast[i]ng the 2 Hulks which lay at Spiking Devil—these Men are not to leave the Service till it is completed & Officers who can be depended on are to oversee them as the Work of the Army constantly suffers by this Means" (MHi: Heath Papers).

5. Capt. Jotham Horton of Boston, who had been a first lieutenant in Col. Richard Gridley's artillery regiment from April to November 1775, was commissioned a captain-lieutenant in Knox's Continental artillery regiment on 1 Jan. 1776. Horton was captured at Fort Washington on 16 Nov., and because he subsequently broke his parole, he apparently was unable to assume the captaincy in the 3d Regiment of Continental Artillery that was reserved for him (see Horton to GW, 9 Mar. 1779, DLC:GW).

From the New York Committee of Safety

Committee of Safety for the State of New York.

Sir. Fishkill October 10th 1776.

We received from Mr Tilghman an Account of the enemies Ships having gone up the River—and have dispatched Expresses to General Schuyler and General Clinton agreable to your Excellency's request.[1]

Nothing can be more alarming than the present situation of our State; We are daily getting, the most authentic Intelligence of bodies of Men enlisted and armed in order to assist the Enemy⟨.⟩ We much fear that they co-operating with the Enemy, may seize such Passes as will cut off all communication, between the Army and us and prevent your supplies. We dare not trust any more of the Militia out of this County—We have called for some Aid from the two adjourning ones, but beg leave to suggest to your Excellency, the propriety of sending a body of Men to the high Lands or Peeks Kill to secure the Passes, and prevent Insurrections and overawe the disaffected.[2] We suppose your Excellency has taken the necessary Steps to prevent the landing of any Men from the Ships should they be so inclined as no reliance at all can be placed on the Militia of Westchester County. We are most respectfully Your Excellency's most Obedient & very humble servt

By Order.
Peter R. Livingston, President

LS, in DLC:GW; Df (mutilated), N: New York Provincial Congress Revolutionary Papers; copy, enclosed in GW to Hancock, 11–13 Oct. 1776, DNA:PCC, item 152; copy, DNA:PCC, item 169.

Peter Robert Livingston (1737–1794), a son of Robert Livingston, the third lord of Livingston Manor, was in line to become the fourth lord of the manor until 1771 when his father broke the entail on the estate to prevent the profligate Peter Robert from becoming the principal heir of the family fortune. Along with his reputation as a poor businessman, Peter Robert Livingston also developed a reputation as a radical Whig politician while serving in the New York general assembly from 1761 to 1769 and from 1774 to 1775. He was commissioned colonel of the 10th Regiment of the Albany County militia in October 1775, and he was elected repeatedly during 1775 and 1776 to represent that county in the provincial congress and convention. Named president of the convention on 26 Sept. 1776, Livingston served in that capacity and as chairman of committee of safety until 22 Oct. (see *N.Y. Prov. Congress Journals*, 1:643, 687).

1. Tench Tilghman had written the New York committee of correspondence the previous day, informing it that British warships had passed the obstructions at Fort Washington that morning. "How far they intend going up I don't Know," Tilghman says, "but his excellency [GW] thought for to give you the earliest intimation, that you may put General [James] Clinton on his guard at the High Lands, for they may have troops Concealed on board with intent to Surprize those forts—If you have any Stores on the water Side, you had better have them removed or secured in time—Boards especially for which we shall be put to great Streights if the Communication above should be Cut off" (MH: Sparks transcripts). The committee of safety read Tilghman's letter on the afternoon of this date and approved a draft of a letter to generals Schuyler and James Clinton about the British incursion and measures being taken to defend against it (see *N.Y. Prov. Congress Journals*, 1:669).

2. On this date the committee of safety directed the commanding officer of the Ulster County militia to send 300 to Peekskill and the commander of the Orange County militia below the highlands to call out as many men "as will be sufficient to guard their shores." The commander of the Orange militia above the highlands was instructed to send 100 men to Peekskill, and all rangers raised in Ulster Country were ordered to "repair immediately to Fishkill and be subject to the direction of the committee for inquiring into, detecting and depressing all conspiracies formed in this State against the liberty of America" (ibid.). Fishkill is in Dutchess County.

Robert R. Livingston, who was a member of the committees of safety and correspondence, wrote Tilghman later on this date, and referring to this letter from the committee of safety to GW, he says: "In that we mention the weakness of this state, But still make promises which I am satisfied we shall not perform, I wish no reliance may be made on them I dare not explain myself more fully, as this Letter must Lay a day upon the road, as I find the crews of the [British] ships have already found their way on shore. One regiment at least with a good Engineer might be usefully employed here. If it should be necessary to abandon the country below the high Lands this state may still be secure[.] a Chain of Mountains crosses the Country which with a little labour may be rendered impregnable. If proper magazines are laid up which (if I mistake not) Mr [Joseph] Trumble was ordered to provide I shall not even think a defeat at New York of any great consequence except as it would dispirit friends & encourage foes" (NHi: William Duer Papers).

William Duer, who sat on the committee of correspondence and the committee for detecting conspiracies, also urges the sending of a reinforcement in the letter that he wrote to Tilghman on this date. "There is no Event wh[ich] could have happend that could have given me more Uneasiness than the Passage of the Enemys Ships up the River," he says. "I cannot persuade myself their only design is to cut off the Communication of Supplies by water to our army at Kingsbridge: though that is an Event which will be highly prejudicial to our arms; they certainly mean to send up a Force (if their Ships have not Soldiers already on board) so as to take Possession of the Passes by Land on the Highlands—In this they will be undoubtedly joind by the Villains in Westchester and Dutchess County—it is therefore of the utmost Consequence that a Force should be immediately detachd from the main Body of our army to occupy these Posts—It is impossible for the Convention to draw out a Force which can be depended on from the Counties last mentiond" (NHi: Duer Papers).

To Major General Philip Schuyler

Dear Sir   Head Qurs Harlem Heights Octo: 10th 1776.

I am now to acknowledge Your Favor of the 1st Inst. & to inform You, that the two Sachems of the Cayugas, with Mr Deane the Interpreter, have been with me & spent three or four Days. I shewed them every Civility in My Power & presented them with such Necessaries as our Barren stores afforded and they were pleased to take; I also had them shewn all our Works upon this Island, which I had manned, to give them an Idea of our Force & to do away the false Notions they might have imbibed from the Tales which had been propagated among 'em. They seemed to think we were amazingly strong, and said they had seen enough without Going to our Posts in Jersey or the Other Side Harlem River. They took their Departure Yesterday morning & I hope with No Unfavorable Impressions.

Your Favor of the 6th came to Hand this Day by Mr Bennet; I have communicated the Contents, so far as It respects the Boards, to General Mifflin, who has resumed the Office of Quarter Master General on Mr Moylan's Resignation & the Application of Congress; He will write You to Morrow about them and will send the Sum You require by the Return of Mr Bennet.

It gives me Great Pleasure to hear the Army is so well supplied with Provision & I would fain hope, that if the Enemy do not Effect any Thing in this or the next Month, that they will not attempt to pass the Lakes till Early in the Spring, by Which Time perhaps We may be able to recruit our Army, tho I have My Fears, That the Buisiness will not go on with Ease and Expedition that I could wish. I have done All I could, and urged strongly the Propriety of Giving the Soldiers a Suit of Clothes annually, how Congress will determine[1] I know not; I have also advised the Raising of the Officers Pay.

We are again deprived of the Navigation of this River by three Ships of War, Two of 44 & the Other of 20 Guns with three or four Tenders, passing our Cheveaux de frize Yesterday Morning

And all our Batteries without any Kind of Damage or Interruption, Notwithstanding a Heavy Fire was kept up from both sides of the River.

I have Given Directions to compleat the Obstructions as fast as possible, and I flatter Myself, if they allow Us a little Time more, that the Passage will become extremely difficult, if Not entirely insecure. their Views I immagine are chiefly to cut off our Supplies & probably to Gain recruits. I am Dr Sir Very respectfully Your most Obedt servt

Go: Washington.

LB, NN: Schuyler Papers; LB, DLC:GW; Varick transcript, DLC:GW.
   1. The LB in DLC:GW reads "will determine on the Subject."

General Orders

Head Quarters, Harlem Heights, Octobr 11th 1776.
Parole.   Countersign.[1]
Col. Ewing, Lt Col. Penrose, Major Fitzgereld, Capts. Thorne, Ballard, Packay, and Yates, to sit as a Court of Enquiry into the Conduct of Col. Van Cortlandt, and Major Dey, towards each other; to meet this afternoon at 3'O'Clock, at the Court Martial Room, and make report as soon as possible to the General— Brigade Majors to give them immediate notice.[2]

—— Talmadge Esqr: is appointed Brigade Major to Genl Wadsworth, and is to be obeyed, and respected accordingly.

As there is an absolute necessity for the business of the Army to be carried on with regularity, and to do this, that the officers of each department should have the regulation and direction of matters, appertaining to their respective Offices, in Order that they may become amenable to the public, or the Commander in Chief, when called upon—It is hereby directed by the General, that No Horse, or Waggon, shall be taken by any Officer, of whatever Rank, without an Order from Head Quarters, the Qr Mr General, or Waggon-Master General: But when either are wanted for regimental uses, the application shall go from the Commanding Officer of the regiment, in writing to the Q: M: Gl or W. M. Gl who will issue his orders therefor; and if wanted for the dispatch of public business the application to be made by the Engineer in writing—all Teams belonging to the public, or in their pay, are to be delivered to the Quarter Master General, registered, and under his direction. The Quarter Master General is to take especial Care of all Grain and Hay, belonging to the Public, and see that none of it is delivered, but by his order: And as these Articles are scarce, it is ordered, that all officers, whose duty does not oblige them to be on horseback, dispose of the Horses, or send them out of Camp, immediately; as provender cannot be spared for them on any pretence.

No Boards are to be taken for the use of any Brigade, or Regiment, without orders, nor delivered but by order of the Quarter Master General, who is to make as equal a distribution among the Regiments as may be, and see they are put to the best use possible, and with as little waste, as there may be difficulty in getting them.

Mutual Complaints having been made by Mr Fisk the Engineer, and Mr Kinsey the Waggon Master against each other— A Court of enquiry of 3 Captains, and 4 Subs.—from Genl McDougall's Brigade to sit, and report the matter, with their opinion thereon; to meet to morrow Afternoon at 3 o'Clock, at the Court Martial room.

The General being accidentally prevented, from going to the Alarm-posts this morning; if the weather is fair, he will visit the Troops to morrow morning, accompanied by the General Officers; he hopes the whole line will turn out as full as possible.

The time of the Fatigue Men going out is altered to 8 O'Clock, instead of Seven—The men are to breakfast before they go, as they are not to leave Work on that account. The General hopes the officers will exert themselves, to complete the works, as fast as possible, that the men may be the sooner covered.

Varick transcript, DLC:GW.

1. "Williams' Diary," 49:51, gives the parole for this date as "Sherman" and the countersign as "Floyd."

2. The members of this court of inquiry are Thomas Ewing (1730–1790) of the 3d Regiment of Maryland flying camp troops, Joseph Penrose (1737–1824) of the 5th Pennsylvania Regiment, John Fitzgerald of the 3d Virginia Regiment, Joseph Thorne (1730–1819) of the 2d Regiment of Gloucester County, N.J., militia, Robert Ballard of the 1st Virginia Regiment, and Aquila Paca (1738–1788) and Thomas Yates (1740–1815), both of the 2d Regiment of Maryland flying camp troops. Richard Dey (1752–1811), of Bergen County,

who had been appointed major of Col. Philip Van Cortlandt's regiment of New Jersey militia levies in June 1776, became major of Col. Jacob Ford's New Jersey state regiment on 27 November.

To John Hancock

Head Quarters Harlem Heights
Sir   Octobr the 11[–13]th 1776

I beg leave to inform you, that since my Letter of the 8th and 9th Instt, which I had the honor of addressing you, Nothing of importance has occurred, except that the Ships of War, which I then mentioned, in their passage up the River, took a Sloop that was at Anchor off the Mouth of Spitendevil, and Two of our Row Gallies, which they out sailed. The Crews finding that they could not prevent them falling in to the Enemys Hands, run them near the Shore & effected their own escape. From the Intelligence I have received, the Ships are now laying at Tarry Town, without having landed any men, which seemed to be apprehended by some, or attempted any thing else. Their principal views, in all probability, are, to interrupt our Navigation and to receive such disaffected persons as incline to take part against us. the former they will effect beyond all question, and I fear, that their expectations respecting the latter, will be but too fully answered.

Octr 12th. The Inclosed Copy of a Letter received last night from the Convention of this State, will shew you the apprehensions they are under, on account of the disaffected among them.[1] I have ordered up a part of the Militia from the Massachusetts under Genl Lincoln, to prevent if possible, the consequences which they suggest may happen, and which there is reason to beleive the Conspirators have in contemplation; I am persuaded, that they are upon the Eve of breaking out, and that they will leave Nothing unessayed that will distress us, and favor the designs of the Enemy as soon as their Schemes are ripe for it.

Octobr 13th. Yesterday the Enemy landed at Frogs point about Nine miles from hence further up the Sound. their number we can not ascertain, as they have not advanced from the point, which is a kind of Island, but the Water that surrounds it is fordable at low tide. I have ordered Works to be thrown up at the passes from the point to the Main. From the great number of Sloops, Schooners and Nine Ships that went up the Sound in the Evening full of Men, and from the information of two Deserters who came over last night, I have reason to beleive that the greatest part of their Army has moved upwards or is about to do it, pursuing their original plan of getting in our rear & cutting off our communication with the Country.[2] The Grounds from Frogs point are strong and defensible, being full of Stone fences both along the road & across the adjacent Feilds, which will render it difficult for Artillery or indeed a large body of Foot to advance in any regular order except thro the main Road. Our Men who are posted on the passes seemed to be in good Spirits when I left 'em last night.[3] I have the Honor to be with great respect Sir Your Most Obedt St

Go: Washington

LS, in Robert Hanson Harrison's writing, DNA:PCC, item 152; LB, DLC:GW; copy, DNA:PCC, item 169; Varick transcript, DLC:GW. Congress read this letter on 15 Oct. and referred it to the Board of War (*JCC,* 6:875).

1. See the New York Committee of Safety to GW, 10 October.

2. General Howe explains his strategy in a letter to Lord George Germain of 30 Nov. 1776: "The very strong positions the enemy had taken on this [Manhattan] island and fortified with incredible labour determined me to get upon their principal communication with Connecticut, with a view of forcing them to quit the strongholds in the neighbourhood of King's Bridge and if possible to bring them to action. All previous arrangements being made, the army embarked on the 12th October in flatboats and other craft, and pressing through the dangerous navigation of Hell Gate in a very thick fog, landed on Frog's Neck near the town of West Chester about 9 in the morning. . . . Lieutenant-General Earl Percy remained with two brigades of British and one of Hessians in the lines near Haerlem to cover New York. The army remained in this situation until the stores and provisions could be brought up and three battalions of Hessians drawn from Staten Island, which together with some bad weather intervening occasioned a delay of five days" (Davies, *Documents of the American Revolution,* 12:258–64). For other accounts of the British landing on Frog's or Throg's Neck, see Mackenzie, *Diary,* 1:76–78; Lydenberg, *Robertson Diaries,* 102; *Kemble Papers,* 1:93; Tatum, *Serle's Journal,* 122, and Baurmeister, *Revolution in America,* 58.

3. In the LB the last part of this letter reads: "or is about to do it with an intent (as I suppose) to get in our rear & cut off our communication with the Country; The grounds leading from Frog's point to King's bridge, are strong & defensible, being full of Stone fences, both along the road & across the adjacent fields, which will render it difficult for Artillery, or indeed for a body of foot to advance in any regular way, except through the main road— When I left our people last night they seemed to be in good spirits."

Tench Tilghman, who rode with GW to Westchester County on 12 Oct.

after hearing of the British landing at Throg's Point, wrote William Duer on 13 Oct.: "From the Quantity of Craft of different sorts which were used in transporting the Troops up the Sound I am inclined to think that the greatest part of the Army is removed upwards, and this is confirmed by two Deserters who came over last Evening, who say that two Brigades of British Troops and two Bettalions of Hessians are all that are left. Trogs Neck and Point is a Kind of Island, there are two Passages to the Main which are fordable at low Water at both of which we have thrown up works, which will give some Annoyance should they attempt to come off by either of these ways. From their not moving immediately forward I imagine they are waiting for their Artillery & Stores which must be very considerable if they seriously intend to set down in the Country upon our Rear. The Grounds leading from Trogs Point towards our Post at Kingsbridge are as defensible as they can be wished, the Roads are all lined with Stone fences and the adjacent Feilds divided off with Stone likewise, which will make it impossible for them to advance their Artillery and Ammunition Waggons by any other Rout than the great Roads, and I think if they are well lined with Troops we may make a considerable Slaughter if not discomfit them totally. Our Rifle men have directions to attend particularly to taking down their Horses, which if done, will impede their march effectually. Our Troops are in good Spirits and seem inclined and determined to dispute every Inch of Ground. Our Front is now so well secured that we can spare a considerable number of our best Troops from hence [Harlem Heights] if they are wanted.

"If we are forced from this post we must make the best Retreat we can, but I think this Ground should not be given up but upon the last Extremity. However the General [GW] thinks so well of your hint of laying up Magazines beyond the Highlands, that he has order'd the Commy General to attend immediately to it" (NHi: Duer Papers).

Recruiting Instructions for Colonel Edward Hand

sir　　　　　　Head Quarters Harlem Heights Oct. 11th [1776]
　　You are immediately to Inlist such of your Regiment or any other Troops raised in the Province of Pennsylvania[1] as are able of Body & Willing to enter into the Service of the United States of America upon the following Terms.

　　1st. You are not to inlist any but Freemen able of Body & under the age of 50[2] carefully avoiding all persons Labouring under any Lameness or other Defect of Body prejudicial to the Service. If any such persons or any Boys or decripit persons are brought into the Service the Officer inlisting them will be chargeable with the Expence they may be to the publick.

2dly. You are not to inlist any Deserters from the Army of the King of Great Britain or persons of Disaffected and Suspicious Character—the American Service having already Suffered greatly by the Desertion of such persons.

3dly. you are to inlist Men to serve during the Continuance of the present War between Great-Brittain & the States of America unless sooner Discharged by proper Authority.

4thly. The Men inlisted by you are to be Subject to the Rules & Articles for the Government of the Army published by Congress the 20th Sepr 1776 and are to sign those Articles.

As an Encouragement to such persons as shall inlist in the above Service you are Authorized to engage besides the Pay & Provisions now allowed.

1st. Each Soldier shall Receive 20 Dollars Bounty Money on being approved by a Majr Genl a Brigr Gen. or Colo. Comdt of a Brigade.[3]

Secondly—He shall also be intitled to 100 Acres of Land at the expiration of his inlistment & in Case of his Death in the Service his Representatives will be intitled thereto.

When any Person is enlisted you are as soon as convenient to take him to some person duly Authorised by the above Articles to take the Oath there Prescribed.

LB, in Thomas Mifflin's writing, DLC:GW; Df, in Joseph Reed's writing, DLC:GW; Varick transcript, DLC:GW. The LB includes some draft changes. The draft in Reed's writing omits the last paragraph. For other significant differences in wording between the LB and draft, see notes 1, 2, and 3.

1. In the LB the words "or any other Troops raised in the Province of Pennsylvania" are inserted above the line. In the draft an almost identical phrase was inserted above the line and then changed to read: "or from the flying Camp or Militia of the State of Pennsylva."

2. The draft reads: "but Freemen above the Age of 17 & under 50." The LB originally included the same wording and then was changed to read as it does here.

3. Both the LB and draft originally read: "20 Dollars Bounty Money on passing Muster" before being changed to the present wording.

To Major General William Heath

Dr Sir,   Haerlam Heights 11th Octr 1776

The Ships which have got up the River with their Tenders (and now two of our Row Galleys) must be well attended to, or they may undertake something against our Stores, Craft, or &ca at Spiten devil—delay no time therefore in having some Work thrown up at the Mouth of that Creek for the defence of what lyes within, & to prevent Surprizes.

A Small number of Troops Imbark'd on Long Island yesterday (behind Montrasors Island) and appeard to steer to the Eastward—How far they went I know not—they were Hessions & of those I saw not more than a hundred—It might not be amiss to inform Gen. Lincoln of this but in such a manr as to occasion a good look out along the Sound without spreading an alarm.[1] I am Sir Yr Most Obedt Servt

Go: Washington

ALS, MHi: Heath Papers.

1. Samuel Blachley Webb wrote to Benjamin Lincoln on this date: "I am directed by his Excellency [GW] to inclose you some minutes delivered him by the Commissary; he conceives the Stores and Provisions to be in very great Danger, and would have every method taken for their Security. He desires you will as soon as may be have the Regiments mentioned Posted in such manner as may be of the greatest Security to that part of the Coast where Stores are hourly collecting" (Ford, *Webb Correspondence and Journals*, 1:170).

From Major General William Heath

Dear General   Kingsbridge Octr 11th 1776

I have Just Received the Honor of yours of this Day's date, and am fully Convinced that a Work should be thrown up without the Least Loss of Time at the mouth of Spiten devil—If Colonel Putnam and Colo. Knox Can be spared a few hours I wish Your Exellency would please to Send them Here in Order to Trace out a Proper Work, and Determine what Ordnance will be necessary to be Mounted at the Mouth or on the Heights, on the North River, I have Sent to General Lincoln desiring him to be here as Soon as Possible when I shall Communicate to him what your Excellency has Directed, Which I shall Aim to do in Such Manner, as to rouse to Vigilance and avoid alarm.[1] I have the Honor to be with great Respect Your Exellencys Most Humble Sert

W. Heath

ADfS, MHi: Heath Papers.

1. GW received this letter the next day, when Robert Hanson Harrison wrote Heath that GW "has given Orders for all the Regiments to be under Arms here that they may be ready to Act as Occasion may require—he wishes you to make such disposition of the Troops on your side & of the Two Militia Regiments that are posted opposite to this as you think necessary and begs & Trusts that every possible Opposition will be given to the Enemy. God bless & lead you on to Victory. . . . [P.S.] His Excellency would beg your attention to one thing Viz., that you will take proper precautions against a Feint & watch the Enemy's Motions—they perhaps may make a feint to land at Frogs point to draw your attention that way & slip down when it is high water towards Morrissania with a view of getting in your Rear—Guard agt that" (MHi: Heath Papers).

From Edmund Randolph

Dear Sir   Wmsburg [Va.] Octr 11. 1776.

I congratulate your Excellency, as a Friend to the Reputation of Virginia, and the Interests of the Continent, that Colo. Harrison is again restored to the Councils of America. During his Absence at the Northward, he had been appointed one of our privy Council, but refused to qualify, as such. This afforded him an Opportunity, to vindicate himself from those malicious Insinuations, which first brought about his Disgrace. For he informed the Assembly, that his Honour, which had been so deeply wounded on a former Occasion, forbid him to accept any Office whatever, until the Stigma, impliedly fixed upon his Character by recalling him Home, was wiped away. His Defence, if that could be called a Defence, the Object of which was to efface unworthy Impressions, made by Accusers, who whispered Poison, and dar'd not shew themselves in open Day—was spirited without any Degree of Bravadoing, and satisfactory even to those, who were prejudiced against him. With this happy Revolution in their Opinion of an honest, and able Statesman, the Senate and House of Delegates, in the whole amounting to seventy four Members, have sent him back to Congress, in the Room of Mr Jefferson, who has resigned, with a Ballot of 69 to 5. These five are supposed to be the Remains of a certain Party, not unknown to your Excellency. Nor was this all. they farther thanked him for his past Services Nem: Con: In short, his late Disappointment has served to raise his Credit to a higher Pitch.[1]

Our Soldiery are in a Situation, truly distressing to themselves, and the Country. To themselves, as they are now labouring under severe Autumnal Disorders, many of which prove Mortal, and to the Country, as we are apprehensive, that the upland People, on whom we chiefly depend for the Recruits, should be disgusted with the Service in the lower Parts which engender such Maladies. From what Cause the present general Sickness proceeds, I know not: but Wmsburg, which has hitherto been proverbial for general Health, is now notorious for the Contrary. The Assembly talk out of Doors upon the Subject of new Levies: but for God's Sake from whence are they to be obtained? I hear, that our second Regiment, whose Term of Inlistment expired in September last, has little Prospect of Renewal: An ungenerous Neglect prevails in the upper Counties concerning the Defence of the lower. To be ingenuous, I am afraid, we can get neither Clothing or Arms for any more Troops. I am Dr Sir yr Excellency's much oblig'd affte Servt

Edm: Randolph

ALS, DLC:GW.

1. Benjamin Harrison was not reelected a delegate to the Continental Congress by the Virginia convention on 20 June 1776, in part at least because it was rumored that he had influenced Congress to appoint his son-in-law, Dr. William Rickman, as physician and director general of the Continental hospital at Williamsburg instead of the Virginia committee of safety's choice, Dr. James McClurg (see Scribner and Tarter, *Revolutionary Virginia*, 7:557–58, and William Fleming to Thomas Jefferson, 27 July, in Boyd, *Jefferson Papers*, 1:474–76). Harrison's omission from the delegation may have been engineered, as Randolph and some other contemporaries believed, by a hostile political faction (see Randolph to Jefferson, 23 June 1776, ibid., 407–8; and Edmund Pendleton to Jefferson, 22 July 1776, ibid., 471–72; and Benjamin Harrison, Jr., to Willing, Morris, & Co., 29 June 1776, cited in Scribner and Tarter, *Revolutionary Virginia*, 7:560–61, n.9). Prominent among Harrison's political enemies at this time was Richard Henry Lee, with whom Harrison had disagreed on western land policy and the pace of the movement toward independence (see source note in Boyd, *Jefferson Papers*, 2:16–18).

Harrison was appointed to the Virginia council by the convention on 29 June 1776 (see Scribner and Tarter, *Revolutionary Virginia*, 7:655). The general assembly elected him a delegate to Congress on 10 Oct., and the house of delegates then "*resolved unanimously*, that the thanks of this House are justly due to the said *Benjamin Harrison*, for the diligence, ability, and integrity, with which he executed the important trust reposed in him as one of the delegates for this country in the General Congress. The Speaker accordingly delivered the thanks of the House to the said *Benjamin Harrison* in his place, who expressed the great pleasure he received for this distinguished testimony of his country's approbation of his services" (*Va. House of Delegates Journal*, Oct.–Dec. 1776 sess., 7–8; see also *Va. Senate Journal*, Oct.–Dec. 1776 sess., 4–5). The Latin phrase *nemine contradicente* means that the action was taken without dissent.

To Major General Philip Schuyler

Dear Sir   Head Qutrs Heights of Harlem Octo: 11th 1776.
    I this Morning received Your Favor of the 7th inst., and am to inform You, That It is not in my Power to supply You with a single Nail, nor are they to be procured in Philadelphia, as General Mifflin tells Me, Who has just returned from thence. For Want of them, we are building here, Huts of sod, Logs &ca to cover the Troops & Which I am in Hopes will make a tolerable Good shift.
    Since My Letter of Yesterday, Nothing has occurred & I have only to add That I am Dr Sir, Your most Obedt servt
                                                        Go: Washington

LB, NN: Schuyler Papers; LB, DLC:GW; Varick transcript, DLC:GW.

From Jonathan Trumbull, Sr.

Sir   New Haven Octobr 11th 1776
    In Consequence of your favour proposing a Descent on Long Island;[1] Altho I was so Unhappy as not to be Able to Meet Generals Clinton & Lincoln at this place as requested, I Applied to the State of Rhode-Island, And Obtain'd their Consent & Orders that Colo. Richmond and such part of his Battallion, as shall not inlist on board the Continental Vessells, should Assist in the Enterprise.[2] Coll Richmond will Accordingly begin his March this day for New London & bring with him the Whale Boats Collected in Massachusetts Bay & Rhodeisland to the Number of between 80 & 90 which it is Apprehended will be of great Use to the Troops Ordered on this service, especially to Secure & Assist their Retreat should it be attempted to be cutt off—When Coll Richmond Arrives at New London he has Orders to put himself Under the Command of such General Officer as your Excellency shall Appoint.

I have this day Conferr'd with Colls McIntosh and Livingston on the Subject,[3] they Inform me they are Supplied with Provisions and Ammunition for their purpose, & only want such a Number of Water Craft, as with the Whale boats Divided into three parts, that in the whole may be sufficient to Transport 12 hundred Men, As he means each division to be so placed at the in letts to the Island, as if cut off from one he may resort to the Other to make his retreat sure, if Necessary. These I have Ordered for him and dare say will be provided, & ready without delay—The Number of Men he proposes to set out with will doubtless be Sufficient for his first Attempts, But what reinforcements will be Necessary soon to follow to Answer every purpose, your Excellency will Judge; they may be thrown Over from Stamford Or Norwalk very soon if placed there—I am Apprehensive least some difficulties may Arise with respect to the Command of this Detachment. Coll McIntosh is a Superior Officer to Lieut. Coll Livingstone & Richmond is Superior in Rank to both. Coll Livingston Appears to be a Young Gentleman of real Spirit and Abilities and has every Advantage, in his knowledge of the Island & the people there. The Other Gentlemen have also their Merrit; may not a difficulty Arise as to the Command, I hope there will not. As the Gentlemen are all well disposed I hope they will Coopperate to the best Advantage in the Whole—What is further Necessary to render their Operations effectual you will please to Consider & direct.

Our Naval Expedition Against the Ships of the Enemy in the sound is still in Contemplation, and preparations are making for the same as fast as we can, Commodore Hopkins writes me the 5th Instant that the Alfred and Hampden are ready, & that the two New Frigates there would be ready in About a Week if they can be Manned Neither of them having more than half their Compliment at that time—Our Ship & Brigtn. will we trust be ready to join them & when they are equipped[.][4] it is proposed that they first Attack the two Frigates that Infest the Coast & sound, if they or either of them shall Appear in their way, Otherwise they will proceed directly up sound and Give the best Account they can of the Ships this side Hell Gate which is the principal Object.

I am now Informed that the two Frigates & the Alfred are

Manned from Coll Richmonds Regiment which I hope will prove true but if not am in hopes they may be Compleated by Volunteer⟨s⟩ from Rhodisland & New London. but if they should still fall short of their full Compliment, I beg leave to Suggest to your Excellency Whether they could not without Inconveniency be filled up from some parts of your Army, Unless the Row Gally men by the Enemies Ships passing up North river are rendered Useless, in which case they may be Ordered to some proper place along sound for Commodore Hopkins to take them in. I have given Commodore Hopkins the Utmost Assurance to give him all possible Intelligence from time to time of the Enemy Ships of Force this side Hell Gate, that he may be Apprised What he has to Encounter,[5] to that purpose I beg leave to Suggest to your Excellency to Give Orders to such Commander of the Guards or Posts in sight of the Enemy Ships to give me Intelligence of their force situation & Motions, or whether & when joined by any Other of the Enemies Ships thro' Hell Gate.

I have heard that one 24 Gun Ship of the Enemy has allready passed thro' to them. Since my last from Commodore Hopkins, am Inform'd That the Columbus Capt. Whipple has Arrivd in Port at Rhodisland[.] have wrote to him to take her with him which will make considerable Addition to his force, please to Afford me your Advice & fullest Information.[6] I Cannot but flatter my self with strong hopes of Advantages to be derived from this Adventure of Our Ships, As well as the Expedition to Long Island; Secrecy in both is of Utmost Importance. I am with great Esteem and Regard Sir—Your most Obedient humble Servant

Jonth; Trumbull

LS, DLC:GW; LB, Ct: Trumbull Papers.

1. See GW to Trumbull, 30 September.

2. Trumbull wrote Nicholas Cooke about the proposed Long Island expedition on 1 Oct., and Cooke replied on 5 October. For Cooke's letter, see "R.I. Revolutionary Correspondence," 173–74.

3. William McIntosh (1722–1813) of Needham, Mass., commanded one of the regiments of Massachusetts militia reinforcements under Gen. Benjamin Lincoln that recently had arrived at Fairfield, Conn., on their way to New York. For the proposed Long Island expedition, McIntosh apparently was put in command of two militia regiments (see GW to McIntosh, 21 Oct.). McIntosh served as a militia colonel from 1775 to 1782 and as a member of the Massachusetts house of representatives at various times between 1775 and 1804. He represented Needham at the state ratification convention in 1788.

4. For Esek Hopkins's letter to Trumbull of 5 Oct., see Clark and Morgan, *Naval Documents*, 6:1134–36. The two new Continental frigates were the *Warren* and *Providence*. The Connecticut naval vessels were the ship *Oliver Cromwell* and the brig *Defence*.

5. See Trumbull to Hopkins, this date, ibid., 1219–20. This naval expedition was soon canceled, because on 10 Oct. the Continental marine committee wrote to Hopkins ordering him to sail with his ships to Cape Fear, N.C., to reduce a British fort said to have been built there (see ibid., 1202–3).

6. Abraham Whipple, commander of the Continental navy ship *Columbus*, arrived at Providence on 29 Sept. from a voyage during which he had captured four British prizes (see the *Providence Gazette; and Country Journal*, 5 Oct.).

General Orders

Head Quarters, Harlem Heights, Octobr 12th 1776.
Parole　　　　　　　　　　　　　　　　　　　Countersign
The General orders, that one man from every Mess, be kept cooking, till there are provisions dressed for three days—The Butchers are also to keep killing.

Varick transcript, DLC:GW.

Letter not found: from the Board of War, 12 Oct. 1776. On 22 Oct. Robert Hanson Harrison wrote to the Board of War: "I am directed by his Excellency, whose business has called him from hence, to acknowledge his receipt of your Favors of the 12th and 15th Instt, and to inform you in Answer to the first, that he will mention the case of the French Gentn to Genl Lee, and obtain his Opinion as to the best mode of providing for 'em in a usefull way. The Horses belonging to the Light Dragoons, who were taken, he thinks will be very serviceable, and he will write to Genl Ward or One of the Agents to purchase them" (DNA:PCC, item 152).

To Nicholas Cooke

Sir　　　　　　　Head Qrs Harlem Heights Octr 12[–13]th 1776
The situation of our Affairs and the approaching dissolution of the present Army, calling for every possible exertion on our part to levy a new one; and presuming that your State are about to make an arrangement of Officers for the Quota of Troops they are to furnish, and that they may wish to know those belonging to them who have served with reputation and bravery;

I have thought it expedient, to obtain a return by such means, as seemed most likely to be well founded. to this end I have made enquiry, and the inclosed list which I have the honor to transmit you, comprehends the Names of those, who in public estimation, and that of the Generals under whom they have more particularly acted, have behaved themselves well & to good acceptance, and whose past conduct give a reasonable hope, that their future will render material services to their Country.[1]

The advantages arising from a judicious appointment of Officers, and the fatal consequences that result from the want of them, are too obvious to require arguments to prove them; I shall therefore beg leave to add only, that as the well doing— nay the very existence of every Army to any profitable purposes, depend upon it, that too much regard cannot be had to the chusing of Men of merit, and such as are not only under the influence of a warm attachment to their Country, but who also possess Sentiments & principles of the strictest honor. Men of this Character are fit for Office, and will use their best endeavours to introduce that discipline & subordination which are essential to good order, & inspire that confidence in the Men, which alone can give success to the Interesting and important contest in which we are engaged. I would also beg leave to subjoin, that it appears to me absolutely necessary, that this business should have your earliest attention, that those who are nominated, may employ their interest and influence to recruit Men out of your Corps that are now here without loss of time.

In respect to the Officers that were on the Canada expedition, their behavior & merit, and the severities they have experienced, entitle them to a particular notice in my opinion—However as they are under parole,[2] I would recommend that Vacancies should be reserved for such as you think fit to promote, not wishing 'em to accept Commissions immediately or to do the least act, that may be interpreted a violation of their engagement. their releasement I hope, will be soon obtained, as I think 'em entitled to the first exchange, and which I have mentioned to Congress.

I flatter myself that the freedom I have taken in the instances above mentioned, will have the indulgence and pardon of your State, when I assure you, that the List which you will receive, is

not intended to exclude Gentlemen of greater merit or transmitted with other views, than to assist you, and of promoting
the general good, and also, that the measure has been recommended by a Committee of Congress who were pleased to honor
me with a visit. I have done the same to Governr Trumbull at
his particular request, and the Officers are makeing out a return
to be laid before the Assembly of the Massachusetts bay of the
same nature so far as it concerns the Officers from their state.

On the morning of the 9th Instt Three of [the][3] Enemy's
Ships, Two of 44 and One of 20 Guns with three or four Tenders
ran up the North River without receiving any interruption from
our Chevaux defrise, or apparent damage from our Batteries,
tho a heavy fire was kept up against them from each side of the
River. They are laying at Tarry Town from 25 to 30 miles above
this, & out sailing Two of our Row Gallies in their passage up,
they fell into their Hands. the Crews escaped.

I like to have omitted mentioning of a paymaster to each Regiment, who, I perceive, are not noticed in the List transmitted
you. Congress by a late Resolution have allowed such an Officer
with Captains pay,[4] and as their duty will be not only to receive
the Regiments pay but to keep accounts of their Cloathing, and
every other incidental charge, I would beg leave to recommend
that attention should be had to their Appointment, and that persons may be nominated who are well versed in Accounts & who
can keep them in a fair and proper manner. I am led to advise
this precaution to be used, because it will be an Office of a good
deal of consequence, & because in several instances in the present Army, where the appointments were made in consequence
of recommendations from the Field Officers, persons have been
put in, who so far from being Accountants, and answering the
designs of Congress can scarcly write their own Names.

13 Octobr. Yesterday the Enemy landed at Frogs point about
Nine Miles from hence up the Sound. their number we cannot
ascertain as they have not advanced. the point is rather an
Island, as it is surrounded with water on every high tide. From
the great movements of Ships & other Vessels up the sound in
the Evening with Troops in, and the information of Two deserters who came out last night, there is strong reason to believe,
they mean to land and to pursue their former Scheme of getting
in our rear & cutting off the Communication with the Country.

I have ordered some works to be thrown up on the passes leading from the Sound where they are landed, and from the situation of the Grounds thro which they must pass, if they pursue
their plan, I would fain hope they will sustain considerable Loss
if not a repulse. I have the Honor to be with great esteem Sir Yr
Most Obedt Servt

Go: Washington

LS, in Robert Hanson Harrison's writing, R-Ar; LB, DLC:GW; Varick transcript, DLC:GW.

1. The enclosed undated return of Rhode Island officers recommended for
the new establishment includes names for most but not all of the commissioned
and staff officer positions in the two regiments that Rhode Island was to raise.
Several of the second lieutenant and ensign positions are left blank, and the
only staff officers recommended are the two regimental quartermasters. Daniel Hitchcock and Christopher Greene are nominated to command the regiments. A note on the reverse of the document reads: "Colonel [James Mitchell]
Varnum would have been recommended for a Colonel of one of the Regiments, but he refuses to serve" (R-Ar). For Nathanael Greene's role in preparing this list and his comments on it, see his letters to Cooke of 11 and 16 Oct.
in Showman, *Greene Papers*, 1:313–16, 317–18.

2. The LB reads "under their paroles."

3. This word appears in the LB.

4. For this resolution of 16 July, see *JCC*, 5:564.

From Major General Nathanael Greene

Fort Constitution [Fort Lee, N.J.]

Dear General   Octo. 12th [1776] 5 OClock
    I am inform'd a large body of the Enemies Troop have landed
at Froggs point. If so I suppose the Troops here will be wanted
there. I have three Brigades in readiness to reinforce you; General Clintons Brigade will march first. General Nixons next and
then the Troops under the command of General Roberdeau. I
dont Apprehend any danger from this quarter at present[.] if
the force on your side are insufficient I hope these three Brigades may be Ordered over and I with them and leave General
Ewings Brigade to Guard the Post. If the Troops are wanted
over your side or likely to be in the morning, they should be got
over in the latter part of the Night as the Shiping may move
up from below and impede if not totally stop the Troops from
passing.[1] I wait your Excellencys further commands. Should be

glad to know where the Enemy has landed & their numbers. I am with great respect Your Excellencys Obedient Servant

                                              N. Greene

N.B. The Tents upon Staten Island have been all Struck as far as discovery has been made.

ALS, DLC:GW.

1. Gen. John Nixon's brigade crossed the Hudson River on the night of 13 Oct. to reinforce Heath's division (see Greene's orders to Nixon, 13 Oct., in Johnston, *Campaign of 1776*, pt. 2, 144). Much to Greene's disappointment, he and the rest of his division remained in New Jersey (see Greene to Nicholas Cooke, 16 Oct., in Showman, *Greene Papers*, 1:317–18).

From Robert R. Livingston

Sir: Oct. 12th, 1776

I should do injustice toward the politeness & attention with which your Excellency has been pleased to listen to the crude opinions which I have some times offered if I did not (without any appology) deliver my sentiments on the present alarming state of this Colony & submit to your Excellencys better judgment such measures as will (in my Idea) be most likely to eleviate the evills I apprehend. While the army remained at New York I saw the possibility of their retreats being cut off & moved & got such a resolution in our Convention as I thought would contribute to your Excellencys satisfaction on their head—Since I was persuaded then & the (event has justified that persuasion) that your Excellency saw the danger & remained in New York till the propriety of removing should be thought in compliance with the prejudices of others & least you should be charged with unnecessarily abandoning that City. Since upon experiment it appears contrary to the general sentiment that the obstructions in the river are ineffectual the present situation of the army tho not exactly similar bears some resemblance to that in which it was at New York.

The enemy may still land above & reduce your Excellency to the necessity of attacking them at their Landing or of suffering them to seize upon advantageous passes from which it will be impossible to dislodge them for such is the peculiar situation of the Country & the vicinity of the sound will it be very difficult so to station themselves as to cut of all supplyes going to your camp or at least render them extremely hazardous. This too may in my opinion be done with a part of their forces while the remainder having by this means their retreat secured may ravage the Country, encourage the disaffected & by their assistance without danger carry their arms even to Albany, which would greatly endanger the northern army who for want of teams hors's &c which are not to be procured in that almost uninhabited country could not remove any part of their stores if so or even so much provision as would subsist them on their way down if they attempted to march to Albany. Stay they could not, nor would any other means be left them but to retreat in to New England without artillery, stores or provisions in which case their strength would soon be disipated by desertions or the whole to be obliged to release separate for want of the necessary stores. It may be asked whether these passes can not be secured by the militia of our states. I assure your excellency as an undoubted fact that we have already made our utmost exertions that our secret enemies are numerous & implacable that the whole force that we have ventured to call out on this occasion is three hundred men & that we have little reason to expect that even these can be obtained,[1] add to this that the western part of Connecticut are by no means to be depended upon.

In this situation I humbly conceive that two things are necessary, one of them I suggested long since to our Convention who approving the same it was mentioned to your Excellency & not carried into execution for reason which had then great weight, but from an alteration of circumstances do no longer operate, I mean the marching a body of force from New England either militia or others to Beron river or some other strong grounds that commands the passes into Connecticut.[2] This I believe may now be done without any great difficulty only by collecting the troops that are scattered along the sound.

The next is to order up one or two regiments to secure the passes in the highlands & at the same time to form a strong camp a little above where the ships now are which may from the nature of the ground be done with out any great numbers of men & who w'd make it dangerous for an enemy to have them on their rear, this indeed will lesten the army at New York but it will at the same time add to their real strength since it will

either reduce the enemy to the necessity of marching the lines
in front or if they sh'd Land above expose themselves to the
danger of being hemmed in by three armies. This I dare say
they will not attempt & I promise myself much from the bear
reputation of three such bodies besides that they would enable
you [to] collect a new army in case of a defeat below.

I dare say your Excellency sees the necessity of carrying up
magazines of provision & materials for Barrackes in some part
of this Country that the want of them should not in case of any
unfortunate accident oblige the army to separate. Where not the
treasury of this state exhausted by the uncommon expence to
which we have been put by the disaffection of our own people,
the debt that is due from the Continent & the disappointments
we have met with in not being able to strike money yet, the Convention of this state would have at their own risque have done
some thing therein. Your Excellency sees the opinion I have of
your patience & good nature in my venturing to obtrude upon
them these crude & hasty remarks, yet I may possibly find some
excuse for them as my anxiety for the success of the great cause
in which your Excellency is engaged to support & my knowledge of a Country which your Excellency had no leisure to
explore.

                                    ROBERT R. LIVINGSTON.

Life in Letters: American Autograph Journal, American Autograph Shop, Marion
Station, Pa. (1938), 1:6–8; ADf, sold by Argosy Book Store, Inc., item 385,
catalog 448 (1959). GW sent Jonathan Trumbull, Sr., a copy of this letter on
15 October.

1. For the calling out of these militia reinforcements by the New York committee of safety, see the committee of safety's letter to GW of 10 Oct., and
note 2.

2. For the New York convention's earlier proposal to form a camp of 6,000
men on the Byram River along the border between New York and Connecticut, see the convention's letter to GW of 16 July and GW to Jonathan Trumbull, Sr., 19 July.

From Colonel Joseph Phillips

                                       [c.12 October 1776]
The Address of Joseph Phillips, Colonel of a Battalion of Jersey Levies, Sheweth: That your Excellency's adressor, hath
viewed with infinite regret, the Enemies Ships of War passing

by us up the North River, opposite Mount Washington, with impunity: owing in a great measure, he humbly conceives, to the bad Construction of some of our Batteries, & the want of others in more suitable places: To remedy which, he begs leave to propose, that he (with the fatigue Men of Genl Heard's Brigade if your Excellency pleases) will finish the Battery on the Rocks near the River side, which he began in July last; & will also construct & compleat another small one for four Guns, a little above, nearer Mount Washington, that will rake or scour the River side both up & down; the Embrasures of which, made so, that a piece of Ordnance may either be elevated or Depressed, as occasion may require. Your Excellency's Addresser, with very great deference, is Confident that Cannon planted & properly Mann'd at the proposed Batteries, will annoy the Enemies Shipping abundantly more than those at any other place or places contiguous to our Vesseaux De Frize.[1]

Your Addresser begs leave to mention that he hath some little experience in the Engineers Branch that he acquired in the course of Five Years that he served His Britanic Majesty last War, tho' not immediately employed as an Engineer, yet under the special instruction & direction of Capt. Harry Gordon on the Ohio, & Col. Patrick Mackellar &c. in the West Indies, having served with them at the Seiges of Martinico & Havannah.[2] He hath no sinister, or Ostentatious motive that influences him, his only ambition is to contribute his Mite, to the service of his Native Country, and merit your Excellency's approbation—for whom he possesses the most profound regard & Esteem And is His most Obedt humble Servt

Jos. Phillips

ADS, DLC:GW.

1. Robert Hanson Harrison replied to Phillips on this date: "I have it in charge from his Excellency, the Commander in Cheif, to return you his most thankfull acknowledgments for the proposition contained in your address and to inform you, that he not only approves of the same, but wishes you to proceed with the Works which you have mentioned. The generous motives which Induced you to lay the measure before him in his estimation do you the highest honor & are such as he would be happy to see prevail generally thro the Army" (DLC:GW).

2. Harry Gordon (d. 1787), a Scottish engineer who helped to build Braddock's Road in 1755 and was attached to the Royal American Regiment the following year, began supervising the construction of Fort Pitt at the Forks of

the Ohio in September 1759. Patrick Mackellar (1717–1778), another Scottish engineer who had served on the Braddock campaign, was appointed chief engineer of the frontier forts in 1756. Mackellar acted as chief engineer for Gen. Jeffery Amherst at the siege of Louisburg in 1758 and for Gen. James Wolfe at Quebec in 1759. During the winter of 1762, Mackellar conducted the siege operations for Gen. Robert Monckton's expedition against Martinique in the West Indies, and the following spring and summer, he served as chief engineer for the earl of Albemarle's successful attack on Havana, Cuba. Gordon also participated in the siege of Havana. After the French and Indian War, Gordon and Mackellar both had long and distinguished careers in the British corps of engineers. Gordon served in the West Indies from 1767 to 1773, and during the campaign of 1776, he was chief engineer in Canada, a position that he soon resigned over a question of rank. Gordon returned to the West Indies in 1783 and died on his way to England four years later. Mackellar served as chief engineer at Minorca from 1763 until his death fifteen years later, rising to the rank of colonel of engineers in August 1777.

General Orders

Head Quarters, Harlem Heights, Octob: 13th 1776.
Parole.   Countersign.[1]

The General expressly orders, that the men have four days provisions *ready dressed,* at all times, for which purpose the[2] Commissaries, or the Deputies, are to keep the Butchers constantly killing, till such supply is had, and one man from every Mess is to be kept cooking—The commanding Officers of regiments, and others, are most earnestly requested to see this order carried into immediate execution.

Supplies of Ammunition may now be had, so that any Officer who now neglects getting what is necessary, must be accountable to his Country, and the men under his command.

When any Regiments are about to march, they are to have their Tents struck, rolled up, and a Guard under the Command of a careful Officer, to attend them, and the Baggage; who is not under any pretence to leave them, without orders.

As the Enemy seem now to be endeavouring to strike some stroke, before the Close of the Campaign, the General most earnestly conjures, both Officers and Men, if they have any Love for their Country, and Concern for its Liberties; regard to the safety of their Parents, Wives, Children and Countrymen; that they will act with Bravery & Spirit, becoming the Cause in which they are engaged; And to encourage, and animate them so to do, there is every Advantage of Ground and Situation, so that if we do not conquer, it must be our own faults—How much better will it be to die honorable, fighting in the field, than to return home, covered with shame and disgrace; even if the cruelty of the Enemy should allow you to return? A brave and gallant behaviour for a few days, and patience under some little hardships, may save our Country, and enable us to go into Winter Quarters with safety and honour.

The marching of some troops to Kingsbridge, makes it necessary to reduce the Picquet to 600 Men, and the Fatigue proportionably.

Varick transcript, DLC:GW.

1. "Williams' Diary," 49:52, gives the parole for this date as "Juniper" and the countersign as "Lee."

2. The copyist inadvertently wrote "they" in the manuscript.

From William Fitzhugh

Dear Sir   Annapolis Maryland October 13th 1776.

I had the Honor to recieve your favr of the 5th Inst. & am much Oblig'd to you.[1]

I hope you will forgive the trouble I have Given, & may Hereafter Give you by recommendations, & Shew no more regard to them, than you think, or may know they Deserve, As in my Scituation, I have many Applications, which might be thought unfriendly to reject, you may However, be Assur'd, That I will not Name to you a man whom I do not know or believe to be Worthy.

I Suppose Lieutenant Steward If he Deserves it, will be promoted in the Corps to which he belongs, & wth respect to Wilkinson, who I verily believe is a young Fellow of Great Merit, I will Endeavor, as you are Pleas'd to Advise, to get Him Provided for in The Battalions to be rais'd Here, But in the Intrim, As I presume you have frequent Communication wth General Gates, or the Commanding Offr of the Northern Department, I shou'd be much Oblig'd to you for Making mention of Him, refering to His Conduct & Behaviour.[2]

This Convention have now Sent Commissioners to your Camp, to Incorporate our Independant Compys & to form into Battalions, Such of Our Flying Camp as will Enter, on the Terms & Conditions, Directed by Congress, for the Continental Army, And Carry wth them, Blank Commissions, for such Officers, who will Continue, or may be promoted: I cannot say, that Confering such a Trust, was Intirely Agreeable to Me, But as it cou'd not be Avoided, I mov'd for & Carried, an Instruction "That the Commissioners be Instructed to Consult with & Take The Advice of His Excellency Genl Washington respecting the Promotion or Appointment of Officers:["][3] This I Immagine, will Guard against an Evil, which their want of Experience & knowledge in Military Affairs, Perhaps cou'd not have been Avoided; As my Particular friend Genl Beall is of the Flying Camp, & The Term of their Service will Expire on the first Day of December Next, I cou'd Wish to have had Him Appointed Collo. of the Incorporated Independant Compys, But it was thought it might be Injurious to the Field Officers of Collo. Smallwoods Regiment, However, If a Battalion is form'd out of The Flying Camp, & remainder of the Independant Compys now with you, For the Continental Service, The Brigadier (If He will Accept it) Ought of Course to have the Command. It wou'd be a Pity, & a real Loss to the Service, If so Valuable an Officer as Beall, Shou'd be Discharg'd from it, As must be the Case, at the Expiration of the Term of the Flying Camp, Unless some provision is made for Him; I believe this Gentleman had the Honor to be known by you in former Service, & therefore will not Say more of Him at Present, His Brigade Majr is a Brave young Man, & I hope will be provided for in the New Corps.[4]

I am Glad your Loss on Evacuateing New york, was not Greater than you mention, It is Less than I fear'd and Expected; I never look'd on New york, As a Place Tenable against an Enemy Commanding the Water, Even, If their Land Force had been Inferior to what it was, & I heartily rejoyce, at your having made so Good a Retreat from it, But am Still Distress'd to think of your Winter Quarters, Considering the Want of Tents warm Cloathing, &c., Yet, As Many reinforcements are going to you, & I trust will be provided with every thing Necessary, I Doubt not, but that you will be able to keep your Adversaries within Due

Bounds this Campaign, & that they will be Sick of their Enterprize Before the Middle of next Summer.

I am Sorry to find that the Delay of Congress, to Settle a Confederation has Created some Jealousy & Uneasiness, But hope it will not be Attended by any Evil Consequences; I believe Our Convention now Setting, will Remonstrate with Congress, on the Subject of Crown Lands in the Different States, not Already Granted or Located. As there is an Oppinion Held up, That all such Lands, Ought to be Apply'd, to Defray the Genl Expence of the United States in the War.

We have Order'd Eight Battalions for the Continental Army, Including Our Troops already Sent, or Such of them as will Engage During the War, to be rais'd Immediately, & have no Doubt of their being Compleated in Proper time, As the Inhabitants of This State Appear to Me, to have a Warm Zeal for the Cause of America.

I was Apply'd to by many Members of Convention to go as one of the Commissioners to New york, & Shou'd have been Exceeding Happy in the Oppertunity, of Paying my Personal Respects to you, But am so very blind, that I can Scarcely Walk aCross a Room, & as Matters of Importance must come on, in the Formation of a New Government, Which is now under Consideration, I Did not think Myself at Liberty, or that it wou'd be prudent to leave the Convention at this time, & Therefore Declin'd it.

Mrs Fitzhugh is now with Me, & Joins in Affect. Complts & best Wishes for your Health & Success. I have the Honor to be With sincere Regard Yr Excellencys Affectionate & Oblig'd H. Sert

Willm Fitzhugh

P.S. Permit Me to recommend to your Countenance & Favor, Capt. Thomas Smyth Junr of Collo. Richardsons Battalion Flying Camp. Formerly a Lieutenant in Collo. Smallwoods Regiment, He is a Son of My Particular friend Thomas Smyth Esqr. of Chester Town (who is now a Member of Our Council of Safety & Convention) And is a Brave & Worthy young Gentleman.[5]

This Will be Deliver'd to you by Thomas Contee Esqr. Who

goes to the Camp as One of Our Commissioners. I beg leave to Introduce Him to your Usual Civility.[6]

The Inclosed is a Part of Our Commissioners Instructions, refer'd to in this Letter.[7] Dear Sir yrs Affectionately

Willm Fitzhugh

ALS, DLC:GW.

1. This letter has not been found.

2. James Wilkinson (1757–1825), an indefatigable schemer and self-promoter best known for his unscrupulous postwar business and political activities on the western frontier and his deep involvement in the Aaron Burr conspiracy, was at this time a brigade major in the northern army. A native of Calvert County, Md., Wilkinson studied medicine at Philadelphia before enlisting as a private soldier in Capt. William Richardson's independent Maryland company during the spring of 1775. In September 1775 Wilkinson joined Col. William Thompson's rifle regiment at Cambridge, Mass., as a volunteer, and from November 1775 to April 1776 he apparently served in some capacity on Gen. Nathanael Greene's staff. Commissioned a captain in the 2d Continental Regiment in March 1776, Wilkinson accompanied his regiment that spring to New York and then to Canada, where in June and July he acted as an aide-de-camp to Gen. Benedict Arnold. General Gates appointed Wilkinson a brigade major in the northern army on 20 July and assigned him to Mount Independence near Ticonderoga. Although Wilkinson was made lieutenant colonel of Col. Thomas Hartley's Additional Continental Regiment on 12 Jan. 1777, he resigned that commission the following April in order to remain with the northern army as an aide-de-camp to Gates (see GW to Hartley, 9 April 1777, DLC:GW). In May 1777 Wilkinson became deputy adjutant general of the northern department, and as such he carried Gates's dispatches concerning the British surrender at Saratoga to Congress in late October. Congress rewarded Wilkinson for that service by brevetting him a brigadier general on 6 Nov. 1777, and on 6 Jan. 1778 it elected him secretary to the Board of War (see *JCC*, 9:851, 870; 10:24). Widespread resentment in the Continental officer corps at Wilkinson's being given so high a rank for so little cause obliged him to resign his brevet commission in early March 1778, and at the end of that month Wilkinson also resigned as secretary to the Board of War because of a bitter quarrel with the board's president and his former mentor, General Gates (see ibid., 226, 297, and Henry Laurens to Wilkinson, 31 Mar. 1778, in Smith, *Letters of Delegates*, 9:359). On 24 July 1779 Congress chose Wilkinson to be Continental clothier general (see *JCC*, 14:883–84). Although Wilkinson's consistent neglect of that office greatly displeased GW, he did not resign until March 1781 (see GW to William Heath, 18 Nov. 1779, MHi: Heath Papers; GW to Samuel Huntington, 24 Mar. 1781, DNA:PCC, item 152; GW to Wilkinson, 24 Mar. 1781, DLC:GW; and *JCC*, 19:313).

3. For the Maryland convention's resolution of 9 Oct. authorizing these commissioners and incorporating the instruction moved by Fitzhugh, see DNA:PCC, item 70. Fitzhugh enclosed a separate copy of that instruction with

this letter (see note 7). The four commissioners appointed were James Lloyd Chamberlaine, Benjamin Rumsey, Thomas Contee, and John Hanson, Jr.

4. Daniel Jenifer Adams (1751–1796), of Charles County, Md., who recently had struggled to discharge a large debt that he owed GW for flour sold in the West Indies, was commissioned a third lieutenant in Rezin Beall's independent Maryland company on 2 Jan. 1776, and on 27 Aug. Adams became brigade major of the Maryland flying camp. Named major of the 7th Maryland Regiment on 10 Dec. 1776, Adams served with that regiment until he resigned his commission on 1 June 1779.

5. Thomas Smythe, Jr. (1757–1807), who had been appointed a first lieutenant in Col. William Smallwood's Maryland regiment on 14 Jan. 1776, served from July to December as a captain in Col. William Richardson's 4th Regiment of Maryland flying camp troops. On 10 Dec. Smythe became major of the 5th Maryland Regiment, from which he resigned on 12 Mar. 1778. He represented Kent County in the lower house of the Maryland assembly in 1782 and 1783. Thomas Smythe, Sr. (1730–1819), a Chestertown merchant and planter, represented Kent County in several Maryland conventions between 1774 and 1776. A major in the county militia, he owned a shipyard where he apparently built vessels for the state during the war.

6. Thomas Contee (1729–1811), a Prince George's County, Md., tobacco trader and planter who resided at Brookefield, his family estate near Nottingham, was an uncle of Alexander Contee Hanson, GW's assistant secretary at this time. Contee repeatedly served in the Maryland assemblies and conventions between 1769 and 1778, and he was a member of the council of safety from 1776 to 1777. A major in the county militia by 1776, he was promoted to lieutenant colonel during this year.

7. The enclosed copy of this instruction, most of which Fitzhugh quotes in the fourth paragraph of this letter, is in DLC:GW (see note 3).

From Major General William Heath

Dear General   Kingsbridge Octr 13th 1776

I would have wrote your Excellency Earlier this morning, But have waited to have Intelligence from the Two Regiments near frogs Point, which I have but Just Received, a Large number of vessells, Ships, Brigs, Schooners, Sloops Lighters &c. Saild through Hell gate yesterday afternoon, and Came to anchor last night off Frogs Point, where they still remain, during the night, Lanthorns were Lighted and hung out at their Yard Arms which made a very Extraordinary Appearance, There has been no movement this morning, but all Still & Quiet both at Frogs Point, and Morrisania and but few Troops have been Seen at frogs Point[.] whether, this Manœuvre is a Fient or not is yet Uncertain, I Beleive our Readiness to meet them yesterday at the Bridge & Pass over the Marsh has Disopointed them, a Small work has been Thrown up at each of the before mentioned Posts—I shall order a Reinforcement to Support those Posts—every Occurrunce worthy of notice shall be Immediately Transmitted to Your Excellency. I have the Honor to be with great respect your Excellency's most Huble Servt

W. Heath

ADfS, MHi: Heath Papers.

This letter apparently is a reply to the letter that GW's aide-de-camp William Grayson wrote to Heath on this date, informing him "that his Excy [GW] (as the enemy did not attempt a landing at Morissania this morning) thinks it would be adviseable to send a stronger force towards the two passes near the Enemy, where our Men were posted yesterday; & also to throw up some works for their cover & defense; He also recommends strongly to your attention, the keeping a good look out at Pell's point, at the mouth of East Chester creek, & at Hunt's & Willet's points, for the sake of gaining intelligence these posts to be considered as look outs only; Should the Enemy make any movement you will immediately communicate it to Head Quarters, You will write to the Genl by return of this messenger, & let him know what has happened since" (MHi: Heath Papers).

Joseph Reed wrote Heath on this date: "It being necessary since the late Movement of the Enemy to form some Plan the General [GW] proposes a Meeting of the General Officers this Day at 12 oClock at or near Kingsbridge" (MHi: Heath Papers). Heath says in his memoirs: "The General Officers of the army were this day [13 Oct.] in council at our General's [Heath's] Quarters" (Wilson, *Heath's Memoirs*, 81). No minutes have been found for this council of war.

To Colonel Thomas Tash

Sir   Head Quarters 13th Octo. 1776

Since I wrote you by Lt Colo. Welch upon the Subject of fixing on Quarters for your Troops,[1] I have received from the Committee of Safety for this State such an Account of its alarming Situation owing to the numbers of disaffected, together with the little Confidence that can be placed on the Militia of some of the Counties,[2] that I find it necessary to order a part of the New Hampshire Troops to their Assistance, and do therefore direct you to march your Regiment with all possible dispatch to Fish Kills, where you will receive further directions from the Committee—I think it will be proper to send an Officer forward to give the Committee notice of your coming, that they may Assign you the places where it will be most suitable to post your Men.[3] I am sir Your most Obed. Servt

G.W.

⟨P.⟩S. do not delay ⟨y⟩our march a moment, nor the sending an Officer ⟨to⟩ the Convention of this State now setting at The Fish Kills.[4]

LB, in Tench Tilghman's writing, DLC:GW; Varick transcript, DLC:GW.

1. This letter has not been found. Joseph Welch (Welsh; 1734–1829) of Plaistow, N.H., served as a member of the New Hampshire provincial congress during 1775, and he was named one of the colony's two paymasters for its Continental troops in June of that year. The following August Welch became major of Col. Josiah Bartlett's militia regiment, and on 17 Sept. 1776 he was appointed lieutenant colonel of Colonel Tash's regiment of reinforcements. During the fall of 1777 Welch commanded a regiment of New Hampshire volunteers who reinforced the northern army at Saratoga.

2. See the New York Committee of Safety to GW, 10 October.

3. Tench Tilghman informed William Duer on this date of GW's orders to Tash (NHi: Duer Papers), and Robert Hanson Harrison conveyed the same information in his letter to Duer of 14 Oct. (NN: Emmet Collection). Duer replied to Tilghman on 14 Oct. that Tash's regiment "will be of great service to prevent at least a Revolt, though It will not be strength enough to occupy the Passes through the Highlands" (NHi: Duer Papers).

4. Tash's regiment marched from Greenwich, Conn., on the morning of 14 Oct. (see Tilghman to Duer, 15 Oct., NHi: Duer Papers). Five or six companies arrived at Fishkill by 16 Oct., only to be sent back to the "South Entrance of the Highlands" (Duer to Tilghman, 16 Oct., NHi: Duer Papers).

From Jonathan Trumbull, Sr.

Sr   New Haven Octor 13th 1776

Since mine of the 11th Instant by express have Received pretty Sure Intelligence that a plan is forming by the Noted Majr Rogers a famous Partisan or Ranger in the last Warr now in the Service of Genl How on Long Island where he is Collecting a Battallion of Tories with Such as he can procure from the Main many of which we understand have lately Stole over to join him and who are perfectly acquainted with every inlet and avenue into the Towns of Greenwich, Stamford & Norwalk where are Considerable quantities of Continental Stores, the designe of Rogers as far as we can learn is from Huntingdon to make a Sudden discent in the Night more especially on the

Town, of Norwalk, not only to take the Stores there but to Burn & destroy all before them there, It is to be noted that about two hours will bring them over in the Night from Huntingdon to Norwalk or the other Towns mentiond in & near which are many Tories expected to join them, The Militia lately returned into those Towns & others near are mostly Sick and Infirm— I have understood ⟨that⟩ the New Hampshire Militia on their way for your Army ⟨were⟩ ordered to be Stationd for a while at Norwalk & Greenwich or Horseneck but find now they are all moved forward from Norwalk, I thought ⟨it⟩ my duty to acquaint your Excellency with every Intelligence from the Enemy & of their designes that you might take Such Steps as you Should think proper to counteract them[.] The Towns mentiond are much Alarm'd especially Norwalk who have taken an active part In bringing of Inhabitants, Stock, & Stores from Long Island and are particularly threatned with reprisals, being made upon them[.] I have orderd Capt. Niles in the Spy to Cruise along the Sound as far Westward as it will be Safe for him to goe which is perhaps as far as Byram River,[1] he is now in that quarter, I understand there is two Small Privateer Sloops now at or near Norwalk (viz.) Capts. Rogers & Pond[.] the one believe belongs to the State of New York the other Continental, but am Informed they are about leaving that Station[.][2] if they with Niles were to Cruise back & forward along ⟨the⟩ Sound & towards the Western part they might be of Special Service to prevent any Sudden Incursion of parties of the Enemy from Long Island as well as be Safe Convoys for your Stores along the Coast to Byram but Niles only can be under my direction[.] your Plan for a discent on Long Island is ripening as fast as possible to be put in execution, & as far as I Can learn by Colol Livingston he cannot make out of those assigned to him above Eleven or *1200* Men[.] wheather he ought not to be joind or reinforced by as many as to make up two thousand or more must Submit to your Excellency on whose knowledge and judgment I can most Safely relye—I have inclosed the Copies of two Letters discover'd or forced from the possesior for your perusal[3] but the most particular account of Rogers Intentions are from a Friendly woman of good Character who made her escape from Huntingdon a few Nights agoe where Rogers with his Party then was[.] Our Assembly are now Sitting at this place & will have to make out the

Arrangement of the officers for the New Army ⟨before⟩ they rise[.] therefore should be glad your Excellency ⟨would⟩ forward the list desired as soon as may be, as I expect ⟨one⟩ from Genl Gates of those in his Department in a few days.

L (incomplete), DLC:GW; LB (incomplete), Ct: Trumbull Papers. The mutilated words within angle brackets are supplied from Force, *American Archives,* 5th ser., 2:1028–29.

1. The LB reads: "to cruise along the Sound from Norwalk as far Westward as it will be safe for him to go." The council of safety on 2 Oct. ordered Capt. Robert Niles of the *Spy* to "cruise in the Sound betwixt Montack Point and Stamford, in order to watch the movements of our enemies and to give intelligence in the easiest and best manner for the security of the navigation belonging to the United States and of the towns upon the Sound and to annoy our enemies, until further orders" (Journal of the Connecticut Council of Safety, 2 Oct., in Clark and Morgan, *Naval Documents,* 6:1099).

2. Capt. William Rogers commanded the New York armed sloop *Montgomery,* and Capt. Charles Pond commanded the Continental armed sloop *General Schuyler.*

3. The enclosures, which are in DLC:GW, are copies of two personal letters written by Connecticut Loyalists on Long Island to friends at Norwalk: J. Cable to Hezekiah Jarvis, 27 Sept., and Stephen Fountain to Darias Olmsted, 28 September. Both letters contain messages for family members and give only vague intelligence about British military operations. Cable writes: "I Had a Good passage Over to the [Long] Island where I am at present and Am Like to Remain. I am Under Capt. Fairchild in Col: Rogers Battalion of Rangers. . . . I must Own that my wife as well as All Others was Ignorant of my Coming away, which makes me the more Ancious of hearing from Home and Sending home—The whole Say and Desire of the Army is to have the Rebels Stand their Ground and the Jigg will Soon be to an End. . . . we Expect to Remove from flushing to Some Other part of the Island Soon." Fountain, writing from Newtown, laments his misfortune in being compelled "to Leave my Native Shoar to Seek On this Island a place of Refuge from wicked & Ungodly men." He gives highly inflated figures for American casualties in the Battle of Long Island and the current strength of Howe's army. "The 27th Of August Last," Fountain says, "the Loss of the Rebels on this Island was 3550 Kill'd and taken Prisoners—The Loss of the Brittish that they Sustained was 250 Men Kill'd & taken prisoners But Our Army Consists now of Eighty Thousand Besid[e]s Rangers & 200 Transports is Expected in Every Day Laden with Men."

To Major General Artemas Ward

Sir   Head Qrs Harlem Heights Octobr 13th 1776

I have been favoured with your two Letters of the 3d & 6th Instt. in answer to the first, I am not only willing, but shall be much obliged by your Settling with the Gentn to whom Money was advanced for purchasing Arms & for which purpose I have transmitted a List of the Warrants that were drawn in their favor. Before I left Cambridge some of the Gentlemen, (three, four or more of them) accounted with me, but having sent away my Book, in which their Names and the ballances they paid in, were entered, some time before the evacuation of New-York, I cannot particularise them, and therefore have forwarded a List of the whole.[1]

In respect to the latter, and the Invoice it contains, as the Articles seem all to be necessary, and many of them are much wanted, I think you can not do better, than by ordering them to be sent to the Qr Master General for the use of the Army here.

We are again deprived of the Navigation of the North River, and the Supplies which used to come thro that Channel, by means of the Enemy's fleet, Three of their Ships of War with three or four Tenders having passed our Batteries and Chivaux de frise on the Morning of the 9th without any apparent damage from the former, tho a heavy fire was kept up, as they went by, or any interruption from the latter. they now lay at Tarry Town Twenty five or thirty miles above this.

Yesterday the Enemy landed a considerable body of Men at Frogs point, about Nine miles from hence, up the Sound, and several Vessels following in the Evening with Troops on board, and from the information received from Two Deserters who came out last night, we have reason to beleive, that their Main force is now there, and that they have in view, the prosecution of their Original plan, that of getting in our rear & cutting off our communication with the Country. the place they are at, is rather an Island than a point, on every Flood tide being surrounded by Water. I have posted a part of our force, on the passes leading from it, & have directed some small Works to be thrown up for their security. I am Sir Yr Most Obedt Servt

Go: Washington

LS, in Robert Hanson Harrison's writing, owned (1991) by Mr. Richard Maass, White Plains, N.Y.; LB, DLC:GW; Varick transcript, DLC:GW.

1. GW apparently enclosed copies of the undated "Memo of Moneys paid to purchase arms" between 30 Jan. and 15 June 1776 and the also undated "Memo of sundry payments for Arms Vizt stopped from the Reg[iments of the] old Establishment" between 2 Jan. and 30 Mar. 1776, which are part of a

single document located at the end of the documents for 13 Oct. in DLC:GW, ser. 4. For GW's sending of his headquarters papers to Philadelphia for safe-keeping, see his letter to Hancock of 13 August.

General Orders

Head Quarters, Harlem Heights, Octobr 14th 1776
Parole   Countersign[1]

Col. Bailey's regiment is immediately to join Genl Clinton's Brigade, at present under the Command of Col. Glover—Col. Lippets Regt is to join Genl McDougall's Brigade—Each of these regiments are to take their Tents and Cooking Utensils, and to lose no time[2]—The two Connecticut Regiments, under the Command of Col. Storrs and Major Greaves, (not upon York Island)[3] are to be in readiness to march into Westchester, at a moments warning.

The Brigades which will then remain on the Island, will be in two Divisions; the first composed of Heards, Beall's and Weedon's, to be under the Command of Major Genl Putnam—The second consisting of Lord Stirling's, Wadsworth's, and Fellows's, to be under the Command of Major General Spencer.

Genl Putnam will attend particularly to all the works, and necessary places of defence, from the Line which was intended to be run across from Head Quarters, inclusively up to, and including the Works upon, the Island above that place, as far as hath usually been considered as belonging to this division of the Army—He will also attend particularly to the Works about Mount Washington, and to the obstructions in the River, which should be increased as fast as possible.

Genl Spencer is to take charge of all the Works from Head Quarters, to our front lines, to the South; and attend particularly to all weak places; seeing they are secured as well as time, and circumstances will permit: But as there may be more fatigue Men wanted in one division than the other, they are each to furnish for such Works as the Chief Engineer shall direct; seeing that the duty fall equally upon the officers and men of each division.

A Report is immediately to be made, by the commanding Officers of Regiments, to their several Brigadiers, of the state of ready dress'd Provisions, that if there be any Neglect, or deficiency the one may be punished and the other rectified.

The Court Martial of which Col. Weedon was President is dissolved—A new one to be formed, Col. Ewing to preside.

Varick transcript, DLC:GW.

1. "Williams' Diary," 49:52, gives the parole for this date as "Springfield" and the countersign as "Gordon."

2. "Williams' Diary," 49:53, reads: "to take their tents & cooking utensils along with them & to delay no time."

3. "Williams' Diary," 49:53, reads: "now upon the Island."

Lieutenant Colonel Robert Hanson Harrison to John Hancock

Sir   Head Qrs Harlem Heights Octor 14[–17]th 1776

His Excellency having gone this Morning to visit our posts beyond Kings bridge and the Several passes leading from Frog's point and the Necks adjacent,[1] I have the honor to inform you by his command, that no interesting event has taken place since his Letter by Yesterdays post.

Every days intelligence from the Convention of this State, holds forth discoveries of New plots, and of new conspiracies. Some of the Members seem to apprehend, that insurrections are upon the Eve of breaking out, and have suggested the necessity of seizing and securing the passes thro the Highlands, lest the disaffected should do it.[2] their preservation being a matter of the greatest importance, his Excellency notwithstanding the situation we are in with respect to Troops, has detached Colo. Tash with his Regiment lately from New Hampshire, in addition to the Militia mentioned in his last,[3] with directions to receive Orders from the Convention as to the Station & posts he is to occupy.

There are now in our possession, Several persons, Inhabitants of this State who had engaged to join the Enemy, and who were intercepted in going to them; there are also two, who confess they have been with them and that they had actually engaged in their service; but finding the Terms, (the bounty, pay &c.) not so advantageous as they expected from the information they had received, they were induced to return. As the Affairs of this Government are in a precarious situation, and such as the Convention themselves, seem to think, forbid their interposition, farther than taking measures to apprehend them, His Excellency would wish to obtain the sentiments of Congress and their direction, upon a Subject so extremely critical and delicate, and which in the consideration of it, involves many important consequences.

Your favor of the 9th with its several Inclosures, his Excellency received Yesterday morning by the Express, who proceeded immediately on his Journey.

Octob. 17th. I am directed by his Excellency to acquaint you, that we are again obliged to change our disposition to counteract the Operations of the Enemy declining an Attack upon our Front, they have drawn the main body of their Army to Frogs point with a design of Hemming us in, and drawing a line in our Rear. to prevent the consequences which would but too probably follow the execution of their Scheme, the General Officers determined Yesterday, that our forces must be taken from hence, and extended towards East & West Chester so as to out flank them.[4] Genl Lee who arrived on Monday, has strongly urged the absolute necessity of the measure.[5] It is proposed to leave a Garrison at Fort Washington, and to maintain it if possible, in order to preserve the Communication with the Jerseys. They are landing their Artillery & Waggons upon the point, and there are now several boats passing up the Sound full of Men. I have the Honor to be with the greatest respect Sir Yr Most Obedt Servt

Rob. H. Harrison

P.S. The post having not come in since Sunday till today, has been the occasion of not writing you since that time. he was expected as usual which prevented an Express being sent.

ALS, DNA:PCC, item 152; LB, DLC:GW; copy, DNA:PCC, item 169; Varick transcript, DLC:GW. Congress read this letter and referred it to the Board of War on 21 Oct. (*JCC*, 6:889).

1. Heath says in his memoirs that on 14 Oct. he "with the Generals under his command, reconnoitred the enemy at Throg's Neck; afterwards, the General Officers of the army reconnoitred the various grounds. The same day, Maj. Gen. Lee was ordered to the command of the troops above Kingsbridge, now become the largest part of the American army. But Gen. Washington had

desired him not to exercise the command for a day or two, until he could make himself acquainted with the post, its circumstances, and arrangements of duty. A great number of sloops, boats, &c. were passing the Sound eastward, just at dusk—probably conveying ammunition, provisions, &c. to the troop at Throg's Point" (Wilson, *Heath's Memoirs*, 81). For some of Heath's dispositions on 14 Oct., see his letter to John Nixon of that date in MHi: Heath Papers.

Tench Tilghman wrote Duer on 15 Oct. that he had returned to headquarters the previous evening from Eastchester and Westchester and "there was no Alteration in the Situation of the Enemy except that they had thrown up small Works upon Frogs Point opposite our Works at the two Passes. . . . From the Number of Vessels that have been continually passing up the Sound we conclude that they are transporting Cannon and Stores necessary to enable them to penetrate the Country and set down in our Rear. To hinder them from effecting this, Genl Lee, who arrived yesterday, has taken the Command in that Quarter. He will be posted in such a Situation, with a very considerable Number of Light Troops, that let the Enemy advance by what Road they will, they cannot elude him; if they march in one great Body he can easily draw his Divisions together, if they divide and take different Routs, they will fall in with the different Parties. He will have the Flower of the Army with him, as our Lines in Front are so strong that we can trust them to Troops who would not stand in the Field" (NHi: Duer Papers).

2. See the New York Committee of Safety to GW, 10 Oct., and Robert R. Livingston to GW, 12 October.

3. See GW to Hancock, 11–13 October.

4. See the proceedings of the council of war that met on 16 October.

5. "Genl Lee just now arrived," Robert Hanson Harrison wrote William Duer on 14 Oct., "& is gone after His Excelly" (NN: Emmet Collection).

From Lieutenant Colonel Henry Beekman Livingston

Say Brook [Conn.]
May it please your Excellency.   14th Octr 1776.

Last Wednesday I had a Conference with Governour Trumbull at New Haven,[1] I laid before him the Plan I had formed for our Expedition, which was as follows, we were immediately to engage fourteen Hundred Ton of Vessels, Seven Hundred of which being Sufficient to carry our whole Detatchment, were to be Stationed at Oysterpond Point, with Instructions to wait till farther Orders from us unless disturbed by the Enemies Shiping,[2] when that happened, they were to make some secure Port on the Continent, and whenever Danger disappeared they were to resume their Stations. the Other Seven Hundred Tons are to be Stationed at Satauket about Twenty Miles farther westward with the like Instructions that in case we should be baffled at one Place we may proceed to the other[.] we will have as I am informed by Governour Trumbull Ninety Whale Boats[.] they will Land Nine Hundred Men at a Time, they are not yet arrived at New London but are expected in to Night. To morrow I fancy they will be here. they are to take in our Detatchment and proceed for Fairfield from whence we are to land as many Men as we Conveniently Can on the west side of Huntington in order to cut off the Communication of Three Companies of Troops Stationed at that Place, as soon as this can be effected, the Whale Boats are to Proceid to Mill Creek and Carry across into Southold Harbour[3] where they are to wait for us unless Circumstances permit us with Safety and Secresy to get them into South Bay, if that should be the Case they are to follow us as far as Huntington—and take in our Baggage in Case Necessity should Oblige us to Make a Retreat, Head Quarters on Long Island are now made at Flushing about Twenty Eight Miles from Huntington where a Guard is kept; the Inhabitants are much Oppressed being Prohibited threshing their Grain or Selling their Hay, which Transports are now Loading with at Huntington[.] all the Vessels they Could lay their hands on have been Taken up and ordered to Flushing where their Guard is kept no other part of the Island except that Place and Huntington being Guarded excep[t] a few Men in the Forts Opposite the N. York. Major Rogers is at Huntington tho I cannot hear that he has the Command. The Accounts I have now given You may be depended on, they are given by a Brother to one of our Lieutenants who has been Concealed among them for some time, but has at length made his escape with three others and got Safe to this side, the Enemy were in pursuit of him when he came away, I send you by this Conveyance My Returnes and the Original Papers sent Coll Fanning, of which I formerly sent Copies to Your Excellency being informed by General Clinton of their Consequence,[4] I sent a Party immediately after my leaving New Haven in order to Surprize Coll Fanning and Major Conkling and Seize their Papers[.][5] this was effected, no papers were found on Major Conkling tho I was told he had been very active:

after giving me his Parole he has been permitted to Return again to Long Island. Coll Fanning at his Request, I have permitted to proceid for Convention in order to Clear up his Character, after Exacting his Parole, to take with him and Deliver to Convention the Proofs I had Collected of his being inimical to us—I expect it will be the latter end of the Week before our Descent will be made, I shall with all my Powers forward it— tho' Govr Trumbull is of Oppinion the force allowed is not adequate to the Undertaking tho' I cant help Differing from his Honour in this Particular[.] I enclose Your Excellency his Letter sent me on that Subject with two others intercepted at New Haven and Alluded to in the Governor's Letter,[6] Your Excellency will at once see that they are wrote by some very illiterate Persons who are easily made to believe any thing. I remain your Excellencies Most Obt Humble Sert

Henry B: Livingston

ALS, DLC:GW.

1. The previous Wednesday was 9 October.

2. Oyster Pond Point (now called Orient Point) is at the northeastern tip of Long Island almost directly across the Long Island Sound from Old Saybrook, Connecticut.

3. Mill Creek, which is located about a mile northeast of the town of Southold on the northeastern finger of Long Island, can be reached from Long Island Sound by a short portage across a narrow part of the peninsula. Southold Bay is part of Shelter Island Sound into which Mill Creek flows.

4. Livingston is referring to Oliver De Lancey's orders to Phineas Fanning of 1, 2, 5, and 11 Sept., copies of which he had enclosed in his letter to GW of 24 Sept. (see note 3 to that letter). The enclosed returns have not been identified.

5. Thomas Conkling (d. 1789) the previous day at Saybrook had given his parole of honor not to assist British operations against the Americans. Phineas Fanning signed a similar parole at Guilford, Conn., on 17 Oct. (see Force, *American Archives*, 5th ser., 2:1027, 1104).

6. The enclosed copy of Governor Trumbull's letter to Livingston of 13 Oct. is in DLC:GW. Trumbull had enclosed copies of the two intercepted letters in his letter to GW of that date (see note 3 to that letter).

From Jonathan Trumbull, Sr.

Sir   New Haven Octr 14. 1776

By Capt. Tinker, am inform'd of the Misfortune and Situation of the Row Gallies sent into the Continental Service from this

State[1]—and as Circumstances are alter'd respecting them, since my last to you on the Subject of dismissing their Crews and Arms, must again request your Attention to that Matter[2]—That the Crew of the *Crane,* Capt. Tinker, who escaped, may be dismissed and admitted to return to the Employment of this State, and that if the Crews of the other two Gallies can be of no further Service to you, they likewise may be dismissed, of one or both, as you see fit, as we can employ them to advantage on Board our arm'd Vessels fitting out, into which Service they are desireous of entering[3]—The Gallies being employ'd in the Service of the Continent are esteemd to be at the Continental Care & Risque—This State readily Submit to your Excellencys Direction what is requisite & proper relative to the Men and their Arms. I Am with Esteem & Respect Sir your most Obedt humble Servt

Jonth; Trumbull

LS, DLC:GW; LB, Ct: Trumbull Papers.

1. For the capture of the Capt. Jehiel Tinker's row galley *Crane* by British warships on 9 Oct., see Jeremiah Putnam and Nathaniel Cleaves to GW, that date, and note 3.

2. See Trumbull's second letter to GW of 27 September.

3. The other two Connecticut row galleys were the *Whiting* and the *Shark.*

From Captain Richard Varick

Sir   Albany October 14th 1776 half after three P.M.

I do myself the Honor to inclose Copy of a Letter from General Arnold to General Gates transmitted by the Latter from Tyonderoga & this Moment received in General Schuyler's absence who is now on his Way to Saratoga.[1]

The Lead arrived at Fort George on Saturday last and was immediately forwarded[2]—The powder left this on the same Day and is probably now at or near Fort George, where it will not be delayed a Moment, the commanding officer having General Schuyler's Direction to forward it instantly on its Arrival, to the Army. I am very respectfully Your Excellency's obedient & most humble Servant

Richd Varick

LS, DLC:GW; LB, NN: Schuyler Papers.

1. The enclosed copy of Benedict Arnold's letter to Gates of 12 Oct. contains an account of the defeat of his fleet by the British the previous day at Valcour Island (DLC:GW). Varick also may have enclosed with this letter the undated list of American armed vessels on Lake Champlain that is with the documents for 12 Oct. in DLC:GW, ser. 4.

2. The previous Saturday was 12 October.

General Orders

Head Quarters, Harlem Heights, Octobr 15th 1776
Parole.   Countersign[1]

Col. Joseph Reed's Regiment is to join Genl McDougall's Brigade and Col. Hutchinson's (when the Work he is ordered to execute is finished[)], is to join Genl Clinton's Brigade, at present under the Command of Col. Glover.

Sergeant's, Ward's and Chester's, regiments, and the regiment commanded by Lieut: Col. Storrs, are to form a Brigade & be under the Command of Col. Sergeant.

Col. Storr's and the Regiment under Major Greaves, are to march immediately into Westchester—The first to join the Brigade he is appointed to; the other to join the Regiments commanded by Cols: Douglass and Ely, and with them be under the Command of Genl Salstonstall; as Cols: Horseford's and Major Rogers's Regiments are (but to remain where they at present are, 'till further orders) These five Regiments to compose Genl Salstonstall's brigade.

The other two Connecticut Regiments, encamped upon Harlem River, opposite Head Quarters, are for the present, from their situation, to be annexed to Genl Parsons's Brigade, and be under his command.[2]

The Brigades are now to be formed into Divisions (those on York Island as mentioned in Yesterday's Orders) Nixon's, McDougall's, and that commanded by Col. Glover, to compose one, under the Command of Major Genl Lee—Parsons's, Scott's, and Clinton's another, under the Command of Major Genl Heath—Salstonstall's, Sergeant's and Hand's, another, under the Command of Major General Sullivan; and the Massachusetts Militia another, under the Command of Major Genl Lincoln.

The General in most pressing terms exhorts all Officers commanding divisions, brigades and regiments &c. to have their Officers, and the Men, under their respective Commands, properly informed of what is expected from them; that no Confusion may arise in case we should be suddenly called to Action, which there is no kind of doubt, is near at hand, and he hopes, and flatters himself, that the only contention will be, who shall render the most acceptable service to his Country, and his Posterity. The General also desires, that the Officers will be particularly attentive to the men's Arms & Ammunition, that there may be no deficiency, or application for Cartridges, when we are called into the field.

Varick transcript, DLC:GW.

1. "Williams' Diary," 49:53, gives the parole for this date as "Newmarkett" and the countersign as "Bolton."

2. These orders concern the brigading of eight of the nine regiments of Connecticut militia that were under orders to reinforce the Continental army at New York. Lt. Col. Experience Storrs commanded the 5th Regiment; Maj. Sylvanus Graves commanded the 7th Regiment; Col. John Douglas commanded the 21st Regiment; and Lt. Col. John Ely commanded the 3d Regiment. Obadiah Hosford (Horsford; 1724–1783) was lieutenant colonel commandant of the 12th Regiment, and Zabdiel Rogers (1737–1808) of Norwich was major commandant of the 20th Regiment. Rogers, who had been appointed a major in 1775, was promoted to colonel of militia in 1780. The two regiments assigned to Gen. Samuel Holden Parsons's brigade apparently were Lt. Col. Oliver Smith's 8th Regiment and Lt. Col. Dyar Throop's 25th Regiment, both of which are listed as part of Parsons's brigade in the general return of 3 Nov. 1776. Lt. Col. Jonathan Baldwin's 10th Regiment of Connecticut militia is listed in Saltonstall's brigade in that return (see Force, *American Archives*, 5th ser., 3:499–502).

From Colonel Jacob Bayley

Sr   Fish Kells [N.Y.] October 15th 1776

I was determined to have waited on your Excelencey befor this but am detained here being a Member of the Convention of this State I Send by the Hand of Mr William Wallace an account of the Expence of the Road from Newbury to St Johns.[1] untill we retreated with the Stores Provided to Compleat the Same which were moved on the road thirty Miles I only Charge what was Expended until our return the remaindor I Expended In the Defence of our Frontiers which to us much needed. what Tools we had Provided are kept In Store which I will Make a return of and Dispose of as Directed Two Horses also remaining I will make The best of I am able when I return.

as I Ingaged the hands Immedeate Payment Should be Glad the account Sent or So much as appears reasonable might be Paid Mr William Wallace whose Discharge or Recipt I Elow as my own. I am Sr your Excelencys most obedient Humble Servt

Jacob Bayley

ALS, DLC:GW.

1. In the convention Bayley represented Gloucester County, N.Y., which consisted of the northeastern part of present-day Vermont, including Newbury where Bayley lived. For Bayley's efforts to build a road from Newbury (or Coos as that area was often called) to St. Jean in Canada, see his letter to GW of 15 April 1776. The enclosed undated account, which follows this letter in DLC:GW, ser. 4, lists expenses totaling £982.6.5½, from which Bayley deducted £250 that GW had given to Wallace the previous April, leaving a balance due of £732.6.5½ (see GW to Bayley, 29 April 1776). The expenses are principally for the wages of six overseers at £4 a month and "110 Men Engadged at 3£ pr Month and found in provisions with ½ pint of Rum pr Man each day." Bayley also charged £30 for his "Own Time and Expences in Raising the Men and Superintending the Work" and £22.10 for Wallace's "time and Expence as Clerk and Comisarey."

Letter not found: from John Hancock, 15 Oct. 1776. On 18 Oct. GW wrote to Hancock: "I was Yesterday morning honoured with your favor of the 15th."

Letter not found: to Brig. Gen. Hugh Mercer, 15 Oct. 1776. On 16 Oct. Mercer wrote to GW: "Your Instructions of October the 15th I shall immediately set about observing."

From Richard Peters

Sir   War Office [Philadelphia] October 15th 1776

The Board of War have endeavoured to form an exact Acct of Ordinance Stores, in the several Departments, as well as of those in the Magazine under their immediate Notice here, But from the Want of accurate Returns they have not yet been enabled to accomplish their Design. If these Returns were made

monthly the Board would be enabled in some degree to anti-
cipate the Wants of Amunition in the Army and keep up the
supply as far as may be in their power. I have it in Direction to
request your Excellency will order a Return to be forthwith
made of all Ordinance Stores in your Department and that you
would be pleased to direct as exact Returns to be made monthly
as the situation of the Army will admit. As well as Accounts of
the Men, as to their Numbers and Capacity to do Duty, Returns
should, if possible, be made of their Arms & Accoutriments &
also of the Rations drawn from the Commissary of Provisions as
it has been said that Regiments not half full draw their Rations
as if they were complete; with how much Justice this has been
said cannot be clearly known but if monthly Returns were made
from the Commissaries Office of the Rations drawn by each Regiment, the Returns from the Adjutant General would shew
whether they had exceeded in their Number of Rations what
they were justly entitled to.[1] A List of the Army is making out
wherein at one View every thing relating to each Regiment[2] will
be seen. But the fluctuating State of the Army has prevented
that Accuracy which it is hoped will be shewn in the Millitary
Affairs of the Continent when they shall, by the new Establishment, be put upon a more permanent, & of Course a more respectable Footing. I have the Honour to be with the greatest
Respect Your very obedt humble Servant

Richard Peters Secy

LS, in Timothy Matlack's writing, DLC:GW.

1. Robert Hanson Harrison replied to this letter on behalf of GW in a letter
to the Board of War on 22 October. "In respect to your requisition for an
immediate Return of Ordnance Stores," Harrison writes, "his Excellency [GW]
says It cannot possibly be complied with, in the present, unsettled state of the
Army. in order to effect the good purposes you have in view, he would take the
liberty to recommend the establishing of Magazines of Ammunition & Other
Ordnance Stores in proper places of Security, from whence supplies could be
occasionally drawn. As large Quantities are constantly in demand in time of
War, he does not conceive your provision in these instances can be too great.
he will direct the Regimental Returns in future to include Arms and Accoutrements, and the Commissary Genl to transmit Monthly Lists of Rations. he
thinks the regulation extremely proper, tho he apprehends the information
to be premature respecting the over quantity suggested to have been drawn,
having heard no suspicion of the Sort in this Army of late" (DNA:PCC, item
152).

2. In the manuscript of the LS, the words "to each Regiment" are inserted above the line in Peters's writing.

To Jonathan Trumbull, Sr.

Sir   Head Quarters Harlem Heights October 15th 1776
I was last night favored with your letter of the 6th instant with the return of Prisoners in your State for which I thank you—It is properly made out[1]—Every day's intelligence from the Convention of this State informs of[2] Plots and Conspiracies that are in agitation among the disaffected. The enclosed copy of a letter which I received yesterday from Robert R. Livingston Esqr. one of the Members and who is of the Continental Congress will shew you his idea of the situation of affairs in this Government and their apprehensions of insurrections.[3] The observations he has been pleased to favor me with through the whole of his letter seem to me to be too well founded. The movements of the Enemy, their having sent up some of their Ships in the North River, their landing a large proportion, if not the main body of their Army on Frogs Point (or rather Island as it is surrounded by water every flood tide) nine miles above this on the Sound, added to these, the information of deserters, all afford a strong presumption, nay, almost a certainty, that they are pursuing their original plan of getting in our rear and cutting off all our supplies. Our situation here is not exactly the same as it was at New York. It is rather better. However, as we are obliged to divide our force and guard every probable place of attack as well as we can—as most of our Stores are here and about Kings Bridge, and the preservation of the communication with the States on the other side of Hudson's River a matter of great importance, it will not be possible for me to detach any more assistance than what I have already done for the purpose of securing the passes in the Highlands. I have sent Colo. Tash lately from New Hampshire with his Regiment, upon the business, and as it is of the utmost consequence to possess those passes, and to hold them free and open, I would beg leave to submit to your consideration, whether you can spare any aid upon this interested occasion. I know your exertions already are great, in the Service in this and the Northern Army,[4] and nothing could have

induced me to mention this matter to you, were it not for the alarming and melancholy consequences which will result from the Enemy's possessing themselves of those communications. The Regiment I have ordered up are to receive directions from the Convention, also the Posts[5] they are to occupy, supposing them to be much better acquainted with the places where they should be stationed than I am. If it is in your power to afford any assistance in this instance, you will be pleased to give such instructions to those you send, as you shall judge necessary. I am just dispatching an Engineer to the Convention to throw up some small Works.[6] I have the honor to be with great Esteem Sir your most obedient Servant

Go: Washington

P.S. I have sent two Regiments of the Massachusetts Militia up the River to watch the motion of the Ships and to oppose any landing of men that they may attempt—I am also extending every part of my force that I possibly can towards East and West chester to oppose the Enemy and prevent their effecting their plan of it, if it shall be practicable; but our numbers being far inferior to the demands for men, I cannot answer for what may happen—The best in my power shall be done.[7]

LB, Ct: Trumbull Papers; LB, DLC:GW; Varick transcript, DLC:GW.

1. This letter has not been found, and the enclosed return of prisoners has not been identified.

2. The LB in DLC:GW reads: "mentions."

3. See Livingston to GW, 12 October.

4. The LB in DLC:GW reads: "upon this Interesting occasion. I know your exertions already are great—I know you have a large number of Men engaged in the service in this and the Northern Army."

5. The LB in DLC:GW reads: "as to the posts."

6. GW ordered the French engineer Jean Louis Imbert to assist the New York convention (see Tench Tilghman to William Duer, this date, NHi: Duer Papers, and GW to the New York Convention, 17 Oct.).

7. The LB in DLC:GW reads: "the most in my power shall be done." William Duer wrote Tench Tilghman on 17 Oct. that he had been informed "that the Guards who were sent to watch the ships are extremely negligent—All the Coast from Tarry Town to Peeks Kill is I am told destitute of Guards—Several Disaffected Persons have join'd the Enemy, and a considerable Quantity of cattle has been carried off—It is said that application was made to the officer commanding in that Quarter, who arg'd that he had no orders for watching the Shores[.] I know not how to believe this, though it is transmitted through a channel I can hardly suspect of Misrepresentation" (NHi: Duer Papers).

General Orders

Head Quarters, Harlem Heights, Octobr 16th 1776.
Parole Burlington   Countersign Boston.

Varick transcript, DLC:GW.

Council of War

[16 October 1776]

At a Council of War held at the Quarters of General Lee 16th Oct. 1776.

Present. His Excelly General Washington[,] Major Generals Lee[,] Puttnam[,] Heath[,] Spencer[,] Sullivan[,] Brigadi[e]r Generals Ld Stirling[,] Mifflin[,] McDougal[,] Parsons[,] Nixon[,] Wadsworth[,] Scott[,] Fellows[,] Clinton[,] Lincoln[,] Colo. Knox, Commandr of Artilly.

The General read sundry Letters from the Convention & particular Members &c. of the Turbulence of the disaffected in the upper Parts of this State—and also sundry Accounts of Deserters shewing the Enemy's Intentions to surround us.[1]

After much Consideration & Debate the following Question was stated—Whether it having appeared that the Obstructions in the North River have proved insufficient & that the Enemy's whole Force is now in our Rear at Frog Point, it is now deemed possible in our present Situation to prevent the Enemy cutting off the Communication with the Country & compelling us to fight them at all Disadvantages or surrender Prisoners at Discretion.

Agreed with but one dissenting Voice, viz. Genl Clinton that it is not possible to prevent the Communication & that one of the Consequences mentioned in the Question must certainly follow.

Agreed that Fort Washington be retained as long as possible.

D, in Joseph Reed's writing, DLC:GW; Varick transcript, DLC:GW.

Heath writes in his memoirs that on this date "two works were discovered on Throg's Neck, nearly finished. The General Officers of the army rode to reconnoitre the ground at Pell's Neck, &c. and it was determined that the position of the American army should be immediately changed; the left flank to be extended more northerly, to prevent its being turned by the British" (Wilson, *Heath's Memoirs*, 81–82).

Tench Tilghman wrote William Duer on this date: "I have yours of the 14th, which is principally taken up with pointing out the necessity of securing a proper place of retreat beyond the Highlands, should any accident befall the army. I cannot speak positively, but I am inclined to think the expediency of such a measure is in deliberation before a council of war held this day at *King's Bridge*. I know some of our ablest heads are clearly for it" (Force, *American Archives*, 5th ser., 2:1077).

1. See the New York Committee of Safety to GW, 10 Oct., and Robert R. Livingston to GW, 12 October.

From Brigadier General Hugh Mercer

Sir   Amboy [N.J.] October 16. 1776

General Green has informed your Excelleny that a party pass'd over last night to Staten Island with a view to attack the Enemy, at the east end near the Watering Place—as we advanced towards Richmond Town information was given, that some Companies of British & Hessian Troops, were stationed there—surprising them was therefore the first object, which was effected this morning at break of day—Well disciplined Troops would have taken the whole without the loss of a man—but we only took about twenty prisoners, partly Hessians & English— eight Hessians & nine British, one of those wounded, & besides these two mortally wounded left at Richmond Town—We lost two men in the Action—What we have collected of intelligence from the Prisoners, is enclosed.[1]

Your Instructions of October the 15th I shall immediatly set about, observing with the utmost diligence and Punctuallity[2]— Col. Griffin receivd a Wound in the Heel in the Action of this Morning & Lt Col. Smith of the flying Camp was slightly wounded in the Arm[3]—I shall send the Prisoners on to Philadelphia. I have the honour to be Sir Your Excellencys Most obed. Set

H. Mercer

LS, DLC:GW. The last two sentences and the closing are in Mercer's writing. Although Tench Tilghman docketed this letter in part "Ansd 18th," that reply has not been found.

1. Nathanael Greene accompanied Mercer and the raiding party to Staten Island, but he was obliged to leave before the attack because about eleven o'clock at night he received orders from GW directing him to come immediately to Harlem Heights. For GW's limited involvement and a somewhat fuller

account of the raid, see Mercer to Hancock, 17 Oct., DNA:PCC, item 159; see also Mackenzie, *Diary,* 1:80.

The enclosed examination of one Hessian and two British prisoners, dated 16 Oct., is in DLC:GW. Robert Holbrook of the 14th Regiment says: "There were about 1500 [troops] on the Island at first—about 10 days ago the greatest part of the Hessians embark'd. . . . Genl How has 22000 including Hessians & all other Troops—Some new Troops landed last Monday [14 Oct.]—the Army in good Health—& plenty of Provisions—all Salt on the Island—they expect 15000 Hessians every day—but no English Troops—the only reinforcement is the 6th Ridgment about 150—Hessians in the Army supposed to be 15000."

Peter Gee of the 6th Regiment says: "150 of them landed on Staten Island last Monday from the Chambury, Transport—left England the 3d July[.] 20 Sail Came out with them 2 Men of Warr & 18 Provision Vessels—they were makeing great preperations in England, recruited very fast—but expected the Press [impressment] to break out—about 700 Hanoverians came out, as many more expected, some of them lay at Plymouth—the greatest part of the Hessians left the Island—a great many Sick on the Island—the number in the Fort not known supposd about 600—only two pieces of cannon in the Fort—expected a reinforcement of the regulars."

Christian Guiler, a Hessian private, says: "Tis 8 Years since he left his own Country[.] allmost all thier Troops is with Genl How—12000 of them have come, expect more—expected if taken Prisoner to have Mercy Shewn him if we were a Christian People—that he was brought from his Country by force, that detachments were sent through thier Country & if thier Parents interferd were put into Jail—were told they were to be Garrision'd in England—but affter 3 days arrival in England were orderd to embark for America to thier great disappointment, & against thier Will[.] were guarded to thier Ships—they saw no papers of any kind among them from us—if they knew that they would be well treated by us, would all lay down thier Arms—have no desire to return to thier Ridgments again—are much pleasd & happy with the treatment they have recievd—and are very thankfull for the same."

2. These instructions have not been found. Mercer says in his letter to Hancock of 17 Oct. that "General Washington's Orders, which I recieved that night [15 Oct.], immediatly to form a new Arangement of the troops in New Jersey oblidged us to return to Amboy" the following morning (DNA:PCC, item 159).

3. Samuel Griffin was deputy adjutant general of the flying camp. Jonathan Bayard Smith, whom Congress had appointed deputy mustermaster for the flying camp on 9 July, resigned that office in a letter to Hancock of 25 Sept., and Congress accepted his resignation two days later (see *JCC,* 5:529, 830; and Smith to Hancock, 25 Sept., DNA:PCC, item 78). Smith returned to Philadelphia by 2 Nov. when he served as secretary of a citizens' meeting regarding the new state constitution and the impending elections to the general assembly (see Force, *American Archives,* 5th ser., 3:483–84). Smith was elected a delegate to the Continental Congress on 5 Feb. 1777.

From Major General Philip Schuyler

Dear Sir   Saratoga [N.Y.] Octr 16th 1776

I am honored with your Excellency's Favor of the 10th & 11th Instant; I am very confident the Manner in which you have treated the Cayuga Sachems, will be attended with very salutary Consequences.

By a Person from your Camp, who left it since the Ships of War passed your Cheveaux de Frize, we were informed that all the Craft that could be procured, were employed in carrying Stone to compleat the Obstruction in the River; Your Letter gives me Hopes that those that are passed, will be prevented from returning.

Since the Letter of General Arnold's transmitted you by Capt. Varick, I have not had a Line from Tyonderoga,[1] I have Hopes that the Enemy will not renew their Attack on our Fleet; The Ammunition arrived at Tyonderoga last Night.[2]

I shall dispatch a Messenger to Boston for Nails, and hope to receive a Supply from thence.[3] I am Dr Sir with Every sentiment of Esteem & respect Your Ex: Most Obedt Hume Servant

P. Schuyler

LS, DLC:GW; LB, NN: Schuyler Papers.

1. Arnold's letter to Gates of 12 Oct. regarding the defeat of his fleet at Valcour Island the previous day was enclosed in Richard Varick's letter to GW of 14 October.

2. Gates wrote Schuyler from Ticonderoga on 15 Oct. informing him that "part of the Lead, about Three Tons is arrived" (DLC:GW).

3. See Schuyler to the Selectmen of Boston, this date, in Force, *American Archives*, 5th ser., 2:1087.

From Major General Philip Schuyler

Saratoga [N.Y.] Octo. 16. 1776

Dr Sir   Six oClock Afternoon

Inclosed you have Copies of Letters from Generals Gates and Arnold, announcing the total Destruction of our Fleet on Lake Champlain.[1] I shall write to every State nearest me to march up their Militia to support our Army as the Enemy will doubtless very soon attack it, and do every thing in my Power to prevent their penutrating into the Country, should our Army be obliged to give way which I have good Hopes will not be the Case. I am Dr Sir Your Excellency's most obedt hum. Servt

Ph: Schuyler

LS, DLC:GW; LB, NN: Schuyler Papers; copy, enclosed in Harrison to Hancock, 20 Oct. 1776, DNA:PCC, item 152; copy, DNA:PCC, item 169.

1. After Arnold's fleet was defeated at Valcour Island on 11 Oct., it attempted to escape the pursuing British vessels by sailing south on Lake Champlain, only to be caught and attacked about ten miles north of Crown Point on 13 October. Arnold, who reached Ticonderoga with many of his men after beaching and burning his flagship and four smaller vessels, wrote Schuyler on 15 Oct. describing the action. "Of our whole Fleet," Arnold says, "we have saved, only two Gallies, two small Schooners, one Gondola and one Sloop. . . . The Enemies Fleet were last Night three Miles below Crown Point, their Army is doubtless at their Heels, we are busily employed in compleating our Lines, Redoubts, which I am sorry to say are not so forward as I could wish, we have very few heavy Cannon, but are mounting every Piece we have, it is the Opinion of General's Gates and Sinclair [Arthur St. Clair], that eight or ten Thousand Militia should be immediately sent to our Assistance, if they can possibly be spared from below. I am of Opinion the Enemy will attack us with their Fleet, and Army, at the same Time, the former is very Formidable. . . . The Season is so far advanced, our People are daily growing more healthy, we have about nine Thousand effectives, and if properly supported, make no Doubt of stopping the Career of the Enemy." The enclosed copies of Arnold's letter and Gates's covering letter to Schuyler of the same date are in DLC:GW.

To Jonathan Trumbull, Sr.

Sir   Head Quarters Heights of Harlem October 16th 1776

I have been favored with your several letters of the 11th and 13th instant with their enclosures. The first I received would have been answered sooner had I been able to have furnished the necessary intelligence respecting the Enemy's Ships of war in the Sound above Hell Gate. This induced me to detain the Express a day, in expectation of gaining a more certain information of this fact than what had then come to my knowledge—By some deserters who came ashore from their Shipping at Frog's Point yesterday, and who, from what I could discover, on their examination, I think, in this instance, are deserving of credit, I am acquainted, that there are now between Hell Gate and Frog's Point, five Ships of war—The Foy [Fowey] of 24 Guns—the Le Brune of 32—the Carysfort of 28—the Niger of 32 and Halifax of 16; and that the Mercury and one other Ship are cruising off Block-Island—Whether their number may be augmented or diminished in a short time, is more than I can say; though I must observe the Enemy's Frigates of 28 Guns (as we have found from experience) are now [not] deterred[1] from passing through Hell Gate—I would therefore strongly advise, in case an attack on the Ships of war near Frog's Point, should be determined on, that Tenders or other small craft should be sent ahead for the purpose of discovering with certainty the number and strength of the Enemy who, from the circumstance I have mentioned, may be easily reinforced—As to furnishing any Soldiers from this Army toward manning your Ships, it is what, I am sorry, under the present appearance of things, I cannot comply with, the Enemy being too powerful on this quarter to admit of any diminution of the Troops who are to oppose them. For this reason also I cannot afford any reinforcement to Colo. Livingston to augment his Detachment from twelve hundred to two thousand, which you think would be necessary—Indeed, as we have received information that the Enemy have been considerably reinforced by the arrival of Hessians, and as they have, from accounts, drawn almost their whole force to Frog's Point, I think it would be highly advisable (unless the expedition to Long Island is in such forwardness as to be carried into execution immediately) to send forward the two Massachusetts Regiments who were detained for that particular service. Should it be determined to proceed to Long Island, I cannot interfere by any means to give the command to a young Officer.

With respect to the Stores at Norwalk and the other Towns you mentioned, I have ordered them from thence, thinking this method more eligible than to furnish Troops, of which we are in such want, for their defence—I did myself the pleasure of writing to you a few days ago, which I imagine you have received.[2] I am Sir with great Respect Your most obedient Servant

Go: Washington

P.S. I have just received the examination of another deserter who says he came away from the Dolphin, last Thursday, a sixty gun Ship in the Sound above Hell Gate; but this I am in doubt about:[3] At any rate I imagine, if it is true, it must be known to you by information of the inhabitants living on the Sound.

G.W.

LB, Ct: Trumbull Papers; LB, DLC:GW; Varick transcript, DLC:GW.

1. The LB in DLC:GW reads "nor deterred." The Varick transcript reads "not deterred."

2. See GW to Trumbull, 9–10 October.

3. The previous Thursday was 10 October. The British warship *Daphne,* which had arrived at New York on 3 Oct., was a small frigate carrying twenty guns.

General Orders

Head Quarters, Harlem Heights, Octobr 17th 1776.
Parole.   Countersign

There are a number of priming-Wires and Brushes in the Commissary's Store, near Genl Spencer's Quarters, and at Kingsbridge; in the latter a number of Pouches, which are to be distributed among the Brigades. The Brigadiers are desired to send to those places, where they may receive priming-Wires and Brushes; the Pouches are to be divided, and each Brigadier is to send for his proportion, as soon as possible and have them filled with spare Cartridges.

As the Movements of the Enemy make an Alteration of our position necessary, and some regiments are to move towards them, the commanding and the other Officers of regiments, are to see the following Orders punctually executed.

The Tents are to be struck, and carefully rolled, the men to take the Tent poles in their hands—two Men out of a Company with a careful Subaltern, to go with the Baggage, and not leave it on any pretence—No Packs (unless of Sick Men) Chairs, Tables, Benches or heavy lumber, to be put on the Waggons—No person, unless unable to walk, is to presume to get upon them—The Waggons to move forward before the regiments, the Quarter Master having first informed himself from the Brigadier, or Brigade Major, where they are to pitch—Every Regiment under marching orders, to see they have their Flints & Ammunition in good order and complete.

Lieut. Nevins of Col. Tylers regiment is to do the duty of Captain, in the room of Major Chipman lately promoted.[1]

Daniel Lyman Esqr: is appointed Major of Brigade, to Genl Fellows, and is to be respected accordingly.[2]

A General Court Martial whereof Col. Ewing was President, having convicted Lieut: Pope of the Rangers, of the scandalous Crime of "Conniving at plundering—contrary to frequent and express orders," and sentenced him to be cashiered; The General approves the sentence, and he is accordingly cashiered. The same Court having convicted Corporal Geo. Wilson of "plundering Mr Bushey's House at Harlem"—and sentenced him to receive 39 Lashes—The General approves the sentence, and orders it to be executed to morrow on the parade, before the Guards march off—The Provost Marshal to see it done.[3]

Col. Weedon's and Col. Reed's Regiments to join Lord Stirling's Brigade immediately.

Major Parker of Genl Heard's Brigade to attend the Works, and be execused other duty.[4]

Varick transcript, DLC:GW.

1. David Nevins (1747–1838) of Norwich, Conn., who had served as an ensign in the 6th Connecticut Regiment during 1775, was appointed a first lieutenant in the 10th Continental Regiment on 1 Jan. 1776.

2. Daniel Lyman (1756–1830) of Durham, Conn., who had left Yale College during the Lexington alarm in April 1775 to join Benedict Arnold's New Haven Volunteers, returned to Yale earlier this year and finished his degree before this day's appointment as brigade major. In the spring of 1777 Lyman was commissioned a captain in Col. William Lee's Additional Continental Regiment, and in May 1778 he became an aide-de-camp to General Heath, in which capacity he served until the end of the war. In 1790 GW appointed Lyman surveyor and inspector for the port of Newport, and from 1812 to 1816 he was chief justice of the Rhode Island supreme court.

3. The copyist inadvertently wrote "Pove" on the manuscript. Jacob Pope of Massachusetts, a second lieutenant in the 21st Continental Regiment who had been detached to the corps of rangers commanded by Maj. Andrew Colburn, was tried on 15 October. At the trial John Bushing testified: "My House is down by the 8 Mile Stone [on the post road]. The Day after the Army retreated from [New] York, I left the House & left most of our articles in the House. I heard that the Rangers had a Number of Things & apply'd to Lieut. Pope to get them. Lieut. Pope appeared quite willing to have the men searched. I found an old Chest, 20 lb. yarn, a Pot, an Ax & two or three other Trifles in the Quarters of the Men. I took them away without opposition. Lieut. Pope told me he had taken a Gun out of the House, but told me I should not have it unless I gave him five Dollars or got an Order for it from the General. I accordingly got an Order & then Lieut. Pope told me he had sent the Gun beyond Kingsbridge & gave me an Order to get it. Lieut. Pope appear'd quite willing to have me take away every Thing I found, except, the Gun, which he made no Difficulty about, after I had the General's Order."

Capt. Lemuel Holmes of the rangers testified that Pope had removed the articles from the house to "save them for the Owners or the Continent," and they subsquently had been inventoried and sent to headquarters. Holmes added, however, that "Lieut. Pope shewed me a Gun & said he thought that was his Property." Both a sergeant and Adj. Thomas U. Fosdick then testified that Pope paid $5 to Corp. George Wilson for a coat and jacket that had been taken from Bushing's house. Pope admitted buying a coat from Wilson, but he denied knowing it was plunder. After the court found Pope "guilty of Conniving at plundering," it proceeded that same day to try Wilson who pleaded guilty to the charge against him. The court not only sentenced him "to be whipped thirty nine Lashes" but also "in future that he do Duty as a Private Centinel" (see the court-martial proceedings, 16 Oct., DLC:GW).

4. Samuel Franklin Parker (1745–1779) was appointed a captain in Col. David Forman's regiment of New Jersey militia levies on 14 June 1776, and he became major of the regiment on 10 July.

To Colonel Jacob Bayley

Sir   Head Quarters Harlem Heights 17th Octob. 1776

I have yours of the 15th Inst. by Mr Wallace with an Acct of the Expence incurred in cutting a Road from Coos to St Johns, the Amount of £982.16.5½ lawful Money.[1] There are some few Errors in casting out the different Articles but they may be easily rectifyed when a Settlement is made.[2]

I have it not in my power to make Objections to any part of the Account, as I cannot but suppose that it is all just and what has really been paid or agreed to be paid, but proper Vouchers should accompany all public Accounts, and these Mr Wallace tells me you can furnish. The most material is a Muster Roll of the Men employed, shewing the time of their Engagement for the Service and that of their Discharge. It is probable no Receipts may have been taken for some of the Articles, but you will please to furnish them for as many as you are able. I beg I may be clearly understood. I do not call for Vouchers, because I suspect you of charging more than is justly due, but because it is necessary that they should accompany all public Accounts that pass thro' my Hands. When this is done the Acct shall be adjusted and paid by Sir yr most obt Sert.

LB, in Tench Tilghman's writing, DLC:GW; Varick transcript, DLC:GW. The LB is addressed "To Colo. Bayley at Fishkills."

1. Tilghman apparently misread the account total "£982.06.5½" as "£982.16.5½." (see Bayley to GW, 15 Oct., n.1).

2. Bayley's account is corrected in three places apparently by someone at GW's headquarters. The total wages for 110 men working 45 days (a month and a half) at £3 each a month is computed as £490 when the correct amount is £495. Errors are also made in computing the hire of a man and a packhorse for 6 days at six shillings a day, which is given as £3.12 instead of the correct amount of £1.16., and the traveling expenses of 19 men for 40 miles at two pence a mile, which is given as £5.18.4 instead of the correct amount of £6.6.8 (see Bayley's undated account with his letter to GW of 15 Oct. in DLC:GW, ser. 4).

To Nicholas Cooke

Sir   Head Qrs Harlem Heights Octobr 17th 1776

On Monday last I was honoured with your favor of the 5th Instt[1] and beg leave to inform you, that the reasons which you assign for countermanding Colo. Richmonds march appear to me strong & substantial; As to the expedition to Long Island, it is impossible for me to give any direction about it, It must be governed by a variety of circumstances; nor will it be in my power to appoint any person to command it, the situation of our Affairs here requiring the presence of every Officer of the least merit for the Government of this Army.

In respect to your request, to have a List of Officers transmitted who have served to good acceptance, I am happy that I had anticipated your views & those of your Honble Assembly in this Instance before the receipt of your favor. I wrote you fully on this Subject in a Letter I had the honor of addressing you on the 12th, sending you a List of such Officers as were particularly recommended for the Two Battallions you are to raise, to which I beg leave to refer you as it contains my sentiments at large. I have the Honor to be in haste with great Esteem Sir Yr Most Obedt Servt

Go: Washington

LS, in Robert Hanson Harrison's writing, R-Ar; LB, DLC:GW; Varick transcript, DLC:GW.

1. The previous Monday was 14 October.

To the New York Convention

Gentn　　　　　　　Head Qrs Harlem Heights Octobr 17th 1776

Judging it a matter of the utmost importance to secure the passes thro the Highlands, I have sent up Monsr Imbert, a French Gentlemen, who has been placed in the Army as an Engineer by Congress, in order to take your directions respecting the passes & such Works as you may esteem necessary to preserve them. As the situation of Affairs in this State is rather alarming, I would beg leave to recommend your earliest attention to this Business, & that no time may elapse before the Works are begun. I have no acquaintance with Monsr Imbert, & his abilities in his profession remain to be proved; However I trust under your care and advice that whatever may be essential will be immediately done.[1] I have the Honor to be &c.

G.W.

I can spare no Other Engineer having but one besides.

LB, in Robert Hanson Harrison's writing, DLC:GW; Varick transcript, DLC:GW.

1. William Duer apparently had assumed that Thomas Machin, who was stationed at forts Montgomery and Constitution, would be given this task, instead of Jean Louis Imbert, a recently arrived French officer whom Congress had recommended to GW as an engineer on 19 Sept. (see *JCC*, 5:783; Richard Peters to GW, 20 Sept., cited in GW's first letter to Hancock of 7 Oct., n.4; and Duer to Robert Hanson Harrison, 15 Oct., NHi: Duer Papers). Tench Tilghman wrote Duer on this date that GW "has had no great experience of the abilities of Mons. Imbert the French Engenier who goes up with your Express, but he thinks it would be of Service to you if Mr Machin could Spare time to Step over & point out to Mons. Imbert the Kind of work, that will be most advantageous & soonest Constructed So as to answer the desired purpose. I mention this because Imbert in Some works he began here went upon too large a Scale & with more regularity than is necessary in this rough Country, perhaps he wanted to Shew his Skill he would have been too tedious—You must endeavor to procure him an interpreter, otherwise he will be much at a loss to direct the working Parties" (MH: Sparks transcriptions). Duer replied to Tilghman on the following day: "I observe what you mention with Respect to Mr Imbert, and shall give such hints to the Committee of this Convention who will cooperate with Mr Imbert in erecting his Works as may be Useful. . . . I have convers'd a good deal with Mr Imbert this Evening; whether or not he is an Engineer, I am not able to determine; but he appears to me a judicious and sensible man" (NHi: Duer Papers).

Imbert accomplished little in the highlands before he returned to Philadelphia in early November carrying a letter of recommendation from Charles Lee to Benjamin Franklin dated 6 November. "Whether He is a great Engineer or no I cannot pretend to say," Lee writes Franklin from Philipsburg, N.Y., "as He has had no fair opportunity of displaying his talents. The few small works He has thrown up have been in haste, at the same time labouring under the disadvantage of not being able to explain himself to the workmen. From the little I can judge of him He is a Man of capacity and knowledge, and I am told by his Countrymen that his Fort lies in surveying Georgraphically and military a Country. I know not any kind of Officer more wanted in America than a Military Surveyor of those parts which are likely to be the scene of action. General Washington and Myself have therefore concurr'd in opinion that He shoud begin with the Jerseys and if He gives satisfactory proofs of his talents in this line, to recommend him to Congress for this important Office" (Willcox, *Franklin Papers*, 23:3–4). Congress apparently did not offer Imbert such an office, however, and in the spring of 1777 he returned to France, citing ill health as his reason for leaving America (see Imbert to Congress, 6, 12 April 1777, DNA:PCC, items 41, 42).

General Orders

Head Quarters, Harlem Heights, Octobr 18th 1776.
Parole Stamford. Countersign France.

As the Brigades of the Army now move at such distance from each other, that a punctual attendance, at Head-Quarters, for Orders, cannot be expected—One Brigade Major from each Major General's division, is to attend, as early in the day as he can—the several Brigade Majors, or Adjutants who act as such, are to attend him at a stated hour, and then distribute the Orders through the several Brigades, and Regiments, as fast as possible.

Varick transcript, DLC:GW.

To John Hancock

Sir Harlem Heights Octobr the 18th 1776

I was Yesterday morning honoured with your favor of the 15th with the Resolutions of the 11th and 14th. the latter by which Congress have authorized me to appoint Monsr Pennet a Brevet Aid De Camp, claims a return of my acknowledgements.[1]

Last night I received a Letter from Mr Varrick, Secretary to Genl Schuyler, inclosing a Copy of One from Genl Arnold to Genl Gates. The Intelligence transmitted by Genl Arnold being of an extremely interesting and important nature, I thought it adviseable to forward the same immediately by Express—you have a Copy herewith which contains the particulars and to which I beg leave to refer you.[2]

The Accounts transmitted yesterday by post, will inform you of the movements of the Enemy and of the measures judged necessary to be pursued by us to counteract their designs. I have nothing to add on this Head, except that Ten or Eleven Ships which have been prevented passing Hell Gate for Two or three days for want of Wind, are now under way & proceeding up the Sound—Among them there appear to be two Frigates, the rest probably have in Stores &c.[3]

Inclosed is a Copy of the last Genl return I have been able to obtain. It only comes down to the 5th Instt.[4] the situation of our Affairs & the almost constant necessity of sending detachments from one place to another, to watch the Enemy's motions have prevented the Officers from making them with regularity. I have the Honor to be with great esteem Sir Your Most Obedt St

Go: Washington

LS, in Robert Hanson Harrison's writing, DNA:PCC, item 152; LB, DLC:GW; copy, DNA:PCC, item 169; Varick transcript, DLC:GW. Congress read this letter on 21 Oct. and referred it to the Board of War (*JCC*, 6:889).

1. This letter has not been found. For Congress's resolution of 14 Oct. concerning Pierre Penet, see ibid., 869–70. On that date Congress also resolved in response to GW's letters to Hancock of 7 and 8 Oct. that the states in which prisoners were held should furnish Congress with accounts of the expenses incurred in that regard and that $500,000 be sent immediately to the paymaster general to pay bounties to soldiers reenlisting for the duration of the war (see ibid.). The resolutions of 11 Oct. apparently were the ones that Congress passed on that day giving GW permission to release Chambault and asking him to use every means possible to obstruct the Hudson River in order to prevent the British warships above Fort Washington from receiving any aid (see ibid., 866).

2. Arnold's letter to Gates of 12 Oct., a copy of which Richard Varick enclosed in his letter to GW of 14 Oct., contains news of the American defeat at Valcour Bay. The copy of Arnold's letter that GW sent to Hancock is in DNA:PCC, item 152.

3. These transports carrying Hessian soldiers from Staten Island had been trying since 13 Oct. to sail up the East River and pass through Hell Gate to the army at Throg's Point, but the lack of sufficient wind delayed them, because it was, Frederick Mackenzie says, "very dangerous to attempt going through Hellgate with those large vessels, with the tide only" (Mackenzie, *Diary*, 1:78–

80). On 17 Oct. the sloop *Senegal* got through Hell Gate "with much labor and danger," touching the shore several times on the way, but this morning the warship *Rose* made the passage "without any difficulty, having a fine wind, & favorable tide." The transports soon followed, and the Hessians joined Howe's army later this day (ibid., 81–82).

4. The general return of GW's army for 5 Oct. shows that he had under his immediate command 1,499 commissioned officers, 229 staff officers, 2,164 noncommissioned officers, and 25,735 rank and file, of whom 14,145 were present and fit for duty, 4,738 were sick present, 3,209 were sick absent, 3,982 were on command, and 127 were on furlough. Attached are returns for Knox's artillery regiment, which had a total of 1,160 officers and men, and for the Connecticut and Rhode Island militia, which reported having 179 commissioned officers, 24 staff officers, 332 noncommissioned officers, and 1,774 rank and file, of which 1,275 were present and fit for duty. A note at the end of the return reads: "N.B. Gen. Lincoln's Militia from Massachusetts, computed at 4000, so scattered & ignorant of the Forms of Returns that none can yet be got—The Magazines of Provisions being formed along the Sound & among People of an inimical Disposition it is absolutely necessary they should be well guarded—Two Regimts of New Hampshire Militia on Command—one at the White Plains the other at the Fish Kills—under the like Circumstances. The moving State of the Army has prevented Returns being made since the above Date" (DNA: RG 93, Revolutionary War Rolls, 1775–83; see also Force, *American Archives*, 5th ser., 2:907–10).

Letter not found: to Brig. Gen. Hugh Mercer, 18 Oct. 1776. Mercer's letter to GW of 16 Oct. is docketed in part "Ansd 18th."

To Samuel Washington

Dear Brother,   Heights of Haerlem 18th Oct. 76.
    Your Letter of the 26th Ulto intended to have come by Captn Thomas Rutherford was delivered to me by Mr Vale. Crawford who will also be the bearer of this Letter to you.[1]
    I wrote you last Week under cover to Lund Washington (who I desired to forward it by a safe hand) a long Letter, containing a full Acct of our Matters in this Quarter;[2] to this, & the bearer, I must refer you for further particulars; as the present critical Situation of our Affairs scarce allows me time to read, much less to write Letters, altho^ I have no pleasure or gratification here equal to that of hearing from my friends.
    We are, I expect, upon the Eve of something very important; what may be the Issue; Heaven alone can tell, I will do the best

I can, and leave the rest to the supreme direction of Events. My sincere good wishes attend you, and my Sister and Family and all friends and be assured that with the most unfeigned Love I am and ever shall be Yr Affecte Brother

Go: Washington

ALS, PWacD: Sol Feinstone Collection, on deposit PPAmP.

1. Samuel Washington's letter to GW of 26 Sept. has not been found. Thomas Rutherford of Berkeley County, Va., in 1750 sold GW the rights to a 443-acre tract of land on Evitt's Run in Frederick County, the first of the several Shenandoah Valley tracts that GW ultimately bought. A lieutenant in Capt. John Ashby's company of rangers during the early years of the French and Indian War, Rutherford became an Indian agent in 1757 and a deputy commissary the following year. From 1761 to 1769 he represented Hampshire County in the House of Burgesses. On 12 April 1776 Rutherford contracted with the Virginia council of safety to furnish arms for public use, and on 17 Dec. 1776 the state council gave him £250 for the establishment of a gun factory in Shepherdstown (see *Journals of the Council of State of Virginia*, 1:258, 286, 383, 388, 2:63).

2. See GW to Samuel Washington, 5 Oct., and GW to Lund Washington, 6 October.

General Orders

Head Quarters, Harlem Heights, Octobr 19th 1776.
Parole.   Countersign.

Varick transcript, DLC:GW.

From Nicholas Cooke

Sir,   Providence, October 19. 1776

Your Letter, requesting an Account of the Prisoners in this State, I have duly received;[1] and ordered the Sheriffs of the several Counties to make Return to me of the Number of Prisoners in their respective Counties, and of their different Stations, which Return has not been yet made. I also wrote immediately to Governor Trumbull of Connecticut, to know where their Prisoners were to assemble, that they might both go together, but have had no Answer,[2] but shall endeavour to forward them when I shall receive Information from him—Since which I have received a Letter from the Captain of the Syren Frigate, off

Block-Island, that he had a Number of Prisoners on Board, taken in Merchant Ships, whom he has Orders from Lord Howe to exchange for others of equal Stations.[3]

I inform Your Excellency that a Prize Ship is brought in here, having a Quantity of Blankets, some coarse woollen Goods, Linens and Shoes, which the Owners of the armed Vessel who took her, are desirous may be purchased for the Use of the Army; and in Order that those Goods may not be scattered, they propose that they be all put up in One Lot together; and that no Stranger be allowed to bid them off, unless he shall produce Orders from You or the Congress that he is making Purchase of them for the Army—I should be glad, if Your Excellency should think proper, that You would appoint Somebody immediately to purchase the same. If You should make any Appointment for that Purpose here, I would just inform that Messrs Clark and Nightingale Mr John Brown and myself are all interested in the Privateer, and therefore not so suitable for such Appointment as others. Mr Daniel Tillinghast here is the Continental Agent, and I believe a good Man.[4] I am Your Excellency's most obedient and most humble Servant.

L, DLC:GW.

1. See GW to William Bradford, 29 September.

2. See Cooke to Jonathan Trumbull, Sr., 10 Oct., in "R.I. Revolutionary Correspondence," 174–75.

3. Capt. Tobias Furneaux of H.M.S. *Syren* wrote Cooke about this matter on 11 Oct. (see Clark and Morgan, *Naval Documents*, 6:1216).

4. The British ship *Thomas*, commanded by Capt. Thomas Bell, was sailing from London to Quebec when it was captured on 21 Sept. by the Rhode Island privateer *Hawke* commanded by Capt. Arthur Crawford (see libel against the prize ship *Thomas*, 9 Oct. 1776, in Clark and Morgan, *Naval Documents*, 6:1175). On 23 Oct. Congress requested Cooke immediately to purchase all the blankets and coarse cloth "at continental expence, for the use of the army under General Washington's command" and ordered that the blankets be sent to GW and the cloth made into clothing for the soldiers at the direction of Q.M. Gen. Thomas Mifflin (*JCC*, 6:897). Delegate Robert Treat Paine of Massachusetts sent a copy of that resolution to Cooke, who on 25 Nov. wrote Paine, informing him that Mifflin, in consequence of Cooke's letter to GW of this date, had appointed a gentleman in Providence to purchase goods from the captured ship and that person had "accordingly bought the Blankets being near Three Thousand, Three large Hogsheads of stout Shoes being the whole of that Article, and Three or Four Hogsheads of Camp-Kettles, and is now in Treaty for a large Quantity of coarse Cloths—Linens and Stockings for the same Purpose" (Clark and Morgan, *Naval Documents*, 7:275).

Letter not found: from Jonathan Trumbull, Sr., 19 Oct. 1776. On 22 Oct. Robert Hanson Harrison wrote to Trumbull: "I have the honor, by his [GW's] command, to acknowledge his receipt of your several favors of the 19th & 21st instant" (Ct: Trumbull Papers).

General Orders

Head Quarters, Harlem Heights, Octobr 20th 1776.
Parole   Countersign

Varick transcript, DLC:GW.

Lieutenant Colonel Robert Hanson Harrison to John Hancock

Kingsbridge Octob. 20th 1776
Sir   ½ after 1 OClock P.M.

I have it in command from his Excellency, to transmit you the inclosed Copies of dispatches which just now came to Hand & which contain Intelligence of the most interesting and important nature, respecting our Affairs in the Northern Department.[1] His Excellency would have wrote himself, but was going to our Several posts, when the Express arrived.[2]

The Enemy are pursuing with great Industry their plan of penetrating the Country from the Sound, & of forming a Line in our Rear. They are now extended from Frogs point to New Rochelle, from whence it is generally conjectured they mean to take their Route by way of the White plains & from thence to draw a Line to the North River. We on our part, have drawn our whole force, except the Regiments intended to Garrison Fort Washington, from the Island of New York and have possessed ourselves of the Heights, passes and advantageous Grounds between New Rochelle, where the Van of their Army now lies, and the North River. They will in all probability attempt to effect their purpose by moving higher up, if they do, our Forces will move accordingly, it being a principal object to prevent their out flanking us. On Friday One of their Advanced parties near East Chester fell in with part of Colo. Glovers Brigade & a smart &

close Skirmish ensued, in which I have the pleasure to inform you our Men behaved with great coolness & Intrepidity and drove the Enemy back to their Main body.[3] I have the Honor to be in haste with great esteem Sir Yr Most Obdt St

Rob. H. Harrison

ALS, DNA:PCC, item 152; ADf, DLC:GW; copy, DNA:PCC, item 169; Varick transcript, DLC:GW. Congress read this letter on 21 Oct. and referred it to the Board of War (*JCC*, 6:890–91).

1. Harrison enclosed copies of Arnold's and Gates's letters to Schuyler of 15 Oct. concerning the destruction of Arnold's fleet and Schuyler's second letter to GW of 16 Oct. which covered the copies of those letters that GW received on this date. The copies of Arnold's and Gates's letters that Harrison sent to Hancock are in DNA:PCC, item 152.

2. The following day Harrison wrote a brief letter to Hancock from Valentine's Hill at Mile Square in present-day Yonkers, informing him that GW was "absent on a visit to the Several posts on the left of our Lines & at the White plains" (DNA:PCC, item 152). GW moved his headquarters from Harlem Heights to Valentine's Hill on that date.

3. On the morning of 18 Oct. General Howe moved the major part of his army from Throg's Neck to the Pell's Point peninsula (now part of Pelham Bay Park) located about three miles to the north up Long Island Sound. An advanced force composed of grenadiers and light infantry embarked on flatboats at daybreak and moved up Eastchester Bay to the mouth of the Hutchinson River, where about eight o'clock in the morning they landed on the western shore of Pell's Point peninsula. The advanced force was soon joined there by the main body of Howe's army, which marched north up Throg's Neck and ferried across the mouth of the Hutchinson River using the advanced force's flatboats. The British then marched up Pell's Point peninsula, and by nightfall they occupied a front about two miles in length "with the left upon a creek opposite to East Chester and the right near to [New] Rochelle" (William Howe to George Germain, 30 Nov., in Davies, *Documents of the American Revolution,* 12:258–64; see also Lydenberg, *Robertson Diaries,* 103–4, and Baurmeister, *Revolution in America,* 59–60). Howe's main army remained in that position until the morning of 21 Oct. when it again moved north toward White Plains.

On the march north from the landing place at the mouth of the Hutchinson River, the British advanced guard encountered opposition from Col. John Glover's brigade, which consisted of about seven hundred and fifty men. Concealed in woods and behind stone fences, the Americans harassed the British column, inflicting some casualties before being forced to retreat by the enemy's greatly superior numbers. For accounts of this skirmishing, which occurred during the late morning and early afternoon of 18 Oct., see particularly Extract of a Letter from Fort Lee, 19 Oct., in Force, *American Archives,* 5th ser., 2:1130–31; Extract of a Letter from Colonel Glover, 22 Oct., ibid., 1188–89; Extract of a Letter from a Gentleman in the Army, 1 Nov., ibid., 3:471–74; Wilson, *Heath's Memoirs,* 83; Lydenberg, *Robertson Diaries,* 103–4; and William

Howe to George Germain, 30 Nov., in Davies, *Documents of the American Revolution,* 12:258–64. Glover says that he "had eight men killed and thirteen wounded, among whom was Colonel [William] *Shepard*" (Extract of a Letter from Colonel Glover, 22 Oct., in Force, *American Archives,* 5th ser., 2:1188–89). William Howe says that on his side "three soldiers were killed and about twenty wounded." In addition, Lt. Col. Thomas Musgrave of the 1st Battalion of light infantry and Capt. William Glanville Evelyn of the 4th Regiment were wounded, the latter fatally (Howe to George Germain, 30 Nov., in Davies, *Documents of the American Revolution,* 12:258–64). For GW's praise of Glover's men for this action, see General Orders, 21 October.

To Robert R. Livingston

Dear Sir,   Mr Lowe's 20th Octr 1776.

I wish I had leizure to write you fully on the subject of yr last Letter[1]—the moving state of the Army, and the extreame hurry in which I have been Involved for these Eight days, will only allow me time to acknowledge the receipt of yr favour, and to thank you (as I shall always do) for Any hints you may please to communicate, as I have great reliance upon your judgment; & knowledge of the Country, (which I wish to God I was as much master of)—Drain'd as Connecticut is of Men, I have nevertheless recommended to the Govr of it the advantages which would result from a Body of Mens moving towards the Enemy's right[2]—but whether it will, or can be done, is more than I am able to say. A Regiment is gone to the Highlands to be under direction of your Convention.[3]

Let me Intreat you my Dear Sir, to use your Influence to send, without delay, Provisions for this Army, towards the White Plains—upon a strict scrutiny, I find an alarming deficiency herein, occasiond by the Commissary's placing too much confidence in his Water Carriage, and the Stock he had laid in at the Saw pits &ca (which but too probably may be cut of from us, altho^ upon the first knowledge I had of Its being there, I ordered it to be remov'd)—We want both Flour, & Beef; & I entreat your exertions to forward them. I must also entreat you to send us a Number of Teams the more the better to aid in removing the Army as occasion requires. We are amazingly distress'd on Acct of the want of them—We can move nothing for want of them—In short Sir, our Situation is really distressing.[4] I have orderd Lord Sterling with upwards of 2000 Men to the White

Plains to prevent the Enemys taking possession of it, & for security of Our Stores there; but the Troops were obliged to March without their Tents, or Baggage. In exceeding great haste, & much sincerety I am Dr Sir Yr Most Obedt and obligd Sert

Go: Washington

ALS, MWiW.

GW apparently wrote this letter at Isaac Low's house, which was adjacent to recently constructed Fort Independence in Westchester County about a mile northeast of King's Bridge or, in present-day terms, near the south end of Jerome Park Reservoir in the Bronx. The British army dismantled Low's house later in the war to obtain materials for building and repairing barracks at Laurel Hill on Manhattan Island (see Coldham, *American Loyalist Claims*, 296).

1. See Livingston to GW, 12 October.
2. See GW to Jonathan Trumbull, Sr., 15 October.
3. See GW to Thomas Tash, 13 October.
4. Tench Tilghman wrote William Duer on this date: "To be obliged to follow an enemy whose route is a Secret to us, is not a little distressing especially as we have not Wagons sufficient to transport our baggage & provisions. the latter must be particularly attended to or the army must perish—Upon a survey of our Stores we find we are not so fully stocked as could wish[.] Flour is what is most likely to be wanted, his Excellency [GW] therefore calls upon your convention in the most pressing manner & begs you will set every engine at work to send down every barrel you can procure, towards the army always advising the persons who conduct the Wagons to enquire how far & upon what roads the Enemy are advanced lest they fall into their hands[.] All the Cattle that can be collected you will please to have drove down using the same precautions when they come near the advanced posts—The General [GW] has given orders for the removal of all our Magazines from the Sound, but the enemy have such an advantage by the command of the water that possibly some may be intercepted, it therefore behoves us to double our diligence in procuring supplies from every quarter that remains open—The commissary General [Joseph Trumbull] is sent for from the Eastward, his presence will be of great service but in the meantime great dependance must be put upon the exertions of all our friends in your Quarter" (MH: Sparks transcripts).

To Joseph Trumbull

Sir   Head Qrs Kings bridge Octob. 20th 1776

This is designed to inform you of our alarming situation on account of the state of our provisions. From the best intelligence I have been able to obtain, there are not more than Fifteen hundred Barrells of Flour here and at our posts on the Island of

New York (including three Hundred that came from the Jersey's last night) and about Two Hundred Barrells of pork; nor do I learn that there are many or but very few Live Cattle collected at any place within the Neighbourhood. The passage across the North River is precarious, and much, if not entirely, in the Enemy's power & but little or no dependance should be had in supplies from that Quarter. I must therefore request and entreat your every possible exertion to have large quantities of Cattle & other provision carried to the interior parts of the Country with the utmost expedition out of the reach of the Enemy, who are trying to penetrate from Frogs & pells points & New Rochelle,[1] and to form a line in our Rear, from whence proper Supplies may be immediately drawn for the Subsistence of our Troops— If this is not done—I fear—I am certain that the fatal consequences attendant on Mutiny and plunder must ensue—indeed the latter will be authorized by necessity. I cannot undertake to point out the places where stock should be driven to—But I must urge you to have a sufficiency in our Rear & also of Flour which may be drawn or moved farther back as occasion may require[2]—If the Enemy advance from the Sound, so must we. they must never be allowed to get above us & possess themselves of the upper Country, if it is possible to avoid. As soon as I heard of their landing at Frogs point and of their plan to get in our Rear, I gave orders for the Removal of the provisions & Other Stores from Biron River &c. into the Country[3]—to the White plains as the first & most convenient stage—Whether they have, I have no certain information—but supposing they have, It is most probable what are not immediately expended must be pushed forward, as every movement of the Enemy indicate their determination to get behind us & most likely by that Rout. In a Word Sir, let Nothing be omitted, to hasten supplies of Cattle &c. in our Rear, as I have mentioned, or events the most alarming & injurious not only to this Army but to the liberties of America may follow.[4] you must not stop on account of expence, nor to collect large Quantities before they are sent off. Ten in a drove will be of material consequence. I have ordered a respectable force for the protection of the provisions now at the plains. I am Sir with great esteem Yr Most Obedt Sert

Go: Washington

LS, in Robert Hanson Harrison's writing, Ct: Trumbull Papers; LB, DLC:GW; Varick transcript, DLC:GW. The LS and LB differ in wording in several parts of the text. The most significant variations appear in notes 1, 2, 3, and 4.

1. The LB reads: "to penetrate from the sound."

2. The LB reads: "I cannot undertake to point out the particular places where Stock should be drove to—But it is absolutely necessary that large Quantities should be kept in our Rear, to be killed or moved as occasion may require."

3. The LB reads: "As soon as I heard that they had landed at Frogs point, and that they had digested a plan of getting into our Rear, I gave Orders that the provisions and Other Stores should be removed from Norwalk &c. into the Country."

4. The LB reads: "In short Sir, I beg that you will have Supplies immediately in our Rear, to be drawn or moved back as circumstances may be, or the most fatal and alarming consequences to this Army and the liberties of America may & will in all probability follow."

APPENDIX

Routine Documents Omitted from This Volume

These documents, which include routine letters of introduction and recommendation, routine administrative correspondence, a routine letter of resignation, and personal appeals to which GW made no significant reply, may be found in the CD-ROM edition of the Washington Papers.

From Brig. Gen. Nathaniel Heard, 13 August 1776 (LS, PHi: Gratz Collection; Sprague transcript, DLC:GW).

From Josiah Martin, 16 August 1776 (ALS, DLC:GW).

From the Maryland Council of Safety, 24 August 1776 (LS, DLC:GW; LB, MdAA).

To Maj. Gen. Horatio Gates, 31 August 1776 (LS, NHi: Gates Papers).

From Col. Paul Dudley Sargent and Maj. Jonathan Williams Austin, August 1776 (DS, DLC:GW).

From Silas Deane, 15 September 1776 (Wharton, *Diplomatic Correspondence*, 2:145).

From Ruthey Jones, 15 September 1776 (ALS, DLC:GW).

From Alexander John Alexander, 20 September 1776 (ALS, DLC:GW).

From Brig. Gen. Samuel Holden Parsons, 3 October 1776, (ADS, MHi: Heath Papers).

From Maj. Gen. William Heath, 4 October 1776 (ADfS, MHi: Heath Papers).

From Capt. Andrew Long, 14 October 1776 (ALS, DLC:GW).

From James Bowdoin, 17 October 1776 (ALS, DNA:PCC, item 78; ADfS, MeB).

Index